THE CONQUEST OF TEXAS

The Conquest of Texas

Ethnic Cleansing in the Promised Land, 1820-1875

GARY CLAYTON ANDERSON

UNIVERSITY OF OKLAHOMA PRESS : NORMAN

ALSO BY GARY CLAYTON ANDERSON

Kinsmen of Another Kind: Dakota-White Relations in the Upper Mississippi Valley, 1650–1862 (Lincoln, Neb., 1984; St. Paul, 1997)

Little Crow, Spokesman for the Sioux (St. Paul, 1986)

(Edited with Alan R. Woolworth) *Through Dakota Eyes: Narrative Accounts of the Minnesota Indian War of 1862* (St. Paul, 1988)

Sitting Bull and the Paradox of Lakota Nationhood (New York, 1996)

The Indian Southwest, 1580–1830: Ethnogenesis and Cultural Reinvention (Norman, Okla., 1999)

Publication of this book is made possible through the generosity of Edith Kinney Gaylord.

Illustrations and maps are published with the generous assistance of the Graduate College of the University of Oklahoma.

Library of Congress Cataloging-in-Publication Data

Anderson, Gary Clayton, 1948–
    The conquest of Texas : ethnic cleansing in the promised land, 1820–1875 / Gary Clayton Anderson.
        p. cm.
    Includes bibliographical references (p.   ) and index.
    ISBN 0-8061-3698-7 (alk. paper)
        1. Texas—Race relations—History—19th century. 2. Racism—Texas—History—19th century. 3. Violence—Texas—History—19th century. 4. Forced migration—Texas—History—19th century. 5. Mexicans—Texas—Social conditions—19th century. 6. Indians of North America—Texas—Social conditions—19th century. 7. Texas Rangers—History—19th century. 8. Texas—History, Military—19th century. 9. Texas—History—To 1846. 10. Texas—History—1846–1950. I. Title.

F395.A1A53 2005
305.8'009764'09034—dc22
                                                                    2005041772

The paper in this book meets the guidelines for permanence and durability of the Committee on Production Guidelines for Book Longevity of the Council on Library Resources, Inc. ∞

1 2 3 4 5 6 7 8 9 10

To Chas, a son-in-law of extraordinary kindness, wonderful humor, and absolute loyalty—may he ever be an angel on the shoulders of his children

CONTENTS

ILLUSTRATIONS

Toshewa (Silver Brooch), Penateka Comanche chief
Asahabit (Birch Chief), Comanche advocate of peace
Quanah Parker, young Naconi Comanche leader
Kicking Bird, Kiowa chief
Satank (Sitting Bear), Kiowa chief
Satanta (White Bear), Kiowa chief
Satanta's youngest daughter
Big Bow, Kiowa leader
Lone Wolf, Kiowa leader
Sitting-in-the-Saddle, Lone Wolf's son
Captured Comanche women: Wappah, Marnme, and Qnamothkee
Agent Lawrie Tatum and ransomed Mexican captive boys

Maps

THE CONQUEST OF TEXAS

INTRODUCTION
DEMYTHOLOGIZING TEXAS

The shingle said, "Gone To Texas." Posted on a log cabin door in the antebellum South, the message signaled a slow but steady migration of southerners into the new, promised land of Texas. The men were mostly farmers. Dressed in home-spun, they trudged alongside ox-drawn wagons, their womenfolk, children, and African American slaves walking behind, trying to stay out of the wheel ruts. Most could read and write, but only a few left diaries. Most had debts; honest and hardworking—but money poor—they hoped to pay off what they owed in far-away Texas. Nearly 30,000 Anglo-Americans arrived in the decades of the 1820s and 1830s; the population jumped to 160,000 by 1845 and to an astonishing 600,000 by the time of the Civil War. People moved to early Texas because they thought they could acquire land easily, get out of debt, and prosper.

Texas was an inviting land. Most early pioneers avoided the heavily forested "Big Thicket" along the lower Trinity and Neches rivers, entering instead the rolling prairies and piney woods just south of the great bend of the Red River. Clusters of pine often predominated here, intermixed with stands of magnificent post oak. The Red, like many other streams in Texas, originated far to the west, mixing with other stream courses and rivers until eventually disemboguing into the Gulf of Mexico. The river's placid nature changed during the torrential rain-falls of spring. Flooding became so severe at times in Texas that the floodplain of the Red River—as well as those of the Brazos, Trinity, and Colorado rivers—extended for miles. But even floods proved a boon, producing alluvial valleys that had only to be broken, plowed, and planted.

Early "Texians," as these settlers styled themselves, had little difficulty in building cabins and raising enough corn to survive the first year. They usually chose to live in the river valleys, where the soil was good, leaving much of the up-country between the rivers unsettled. While waiting for crops, these pioneers hunted pronghorn antelope, deer, and turkey. And as late as the 1820s, herds of bison often ventured off the plains into central Texas. Many an early settler in later life would muse about his youth, when he could bring down several ducks or geese with one shot or fire into a herd of deer and feel certain of success.

Cornfields and hogs provided staples of cornbread and bacon, but Texans came to grow cotton, a cash crop that supported the economy well into the twentieth century. Early pioneers in the 1820s introduced a few African American slaves for labor. After Texas secured independence from Mexico in 1836, the number of slaves escalated dramatically, until they constituted nearly one-third of the population by 1860 (and became the most valuable asset in the state). With black slaves to do the field labor, Texas was every bit the promised land anticipated by the hopeful southern emigrant who hung out a shingle announcing his departure.[1]

Faith in that promise persists in Texas culture today. Many Texans still see their state as grander, more righteous and hallowed in its history, than any other part of North America. Texas is the land of giants—Stephen Austin, Sam Houston, Mirabeau Lamar, Davy Crockett, William Barret Travis, John Hays, and James Bowie—all male, all white, and all heroes in a society that still worships heroes. Their history is likewise heroic. Working against immense odds, these men carved a nation—the Texas Republic—and later a state out of what they saw as a wilderness.

Therein lies a problem. Texas was not a wilderness open for the taking. American Indians lived in Texas, and they wished to preserve their claim to this land for the benefit of their progeny. To be sure, the Texas tribes had experienced many evolutionary changes. The initial, indigenous inhabitants—Jumanos, Coahuiltecans, Tonkawas, Karankawas, Apaches, and Caddos—had faced decline and, in some cases, near extinction. But the more mobile Comanches and Wichitas inhabiting northern, central, and western Texas remained strong well into the nineteenth century. Together, the indigenous populations numbered thirty thousand people in 1820. In the decade that followed, another ten thousand American Indians migrated to Texas from the American South and the Midwest. Identified in history as "immigrant" Indians, they too sought homes in a promised land.

The region's written history began when Spaniards entered Texas, exploring the Panhandle and the northeastern woodlands simultaneously in 1541. Missions and presidios (forts) followed, San Antonio being established in 1718. While the Spanish population was only five thousand in Texas proper (Spain had defined Texas as the region between the Nueces and Red rivers), several Hispanic hamlets sprang up along the lower Rio Grande, from Matamoros to Laredo, supporting cattle and sheep herds in the interior both above and below the river. These new communities, given the substantial distances that separated them from Mexico City and the resultant isolation from the seat of Spanish government, often developed a sense of independence. Some residents, for example, saw themselves as Tejanos rather than as Spaniards.

This sense of a Texan identity expanded after Mexico gained its independence in 1821. During Mexico's early development—one dominated by divisive politics and discord—Tejanos generally enjoyed excellent relations with nearby Anglos in Louisiana; much of the commerce that originated in Texas was tied to New Orleans or other northern gulf ports. Many Creole Tejanos from northeastern Texas in particular had much more in common with Louisiana than with Mexico. Not only was Mexican political authority distant and in disarray, but local authority in Texas remained stubbornly aloof from Mexico City and focused on regional development.

Despite considerable ambivalence, some important Tejanos supported the Anglo-led revolution that began in 1835. The promises of liberty, equality, and free trade transcended ethnic differences, at least at first. The fact that Texans preached the rhetoric of eighteenth-century liberalism and capitalism helped ease the break from Mexico by emphasizing natural rights and freedom, in essence utilizing the political rhetoric of the American Revolution. Their efforts minimized the emergence of Mexican nationalism among the Tejano minority; in some communities, nationalism never emerged at all, as some Tejanos identified themselves as Americans.

Mexico, however, had hardly been repressive. Much like Great Britain in its dealing with American colonists in the 1770s, Mexico seldom restricted development in its northern states. Indeed, it passed one of the most liberal land colonization policies in the world and turned the implementation of this policy over to state governments in the 1820s. Each Anglo settler in these early years who left the United States for Mexican Texas was given nearly five thousand acres of land, free! Taxes, with the possible exception of a few import duties, were nonexistent; military service was voluntary; and, although Mexico was a Catholic nation, very few clerics ever ventured north of the Rio Grande to convert the largely Protestant Anglo majority. Finally, Texans, unlike American colonists prior to 1776, even had representation in the Mexican state government of Coahuila-Texas.

In retrospect, rather than a fight for liberty, the 1835 Anglo-led revolution was a poorly conceived southern land grab that nearly failed. Texans had an overwhelming desire to expand slavery (an institution that Mexico had outlawed) and to use slave labor to increase profits made from cotton production.

Many American politicians, particularly those from the North, recognized the conspiratorial nature of the revolt and initially kept Texas from joining the American union. Texas formed a republic in 1836 and remained separate from the United States for nine years. During that time, Texas constantly feuded with Mexico, creating a "culture of war," or a persisting belief that violence against people was necessary for nation building.

The new republic raised voluntary armed forces to defend itself, and other paramilitary units formed independently. Texas became "militarized," as sons and fathers expected to fight and often embraced the opportunity. The rise of "Manifest Destiny" in the United States in 1845 further invigorated this militancy, and many Texans volunteered to fight in the Mexican War of 1846–1848. The war finally brought Texas into the union, along with other vast lands across the American West.

Yet Texas remained unique in comparison to other western U.S. territories and states. The Texas state government that emerged in 1845 retained control over public lands, including the vast prairies and plains to the west of the settled areas, even after entering the union (the only state added after the revolution to retain such control). From the 1840s onward, the Texas state legislature debated what to do with these lands. Gradually, state legislators in Austin claimed complete sovereignty and denied the claims of other deserving groups, including large populations of American Indians, many of whom were indigenous to Texas. State legislators even tried to convince the U.S. government that Texas owned the eastern half of what would become New Mexico, lands also claimed by Indian nations.

American Indians never relinquished their claim to Texas or the Great Plains. They fought the newcomers' advance into central and West Texas almost from the beginning of Anglo settlement. Fighting during the 1820s was initially limited to conflict with the small, depleted tribes of the Colorado and Guadalupe river valleys, known as Tonkawas and Karankawas. Most of these Indians were quickly forced into Mexico or westward, beyond the settlements.

As Texans moved up the Brazos River and southward from the Red River, however, they soon clashed with settled farmer Indians, such as the Wichitas and the Caddos. These peoples already had forfeited land to invading Indians from the East, the so-called immigrant bands—Cherokees, Choctaws, Creeks, Seminoles, Kickapoos, Shawnees, and Delawares—and were reluctant to retreat any farther into the interior. The ethnic milieu found in northeastern Texas in the 1830s was, in terms of the multiplicity of languages and lifeways, truly unique.

Texas formally expanded Indian warfare to the plains in 1839. Here, large numbers of immigrant Indians, renegade groups from Indian Territory, and Americans and Tejanos all interacted with the Comanches, Apaches, and Kiowas of the plains. These Plains societies had created an extremely successful political economy that depended on hunting, horse raising or stealing, and trading. Comanche lands extended deep into central Texas, including much of the Guadalupe and Colorado River watersheds.

Many of the newcomers from the East who mingled with the Comanches and Apaches promoted trade, but Texans fumed over such behavior, believing that it encouraged the selling of firearms. Texans, never a part of this economy, soon sought its destruction. Simultaneously, Texans moved up the Colorado River, challenging the Comanches for the hunting grounds that existed in its watershed.

Soon, the decade-long conflict with Mexico (1835–1845) merged with the violent and continuous wars with Indians. The struggle became an ethnic and racial feud that resulted in unimaginable destruction and the loss of thousands of lives.

Texans remained in a virtual state of war for nearly fifty years, the longest continuous struggle of its kind in American history. Indeed, the fighting subsided only with the defeat of the Comanche and Kiowa during the Red River campaigns of 1874–1875. Although the following statement may seem "presentistic" to some, in hindsight the conflict can be seen for what it was: an Anglo-Texas strategy and a policy (at first haphazard, debated, and even at times abandoned) that gradually led to the deliberate ethnic cleansing of a host of people, especially people of color.[2]

Taking such a view of history warrants explanation. While mostly ignored, a few scholars have suggested that Americans practiced genocide on Indians in certain regions of the United States, including Texas. I argue, however, that the situation in Texas fails to rise to the level of genocide, if genocide is defined as the intentional killing of nearly all of a racial, religious, or cultural group. I seek to draw an important distinction from it. Rather, Texans gradually endorsed (at first locally and eventually statewide) a policy of ethnic cleansing that had as its intention the forced removal of certain culturally identified groups from their lands. These target groups included Indians, especially, and to a smaller degree Tejanos. The story that follows is mostly that of the struggle between Texans and Indians.

Texans would have been pleased had the groups they wanted removed simply left without violence. But these groups did not. The conflict in Texas was over land; indiscriminate killing, while common during the fighting, never became prolonged, strategic, state policy on either side. Indians, for their part, practiced raiding and kidnapping on a large scale, but an accommodation with Americans in Texas was always possible. Comanches and Kiowas mostly raided weak societies, such as the Mexicans along the Rio Grande and south of it, because the Americans in Texas were better armed and capable of defeating the Indians' best efforts. The ethnic conflict continued in Texas because Anglos wanted it to; ethnic cleansing, not genocide, became state policy.

Recent studies in Yugoslavia and elsewhere reveal that political elites often direct the actions of paramilitary groups involved in ethnic cleansing. The situation was similar in Texas, where politicians supported Texas Ranger units that became the agents of ethnic cleansing. Rangers did act occasionally on their own, and politicians found them difficult if not, at times, impossible to control. Nevertheless, many politicians in the state had been rangers, and the paramilitary groups that forced removal or committed the occasional genocidal act were an extension of the Texas political system.

Anglo political elites likewise encouraged a great distrust of "the other" (which could be Indians or Tejanos), even at times in speeches individually calling for the extermination of Indians. Texas politicians urged on rangers, supported them with racially charged orations, and even belittled and coerced U.S. Army officers to the point that they too joined the violent crusade to rid the land of Indians and, at times, Tejanos.

The struggle in Texas was also heavily influenced by American Indian policy. During the administration of President Andrew Jackson, Congress passed a removal bill in 1830 in which the government forced most Indians from eastern states to areas west of the Mississippi River. Individual Indian families were allowed to stay on their lands if they agreed to become citizens of the state in which they lived and to take up farming. The government's goal was to remove "tribal" groups to the West. This removal policy at times may have approached ethnic cleansing, but mostly it did not, because it generally was designed to force assimilation. In many ways, it was an extension of the nineteenth-century doctrine of American liberal ideology that forced people to conform to the land settlement patterns created by the U.S. government, emphasizing small farms rather than large communal holdings.

Regardless of the intent of national policy, the Texas government clearly took a different view. It encouraged Texas Rangers, the enforcement arm of Texas policy, to attack Indian villages filled with women and children—the usual victims of ethnic cleansing. Rangers killed indiscriminately, they robbed, and they raped. Their goal was to spread terror so that neighboring Native groups would leave. As in Yugoslavia, they were quite successful at this business.

Texans openly embraced this ranger activity. Rangers soon became steeped in the heroic platitudes that made them legends in their own time; many went on to careers in politics, and a few dozen left memoirs. The Texas Rangers were mostly adventurers rather than settlers, seeing the rather aimless, mobile life of a ranger as more glamorous than picking cotton. Such men, often called to duty in a saloon, responded quickly to a threat and demonstrated boldness and courage equal to the best-trained troops.

As volunteers, rangers agreed to serve for limited terms—anywhere from a few weeks to six months. They provided their own horses and received a mere dollar and a quarter a day or frequently only their meals as compensation. Seldom possessing uniforms of any sort or even having an interest in sporting such garb, rangers could easily be recognized by their swagger, large floppy hats, heavy rifles, and occasionally swords. After 1840, no self-respecting ranger would ever be caught without a Colt five- or six-shot revolver strapped to his side, a most effective weapon that dramatically changed Indian warfare on the plains.

Some rangers were fine troops: well mounted, well led, and disciplined. Others were quite the opposite. Successful ranger captains such as John Coffee Hays refused to take ruffians. Hays maintained a healthy respect for the law, and his men gave good service. Other rangers, organized by local judges or politicians (often for show), stayed mostly at home, strutting in front of the young ladies-in-waiting in the small hamlets that dotted the lower Brazos and Colorado valleys. They seldom left the counties where they served.

A third type of ranger veteran, unfortunately, saw a term of service as an opportunity to pillage Indian or Mexican towns. The leaders of such groups promised pay in the form of scalps, hides, horses, and mules, all marketable in the cash-strapped Texas economy. Filled with hatred and malice, members of such groups seldom took prisoners or even asked whether the Indians they attacked were friendly or hostile. Rangers, then, could be brave defenders of the republic, rather harmless stay-at-home show-offs, or (more often than not) brutal murderers.

As rangers slowly cleared the West of Indians, politicians realized that large masses of land were becoming available for settlement. All of what is today central and West Texas—including the now famous Crawford Ranch, the beloved home of President George W. Bush, as well as the ranch once identified as the "Western White House" when Lyndon B. Johnson served in office—was taken from Indians without the formality of treaty negotiations. Some Texas politicians, less reactionary, tried negotiating with the various tribes. A few even wrote treaties that contained boundaries that in essence granted Indian ownership to land. The attempts to create boundaries or to agree to any line separating Indian and Texan ownership of land produced hot debates in the Texas legislature. In the end, Texans refused to accept a boundary that separated Indians and Anglos. Eventually it became impossible politically to suggest that Indians had legitimate rights to land.

Even the federal government, which entered Texas to solve the "Indian problem" in 1849, would ultimately adopt ranger tactics and endorse ethnic cleansing. While trying to effect a peaceful solution in the early 1850s, the U.S. government established two small reservations for the Texas tribes along the upper Brazos River. Texas Rangers ultimately broke up the reservations. Some of these so-called rangers were clearly renegades who rustled livestock on the side under the guise of enforcing the law. Soon thereafter, the U.S. Army declared all Indians in Texas to be hostile and herded those that could be caught onto reservations in Indian Territory. A primary reason for the organization of the newly invented First and Second United States Cavalry in 1855 by Secretary of War Jefferson Davis was to search out and destroy villages of Comanches, who refused to accept this ultimatum.

It is evident that as the Civil War approached, Texas was a very violent place. The war only exacerbated this circumstance. Texans mostly blamed Indians for the violence—an unfair indictment, since a series of terrible droughts had virtually incapacitated the Plains Indians, making them incapable of extended warfare. Violence in Texas during the war and in its aftermath was mostly locally manufactured, the product of conflict originating out of the debate over secession, which Texans were divided over, and a result of the large numbers of so-called bush-men, many of whom were draft dodgers, and rustlers who had invaded the state. They would continue to create havoc into the 1870s, when the Indians were finally defeated, and thereafter.

An accurate history of this entire story has largely eluded historians. The first generation of historians lived the events that they described. Among them was John Henry Brown, whose two-volume *History of Texas from 1685 to 1892*, published in 1893, became a classic. Brown had been a Texas Ranger in the 1850s. Deeply involved in the attacks on the Texas Indian reservations in 1858 and 1859, he solemnly served as the first hagiographer of the rangers. And Brown's version of history influenced nearly every writer that followed.

Brown was also strongly influenced by John Wesley Wilbarger, who had published *Indian Depredations in Texas* four years earlier.[3] Wilbarger came to Texas in the 1830s with his brother Josiah. Soon thereafter Josiah was scalped and left for dead by Indians. John Wilbarger, reeling from the experience, became an avid Indian-hater who during his long life recorded nearly every major and minor clash that occurred between Indians and Texans. His *Indian Depredations* methodically lists casualties on both sides, complete with names and dates. Nearly two hundred engagements are recorded (some entries, a mere half page in length, describing an Indian attack on an isolated ranch or farm), giving complete details of casualties on both sides.

Wilbarger's book is understandably racist and biased, but it provides the most complete listing of casualties available, starting in 1823 and ending in 1875. Surprisingly, however, the casualty numbers that he offers run completely counter to the standard interpretation of Texas history—that Comanches and other Indians killed hordes of Texan settlers and raped and pillaged their way across the frontier for five decades. Adding up Wilbarger's numbers of killed on each side, the reader soon ascertains that Indians more often suffered at the hands of Texans than vice-versa. Indeed, Wilbarger's numbers show that roughly four hundred Anglos and African American slaves lost their lives during the fight for Texas (some deaths clearly being the work of renegades); Indian losses, however, ranged from seven hundred to a thousand people. Even so, Wilbarger's numbers fail to include Indians killed in ranger attacks on their villages or by the U.S. Army.

Texas Rangers carried the fighting to Indian villages early in the war. One classic description recited by Wilbarger is example enough of their tactics. As rangers hit a Comanche village in 1839, they "charged and fired a volley into the tents and wigwams, killing indiscriminately a number of all ages and sexes." As the carnage continued, the rangers saw "women screaming, and children crying—all running hither and thither and against and over each other in their flight." Wilbarger remains silent on how many Indians died during such an attack, even as he wallows in the success of the expedition: "Little did these blood thirsty monsters think they could or would be sought out in their distant home."[4]

Wilbarger also does not count the hundreds or thousands of Indian deaths resulting from the army's attack on Comanche towns, starting in the late 1850s and lasting into 1875. Many Indians clearly starved to death in the aftermath of these attacks, when they returned to their villages in winter to find that their tents and carefully packaged dried bison meat had been burned or stolen. In reality, the number of Indian casualties reported by Wilbarger should likely be doubled or even quadrupled.

Since Wilbarger also included dates for each engagement, time lines for the Texas Indian wars can be established. Roughly half the engagements occurred during the years 1835 to 1843, when Texans were pushing up the Colorado, Brazos, and Trinity rivers, seizing the country around what would become Austin, Waco, and Dallas. Here, Comanches, Wichitas, and Caddos made a stand—and lost. Surprisingly, there were exceedingly few engagements in the late 1840s or into the early 1850s, when the army arrived in Texas. Fighting resumed in 1857 and continued into 1860, lapsed then, and broke out again after 1864. Over a third of the engagements Wilbarger reports occurred during these periods. The final struggle opened in the region of the Panhandle and lasted throughout 1874–1875. Texas state militia troops had nineteen engagements with Indians during these years, although the U.S. Army bore the brunt of the fighting.

Drawn to the dynastic elements inherent in the birth of the republic and the many battles that were fought in the late 1830s, 1850s, and 1860s, the first generation of modern twentieth-century Texas historians wrote epic tomes that glorified the lives of the Texas heroes who fought against Indians. Historians Walter Prescott Webb, Eugene C. Barker, and Rupert N. Richardson all viewed the ethnic fighting over land in Texas as little different from the story of the American frontier—as part of nation building.[5] Much of this interpretation still exists in some histories and is especially prevalent in Hollywood movies depicting the region, an excellent example being *The Searchers* (1956), with John Wayne. Somewhat dated but still a classic, the film's plot centers on a raid on a Texas ranch, the massacre of a family, and the captivity of two young girls, the eldest being brutally raped and murdered by the Indians.

Many recent revisionists have moved beyond this hagiography, yet the new revisionist historiography is narrowly focused (often on ethnic groups), and it is tangential to the Texas story. Some new tribal studies outline the history and culture of the Comanches, Caddos, Wichitas, Texas Cherokees, and even the less-known Tonkawas and Karankawas.[6] Such studies are usually interrupted by the Texas Revolution, some concentrating on the Spanish and Mexican periods and others on the Texas conflict with Indians during the Civil War and thereafter. As a result of the growing interest in social history, recent biographies of major characters such as Stephen Austin and Sam Houston focus on family life and politics, if not ignoring Indians or Indian policy completely.[7]

Tejano historians, or those who address the Hispanic aspect of early Texas history, have offered many insightful additions to this historiography. Much scholarship now views Tejanos as willing partners with Anglos or at least as sympathetic to local government rule—a fresh view, given the near absence of such people from most Texas histories. Today, the historic Tejano community is often portrayed as "an entity different from Mexico" and Tejanos as people who occasionally even supported capitalism and slavery in Texas. Some built and maintained successful communities—especially along the Rio Grande and at San Antonio, Goliad, and Nacogdoches—and contributed politically and socially to the emergence of Texas. Others fled back to Mexico in the face of growing racial prejudice and adversity.[8]

The history of these Tejanos, as well as that of Indian peoples, has often constituted a nearly separate story. As Tejano historian Jesús F. de la Teja has rightly pointed out, much of the newest history of Texas, including even the most widely used college-level textbooks, "almost completely ignores Tejanos" and their role.[9] Yet during the struggle over the conquest of Texas, Indians played a greater role in trying to turn back the Anglo tide than did Tejanos: Indians fought more battles with Anglos, and the Indians were simply better armed. The Indian wars in Texas went on for virtually fifty years. While historians can no longer ignore the Tejano contribution to the history of early Texas (this study attempts to include them), Tejano history is much more dynamic in the twentieth century, when Tejanos fought to regain their lost heritage in Texas. Despite such a caveat, it seems almost incomprehensible to write any early Texas history without including Tejanos and Indians at every turn.

Just as unthinkable is a history of Texas without the most recognizable icon of the state's past—the Texas Rangers. The rangers sit at the apex of a mythological Texas, being the foundation, to a degree, to the hagiography that dominates the region's nineteenth- and even twentieth-century history. The memoirs of various rangers suggest that they never ran, even when facing massive odds; and unlike the martyrs of the Alamo, the rangers always won their battles. In one study, published in 2002, noted historian Robert M. Utley offers a modern portrayal of this group of men. While acknowledging the often brutal tactics of the rangers, the author equates them with the Sons of Liberty, or the Minutemen of the American Revolution. The chapters on ranger tradition argue that rangers were "citizen soldiers." Thus, "By heritage . . . they were fighters. They made up a society that prized virility, valor, and fortitude, and they stood ready to take up arms when called." As the prosecutors of law and order in Texas, Utley asserts, they took up those arms in the name of justice.[10]

Those on the receiving end of such "justice" were often American Indians or Tejanos. To justify the actions of Texas Rangers, who have always been portrayed as heroes in Texas history, accounts such as Utley's tend to vilify the rangers' opponents, mostly Comanche Indians, as incarnations of the Devil. Comanches, according to this view, made war their "greatest obsession," preying on everyone "from infants to old people, of both sexes, by rape, pillage, torture, brutal treatment of captives, and frightful butchery of the dead."[11] Even today Texas historians find it exceedingly difficult to see the raping and pillaging of Indians and Tejanos by Texas Rangers as anything other than justifiable combat or the acceptable behavior of "boys being boys." Few historians when surveying this conflict have moved much beyond Brown and Wilbarger.

Perhaps inevitably, historians who buy into the benevolent-ranger mythology simplify the motives and goals of Tejanos. Utley, to take one example, states that Tejanos "called themselves Mexicans, they spoke Spanish, their loyalties ran to Mexico, and their culture was largely Mexican."[12] In reality, Hispanic Texans called themselves Tejanos, their loyalties were divided, and their culture was in transition (as are all cultures), with some embracing the economic ideology of Anglos and some wishing to remain in a precapitalistic state.

Fortunately, a number of Texas historians have joined together to offer a new synthesis of Texas history, one that is objective and fair in terms of the material covered; but this new approach still has difficulty in giving Indians their due as people. Robert Calvert and Walter Buenger, in an essay entitled "The Shelf Life of Truth in Texas," explore the mythology that is so strongly represented in the corpus of Texas history. To prove the point, they collected essays from like-minded revisionist scholars and produced an anthology entitled *Texas through Time,* which they describe as a "new synthesis."[13] Various historians in this anthology offer essays on "Texas Mexicans" (or Tejanos), "African Americans in Texas," and even "Texas Women." But there is incredible irony in this new history—somehow the first occupants of Texas, the American Indians, got left out. It is as if the editors had difficulty dealing with the fate of the Texas Indians and their humanity; indeed, the editors seem to say that if Indians could not be projected as culturally viable people, who made a contribution, then ignore them.

One of the members of this new school (a contributor to *Texas through Time*), Randolph B. Campbell, recently published the first new Texas history textbook to appear in many years. Campbell describes the Tejano elites as people who dreamed of "a dynamic, capitalistic northern Mexico," connected in commerce with the United States. This is certainly a revisionist view. Campbell's discussion of Texas Indians appears mostly in a section devoted to the frontier. Here the author shows sympathy for Indians, primarily in his discussion of the failure of the state to recognize Indian claims to land. While this is a good beginning, Indians appear in the text only modestly thereafter. Unfortunately, despite an attempt at being even-handed, in what amounts to a conclusion, Campbell utilizes the same rhetoric as many authors who have preceded him: when all is said and done, he concludes that Indians left behind a trail "of theft, rape, murder, and mutilation." Rangers and soldiers never did such a thing; they were the protectors of an advancing civilization.[14]

Unfortunately, then, Texas history even today is dominated either by the hallowed, nationalistic rhetoric of nation building or by individual studies of ethnic or racial groups who seemingly were denied a place in the nation being built. It is exculpatory history, at least in terms of Anglo guilt. In describing Anglo settlement (1821–1833), the Texas Revolution (1835–1836), the establishment of the republic (1836–1845), and early statehood (1845–1875)—most histories either tell the story of disconnected groups of victims or depict Anglo actors striding boldly across a grand Texas stage. They are, in a word, "heroic" figures. They are the defenders of the Alamo, the writers of the Texas Declaration of Independence, the martyrs of the attack on Judge Parker's Fort, and, of course, the Texas Rangers.

The historiographic problem is likely a result of the traditional way in which late-twentieth-century historians have examined Texas history: part by part, age by age, and group by group. Perhaps this explains why the most widely read general synthesis of this story (Calvert and Buenger's edited volume and Campbell's text have yet to change this) is still T. R. Fehrenbach's *Lone Star: A History of Texas and the Texans* (1968). This readable albeit hefty tome has sold thousands of copies since it first appeared. Numerous reprints have been issued, most recently in 1997. In Fehrenbach's section on the Texas frontier—one entitled "Red Niggers, Red Vermin"—he argues that early Texans were justified in taking the land, an act that "cannot be fairly rejected or criticized by those who failed to share the Texan experience."[15] Fehrenbach commonly uses the term "savage" in describing Texas Indians. An individual Indian, almost always assumed to be a Comanche, was incapable of compassion and was immersed in a lifestyle of butchery and lust. Texans, who might have been brutal at times in conquering the land, nevertheless represent the inevitability of human progress. They killed for the sake of advancing civilization, never once committing a massacre, while Indians "murdered and raped" because they represented a flawed humanity.

In all fairness, Fehrenbach's popular study represents an approach that most academics have long since relegated to unused bookshelves. Yet general studies of the conflict over the promised land of Texas that would replace Fehrenbach's volume have not appeared.

Some newer histories have occasionally distorted the story even more in the other direction—toward what is generally called "victim history."[16] Fodder for this school is David E. Stannard's recent *American Holocaust: The Conquest of the New World* (1992), in which Stannard extends the genocide theme to the entire Western Hemisphere. Such books turn isolated events into trends and blame all Euro-Americans for consequences that chronologically span four centuries and involve a multitude of factors.[17]

Fehrenbach and Stannard, then, represent the narrative poles around which general Texas histories tend to cluster even today—inevitable progress obtained at unfortunate (often unavoidable) costs, versus horrific and deliberate genocide. The book that follows is not an academic conversation with either Fehrenbach or Stannard but rather an effort to create a new paradigm for understanding the violence that dominated Texas history, especially along its frontier, by utilizing the more moderate and well-understood process of ethnic cleansing. And much like the Europeans and Asians of more recent times, some of whom saw ethnic cleansing as a regrettable necessity, Texans struggled with the implementation of the policy. Indeed, some earnestly fought to overcome the deep-seated racism that gripped their society; but they were in the minority.

This work also attempts a new cultural conversation to advance our understanding of ethnic conflict in the American West. Comanches became excellent breeders of horses, building a political economy that benefited Anglos, especially those on the high plains and in New Mexico, but one that was based, to some degree, on raiding. Caddos and Wichitas were fine farmers even though they never cropped cotton. These same Caddos and Wichitas often served as scouts for rangers and the army. Cherokees built towns, farms, and even schools in Texas. And despite scholarly arguments to the contrary, Tejanos often taught Anglos how to be cowboys and wanted to become respectable ranchers themselves, exporting their mutton and beef to the United States. All of these groups made contributions to Texas history; they can no longer be dismissed as simple murderers and rapists.

Why, then, did most Anglos come to condemn Indians and Tejanos despite their important economic contributions? The dominant Anglos had a cultural justification for their racism—non-Anglo ethnic groups possessed different languages, different dress, different economies, and different religions—in short, different cultures that Anglos marginalized in terms of their value. The justification for attacks upon such non-Anglo groups evolved out of an imagined fear that such groups would somehow pollute what Anglos perceived as their superior culture. Nonconformity to an Anglo-southern culture offered the ultimate rationale for the seizure of Indian and Tejano land and property.

As conflict widened and Indians lost more and more land, they often sought revenge upon Texas settlements. Comanches rightfully became convinced of Texans' inhumanity, and the deadly actions of their war parties (while universally overplayed by Texas politicians, newspaper editors, and even twentieth-century historians) has had a dramatic impact on the Anglo-Texan psyche, both then and now. Comanches did raid ranches and farms. The raids on the Parker, Lockhart, and Webster families between 1836 and 1838 resulted in eighteen deaths and the carrying into captivity of a dozen women and children. These rather minor raids, in comparison to ranger attacks on Indian villages, were the most destructive on record. But they provided the foundation for a growing folklore and mythical literature that depicted the savagery of Indians and the utter helplessness of the Texas frontier family. Texas newspapers reprinted the hellish stories that emitted from these raids, embellishing them and continuing the myth of the poor, noble, embattled Texas frontiersmen.

The role of this folklore became apparent by the 1850s. Despite the success of the U.S. Army in ending depredations, newspapers in the state launched a massive campaign condemning the army for its failures. Most readers accepted the charge that depredations continued unabated: that a hundred thousand animals had been stolen from Texas farms and ranches and that hundreds of people had been killed by Indians. Many Texans at the time failed to recognize that law and order was collapsing in northwestern Texas as well as in the trans-Nueces region, the lands between the Nueces River and the Rio Grande.

A whole host of men participated in this chaotic bloodshed. These included many Anglos (some of whom were pioneers but mostly Texas Rangers), some mixed-blood Indians from Indian Territory, and Tejanos from southern Texas and northern Mexico who fought to regain or retain their lands and property. The outbreak of the Civil War only expanded this violent and lawless situation.

If the history of Texas is to be chronicled with some degree of objectivity, it first must be placed within the context of these many ethnic and culturally diverse groups. There must be an alternative to Fehrenbach, who hails the triumphant Texan, as well as to Stannard, the excoriating revisionist. Historians must retell Texas history as it really is, an unfolding of interconnected events driven by racial prejudices born of cultural conflict, unfamiliar lifestyles, disparate political and economic goals, and, on the part of Texas officials and leaders, overly strong commitments to land development and nation building.

What is more, approaching objectivity in Texas history requires recognizing that all the peoples in Texas possessed goals and motives that approached, at one time or another, righteousness as well as malevolence. When analyzing these motives and goals, a thorough historian must don many hats: the warbonnet, the sombrero, the Stetson, and the cockaded cavalry fedora. Texas history must also go beyond assuming that all subgroups in Texas—Indian, Tejano, or Anglo—uniformly had common goals just because they may have had similar ethnic identities. Texans were seldom unanimous in the development of an Indian policy or in support of ethnic cleansing (even though those supporting ethnic cleansing won out); and Texas Indians were never united in any defense of their lands or a raiding lifestyle. In what will surprise some readers, many Indian leaders worked to suppress bloodshed. For their part, Tejanos were the most disunited of all: some were monarchists, some aristocrats, some successful ranchers, some liberal revolutionaries, and some simply *vecinos,* or commoners, tired of the trials of life under Mexican rule.

Then as now the inhabitants of Texas faced circumstances and choices that had wished-for as well as feared consequences. Nothing was inevitable. Many people in Texas, including Indians who had experienced centuries of contact with Spaniards, were already in various stages of acculturation when Anglos arrived—change was under way. Left alone, both Tejanos and Indians would have acculturated much of what has become Texan. Many Tejanos had already embraced republican capitalism. And Indians likely would have willingly discarded the warbonnet for the broad-brimmed felt hat over time. The story of Texas might have been different.

Today, the Texas story can no longer be depicted as a righteous conquest by a courageous few bringing civilization to a "wild" land. The many different voices and cultures that constitute Texas history make for a more demanding tale, a history that starts to make sense only when the very roots of the conflict are exposed. Texas promised much to many. The contest that resulted proved an angry and brutal one. And as is true with most historical drama turned violent, the battle over Texas land had much more to do with conquest than liberation, more to do with extreme racial hatred and commitment to martial violence than economic needs.

1

AT THE DAWN OF THE
AMERICAN INVASION

The year was 1815. The weather for June was hot and dry, as a drought had hit the great plains of Texas. Riding over yet another rise in a seemingly endless prairie, a tired Reuben Ross and his trading party suddenly saw a massive camp of more than five hundred bison-skin tepees before them in a beautiful valley. The town covered several miles of the upper Brazos River. Ross was startled and pleased. He had discovered the main encampment of some of the most powerful Indians in Texas and, in terms of livestock, some of the richest.

Each circular tepee stood sixteen feet tall, with a ground diameter of twelve feet. Most had bison hides stacked eight or nine deep inside to make for comfortable bedding. In and about the tepees, campfires were clustered, with copper kettles hung over them in readiness for the midday meal. Children, half-naked owing to the heat but healthy and well fed, scurried around the camp. Ross could see that these were a successful people.

The Comanches were busy putting in a stock of bison meat. Everyone in camp seemed busy. Next to the tepees, young women tended racks hung with fresh meat, drying in the wind. Built six feet off the ground, the racks were high enough to keep the hundreds of dogs milling greedily about from grabbing a morsel. Intermixed were large frames where other women stretched and cleaned hides. The idyllic scene likely distracted Ross from an obvious reality—the butchering produced a considerable odor, and the women who did it, despite their dexterity, often had their deerskin frocks covered with blood at the end of the day.

Shifting his view to the horizon, Ross saw what he and his friends had come for. Along the far ridges and beyond he could see horses, thousands of them—perhaps twenty thousand animals in a camp that size. Boys tended these animals, the older ones of twelve or thirteen giving orders, but many younger lads only five or six years old following them. Ross could not be sure, but the camp seemed to hold at least five thousand people.[1]

Comanches were sturdy people, strong, independent of will, and committed to their freedom and their plains lifestyle. At times, they ate mostly bison meat for sustenance. The women boiled it, served it in a soup, or handed it out as jerky. Comanche camps seemed disordered to the common observer, but senior women directed the labor necessary for food, clothing, and housing. The women who ran the camp could be distinguished by the orders they gave and the clothing they wore. Most had some jewelry and often a blanket to cover their simple deerskin frocks and leggings. Those with greater status might wear a cloth over one shoulder, like a sash.

Men lounged around the camp seemingly uninterested in domestic affairs. This attitude changed when hunting or raiding parties left. Then they dressed for the occasion, donning a breechcloth and decorative leggings that stopped below the knee and turned into moccasins. During winter, they wore bison-skin coats with an attached hood. Comanche men took obvious pride in their weapons. Typically, each carried a bison-skin shield nearly four feet long, a knife, a quiver with arrows and bow, and a long lance. They favored close combat and occasionally clashed with other tribes, as cavalry on the plains had done since the early 1600s to protect their hunting ranges. By the time Ross found them, a few had acquired short trade muskets. The chiefs especially carried these arms for status. They also wore magnificent headdresses with eagle feathers, the train of which sometimes reached the ground and included the hair of their several wives, woven in.

Seldom did Plains Indian villages reach the size that Ross observed; June was a special time when many bands of Comanches came together to hunt, feast, and dance. Other Indian bands that lived nearby or visited the Comanches were not as numerous. Nevertheless, likely nowhere else in America did so many different kinds of Indians come together to talk and barter. Ross was surprised to see so many others in the Comanche town, including Kiowas, Wichitas, Delawares, and Lipan Apaches. And farther east, back in the wooded river valleys of Texas, were others—Caddos, Karankawas, and Tonkawas—whom Ross had passed before entering the plains.

All of these peoples possessed a belief in themselves, their way of life, and their religion. Though they never built churches, they knew the afterlife well. They had a sense of morality—they knew what actions were necessary to preserve themselves and their society and to reach their utopian life beyond death. Texas Indians were quick to defend this way of life. Conventional pioneer wisdom often said that no one ever saw an Indian more self-assured than a Comanche sitting astride a horse, whether in war or on the hunt for bison.

Some Native Texas groups were less militant than the Comanches, more prone to nurture their farms and sedentary towns nestled in the river bottoms Ross had crossed before entering the plains. These people held Green Corn ceremonies that represented a cultural richness in religion, folklore, and social organization that was six or seven centuries old. They farmed and hunted. On the coast were superb fishermen. Overall, the first occupants of Texas were successful people. They shared their food, raised their children to be fiercely protective of their way of life (rebelliousness was not tolerated), and survived and prospered in a land that required endurance, fortitude, and organization.

The Comanches were actually the last indigenous group to arrive in Texas, having migrated into the plains around 1700. Apaches, Wichitas, Caddos, Tonkawas, and Karankawas had been there for centuries, and most had had extensive contact with early Spaniards. Those living in East Texas had known Frenchmen. Intertribal warfare and conflict with invading Spaniards had existed early on, but contact also had led to exchange or, as Europeans called it, "trade." While Spanish missionaries sought to convert the Native societies, most of the Franciscans had little success. The Wichitas and Caddos were too far north of the mission enclave at San Antonio, which eventually became the Spanish capital of Texas, and the Apaches, Tonkawas, Karankawas, and Comanches were too mobile and too independent. Karankawas lived along the gulf coast on sea animals and deer and seldom settled in one locale long enough to listen seriously to a sermon.

Nevertheless, prosperity from commerce affected everyone in the region, Spaniards and Indians alike, and ultimately Spain gave up trying to conquer Texas. Instead, it agreed to a negotiated peace with the tribes. The agreements that Spanish officials brokered with Comanches, Wichitas, Tonkawas, and Apaches in the 1780s led to the expansion of Mexican ranching in southern Texas as well as the development of larger Indian livestock herds. No other Indians had as many horses as did the Comanches, and they, along with their Wichita and Caddo neighbors, even learned to breed mules, an increasingly important commodity in the American market after 1815.[2] This peace, broken occasionally by small raids, remained in place until 1810, when the war for independence began in Mexico.

Given the presumption of Indian "savagery," a view held by many Texans in later years, it seems almost heresy to suggest that the Indians of the southern plains built a political economy that thrived on an ordered and at times peaceful acquisition of wealth. But that is what happened in the late eighteenth century.[3] Wichitas and Caddos were excellent farmers who produced bountiful crops, and most of the Plains people who avoided agriculture had mastered pastoralism, raising both horses and mules. They also took hundreds of bison for meat each year, preserving the hides and drying the meat into jerky. Plains Indians produced hides, tallow, jerky, and livestock, which they commonly exchanged at San Antonio, Laredo, or Santa Fe, New Mexico, and these products rapidly found their way into the Spanish economy.[4]

Intertribal commerce also prospered. One Indian group would have a surplus of bison meat, robes, and horses, while another would have large quantities of corn, beans, and melons; Spaniards manufactured goods that also entered this market. Applying market value to such items proved impossible, and Indians and Spaniards alike exchanged them, enhancing each other's diet or lifestyle and thereby preserving alliances.

Chiefs, or senior men within the Native societies, controlled the process of exchange through councils, negotiating agreements with other Indian groups and Europeans. These men acquired their authority initially through a demonstrated bravery in war. Once their leadership was recognized, they maintained their authority through the redistribution of goods to their people, which gave them greater status and political power. Such success among Plains people also led to the acquisition of wives, sometimes nearly a dozen.

Fundamentally, chiefs often opposed war, at least with exchange partners, because it disrupted the economic system that they had created. Indeed, chiefs often bonded themselves to their fellow exchange partners (senior leaders in other villages or European towns) through alliances. Such agreements were negotiated and maintained by the giving of presents. Reciprocal relationships were so important in the Southwest that Spaniards had to agree to honor them or face war. The same held true for the various tribal societies that created such bonds.

Raiding, or warfare of any kind, was thus reserved for peoples who lacked a reciprocal or economic relationship. For the Comanches, this included their enemies: Pawnees, Arapahos, Cheyennes, and Osage Indians to the north and Tonkawas and sometimes Lipan Apaches to the south. Wichitas and Caddos had the same enemies and often joined the Comanches. After 1810, such raiding was extended to northern Mexico.

Warfare was also more frequently conducted by young men who were seeking status, hoping to acquire power and wives in Plains society. Tension, then, existed within the Plains communities, often driven by honor and shame, violence and kinship, and diplomacy and war, the dichotomies of Indian life.

As the process evolved, particularly among the Comanches and Wichitas, tribes became wealthier and more socially stratified. European wares enhanced this new socioeconomic formation, as manufactured goods became marks of distinction and status. Thus, Texas Native societies learned to reach out to Europeans and Americans such as Ross. Indeed, as early as 1790, several Americans who were connected with the horse trader Philip Nolan had penetrated the plains to attend Indian "exchange fairs." They left few records but imported thousands of horses into the Louisiana market until Nolan was killed by a Spanish patrol in 1801.

Even as exchange helped sustain political hierarchies in Indian communities, it augmented cultural diffusion. Ideas and mores common to both Indians and Europeans found their way into Spanish and Indian towns. From 1786 to 1810, Indian diplomatic and exchange missions freely entered Spanish towns, where leaders held councils as Indian women hawked their goods and talked with the local citizenry. The Spanish benefited from these relationships to such an extent that Spanish ranchers expanded well up the Rio Grande valley and spilled over into the Nueces River valley of southern Texas by 1800. Some Spanish ranchers even marketed their expanding cattle herds in Louisiana.[5]

Spaniards dubbed the period of prosperity the "false peace," since a few disgruntled Comanche and Wichita young men occasionally defied their chiefs and launched a raid or two, mostly to acquire horses. Chiefs, hoping to maintain peace, would occasionally return the animals to the Spaniards. These restitutions indicate a surprising level of mutual respect in the way Indian and non-Indian groups interacted. In a council at San Antonio with Governor Antonio Cordero in 1807, leading Comanche, Wichita, and Lipan Apache chiefs spoke at great length of their appreciation for the state of affairs. "I cannot express to Your Lordship," Governor Cordero wrote to the commandant general, "the energy with which they spoke against the evils of war, the sane morals they set forth, and the opportune remarks they made on this matter." Their speeches, he said, left him "impressed and aware of the injustice that is done" to the Indians "in considering them nothing but savages."[6]

In some regards, the Spanish had little choice other than to accept the false peace. Demographically, American Indians were the most populous people in Texas in 1820; some thirty thousand indigenous Natives, the majority of them hard-riding Comanches, called it home. Probably forty thousand Comanches had inhabited Texas in the 1780s, when the peace was established. But epidemics of smallpox had struck in 1781, 1800, and 1816, lowering the Comanche population to roughly twenty thousand by 1820. Their numbers declined to about twelve thousand by the 1830s and 1840s, primarily because of more epidemics, including the first reported incidents of cholera.

The farming Indians of Texas, such as the Wichitas and Caddos, were perhaps the most productive despite small populations. They had suffered from the same epidemics as the Comanches, their numbers plummeting to about five thousand people in 1820. They lived in a half-dozen towns spread out along the Brazos, Trinity, and Red rivers. The Caddos, who numbered perhaps two thousand, had fractured into eastern and western villages, the easternmost establishing farming communities along what would become the Louisiana border, while the western Caddos had moved into the Neches and Trinity river valleys. The severe drought of 1806 to 1821 had damaged their economy; crop failures were common during this period.[7]

When crops failed, the farmer Indians turned to hunting, entering the plains to take bison. These animals had roamed the plains in the millions of animals in earlier centuries, but they also had been affected by the severe drought of the early part of the century. The hide trade was a second factor in the decline of bison, as thousands of animals were slaughtered each year for their hides by the 1830s. This hunting domain of the southwestern Texas Indians extended from the Arkansas

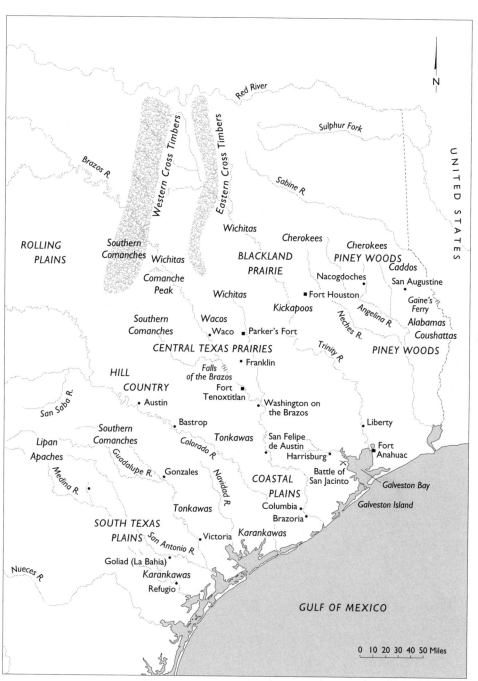

N

Red River

Sulphur Fork

Brazos R.

Western Cross Timbers

Eastern Cross Timbers

Sabine R.

UNITED STATES

ROLLING
PLAINS

Southern
Comanches   Wichitas

Comanche
Peak

Wichitas

Wichitas

BLACKLAND
PRAIRIE

Cherokees

Cherokees

PINEY WOODS

Caddos

Nacogdoches

San Augustine

Fort Houston

Gaine's
Ferry

Kickapoos

Angelina R.

Neches R.

Alabamas
Coushattas

Southern
Comanches

Wacos

Waco   Parker's Fort

CENTRAL TEXAS PRAIRIES

Franklin

PINEY WOODS

Trinity R.

Falls
of the Brazos

HILL
COUNTRY

San Saba R.

Austin

Fort
Tenoxtitlan

Washington on
the Brazos

Bastrop

Liberty

Lipan
Apaches

Southern
Comanches

Colorado R.

Tonkawas

San Felipe
de Austin

Fort
Anahuac

Guadalupe R.

Harrisburg

Medina R.

Gonzales

Navidad R.

Battle of
San Jacinto

Galveston Bay

COASTAL
PLAINS

Galveston Island

Tonkawas

Columbia

SOUTH TEXAS
PLAINS

San Antonio R.

Victoria

Karankawas

Brazoria

Nueces R.

Goliad (La Bahia)

Karankawas

Refugio

GULF OF MEXICO

0 10 20 30 40 50 Miles

Texas, 1820–1840

River nearly to the Rio Grande, some one thousand miles. It was nearly as wide, beginning in central Texas and extending into the foothills of New Mexico.

The Apaches who had once inhabited much of that domain had been pushed deep into southern Texas and northern Mexico by the Comanches by 1820. They occasionally allied with yet another group, the Tonkawas, a small tribe of southeastern Texas. To the east of the Tonkawas, along the gulf coast, lived a final survivor of the early Spanish missions—the Karankawas. Living in small bands that mostly fished and hunted deer, the Karankawas numbered only a few hundred by the time of Anglo occupation in 1820.

In retreat, Apaches had built strongholds in the mountains of southeastern New Mexico and along the Rio Grande and Nueces rivers. By the period of Anglo settlement, only a few Apache bands, called mostly Lipan Apaches, remained in Texas; one or two of these bands tried to maintain friendly relations with Texans. The animosities that had characterized Apache-Comanche relations early on had subsided by 1820, but Apaches would occasionally act as guides for Anglo or Mexican military forces against Comanche towns.

The Comanche people who had inherited the bison-hunting lands of the southern plains constituted twelve bands, broken geographically into southern and northern groups. The southern bands comprised the Penatekas ("Honey Eaters") and the Hois ("Comanches of the Woods"). The northern Comanches, generically designated as Yamparicas by the Spaniards, were divided into three major bands and a number of smaller ones. The three main groups included the Tanimas (or Tenawas), Kotchatecas (or Cuchanticas), and Quahadas (also called Naconis). Americans later corrupted these names, creating a number of variants, some of which were almost unrecognizable.[8] The southern Comanches faced the reality of diminishing bison herds first, as the surviving animals moved northward, away from central Texas. By the 1850s, when at most only a few million animals remained, a number of southern Comanches joined northern bands.

Comanche pride in themselves and their society held them to a strict code of conduct—one, for example, that generally prohibited the consumption of alcohol, at least prior to the reservation period starting in the 1850s. A Comanche man needed to prove himself to acquire a wife and thus a family and, ultimately, standing in the society. When a young man failed or became deformed by a wound, he often killed himself rather than face the rebukes and ridicule of his people. Comanche men never surrendered to an enemy under any circumstances. Partly this was because the society practiced patrilocal marriage; a young man lived in the kin group of his father and thus had uncles who constantly judged his development. To let them down was unthinkable.

Wichita and Caddo communities, nestled along the timbered river valleys of central and northeastern Texas, possessed a worldview that was more sedentary and associated with agricultural celebration. The sandy-loam soil of their river valleys required little tilling for the patches of corn, beans, squash, and pumpkin that they grew. Commonly, they planted corn first, then allowed the bean plants to crawl up the cornstalks. This allowed for an easy harvest: women pulled up the plant intact and carried it back to their house. The cornstalks were fed to the horses. Because they could harvest two crops a year, Wichitas and Caddos usually produced an excess of food that could be exchanged with Comanches or others.

In 1820 the main eastern Caddo village of some four or five hundred souls was located just beyond the junction of the Sabine and Red rivers near Caddo Lake in Louisiana. Many of the men and women in the town were part French or part African American. Western Caddos had moved into central Texas in the late eighteenth century, some intermarrying with Wichitas, who had similar agricultural settlements.[9] One such band, the Kichai, was part Caddo and part Wichita. The western Caddos, unlike their eastern relatives, maintained some distance between themselves and the advancing Americans, whose liquor and diseases slowly decimated the eastern group.

Wichitas, closely related to the Caddos in language and culture, had permanent villages along the Red River in Texas well before Spanish contact. Intertribal warfare with well-armed Osages and Pawnees to the north, however, had pushed some of the Wichitas into central Texas. By 1820, two main Wichita towns existed along the Brazos River, one being occupied mostly by Tawakoni Wichitas and the other by the Waco Wichitas. (The latter would later give up their name and village to what became Waco, Texas.)

To the north, Taovayas Wichitas formed several villages along the Trinity River and tributaries of the Red River. These towns held the majority of the Wichita population. One large group, however, had moved into the region near the Wichita Mountains of southwestern Oklahoma and founded a famous town that U.S. Army troops first visited in 1834. Many different Indians, including some northern Pawnees (or Black Pawnees, as the French called them), also occasionally visited the Wichitas. These northern Wichitas had considerable trouble maintaining recip-rocal relationships with both the Comanches and the Pawnees because the latter two tribes were constantly at war.[10] Some southern Wichitas accordingly chose sides; a good many ran with Comanches, even joining Comanche war parties, while others slowly moved south.

Both Wichitas and Caddos had a matrilineal social system in which senior women possessed significant power. Married Wichita and Caddo men lived with their wives' relatives in houses where they owned practically nothing. They did join male societies that promoted hunting and even raiding, but their sedentary village life encouraged a domesticity that tempered the urge to fight. Wichita and Caddo leaders often promoted exchange fairs and peace. They possessed a rich village life that offered ceremonies befitting the agrarian nature of their existence. Religious elites decided when to bless the corn seeds for planting and directed Green Corn ceremonies to offer praise to the first fruits of the season.

Politics often became a favorite topic of discussion when Comanches and Kiowas joined Wichitas and Caddos at these exchange fairs. The fairs were grand gatherings, as boys and young men played ball games, women showed off their pottery and basketry, and men hosted feasts for their counterparts. These fairs started in late May and often continued into the late summer. They coincided with the several harvests that occurred, which encouraged dances and general celebration. Dancing naturally led to courting, although a young Wichita woman usually married the man chosen by her parents.

Despite their generally peaceful inclinations, Wichitas would fight when they had to. They built their villages like fortresses, with underground bunkers to protect women and children but leaving their horse herds and their crops susceptible to raiders. This sedentary and defensive lifestyle left the Wichitas increasingly dependent upon the Comanches as the nineteenth century wore on.

While intertribal warfare occasionally flared up, European-introduced diseases destroyed far more Texas Indians than did fighting. Like all Indians of North and South America, the Indians of Texas had only minimal immunities to diseases such as smallpox, cholera, measles, and mumps. The first such pathogens probably came with De Soto and Coronado in 1539, and the epidemics that followed were especially harmful to the more settled agricultural towns. But epidemics decimated hunting peoples as well, especially the Karankawas and Tonkawas. Their populations of a few hundred people were so small by 1820 that they could not challenge early American settlement.[11]

The Native history of Texas certainly would have been less complicated had not another ten thousand Indians begun migrating into the region before and after Mexican independence in 1821. These "immigrant Indians" often settled into town sites that Caddos had abandoned in northeast Texas. The entire list of all the different immigrant bands that entered Texas—some for very short periods of time—would fill a page, but the most important included Cherokees, Creeks, Choctaws, Chickasaws, Seminoles, Kickapoos, Shawnees, Delawares, Alabamas, and Coushattas. Another hundred thousand eastern Indians were removed into Kansas and Indian Territory from the states east of the Mississippi River by 1840. Combined, these groups had a profound impact on the region, often vying for the resources of the indigenous groups, such as the Comanches, and causing conflict.

In dress, the immigrants looked far different from the indigenous groups. Most immigrant Indians used a combination of costume, mixing English, French, Spanish, and Indian fashions. Their men preferred cloth shirts to buckskin; sashes, turbans, and pants to feathered headdresses and breechcloths; woven blankets to buffalo robes. Immigrant Indian women often donned large calico dresses that they purchased in

Anglo towns, in the southern style. This was mostly impossible for Plains Indian women, who received a cloth dress only after a male raider had taken one from an Anglo victim, which became a common occurrence along the Texas frontier.

Both men and women of the immigrant tribes wore an abundance of jewelry. The more status the person acquired, the more prone to show it through adornment. Large, copper earrings were common, as were bracelets. The bracelets came in many different sizes so that they could extend up the arm nearly to the elbow. Wichita and Caddo women also wore earrings and bracelets, but what made their appearance more striking was the use of tattoos. The more status a senior Caddo or Wichita woman had—and some wielded considerable influence—the more tattoos she displayed on her body.

Immigrant Indians had varying views about economic development. Some were interested only in hunting and trading; others were dedicated farmers. Most of the men who came to Texas preferred to hunt because their womenfolk did the farming, but some worked at both. Their women, coming from a matrilineal system similar to that of the Wichita and Caddo people, kept clean, large houses, some of which were made of logs and others of pole and thatch. Cherokee women brought livestock and swine into Texas; from the milk of their cows, they made cheese. Chicken houses were common in all their towns. In fact, many of the towns of immigrant Indians looked much like the European peasant hamlets of the eighteenth century.

More important, immigrant tribes knew the value of land in terms of dollars. They even had some experience in processing deeds and general legal work. Having been exposed longer to Americans, most had already become acculturated to some of what was a southern lifestyle, including racist views of African Americans. Some immigrant Indians held slaves who paid for their keep with monthly payments of tribute. Other immigrant Indians looked down upon Plains Indians, such as Comanches, believing them to be unsophisticated and "savagelike."

Immigrant tribes, then, had many different voices and worldviews. Most had a number of Anglos who came and went at their towns. Some of these men had married into the tribe and produced families, promoting factionalism because mixed-bloods, full bloods, and Anglos often had differing views on political and economic issues. Anglos often pushed for the recognition of a market economy. Mixed-bloods occasionally followed the advice of their Anglo fathers, embracing negotiation, land sale, and the market economy that existed around them. But blood quantum could just as easily be deceiving. Cultural values were often determined by the experiences of the individuals involved. As a result, the immigrant Indians of Texas, who lived in perhaps twenty to thirty large and small communities, were a diverse lot.

Not unlike Anglos of the same period, some of the immigrant bands that voluntarily removed from the American South saw Texas and the western plains as offering new opportunity. The leaders of these groups were energetic men who recognized that the game herds of the East, even those of Arkansas, Louisiana, and East Texas, had been decimated. Some were colorful, spoke many different languages, and possessed political and economic savvy that rivaled that of Anglo pioneers. Sporting names such as Black Beaver, Jesse Chisholm, Delaware Jim, Shawnee Bob, Jim Pockmark, Jim Shaw, Bowles, and Big Mush, they had to reorganize fractured groups or bands in Texas or Indian Territory, doing so by the force of their personality. Some, despite being encouraged to go West by the United States, maintained at least a marginal degree of loyalty toward Americans, but good relations with Texans would be more difficult.

Conversely, some immigrant Indians, both full- and mixed-bloods, blamed Americans for all their troubles, and many came to despise Texans. A few Shawnees and Kickapoos—remnants of Tecumseh's confederacy—who came to Texas were militantly anti-American. Tecumseh's Shawnee warriors had joined the British during the War of 1812. After their forces were crushed in 1814 near Detroit, many of these Indians fled to Canada. By the 1820s, small numbers trickled back into Kansas and Indian Territory and eventually into Texas. Even more anti-American were the bands that came out of Florida, such as Wild Cat's Seminoles. These Indians distrusted and disliked Americans so much that they fled to Mexico.

Immigrant Indians brought with them a complex and shifting set of prejudices. In the 1820s, immigrant Indians would at times fight Caddos, Wichitas, and Comanches and at other times trade with them, help alienate them from Americans and Mexicans, and mingle with them in their towns. The same could be said about the immigrant Indians' relationships with Texans and Tejanos. Their behavior exhibited few stereotypical patterns, and they increasingly became the wild card in Texas politics. The whole question of Texas independence would become inextricably interwoven with the immigrant bands. These groups could have easily determined whether Anglo-Texans won or lost their war for independence in 1835–1836.

Chief Bowles's Cherokee band of over a thousand people constituted the first immigrants to build a permanent town in East Texas. Rendezvousing at Pecan Point along the Red River in 1820, Bowles's people moved south to a point thirty miles northwest of Nacogdoches and built a series of hamlets. Their houses, built in the old "French" style (placing the logs vertically in the ground) made the community look like a European settlement. Most Cherokees preferred a sedentary life, but others used villages in Texas only as a staging area to enter the plains and trade and hunt. A number became excellent guides and trackers.[12]

Bowles came to represent the immigrant Indians. His village was a mixture of people, full-blood and mixed-blood, some of whom spoke English. Bowles exemplified this ethnic mix, likely being Anglo-Cherokee. His early life in the east is unclear, but he lived for a time near Mussel Shoals in Tennessee. After clashing with settlers—a fight in which several men were killed—he felt compelled to move west with his party. When he arrived in Texas, Chief Bowles was already in his mid-sixties, but he was a formidable man: tall, handsome, and intelligent. He had learned much of frontier politics while shuffling from place to place in Tennessee.[13]

Bowles tried to build alliances with the other immigrant bands. Many, the Delawares and Shawnees especially, used Bowles's hamlet as a point of rendezvous, a place where news could be heard and issues discussed. Some followed the Cherokee example by bringing their families into Texas in the mid-1820s; others left dependents behind in Arkansas or Indian Territory. These allies of the Cherokees numbered minimally two to three thousand people in the 1820s, and their populations increased as Indian removal forced more eastern Indians west during the next decade.[14]

Given the large component of mixed-bloods who lived in their communities, these people knew much about Anglo-Americans and Texas. They also possessed a strong sense of geography, having moved nearly halfway across the continent. Hunting in the West and traveling to Mexico City did not frighten them. Most entered Texas knowing that Mexico was giving land to settlers, and almost every immigrant band sent representatives to Mexico City to seek land from authorities there. They even knew of the formation of Indian Territory (Oklahoma), which Congress authorized in 1825, and knew also that the U.S. government was about to force the removal of American Indians from the South to these western lands. Little escaped Bowles and others like him.

Early on, many Tejano traders made common cause with Texas Indians. During the late eighteenth century, considerable numbers of Mexicans had fled the lower Rio Grande valley to live in Indian camps. Others had been captured by Comanche or Wichita raiding parties and adopted into these tribes. In any given Comanche town by 1800 it was likely that fully one-quarter of the population possessed some Spanish blood.[15] Most Comanche, Kiowa, Wichita, and Caddo chiefs were fluent in Spanish, the lingua franca of the southern plains. Spain and later Mexico looked with disdain, however, upon Spaniards or Mexicans who had "gone native." Both the Spanish and the Mexican government tried to regain Spanish-speaking adults and children who were living among the Plains peoples, but many refused the offer of repatriation.

Spurred by the fur trade, adventure, and the belief that considerable riches awaited them, Anglo explorer-traders entered "Spanish" Texas in considerable numbers after the close of the War of 1812. These explorations, along with the growing revolutionary infighting in Mexico, made it difficult for Spain and later Mexico to reestablish the reciprocal exchange ties that had characterized the "false peace" that existed between 1786 and 1810. Manufactured goods were being carried into Plains Indian camps by Americans; Spain lacked access to these goods (most of which were manufactured in England or the United States) and generally denied its citizens the right to trade with Indians. As the false peace fell apart, the destruction of Tejano ranches in the south escalated.

Ross's party of 1815 entered Spanish Texas illegally. Perhaps not surprisingly, it was apparently sanctioned by U.S. officials in Louisiana, since Ross gave his journal to Major William Trimble at Fort Jesup upon his return. Some Tejanos from Nacogdoches joined Ross. Although his journal fails to identify his associates, they likely included Bernardo Gutiérrez de Lara, Peter Ellis Bean, Francisco Ruiz, and perhaps some of the Nacogdoches fur traders who had once partnered with Philip Nolan.

Ross and his party moved sixteen mule loads of goods west that summer—no doubt including guns, ammunition, and such items as blankets and kettles. Although no entries in Ross's journal suggest that he encouraged the Comanches to raid Tejano ranches in southern Texas for more animals, it was from these ranches, as well as others along the Rio Grande, that considerable numbers of Comanche livestock, as well as people, would eventually come.[16] Thus, Anglos and Tejanos had established a pattern of trade in Plains Indians towns that others would follow, including many immigrant Indians.

Over the next few years, reports of other Mexican revolutionaries and Anglo-Americans being involved in the western trade continually surfaced. A combined group again reached western Comanche towns in 1818, one party under the command of the American Benjamin Milam, who would later take his place in Texas history in the storming of San Antonio at the outset of the Texas Revolution. Another brigade, consisting of twelve men, reached the Kiowas and Plains Apaches in 1819. Spaniards complained vigorously of these intrusions into their lands, noting by 1820 that most northern Indian camps contained "renegades" (Anglo-Americans, for the most part) who worked with "revolutionaries" (who were clearly Tejanos) and other Mexicans.[17]

This plains trade grew in value with each passing year. A Spanish official estimated that in 1820 alone the Tejano citizens of Nacogdoches had moved $90,000 in goods "supplied by merchants of Natchitoches and New Orleans." The content of the trade was a particular cause for concern: the traders carried west mostly "arms of good quality, double-barreled guns, lances, and a great quantity of ammunition."[18] One American, a Captain Trimble, admitted to seeing "an extensive traffic in horses and mules" resulting from exchanges with the Comanches, with many of the animals coming from Mexican ranches. American demand for mules especially increased as new cotton lands were opened in the South. The demand also doomed attempts by Mexico, after 1821, to create a workable Indian policy, one modeled on the older reciprocal relationships that had tied the plains economy to Spanish and, later, Mexican towns to the south.[19]

American traders such as Jacob Fowler very much hoped to alter the older exchange economy, intending to instill instead a sense of market economics. Fowler's attempts to attach certain values to trade items in the autumn of 1821 caught Comanche leaders by surprise. They demanded presents of Fowler that were needed for redistribution among their following. When Fowler refused, the Indian chiefs became combative.[20] More Fowlers would come onto the plains by the 1830s, making it difficult for Plains Indian leaders to maintain their status and political positions. This was no less the case after ever larger brigades of immigrant Indians reached the trade fairs, some of these newcomers moving in with the Comanches. And as chiefs could no longer restrain their young men from raiding, they either led raids or lost influence, making the plains a more violent place than ever before.

Fowler's efforts also presaged a gradual shift on the part of American commercialists away from Indians and their horse-and-hide economy, a condition that led to considerable confrontation along the emerging Santa Fe Trail, which opened in 1821. The route connected Missouri with New Mexico and cut across Comanche/Kiowa lands.[21] The early profits from New Mexico attracted large numbers of American and Mexican entrepreneurs, and many thereafter wished to avoid Plains Indians and the presents that had to be offered to the chiefs. Some forty wagons left Missouri in the early days of May 1824 alone, and they returned four months later with a 50 percent profit.[22] Soon, activity along the trail expanded southward into Chihuahua. Here, the horse-and-mule trade prospered as Americans and Mexicans both drove many herds north, through New Mexico and northeastward into Missouri, crossing Comanche lands.[23]

Given the serious disruption of the economy of southern Texas by Indian raiding, in late 1821 the San Antonio town council sent Manuel Barrera north to cajole Indian leaders at the Waco Wichita town, where a conclave of Native people had gathered, many from the plains. Attempting to reestablish the "false peace," Barrera promised these Indian leaders many presents. But Texas, which had been torn up from the civil war attending the struggle for independence, failed to deliver on Barrera's promised "grand gifts." Such would be the story of Texas for the next decade; ironically, a Plains Indian economy tied increasingly to markets in the eastern United States (and Texas) became somewhat isolated and incapable of operating within that market.

Many other Mexican agents followed Barrera, all of them bent on subduing the northern Indians and bringing prosperity back to northern Mexico and Texas. But during the period of the early Mexican Republic, the economy and the political structure of the region never recovered to the point where the goods necessary for exchange and political order existed to make it work. The Tejanos, the first successful European settlers of the region, found themselves increasingly marginalized, both economically and politically, in a land where power and influence increasingly fell to invading Anglo-Americans, immigrant Indians, and Plains tribes.

Texas soon became a place like no other in North America. Its lands harbored a growing Indian ethnic milieu after 1820. Pressing in from the east were Anglo-Americans, mingling with the few Tejano inhabitants who remained. Crossing into Texas from Arkansas were immigrant Indians possessing many of the same hopes and desires as their southern Anglo counterparts. To the west and in central Texas were Comanches, Wichitas, and Caddos concerned about their homeland and prepared to defend it. And in the south, mostly, were pockets of Tejanos—the largest group having consolidated at San Antonio—hoping without much hope to reestablish a prosperous Texas. Had Mexico been able to offer all these people a stable government, law, and order, perhaps the later clashes could have been averted. Confusion and disorder reigned almost from the start, however, and substantially greased the slope that led to violent conflict.

Various ethnic groups started fighting over land in Texas almost immediately after the emergence of a new independent government in Mexico City in 1821. Mexico's eventual outlawing of slavery, its futile attempts to sort out the confusing and sometimes archaic land grant system, the growing political chaos in Mexico itself, and a failed Indian policy left Texas vulnerable to confusion and violence. While a serious debate over the future of Texas always seemed in the offing, the new republics of both Mexico and later Texas ultimately failed to find the answers that could bring peace and prosperity. Texas, a land of so much promise and of so many different peoples, soon confronted a spiraling, ever more violent, ethnic and racial war.

2

THE TEXAS CREED IN A
TEJANO AND INDIAN LAND

One trail that early Anglo pioneer wagons used to enter Texas meandered through Louisiana northward to the Sabine River, a rapid stream with steep banks. The river served as the boundary line separating Mexican Texas from the United States. Once across, the pioneers found a well-marked road into Nacogdoches, the most important community in East Texas. Houses, occupied mostly by Tejano families, graced the road every mile or two along the way. The Anglos called the inhabitants of the houses "Creoles," a term that reflected their European lineage. Some Creoles profited from the migration by providing travelers with bed and board for twenty-five cents a night. A few Creoles ran "public houses," where homemade whiskey or cheap imported claret wine could be purchased for a few cents a glass.

Nacogdoches must have seemed unusual to the entering Americans as they encountered the myriad of people that characterized Texas in the 1820s. A small but enterprising American population sat at the top of the social ladder, outnumbered in every respect by people of color. Indians lounged in groups on nearly every street corner. Almost every evening in summer they played ball, or lacrosse, to entertain the citizenry. This game was practically the only show in town, other than the small Tejano band that marched down the main street on holidays.[1] The Tejanos were a mixture of mestizos (Indians and European blood combined), Creoles from Louisiana, and a few Mexicans: some soldiers, a few government officials sent from the heartland of Mexico, and some settlers and traders.

Little did the denizens of this fledgling community sense that it was being invaded by people who believed themselves superior to the local citizenry—as the Anglo interlopers wrote in their diaries, journals, and letters home. Some Anglos distinguished themselves by their dress. The most stylish wore "Quakerish" stovepipe top hats. Though most were southerners, a few (such as leading citizen Frost Thorn) came from New York, and the only doctor in town (J. H. Miller) hailed from Baltimore. Some of the Anglo pioneers who came through wore clothing of homespun, but they too had a determined look; they came to build better lives and looked down upon people they judged of less accomplishment, especially the smallish, dark-skinned Mexican soldiers and the seemingly placid Indians.

A minority in the 1820s, the Anglos would increase in both numbers and precedence through the decades that followed. In the process they would slowly reveal a new creed for Texas, founded on the belief that certain races of people were more accomplished and more justified in inheriting the land than were others. Anglos thought they possessed superior institutions—political systems that were presumed to be democratic, Protestant religions, and a driving certainty of "exceptionalism," the sense that such an ordained race could do no wrong. The Texas creed contained one other canon: that Anglos were justified in using violence (indeed, one's honor demanded it) to create and sustain Anglo dominance.

As the great Anglo migration to Texas got under way, Nacogdoches represented the cultural and demographic reality of Texas. Despite Anglo disdain, each of the three cultural groups widely represented in the town—Anglos, Mexicans, and American Indians—had much to do with determining Texas's history, for all three had a sense of nationhood and all three had developing political economies. Just the same, all three possessed factions, or at least ethnic subgroups.

Among the American Indians of East Texas alone, for example, more than a dozen languages were spoken. Indians in Nacogdoches frequently communicated through signs, even when bartering among themselves for blankets or kettles. American Indians dominated most of the land in 1820, but they lacked a sense of unity and occasionally fought among themselves.

Tejanos had a better sense of cultural identity and had established institutional processes of government, but class consciousness divided them. Some were poor peasants imported originally for military service, while others were elites who honored an age-old caste social system. Many others fell somewhere in between. Regardless of the official backing of the government of Mexico, they lacked the authority and the manpower to rule the land.

The newly arriving Anglos possessed the clearest sense of identity, which gave them an advantage in the quest for control of the land. Anglo debates centered on such issues as land allocation, taxes, and law and order, rather than one's position in society or one's tribal affiliation. Nevertheless, Texas Anglos were divided too. Some came from the upper South, while others were from the lower American states. Texas Anglos soon found themselves at odds with the Americans who began to occupy Indian Territory to the north and, after Texas statehood, with the U.S. Army, which attempted to halt the violence in Texas. The historical evolution of these differences—especially those between Texans and Americans—had much to do with shaping a clear and distinct Texan identity and has some repercussions even today.

One of the shortfalls of most Texas history, then, is the belief that some sense of commonality existed within each of these three cultures, that the story of Texas is a simple one in which Indians fought Texans and Mexicans quietly receded into the background. In reality, the early history of Texas is characterized by dramatic mobility within and among all three cultural groups, as land changed hands and conflict ebbed and flowed. Nothing resembling a dominant culture existed until the Mexican War of 1846; the diversity of peoples created anxiety and insecurity, which led to violence among the Anglo, Indian, and Tejano cultural groups.

Tejanos constituted the second largest population in 1820. Roughly four thousand to five thousand Spanish-speaking people were scattered throughout both southern and northern Texas (excluding the region that would become El Paso), but they too had different origins. Some fifty-five early settlers of San Antonio had come from the Canary Islands, and their descendants played major roles in the city's development. Those Tejanos living in and about Nacogdoches—with the exception of Mexican army troops—generally came from old-line Creole families, being of Spanish blood mostly but having occasionally intermarried with early French settlers or Indians. The majority, especially those in the Nueces River valley and north of it, were mestizos (or mixed-bloods), with origins in Mexican Indian society. Though all increasingly called themselves Tejanos, in reality, distinctions based on a Tejano's politics, his birth, and his blood defined and separated the Tejano community into various factions.

The Anglo community that slowly evolved in Texas came to view itself as standing apart from the American cultural majority from which it had come. Anglo-Texans soon called themselves "Texians," denoting their struggle for a new identity, separate from whatever state a Texian had originally hailed from. They were certainly different from the people who lived north of the Mason-Dixon line. Most early Anglo-Texans had come from a southern agricultural background and had considerable experience in taming a land. They were an independent lot—especially their women. Most Anglo females in Texas had learned the use of firearms at a young age; they may have feared Indians, but they had a strong sense of survival.

The history of all these people was driven by the evolving notions of race that existed in early-nineteenth-century North America. Anglos were originally viewed by Tejanos as progressive and forward looking, and indeed many early Anglo-Texans respected Tejano traditions (perhaps out of necessity), even marrying into leading families. Likewise, Anglo-Texans initially got on well with many Indian bands. But the attitudes that Texans brought with them, the cultural baggage that made them unique, changed over time. As they became demographically stronger, Texans were far less willing to tolerate other cultural groups.

Anglo-Texans remained more respectful of elite Tejanos than of commoners. The majority of the elite Tejanos lived in and about Mexican towns, such as San Antonio, Goliad, and Nacogdoches. Some (perhaps two or three dozen) owned landed estates, or *latifundios*. The vast majority of Tejanos, however, lived and worked on much smaller rancheros. The owners of the small ranches—especially north of the Rio Grande in Texas—were often identified as *rancheros,* and they occasionally employed vaqueros to tend their stock. Still other Tejanos worked as day laborers or as tradesmen in the few towns that came into existence after 1750. A number worked as carters, moving goods north and south, along the coast and to inland towns; they may have been judged as having the least visible means of support.[2]

Ironically, many Tejanos (perhaps even a majority of them) likely supported the Texas Revolution in its early stages or at least remained neutral. Members of some elite families joined in the defense of the Alamo and fought alongside Texans at the battle of San Jacinto. Liberals, they saw in the Texans' move for independence the vestiges of a political and economic system that emphasized local control rather than federal meddling, as well as capitalism and cotton production. These Tejano liberals found considerable support for their cause in the northern Mexican communities of Saltillo, Parras, and Monclova, where other liberal merchants resided.[3]

Most Tejanos eventually discovered that their support did little to protect them from the aggressive Americans who invaded Texas. Some Tejanos in the vicinity of Goliad lost their lands in the late 1830s; others faced the loss of land and property after the Mexican War of 1846–1848, when Anglo-Texans charged them with disloyalty. Despite such setbacks, some regrouped, returned to Texas in the 1850s, and fought for their lands in the court system. They formed the foundation of the modern Tejano community that thrives in the region today.[4]

Certainly the failure of Tejanos to defend themselves successfully against Indians or to stand up to dictatorial Mexican politicians had much to do with the growing Anglo resentment toward and displacement of these people. There was a certain belief in the Anglo community that those who could not defend themselves were unworthy people; they had no honor. Nevertheless, these same Anglos hated American Indians who could, and usually did, defend themselves. To comprehend the Anglo settler in Texas, one must first understand the American South and its political and racial worldview.

The southern Anglo mindset had more to do with the cultural assumptions that these people brought to Texas than with the people they met there. Their beliefs were driven by a strong commitment to material gain, which in turn was interconnected with the institution of slavery. To defend the institution, a code emerged that led to extremely racist views regarding people of color. The code was perceived as righteous and morally correct because it helped define a higher form of civilization deemed superior even to that of the increasingly industrial northern states.

Yet the United States, which Texas ultimately joined, had adopted a constitution that offered some protection for people of color like those encountered in Texas. Even in southern states such as Louisiana, Spanish and French Creoles had basic civil rights. For Indians, federal protection came in the form of control over land distribution and Indian policy, beginning with George Washington's Intercourse Acts, which attempted to protect Indians from Anglo aggression. Such rights were firmly entrenched in the liberal ideology of the American Revolution.[5]

Thomas Jefferson helped mold this liberal racism (some might say the fiction of it), putting it to paper in his *Notes on the State of Virginia,* a defense of America against European criticism. The Indian, Jefferson said, was "brave, when an enterprise depends upon bravery"; and he would "defend himself against a host of enemies, always choosing to be killed rather than to surrender." (Jefferson may easily have been writing about the Comanche Indians.) This same Indian, Jefferson added, was "affectionate to his children," and above all, "his friendships are strong and faithful to the utmost extremity."[6]

Jefferson's Indian nevertheless lacked law, order, and a sense of moral purpose. Perhaps an instinctive democrat, the Indian possessed few political institutions and lacked the maturity to join the ranks of the new republican system. To liberal Jeffersonians, the Indian was the "noble savage": childlike, simple, and nonsensical in terms of government and religion. This rendered the Indians' total immersion into the American system problematic. And this view, in turn, negated much of what Jeffersonian politicians said in reality about the goodness of Indians.[7] But the mythology of the noble savage hung on, especially in the East, where the Indian was mostly extinct or removed.

The literature of the time, especially a series of novels written by James Fenimore Cooper, reinforced Jefferson's views to some degree but added ambiguity. To Cooper, the Indian was noble and ignoble at the same time. He came out of the forest, isolated from the elements of progress—state creation, democracy—that defined European America. Cooper never lingered long in debating the ultimate destiny of the Indian—he would simply fade away, into the forest, the paradox of his goodness or badness left unresolved.

Critics of Cooper's ambiguous Indian abounded. One, the powerful Democratic senator Lewis Cass of Michigan, served as Andrew Jackson's secretary of war and implemented Indian removal. Cass thought that Americans could ill afford Cooper's latent romanticism. In Cass's opinion, the Indian increasingly became Cooper's violent nationalist, Magua, rather than the placid, noble Uncas.[8] Cass, being from a new state with Indian populations, generally represented the views of those in the West, where Indians still existed in number and held significant resources in the form of land.

The demise of the portrayal of the noble Indian may have been partly a matter of greed—Anglo Americans wanted the Indians' land. Yet it also can be explained in part by the rise of rabid racism in the nineteenth century—whether toward Indians, Mexicans, or blacks. Reflecting this racism was a rash of new, romantic literature. The captivity narrative—often a short re-creation of some supposed

Indian attack—became a staple of American reading. It displayed the Indian in all his villainy, replete with the stock sensationalist conclusion that female captives suffered the "fate worse than death," or rape, when in Indian hands.[9] This theme, although at times hidden by innuendo and supposition in the narratives, did much to devalue the nobility of the mythological Indian even as it underscored the heroic duty of the American male to protect—some might say control—American womanhood.

The ultimate male role model for this duty was none other than Daniel Boone, introduced by John Filson in *The Discovery, Settlement and Present State of Kentucke* (1784). Filson's work led to a cottage industry of pamphlets and books about the frontier and Indians. In them, the "Boonesque" character acquired his goodness while conquering the wilderness; he brought order to the land while serving as the sword of progress. The Indian, by contrast, opposed progress, sought revenge, scalped people, and mistreated women—or so the fable went.[10]

Beginning in the 1820s, with the American push into the West (including Texas), a transition occurred in which the "noble savage" became the "savage less noble" and, eventually, at least to some Anglo observers, simply the "savage." When circumstances narrowed, when people fought over land in Texas, when cupidity begged culpability, it was far too easy for racial bias to render the Indian—and by racial similarity and color, the Tejano—as not only a nuisance, but a malevolent one at that.

Much of the American upper South—Kentucky, Tennessee, Missouri, and Arkansas—embraced this view of the Indian. The region had nurtured men like Boone to carry the torch of civilization: to explore, to hunt, to fight Indians, and to find the trails that opened land for settlement. During the early development of Texas, the upper South provided the majority of Anglos that settled in the colonies of Stephen Austin, Green DeWitt, and other land agents along the lower Colorado and Brazos rivers. Among them was the famous James Bowie, who had migrated to Texas in the 1820s, carrying his "Bowie knife." But these were unsettled people, often mobile and seldom satisfied with their situation.

A region unique in the eastern United States, the upper South was somewhat late in the development of a successful market economy. It had a population seething with restless men and women who were good at settling a new land. Consisting mostly of yeoman farmers of Scots-Irish and German descent, they established small grain and pig farms but often survived by the skill of the hunt. Almost all carried rifles (generally the long rifle that had been successfully wielded at the battle of New Orleans). Many of these men would provide much of the firepower for Sam Houston at the battle of San Jacinto when Texas gained its independence.

After the republic was established in 1836, a huge number of people entered Texas from the lower South. Whereas Mexico had tried to ban slavery, the laws of the new Texas republic embraced it. People from South Carolina, Alabama, Georgia, Mississippi, and Louisiana poured into the Texas gulf plains, bringing the cotton culture that would soon dominate the state. Some moved up the river valleys, opening lands to cotton and slavery; others remained in the east, where they attempted to re-create Georgia and Alabama in the patchy post oak and piney woods. The greatest influx from the lower South came in the 1840s and 1850s, when the Texas population exploded. Despite their southern origins, of the 600,000 people calling Texas home in 1860, a mere 21,878 owned slaves, and the vast majority of slave owners possessed ten or fewer.[11]

While considerable recent literature has emphasized the growing social and political power of the southern plantation-owning elite, in reality (in terms of property equality), little difference can be found between the rural make-up of the South and the North. Most slave owners in the South (similar to circumstances in Texas) owned fewer than five slaves, and less than 3 percent of slaveholders owned more than fifty slaves. Slaveholding, then, was a middle-class occupation; it became a significant part of status for all white southerners. By the Civil War, some 27,000 southern doctors, teachers, lawyers, and tradesmen owned slaves.[12] In Texas, despite their lack of interest in cotton farming, both Stephen Austin and Sam Houston owned slaves, who served mostly as servants.

Just the same, southerners owned slaves mainly because it was profitable to do so; the majority of slaves worked in the fields. An acre of land in Texas produced six hundred pounds of cotton, and on average, a healthy black field hand could pick roughly eight bales a year, worth upward of $50 a bale. But slaves were expensive, often costing more than $2,000 each. The average Texas slaveholder made a good profit in cotton only when the plants produced well and transportation to market was affordable. This translated into having access to riverboat transportation.

In Texas, cotton production boomed between 1836 and 1860, remaining the most important aspect of the economy well into the twentieth century. The 1850 census showed twelve thousand farms in Texas, most of which had three times the acreage of an average farm elsewhere in the United States. Yet most Texas farms produced less crop than a farm in Ohio. Perhaps this relatively low production resulted from a combination of problems with transportation and the precapitalistic nature of settlers from the upper South—or it may suggest that slave labor was inefficient. Regardless, Texas produced some 58,000 bales of cotton in that first census year, and when planters from the lower South moved into the region in the following decade, production jumped to an astonishing 431,000 bales.[13] As Texas went through a slow economic transformation between 1830 and 1860—from precapitalistic to capitalistic—people from the lower South generally took charge in the state.

Rapid economic development of this sort also likely had much to do with defining the distinctive "exceptionalism" that came to dominate Texas identity. Everything in Texas was supposed to be bigger and better: the size of the farms, the quality of the land, and the chance for advancement. Given that the restraints inherent in the land policies of the United States never affected Texas, the region became a speculator's dream. The opportunities for the accumulation of wealth in Texas through the ownership of large portions of land and cotton production were so well known in eastern states that they produced a "western fever." Open land, cotton, and slavery in places like Texas, as historian James Oakes has said, "produced a world view that equated upward mobility with westward migration."[14] Those in the forefront of this migration clashed directly with Indians.

Such an argument—that many southerners were restless, expectant capitalists who owned one or two slaves and expected to move west to new lands—is in marked contrast to the older view that most southern slave owners were paternalists who nurtured the relationship between slaveholder and bondsman. Some plantation owners did try to create a paternalistic social order that was inclined to protect slaves from overexploitation. Yet as American liberalism, with its emphasis on freedom and equality, blossomed in the early antebellum period, even southerners who wished to treat their slaves humanely faced a dilemma; how could they embrace the new rhetoric of freedom and democracy and still continue to exploit their slaves? Paradoxically, most came to equate opportunity, freedom, and democracy with slavery and the violence necessary to sustain that social and economic order.

This connection rested on the predominant notion that slaves were degraded individuals or that they originated from a "wretched race" and were thus incapable of the benefits of American liberalism. Such a dehumanizing view led to excessive violence and sexual exploitation. Cruelty became necessary for profit, wealth, and status—and even, so the rhetoric went, for freedom and democracy.

With this necessity came the emergence of a new creed in the South and in Texas, a series of moral absolutes that were racially, economically, and culturally motivated. While some divergence from the creed was allowed, most Texans ultimately came to believe that only white people were capable of enjoying the new liberal freedoms of the evolving nation and that this was the only way to preserve the purity of their cultural improvement on the land. People of color had to get out of the way of liberal, democratic progress.[15]

This early-nineteenth-century creed favored (indeed, preached) an agrarian, or plantation, lifestyle. Within that lifestyle sat a former southerner, with a southern mindset that embraced all Texans, slave owners and slaveless yeoman farmers alike. The creed might have been viewed as a paternalistic necessity by some, while others rationalized adherence as a result of the general economic needs of the region, and still others likely saw the creed as simply part of a general cultural hegemony. Anglo-Texans, after all, were born to dominate people of color, or so the argument went.[16] While the defining elements of the creed would change as Anglos pressed westward into the prairie country, producing a political split by the 1850s in which people of West Texas disagreed with some of the policies advocated by those of East Texas, there was seldom any disagreement over issues such as racial superiority or the need to sustain slavery.

The debate over slavery helped formulate this new creed, but much of its bravado was drawn from a Celtic-influenced tradition heavily reliant on notions of honor. It became a point of southern honor to duel, to gamble, to engage in sport of any sort, and to fight to defend one's honor, to defend one's racial identity, self-esteem, and moral values. As violence toward blacks, Indians, and Tejanos escalated, racial hatred became compatible with honor. Indeed, the white man's honor, the black man's slavery, the Indian's savagery, and the Tejano's passivity and backwardness became embedded in this evolving Texas creed. The code of honor swept Texas into an ever deeper racial cauldron.[17] Fistfights, duels, even the atrocious custom of lynching became honorable events. And the most honorable involved finding an Indian village and killing people—men, women, and children.

In the eastern states, the first casualties of this evolving cultural creed included the southern Indian. Increasingly aware of the crisis over Indian sovereignty to land, many advocates of Jeffersonian liberalism endorsed "voluntary" removal. The idea was simple: approach Indians with treaty offers that guaranteed assistance and help, on the condition that Indians sell their tribal holdings and move into the vast provinces west of the Mississippi River.[18] Voluntary removal set into motion a host of Native peoples who removed from the South, blazing trails into Texas and Indian Territory well before the Texas Revolution.

Voluntary removal led to calls for forced removal.[19] The new southerner—the Scots-Irish or German farmer—soon demanded that the Cherokees, Creeks, Choctaws, and Chickasaws (Indians who had always been accomplished farmers) be moved west, despite the fact that a few members of these societies had opened cotton lands, purchased slaves, and built plantations. Many northerners from the expanding West followed suit, calling for the removal of Kickapoo, Potawatomi, Shawnee, Delaware, and Sac and Fox Indians. Indian removal became a central theme in Texas history throughout the 1830s, 1840s, and 1850s and reinforced notions regarding ethnic cleansing.

The aggressiveness of Texans, their martial mentality and penchant for violence, their individualism and deep-seated racism, and their lust for profit made conflict with Indians almost inevitable. But much the same attitudes existed among many of the settlers who were then opening farmland in Illinois and Wisconsin. And soon the pioneer would covet places such as Iowa and Oregon. While an Indian war might occur in the taking of these lands (and certainly some did), these newly settled areas did not experience fifty years of conflict. Texas was different primarily because Texans and the highly charged elements of their creed were different.

These differences also led to struggles with the more passive Tejanos, whose code was molded more by compliance than rebellion and by the acceptance of a system of social hierarchy. While their numbers remained fairly equal, Anglos and Tejanos could agree on much; but the basic philosophical underpinning of the Anglo-Texan perception of his own supremacy, as it had evolved in the South prior to 1820, would invariably lead to trouble once the Anglo population became demographically more dominant.

Yet choices remained. Elsewhere in the United States, some peoples with differing lifestyles, religions, or ethnic and racial backgrounds managed to live side by side in peace. Many Texans had had contact with peaceful Indians before moving west. Many examples of negotiation existed; representatives of the U.S. Bureau of Indian Affairs were constantly visiting the Indian tribes of the South, and their discussions were often printed in local papers. In addition, some Indians had been close allies of the United States; some had indeed fought alongside Andrew Jackson at New Orleans in 1815.

However, such examples would increasingly be lost to Anglos as they entered the ethnic milieu that typified Texas after 1820. The seeds of cultural supremacy had been too deeply sown to allow for compromise and negotiation.

3

MEXICAN POLITICS AND THE STRUGGLE TO SETTLE EARLY TEXAS

Father Miguel Hidalgo y Costilla, at fifty-seven years of age, had a reputation for being a troublemaker. He had served as the parish priest in the small Mexican peasant town of Dolores for seven years, a job he had been banished to. Like most of his fellow Creoles, Hidalgo blamed his failure on the Gachupin elite who ruled Mexico. They had been born in Spain, to privilege, while Hidalgo had a Mexican nativity. Suffering under this perceived yoke, Hidalgo joined a revolutionary group, meeting at Querétaro, that by 1810 had a plan. In the name of Ferdinand VII, who had been deposed by Napoleon, they would lead Mexico to independence. When the Gachupins in Mexico City heard the news, they sent an army to arrest Hidalgo and his coconspirators.

Seizing the moment, Hidalgo climbed into the small church steeple in Dolores and spoke to the peasantry on September 16, 1810. His entire speech is not known for certain, but he ended with a resounding challenge: "Long live the king of Spain and death to bad government!" Soon the initially confused crowd added to the refrain: "Death to the Gachupins." As bonfires lit up the night around Dolores, a peasant army of fifty thousand Indians and mestizos formed, and then more came. Hidalgo moved to their head and attacked the nearby Spanish stronghold at Guanajuato. The peasants poured into town, attacking, burning, rampaging. In one swift stroke, they overwhelmed the fortified granary that contained the flower of Guanajuato citizenry. The massacre that ensued is often considered the worst in Mexican history.[1]

This slaughter terrified the Mexican elite, and it continued for several months. Creoles, Gachupins, and even some mestizos reacted in horror against Hidalgo and his slaughtering hordes. Fortunately for them, Hidalgo's poorly trained army lost resolve almost as quickly as it had formed. A Spanish force of seven thousand finally routed the peasantry late that fall; the Dolores priest and several of his lieutenants were turned over to the army for execution at Chihuahua in May. A few of his followers continued to fight, however, among them another parish priest, José María Morelos, who sustained a guerrilla war in the south for four more years.

Father Morelos did more to promote the ideology of Mexican liberalism than Hidalgo had done. Morelos fought a series of successful engagements in Oaxaca against Gachupin armies that made him a legend. His many pronouncements also argued for land reform, the right to trial by jury, the abolishment of certain privileges granted to the church, and sovereignty vested in all the people. But he too was captured, dragged into Mexico City, and unceremoniously executed in December 1815.

Hidalgo and Morelos, and their peasant insurrections, had a profound impact on Mexican politics, even in outlying provinces such as Texas. While Creoles in 1821 would eventually force the separation of Mexico from Spain, they did so with the full realization that too much liberal rhetoric could encourage peasant insurrections. Indeed, the coup of 1821 was led by army officers, not renegade priests. The evolving brand of eighteenth-century liberalism that these later men promoted included rights and power for men of reason and property, recognizing the basic caste system that existed below them—mestizos, mulattos, blacks, and Indians, in descending order. Most individuals within these groups were illiterate and considered incapable of self-government.

This is not to say, however, that the Mexican war for independence failed to advance the cause of liberty. The Creoles absorbed at least some of Morelos's rhetoric. When they inherited the country in the 1820s, they sought to end slavery, promote secular education, and deny the Catholic Church certain established privileges. Liberals questioned just who should carry out such reforms. Much of the political debate in Mexico after 1821, and by default in Texas, centered on whether states or the national government in Mexico City should have the power to effect reforms. Federalists (those advocating state power) often clashed with centralists (those who wanted more authority vested in a strong president and the national legislature).

During the last days of the Spanish regime, these debates continued in the hinterland, especially among the few survivors of Hidalgo's insurrection. Among them was Bernardo Gutiérrez de Lara, a Creole who, unlike Morelos, had fled north to Texas with nearly a dozen others.[2] While never recognized diplomatically, Gutiérrez de Lara soon received help from American citizens in the form of money and men to carry on his war for independence. President James Monroe even encouraged U.S. officials to look favorably upon Gutiérrez de Lara's "liberal" cause. With American arms, Gutiérrez de Lara began imitating Morelos's guerrilla tactics. With a small force of Anglos, Mexicans, and Indians, he captured Nacogdoches in 1812 and San Antonio by April 1813.[3] Fighting alongside him was the indomitable Reuben Ross.

The revolutionaries at San Antonio bickered among themselves while a Spanish military force seeking retribution methodically moved northward, pillaging Tejano ranches—often including those of loyalists in their depredations—and executing anyone thought to have supported Hidalgo or Gutiérrez de Lara. For the next eight years, what remained of the revolutionaries occasionally joined with Comanches and Wichitas, whom they recruited with gifts of weapons given in exchange for marketable horses. In turn, the revolutionaries were joined by many adventuresome Americans, including Peter Ellis Bean (who had fought with Morelos), David G. Burnet, Benjamin Milam, James Long, and Ross. Bands of men—mostly Indians but including a few Tejanos and Anglos—attacked ranches and even invaded towns such as San Antonio. Southern Texas was devastated.[4]

The lawlessness and destruction reached such levels that when the last Spanish governor of Texas, Antonio de Martínez, received his commission in 1817, he tried desperately to avoid the appointment. "Since 1813," Martínez lamented, Texas had advanced "at an amazing rate towards ruin and destruction." Spanish army troops scavenged in the streets of San Antonio; the "recklessness and violence of the troops, who, deprived of supplies, [were] naked and starving," drained the few resources remaining in the country. The chain of five Catholic missions that had once dominated the economic life of San Antonio lay in ruin.[5] Spanish Texas, unruly and unprotected, had no future.

This state of affairs seemed destined for change. To the east, the advancing Americans had finally reached Texas. The Louisiana Purchase of 1803 (a deal that brought most lands north of the Red River under U.S. control) resulted in the founding of the state of Louisiana in 1812, and its westernmost settlement, Natchitoches, lay along the central pathway into Texas. Seven years later, Arkansas Territory was established, and in 1821, Missouri entered the union, becoming the second state to be formed west of the Mississippi River. These regions bordering Texas all filled rapidly with settlers and immigrant Indians, many of whom eyed jealously the promised land to their south and west.

It was Moses Austin—a native of Virginia who had lived for many years in Ste. Genevieve, Missouri—who made the first move. The Austins, products of an English background, had migrated to America in the late seventeenth century. Shrewd in business, Moses had left a comfortable mercantile partnership in Philadelphia for adventure and fortune in the new West, opening a lead mine near Ste. Genevieve after his arrival in 1797. His son, Stephen, born four years before, seemed more inclined to study law. Unfortunately, the promise of fortune eluded both father and son; first the War of 1812 and then the panic of 1819 prostrated the family economically. While living in Spanish Louisiana, however, Moses Austin had obtained a Spanish passport, and in December 1820, he headed to San Antonio with a proposal to act as a Spanish contractor to settle American families in Texas.[6]

The scheme had little precedent, and Governor Martínez received Austin coolly at San Antonio. Only the American's Spanish passport saved him from jail. Luckily for Austin, a chance encounter with the Baron de Bastrop, an old acquaintance from St. Louis, resulted in a second audience with the governor. This time, Austin and Bastrop convinced Martínez that settlement was the answer to Texas's turmoil. The governor, who suggested that Austin might carry the title of *empresario,* or land contractor, forwarded the request to the head of the Interior Provinces, General Joaquín de Arredondo, who, despite having never met Austin, surprisingly agreed. Austin was granted the authority to introduce several hundred American families to Texas. Austin never did meet the general. The old lead miner died on his return east, leaving his grant and the future of Anglo settlement to his son, Stephen.[7]

The younger Austin had talent if not timing. He arrived in Texas just as Creole liberal revolutionaries finally seized control of the federal government in Mexico City and proclaimed independence from Spain in 1821. As this news reached Texas, the first vanguard of Americans, mostly poor farmers from the upper South recruited by the older Austin, crossed the Sabine River in November 1821 and headed into the rich bottomlands along the lower Brazos and Colorado rivers. They had little if any direction and settled where they wished. In addition, their right of occupancy was based upon a tentative grant from a now-defunct government.

Soon reaching his father's colony, Stephen Austin had high hopes that the original plan could be implemented. Austin came to believe strongly in the promised land of Texas and in the rights of Anglos to settle that land, to accumulate wealth, and to use slavery and capitalism to succeed in their endeavor. Informed that all land grants would now become the province of the new government in Mexico City, Austin headed south; for the next two years he spent little time building his colony. He worked tirelessly to secure the grant that his father had been promised by the old regime.

Mexican politicians debated such "colonization schemes" as they addressed Austin's plan. To some degree, they embraced it and included it in the Colonization Act of 1823. This act exemplified the sense of legacy that the American and French revolutions had brought to Mexican liberalism, that of trying to spread wealth among all people. At least partially, the bill's passage was influenced by Father Morelos, who had popularized the notion that land should be divided into farms and ranches, rather than estates. Anglos who responded to Austin's offer of land benefited from the fact that Mexican liberals in 1823 viewed Americans as people of the same cloth, capable of aiding in the reconstruction of Texas.

Nevertheless, the colonization process drew more heavily on the Spanish experience. The new law allowed Austin to give each family that he settled in Texas one labor of land (177 acres) and one league of land (4,428 acres), the larger being designated for ranching. For his part, Austin received twenty-two and one-half leagues of land for each two hundred families he brought to Texas. But many liberals concluded that land policy should be administered by the state governments that were also taking shape. Soon after confirming Austin as a contractor, the federal government turned the issue of colonization over to the new state of Coahuila-Texas, a joining of two old provinces. Texas, it was felt, lacked the population to be a separate state by itself.[8]

Coahuila-Texas had its own legislature and governmental offices in Saltillo.[9] Despite the lack of a constitution, which would not be adopted until 1827, the Coahuila-Texas legislature passed its first colonization bill on March 24, 1825, using Austin's empresario grant as an example.[10] By this time, Austin had returned to his colony and settled the two hundred families stipulated in the first grant. Following Austin's initial success, the state gave him several more grants. He selected more lands west and east of his original federal grant in 1825, 1827, and 1828. These new grants assured Austin of having the most successful colony in the region; he also attracted the most qualified immigrants.[11]

Nevertheless, Coahuila-Texas gave grants to a host of other applicants, many of whom had fought to help free Mexico from Spain. The most notable of these were Green DeWitt, Benjamin Milam, David G. Burnet, Lorenzo de Zavala, Joseph Vehlein, Sterling Robertson, and Hayden Edwards. Along with Austin, all of these men issued titles to settlers, some fulfilling their contracts to a much greater extent than others. Most, however, found it easier to issue titles than to recruit and keep colonists on the land, especially given the growing hostility of Indians who traversed Texas.[12] At this early date, most Comanches and Wichitas still admired the Americans, but the chiefs found it increasingly difficult to control young Comanche warriors who spotted herds of livestock, which had become the lifeblood of the plains economy.

A clash between the newly arriving colonists and the Indians seemed inevitable. The departing royalist governor, Martínez, even predicted it unless certain key changes occurred in Mexican Indian policy. Being a nationalist, he argued that Mexico must replace the foreign (meaning American) traders who frequented Comanche and Wichita camps, such as Ross, with Mexicans. Indians, Martínez felt, understood loyalty above all and would join and protect those who consistently aided them. Allowing Americans continued access to Plains Indians, he believed, would spell Mexico's doom.[13]

Mexican general Don Gaspar López, at Monterrey, agreed with the departing governor. Studying the situation, he had learned that Nacogdoches, which had been abandoned during the revolutionary period, was quickly being resettled in the early 1820s by an influx of Americans, Creoles originally attached to Louisiana, mixed-bloods, Indians, Tejanos, and a variety of others of what he considered questionable character.[14] Most were involved, to one degree or another, in a mercantile trade involving livestock, and they had little loyalty to the new Mexican state. Worse, Mexico had no troops in the region to control the town.

Neither of these two officials fully comprehended the extent of the expanding American trade on the plains. To have dislodged the Americans by this late date may, in fact, have been impossible. This became a stark reality in 1822, when several hundred Comanches seized Austin and his traveling companions along the Rio Grande. The empresario boldly announced that his party consisted of "their friends the Americans," the same people who brought them trade goods. This saved their lives and brought the return of their property.[15] American influence was growing on the plains, and it gnawed away at older economic and diplomatic relationships that Mexico was hard pressed to reestablish.

General Anastacio Bustamante, who commanded the Mexican army, saw the need to bring back the "false peace" and its benefits. But massive numbers of presents cost money, expenses that Mexico could ill afford, and the economy of southern Texas had so suffered that the state of Coahuila-Texas could offer the Indians little in exchange for their goods. Comanches, having no reason to leave Mexican live-stock alone, expanded the scope of their raiding operations south of the Rio Grande valley. By 1824, Wichitas had either joined them or were sending their own parties south.[16] As ranch after ranch in southern Texas and northern Mexico suffered losses and thus possessed fewer pickings, Comanches moved deeper into Mexico, raiding southward hundreds of miles into Coahuila and Chihuahua.

These war parties acted unpredictably, some stealing a few animals and others committing more violent acts. A Comanche war party of over a hundred men struck near Monclova, Coahuila, over Christmas of 1821–1822. The group soon broke into smaller bands, with some Indians returning to the Rio Grande to "run mustangs," while others extended their raiding nearly to the coast.[17]

Despite these raids, Mexican authorities continued to negotiate with Comanche leaders. Yet conditions had changed in the years after 1810. While Mexico could hardly protect itself from raiders, the leading chiefs of the Comanches and Wichitas had difficulty in controlling their warriors and often said so in councils. Chiefs, with-out presents to give their young men, found their positions compromised.

The problem was complicated further by the large number of Hispanic people who now lived with the Comanches and Wichitas and felt no loyalty toward Mexico. In a conference held at San Antonio in December 1822, several leading Comanche chiefs admitted to a loss of political power. "It is not possible for them to contain the bad Indians," reported the new governor, José Felix Trespalacios, "as they said to me that among the Indians there are *ladrones*" (literally, thieves or worthless men).[18] These ladrones were Tejanos and American renegades. One raiding party reported by General López in 1823 supposedly had "3 Mexicanos" who helped lead the group, serving as guides. The general ordered their arrest—a futile gesture.

Whether these renegades had been captives whom the Comanches and Wichitas had carried off at an earlier date is difficult to determine. A number very likely had been with the American/Mexican brigades that had begun to trade with the Comanches after 1815 and stayed on, marrying Comanche women. At least among the Penatekas, or southern Comanches, renegade-led parties defied the leadership of the main chiefs, some of whom still wished to reestablish the "false peace."[19] Older, established chiefs in particular were more likely to garner influence from distributing presents than from leading war parties. Indeed, some older chiefs were beyond the point where their physical abilities would allow them to make the several-hundred-mile trip into Mexico.

When Mexican "Comanches" failed to know the geography of the lands south of the Rio Grande, the raiding parties took a few *pastores* (shepherds) prisoner and ordered them to locate the best livestock. One such raiding group took an entire "party of *vecinos* [pastores, most likely] . . . to guide the robbery" in December 1824.[20] Just a month later, a pastor came into Santa Rosa explaining that he had been "encircled" by Comanches and forced to take the Indians to nearby horse herds.[21] While the Comanches refrained from harming the young captive, a similar party, working below the Rio Grande in August 1825 near the small village of Palafax, killed five people and carried off six women and children.[22] With the false peace in shambles and Mexicans seemingly incapable of defending themselves, Comanches began losing respect for their one-time friends and commercial partners. Yet few pastores were killed; they were not worthy military opponents.

By late fall of 1825, Indian raiding parties lingered in the Rio Grande valley, almost unopposed. Comanches captured a young Mexican named José Ibarra in November while he tended stock on a ranch just north of what is today Browns-ville, Texas. While the Indians queried the young captive, searching for stock, they encountered several other pastores and captured them as well. As another Comanche party joined the original group, Ibarra recognized that several of the men riding with the Indians were "Spaniards." But as the party headed north, Mexican troops surprised them and recovered the captives as well as several other pastores who claimed to have been forced to join the party.

The recovered Mexican captives provided a wealth of information. From Narcisco Gonzáles, a young man from the town of Palo Alto on the Rio Grande, the Mexican commander learned that some eighty-seven Indians made up the party and that many of them spoke Spanish. They had collected 170 horses from Coahuila and southern Texas. Unlike previous raiders, however, most of these Indians were Yamparicas (northern Comanches). When asked about the number of vecinos or pastores living with this particular band, Gonzáles estimated at least a hundred, if not more. The plains communities where they lived had become extensive markets where corn, milk, and butter were occasionally imported and livestock, weapons, and a host of other items exchanged.[23]

These northern Comanches had learned their trade of raiding into Mexico from the southern Comanche and Wichita bands. A second recaptured Mexican named Toberto Tijerina, who had lived with these Brazos River, or Penateka, Comanches outlined the ethnic mixture of the group: they consisted of "Comanches, Tawakonies [Wichitas], and some respected traders [the word used here is *tallador*] of which he saw of them some physical features. They were those of different nations."[24] The ethnic mix of Texas had been extended to the Plains tribes.[25]

Some Mexican military officers suspected that pastores willingly aided Comanches. In truth, these peasants had scant reason not to. Mexican pastores received very little protection from their government or the owners of the larger Tejano ranches. It was sensible for them to accept a fate of captivity. Usually Comanches treated their Mexican captives quite well; and once in Comanche towns, captives found many Mexicans who had been taken in years past. Some had risen in Comanche ranks to be trusted advisers, prominent warriors, and even chiefs.[26]

Understandably, Mexican elites—especially officials—complained bitterly of such renegades. Even Bastrop, Austin's friend, weighed in, charging that they contributed to the higher level of violence generally associated with raids in the mid-1820s. In particular, Bastrop claimed that they tended to attack helpless women, a new wrinkle that came from "the example & persuasion of the vile Mexicans who had refuge in their [Comanche and Wichita] towns." Bastrop wanted the renegades captured and condemned.[27] As the violence and raiding escalated, Mexican officials debated blame and sought solutions.

Rafael Gonzáles became commandant general of Coahuila-Texas and Nuevo León in 1824. He ordered Mateo Ahumada to organize *compañias volantes* ("flying companies") of cavalry to defend the various Texas communities. While often poorly armed, some companies were patrolling the lands between the Rio Grande and San Antonio by the late 1820s, even though they seldom closed with Comanche raiding parties.[28] These rancheros became an object lesson for the famous Texas Rangers, who would soon take on a similar role. The early Texans who came into the valleys of the Brazos and Colorado rivers had no experience with cavalry tactics and closely observed how the Mexicans performed.

The escalating violence might have been dealt with more effectively had the Red River frontier remained peaceful. In 1822, however, war erupted in western Arkansas and what would soon be designated as Indian Territory, as migrating Cherokees and then Choctaws clashed with Osage Indians over hunting grounds. Soon bands of Shawnees, Delawares, and Kickapoos—moving south from the Missouri River—joined the fray on the side of the Cherokees. Raiding and counterraiding went on for nearly a decade. The result was that more and more immigrant Indians were forced into Texas in the late 1820s.[29]

The intertribal fighting reflected upon the terrible planning of the U.S. government in implementing its removal policy. On arriving in the American West, the immigrating tribes often found that other Indians and even Anglo frontiersmen claimed lands promised to them. Many Indian immigrants (including Bowles's Cherokee band, which crossed the Red River into Texas in 1820) understandably came to view Mexican Texas as being more hospitable. Immigrant Indian settlement in Texas seemed to come into clearer focus when a talented mixed-blood named Richard Fields joined Bowles's emerging town north of Nacogdoches.

Fields was roughly forty years of age when he reached the West. The son of a Scottish trader, Ludovic Grant, and a Cherokee woman, he had grown to maturity in a matrilineal society. His sympathies remained with Indians, especially his mother's clan. But he was fully assimilated into the frontier economy, one of hunting and trading and, as it would seem, traveling. Richard Fields had been everywhere, at times translating for the government with the Chickasaws, opening land in Arkansas for farming, and drifting down into Louisiana, looking for opportunities. He spent many an evening under an open sky. Accordingly, he had the typical frontier look: sinewy, strong, and athletic. He was somewhat of a ladies' man, and he stuck out in a crowd. He would quickly turn Texas upside-down.

Early on, Fields followed his father, turning to the Indian trade. On one venture, he met the legendary Francois Grappe, a part-French, part-Indian upper Louisiana trader who had become the beloved guardian of the eastern Caddo people. Fields was undoubtedly impressed with Grappe's sense of geopolitics; he even married Grappe's daughter, who was part Indian, part French, and part African American. Whether the couple had children or not is unknown, but Fields apparently stayed only a few years with his new family; he was restless and determined to do more with his life. By 1812, he had returned to the East, where he worked as an interpreter. Then war broke out and he joined Andrew Jackson's army, raising a company of Cherokee scouts and serving as its captain. After the war, Fields drifted west, finally arriving in Texas.[30]

Just how Bowles received him is unknown, but likely the young Fields got on well with the old chief, at least at first. Fields may even have been related to Bowles. He definitely would have needed Bowles's support to follow through on his ambitious plans. Fields hoped to benefit from the fluid situation in Texas, especially regarding land. Writing to Governor Martínez in February 1822, he stated a willingness to "fall at the feet" of the governor and wondered what Mexico might do "for us poor Indians."[31] Fields then traveled to San Antonio with several other leaders, including Bowles—a rather obvious indication of Bowles's early support—and met the new governor, Trespalacios. Both men signed a "treaty" that allowed Bowles's Cherokees to reside in Texas. Trespalacios reported that the Indians were "the most industrious and useful of those from the United States," adding that they would surely follow "the course of the [Mexican] empire." But the treaty allowed the Indians only to select land and plant crops.[32] It gave them no title, something Trespalacios lacked the authority to do.

The restless Fields then traveled on to Mexico City and put his case for a land grant to the newly crowned emperor, Agustín de Iturbide, over the winter of 1822–1823. Unfortunately, liberals forced Iturbide to abdicate in March, but nevertheless, the Cherokee agent, with Bowles again at his side, received a letter that gave provisional sanction to Trespalacios's former agreement. Whether he realized it or not, Fields would have to apply to the state government for a land grant, just like the other hopeful empresarios in Mexico City at the time. But as he passed by San Antonio upon returning to Texas in July 1823, Fields failed, seemingly on purpose, to show this letter to local authorities. A year later, he wrote the new political chief, José Antonio Saucedo, that a Comanche raiding party had prevented him from "presenting himself at the capitol . . . so that this government would be satisfied with the papers that I obtained." He assured Saucedo that the supreme government "had conceded to me in this Province land sufficient to establish me with the part of the tribe of Indians [Bowles's Cherokees] who depend upon me."[33]

Fields had used Bowles's Cherokees as a vehicle for what he slowly revealed as a rather grandiose plan of Indian empire. Perhaps he took the idea from the Shawnee Tecumseh, who had tried to forge a pan-Indian alliance in the East after 1800. Tecumseh had traveled south to visit the Cherokees and Creeks to effect such a union in 1811. He urged resistance because the United States would soon take their land. A large contingent of Creeks, called the "Red Sticks," took up Tecumseh's cause and opened hostilities against the United States soon after. Fields had fought alongside Jackson against the Red Sticks, witnessing their utter destruction at Horseshoe Bend in central Alabama in 1813. Jackson forced the Creeks to relinquish 22,000,000 acres as a penalty at the conclusion of the campaign.

Fields clearly had had an epiphany. Texas in 1823 offered him an opportunity to provide a safe home for his Indian brothers and perhaps some glory and honor for Richard Fields. He set about recruiting eastern tribes from the United States that increasingly were losing their lands. He intimated in letters sent east that he possessed "empresario powers." His tone even became revolutionary, as he called upon all "oppressed and dissatisfied Indians to join" him in Texas. Fields was sorely upset with the United States by 1823.

Ironically, despite all of Fields's attempts at manipulation, a Shawnee band of 270 families, or nearly two thousand people, was the first to convince the state of Coahuila-Texas to grant them land. They had an even shrewder negotiator, one John Norton, a Canadian mixed-blood who had fought with Tecumseh. The Shawnees had arrived in Texas in October 1824, and Norton's petition at Saltillo reached state government authorities just at the right time. The Mexican liberal Francisco Ruíz—a man always sympathetic to Indians—was asked by state authorities for an opinion on the Shawnee request. Ruíz visited Norton's Shawnee town, commended the people for their diligence, and helped pave the way for the state land grant, which gave the Shawnees lands on the right bank of the Red River, just above the Great Bend.[34]

The Shawnees had joined what was becoming a mad scramble for land in Texas. The next spring, 1825, a host of grants were issued, often with indecisive boundaries. Despite the competitors, Austin's colony along the Colorado and Brazos rivers grew more rapidly than any of the others, almost doubling in size with every passing year. Not surprisingly, Austin found the notion of granting lands to immigrant Indians from the United States troubling at best. While he wished to remain on good terms with state authorities in Saltillo, he feared the outcome of Indian migration to Texas and quietly made his argument against it whenever possible. Given the fact that the state had given land to followers of Tecumseh, Austin lobbied and received the right to organize militia units. His empresario grant as well as local institutions further implied such a power.[35]

As soon as he possessed the men, Austin commissioned the first militia, or "ranger," companies along the Colorado River. (The term "ranger" had been used in the early U.S. colonies to identify volunteer militias, mostly infantry troops who served for a number of months.)[36] While there seemed to be little threat from the northern Indians—the Comanches and Wichitas had raided Tejano or Mexican ranches and mostly left Anglos alone—Austin and his rangers sought to assert their colony's claim to lands in the lower Colorado and Brazos river valleys. This meant removing the Tonkawa and Karankawa Indians, the original inhabitants, who had remained in the area.

The opportunity to run these people out came after two settlers had been killed. The murderers were never identified, but Europeans had been trespassing on land consistently hunted by the Karankawas in the lower Colorado valley for centuries. The deer populations of the region around the mouth of the Colorado River were still large and provided a primary food source for the Indians, and Texans were also living on deer in the early years of settlement, occasionally competing with the Indians. In the absence of Austin, who was in Mexico City, Robert Kuykendall organized the rangers who stalked the Karankawas. Finding their unsuspecting targets on Skull Creek, a tributary of the Colorado, Kuykendall's men sneaked through the brush to the village's perimeter and all at once fired into the lodges. The Texans murdered nearly two dozen Karankawas in one fusillade—men, women, and children alike.

The Karankawa had remained mostly independent of European intrusion for well over a hundred years. Spaniards had tried to convert them at mission stations at La Bahía and Refugio, but only a few of their number had become nominal Christians. This general Spanish failure had led to a myriad of mythological perceptions of these Indians, including the belief that they were cannibals. Conquering societies, when faced with rejection of assimilation programs, often condemned Native groups as cannibals. It was a practice repeated time and again in South America. Regardless of the truth—and evidence does not support cannibalism—the Texans believed it and justified their attack because, as participant John H. Moore proclaimed, "their cannibalism . . . [was] beyond question."[37]

Texans (particularly young Moore, who had just arrived in the colony) had never witnessed a Karankawa Indian eat anyone. However, Moore hated Indians and soon gained a reputation for being the most efficient organizer of rangers in Texas, killing hundreds of Indians in surprise attacks similar to the one on the Karankawas. Moore and his fellow rangers may have had a secondary reason for the attack. His report of the action indicated that the Texans were nearly out of food, whereas the Karankawa village was well supplied. The years 1821 and 1822 had been dry, and crops had failed. The Karankawa, in contrast to the Anglo-Texans, were excellent hunters and fishermen, and their economy was largely unaffected by the lack of rain. The Texans took what they wanted and scalped the dead, taking trophies that served as topics of discussion around late-night campfires. The massacre of the Karankawas set the tone for the handling of nearby Indians by Austin's colonists.[38]

After his return, Austin used his small ranger force to surround and punish a small Tonkawa band of Indians. He forced the chief to whip several young men for supposedly stealing stock. Once again, the evidence for guilt was lacking. In 1825, Austin's rangers, acting this time on their own accord, overran a Tonkawa camp, killing two people and wounding four. Faced with Wichita and Comanche enemies in the north, the Tonkawas desperately tried thereafter to stay out of the way of Anglo settlers as well as their various Indian enemies, a difficult balancing act. They moved increasingly west and south, out of the central Colorado valley.[39]

Despite their earlier defeat, the Karankawas were not as obliging. They continued to defend their land, particularly the coastal regions where they hunted, fished, and collected various sea foods. Minor clashes with colonists increased, however, as more and more Anglos arrived and settled on the lower Colorado. Feuding over deer occurred continuously, with small hunting parties taking shots at each other. Austin convinced the Spanish priest at Refugio to arrange a treaty with the Indians in September 1824. Some of their leaders apparently agreed to give up land along the lower Colorado and Brazos rivers and to remain west of the Guadalupe River, a rather desolate region that Anglos did not want. But the Karankawas could not survive there and soon returned. Convinced that the Karankawas had broken the treaty, Austin demanded of Mexican authorities in San Antonio the right to force them out. Colonel Ahumada, military commander of Texas, agreed, likely unaware of how determined and brutal the Texans would be.[40]

Rangers under Moore and Kuykendall had little trouble finding the main Karankawa hunting village, located at the mouth of the Colorado River. The rangers launched an all-out assault, and in the ensuing slaughter, the color of the water turned from murky brown to red. Some forty Indians died in a few minutes. As Kuykendall proudly proclaimed, "Indian hunting" had become "sport" in Texas. A few children and females were saved, especially the younger women. Many of the rangers were single, and they described the process of acquiring temporary sexual partners and house servants as "chasing squaws." The few surviving Karankawas fled south, giving up their ancestral lands. In May 1827, Mexican authorities finally orchestrated a treaty in which the Karankawas agreed to stay below the La Vaca River.[41]

The Tonkawas and Karankawas hardly threatened anyone. Austin, however, viewed Comanches and Wichitas in an entirely different light. Writing to militia commander Josiah H. Bell in August 1823, Austin ordered the rangers to watch the Waco Indians. The Wacos had for years courted the Penatekas (southern Comanches), a relationship that produced some intermarriage. While the Wacos remained mostly peaceful, some Waco young men imitated their Comanche friends, joining them on raids in the south. Beyond a doubt, the Wacos saw Texas as their promised land, and they meant to defend it.

Austin's militia, consisting of only fifty to seventy-five men, was capable of destroying the Karankawas but not the more powerful and better-armed Wacos. "I wish if possible to avoid an open rupture with them [Wacos] for six months," he confided to Bell but added that "if they commit any more depredations, the only alternative will be an expedition to destroy their village."[42] Austin obviously understood that the Wacos could stand in the way of his colony's future expansion up the Brazos River. But he had to expand his small army before warring with the Wacos, and temporary negotiation would give him the time he needed.

Over the winter of 1823–1824, several peaceful exchanges occurred between Austin's colonists and the Wacos. Nearly two hundred Indians visited the colony in March, indicating, as one contemporary observer put it, that "they did not come to scear [sic] the Americans from their houses." Instead they wished to exchange corn and beans, of which they had abundant quantities, for manufactured goods.[43] To reciprocate, Austin sent a trading brigade under Thomas M. Duke to the Waco town during the summer of 1824.

Duke found the town's sixty cone-shaped houses—near the present town of Waco, Texas—spread out like the spokes of a wheel around the huge council chamber meant for meeting dignitaries. A main street divided the community in half, or into moieties. This allowed the clan leaders on one side to negotiate marriages with those on the other, thus preventing incest, a strong tribal taboo. Nearby, Duke saw more than four hundred acres of corn, beans, and squash. The "very friendly" Wacos, Duke reported, denied having been involved in the recent thefts of horses near San Antonio, which likely had been perpetrated by Comanches, or in the murder of John Tumlinson, a Texan who had earlier been successful in attacking the Karankawas.[44]

Despite the friendship of the Wacos, conditions in the north deteriorated the next year. The state legislature at Saltillo had continued to hand out land grants in 1825. Increasingly, men with influence or money acquired the grants. The new land brokers included one Hayden Edwards, a Virginian who had patiently waited on the legislative assembly and received the right to settle eight hundred American families on lands west and south of Nacogdoches. The transplanted New Yorker Frost Thorn, who then called Nacogdoches home, had received a smaller grant for four hundred families, to be settled north of Edwards's land. Just what Fields knew about these events, and when, is not clear, but he called an emergency council meeting of all tribes in East Texas. Americans feared the worst, as rumors spread that Comanches, Wichitas, Wacos, Caddos, and Shawnees were all allied with the Cherokees and intended to drive all Americans, including Edwards and Frost and some new colonists, from the region.

Such a notion was ridiculous. Fields had little influence, and Plains Indians were increasingly upset with the invasion of East Texas by immigrant tribes. Nevertheless, the news worried Austin, who now felt strong enough to assail the Indians closest to his colony. He used the threat as an excuse and asked Mexican authorities for permission to drive out the Wacos. Austin got his wish on August 17, 1825. But in what increasingly became typical of Mexico's vacillating Indian policy, the same officials suspended the order a few days later, fearing a general war. By September the campaign was again on, and once again called off. The misunderstandings increased over the winter. In the meantime, the Wacos and Tawakoni Wichitas on the central Brazos quietly harvested their crops and retreated to the north, hearing rumor after rumor of an intended assault by the Texan forces, supported by Mexico.[45]

Colonel Ahumada finally ordered José Miguel Arciniega to Nacogdoches in February 1826 to verify the "hostile projects" of Fields, which supposedly had been aimed "against the new populations of this department." To his surprise, Arciniega found Fields supportive of the Mexican government.[46] The self-anointed Cherokee spokesman claimed that only disgruntled Caddos had joined the Comanches and Wichitas. Nevertheless, Arciniega also heard that some eight thousand more immigrant Indians, supposedly loyal to Fields, were on the Red River and wished to enter Texas. Fields confidently asserted to Arciniega that they were "those which the government of the state of Coahuila-Texas has conceded to me that they . . . come and establish themselves on these lands."[47]

Such news—Arciniega's report and Fields's braggadocio—must have confused Colonel Ahumada. What sort of land grant did Fields have? What new immigrant Indians had been granted entrance to Texas? Given the lack of resources with which to counter Fields, the absence of information regarding Fields's authority, and the continued raids by Plains tribes along the Rio Grande, Ahumada turned instead to Austin. He feared that the situation was getting out of hand in the north, and he once again ordered Austin's rangers to attack the Waco and Tawakoni Wichitas. While the colonel's intentions are unclear, he certainly did not want a unified Indian alliance of Wichitas, Comanches, and immigrant Indians arrayed against him. And with Fields apparently disposed to be friendly toward Mexico, Austin soon surmised that Fields's warriors could be used effectively against the Wacos and Tawakonis, who blocked the Anglo advance up the Brazos River.[48]

In mid-April 1826, Austin wrote to Fields, hoping to coordinate an assault. The Americans would surprise the Wacos while Fields's Cherokees would assail the Tawakoni Wichitas, who had in the meantime moved their town (fearing an attack from immigrant Indians) from the Trinity River to the upper Navasota, some forty miles farther west. Then, together the two armies would "destroy the Toweass [Tao-vayas Wichita] village on Red River." Dangling the carrot, Austin concluded his letter to Fields: "I have no doubt if you turn out in this expedition and destroy the Tawakany village [on the Navasota] . . . that it will be the means of securing you land in the country."[49] Austin, who opposed giving land to immigrant Indians, had few scruples about promising it to schemers such as Fields, if in so doing he could buy their service.[50]

Nevertheless, other delays followed. Austin bided his time by writing inflammatory letters to Ahumada and Saucedo. He indicted the Wacos, Tawakonis, and even the poor Caddo bands—Anadarko, Kichai, and Nacogdoches—calling them raiders who had killed Mexicans and rustled stock. With very little evidence, Austin concluded that all those tribes "are friendly with the Tahuacanoes [Tawakonis], and I believe their destruction to be very important for the common security."[51] Austin's geopolitical maneuvering had only one goal: expel the Indians nearest his colony from their lands. If immigrant Indians or even Mexican troops would help, so much the better. It was classic ethnic cleansing.

Austin's appeal finally bore fruit in May 1826; despite his inability to send Mexican troops, Colonel Ahumada ordered Austin to drive the Wacos from the central Brazos valley. Austin's ranger force, now capable of putting 180 men in the field, stealthily moved up the Brazos River, only to find the Waco town completely abandoned. The Tawakonis had also departed, moving northward and westward, into the valleys of the upper Trinity and Brazos rivers. In an appeal indicative of the value of Waco lands, the ambitious Fields (who had failed to support Austin) asked if his people might occupy the old Waco town site. Ahumada quietly ignored the request, fearing a pan-Indian organization in northern Texas as much as he did the Waco and Tawakoni Wichitas.[52]

To Ahumada's chagrin, Austin's actions threw the relatively neutral Wacos and Tawakonis into the arms of the more aggressive northern Comanches and Taovayas Wichitas. Austin, for his part, cared little about the development of a cohesive Indian policy for Texas. He had clearly helped start a war with the Wichitas in May 1826. Indeed, the expulsion of the Wacos and Tawakonis dashed forever any hope of reestablishing the peace that had existed prior to 1810.[53] Mexican policymakers had vacillated among the once-workable "false peace," a growing belief that the northern Plains Indians must be challenged and defeated, concern over the rise of immigrant Indian power in northern Texas, and the supposed need to assist Austin in the development of his colony. While Austin's colony had prospered, all the other groups had been left dangling in the breeze.

Austin must have been pleased with himself at the outcome of these events. He had convinced Mexico of the danger of groups such as the Karankawas, Tonkawas, Wacos, and Tawakonis, and all had been forced from their land. As a result, vast and extremely valuable new sections of Texas had been opened. The coastal plain along the Colorado and Brazos rivers had been cleared of Indians, and so had the central portions of these valleys. Neither area had been part of Austin's original grant, but both could now be settled. What is more, Austin had learned that he could play one Indian tribe against another and that Mexico would sanction such an effort. While Spain on occasion had tried to protect the rights of Indians, the new state officials of Coahuila-Texas seemed enamored with promoting economic progress, so much so that they sanctioned ethnic cleansing as a viable policy for development.

Those same liberal officials seemed oblivious to other alternatives. An alliance with Fields and the increasing numbers of immigrant Indians might have aided Mexico, even offered a barrier to increased American hegemony. Such a possibility became more remote when news arrived in the colony and at San Antonio of growing unrest in and about Nacogdoches as new forces of immigrant Indians were appearing in droves, asking for land. Fields, who had portrayed himself as a man dedicated to supporting Mexican policy, increasingly represented himself as the leader of the immigrant Indians.

In addition, as this latest development with the immigrant Indians unfolded, the Comanches and Wichitas opened a new offensive in the south. Mexican state officials had their hands full.

4

THE MUDDLE OF
EARLY MEXICAN FEDERALISM

Many of the scheming political players in Texas in the mid- to late 1820s had ambition and nerve, but they worked under a governmental regime that lacked funding and many basic institutions. The legislature of the new state of Coahuila-Texas began meeting at Saltillo in 1824. But the legislators took three long years to write a constitution, and only then could a governor—José Maria Viesca—be elected. During this hiatus, many immigrant Indians and Anglos entered Texas, and the resulting boom in land speculation set the tone for the development of the region for years to come. Fundamentally, the new federalist state government was unprepared to manage this rapid settlement.

In an unorthodox fashion, as the members of the state legislature carved out a constitution, the assembly also passed many new laws before a governor existed to sign them. These included the creation of a state empresario system, under which many land grants were issued. José Antonio Navarro and José Miguel Arciniega, the two representatives from Texas allowed in the legislative assembly, lobbied for many of the land grants, even supporting a host of Anglo applicants. Nevertheless, considerable differences existed among legislators about a variety of other issues—especially Indian policy and slavery, concerns that Anglo settlers watched with interest.

Most Mexican politicians agreed initially that "federalist" (state) laws should predominate in land distribution instead of "centralist" (national) legislation coming from Mexico City. But issues such as national defense proved more problematic. The state defended its right to organize a militia. Federalists, like their liberal counterparts in the United States, believed that a strong national army might be repressive. But the state military commandant at San Antonio, Colonel Mateo Ahumada, had few troops and little money with which to hire them. José Antonio Saucedo, the Texas political chief, who resided at San Antonio, tried to help raise troops but had little success. Without an enforcement arm, the state legislature found it difficult to maintain law and order.

This inability could not have come at a worse time. A crisis regarding the distribution of land in northern Texas had evolved. Many empresario grants had been handed out by the legislature, most to speculators. Thousands of immigrant Indians were entering Texas, and their leaders demanded land. These Indians were ideally suited for military use against the Plains tribes that continued to raid horse herds in the south, but in the Mexican view of the world even the newly arriving immigrant Indians were only partly civilized and thus not unlike those who had followed Hidalgo and Morclos. Many liberals in Saltillo preferred to favor Anglos or even Tejanos—rather than Indians—with land grants.[1]

This left the Anglo settlers as the most logical military allies for the new state. Most hailed from the upper South, a few had military experience in the War of 1812, and all of them, it seemed, owned long rifles. Five or six, mounted on good horses, could go unmolested almost anywhere. These same Anglos had already demonstrated few scruples when it came to destroying Indians living along the coast. Nevertheless, the Anglos living in and about Nacogdoches were a different lot; Colonel Ahumada listened to Stephen Austin when it came to military affairs and recognized the effectiveness of Austin's rangers, but Ahumada soon came to distrust the undisciplined border ruffians who had settled in northeastern Texas. Ahumada's suspicions seemed all but confirmed when news arrived of trouble started near Nacogdoches by an American empresario named Hayden Edwards.

Edwards came to Texas in 1825 with respectable credentials. He had grown to maturity in a wealthy Virginia household, obtained an education, and married well. But his investments in Kentucky had soured, likely as a result of the depression of 1819. Edwards reached Saltillo just as the legislature was handing out empresario grants; he secured a large grant, likely with Navarro's help, that included lands in and about Nacogdoches, extending well west and south of the town. The state required him to settle eight hundred families on the parcel, and he reached Nacogdoches that fall prepared to do business.

Unfortunately, many of the Creole families who lived along the road and back from it claimed to have titles to their farms; others, many of whom were newly arrived Anglo-Americans, simply squatted on land that they then claimed. Worse, Edwards's grant together with the one given to his son-in-law, Frost Thorn, overlapped that of the Indian claim as outlined by Richard Fields. Fields openly claimed in Nacogdoches that Indian lands began along the road west of Nacogdoches and extended northward to the Sabine River and westward to the Neches River.

Even so, Edwards held his ground. He demanded that the older settlers bring in their titles and record them. At times, he threatened to dislodge squatters. Protest letters poured into San Antonio, where Saucedo investigated both sides of the dispute over the summer of 1825. But Saucedo had a limited knowledge of the situation;

he knew that many of the so-called settlers—Anglos, Tejanos, and Indians—were involved in the Comanche plains trade, which he hoped to halt. The most notable of these traders, such as the revolutionaries Bernardo Gutiérrez de Lara, Francisco Ruíz, and Peter Ellis Bean, had returned to Coahuila or San Antonio to work with the liberal government, but hundreds of undisciplined men who had worked with them remained in and about Nacogdoches.

As the struggle over northern Texas continued, some squatters and settlers—Creoles, Anglos, mestizos, and even a few mulattos and free blacks—organized themselves. In November, they signed a petition sent to the Saltillo legislature asking that a slice of Edwards's grant be withdrawn from him and titles issued to them. Making matters worse, the increasingly frustrated Edwards meddled in the December election of the local Nacogdoches alcalde (mayor), the man who controlled the local militia. The struggle convinced Edwards that he might better benefit by selling his entire empresario grant to speculators in the East, an illegal act under Mexican law. Ignoring legality, Edwards left for Virginia in May 1826, intent upon using his many business connections to find investors. Meanwhile, he turned over supervision of his colony to his brother Benjamin. Within a few weeks, news reached Benjamin that the Coahuila-Texas state legislature had rescinded Edwards's entire grant.[2]

This action should have pleased Fields, since it cleared title to lands that his Cherokees claimed and wanted. The Cherokee spokesman continued to inform various immigrant Indians that he had a right to settle them in Texas. In a barrage of letters, he assured Saucedo of his loyalty to Mexico and his growing success in organizing an Indian confederacy. He did have some official authority to act. When Fields traveled to Mexico City in 1823, the soon-to-be-deposed government of Emperor Iturbide had given him a commission granting him authority as "Captain of Indian Towns," a document he displayed from time to time.[3] At most, this was an honorary title, lacking much authority or troops and issued by a government long since out of power. Yet Fields explained the document differently. He argued in theory that it gave him the right to settle Indians in East Texas.

Regardless of the legality, Fields was moving ahead with his plans. A few thousand western Cherokees, under chiefs such as Tahchee and Blanket, had left settlements in Indian Territory, had reached the Red River, and were on both banks of the Red River by 1826. Several thousand Delawares, Shawnees, Kickapoos, Senecas, Piankeshaws, and Potawatomis were also either in Texas or headed south from Indian Territory. Fields reported that eight thousand new immigrant Indians had entered Texas and that more would come.[4] Austin confirmed these numbers in correspondence with Saucedo. The news frightened the Texas political chief, who sent the various reports on to military authorities, including Colonel Ahumada.

The Indian invasion in the north paled, however, in comparison to the assault that Texas faced in the south. The expulsion of the Wichitas from the central Brazos River valley in the spring of 1826 by Austin's rangers had prompted revenge raids that lasted into the fall. The war parties numbered two hundred to three hundred men; many southern Comanches joined the Wichitas. They attacked herders in fields at the San Antonio missions and overran the new colony of Green DeWitt, forcing his settlers to flee to Austin for protection. In the worst attack, Comanches and Wichitas killed seven dragoons guarding a horse herd near San Antonio and then easily beat off the seventy-nine state militiamen sent in relief.[5]

The small dragoon forces, or "flying companies," at Laredo and San Antonio were the only troops available to defend the region. The state legislature had hired Gutiérrez de Lara to build a new force to attack the Plains tribes, and throughout June and July he supposedly recruited troops and purchased horses. By August, however, state officials discovered that Gutiérrez de Lara had absconded with the funds entrusted to him.[6] His only accomplishment was a series of letters written to Richard Fields in which he seemingly convinced the Cherokee spokesman to join in the war. All that the Mexican state of Coahuila–Texas had to do was grant the immigrant Indians some land and, according to Fields, the Cherokees and their allies would fight for Coahuila–Texas against all comers.

With his hopes for land—and thus power—still very much alive, Fields continued to play at his role of military captain and colonizer throughout the late summer of 1826. He occasionally visited the Nacogdoches alcalde, Samuel Norris (whom Edwards had unsuccessfully tried to unseat), solemnly pledging his allegiance to Mexico. "All the newcomers of the different tribes look to this government for protection," he told Norris in late May. Fields seemed even more committed by August. He offered all his warriors "as volunteers . . . to the last drop of our blood for the defense of our country." Such an offer seemed very attractive after Saucedo learned of Gutiérrez de Lara's embezzlement.

Norris finally informed Fields in late September that permission had been granted for Fields to campaign against the western Wichitas and Comanches. The alcalde then added a crucial caveat; Saucedo wanted Fields to hand over the documents regarding the land grant that he claimed to have received in Mexico City, authorizing him to settle thousands of immigrant Indians on the soil of Coahila–Texas.[7]

While this was an innocent request, Fields realized the shaky nature of his supposed grant and that the new Mexican government had never recognized it. This concern on Fields's part became openly clear when an emissary that he had sent to Mexico City returned to the Cherokee towns. The Cherokee diplomat was John Dunn Hunter, a rather famous American who had been taken captive by Indians as a boy and later published his memoirs. The work revealed a man determined to exonerate Indians, in general, from claims of cruelty. Hunter had joined Fields's party in Texas during the summer of 1826 and had agreed to represent Fields and his request for a land grant in Mexico City.[8] Hunter was well known, even in Mexico City, and he presumed that his task would be an easy one.

Whether Fields sensed the reluctance of state officials, such as Ahumada or Saucedo, to support his people's land claim is unclear; what is certain is that Fields came to believe that Hunter could acquire a federal grant from the central government in Mexico City, an act that would have run counter to the powers vested in the new federalist system of government.[9] When Hunter reached the Cherokee towns in October, he sadly informed Fields that centralist officials in Mexico City not only had refused but had been insulting. The federal legislature had long ago stopped issuing land grants within the states.

Fields, not a patient man, saw his whole scheme slip away. In early December 1826, Fields and about a dozen men representing the ex-empresario Edwards imprisoned several officials at Nacogdoches, including Alcalde Norris and the local militia commander, José Antonio Sepulveda. Just as quickly, a few state militia, a handful of citizens, and a contingent of Caddo Indians rescued the state authorities.[10] Hope of defusing the power struggle dissipated when Fields joined Edwards in negotiating a treaty on December 21, calling for the creation of the Fredonia Republic. This document divided East Texas into the "Red Pueblo" and the "White Pueblo" (just where the term *pueblo* came from is unclear, but it obviously meant territory rather than a village), with the Indian lands (the "red") being designated northwest of Nacogdoches.[11]

The overzealous Fields claimed to represent some twenty-six different Indian nations during treaty negotiations, but in reality, few near Nacogdoches joined him, and most opposed him. What is more, he had made a major diplomatic mistake when he took up with a beautiful young Cherokee women, Laulerac, who was Chief Bowles's niece. Bowles supposedly had threatened earlier in the summer to kill Fields if the affair continued. Just when Fields needed support the most, then, he had alienated many Cherokees and Caddos (he had earlier abandoned his Caddo wife) over a romantic escapade. Cherokee tribal leaders Bowles and Big Mush soon convinced the nearby Shawnees, Delawares, and Kickapoos to avoid the brewing confrontation.

The Fredonia uprising attracted at most three dozen men, mostly Anglo ruffians. They soon were forced to retreat from Nacogdoches. As news of the erstwhile revolt reached San Antonio, Saucedo convinced Peter Ellis Bean to go to Nacogdoches and serve as Indian agent for the state. Bean spoke with Bowles and Big Mush and found them compliant. Despite Edwards's attempts to gain assistance in the United States and to solidify the support of other settlers in the region, the rebellion collapsed by late January; in a fit of unnecessary retribution, Indians loyal to Bowles executed both Fields and Hunter.[12]

The uprising, such as it was, had a lasting impact on liberal politicians at the state level as well as on national politicians in Mexico City. It revealed to these men the fluid nature of Mexico's northern border and the state's weakness in protecting that border. In addition, the revolt demonstrated the fickle nature of the loyalty of both Anglos and some Indians in East Texas. Even more concerning for Indians and

Anglos alike, by 1827 some Mexican politicians were beginning to rethink the entire land issue in the north.

Nevertheless, Mexican officials should have taken heart from the fact that the revolt failed because of a lack of support. Austin, for example, had immediately sent a force of mounted men with Bean, supplying more troops than were needed to expel the rebels. Indeed, Austin and his colonists remained loyal to the state of Coahuila-Texas, especially after Austin noted Edwards's "unnatural and bloody alliance with Indians!"

Austin's support, however, came with a price. He had been working on a compromise in the Saltillo legislature that would allow Texas residents to keep their slaves. The federal constitution had outlawed slavery, and the state was busy drafting a similar clause—which the legislature passed but failed to implement in the next year, 1827. Some of Austin's settlers had threatened to return to the United States rather than give up their slaves, a situation that would have crippled his ranger force and thus his colony.[13] Austin had convinced many state legislators of the economic necessity of slavery in Texas, arguing that the region would remain a province of poor herders and malcontents without it and that the loss of his rangers would also hinder development. The ultimate pliability of many legislators regarding this issue helped Austin convince his settlers that their slaves would not be confiscated.

But the Fredonia uprising had failed as well because the thousands of immigrant Indians along the Red River frontier never came to Fields's assistance. Many of them had little in common with Americans like Edwards to begin with; they saw such men as manipulative, land-hungry speculators of the sort that had forced Indian removal in the East. Bowles also helped keep the immigrant groups out of the conflict by working closely with agent Bean. Bean, for his part, continuously promised the immigrants land: just what they wanted to hear.[14]

Even so, the Fredonia fiasco caused an uproar. State officials suddenly realized that rebellion threatened the existence of Coahuila-Texas more than Comanche attacks did. When news of the uprising reached San Antonio, Saucedo and Ahumada organized a force of nearly three hundred state militia. Although lacking horses (thanks to Gutiérrez de Lara) and detained by rainy weather in Austin's colony for three weeks, this force eventually paraded through the streets of Nacogdoches, making a substantial impression.[15] Nearby tribal leaders quickly sought out Colonel Ahumada (who commanded the force), Bean, and Ruíz to discuss peace.

To push his advantage further, Colonel Ahumada arranged an elaborate ceremony in which the Indians had the opportunity to pledge their support. With the troops at attention along the dusty road that led through the center of Nacogdoches, chief after chief stepped forward to met the colonel. The oddity of it all must have impressed Ahumada, as Choctaws and Creeks joined Shawnees and Delawares. Chief Bowles's Cherokees participated, and the chief ceremoniously surrendered Fredonia's captured flags, which no doubt had come from Fields's and Hunter's dead bodies. Several Caddo leaders, joined by a few cautious Wichitas, looked on. To solidify friendship, the colonel encouraged the Caddos and Wichitas to bring in their Comanche allies to join the new alliance.[16]

Ruíz knew the western Indians well, but he had been tainted (in the minds of the Mexican authorities) by his earlier gun-trading activities in West Texas. It took the crisis of Fredonia for state officials to finally turn to him. Rather than wait for the Plains Indians to come in, Ahumada asked Ruíz in May 1827 to travel into the upper Brazos and Trinity river valleys to visit Wichita leaders. Some Wichitas, at least, seemed friendly and wanted peace. They blamed Comanches for recent raids in the south and openly and apologetically told Ahumada that "it had been a long time since they had gone below to raid." Nearly forty Wichitas followed Ruíz back to Nacogdoches the next month to smoke peace pipes with Bean. Once in Nacogdoches, the Wichitas expressed a wish to travel with their friend Ruíz to San Antonio and sign an official agreement.[17] Suddenly it seemed as though Coahuila-Texas might yet reinstate the "false peace" that Spain had once used to bring prosperity to the land.

Ruíz returned to the Wichita towns—high up the Brazos and Trinity rivers and protected by palisades from Austin's ranger army—in June 1827 and coaxed their leaders to San Antonio. The Indian leaders trusted Ruíz, for he had been among them many times. In the council that finally convened at San Antonio, both General Anastacio Bustamante (commanding federal troops in northern Mexico) and Colonel Ahumada attended, along with Saucedo, as well as Ruíz and Bean. After the obligatory smoking of the peace pipe and the long, drawn-out speeches, the group signed a peace treaty that reduced the number of raiding parties that descended upon southern Texas.[18]

The treaty of 1827 was a document written by officials of the state of Coahuila-Texas. The Wichita chiefs promised to "be responsible for robberies . . . castigating the evildoers & delivering up the robbed material to their owners or paying the equivalent for it." Indians would need passports from military authorities to visit Mexican towns, even Nacogdoches, and the same would be true for Tejanos or Anglos who wished to trade with the Indians.[19] The agreement said little about the Anglos in Austin's nearby colony or their expansion northward up the Brazos River. To what degree Indian leaders understood the details is difficult to determine, but most spoke Spanish, and many had bargained with Spaniards or Mexicans before.

Nine chiefs (including a number of significant leaders) signed the agreement, which represented a serious effort on the part of the Indians to reestablish exchange and peace. Young José Maria, who would become a crucially important tribal leader in later years, fixed his mark on the document as a representative of the western Caddos. Menchaca—who often used the Christian name Miguel, suggesting a Spanish mission background—represented the Waco Wichitas, who had been expelled from the central Brazos region. Cibolo Tonto affixed his mark for the Tawakoni Wichitas, yet another group that had been pushed out of central Texas.

Most Comanche band leaders kept their distance from these agreements. Two prominent Penateka chiefs did sign the treaty, though; Quellunes and Incoroy led mobile villages that generally could be found along the central Colorado or the Brazos River. Visibly missing were chiefs from the leading Yamparica bands. The Taovayas—the Red River Wichitas—also seemed to avoid the discussions. The involvement of Ruíz suggests that state officials considered this a limited treaty, negotiated mostly with Indian peoples from central Texas.[20] Most regional politicians and military leaders seemed surprised, however, when raids occurred near Santa Rosa, Presidio Rio Grande, Lampazos, San Fernando, and the small, budding Texan town of Gonzales.[21] In the aftermath, the Waco chief Menchaca blamed the northern Comanches—Yamparicas, especially—who had rejected the 1827 accords.[22]

Even more disconcerting, the peace discussions at both Nacogdoches and San Antonio invariably turned to a debate over land, especially when state officials talked with the immigrant Indians. Representatives of various Shawnee, Delaware, Kickapoo, Alabama, Choctaw, and Coushatta bands openly requested land grants from Coahuila-Texas that summer.[23] Just how many individuals would have benefited from such a grant was relatively unknown, although Fields had reported eight thousand people and Austin put the number at about 1,600 families.

Each of these groups had reasons for moving to Texas. The Kickapoos, in particular, were outraged at the United States for expelling them from their homelands. The Kickapoos had even worked against Edwards because he had "American" followers.[24] Kickapoo hatred of Americans ran deep. When they made their request for land at Nacogdoches, they initially refused to sit in council because the interpreter, Joseph Durst, was supposedly an American. When it was explained that Durst was French, Kickapoo leaders opened the discussions with a torrent of complaints. The Americans, they said, "had moved them from their own country" to a bad country, where "their women and children were dying." The U.S. Bureau of Indian Affairs had failed to provide promised supplies for emigrating tribes. When General Bustamante heard their appeal, he seemed more sympathetic than Ahumada, but he advised them that only state officials, not federal army officers, could grant lands.[25]

For their part, state officials were mostly preoccupied with other issues. The Fredonia fiasco had produced an emerging political backlash centered on the Americans and their relationship with Indians. Some state politicians who supported development in Texas even rethought the general issue of colonization after Fredonia. Some privately questioned the notion that Anglo-Americans would make good citizens; others, in a display reminiscent of the racism of the southern United States, expressed an inordinate fear of the immigrant Indian tribes.[26] Ahumada's views seemed increasingly representative: the Kickapoos, he wrote, were "entirely barbaric" and "very warlike," and they might be "seduced by others [Americans?] who intend our ruin."[27]

Stephen Austin, hardly to anyone's surprise, agreed with part of this assessment. Writing to Francisco Madero at Mexico City, Austin claimed that hundreds of

Shawnees, Kickapoos, Quapaws, and others were gathered along the Red River, ready to descend into the central heartland of Texas. Austin observed that the Shawnees were "known as the party of Tecumseh . . . celebrated for their constant hatred for whites." And he noted that the Kickapoos were "all bad," their customs "barbarous." While the Cherokees already in East Texas were, Austin concluded, "the most advanced in civilization," they too could easily turn to war and, like all Indians, were the hereditary enemies of all whites.[28] Austin, who had previously supported granting land to some immigrant Indians, vehemently opposed it after the events surrounding Fredonia.

The buildup of Indians along both banks of the Red River had reached a point that caused even officials of the United States to fear war. Agent George Gray at Caddo Prairie along the Louisiana frontier wrote to the U.S. secretary of war in June 1827 that Texas and the Southwest seemed like a "whirlpool" that sucked every "restless and dissatisfied" Indian to its "bosom." He noted that "Delawares, Kickapoos, Shawnees, Choctaws and others" were appearing every day, and he concluded, "The feelings, habits and interests of so many discordant groups are so various and clashing that rapine and bloodshed will be the result."[29]

Many of the groups along the Red River, including some Anglo-Americans, continued to hunt. They did so mostly to feed themselves, but competition over game and land invariably led to trouble. Conflict started near Pecan Point in March 1828 when Anglos dispersed some Shawnees living on the south bank of the Red River, well within the grant given the Shawnees in 1825 by the state of Coahuila-Texas, although some officials in the United States claimed the land as part of Miller County, Arkansas, created by the territorial legislature in 1820. Further confusing matters, the U.S. Congress had recently given the land north of the Red River to the Choctaws, many of whom lived along the river.[30]

As tensions reached a breaking point, Wharton Rector, an Arkansas territorial militia colonel, demanded assistance from the U.S. Army at Fort Towson. The fort had been occupied by infantry troops only since 1823, but its commander, Captain Russell B. Hyde, had watched the tensions build along both banks of the Red River for some time. Like many career officers in the army, Hyde had no patience for the nearby Anglos who lived along the Red River because they sold whiskey to Indians and generally caused trouble. He used the occasion to explain the situation in a long, straightforward letter to the War Department in November 1828.

Hyde tersely denied Rector's request for help and lambasted the territorial government in Arkansas and its frontier militia. "The Indians against whom *Mr. Rector had declared war,*" he began, "were none of them within the limits of the United States. They were on the south side of Red River in the province of Texas at least 50 miles above where the Spanish line will strike the Red." What bothered Hyde most was the racist, rapine behavior of Rector and his men, many of whom were typical of the American frontier as well as that of Texas. "If the commanding officer of this frontier is bound to furnish every man with troops who calls on him," Hyde eloquently concluded, "and who wishes to immortalize himself by plundering an Indian town & killing a few women and children, it will be necessary that the force in this section . . . be considerably increased!"[31]

Despite the denial of support from Hyde, Rector raised a force of sixty-three militiamen and marched on the Shawnee town in June 1828. Saber in hand, Rector led his mob to the edge of the community. The Shawnees, who had every right to deny Rector and start a border war, decided to negotiate, despite their Mexican land grant. They had crops that needed time to mature, and they had women and children in their town whom they realized the Anglos would not hesitate to slaughter. They agreed to leave their lands if allowed to collect their corn and other belongings. Rector, being less confident of victory without the backing of the U.S. Army, accepted the offer. But the actions of his gang—the start of ethnic cleansing along the south bank of the Red River—had heightened tensions all along the river's corridor.

This corridor was filling with tribal people as well as Anglos, all looking for opportunities. Fighting seemed imminent in Indian Territory and south of it; the Fredonia Revolt had also demonstrated the tension around Nacogdoches. Thousands of immigrant Indians lived within a hundred miles of the town, all waiting to hear from Coahuila-Texas officials regarding land. To the west of town, Wichitas and Caddos had just signed treaties with Coahuila-Texas, but they still maintained their relationships with the powerful Comanches, some of whom did not want peace. And Austin, manipulating the state legislature, had received three more colonization grants by 1828 for land that he intended to wrest from Indians and settle.

With land disputes and conflict in the offing everywhere in Texas, Mexican officials decided to act. Much of the information regarding the problem came from General Anastacio Bustamante, who knew the Texas situation well. While serving as commander of the eastern interior provinces, headquartered at Laredo, he had received daily reports on the Fredonia rebellion. Like many elite Mexicans, Bustamante concluded that the state government of Coahuila-Texas was relatively helpless in dealing with the invading immigrant Indians and showed little restraint in handing out its public lands.

Throughout 1828, these views circulated in Mexico City, where the central government soon faced a crisis. Even though the first president of the republic, Guadalupe Victoria, served out his four-year term, in 1828 General Vicente Guerrero seized the executive office after the election results indicated that he had lost the presidency by a single vote. General Bustamante became his vice-president. As Guerrero's government moved politically more to the right, toward centralism, the republic became concerned with the expansion of the United States; in Texas, this translated into a growing fear of Americanization.

Guerrero acted first by ordering the formation of a border commission, the *comisión de límites*. The commission's charge was to survey the boundary line that separated Mexico from the United States, a line defined in the Adams-Onís Treaty of 1819. While this objective seemed harmless enough, the boundary commission received additional instructions. Quietly, it was to assess the populations of Texas—including Indian, Anglo, and Tejano—and make recommendations on settlement. Seemingly, the centralists were planning a future military occupation of the region to protect it from Anglo expansion. Impatient and nationalistic, centralists in Mexico City had concluded that the muddle that existed in Saltillo made it impossible for the state of Coahuila-Texas to defend the realm.

According to many centralists, however, concerns regarding defense constituted only half of the problem. The aggressiveness of Anglo settlers and their manipulation—some said bribery—of state politicians to acquire land grants appalled many nationalistic Mexican leaders. Coahuila-Texas seemed to be squandering its birthright. If the state could not police itself, centralists concluded, a stronger hand was necessary.

5

CENTRALISTS AND THE STRUGGLE FOR TEXAS LAND

President Vicente Guerrero selected General Manuel de Mier y Terán to head the Mexican border *comisión* formed in 1828. This man Mier y Terán was ideally suited for the job. Trim, thirty-eight years of age, and a meticulous dresser, he was young enough for the rigors of the campaign, yet he had developed special relationships with high-ranking Mexican officials, including Bustamante. The leaders of Mexico would listen to him.

Most important, Mier y Terán was intellectually inquisitive. He had graduated from the National College of Mines in 1811 and had developed an interest in botany and astronomy. Mier y Terán had embraced the nationalistic fervor that helped bring about Mexican independence, and he had served on the congressional committee that wrote the colonization law of 1823. He likely had met Austin during this time. After finishing the commission's report, Mier y Terán was appointed commandant general of the eastern provinces, taking over the old job of his mentor Bustamante. He would place his stamp on Texas, whether federalists, who feared the growing power of the central government, liked it or not.

To some degree, Mier y Terán represented the new Mexico, that of knowledge and advancement rather than colonialism, religion, and monarchy. Yet he too had survived Hidalgo's rebellion. He held many of the same prejudices common to most Mexican elites. In his reports and diary, he particularly noted the illiteracy and laziness of many Tejanos in Texas and the greed and manipulative nature of Anglos. Yet he wanted what was best for Mexico, and he had a certain sensitivity about the needs of the peasantry and even Indians. His real concern for his country's future led him to fits of depression, for Mier y Terán took his charge seriously. He would determine which lands should be assigned to existing Indians and which to Anglo and Tejano settlers, and he would inform Mexico City authorities on the "level of civilization" of the various Indian tribes in Texas.[1]

Mier y Terán reached the Rio Grande in the spring of 1828 and spent short periods of time at Laredo conferring with General Bustamante and at San Antonio, where he met the new military commander of Texas (who had recently replaced Colonel Ahumada), Colonel Antonio Elozúa. He developed a liking for Francisco Ruíz, who soon joined his party as a guide and interpreter, which helps explain Mier y Terán's growing knowledge of the Indian situation. Moving on to Nacogdoches by May, the general met Agent Bean, who had helped deter the Fredonia rebels. Through Bean and Ruíz, Mier y Terán sent messages to the various tribes, advising them to be patient and to meet him at Nacogdoches.[2]

The Indians arrived for the meeting in their best dress. Mier y Terán recorded the event in his diary, seemingly taken with their diversity despite their lack of what he considered cleanliness. Some had earrings made from metal plates, while others sported tin pendants connected to the "gristle of the nose." But all their spokesmen gave "well studied harangues," speaking with energy and sincerity. "They always began by mentioning the great *being or thing,*" Mier y Terán observed, giving this deity the title "father of men, or *it that is watching over all.*" They talked of support for Mexico, asked for land, and concluded with what Mier y Terán called their "petition of perpetual peace": "We are friends & we live as brothers, but as our lives are short & we do not have a long time to be on the land, we teach our sons to do as ourselves; . . . we ask in the same manner that you teach your sons to be our friends."[3]

Mier y Terán was impressed, more so than he had expected to be. These were civilized people, or nearly so, he thought. While he may have felt otherwise at first, General Mier y Terán soon felt certain that some of the immigrant Indians would help bring stability to the region. The Cherokees, Shawnees, and Delawares living near Nacogdoches numbered nearly seven hundred families, or four thousand people. Most were every bit as industrious as the nearby Anglo-Texans, and they possessed the intellect necessary to "incorporate themselves with the Mexican Nation." The Cherokees had even built schools and were teaching their children to read and write in their own language.[4] The only band that the general initially wished to expel from Texas was the Kickapoos, who he had learned numbered over a hundred families at the time. Mier y Terán described them as "a little less savage than the Comanches."[5]

Over the course of the following weeks, Mier y Terán discovered the basic dilemma facing Mexican Indian policy in the north. He surmised that the immigrant tribes were "not more than factions" of much larger groups, most of their number living in the eastern United States or north of the Red River. Land grants might encourage more migration, perhaps thousands of Indians, and thus more pressure on Mexico to admit them. Nevertheless, the immigrant Indians might offset the growing influence of Americans, whom Mier y Terán distrusted.

The most influential Americans were the empresarios, who numbered well over a dozen by 1828. They were an aggressive and manipulative lot. Indeed, one empresario, David G. Burnet, had just returned from Saltillo, where somehow he had convinced the legislature to cede to him the land taken from Hayden Edwards. This sort of activity constituted the very problem that Mier y Terán hoped to stop. In Nacogdoches, Burnet made common cause with Frost Thorn, who had been connected to Edwards both during the Fredonia plot and through marriage. They, along with Lorenzo de Zavala and Joseph Vehlein, had tied up a huge slice of land in East Texas, much of it coveted by the immigrant bands and other potential settlers.

Anglo-American settlers likely frightened the general to no end. They appropriated land without informing the *alcaldes* (mayors), and they gave little attention to the colonization laws.[6] "The whole population," Mier y Terán concluded, "is a mixture of strange and incoherent parts . . . colonists of another people [Americans], more aggressive and better informed than the Mexican inhabitants, but also more shrewd and unruly." Among them, Mier y Terán found fugitives from justice and vagabonds as well as a few honest men. "But honorable and dishonorable alike traveled with their political constitutions in their pockets, demanding the privileges, authority, and officers which such a constitution guarantees."[7] Although officials in Mexico City were concerned about the situation in Texas, none had arrived at such an obvious conclusion by 1828. Drastic measures were needed to stem the tide toward Anglo mob rule.

While political disorder abounded, the military situation seemed even more tenuous. Colonel José de las Piedras commanded a garrison of troops that had arrived at Nacogdoches just after the Fredonia uprising. They numbered 160 infantrymen and 60 mounted dragoons—when they were all there. But Piedras lacked ammunition and clothing and relied upon merchants at Natchitoches, Louisiana, for supplies. The Americans, by contrast, had seven hundred troops at Fort Jesup, east of the Sabine River, and most of the settlers between Nacogdoches and the Sabine possessed arms. Piedras estimated that the Anglos could collect three thousand men in a few days, making East Texas extremely vulnerable.[8]

As Mier y Terán prepared to return to Mexico City to render his report, he left East Texas to Bean, Ruíz, and Piedras. These men had instructions to build on the successful discussions that had been occurring since 1827. One way was to counsel continuously with the Indians; after the general departed, the agents left for the Cherokee communities to do so. There, Cherokees, Shawnees, Delawares, and Kickapoos joined with representatives of the Alabama, Coushatta, and Caddo people to pledge their allegiance to Mexico. Despite the differences in language and custom, the immigrant Indians seemed to be politically united. It was a festive and peaceful affair, marked by important, symbolic gestures.

Big Mush, the political chief of the Cherokees, opened the discussions. Mier y Terán had sensed the good judgment of this man. Before departing, the general enhanced this leader's prestige by giving Big Mush a baton, a medal, and a pipe, actions that likely irritated Bowles, the military chief. The status symbols seemed to work as Big Mush moved to the front, seemingly speaking for all the Indians. He placed twenty-one lines of white beads, symbolizing peace, on a bison hide that lay in the center of the council ring. Each string recorded a reference to historical events of the past and the agreements that the Cherokees had made to maintain peace.

Other leaders soon followed, several of whom addressed the issue of land. "The Mexicans are our fathers," said Pierna Negra (Black Leg), a younger Cherokee chief, "and we have taken their hand. . . . I was in Nacogdoches and I saw the great captain [Mier y Terán] who came to give us lands." Bean then confirmed what the Indians wanted to hear—that Mier y Terán had come "to give them lands on which they will build towns, grow maize, and raise cattle for their women and children."[9] After all the promises of land, and the impressive visit by Mier y Terán, it is no wonder that these Indian leaders overwhelmingly embraced Mexico. The Shawnee chief probably spoke for all in saying that "the enemies of the Mexicans are enemies of ours." Using the promise of land, Mexico had finally found some Indian allies in Texas.[10]

Meanwhile, General Bustamante had decided to campaign against the Plains Indians who had rejected the peace. The conditions were right, given the calm in northern Texas. The northern Comanches continued to lure some Wacos and Tao-vayas Wichitas into their war parties. Bustamante's decision hinged at least to some degree on information from the Penateka Comanche chief Barbaquista, who confirmed that northern Wichitas were joining Comanches.[11] A combined party of a few Wacos and many Taovayas Wichitas did strike Green DeWitt's small colony, southwest of Austin's settlements, in March 1829, stealing mostly horses.[12]

After the Indian attack—in which no one was killed—Colonel Elozúa ordered Bean to raise the immigrant Indians, commanding them to "attack & destroy in their pueblo the Tahuayasas [Tawakoni Wichitas]." Whether Elozúa knew it or not, these were the same Indians who had signed the treaty in San Antonio in 1827, and they were trying to live by it! It was the Taovayas, living farther north along the Red River, who were most troublesome and seemed most committed to war. Austin likewise called out part of his militia, joining Ruíz, who had been made a lieutenant colonel of state troops.[13]

Colonel Ruíz and the small force of several dozen Anglos went into the field first, converging on the nearly deserted Waco town in May. They found several dozen Wichita Wacos whom the Anglos wished to kill, but Ruíz, respecting the peace treaty, prevented the killing. He had learned that the Taovayas Wichitas had built new, fortified towns well to the north and west and were in constant contact with the northern Comanches.[14] Given their mobility and access to horses, Ruíz concluded that these Wichitas, not the Wacos, were responsible for the raids. Ruíz's failure to destroy the small Waco party, however, outraged the Anglos, who withdrew. Ruíz tried to placate them by arguing that it was wisest to attack the northern Indians in the fall when they returned to their towns to harvest their crops. His advice, while rejected at the time by Austin's troops, would become standard ranger tactics in the future.[15]

Colonel Elozúa mostly agreed. But as he organized men for a fall campaign, a large delegation of over a hundred Comanches and Wacos approached San Antonio. A Waco Indian, speaking for Chief Menchaca, argued in council that the Taovayas Wichitas were guilty of raids, not the Wacos or the Peneteka Comanches—the Wacos and Tawakonis only wanted peace. Despite his orders to make war, Colonel Elozúa felt obligated to smoke with the leaders of the delegation, watching as the smoke rose to the ceiling of the council chamber, signaling a oneness and guaranteeing the truth of each other's words.[16] Just after smoking, however, Elozúa ordered the destruction of the Waco community.

Two weeks later, a force of two hundred rangers from Austin's colony, following Elozúa's orders, hit the Wacos. Learning that most of these Indians had built a hunting camp in the San Saba valley, well west of the Colorado, Austin stalked them, utilizing Tejano and Apache scouts. These Wacos were living on Comanche lands, and they felt safe. But the rangers finally found the Waco town south of the junction of the San Saba and Colorado rivers. Fortunately, the Indians had spotted the Anglo force, and women and children fled as the rangers ordered the charge.

Quickly taking the town, the Anglo-Texans were dismayed to discover that it was nearly abandoned. The troops killed one rather old man and captured a few women and children. This Waco town, made of bison-hide tepees, offered up a store of corn, beans, dried meat, and buffalo robes. The rangers took what they wanted, after which Austin ordered them to burn anything that could not be carried away.[17]

Wacos and other Wichitas angrily retaliated in the late fall of 1829, targeting both DeWitt's and Austin's colonies. They chased herders from their herds and took horses and then briefly shut down the San Antonio to Nacogdoches road.[18] In San Antonio, a desperate Elozúa prodded Bean and Ruíz to use the Indian allies around Nacogdoches. True to their pledges, the Texas Cherokees organized a well-armed force that took the field in the spring of 1830. They needed little incentive beyond the land grant they expected as payment. They also marched off to war with a clear ethnic bias—the eastern immigrants wore manufactured clothing for the most part, rather than skins, and worked in a frontier economy. They looked down on the Wichitas.

The Cherokees had an excellent information network, knowing exactly where to find the Tawakoni Wichita town along the head of the Navasota River, in what would become Limestone County. Here, outcrops of limestone could be mined in sheets and used to cover deep, underground bunkers, which the Tawakonis used to create a dozen or so connected fortresses over which wood palisades were constructed. But on June 21, 1830, led by the old war chief Bowles himself, the Cherokees attacked the town with accurate fire from their long rifles.

Cherokee weaponry wrought havoc on the Tawakoni defenders, who were armed with a few muskets and bows and arrows. Wounded men who fell from the palisades were collected by the women and carried into the underground bunkers. Eventually, the Cherokees stormed the palisades and forced all of the Tawakonis to their last refuge. The dens provided some protection, but then the Cherokees tried to burn the Indians out. The fires likely killed many women and children, who huddled against the walls of what became their tomb. Ultimately, counting thirty-six dead Tawakoni men on the surface, the Cherokees finally sensed that they had satisfied Mexican authorities and broke off the engagement. Their victory brought them many horses, kettles, buffalo robes, and scalps, the common trophies of warfare on the frontier.[19]

As the Tawakoni refugees retreated west after this attack, General Mier y Terán returned to Texas with a substantial military force, recruited in the towns of central Mexico. In the fall of 1830, following Ruíz's advice, the general's troops discovered new Waco/Tawakoni towns recently built on the San Gabriel River, well west of the old Waco town; while few Indians died in the assault, the Mexican force destroyed everything, including fields laden with corn and beans. This food was meant for the lean winter months, and its destruction almost surely led to suffering. In a second attack, Mier y Terán's troops hit the Wichitas again, killing one man, one woman, and four children and capturing nearly two hundred animals.[20]

A much bloodier confrontation was to come. In November 1831, Mexican army troops surrounded a town filled with Wacos and many southern Comanches. This time, the Indians made a determined stand. Both Menchaca, the Waco chief who had spoken eloquently for peace, and Barbaquista, one of the only true friends that the Mexicans had among the Comanches, were killed, along with dozens of other warriors, women, and children.[21] The survivors fell back on their relatives, the northern Taovayas Wichitas, and all thoughts of peace evaporated. In their quest to spare the south from Comanche/Wichita raiding parties, Mexican authorities had attacked the only Indians whose leaders were willing to try to establish peace.

The Mexican, Anglo, and Cherokee campaigns of 1829–1931 devastated the Wacos and Tawakonis. The troops pushed these Indians farther west and north, opening lands for more settlement. While Austin's rangers had begun this process of ethnic cleansing, Mexican authorities, often unaware of which group needed punishment, had carried it a step further. Perhaps worse, at the height of the devastation, in June 1831, a group of American traders introduced smallpox to the Wichita communities. Dozens of people died, many of them young children. The previous decade had been devastating for the southern Waco and Tawakoni Wichita bands. War and pestilence had reduced their populations from perhaps three thousand to less than half that number.[22]

Mier y Terán's troops had played a significant role in punishing the Wichitas, but the general clearly had hoped that a stronger centralist presence in northern Texas would eventually lead to the peaceful organization of the region. To this effect, he wrote a comprehensive report addressing the many problems remaining along Mexico's northern border. His plan called for the reinforcement of military garrisons and for countercolonization, balancing out the rising number of Anglo-Americans with settlers from Germany, Switzerland, and Mexico. Seeing the need to tie Texas economically to Mexico, he also wanted trade policies that allowed coastal shipping to pass easily from Mexican ports south of the mouth of the Rio Grande to the newly opened ports of Brazoria and Galveston in Texas.[23]

After Bustamante took over the presidency of Mexico in 1830, Mier y Terán felt increasingly certain of his authority to make decisions regarding Texas. He selected several strategic places for military posts. A key fort called Tenoxtitlán was constructed at the junction of the San Antonio–Nacogdoches road and the Brazos River. The fort was placed under the command of the capable Colonel Ruíz. Colonel Piedras remained in control of the garrison at Nacogdoches, which Mier y Terán reinforced. Finally, another new post was constructed at the mouth of the Trinity River and commanded by Colonel Juan Davis Bradburn. It controlled the port of Galveston, and its troops patrolled northward from it. Within a year, nearly one thousand Mexican soldiers garrisoned these positions, and General Mier y Terán had seven hundred others on the Rio Grande.[24]

Mier y Terán's strategy seemed even more timely after the newly elected U.S. president, Andrew Jackson, expressed an interest in the purchase of Texas. This infuriated Mexican nationalists, especially President Bustamante, a centralist who feared the rise of U.S. power. Bustamante sent General Mier y Terán's recommendations regarding colonization and trade to the Mexican Congress with his strong endorsement, adding only that all American immigration be ended. The bill to this effect became law on April 6, 1830. The federal law theoretically voided all unfulfilled empresario contracts, even those issued by states such as Coahuila-Texas.[25] Bustamante and Mier y Terán had no doubts of the folly of the federalist experiment and intended to correct it.

Ironically, in the very months during which the Mexican Congress shut down American migration to Texas, speculation in Texas lands reached new heights. Empresarios David G. Burnet, Joseph Vehlein, and Lorenzo de Zavala, realizing that they could no longer recruit Anglo-American pioneers to Texas, tried to emulate Hayden Edwards. They pooled their claims and assigned their grants to the Galveston Bay and Texas Land Company, which was controlled by New York speculators. Much of this land, however, was already occupied by settlers and immigrant Indians.

The directors of the Galveston company had little intention of settling farmers in Texas. Within months, the company offered stock for sale to the public and, more important, sold land scrip that entitled the owner to take up land in East Texas. The speculators ignored the colonization laws of Mexico, national and state, since both sets of laws strictly forbade empresarios from selling land. Thus, as Mier y Terán set out to shut down the frontier in 1830, stock and scrip flooded the market in the United States, sold to potential settlers at prices that ranged from five to ten cents an acre.[26]

As centralists consolidated power in Mexico—and state authority declined—Mier y Terán abandoned his earlier caution regarding giving land grants to Indians. The Cherokees obviously had proved their worth; they would be the counterbalance to the manipulative Anglos. The general ordered that Cherokees, Shawnees, and Delawares receive tribal, or communal, grants.[27] Mier y Terán treated other Indians in a similar fashion. Another Shawnee town, which had combined with some Alabama Indians, was told to select land on the upper Trinity River. Even the Kickapoos, whom the general had initially found wanting, received Mier y Terán's sanction. He wanted them located just west of the Shawnees who were living near Pecan Point, a position that would bring them face to face with the surviving, and angry, Wichitas.[28]

Yet Mier y Terán denied Texas land to some tribal societies—among them Creeks, Chickasaws, Choctaws, Caddos, and, of course, Wichitas. Newspapers in the United States had recently announced the passage of the forced Indian removal bill and that twenty thousand Creek Indians would soon be pushed west. Some of the Creeks had fought against General Andrew Jackson in 1813 (the conflict that Fields had participated in), and General Mier y Terán strongly advised against a Creek grant. The Caddos likewise fell through the cracks. The original inhabitants of East Texas had nowhere to go if they wished to remain in their homeland: some fled into Louisiana to avoid the more hostile immigrant Indians, and others joined the Wichitas.[29]

Despite the land "decrees," issued in the name of the central government of Bustamante, the question of how to distribute the promised lands of Texas remained problematic. Governor José Maria Letona of the state of Coahuila-Texas, now supposedly following Mier y Terán's orders, "commissioned" Colonel Piedras to "put the families composing the Cherokee tribe of Indians into individual possession of lands" in March 1832. This proved difficult, given their communal lifestyle. Exactly a month later, the state political chief, Ramón Músquiz, agreed to handle the administrative aspects of the land grants. Four days later, both the vice president of the republic and Letona literally commanded that the Cherokees and others receive land.[30] But put simply, decrees from centralist military commanders seemingly did not constitute land titles, and surveyors never received the order to mark the lands.

Nevertheless, these promises of land held the allegiance of various Indian groups. Ruíz, who commanded at Tenoxtitlán on the central Brazos, used the promises to recruit Cherokee, Shawnee, and Delaware war parties, with whom he occasionally traveled into the interior to hunt and to confront the Plains tribes. At one point, he even informed a Shawnee war party of the arrival of a large Comanche trading party at San Antonio. Even though Ruíz knew that San Antonio was neutral ground, a place for council and smoke, he failed to discourage the Shawnees, who surprised the Comanches a mere six miles north of the city. In a slaughter that certainly outraged all of the Plains tribes, the Shawnees killed nearly one hundred Indians.[31] The large mass of bodies fed the wolves for days thereafter.

Piedras found immigrant tribes brimming with confidence after the disastrous Comanche defeat. They "wished to repeat the expedition," and Piedras informed authorities in late May that he had called for a general war council. He hoped that some Mexican troops might join his Cherokee, Shawnee, Delaware, and Kickapoo allies. The Tejano populations of San Antonio even took up a collection of money to use in buying powder and lead for the immigrant Indian warriors. Piedras had his force of roughly five hundred Indians ready for action by June; he expected to run the northern tribes out of Texas.[32]

For a short while between 1830 and 1832, Mexican centralists must have thought they had found the answer to the misery that Texas had suffered since 1810. Militarily, centralists had reoccupied Texas and had had some success against the northern tribes. Politically, General Mier y Terán had used the promise of citizenship and the owning of land to gain the support of a broad spectrum of people, many of whom had been slowly and systematically deprived of those rights in the United States. In some ways, he had even moved beyond the liberal rhetoric of Jeffersonian America, to embrace an ethically diverse community of people.

Yet Mexico's weakness as a nation had forced it to endorse a near-genocidal war, mostly against the Wichita Indians; to maintain political hegemony, Mexico had pitted immigrant Indian against indigenous Indian and had anchored tenuous alliances with the promise of land. Worse, the policy was dependent upon a half-dozen immigrant Indian bands that had shifting loyalties and populations. This was a fragile strategy strewn with potholes, both political and military.

In addition, among the various dividends that came with the successful military occupation of Texas was a more forthright relationship with the United States. With at least two presidents—John Quincy Adams and Andrew Jackson—trying at times to purchase Texas, Mexico had looked cautiously at its northern neighbor. Yet with the boundary commission busily doing its job, the time seemed ripe to settle differences and create the legal mechanisms for relations between the two countries. This resulted in the Treaty of Amity, Commerce and Navigation, signed by Mexico and the United States in 1831.[33]

Tariff and trade concerns dominated the first thirty-two articles. Much of the concern centered on regulating the evolving trade between St. Louis, Missouri, and Santa Fe, New Mexico, on what had become the Santa Fe Trail. But the discussions soon turned to the issue of Indian depredations, which were addressed in article 33. Here, the two countries struggled to devise a plan that would end the violence that both Mexican and American teamsters and horse traders using the trail had suffered from Indians.[34]

In a straightforward fashion, article 33 specifically pledged the contracting parties to control the various Indian nations that resided near their common border (the Red and Sabine rivers). This in itself would have been difficult, given the fact that much of the plains—controlled by Comanches, Apaches, Wichitas, Arapahos, and Cheyennes—remained beyond the realm of either nation. Yet the treaty went one step further. Both countries agreed "to restrain by force all hostilities and incursions on the part of the Indian nations living within their respective boundaries." The United States pledged to prevent "their Indians" from attacking Mexico, and Mexico promised to prevent its Indians from committing hostilities on citizens of the United States. In a crucial point, the contracting parties could enter each other's territory to carry out this mission.[35]

The treaty came with much celebration. But just as order seemed to appear out of chaos, as law seemingly replaced corrupt land policy, as military patrols ended the use of Texas as a sanctuary for American criminals, momentous changes altered the entire political landscape. Mexico had moved politically to the right during the centralists' rise to power. But the pendulum swung back during the summer of 1832 as factions, including many groups that still believed that power should be vested in state government, expelled General Bustamante and seized control of the government in Mexico City.

The actions of these federalists plunged Mexico into the turmoil of a new era, that of Antonio López de Santa Anna, the leader of the summer coup. As garrison after garrison fell to the federalists in the south, military order along the northern border of Texas faced a serious crisis. Militant Texans, embracing the new federal cause championed by Santa Anna, challenged the customs collector at Galveston Island and then Colonel Bradburn at Fort Anahuac, on the Trinity River. While General Mier y Terán tried to reason with Austin and restore order, Austin did nothing; soon Bradburn was forced to withdraw.

The general looked with utter dismay at this travesty. Under the banner of federalism, Anglos had forced Mexican troops to retire! Worse, the federalists soon captured Tampico to the south, the general's one base of supply. He rushed to retrieve the situation, but his letters to fellow centralists soon revealed a terrible despair. He could not see Mexico in such a state: lawless, fractured, and unruled. He dressed himself in his finest uniform, walked to the front of the old church of San Antonio de Padilla outside of Tampico, unscabbarded his sword, and fell on it. It was an honorable death for a tired but honorable man.[36]

During these days of turmoil, the American abolitionist Benjamin Lundy appeared at Nacogdoches. He had crossed the Sabine River on June 27 and reached the town on July 1. While he had expected to be challenged by Mexican troops, none appeared. Even in Nacogdoches, the garrison remained ambivalent. Lundy presented himself to the only officer available, Lieutenant Colonel Francisco Medina, who seemed unconcerned by any threat from the United States. Medina gave Lundy permission to travel wherever he wished in Texas.[37]

Lundy found Texas to be socially and ethnically intriguing but in many ways lacking in civility. Mexican troops still could be found in Nacogdoches, as the garrison was augmented by men who had left the fort on the Trinity River. Most of these men, Lundy thought, resembled the vast numbers of Indians—Cherokees, Caddos, Creeks, Seminoles, and Delawares—who thronged into town. Rumors relative to "war and peace" circulated everywhere.

Lundy could hardly help but marvel at the multidimensional nature of the frontier community that unfolded before him at Nacogdoches. In what must have been a comic opera, Anglos, Mexicans, Tejanos, immigrant Indians, indigenous Indians, and slaves all came together to celebrate the Fourth of July. Frost Thorn hosted a dance and a dinner. The local priest offered a morning mass, which was well attended even by Indians, who respected the pomp and piety. The oddly equipped Mexican garrison, now seemingly embracing the federalist cause, paraded down the main street, marching to the tunes of a small band in what little finery they possessed. The troops fired a volley to honor American independence.[38]

As Lundy departed for the east, Mexican military garrisons still seemingly loyal to the centralists abandoned Velasco and Brazoria, and ultimately, Texans challenged Colonels Piedras and Medina at Nacogdoches. The officers retreated from the town with their remaining troops on August 2, 1832.[39] Soon, Anglos in Texas fell into the camp of either "moderates" (those who sought compromise) or "militants" (those who hoped to exploit the turmoil). In December 1832, the politician Sam Houston, once governor of the state of Tennessee but more recently a frontier vagabond from Indian Territory, crossed the unguarded border into Texas. He threw in with the militants, joining the "Great Conspiracy" to wrest Texas from Mexico, as Lundy later labeled the situation.[40]

These "conspirators" possessed one lethal advantage; law and order vanished after 1832 as the political debate between centralism and federalism spread to nearly every province in Mexico. This conflict encouraged Texans to challenge the few Mexican political institutions that still existed, even though the Texans had never been oppressed by them. As revolutionary violence grew, Texas became an uncontrollable land, and Texans embraced a culture of violence in which a violent act became an accepted moral action. The Wacos and the Tawakoni Wichitas had been the first victims of this ethnic violence; others would soon follow.

6

THE AMERICANIZATION OF TEXAS

After nearly four years of living in a drunken stupor, Sam Houston finally had an opportunity to redeem his life. His old friend, President Andrew Jackson, had asked him to go to Texas in the fall of 1832 to report on military and political conditions. Jackson disguised the mission by suggesting that Houston should survey the various Indian tribes there, noting their populations. But Houston went under no illusions. He expected "fighting" there soon, and not with Indians.[1] During the summer and fall of 1832, events would reveal the shrewdness of that assessment. Mexico's grip on the region was crumbling; Americans were crossing the Sabine River by the thousands, entering Texas illegally.

Surprising numbers of these interlopers had checkered pasts, much like Houston's. Jackson understood Houston's desire to start over again, to forge a new life. Jackson had nursed the gallant young Houston back from a near-mortal wound suffered at the battle of Horseshoe Bend in 1813. The two men were fictive father and son. With Jackson's influence, Houston had won the governorship in Tennessee in 1828. At age thirty-five—Houston had sowed considerable wild oats—the newly elected governor had married eighteen-year-old Eliza Allen of Gallatin, Tennessee. And then the trouble began.

The union collapsed, virtually on the wedding night. Eliza loved a man who was much younger than Sam. She had accepted Houston's offer of marriage only after being pressured by her father and uncle. (Historians also have speculated that Houston's war wound, suffered in the groin and quietly called the "running sore," may have shocked the young woman.) The separation prompted Houston to resign as governor and move to Indian Territory. There he settled with John Jolly's Cherokee band, took a mixed-blood Cherokee woman as wife in the Indian fashion, and drank heavily; he was nicknamed "Big Drunk" by his Cherokee friends.[2]

But Houston had spunk and courage—his caning of Congressman William Stansberry attested to that. Using his political connections, in 1831 and 1832 Houston bid on various Indian Bureau contracts to provision the removed tribes, although he mostly lost out to others. Whig congressman William Stansberry pilloried Houston for this activity and also implicated Jackson. Outraged, Houston encountered the unfortunate Stansberry one evening on a dark Georgetown street and beat him nearly to death. Dragged in front of the U.S. House of Representatives by the sergeant-at-arms, Houston was charged with contempt of the House. When ordered to reprimand Houston, the Democratic Speaker, a Jackson crony, instead praised the young Democrat's "outstanding intellect," congratulated him on his magnificent defense of honor, and issued a brief reprimand.[3]

Along with many other Anglo-Americans who joined him that winter in Texas, Houston lived by the southern creed that paired honor with violence. In many ways, this mindset influenced Houston's and Jackson's views of Indians. Once power brokers, they echoed the paternal instincts of southern slave owners. They were "loving fathers" to their "Indian children" but expected a degree of obedience that went way beyond what Indians might logically accept. The paradox of liking some Indians but aiding in the destruction of others is characteristic of both men. Houston even took Indian women as wives—and left them; Jackson used Indians as allies in war and then supported their removal west. In reality, both Houston and Jackson were politicians first and idealists second. Above all, they were southerners and defenders of its creed.

That Jackson and Houston had a plan of sorts for Texas can hardly be doubted. Jackson's efforts as president to purchase the region is evidence enough; he saw the potential for cotton production there. A year after sending Houston into Texas, President Jackson ordered U.S. troops to thrust deep into Indian Territory. First infantry and then dragoons explored the Red River corridor, reaching the Wichita Mountains. The troops supposedly were bringing peace to the land, but Mexican officials knew better. Such troops were the forerunners of U.S. hegemony. They, along with the encroaching Anglo pioneers and the growing numbers of immigrant Indians from the South, spearheaded the future Americanization of Texas.

Nevertheless, the aggressiveness of men like Houston and Jackson posed a problem for empresario Stephen Austin, who still believed in compromise with Mexico. Austin had kept up a respectful dialogue with Mier y Terán over the spring and summer of 1832. Both men were enormously civil and even reflective in their various letters. But the general had consistently refused to consider the political and economic changes that the empresario increasingly saw as essential for the future of Texas. They had reached a respectful impasse when news arrived of General Mier y Terán's death. The suicide must have revived Austin's hopes; Santa Anna's removal of the reactionary centralist General Bustamante from the Mexican presidency would have made Austin even more optimistic.

Austin and his colonists had every reason to expect that Santa Anna's coup would lead to less management of the colony by centralist bureaucrats and, as a result, more freedom for them. Fundamentally, most Texans considered the first step to be separation from Coahuila, or Texas statehood within the Mexican federal system. Separation would allow for a new Texas—a state cast in the image of Alabama or Georgia, complete with slavery and the locally organized slave patrols that were essential for maintaining the peculiar institution. Austin had headed off a previous attempt by the legislature of Coahuila-Texas to make slavery illegal, but separate Texas statehood would give Anglos the chance to control their legislature and keep the institution legal forever.

Texans also hoped that separate statehood would end or diminish the tariff duties collected on imported manufactured goods. South Carolina had recently challenged such duties, provoking a "Nullification Crisis" within the United States between 1830 and 1832. The Carolinians wanted to stop collecting taxes on imported clothing, which they used to clothe their slaves. Despite their failure to convince President Jackson, the debate did not disappear, and newspapers in the United States, as well as many Texans, followed it carefully. Duties on manufactured goods and farm equipment, Austin mused in his letters to Mier y Terán, made no sense when liquor was imported freely.

Finally, Austin wanted the hated April 1830 decree ending Anglo colonization rescinded. He felt that the Fredonia uprising had been led by freebooters, not colonists. Mexico had everything to gain by reopening its northern boundary to men and women of good reputation and industry. Austin was not alone in making such suggestions; on some accounts, he found many capitalistic-minded Tejanos in agreement with him.[4] Texas, Austin hoped, would be Americanized, supposedly for the betterment of everyone. Nevertheless, Austin had no timetable; he was, unlike some of those who plunged into Texas over the winter of 1832–1833, a patient man.

Such patience was necessary, for while Santa Anna's coup had supposedly rid Mexico City's national government of centralists, a few still lingered in Texas. Colonel Piedras's command at Nacogdoches had been broken up, as had Bradburn's troops at Fort Anahuac, but some of their troops had simply removed to San Antonio and were awaiting further developments. As Colonel Francisco Ruíz watched these movements, he decided to evacuate Fort Tenoxtitlán, on the upper Brazos River. Ruíz had federalist sympathies, but unlike Piedras, he had not faced hostile Anglos. Instead, he used a ruse for his movement; he reported that the government had failed to supply him and claimed that he could no longer sustain his men at the fort. Ruíz quietly withdrew the garrison to better quarters in San Antonio in late August.[5]

Ruíz understood Indians most of all; he recognized that the collapse of the Mexican army in Texas meant trouble with the Plains tribes. Perhaps he even feared for his command at Fort Tenoxtitlán, a rather exposed position. Certainly, Ruíz knew that the Plains Indians wanted revenge for the various attacks by both the

Mexican army and the immigrant Indians. By September, large Comanche/Wichita war parties once again were assailing livestock herds in northern Coahuila, overrunning ranches and killing a few herders on both banks of the Rio Grande.[6] When chiefs did enter San Antonio, demanding presents, the new political chief, Ramón Músquiz, who represented the near-bankrupt state of Coahuila-Texas, had nothing to offer. By November Músquiz had concluded that a "general war" existed.[7]

The military situation worsened by the spring of 1833. Mexican colonel don Manuel Barragán reported that some 568 federal troops still remained in the north, mostly located in Coahuila, but they had poor armament and almost no horses.[8] Indian agent Bean at Nacogdoches continued to meet with the immigrant tribes, but without a garrison at Nacogdoches, his influence waned. The Cherokees and their friends seemed more reluctant to go against the Wichitas as they had in the past, most likely because Mexico had failed to grant them land and refused to give their leaders presents.

After the departure of Ruíz and Piedras from the scene in northern Texas, Peter Ellis Bean remained as the only viable representative of Mexico. Bean was not unlike the throngs of Anglo-Americans then entering Texas; he was an opportunist and a land speculator. But he also had connections within the Mexican military establishment. Mier y Terán had assigned Bean to build a small military outpost along the central Neches River in 1831, designed to stop Anglo-American infiltration through what was mostly unpopulated terrain. The post never amounted to much—it consisted of only a few log buildings—and Bean went back to his Indian agent duties after Santa Anna's coup.[9]

Bean certainly understood the concerns that Mexican officials held regarding the border situation. In a futile gesture perhaps intended to impress his superiors more than to accomplish anything, Bean complained vehemently to the U.S. secretary of war, Lewis Cass, about the large numbers of immigrant Indians who were coming into Texas. Bean wrote, "Not less than 700 Indians have introduced themselves in this territory" during the spring of 1833. Some were Seminoles, others Creeks and Choctaws; many wished to hunt in the west, but others thought of settling in Texas permanently. Preventing this migration, Bean argued, was "demanded by the existing treaty" (referring to article 33 of the 1831 treaty).[10] Cass was busy at the time, ironically focusing on Indian removal then under way in the East, which caused more dislocation and growing violence in Indian Territory.

The Jackson administration resolved to end the confusion that existed in Indian Territory. Eastern Indian tribes were resisting removal precisely because of the confused situation that Bean outlined. The U.S. Senate created a commission to address the problem in 1832 and gave the commission funding and authority to negotiate treaties. But establishing order in Indian Territory and securing the border with Texas was assumed to require more and better-equipped troops. Jackson's War Department responded by ordering a newly recruited regiment of mounted dragoons, some six hundred strong, to Fort Gibson. Such a force by itself would eventually outgun the entire Mexican army in the north of Texas.

Mexican officials initially knew little about the new dragoon force, but it complemented a sizeable U.S. military buildup west of the Mississippi River. The infantry garrison at Natchitoches, Louisiana, was often several companies strong. More U.S. infantry troops had settled into Fort Towson, just north of the Red River, a location that was intended to bring order and peace to the Red River corridor. The mounted dragoons, operating out of either Fort Towson or Fort Gibson, in northeastern Indian Territory, could easily reach the Plains Indians (Comanches and Wichitas) who were at war with Mexico. Under the 1831 treaty, the United States was obligated to enforce Mexico's position against the Plains tribes, and if these tribes supposedly left U.S. territory to attack Mexico, U.S. troops were even authorized to enter Mexico to do so!

But Mexican military leaders soon recognized the irony of such a situation. Mexico had struggled for years to prevent traders from the United States from reaching the Plains tribes with guns and munitions, which they exchanged for Mexican livestock taken in raids. The American push might lead to peace treaties with the Plains tribes, which would only invite more commerce, resulting in more destruction in southern Texas and northern Mexico. Could the Americans be trusted to act in Mexico's interests?

The new commission created by the U.S. Congress had little understanding of this complex situation. It simply proposed to solve the land disputes in Indian Territory and end the intertribal fighting that had resulted from removal. In typical bureaucratic fashion, the commission included poorly informed eastern politicians. Named the Stokes Commission for Montfort Stokes of North Carolina, it contained two other members: Henry R. Ellsworth and John F. Schermerhorn. They established a headquarters at Fort Gibson over the winter of 1832–1833. The commissioners did consult with the various military commanders at Forts Gibson, Towson, and Jesup, as well as with Indian agents F. W. Armstrong and Jehiel Brooks.[11] Brooks, who handled the affairs of the Louisiana Caddos, had feared for some time that his Caddos would "destroy the white settlements" in Louisiana if something were not done to prevent Anglo-American settlers from encroaching on their lands.[12]

Similar problems existed north and west of the Caddo on lands set aside for the removed Choctaws. Because of transportation problems, promised rations arrived in a piecemeal fashion, and when Agent Armstrong handed out money as annuities, whiskey peddlers swarmed into Choctaw country, resulting in binges that endangered Indians and anyone nearby.[13] The army disliked playing policeman, and officers often refused to enforce the Intercourse Acts, which prohibited such sales on Indian land.

At Fort Gibson, Colonel Matthew Arbuckle concluded that the liquor was not as serious as the split brewing within several of the various removed tribal societies. Most full-bloods who had been removed to the West exhibited "much displeasure towards the United States." Some openly stated that when relatives arrived from back East, they would "take satisfaction" upon the Anglo-Americans nearby and the various mixed-bloods who supported them. In a word, Indian Territory was a mess, filled with disgruntled people, most of whom were heavily armed.[14]

The commissioners, once at Fort Gibson, confirmed much of what the army officers and agents had already reported. They found "war parties out" in nearly every direction. A Delaware party had just returned from destroying a Pawnee village, and a group of twenty-eight Shawnees, hunting in the west, had just fought with over three hundred Comanches. The Shawnees, better armed and determined, claimed to have killed seventy-two Comanches while losing only seven men.[15] While the numbers may have been exaggerated, there was no question about the military capabilities of the Shawnees and their friends; they had fought the U.S. Army during the War of 1812, and Comanches did not frighten them.

While military threats and presents helped the commissioners end the Chero-kee/Osage feuds in northeastern Indian Territory by 1833, the ultimate challenge for the commission (one increasingly feared by Mexico) was to make peace between the western tribes and immigrant bands such as the Shawnees.[16] On the plus side, Congress had appropriated funds for presents and was prepared to agree to treaties that allocated annual supplies of food, called annuities. A far greater negative, how-ever, was the fact that U.S. officials knew little about the western Plains tribes. Many immigrant Indians were in Texas, beyond the reach of the commission, and Comanches and Wichitas remained in moving camps south and west of the upper Red River.[17]

Houston's job supposedly was to make contact with these people and explain the peace plan. By December 1832, he had disposed of his possessions in Indian Territory—and, according to folklore, had abandoned his Cherokee wife—and headed south.[18] Using information readily available, he reported on the various Pawnee and Wichita bands (mostly unaware of the differences between them) and suggested a total population of over thirty thousand. Regarding the Comanches, he failed to recognize the distinct difference between the northern Comanches, whom he called "Amparacas" (for Yamparicas, the Spanish term), and those bands that lived symbiotically with the Texas Wichitas. Houston placed Comanche populations at roughly fifty thousand. His population figures were grossly inflated and his informa-tion worthless.[19] Houston did suggest that the Plains Indians were open to approach by Anglo-Americans, which was welcome news to some degree.

Houston displayed a profound ignorance of Texas tribes, but then, he was distracted. More likely his immediate interest was the potential for land speculation and politics.[20] Not long thereafter, Houston abandoned Indian issues and prepared himself to run as a representative of the San Augustine district in East Texas. Texans were organizing, and Houston wanted to be a part of the process.[21]

With good reason, the Stokes Commission ignored Houston's reports—they may never have even seen his figures. Much better information came from men such as Arkansas native Albert Pike, who had spent time with the Comanches.[22] The "northern Comanches," as he called them, had little in common with the smaller bands of the same people who lived along the upper Brazos River. The Wichita, in turn, Pike described as being anti-American, outraged over the various campaigns launched against them by Austin's rangers as well as immigrant Indians and Mexican troops. Forced from their homes along the central Brazos River, these Wichitas were said to be poisoning the mind of any Plains Indian who would listen. Pike suggested that a massive show of force—literally an invading army—would be necessary to overawe them.[23]

Taking Pike's advice, Colonel James Many, stationed at Fort Towson, launched the first U.S. military expedition up the Red River in April 1833. Many, who would acquire a long record of steady service in the West, developed an extraordinary knowledge of Indian affairs; the more he learned, the more sympathetic he became toward Indians and their plight.[24] He eventually came to view the Texas creed as sanctimonious, primarily because of the way Texans mistreated Indians, an attitude held by a number of his fellow officers. (In later years, Many even came to dislike the affable Houston.) Many's infantry force was halted by severe flooding along the Red River corridor that spring, and he was forced to turn back.

Colonel Many's efforts symbolized the growing restlessness of Anglo-Americans. Many had concluded that if immigrant Indians from the southern United States could hunt and trade on the plains, his army troops could certainly campaign in the region. And events in Indian Territory had made it essential to learn more about the Great Plains, especially the region's Indian inhabitants and geography. By fall of 1833, it became common knowledge in the West that the army would try again in the following year.

To what degree this impending campaign had an impact on events in Texas is uncertain, but the Anglo population was growing as restless as the U.S. Army. They had rallied around the "liberalism" of Santa Anna and called for sweeping govern-mental change. In October 1832, a number of prominent Anglo-Texans wrote and signed the first petitions that called for the revocation of the April 1830 law, for duty-free trade, for protection against Indians, and for separate statehood for Texas. While the petitions bordered on treason, many Tejanos in San Antonio supported these grievances. The *ayuntamiento,* which they controlled, sent petitions on to the general government, complaining (albeit in more conciliatory language) of many of the same problems.

Tejanos including Juan Seguín, who served at the time as the alcalde of San Antonio, and a number of elites such as Antonio Navarro and Miguel Arciniega openly supported the Anglo reforms and federalism in general. But others were not in agreement. The political chief, Ramón Músquiz, increasingly distanced himself from Seguín but soon found that the state government could offer little in the way of sup-port for a more cautious course. With local authorities divided, the state government slowly fractured. By 1833, federalist-leaning state politicians were fighting with centralist state leaders over such mundane issues as where the state capital should be located. The shouting match in Coahuila reaffirmed to many Anglo-Texans that Mexicans could not govern.[25]

Meanwhile, Texans continued to form committees and write petitions. Men bent on confrontation or looking for opportunities—many of them new arrivals—controlled the convention of April 1833. Houston, who finally had been elected as the delegate from San Augustine, was prominent among them. Less willing to compromise and at times downright demanding, the representatives pressured Stephen Austin to carry their grievances to Santa Anna in Mexico City. These efforts virtually bypassed all duly appointed local and state Mexican authorities, even elite Tejano friends of the colonists in San Antonio; Anglo-Texans were pushing the issues.[26]

Austin reached Mexico City during the summer but soon found that Santa Anna had left the new government in the hands of his vice-president, Gómez Farías. A liberal nationalist, Farías harbored suspicions of Austin and all Texans, especially their argument for separate statehood and their defense of slavery. Frustrated, Austin finally wrote to the ayuntamiento in San Antonio—which he considered friendly—that it should take the lead in separating Texas from Coahuila. Most Tejanos would not do this, and someone in San Antonio forwarded the infamous letter to Mexico City. Farías, angered by the betrayal, then ordered Austin's arrest.

The seizing of Austin on January 3, 1834, outraged Anglo-Texans, but they did little about it. Cholera had appeared in San Antonio and had spread northward.[27] Perhaps more important, over the winter some of the most militant of the Texas delegates who had signed the petitions were gone, including Houston, who had traveled to Washington, D.C., to report to friends, including the president.

Houston returned in May 1834 but stayed for several months in the small town of Washington, Arkansas, some ten miles from the Texas border. While his actions and tenure there remain mostly a mystery, he did know about a massive display of force by U.S. troops that was being organized in Indian Territory. While in the East, Houston must have seen the orders for the units to march. It was anticipated that this army would enter Texas. Houston had picked a spot that was at the crossroads of all information coming in and out of both Texas and Indian Territory. He obviously expected war in Texas that summer of 1834. Indeed, he told friends that he would join in "Indian councils" in Texas in June.[28] Washington officials likely saw him as an asset during such talks given his earlier experience with the Cherokee.

Colonel Henry Leavenworth took more time than expected, however, in organizing his campaign. More important, during the planning stages, the decision was made to ask Mexico for permission to enter its territory rather than rely on the vague language in the 1831 treaty. Commissioner Stokes then belatedly decided to seek such permission by letter, sending off the request in May 1834 to San Antonio officials.[29] Since theirs was a mission of peace, the commissioners could hardly understand why Mexico would fail to cooperate. Stokes had little idea of Mexico's ongoing policy of using immigrant Indians against the Plains tribes.

The commission's request reached Colonel Juan Nepomuceno Almonte in San Antonio. His reply shocked the commissioners: Almonte had no authority to allow U.S. troops into Texas, and he had no interest in peace with Comanches. "Far from being friendly," the Mexican commander wrote, all the Plains people were warlike and enemies.[30] Colonel Leavenworth, likely as surprised as the commissioners by the reply, decided against violating Mexico's sovereignty, at least in 1834.

Even so, more than five hundred men under Leavenworth set out from Fort Gibson in mid-June 1834. This would remain the largest number of U.S. troops deployed on the plains for many years to come. Colonel Henry Dodge, who commanded the dragoons, had dressed his men (a dandy lot) in short, black jackets over the typical infantry blue pants, and their hats sported a long black plume, likely of imported ostrich. Such dragoon units would have a special place in the army until formal cavalry units were created in the 1850s. If Mexico needed any notice as to the growing penetration of the region by their neighbors to the north, this army was certainly it.

Surprisingly, Stokes and Schermerhorn stayed behind. Perhaps they waited for orders from Washington, giving them permission to enter Mexico, or still hoped to gain such permission from Almonte for the planned incursion. In the meantime, the troops were poised to cross the Red River to where Comanches and Wichitas were sure to be found in large numbers. Houston's expectation of attending negotiations on the Trinity River fit well into such planning. The commissioners' decision left the entire affair in the hands of the military officers. Capable men, these officers took their charge of overawing the Plains Indians seriously. Indeed, Dodge's troops traversed much of southwestern Indian Territory, mapping the region and learning much about the tribes who lived there. What is more, Dodge started a dialogue with these Indians that continued for years to come.

The military leaders of the expedition constituted a who's who of the most notable officers in the army at the time. Leavenworth already had a distinguished career, and Dodge would be one of the few officers in the history of the American republic to be voted a sword by Congress. The dragoons under Dodge had other noted officers, including Lieutenant Colonel Stephen Watts Kearny and Major Richard B. Mason; both would later help bring California into the union. (Both also would die relatively young, a decade before the Civil War—Kearny of a mysterious illness contracted in Mexico.) Perhaps more notorious was Captain Nathan Boone, the son of Daniel Boone. Young Boone already had a reputation as a fearless woodsman; he was eager to visit the Great Plains.[31]

A number of other distinguished men joined the force to see the West. Artist George Catlin and botanist Carl Beyrick sketched landscapes and studied plants.[32] Catlin's paintings of the event would later captivate many, both in the United States and in Europe. But the most important civilians included a large contingent of full-blood and mixed-blood scouts: Black Beaver (a Delaware) and Jesse Chisholm (of Scots-Cherokee descent) were the most noted. Superb trailblazers, both had traveled to the Pacific Ocean and back; both later served as guides for California-bound immigrant trains. Black Beaver spoke many different Native languages, as did Chisholm, including Comanche. And both were honorable, enjoyable men, whom many army officers came to appreciate. Captain Randolph B. Marcy would later immortalize Black Beaver as "perfectly reliable, brave, and competent. His reputation as a resolute, determined, and fearless warrior did not admit of question, yet I have never seen a man who wore his laurels with less vanity."[33]

Unfortunately, the troops—traveling in the hot July weather in their beautiful dark, woolen uniforms—soon came down with "bilious fever, and fever and ague." The epidemic resembled the cholera that had spread northward from San Antonio, and under the bright plains sun, man after man fell.[34] A crisis loomed when the full party reached the Washita River. Nearly half of the men, including Leavenworth, were sick. Leavenworth ordered Dodge ahead, pushing through the ten miles of brush called the Cross Timbers onto the open prairie. Here, on July 14, the dragoons met thirty Comanche hunters, led by His-oo-san-ches ("Little Spaniard"), a renowned warrior of Mexican descent.

From these Comanches Dodge learned much, and he visited their town of two hundred lodges.[35] The colonel was astonished at the large numbers of "Spanish women" living among them; he failed to understand that thousands of Mexican women and children had been taken captive in decades past. The women gave the camp a Hispanic flavor as they scurried about in long dresses, openly speaking the Spanish language. The men, by contrast, were quick to display their Comanche pride. His-oo-san-ches boasted that they were "the largest band, the proudest and the boldest." This Mexican Comanche had found it easy to become part of—indeed, a leader of—a Plains Indian community.[36]

On July 30, Dodge and 183 dragoons finally reached the Taovayas Wichita town, nestled under a granite ledge at the foot of the Wichita Mountains. The houses were large, conical, and thatched with grass; scaffolding attached to the houses was used for sleeping in the warm summer nights. Nearby, women attended drying rakes that held bison meat and frames used to stretch hides. Dodge and his men could see many hundred dogs running about, intermixed with children of all sizes.

The Wichita people were excellent farmers. Large cornfields stretched out in front of the town, fenced with brush and revealing an occasional scarecrow to keep the birds at bay. Watermelons and squash were intermixed with the corn, and beans were planted at the base of the corn plant, trellised up the stalk. Avenues meandered out from the town. Along the main lane, the Wichita elders soon gathered, nervously awaiting the approaching U.S. forces.

Dodge intended to overawe these Wichitas, but he also wanted peace. The colonel could see that unlike the Comanches, the Wichitas feared the U.S. Army, probably because of lessons learned from immigrant Indians who had come among them or as a result of Texas Ranger raids.[37] Dodge quickly convinced the elders that his dragoons came on a mission of peace. Once in council under a large arbor made of brush, the Wichita elders listened intently as Dodge asked them to stop fighting the immigrant Indians. They agreed, of course, eyeing all the time Dodge's large, well-armed force.

That show of force was essential, for the level of distrust among the various tribes was profound. Comanches, Kiowas, and Wichitas—all present for Dodge's final address—viewed the Osages, Cherokees, and Choctaws with considerable suspicion even though they often admitted such people to their trade fairs. Other immigrants such as Shawnees, Delawares, Seminoles, and even a few Kickapoos remained on both sides of the issue, working easily at times in the frontier economy of eastern Indian Territory and occasionally traveling to exchange fairs held in far-off Comanche camps. Dodge finally convinced a small delegation to accompany him back to Fort Gibson, including fifteen Kiowas, the Comanche His-oo-san-ches and a few of his friends, and two Wichita leaders. These men made the long trip back to Fort Gibson likely out of curiosity, but Dodge had also made it clear that more presents would await the delegates in the East.[38]

The Plains delegates played their role perfectly at Fort Gibson, convincing the U.S. commissioners that peace with the Plains tribes was possible. Over the winter, government officials pondered just how to bring about that desired end. Newly promoted Brigadier General Arbuckle, commanding at Fort Gibson, wanted "a more particular arrangement," in which large numbers of leaders from all the Plains tribes would meet representatives of the immigrant groups and the United States.[39] Secretary of War Cass agreed and authorized the spending of $10,000 for presents. Arbuckle thought the agreement could be signed that coming summer of 1835, and Cass appointed Stokes, Armstrong, and Arbuckle to negotiate it.[40]

The chances for success improved dramatically when Holland Coffee met with Captain John Stuart, from Fort Towson, in March 1835. Coffee, a trader, had pushed up the Red River the fall before and had constructed a new trading post some seventy miles west of where the Washita River enters the Red. Probably on Cache Creek, the post boasted a four-sided palisade wall of "one hundred feet square," within which Coffee kept his goods. While twenty or so Anglos had joined his brigade, he had also recruited about a hundred Indian hunters, mostly Cherokees, Choctaws, Shawnees, and Delawares. With such support, Coffee could hold his own against any of the Plains bands.

Over the winter, Coffee had held "almost daily intercourse" with representatives of the Comanches, Kiowas, and Wichitas. They initially distrusted him—and his immigrant Indian hunters. The best evidence of their suspicion, Coffee thought, was the fact that they came in large numbers and well armed. But by spring, these Indians appeared in smaller groups; most apparently feeling safe, they entered his compound to exchange a few horses, bison meat, and hides for sugar, coffee, munitions, and a few guns. Coffee learned that Dodge's expedition had had a startling impact but that the Indians expected other meetings and more presents. Coffee carefully explained to Captain Stuart the etiquette of the plains; peace treaties had to be reinforced with presents on a yearly basis. Dodge had promised more presents, and without them the Indians would be "disappointed . . . faithless and disaffected."[41]

Yet Coffee knew how difficult maintaining peace would be. Around his post were Delawares, Shawnees, Choctaws, Comanches, Kiowas, and Wichitas, all with competing interests. To the east, a large body of migrating Creek Indians had settled near Doaksville (on Choctaw lands) to send hunters into the west, and others had encroached upon land assigned to the Seminoles along the Canadian River. The most identifiable culprit was "General" Chilly McIntosh's band. The son of the famous Creek leader William McIntosh, who had been assassinated by his own people for selling Indian lands in Georgia, McIntosh had many enemies.

With the prospect for conflict escalating, both the commission and General Arbuckle spent most of the fall of 1834 and spring of 1835 removing the various interloping groups. The most defiant band seemed to be Delawares who grazed "immense droves of horses," animals that they had obtained from the Comanches, on the lands of other Indians. With long rifles purchased through their horse-trading ventures, they also killed "hundreds" of deer, bears, and turkeys—game coveted by a variety of people.[42] The Delawares had grown wealthy and defiant and moved to assigned lands only after repeated threats.

With such minor victories, the commission worked on doggedly, planning for more councils in 1835. General Arbuckle assisted by ordering Major Mason's two platoons of dragoons to find a locale for a council chamber that all the various parties could reach. Mason's troops moved up the Canadian River in July 1835, selecting "Camp Holmes" on Little River, about thirty miles southeast of present-day Oklahoma City, Oklahoma.[43] Over the next several years, this became a place where Plains Indians, immigrant Indians, and U.S. officials came to talk.

Almost simultaneously, another dragoon expedition under Colonel Dodge moved westward along the Arkansas River, some 150 miles to the north, encountering Cheyennes and Arapahos near the newly created Bent's Fort, a trading post, in southeastern Colorado. Even as Dodge's council with these tribes ended, a large party of northern Pawnees and Arikaras appeared and offered to make peace. While Dodge seemed overwhelmed with his success, he learned that these more northern Plains tribes fought constantly with the Comanches, Kiowas, and Wichitas who were at Camp Holmes. U.S. officials were finally getting a true picture of the complex geopolitics of the plains.[44]

Meanwhile, at Camp Holmes, Major Mason discovered that more Indians had camped in the vicinity than had been anticipated and that they wished to be fed. On July 8 a few started leaving, disgusted.[45] When Mason finally informed the remaining Indians that the commissioners would arrive on August 20, grumbling arose from the ranks. "They are so entirely ignorant of the whites," a somewhat dejected Mason concluded, "that they cannot comprehend why it is that we are so very desirous of keeping them here to make a peace." They assumed that Mason had organized a "deep laid plot" to destroy them. Indians, including some Osage leaders, helped spread the conspiracy theory.[46]

General Arbuckle and Stokes finally departed for Camp Holmes on August 6 with representatives of the Creeks, Cherokees, Senecas, Delawares, and Choctaws in tow. Even as various chiefs of the immigrant Indians and a handful of Comanche and Wichita leaders agreed to terms on August 23, rumors and fears eroded the very peace being agreed to. In exchange for annuities, the treaty prohibited attacks on Santa Fe Trail wagon trains while granting permission for the immigrant tribes to hunt west of the Cross Timbers. The latter condition, demanded by the immigrant tribes, would cause endless trouble.[47]

Arbuckle and Stokes hailed the agreement, and so did their superiors in Washington, D.C. Newspapers reported that Indian Territory was completely pacified.[48] Yet within weeks, rumors of dissatisfaction surfaced. Osage leaders, jealous and increasingly isolated, did their best to convince the western tribes that the U.S. officials meant to "entrap [them] and finish them off."[49] Then Comanches and Wichitas became outraged when immigrant Indians invaded bison-hunting grounds west of the Cross Timbers—their agreement to allow such hunting obviously had not been thoroughly explained. Perhaps as damaging, U.S. officials learned that the few Comanches who had sought Mexican counsel at San Antonio had been told that the Americans wished only to "make war upon them and cut them off."[50]

Colonel Almonte, back in San Antonio, obviously must have viewed these troop movements with considerable suspicion. The U.S. Army forces had traversed the entire length of the northern border of Texas, and they were dealing directly with the hated Comanches and Wichitas. But the Mexican colonel had no troops with which to counter these movements. His only response was to organize a small party intended to dislodge the Indian trader Coffee from the Red River, as his post was believed to be on the southern bank, in Mexican Texas.[51]

Almonte held out some hope for military assistance when General Santa Anna began to reorganize the shattered government in Coahuila-Texas. Perhaps surprisingly, however, the general's efforts at first seemed to suggest compromise. He allowed the state governor to appoint Seguín as the interim political chief in Texas because Músquiz had become increasingly anti-Texan. Texas also received the right to use English as an official language. This at least suggested state support for the arguments of Anglo-Texans and perhaps even the willingness of the federalists to stand up for more liberal government. Seguín was a Federalist, endorsed capitalism, and supported Austin and his colonists.[52]

Texas communities had prospered, and this wealth made it both more difficult and more important for Texans to push issues that might lead to a break with Mexico.

The slave population had reached nearly five thousand, and prime field hands were worth between $2,000 and $3,000.[53] Austin's "capital," San Felipe de Austin, boasted a population much larger than San Antonio by 1834—three thousand people, at least—and colonists had moved well up the Brazos River, opening farms and ranches. Nacogdoches also had grown. As one American traveler put it, the town was emerging from its frontier status, with settlers constructing "a number of elegant, framed houses" and two new hotels. Commercially, the town bustled with activity.[54]

Colonel Almonte, a staunch Mexican nationalist, confirmed what he believed was a general complacency in Texas after he visited Nacogdoches in the summer of 1834. His "Statistical Report on Texas" offered information on both the demographic and the political status of the three main districts—San Antonio, the central Brazos and Colorado valleys (Austin's colony), and Nacogdoches.[55] Almonte concluded that only the men from the Brazos district ("and they are few") were promoting the idea of separate statehood for Texas. Most Tejano leaders from San Antonio—Seguín, Ruíz, and a few others likely exceptions—seemed uninterested in the issue or opposed to it, and most of the authorities in Nacogdoches also saw little need for a separate state. Almonte, then, saw a divided population, and consequently one that could be easily controlled.[56] The Indian situation and the lack of Mexican troops in Texas was another story.

Almonte's information on Indians came mostly from Bean, who had been busy. Bean had recognized the growing impatience and distrust of the immigrant Indians and had once again quelled these concerns by convincing them to petition state officials for land in the fall of 1833. In their petition—one signed by "Col. Boles, John Boles, Richard Justice, Piggion, Andrew Mcbann and Eli Harlin"—they methodically outlined their boundary. It commenced at the ford of the San Antonio Road on the Trinity River, running up the road to where it met the Angelina River, and thence moved north before cutting overland in a northeasterly direction to the Sabine River. From the Sabine, it ran due west to the Trinity, following the course of the river back to the original point. The claim included roughly three thousand square miles of East Texas. The Cherokees had selected a Tejano, Don Manuel de los Santos of Nacogdoches, to act as their land commissioner, and their petition asked that the land to be granted "in common."[57]

During his trip north in 1834, Almonte seemed supportive of the Indian claim.[58] In meetings with a large group of Choctaw Indians, he found them "extremely attached to us"; they were "good warriors . . . and agriculturalists." He felt that the government should "agree with the state on the method of placing" tribes such as the Choctaw on land "in the knowledge that those are enlisted to serve as allies of the Mexicans." The Choctaws had even offered to fight the Comanches—even though some Choctaws worked for Coffee at Comanche trade fairs.[59] Thus, when Almonte met the "ringleaders" of the "Cherokees, Shawnees, Kickapoos, Creeks,

Delawares, Choctaws, [and] Nacogdoches [Caddos]" on May 29, 1834, he, like Mier y Terán, promised land in return for Indian fidelity.[60]

But once again, it was unclear who actually possessed the authority to distribute this land—nowhere in Mexican law did military officers possess such power. In addition, General Santa Anna soon began consolidating power, dissolving the various state governments. With the demise of the legislative body and the emergence of dictatorship in Mexico City, thoughts of land distribution for Indians ended. The prevailing view among many Mexican national politicians, including the influential conservative Lucas Alamán, was that Coahuila-Texas had mishandled its public lands and that many grants should be rescinded.[61] Such a view undoubtedly was unsettling to Anglos, especially those who had land titles that derived from state empresario grants.

The shifting political winds, the expanding Anglo-American presence, and the rise of Santa Anna caused Almonte to undergo a dramatic change of heart that became evident by the late fall of 1834. He wrote several letters to officials in Mexico City in which he inexplicably reversed himself; he came out against Indian land grants, even to the loyal Cherokees. Almonte reasoned that the Anglo-American advance into Indian Territory and the U.S.-brokered peace between the immigrant Indians and the western tribes would bring disaster to Mexico that would end in a united Indian campaign against Mexico, supported by Anglo-Texans, who the colonel concluded were "hostile to all Mexicans."[62] As Almonte came to this conclusion, Sam Houston was involved in trying to create just such a scenario.

While the winter months of 1834–1835 had provoked considerable soul-searching for Colonel Almonte, it also worried Anglo-Texans and their liberal Tejano supporters. All plans for the future development of Texas were thereafter subject to review by General Santa Anna. He seemed determined to turn states into provinces, sapping the power of federalism and then ruling the provinces from Mexico City. The new regime was thought capable of even forcing Anglos from Texas—certainly there was talk of removing those who had arrived illegally, including the likes of William Barret Travis and Sam Houston.

These were certainly dark days for empresario Stephen Austin, who had put considerable personal effort into the development of his colony. In December 1834, Santa Anna finally released Austin from jail in Mexico City on bond. Forced to remain in the capital while awaiting trial, Austin underwent a conversion; he became more militant (albeit understandably unwilling to put these views to words in letters to friends that might be intercepted). Santa Anna's general amnesty allowed Austin to proceed home in September 1835. After reaching his colony, he learned that a "War Party" had emerged that backed paramilitary activity, and Austin was prone to join them.

Many militants were determined to implement the Americanization of Texas by force, to drive from the land those who opposed home rule (in other words, statehood) and slavery. While Mexican centralists posed the most obvious obstacle to this scheme, a general concern existed among Austin's colonists regarding the vast number of Indians who remained in the region. Some could be co-opted through negotiation, others might easily support Mexican centralists in a confrontation, and still others were decidedly anti-Anglo. And some Texans even spoke up in favor of an American system of government, perhaps even annexation to the United States. As Austin tried to reassert leadership in his colony, then, many issues and strategies were unresolved.

But others seemed clearer. The three years following the collapse of the Mexican army's occupation of Texas had brought massive migration, increasing the Anglo population by perhaps a third so that it stood at nearly thirty thousand, many of them armed. Mexico's neighbor to the north seemed more aggressive, willing to deploy its army perhaps even on foreign soil in the West. By 1835, Americanization had become a force to reckon with, and the Anglo-Americans, who increasingly called themselves Texians, would be difficult to remove from Mexican Texas.

7

THE TEXAS CREED
AND THE CLOUDS OF WAR

The vast majority of Anglos who came to Texas were capable with a rifle. While some (particularly the early families that entered Austin's colony) preferred a pastoral life, most were wedded to the southern-derived creed of honor and bravery. They were willing to fight for their sense of liberty, which placed an inordinate emphasis upon defense of family and state—which, in turn, demanded the preservation of one's honor—and was anchored by the notion that slavery produced a cultured and refined society worth defending. The more brash among them adhered to a sense of destiny, exemplified especially in the lives of men such as Travis and Houston. While Stephen Austin may have been the Anglo "father" of Texas, William Barret Travis and Sam Houston, through their sacrifice and military skills, were soon to be seen as its heroic saviors.

Both Houston and Travis had come to Texas late, during the illegal migrations in 1832 and 1833. They both had suffered failed marriages and saw in Texas a chance to recoup their positions in a society that honored familial and economic accomplishment. Houston and Travis expected to fight; indeed, unlike Austin, they both schemed to promote revolution of one sort or another. After Travis left his wife and children behind in Alabama, he swore that he would do something great and honorable in Texas or die trying. In reality, both men would sell their souls to redeem their failed lives, and military adventure offered the main chance to achieve this goal.

Yet the opportunistic personalities of Houston and Travis did not fit every Texian, or "Texan," as this nationalistic group of Anglos would soon call themselves: some talked of war. Fortunately for both Houston and Travis, General Antonio López de Santa Anna was the one to precipitate the crisis in Texas when he militarily reoccupied that northern province in the fall of 1835. The Mexican general had his own principles of honor and glory, formed over years of struggle within the Mexican army. Decidedly not a liberal, Santa Anna was born in 1794 to some of Hidalgo's despised Gachupin parents near Vera Cruz. He had been to Texas before, fighting for Spain at the battle of Medina River in 1813, when the Spanish defeated Gutiérrez de Lara and his Anglo-American friends who had pronounced for Hidalgo. Santa Anna's support for Emperor Iturbide demonstrated a commitment to monarchy rather than democracy, and his willingness to install himself as dictator surprised few. A good organizer, he at times could be a poor general; he had very little concern for the welfare of his troops.[2]

Santa Anna had well-trained subordinates, however, most of them educated at the Mexican Military Academy. The general picked his brother-in-law, General Martín Perfecto de Cós (commander of the Eastern Internal Provinces), to march on San Antonio. Cós immediately concluded that to establish law and order, certain Anglo agitators would have to be arrested or expelled from Texas. The necessity for this strategy became even more obvious after he sent a small garrison to reoccupy the old fort at Anahuac and Texans under the leadership of Travis attacked and repelled the Mexican forces. The general demanded that Texans arrest Travis and many others; this, however, Texans (including Austin), would not do. The Texas creed would not allow them to give up their own. When Cós occupied San Antonio with a twelve-hundred-man army in October 1835, a clash seemed certain.

As Mexican officials concentrated on the treasonous activities of Texans, the leaders of the immigrant Indians became sullen and increasingly suspicious of everyone. Chief Bowles, who had lived on his land peacefully for fifteen years, complained vigorously of his "white neighbors" in the spring of 1835, accusing them of "killing and marking his cattle."[1] Texans had surveyed three *sitios* of land on Frost Thorn's empresario grant west of the Angelina River (roughly twelve thousand acres of land) and had reached the outer limits of the Cherokee town, trying to run the placid Chief Big Mush off his farm.[2]

With Bowles angry, rumors spread rapidly of his supposed involvement with other Indians who might be plotting massacre. In reality, Bowles met with a handful of Tejano citizens who were suspected of plotting against Texans that summer. An ethnic polarization seemed to be forming near Nacogdoches, as Texans, Indians, and Tejanos plotted and schemed against each other. The local sheriff arrested and questioned several Tejanos, but the investigation revealed little. The information he collected did, however, reveal the activities of one Benjamin Hawkins, a peaceful man then living in Bowles's village.

Ironically, Hawkins (a mixed-blood Creek leader) had paired up with Sam Houston to speculate in land. The son-in-law of William McIntosh and the brother-in-law of Chilly McIntosh, Hawkins had been heavily involved in land speculation for many years, likely becoming Houston's partner when Houston was living with the Cherokees in Indian Territory in 1829. Hawkins had money. He had purchased 3,770 acres of land and built a plantation in Shelby County, Texas, east of Nacogdoches. He and Houston realized that as Indian removal played itself out, the removed tribes would receive huge cash annuities for their land. It made more sense to sell land to rich Indians than it did to offer it up to poor southern whites, who had little cash and expected to get farms in Texas for virtually nothing.[3]

Yet Hawkins, like Fields before him, made a grievous error while at Bowles's village. He apparently claimed the ability to bring twenty-five thousand Creek Indians into Texas—some (such as his relatives the McIntoshes) doubtless migrating from Indian Territory, and others likely coming from the many thousands of Cherokees about to be removed from Georgia, North Carolina, and Tennessee. Houston clearly signed off on this plan, although he later publicly disavowed it. Some evidence even suggests that the former Tennessee governor hoped that a rush of immigrant Indians into Texas might start the fighting he desperately hoped for. Whether Hawkins unveiled this plan entirely at Bowles's town is unknown, but the news became common knowledge across Texas. His visit and his meeting with various Tejanos led Texans to conclude that he intended to "raise the Indians."[4]

While Anglos fretted over Indian conspiracy, agent Bean at Nacogdoches tried desperately both to maintain order and to placate the new authorities in Coahuila-Texas. He continued to vouch for the reliability of the immigrant tribes, reporting that five hundred men from their towns had agreed to campaign against the Comanches. Bean was also trying to prevent the Creek migration to Texas. Hawkins and another speculator, Archibald Hotchkiss, had offered $20,000 for the land grant given to General Vicente Filisola in 1831, much of this land within the Cherokee claim. Likely at Bean's urging, Houston, Henry Raguet, John Forbes, and several other Nacog-doches citizens signed a petition sent on to Andrew Jackson, protesting the sale. Houston must have blushed as he signed the document; he certainly played all sides![5]

General Cós and Bean both also believed that the Americans on Red River were a serious threat.[6] Bean especially condemned the trader Coffee, who handed out munitions to the Comanches on a daily basis. Worse, some spies had reported that Coffee had unique spiritual powers; the nearby Comanches called him "the wizard." Coffee was a master at old fur-trade tricks, such as lighting a cup of brandy on fire in front of an Indian delegation and then threatening to do the same to all the rivers if the Indians misbehaved.[7]

When he learned of Coffee, General Cós demanded that Bean arrest the trader, as the general intended to arrest other troublemakers.[8] But Bean, like Houston, also could play several sides. Virtually on the same day as Cós's order arrived (June 12, 1835), Bean entertained a young lieutenant in the U.S. Army, Henry Swartmont, who had entered Texas illegally to gain information regarding Mexico's attitude toward the U.S. military activities along the Red River corridor. Coffee, Swartmont argued to Bean, had helped the peace process and deserved protection from both the United States and Mexico. Bean coyly informed the lieutenant that Mexico had no money with which to campaign against either Coffee or any of the Plains bands.[9] Bean would certainly not disturb Coffee.

Bean's increasing cooperation with Americans suggests much about the shifting fortunes of politics and military affairs in East Texas. Although an American, Bean had dedicated much of his adult life to fighting for Mexican liberalism. He had joined Father Morelos in the war for independence, rising to the rank of colonel. In the process, he had become close friends with Morelos's son, Juan N. Almonte. Bean at one point had convinced Almonte to support the immigrant Indians' land claim, and Almonte's turnabout likely bothered him. Almonte's support of the centralists' cause probably brought further confusion; Almonte had joined General Cós's army by fall. Bean, then, like a number of Texans and Tejanos, undoubtedly did considerable soul-searching that summer.

Bean, although he never said so in reports to San Antonio, could also sense the growing Anglo militancy in Texas. Militia units were organized in several communities, ostensibly to fight Indians. One came together in Sterling Robertson's new colony that spring, perhaps intent on repelling the Creek invasion. Every authority, Mexican and American, had heard of Hawkins's plan. The rangers of Robertson's colony also had made contact with rangers in Austin's colony to the south, each group pledging to support the other.

Acting on its own volition and without provocation, the rangers from Robertson's colony made an unprovoked attacked on the Kichai village—mostly Caddos—along the central Trinity River in May 1835. The rangers stormed the town and burned it, "killed a number" of Indians, and wounded many others. While the Texans had complained of minor depredations, the sole purpose of the raid seems to have been to acquire animals to sell for profit, as the rangers carried off fifty horses.[10] Such attacks had a secondary motive, though; they drove the Indians farther north and west.

At this point, thirty to forty men from Austin's colony participated in the pillaging. The various small companies were led by Edward Burleson, Robert M. Coleman, and the infamous John H. Moore. These men, mostly from Kentucky and Tennessee, were highly proficient with long rifles. Most had joined the ranger forces for the booty that came from attacking Indians. Such men were mostly adventurers—young and aggressive and prone to quick, violent acts. Just north of the San Antonio–Nacogdoches road, the ranger army captured two Cherokees, a Caddo, and several Indian women—a small hunting party.

Such parties came and went along this road by the dozen, most expecting to see Texans or Tejanos and prepared to interact with them in a friendly fashion. But this encounter became suddenly different. As Captain Edward Burleson described the scene, the rangers in a "democratic fashion" voted to execute the Indian men, the tally being two to one in favor. After killing the men, the bloodthirsty rangers carried off the women likely for pleasure. One ranger with the company described his fellows as, as much of a "*don't care* a looking company of men as could be found on the top of the ground."[11]

The various haphazardly led companies proceeded farther, beyond the head-waters of the Navasota River, and Coleman's ranger company collided with a hundred well-armed Wichitas and Caddos bent on revenge for the attack on the Kichai town. Many Indians died that day, but they kept coming, fighting with a ferocity that surprised the Texans. While the Indians suffered many dead, Coleman's party had four men seriously wounded and one killed. Fearing more casualties, Coleman ordered a retreat, sending for reinforcements from Moore and Burleson.

Fleeing south, Coleman's company reached the fort that had been completed the year before by Silas M. Parker on the upper Navasota River. This stockade, which housed eight or nine families, was seventy-five miles north of Austin's original colony. After the battles with the Wichitas and Caddos, the Texas rangers used the fort as a base of operations. In late July, after Moore's and Burleson's companies joined Cole-man, the Texans at Parker's fort numbered more than 150 men and once again assailed the northern Indians.

Riding north under the command of Moore, Burleson, and Coleman, the force sought out Indian villages wherever they could be found. They discovered a few Tawakoni Wichitas near their old town on the Navasota River, but these Indians took flight. At the Trinity River, the hard-riding rangers quickly attacked another Wichita town, leaving several dead. Finally, upon reaching the forks of the Trinity near modern Dallas, the party burned the town of the displaced Wacos. One poor Waco woman, taken captive by the rangers, was so distraught that she killed her infant daughter and tried desperately to commit suicide. While she was in agony from her wounds, a ranger dragged her to a riverbank, forced her to kneel, and cut off her head with a sword. Rangers then threw her body into the river.[12]

Mexican officials in the south knew little of these assaults. Bean knew of them and realized that several of the men executed by the rangers were from Chief Bowles's village. Bowles's young Cherokee warriors demanded revenge despite the fact that the victims had been running with, as one observer put it, "hostile Caddos."[13] This would have been an ideal time to build a Mexican alliance of immigrant Indians against the Texans, but by July 1835, Bean seemed unwilling to do so. Indeed, Nacogdoches political chief Henry Rueg, Bean, and others warned Bowles to remain at peace. While Rueg wrote to the ayuntamiento at San Augustine that he expected "an upcoming Indian war" that summer, Bean helped prevent it.[14]

To be certain, the brutal strikes on the Caddo and Wichita communities—attacks that help explain the famous assault by Indians on Parker's Fort the next year—came at an auspicious time for the Texans. The attacks demonstrated the ability of Anglo colonists to punish the tribes in their towns at a time when Mexico had supposedly abandoned them. The assaults, and Bean's careful advice, neutralized the immigrant villagers as well as the Caddos and Wichitas, allowing many of the men who had marched on the Indian communities to turn their attention to General Cós. By late July, they did.

Cós's demand that the Texans arrest several Anglo troublemakers, including especially Travis, fell in front of a new Texas convention, called a "Consultation," which met in November 1835. Austin, who had arrived two months before, joined the discussions thoroughly convinced that Texas must resist Santa Anna. An opportunity soon surfaced. On October 2, rangers under "Colonel" Moore clashed with Cós's troops near Gonzales. The engagement sprang from the refusal of the Texans to give up the old cannon that sat in the town square. With a rabble forming under leaders such as Moore and Burleson (who had just finished burning Indian villages in the north), together with James Bowie and Austin, this so-called Army of Texas laid siege to San Antonio on October 15.

Given the circumstances, the immediate concern of the Consultation was to justify such actions. The group did so in a unanimous, but ambiguous, declaration issued on November 7. The declaration openly stated that hostilities were begun to protect the rights of the state of Coahuila-Texas, which were guaranteed under the Mexican Constitution of 1824 but were being trampled by military despotism. The hostilities opened by Texans, the document further stated, were aimed at defeating centralists, and the Texans welcomed with open arms Tejano federalists. The appeal, while much debated, had an immediate effect, as it was issued just after General Cós had publicly humiliated Juan Seguín and other Tejano federalists in San Antonio; Cós had identified the Sequín family as disloyal and had run Juan's father out of town.

As fighting erupted, Seguín brought thirty-five mounted Tejanos over to the Anglo cause. Plácido Benavides arrived at the scene of battle with thirty mounted rancheros from Victoria, and these men—the only mounted troops in the Texas army familiar with the region south of San Antonio—cut Cós off from supplies available on the coast and from the south. The Tejano force likewise burned much of the grass between the Nueces and the Rio Grande, the scorched-earth policy making it difficult for a Mexican relief column to reach San Antonio.[15]

Despite the Tejano reinforcements, which soon reached roughly 150 men, the Texas army faced a formidable opponent. Cós had consolidated more than 600 soldiers in San Antonio over the summer and fall.[16] While poorly trained and not heavily committed to the cause, they were dug in. Moreover, Cós's cavalry was a unit dedicated to defending Texas. The Texan/Tejano force seldom reached more than half the number of Cós's troops. While Tejanos seemed committed to the cause and Indians were quiet in the north, such good fortune could not defeat a large army.

The members of the General Council of the Consultation, which ruled Texas until the declaration of independence in early March 1836, came to two obvious conclusions: they needed to recruit men and arms in the United States (and possibly bring in the U.S. Army), and they needed to maintain peace with the northern Indians because those Indians could descend on the farms and ranches of Texans while the men were away fighting General Cós. The task of going to the United States was quickly handed to Austin, William Wharton, and Branch Archer. The job of placating the Indians fell to Houston almost by default. Having good relations with the Cherokees, he well realized that they might bring a thousand warriors to bear arms for either side.[17]

The immigrant tribes obviously wanted some resolution of the land situation. A few leading Texan revolutionaries supported land cessions to Indians, arguing that Indians had as much right to Texas land as Anglos did and that land had been promised (indeed, supposedly granted) by Mexico to these tribes. Houston agreed, believing further that a land grant would help mold an alliance or at least keep the tribes neutral. But other Texans remained more circumspect, taking the more recent view of Mexican centralists—that under the treaty of 1831 the United States was obligated to stop Indian migration to Texas. Especially troubling was the rumor that Benjamin Hawkins wanted to move twenty-five thousand southern Indians into Texas.[18]

Interpretations of the treaty of 1831 produced many curious scenarios. Jackson, for example, could use a ruse such as Indian war on Anglo-Americans in Texas to justify sending troops across the Sabine River. Jackson, like most Democratic politicians, had often displayed an interest in adding Texas to the union. Texas revolutionaries fully comprehended that the treaty of 1831 offered a pretext for an all-out invasion by the United States.[19] Jackson had the troops in Louisiana and Indian Territory to accomplish such a plot.

Meanwhile, the General Council worked both to overawe the Indians of northern Texas and to make allies of them. In late October, the council commissioned Silas Parker as superintendent of rangers (a logical move, as Parker's stockade had in effect become a ranger fort despite its small civilian population). He was to send patrols between the upper Brazos and Trinity rivers into the lands adjacent to his fort.[20] In early November, well aware that Cós still held San Antonio and that he might persuade the Indians to join him—they had fought with Mexico in the past—Houston met with Bowles and Big Mush at Nacogdoches, openly promising that the new Texan government under the Consultation would honor their claims to land.

A few days later, Houston put this promise in writing, assuring Chief Bowles that "your land is secured."[21] Coming as it did from Houston—a man who was a friend of the Indians, had married a Cherokee women in Indian Territory, and, according to Chief Bowles, had also taken one of his daughters as a wife sometime after arriving in Texas—what better guarantee could the Cherokees receive? (Ironically, at the same time, George Pollitt, head of the Nacogdoches ayuntamiento, wrote to Houston complaining that "some scoundrell [sic] had surveyed a part of Bowles's land.")[22]

Given Houston's supposed success, the General Council passed a resolution stating that both the Cherokees and their associated bands, "twelve in number," would receive land "included within the bounds hereafter mentioned from the Government of Mexico, from whom we have also derived our right." The council then identified the Indian claim, outlining its boundaries much as the Cherokees had done on numerous other occasions.[23] Presiding officer Henry Smith, likely in response to Pollitt's letter, then asked that the council act to prevent other Texans from surveying Indian lands. This too passed, and a halt to surveying in Thorn's empresario grant was ordered.[24]

Unfortunately for the Indians, two events soon interceded. First, Henry Raguet wrote Houston on December 3 that some "two hundred voters and their familys [*sic*]" occupied the land proposed for the Indians. While this number was likely an exaggeration, Raguet counseled Houston to stop mentioning the borders of the Indian claim and to be more discreet with the whole negotiation.[25] Second, this information reached the General Council just after a hard battle had concluded at San Antonio. General Cós, low on supplies, had surrendered his entire force. The rush to concede land to Indians quickly subsided.

While the council intended to purchase Indian neutrality, with the fall of Cós that end could be approached more cautiously. Soon the council warned Houston and others working on the negotiation that "all honest claims of the Whites" must be protected.[26] By mid-January, Houston discovered that his friend Bowles had learned of the change. The chief had also discovered that no one intended to enforce the ban on surveying, which began again within the Indian claim. Houston feared an outbreak if a treaty was not signed. When Houston sent a friendly letter to Bowles asking if he might be willing to assist the Texans militarily, Bowles failed to respond.[27] In early February 1836, Chief Bowles refused to even meet with Houston in Nacogdoches.[28]

Just as negotiations seemed to be breaking down, rumors flashed across Texas of a Mexican counterinvasion. General Santa Anna had organized an army of several thousand men to retake Texas. The revolutionary pendulum had swung once again back the other way. In late February, a much graver Houston traveled to the Cherokee town, hat in hand, hoping to find Bowles willing to listen to him. Houston used all his persuasive abilities to bring the immigrant Indian leaders to terms. While the General Council had advised against the granting of land, such advice now seemed obsolete. The Cherokees led the delegation of associated bands, which included Shawnees, Delawares, Kickapoos, Quapaws, Choctaws, Biloxi and Ioni Indians, Alabamas, Coushattas, and the Caddos of the Neches River. The parties signed a treaty accord on February 23, 1836.[29]

The treaty contained thirteen articles, some contradictory, which was perhaps inevitable given the many claims in northern Texas. Article 3, for example, said simply that other land grants—supposedly those issued to empresarios—were not affected by this treaty. Did this mean that such grants were valid or invalid?[30] Despite the unfinished nature of the treaty, it accomplished what it was intended to do. The Cherokees and the other immigrants agreed to neutrality at a time when Texans needed a peaceful northern frontier.

Just ten days after the signing of the Cherokee treaty, on March 2, 1836, Texans declared their independence at Washington-on-the-Brazos, creating the Texas Republic. Much like Jefferson's declaration (written sixty years before at Philadelphia), the document contained a list of charges: Mexico had abandoned federalism for despotism, it had failed to protect the lives and property of citizens, it had tried to enforce decrees by the use of armies, and—in an interesting twist—it had incited Indians to massacre the white inhabitants. The document then called for a separate and independent Texas. The declaration, after very little debate, was signed by fifty-nine men, including José Antonio Navarro and José Francisco Ruíz, both federalists and Tejanos.

It is highly unlikely that such a meeting, which occurred on the central Brazos River, could have even occurred had an Indian war broken out to the north. It also seems obvious that such a war would have been under way had the rangers under Moore and Burleson remained active in the region and Houston remained elsewhere. But Houston and Texas would soon face their gravest test. Houston had politically given the republic a chance to write its declaration; Texans would now have to earn their right to separate from Mexico on the battlefield.

Chaos rather than order had attended the declaration of Texas's independence. Most of the delegates to the convention were relatively new to Texas, primarily because the previous Consultation had made a mess of things. Prior to the declaration, the political body had appointed a number of military officers, for the most part called colonels, several of whom were incompetent and determined to make their own war. It had also supposedly handed over the Texas army to Houston, who was commissioned as a general. But the colonels failed to listen to the general. Thus, two small Texan armies, ignoring orders from Houston, marched south to the Nueces River intent on plundering Mexican border towns. Other Texan garrisons, of roughly one hundred and three hundred men respectively, held San Antonio and Goliad.

At San Antonio, the Tejano population remained supportive of the Texan cause. Some of the troops in the city's garrison, housed in the old mission called by then the Alamo, were Tejanos. They were pleased to hear of support coming from Saltillo and Monclova, where the state legislature had been disbanded but had voiced considerable concern regarding Santa Anna's growing attack on federalism. The governor, Agustín Viesca, continued to plot with Austin and encouraged federalists to defy General Cós's order prohibiting men of Coahuila from crossing the Rio Grande to aid in the Texas revolt.

Despite this defiant Tejano support, conflict erupted between Texans and Tejanos at Goliad and elsewhere. Phillip Dimitt seized command of the republic's volunteers at Goliad and prepared to defend it. But he gained a brutal reputation by impressing Tejanos for labor, using them to dig trenches.[31] When Governor Viesca arrived in Goliad from Saltillo, Dimitt even insulted the governor, causing Austin to demand Dimitt's retirement from service.

It was amid such bickering, confusion over command, and growing distrust that General Santa Anna marched his army north to San Antonio in midwinter despite the lack of grass for his animals. His tired troops, many of whom were without shoes, had reached the Leona River (eight miles south of town) early on February 23. Late that evening, led by a regimental band, the Vanguard Brigade entered the outskirts of San Antonio. Unlike the army of six hundred (mainly convicts) that General Cós had had to rely on to defend the city a few months before, Santa Anna's advance force numbered roughly three thousand men.

The appearance of Santa Anna's troops at San Antonio startled Travis and the Texan defenders of the Alamo, who barely had time to close the gate to their partially prepared fortress. Within hours, Santa Anna began a siege of the small garrison, which numbered a mere 150 men. The Mexican general supposedly fired on the state flag of Coahuila-Texas with its two stars, one representing Coahuila and one, Texas. As more of Santa Anna's troops arrived during the day, the general unfurled his own flag, the blood-red ensign that signified the Degüello. With its skull and crossbones prominent, the flag meant that the Mexican forces would give no quarter unless the Texans immediately surrendered.

Discussions went on in the Alamo throughout the afternoon. This time, many of the Tejanos, who watched nearby, could do little to help, and they fled from the town. Indeed, some Tejanos inside the Alamo took advantage of a supposed offer of amnesty to Mexicans to leave the fort. Seguín and several of his men, however, remained under arms; a few would eventually charge through the Mexican besieging forces with the last, fleeting appeals for help from Lieutenant Colonel Travis, who commanded inside. He had been ordered to retreat by Houston but like so many Texan officers had ignored the general of the Texas army.

The men in the Alamo did not wish to die; they likely believed that they held a strong position, since the Texans had needed nearly two months to take the fortress earlier. Some no doubt felt that reinforcements would arrive to save them. Travis, moreover, could hardly have expected to be allowed to live had he surrendered; he headed the list of insurrectionists who had brought trouble to Texas, and he knew it. Nevertheless, late in the afternoon of February 23, Travis sent Albert Martin out to talk with the Mexicans under a flag of truce.

Martin was a loyal and dedicated man. He met the indomitable Colonel Almonte outside the walls and asked for conditions. Almonte, somewhat sympathetic toward the Texas cause and hopeful of a peaceful resolution, nevertheless had to follow Santa Anna's orders. The general wanted surrender immediately, without terms, or the Texans would be destroyed. While yet another "colonel," James Bowie (who had married a Mexican woman and seemed convinced that surrender was the only alternative), wanted to accept the offer, he lay sick and near death from what was likely either typhoid or cholera. Travis elected to fight. During the night, he composed his first of several appeals to the people of Texas. It concluded with a resonating declaration that was pure Travis: "I shall never surrender or retreat. . . . Victory or Death!"

Travis expected help from the garrison at Goliad, where Colonel James Fannin—the only man in Texas with formal military training—had recently taken command. Fannin had studied for two years at West Point. Unfortunately, he exhibited indecision and caution when he received Travis's appeals for reinforcements on February 25. Other Tejanos escaped the Alamo on February 29 with news that the garrison still awaited relief. Not until early March did Fannin order a march, but then he countermanded it, reconsidered it, and finally did nothing. By March 3, the last regiments of Santa Anna's infantry had arrived, building the general's assault forces to 2,600. While junior officers wished to wait until twelve-pound cannon arrived to destroy the walls of the Alamo, Santa Anna was impatient and ready to attack.

The leaders of the Anglo community in Texas would soon face their gravest hour. But this coming time also would be one of growing uncertainty for thousands of Indians, Tejanos, and Mexicans and their chiefs and leaders as well. Increasingly, personalities and defense of honor rather than law, order, or debate played a crucial role in determining the outcome of events all across Texas. Bean and Bowles, Houston, Cós, and Austin, and Travis and Santa Anna slowly became locked into a struggle that left little room for compromise or peace. And a complex set of rivalries over land and politics, the debate over Texas independence, and the fundamental belief of many Tejanos in federalism within the Mexican system had produced a sometimes-confusing series of events that would unfold at breakneck speed over the next few years.

For Indians, the honor and duty required of men in defense of their communities would lead to violent acts of revenge. Chiefs who might still remember the old times of the "false peace" could not restrain young men who saw their wives and daughters butchered and their children facing starvation after rangers had burned villages and destroyed crops. The choices for the Tejano community must have been even more difficult—federalism seemed nearly dead, buried by the dictator Santa Anna. But would a new political system under Anglo-Texans guarantee their rights?

As this ever-tightening web of ethnic conflict and intrigue unfolded—as the men at the Alamo faced their martyrhood, as immigrant and Plains Indians considered their choices, as Houston and Santa Anna raced to meet their destinies—the cultural circumstances, the ethnic and racial differences and the personalities that drove Texas history, soon led inexorably to war. Men such as Moore, Burleson, Dimitt, Bowie, and Travis—men of the South who put honor, chivalry, and a belief in the inevitable righteousness of Anglo rule above all else—rose to defend Texas. And Santa Anna marched to strike them down. In this increasingly opaque struggle, notions of "loyal" Tejanos and Indians became obscured by the myopia of war. Texans soon concluded that only their beliefs, though at times prejudicial, hateful, and violent, were glorious and righteous.

8

REVOLUTION AND THE "RUMOR" OF INDIAN WAR

Quietly, just after midnight on March 6, Santa Anna's officers roused the infantry troops from their slumber. It had been cold and damp, as a norther had swept through San Antonio a week before, chilling the troops. But officers ordered them to leave their overcoats. The men were checked to make sure they had shoes and sandals, however; an outcry from stepping on a thorn or sharp stone could give away their position. Not even smoking was allowed, for fear the Texans inside the Alamo would smell the aroma. Slowly the troops moved closer to the walls of the fortress, taking up positions in trenches and in the *jacales* (small Tejano houses) that the Texans had mostly burned. At 5:30 A.M., a Mexican bugler sounded the call to arms, the military band belted out the song that announced the Degüello, and the troops rose in columns, advancing on the Alamo from all four directions.[1]

The startled Texans, who had sought the heat of their barrack fires that night, hardly reached their positions on the walls. They were thinly placed; after a handful of reinforcements had reached the fortress in late February, the Texans mustered just over 180 men, not enough to fill all the gaps. Worse, the many cannons along the walls could be fired only once because the defenders were too few to man them properly. And in the dark the Texans could see virtually nothing. Above the sound of the band, canteens rattled and the Mexican troops, in their adrenaline-charged euphoria, began a slow cheer that grew into a roar as they advanced.

Hearing the noise and sensing the shadows, the Texans ignited their cannons, which were filled with broken metal, pieces of horseshoes, and the like. Each charge tore holes in the Mexican lines, leaving ten or twelve men headless or armless and dying. In some Mexican regiments, the first line all but disappeared, but others collected their scaling ladders and pressed on. The Mexicans fired back with their British-made

"Brown Bess" muskets; a ball struck Travis between the eyes, nearly decapitating him. Soon there was mass confusion.

Mexican infantry reached all four walls, but they were in disarray, confused; unit integrity was almost gone. A few had tried to scale the heights in the dark. Texans at first had the advantage, firing at point-blank range with cannons and muskets. Swords flashed at the tops of the walls as the combat became hand-to-hand. In the confusion, some Mexican troops shot or bayoneted their own men, for no one could tell who was who.

The north wall was the easiest to penetrate, but here, too, the first assault wave had broken down. Santa Anna, realizing the need, committed his reserves. They hit the north wall, which in spots had been completely broken down during the earlier fight with General Cós. Lieutenant Alamaron Dickenson, an engineer of sorts, had repaired the walls with horizontal logs filled in between with dirt. But the logs could be climbed, and a few Mexican troops soon vaulted into the compound and opened the north gate. This made the other walls indefensible.

Texans, outflanked and choking from the smoke, ran to the chapel and huddled inside the barracks. Mexicans turned the Texans' own cannons on them and blew open the doors. While the attackers had breached the north wall in only twenty minutes, they took nearly two-thirds of an hour to clear the buildings; the fighting inside was vicious. Bowie, too sick to fight, was murdered while still in bed.

A few Texans (supposedly, seven) surrendered. Reputed to be among them was the former congressman and American folk hero Davy Crockett. As dawn crept over the mission chapel, they were put to death, either by firing squad or by being hacked to death with swords.[2]

At sunrise, the Alamo was a mass of smoke and dead bodies. Mexican soldiers picked through the remains, mutilating and bayoneting anyone who showed signs of life. A handful of Texans did survive, however—including Susanna Dickenson, the young wife of Lieutenant Dickenson, and Travis's slave, Joe. They had stayed in the chapel and, along with a few children, were brought in front of Santa Anna. The general allowed them to leave. They carried the news of the defeat to Houston, who lingered at Gonzales to the north.

Rumors, innuendos, and belatedly even some truth spread the news of the defeat northward into the Texan settlements. The 182 or 183 killed quickly passed into immortality. In this romantic era, not surprisingly, a comparison was soon made to Thermopylae, where a handful of Spartans and Greeks had tried to halt the advance of the Persians in 480 B.C. and a single Spartan had survived to tell the tale of defeat. As Texans saw it, "Thermopylae had her messenger of defeat—The Alamo had none!" While Texans elevated the number of Mexican casualties from 2,000 to 3,000, to 5,000, and then to 8,000, in reality Santa Anna had lost 521 men, mostly because he refused to wait for his heavy guns. But other Mexican troops were wounded and dying, and the general had barely more than a regiment or two (perhaps 1,500 men) to press the attack northward. He incorrectly assumed that this battle, this bloody and final sacrifice at the Alamo, would end Anglo-American resistance in Texas.

To the south, Santa Anna's subordinates were more cautious but just as successful. The Texan General Council had commissioned Colonels James Grant and Frank W. Johnson to carry the war to the Mexican heartland. The campaigners likely had plunder in mind. But some of these men mutinied and returned to Goliad, where Fannin remained with a force of over three hundred Texans. General José Urrea and five hundred Mexican dragoons, scouting along the coast, overtook Johnson and Grant and slaughtered their two small commands, totaling sixty men, near San Patricio.

And still Fannin dallied, even after he had learned of the destruction of the Alamo and of Houston's order to fall back to Victoria. When Fannin finally decided to abandon Goliad on March 19, he had waited too long. Urrea caught the unsuspecting army on the open prairie. Urrea's spy network of Tejano vaqueros (alienated by Phillip Dimitt) had proved invaluable to the Mexicans in revealing Fannin's movements. After a few hours of fighting under a blazing sun without water, Fannin surrendered. Urrea initially treated the Texans as prisoners of war, but he received orders from Santa Anna to execute them all. The Mexicans divided Fannin's army into four groups, marched the 350 Texans out of Goliad, and shot them down along the road. Only a dozen or so survived. This left Texans with a force of only 300 to 400 volunteers and a determined battle cry: "Remember the Alamo, and remember Goliad!"

Despite Travis's obstinate refusal to surrender—some of his martyred men certainly had wanted to—the sacrifice at the Alamo did, to some degree, benefit the Texan cause by awakening more-conservative Texans to the fact that this was a life-and-death struggle. The battle at the Alamo had weakened and delayed Santa Anna's army; however, it had also produced a panic. The disasters at the Alamo and Goliad prompted a massive exodus of Texans. Many of those in flight were able-bodied men who wished only to protect their families. Well over five thousand people along the Colorado River alone abandoned their farms and fled toward Louisiana. Thousands more started an exodus along the Brazos and Trinity rivers. An army of many thousand could have emerged from those refugees, but they fled instead.

Santa Anna had given no quarter in the battles, and Texas civilians expected the worst. Even those who surrendered had to expect execution. After March 20, scared Anglo men, women, and children burned their farms, hoping to deny the advancing Mexican army food and shelter, and turned north. The exodus became known as the "runaway scrape." Seguín's small force of Tejanos patrolled ahead of Santa Anna's troops, warning Texans and helping them flee.[3]

General Houston found solace in the reported loss of perhaps a thousand Mexican troops who had been killed or wounded. Santa Anna had to bury his dead and reorder his command. But Houston may not have been ready to take the battle to Santa Anna; rumors swirled that he had been drunk during the Alamo's last days.

When sober, he did have a good argument to present to the three hundred to four hundred Texans who followed him. Fannin and Travis had disobeyed orders, he preached, and were good examples of how not to fight in the future. While many of Houston's men in the days to follow would fume over the supposed cowardice of their retreating "general," Houston kept most of his troops intact as he waited for an opportunity to strike Santa Anna.

Given the impossibility of holding elections, the founding fathers created an ad-interim government that would guide Texas through the coming spring and summer. This governing body elected land speculator David G. Burnet as president despite his general dislike of Houston. Samuel P. Carson agreed to be secretary of state; Thomas J. Rusk, a South Carolinian lawyer and to some degree a protégé of John C. Calhoun's, served as secretary of war. Lorenzo de Zavala, another empresario, reluctantly agreed to the mostly symbolic post of vice president. Zavala would serve Texas loyally through the spring and summer crisis of 1836, helping to rally Tejano support to the cause, but he left government that fall somewhat disappointed in the new republic he had helped create. He soon thereafter died of pneumonia. Texas, to Zavala, had become far too Anglo in a short time.

For its headquarters the new government selected Harrisburg (a location presently within the city limits of Houston, Texas), primarily because of its proximity to water transportation and the United States.[4] From the beginning, the government coveted aid from the United States, and Burnet and his cabinet used every means available to get assistance. One approach entailed cultivating General Edmund P. Gaines, the new commander of all U.S. troops in Louisiana. Burnet and Carson knew that Gaines had a brother in Texas who operated a ferry along the Trinity River; indeed, James Gaines had served on the committee that had written the Texas Declaration of Independence and had been one of the first Texans to sign it.

But General Gaines's connection to Texas went even deeper. The general's nephew and namesake (son of ferryman James Gaines) had joined Houston's army.[5] In other words, at its most critical hour, Texas had an advocate in the U.S. Army; General Gaines would play a crucial role in Texas affairs. An experienced soldier, independently wealthy, and politically connected, he also believed in American destiny, and he took a rather dim view of Indians who stood in the way of American progress.[6]

Burnet could not have found a better general to scheme with. Given the loss of troops in the south, Burnet realized that the most immediate help existed in the U.S. military units stationed along the Texas frontier. Colonel James Many had some three hundred men at Fort Jesup; Secretary of War Lewis Cass had ordered General Gaines to the region with reinforcements on January 23, 1836, increasing the infantry regiments substantially. In his message, Cass, an avid expansionist, had commanded Gaines to enforce the treaty of 1831, preventing "by force, all hostilities and incursions on the part of the Indian Nations." The order gave Gaines permission to cross the border if Indians in the United States started attacking civilians on the other side.[7]

General Gaines felt perfectly comfortable in starting the Mexican War well before James K. Polk considered the possibility. Oddly, what stood in the way was Sam Houston's advocacy of a Texan-Indian alliance. In mid-March, General Houston, while still in full retreat, wrote several feverish letters to Burnet: "We must have the friendship of the Comanches and other Indians," he concluded. Houston wanted agents sent into the upper Brazos region with the intent of convincing Comanches to raid down the Rio Grande below Laredo. Disrupting the "Laredo route," as he put it, would hinder Santa Anna's advance. Houston then demanded that the ad interim government "ratify the Cherokee Treaty."[8] Houston fought alongside Indian allies at the battle of Horseshoe Bend and understood that with Comanches and Cherokees as allies, the revolution could be saved despite the foolishness of Travis, Fannin, and their bands of martyrs.

Burnet had other ideas. Once president, he hired Michael B. Menard from Nacogdoches as Indian agent for northern Texas, ordering him to open negotiations with the Cherokees. "But I must enjoin you," Burnet wrote, "to avoid with great caution entering into any specific treaty relating to boundaries that may compromise the interest of actual settlers." Menard had orders to tell the chiefs that the government was far too busy with affairs in the south to take up such issues.[9]

A second blow to Houston's hoped-for alliance came as rumors of a Mexican-Indian alliance swept Texas. Thomas Jefferson Green, another Carolinian who fancied himself a general in the Texan army—although he had managed to avoid most of the fighting—started these rumors by reporting to officers at Fort Jesup on March 11 that a "blank commission" had been issued by Santa Anna to recruit the immigrant Indians.[10] Once started, the cry of "Indian outbreak" reverberated across the land.

More inflammatory information came from Henry Raguet and John Mason, members of the Committee of Public Safety at Nacogdoches. Mason claimed in letters sent directly to Fort Jesup that "various tribes of Indians" from the United States had arrived near Nacogdoches, intent upon slaughtering the Texans. He identified some as the hated Fox and Sac, who four years before—under the leadership of the infamous chief Black Hawk—had rebelled in present-day Wisconsin, Illinois, and Iowa.[11] Mason appealed to General Gaines's "principle of humanity," calling upon the general to send troops to Nacogdoches as quickly as possible.[12]

General Gaines considered all these reports as he traveled west. Not surprisingly, given the sources, he took the bait. Along the road, he wrote to Cass that the situation might require "crossing our supposed or imaginary national Boundary and meeting the savage marauders wherever [they are] to be found."[13] Once in western Louisiana, Gaines rushed to raise state militia troops, since the U.S. Army forces there were still roughly a thousand men and not up to the task of warring with Mexico. Gaines demanded two brigades from the governors of Louisiana and Mississippi. The treaty of 1831, Gaines stated, must be enforced; Indians from the United States had to be prevented from slaughtering innocent Texans.[14]

The Burnet government did its best to urge the U.S. Army onward. Secretary of State Carson (then at Liberty, Texas) pleaded with Gaines to cross the Sabine River and save the settlements. Burnet wrote numerous epistles to the various committees of vigilance, calling on them to "stir up the people" and save Texas.[15] These committees, organized generally to defend individual communities, soon saw Indians behind every tree. By April 10, the committee from Nacogdoches sent a frightful warning east: "the whole country is in a panic."[16] The settlers abandoning their farms and homes had been led to fear the tomahawk, not the Mexican bayonet.

The exaggerated rumors of Indian war came from several sources. One Charles Sims, who lived near the Cherokee and worked for the Nacogdoches ayuntamiento as an Indian agent (Sims had married *regidor* George Pollitt's daughter), suddenly claimed the Cherokees wanted war. Supposedly, Cherokees had killed a Texan and anticipated joining some "1700 Indians" who were then a hundred miles west of town. The Indians consisted of "Caddoes, Kechies [Kichais], Ionies, Tawakonies, Wacos, and Comanches." Agent Menard, Texas president Burnet's man, solemnly confirmed the information. Mason hurriedly rode to Fort Jesup, arriving on April 12. He delivered the Nacogdoches committee's petitions and prayers personally to General Gaines: "You know our condition. Comment is useless. Many Women and Children must fall victims to the merciless enemy."[17]

Gaines, who had reached the fort that evening, quickly spoke with a variety of informants, including one Miguel Cortinas, a Tejano ne'er-do-well who earlier had been accused of plotting with the Cherokees. But Cortinas had been living in Louisiana, and later evidence would suggest that he had little, if any, influence with the immigrant tribes. Cortinas nevertheless informed the general that his brother, Eusebío, had a commission from General Cós to raise the Cherokee Indians against the Texans. Chief Bowles, Cortinas claimed, had been made a lieutenant colonel in the Mexican army.[18] Gaines immediately feared that this unholy alliance would bring in the removed Indians of Indian Territory. "Many of the Indians from our side of the Texas line will unite with the victors in the bloody conflict now raging there," he quickly scribbled in a note to General Arbuckle on April 12, while pleading for more troops.[19]

If Gaines had any doubts about Cortinas's claim, Mason, from the Nacogdoches Committee of Public Safety, filled in the details. The hostile Indians, he told Gaines on April 13, were only sixty miles north of Nacogdoches, and the town had been evacuated, the people "leaving everything behind." The two hundred or so armed men in Nacogdoches would gladly sacrifice themselves (suggesting another "Alamo") as a rear guard to protect refugees as they fled to the sanctuary of Louisiana. The Sabine River was swollen, however, and Mason begged Gaines for men to move the families to safety. "The road from Nacogdoches to the Sabine," Mason wrote, "is one unbroken line of women & children on foot with nothing but their clothing."[20]

Meanwhile, Mason's rhetoric—of fleeing refugees—had become reality in the regions south of the Colorado River. General Houston had heard the news of the Alamo's fall on March 11, but the scope of the disaster set in only after he had met Susanna Dickenson and the slave Joe. Santa Anna's psychological warfare in releasing the survivors to carry the news north had an impact, although what kind of impact is open to debate. While Mexican sources claim that the civilians were treated well, Houston had another story.[21] "One American female," Houston wrote of the group on the 13th, "the wife of Lieutenant Dickerson [*sic*], *dishonoured!*"[22] Dishonor or no, Houston continued to retreat.

Although his forces were girded for a fight, Houston ordered his four hundred men northward in retreat, eventually crossing the Brazos River after receiving word of the destruction of Fannin's troops. Across the land, fires burned throughout the nights as houses and barns and haystacks were consumed. Houston's men even set the ferries ablaze to slow the Mexican advance. The Texas general finally halted in mid-April, encamping some thirty miles north of San Felipe de Austin along the north bank of the Brazos. His men became so incensed by his inactivity that some units became defiant and mutinous, determined to fight the Mexican forces south of them. A crisis loomed as Santa Anna reached the lower Brazos on April 12. There, the Mexican general learned that Burnet's government remained at Harrisburg.

As Mexican victory seemed imminent, Burnet, Carson, and Mason worked feverishly to convince General Gaines to cross the Sabine River and save Texas. U.S. troops seemed the only salvation, as Houston apparently would not fight—despite several barbed letters from Burnet goading him to action. Carson rode into Fort Jesup on the evening of April 13 to join the lobbying party led by Mason. Early the next morning, at 2:00 A.M., a fast rider came in to inform Gaines that fifteen hundred to two thousand Indians in conjunction with a force of a thousand Mexican cavalry were just sixty miles from Nacogdoches. Carson soberly told Gaines that surely some three hundred Anglo families had already been slaughtered. Gaines immediately ordered thirteen infantry companies with two pieces of artillery to invade Texas even though clashing with Mexican troops would mean war for the United States.[23]

Secretary Carson seemed giddy over the apparent success of implicating the Indians. To Burnet he wrote that the movement of the U.S. troops "shows the wisdom of our decision upon the proposition of [Henry] Smith and others [Houston] to bring Indians to our aid." Obviously such Indian allies would have muddled the situation. Gaines had informed Carson that "should he be satisfied of the fact that the Mexicans have incited *any Indians,* who are under the control of the United States," Gaines would consider that situation a violation of the treaty of 1831. Thus, as Carson put it, the Texans had only to "satisfy Genl. Gaines of the fact" that Cherokees, Caddos, Comanches, and others were in league with Mexico, a proof Carson felt confident of being able to provide.[24]

With continued flooding, Gaines's troops took several hours to cross the Sabine. But as the morning sun rose and Gaines watched the troop movements from the west bank, he suddenly developed a modest case of cold feet. While many "Texian women and children" were fleeing in "great panic" into Louisiana, he later wrote, he noticed the total lack of wounded people. The panic proceeded "under circumstances which seemed to afford no conclusive evidence of a *spirit of general hostility* towards the inhabitants." With suspicions mounting and cognizant of the fact that Cass had granted him the discretion of crossing the border only if "armed bands" could be detected and clearly identified, Gaines halted the advance. He then ordered a mounted patrol to scout into East Texas. Gaines delayed reporting his findings to Cass for five days, waiting anxiously for the evidence necessary to start his war.[25]

As the general waited, dispatches from the north weakened the Texas plot. Holland Coffee continued to meet and smoke with large numbers of Comanches and Wichitas. At times, U.S. military officers joined him. The concern of these Indian leaders had much more to do with the invasion of their lands by Delawares, Shawnees, and Cherokees (attached to Coffee) than anything going on in Texas. The U.S. Army distributed presents, but the rift between the immigrant Indians and the Plains tribes continued to fester; hunting was becoming a difficult business for the Plains tribes, who had to compete with the many immigrant groups who had come into their land.[26]

Other traders joined the diplomatic corps negotiating with the Plains Indians. Pierre L. Chouteau, of the famous St. Louis trading family, agreed to lead one of these parties. He entered western Indian Territory in early spring 1836 and traveled up Cache Creek into the Wichita Mountains, then west, where he found camps of Wichitas, Kiowas, Comanches, and Plains Apaches. All these people accepted his gifts from the "American Father" and agreed to meet General Arbuckle at Fort Gibson. In his final report, Chouteau confirmed much of what U.S. officials already knew; the Indians living in the Red River corridor remained at peace.[27] Ironically, as Burnet and Carson tried desperately to create an Indian war, none of the Indians most capable of doing it would cooperate.

Not surprisingly, the evidence that Gaines so desperately sought rapidly unraveled. Chief Big Mush sent a hurried note to the Nacogdoches Committee of Vigilance and Public Safety on April 13 noting the surprise of his people at the departure of so many of his Anglo-Texan neighbors. "Some mischief making person" was clearly at fault, he wrote. Big Mush had learned that this person—he likely meant Sims—had represented the Cherokees as being "assembled in hostile array," which was a complete fabrication. No Texan had been killed or even threatened, and hordes of western Indians were not massing west of Nacogdoches, at least to Big Mush's knowledge.[28]

While the Committee of Vigilance and Public Safety at Nacogdoches knew as early as April 13 that the rumors of Indian attack were largely untrue—a fact that went unreported to General Gaines—the voluntary Tejano compañia volante headquartered at Nacogdoches still remained a potential threat. These Tejanos, born and bred along the Louisiana–Texas border and connected as much with French-speaking people as with Spanish speakers, seemed ambivalent toward Santa Anna's cause and supported local political control, but suspicions mounted on both sides as Tejanos and Anglo-Texans eyed each other.

Fortunately, the Tejanos and their Anglo neighbors had known each other for a decade or so, and on April 14, Tejano commander Vicente Córdova met Robert Irion, chair of the Nacogdoches committee, and they worked out their differences. Three days later, the Tejanos had convinced Irion of their total lack of interest in supporting Santa Anna, and Córdova and the nearly two hundred Tejanos in his force pledged to protect the property of all citizens in and about Nacogdoches. The agreement allowed Irion to send two hundred well-equipped soldiers to Houston's camp.[29]

Córdova's actions seemed logical at the time. Many Nacogdoches Tejanos, dissatisfied with the chaos in Mexico City and the rise of centralism, openly embraced Texas independence. The land was open and vast, and contact between Nacogdoches and Mexico City had been infrequent at best. Córdova and his fellow Tejanos had always had more contact with Louisiana than even southern Texas. They were an ethnic group unto themselves, quite separate in many ways from Mexico, and were willing to protect everyone's property in exchange for recognition of their rights under the new Anglo-Texan regime. Like many members of the San Antonio Tejano community, they leaned toward the liberal capitalistic views of most Americans rather than the conservative centralist ideology that had come to characterize Mexico.

By April 20, the upshot of all this maneuvering seemed obvious even to the sympathetic Gaines: Burnet and Carson had conspired to convince him to invade Texas. James Gaines later revealed in a letter that the scheme had been hatched by the ad-interim government. The ferryman even identified two key agents, Martin Palmer and Samuel Benton, who had been ordered to begin the rumors of Indian war. Gaines metaphorically blamed these men for "blowing the very trees up by the roots . . . [bringing] every settlement . . . to the point of breaking up." He also blamed Bowles and Bean—whom he identified as being "of the Santa Anna corps"—as men who confirmed and recirculated the rumors of Indian war.[30] In retrospect, James Gaines realized that rumors had done more harm than good in causing Anglo-Texan civilians to flee.

The folly of the Burnet-Carson scheme became even more apparent after the patrol sent by General Gaines returned from Nacogdoches. Lieutenant J. Bonnell, who led the patrol, had expected to find hard fighting in and about the Texas town, but instead he had found the Indians entirely peaceful. When Bonnell had asked the Caddos whether the Tejano Cortinas had tried to recruit them, the chiefs had told Bonnell that they did not know a Cortinas. Bonnell ultimately learned that one Manuel Flores had received a letter from the Mexican consulate in New Orleans but that those authorities had exhorted him to keep the Indians in the region quiet and not provoke them to war.[31]

After Bonnell's arrival on the morning of April 20, General Gaines penned a long report to Cass. Despite the lack of an Indian uprising, the general still depicted the mysterious Cortinas as an enemy agent sent by Mexico to raise the Indians—an obvious lie. Amazingly, he called upon the U.S. government to send more troops. Cass asked Congress for $1 million to pay for the deployment of additional forces, but he also advised Gaines soon thereafter that President Jackson desired peace with Mexico, since abolitionists were carefully watching the administration and a presidential election was a mere seven months away. Gaines had authorization to advance only as far as Nacogdoches, and only if the "contending parties" invaded that space.[32]

As Gaines lingered at the Sabine River, Santa Anna made a momentous decision. Still on the Brazos but apparently unaware of Houston's location, the Mexican general marched eastward on the ad-interim government's base. On April 15, with about a thousand men, the Mexican general captured Harrisburg. He barely missed Burnet, who had embarked by ship for Galveston. Santa Anna continued down Buffalo Bayou in hopes of seizing the vessel where the bayou narrowed. Meanwhile, the reinforced troops of General Houston broke camp and reached the destroyed Harrisburg on April 18. Two days later, the advance scouts of Houston's army, now numbering nine hundred men, clashed with Santa Anna's rear guard.

The engagement surprised the Mexican general, who had concluded that armed resistance in Texas had collapsed. Santa Anna sent an urgent rider south to his able relative General Cós (whom the Texans had recently paroled), ordering Cós to bring up the five hundred reinforcements that had been held in reserve. Santa Anna then took up a defensive position along the bank of the lake formed by the bayou and the San Jacinto River. After marching all night, Cós's exhausted men arrived about noon the next day, April 21. Since swampland prevented Houston from enveloping the Mexicans, Santa Anna's confidence in his strong position seemed warranted.

Houston likewise set up camp and called a council of war. Most of his officers hoped to provoke the Mexicans into a frontal assault. Santa Anna outnumbered them nearly two to one, and most of Houston's military advisers were uncertain as to how the Texan army would perform. Many of the recruits were raw, fresh from the United States. A small contingent of Indians, including the indomitable Creek Benjamin Hawkins, had joined the group, and Seguín was there at the head of some twenty-five Tejanos. Although Houston initially ordered these men to guard the baggage train in the rear, after they protested, the general reassigned them to the front lines. They were as anxious to fight Santa Anna and Cós as were the Anglo-Texans.[33]

As his officers argued, a nearly sober Houston, who had often been criticized for indecisiveness in the past, ordered a silent assault at 3:30 that afternoon, hoping to catch the exhausted Mexicans in their traditional siesta. The strategy worked marvelously. The Texans hit Santa Anna's troops before most could reach their stacks of muskets, which had been tied together to prevent accidental discharges. Most Mexican officers failed to give a command, soldiers ran hither and yon, and mass chaos ensued.

The actual battle, called San Jacinto after the nearby river, lasted eighteen minutes, but the slaughter of Mexican troops went on for two hours. When a few of Houston's officers tried to stop the killing, their own men threatened them. Even the Tejano participants joined in the carnage as payback for the insults at San Antonio.[34] Roughly 630 Mexicans died in the conflict; many were shot in the back while fleeing. Lying wounded on the ground were another 200, most of whom later died. The Texans lost 9 men, with several dozen wounded—including Houston, who took a ball in the leg. Among the roughly 700 Mexican prisoners was Santa Anna, who tried to escape dressed as a common soldier. Brought before Houston, Santa Anna readily agreed to grant Texas its independence.

The indisputable victory at San Jacinto proved the undoing of the remainder of the Mexican forces in Texas, commanded by General Vicente Filisola. By late May, these garrison troops had retreated to the Rio Grande. While most Texas soldiers wanted to execute General Santa Anna, Houston and Burnet prevented this and instead negotiated two treaties with him. In the first, Santa Anna agreed to Texas independence, and in the second—a secret compact—Santa Anna promised to work for a permanent peace if he was returned safely to Mexico. Neither agreement did much good, for the Mexican Congress rejected the actions of the disgraced general. Texas would continue to be at war with Mexico for nine more years.

In the aftermath of the battle, Burnet ordered Secretary Rusk to take command of the army because Houston's wound needed time to heal. Burnet then called for elections on September 5; Texans would decide who would lead them and whether they would ask for admission to the United States. Over the next few months, settlers went back to their destroyed homes and began to build anew. Other Anglo-Americans, searching for cheap land, flocked into the new republic.

Much remained undone, however. The U.S. government was then implementing the final stages of its Indian removal policy, pushing most of the remaining Indians off their lands in Tennessee, Georgia, Alabama, Mississippi, Michigan, and Wisconsin. Everyone expected trouble. The rumors of Indian conflict that had been clumsily begun during the revolution continued all across the Texas frontier. Once the rumors regarding Mexican agents and Indians had been created, the argument seemed so compelling that even rational men could hardly question the notion. The final stages of Indian removal, a new wave of Anglo immigration into Texas, and the continued plotting of Mexico to regain Texas gave the officials of the emerging Texas Republic much to worry about for years to come.

Much of the success or failure of Indian policy in Texas rested with the government of the republic. By late May, the ad interim government had set up a joint committee to discuss Indian affairs. After looking at all available evidence, the committee concluded that a group of "hostile tribes," consisting of the "Caddo, Wacos, Tiwachanes [Tawakonis], Keechies [Kichais], Ionies and Pawnees [Wichitas]" remained poised on the northwestern frontier, threatening the very existence of the new republic.[35]

Many Caddo young men had in fact joined their western relatives living near the various Wichita towns. Justifiably angry over the loss of their land and seeking revenge for the attacks on their towns by rangers the year before, a party of Caddos joined other Wichitas and Comanches in overrunning settlements along the Navasota River on May 9. The most destructive assault occurred at Parker's ranger fort near the river's headwaters. Because the place was known to have harbored the rangers who had raided Wichita and Caddo towns the summer before, the Indians tore it apart, killing five men and taking five women and children captive.[36]

Other attacks occurred during the same week on Little River and just west of Nacogdoches, where Caddos and Wichitas killed two or three more Texans.[37] Most Texas officials feared that the violence would encourage the newly arriving immigrant Indians to cross into Texas and join the marauding Wichitas and Caddos, the entire group fighting for Mexico.[38] The attack prompted an urgent letter from Houston, asking that General Gaines send U.S. troops directly into Nacogdoches to defend the settlements. Houston had heard that nine Texans had been killed (these numbers included those at Parker's Fort), and he fully expected more raiding. Gaines, he wrote, should occupy the town and "save Texas."[39]

General Gaines did order a dragoon company stationed at Fort Gibson to march overland to Fort Towson, near the Red River. He hoped that the deployment would open a road southward through north Texas, following the upper Sabine River to Louisiana.[40] With troops capable of entering East Texas from either Fort Towson or Fort Jesup—logical points at which to keep reserves—Gaines in early July ordered the dragoons to enter Nacogdoches and build a blockhouse for protection. While of dubious legality—Texans, of course, did not mind—Gaines's actions clearly gave the U.S. government a foothold in Texas. Lieutenant Bonnell, who commanded the expedition, soon reported a host of rumors—most of which he did not believe. But by this time, the destruction of Parker's Fort had been confirmed, and Gaines anticipated an Indian war.

After collecting all this information, Gaines then asked the U.S. War Department for more troops. His pleas reached a crescendo on August 10: "I have received information, the truth of which I cannot doubt," he wrote, that Texas Indians had joined with those "of our side of the unmarked but supposed boundary." These Indians were "engaged by the authority of Mexico to aid in the war of extermination against Texas." The Indians would eventually overrun the small garrison at Nacogdoches; Gaines continued by asserting that all of western Louisiana (prime cotton-producing land) was in jeopardy. Finally, Gaines argued that the possibility of plunder would tempt even immigrant Indians, who "have pretensions to civilization" but "assume the garb and character of savagery."[41] Unfortunately for him, the militias of both Arkansas and Louisiana still showed little interest in "saving" Texas.[42] Gaines wanted federal troops.

The belief that Texas needed saving grew as rumor spread across the land. Indian agent Menard, passing himself off as a "Mexican agent," reported that Chief Bowles had been encouraging a union with Mexico against Texas.[43] By July, General Rusk accepted such rumor as fact, and as commander of the Texas army, he issued a proclamation addressed to the "People of Texas." He unabashedly warned that "agents with large sums of money" had recently granted commissions to Indian leaders in the Mexican armed forces "in order to induce them to commence an indiscriminate massacre of your wives and children."[44] The news worsened when an American living in Matamoros reported that "6 or 7 chiefs" of the Cherokee and other tribes had arrived to confer with General José Urrea, the commander who had slaughtered Fannin's men at Goliad.[45] No names were provided, but one was later assumed to be Bowles.

With rumors of Mexican-Indian invasion spiraling out of control, Anglo-Texans at Nacogdoches prepared to defend themselves. They began slowly by disarming individual Tejanos, although initially they left the old compañia volante unchallenged.[46] While most of the Tejanos living near Nacogdoches remained loyal, suspicions and rumors continued to condemn them. As many Tejanos saw land claims (some likely undocumented) fall into the hands of Anglos, their sympathy if not outright loyalty shifted away from the Texan cause. Eusebío Cortinas, for example, had become disillusioned—especially after being named as one of the six or seven men seen in Matamoros. A few Tejanos near Nacogdoches moved back to Louisiana. A handful of others moved northward to the vicinity of Bowles's village, while still others joined the Wichitas and Caddos in the west, decisions that Texans thought were tantamount to siding with Mexico.[47]

According to Menard, on August 9 Bowles supposedly proclaimed his loyalty to Mexico and indicated that a large force of Indians was forming on the upper Trinity River to assault Texas. This information reached General Gaines a mere day after its collection. In his usual bombastic fashion, the general exaggerated the situation in his report; some "4,000 Indians, Comanches, Pawnees, & others, with some Caddoes, & Cherokees" were waiting for the Mexican army and would soon sweep down and destroy everything in their path, including Nacogdoches.[48]

Four thousand Indians indeed! To what degree Gaines believed his exaggerated rhetoric is anyone's guess. He certainly had poor intelligence and gave too much credence to Menard and Miguel Cortinas. While the Caddos and Wichitas were upset, and even a few Cherokees seemed to defy the peace called for by Chief Big Mush, such an Indian alliance simply did not exist. As for the number reported, four thousand warriors could have been obtained only by including the Plains tribes, the very Indians who saw the immigrant Indians as a threat rather than as allies.

Just how many Indians lived in East Texas was disputed. Menard quietly put together a census in late July that he likely meant only for Burnet's eyes. This census demonstrates the folly of Gaines's reports. Menard estimated that 1,230 warriors lived in East Texas, including ten immigrant Indian bands and two Caddo towns. The Kickapoos, at 180 men, had the largest force, the Cherokees being second with 140. The total population was roughly 7,500 people, mostly immigrant Indians.[49]

Despite the tribal factionalism that existed within these groups, the rumors of a monolithic Indian conspiracy remained so vivid in the minds of most Anglo-Texans that they refused to believe evidence to the contrary. Texas leaders were eager to fan the flames of rumor. What is more, learning that the debate under way in the U.S. Congress over the annexation of Texas was running against them, many Texans were convinced that if the U.S. Army occupied Texas, annexation might become a fait accompli. Thus Gaines, Rusk, and even the supposedly pro-Cherokee Houston all fed the rumor mill, distorting truth, hoping to force the hand of the United States.

Houston, however, was willing to weigh other options, for he recognized the potential for peace with Indians. An Indian war might bring annexation, but it also would cause serious disruptions along the frontier and perhaps even in the small fledgling Texan cotton communities well to the east. This central dilemma dominated Texas politics for decades to come and would tug, one way or the other, on almost every Texas politician; peace produced through compromise and negotiation would lead to concessions to Indians and perhaps regulation of Anglo expansion, while war (and its attending disruptions) offered political opportunities and untold advantages for land speculators and frontier rowdies.

Sam Houston hoped to solve the dilemma. Fully recovered from his wounds by early August, he announced his candidacy for president of the new republic. While Stephen Austin and others also ran, everyone knew that Houston, the hero of the battle of San Jacinto, would win in a landslide. Given this knowledge, Houston set out to design a workable Indian policy even before the elections, scheduled for September 5. One of his first decisions was to hire William Goyens as Indian agent to the Cherokee, replacing the undependable Menard.

Goyens, a mulatto blacksmith and Indian trader, had come to Nacogdoches in 1820 from North Carolina. He had lived with the Cherokees for some time; Goyens had learned their language even better than Houston, and he had served as Houston's interpreter during the 1836 treaty negotiations.[50] Houston's appreciation of Goyens, a hardworking and decent man, says much about the general's views on race. Houston, somewhat like Jefferson, held paradoxical views on slavery. Houston had grown up in a society that was dependent upon the institution, and he owned slaves (mostly household servants), but he found slavery to be degrading and morally questionable. It was this ambiguity in Houston's character that allowed him to employ Goyens, who would serve the cause of peace.

A workable peace with the northern Indian tribes became more necessary than ever after Houston learned that the U.S. Congress would not even consider Texas annexation after Daniel Webster and John Quincy Adams came out against it. Even Houston's old mentor, President Andrew Jackson, backed away. Jackson understood that supporting annexation would damage the chances of his hand-picked candidate for president that fall, the Democrat Martin Van Buren. Houston realized that with the election only months away and knowing that everything might change in its aftermath, he needed to be flexible.

Houston's ambiguous understanding of slavery and race brings into question his longstanding reputation as a friend of the Indian. He had adopted what Anglos perceived to be the Indians' loose moral standards, and he had spent many hours smoking, listening to Cherokee elders, and showing sympathy for the plight of the various immigrant tribes. But above all, Houston was a politician—and a pragmatic one at that. If he could draw the U.S. Army into Texas through Indian war and thus force Congress to sanction annexation, he would do it. If not, he would pursue peace with the Indians.

This was a dangerous game, well suited to the gambler that Houston was. And it smelled of the same tactics that his old nemesis, Burnet, had employed during the revolution.

The scheme began when Houston received a discouraging letter from Bowles, dated August 16, 1836. Bowles had heard that all of his people would be killed, "by both red and white" men. Houston rushed to quiet Bowles, offering the olive branch and pleading that Bowles and his Cherokees remain at peace.[51] Simultaneously, Houston wrote to Lieutenant Colonel William Whistler, the U.S. officer who had taken command of the stockade at Nacogdoches. He reported to Whistler that a Texan recently had been killed, supposedly by Cherokees. The United States, Houston argued, was bound by "convention" to defend Texas against the Cherokees. He wanted Whistler to commence "early action" immediately.[52]

Going a step further, Houston issued his own proclamation to the people of Texas on August 29. "Some Cherokees with the notorious *Cortinas* have just returned to the Cherokee village from Matamoros," he warned, after having supposedly enlisted the aid of the "Prairie" Indians in a war on Texas. (Interestingly, Houston failed to mention the letter from his friend Bowles.) Houston called for rangers to organize and defend northern Texas.[53] On the same day, he apprised General Gaines that Indians had converged on the upper Trinity River and that Mexican agents had incited them. "I rely more upon your facilities to give us Independence than upon any other assurance," he coyly mused, stroking Gaines's ego.[54] Two days later, Houston gave his hastily organized rangers their marching orders: "Do not be first to make a quarrel with the Indians. Let the [U.S.] Dragoons make a report before you go into the limits of the [Cherokee] nation."[55]

Unbeknownst to Houston, Whistler at Nacogdoches with his dragoon command had already ordered such a report, sending Major Ben Riley on a northern scout. Like Bonnell, Riley found no hostile Indians, Cherokees or otherwise, noting only that a deluge of liquor pouring into the region had made the Caddos "incapable of the smallest exertion."[56] This new information put an end to Houston's most immediate scheme. While Houston continued to emit dire warnings of Indian war into mid-September, Colonel Whistler increasingly ignored him. Indeed, the colonel asked General Arbuckle—Gaines had been ordered east—if he might evacuate Nacogdoches. "No necessity exists for the 7th Infantry to remain here," the colonel wrote; indeed, in Whistler's opinion, "no necessity has ever existed for our occupying Texas." Arbuckle, who by this time was on to Houston's maneuvering, concurred.[57] The Seventh Infantry was quietly withdrawn from Nacogdoches before Christmas.[58]

As the campaign to entice the United States into Texas collapsed, Houston inaugurated an amazing change in Texas Indian policy—one devoid of war rhetoric. That fall, he opened negotiations with both the Cherokees and the Shawnees, signing an agreement in which Houston's Indian allies would provide twenty-five rangers to patrol the regions northwest of their villages, keeping the Caddos and Wichitas at bay. The republic agreed to pay them $10 per month and allowed them to keep any booty that might come from assaults on "wild" Indians. Each "Indian" ranger was to place a white feather on his head to identify himself as friendly.[59] Flushed with this success, Houston even attempted to open negotiations with the Wichitas and Comanches: the "wild" tribes, as he called them.[60]

With negotiations under way and Houston's election to the presidency of the republic accomplished, he then engaged the new Texas legislature in a debate over Indian policy. On October 20, 1836, Representative Isaac Burton, taking up the challenge, introduced a resolution calling for the creation of a permanent committee to examine Houston's actions and to make further recommendations. In particular, Burton wondered what to do with the "Indians from the United States, now in Texas." The key question, according to Burton, rested on whether they had conspired with Mexico or not.[61]

Two days later, Houston went before the same body and presented his inaugural address, calling for "peace and amity." He asked that the republic's new congress let him create trade houses of the sort that he had already begun northwest of Nacogdoches, which would lead to commerce and friendship. Texans, he argued, should abstain from aggression and live peacefully with their Indian neighbors.[62] This looked much like the policy of the United States: negotiation, treaties, and, if necessary, peaceful removal.

Houston's policies came before the full congress in the form of a resolution on November 8. Prepared by the chairman of the committee, Edward Burleson, this measure specifically gave the republic's president the authority to erect trade houses wherever necessary, to employ troops (even from Indian tribes) in such numbers as were needed, to make treaties, and to employ Indian agents.[63] Over the next four days, the debate over the resolution revealed a clear division within the newly created Texas Congress.

Some representatives, such as Houston's friend Branch T. Archer, argued that the president should be given a free hand. Archer represented a minority, however. Others, such as Burleson (who adamantly hated the Indians and was no friend to Houston), saw Houston's plan as a delaying tactic that would pacify the Cherokees and Shawnees to buy Texas the time it needed to establish itself. Finally, a third group openly criticized negotiations and the idea of employing Indian rangers: "Who can confide in them?" Burton argued. "What was their conduct at Matamoros? They joined the Mexicans. Who would think of trusting the frontier to those treacherous butchers?" While the resolution regarding trade houses passed, primarily due to Houston's overwhelming popularity, opposition to negotiation mounted.[64]

The factionalism became even more apparent when Houston asked the Texas Senate to confirm the treaty that he had negotiated with the Cherokee during the days of turmoil before the loss of the Alamo. "You will find upon examining this treaty that it is just and equitable, and perhaps the best which could be made at the present time," the president declared. Houston acknowledged that some Cherokees had been plotting with Mexico and that some would probably join a Mexican force were one to appear in Texas, but he asserted that the majority would remain peaceful and should be given lands. The treaty even dealt with the objections of Anglo-Texans near Nacogdoches, since it granted only "usufructuary rights," and the Texas Congress could settle all land claims within the Cherokee district even after ratification.[65]

The logic of these arguments failed. Indian haters and land speculators, led especially by David Burnet, had no intention of giving Indians land. Further problems for the treaty appeared when a military agitator named Felix Huston revealed that Indians, believed to be Cherokees, had negotiated with General Urrea in Matamoros in early December 1836. The consul for the United States seemed to confirm the visit, even though the identity of the Indian party remained mostly a mystery. Huston's news tipped the scales against the Cherokee treaty. The Texas Senate rejected it.[66]

While the senate's actions created a problem for Houston's policy of negotiation, the president still hoped to convince the majority of Texans to respect Indian claims to land in East Texas. And it still seemed likely that the United States would eventually annex Texas, taking the issue of Indian lands out of the hands of the fledgling Texas Republic. The Texans did not see how the United States could turn down one of the fairest portions of North America over such an innocuous issue as slavery. Obviously, annexation would bring the U.S. Army to Texas and would solve the "Indian problem" militarily. In the meantime, Houston would emulate the U.S. government in organizing Indian agencies, creating boundaries and trade houses, and gaining the trust of the tribes.

Houston had reason to be optimistic. Texas had a plethora of land. If the Cherokee treaty was inoperable, other land arrangements could be made. Indians in the southern United States had been moved mostly to other lands without violence, and he did not see why Texas should be any different. Nevertheless, what the hero of San Jacinto failed to realize was that a cancer was slowly engulfing Texas, making negotiation difficult if not impossible. Texans soon embraced a nearly endless pattern of conflict; the resulting struggle would lead to "ethnic cleansing." A culture of violence would stalk the land, deifying the makers and martyrs of this promised land and plunging Texas into decades of despair.

While cultural and ethnic differences were the underpinning for this cancer, the various rumors begun by the Burnet government during the revolution hastened along the disease. Adding to the difficulties was the land speculation spawned by the empresario system and continued on a grander scale after the revolution. As choices narrowed, ethnic polarization among and between Indians, Tejanos, and Anglos grew, and the proponents of negotiation were slowly hounded into silence by the beating of infantry drums.

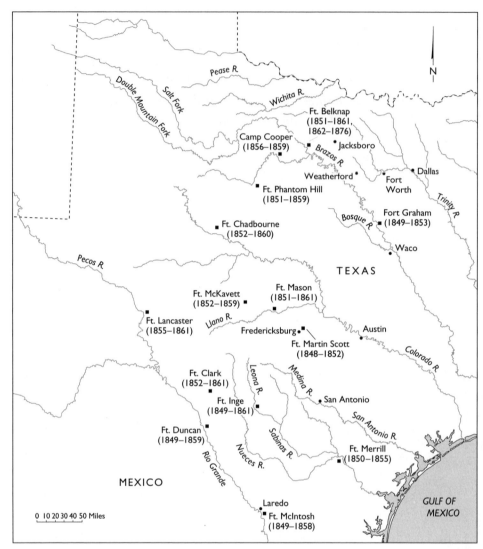

The Texas frontier, 1849–1861

9

INDIAN INTRANSIGENCE

Most of the rumors of Indian war, circulated during the weeks after the Alamo fell, were just that—rumors concocted to bring the U.S. Army into Texas. Worse, Burnet never really considered negotiating with Indians. He had larger fish to fry, or so he thought. The agents he employed had only one goal: hoodwink General Gaines and convince the general to save Texas. It came as a surprise, then, when the republic became entangled in a series of clashes with Indians in late spring of 1836.

The fighting erupted piecemeal, without a declaration. Texans hardly knew that their actions had increasingly infuriated the Plains tribes. Wichitas and a few Comanche allies had committed depredations near Bastrop and Gonzales in the years before. These raids usually amounted to horse and mule rustling. The fighting had been more vicious in the Navasota and Brazos river valleys, where rangers had burned Wichita and Caddo villages. But as the revolutionary campaigns against Mexico ground down, Plains Indians dramatically escalated their raids on Mexico and on Texans. Ranger paramilitary units operating on their own struck back, searching for unprotected Indian villages and occasionally finding them. When they found a target, they killed and burned with impunity. Before Texas knew it, an Indian war had started that went on into the early 1840s.

As the conflict widened, women and children increasingly became victims on both sides. This infuriated Texans, who concluded that white women when taken captive were raped. Suffering the "fate worse than death" became a dreaded fear in every Texas home. But Plains Indian warriors reacted no differently. They came to see Texas Rangers as brutal murderers; rangers even shot down women and children, conduct unheard-of among Plains societies. Cultural variations—stark and compelling under normal, friendly contact—were exaggerated and expanded upon during a time of increased conflict.

The first Indian onslaught was wreaked upon a group of unsuspecting English-men whom the Indians assumed were Anglo-Texans. The isolated attack was hardly publicized in Texas because it occurred while Santa Anna marched on Harrisburg. The new English immigrants had opened irrigated farms on Los Moras Creek, a small tributary of the Rio Grande that enters the river just above Eagle Pass. John Charles Beale had recruited these settlers in 1835 after he received a land grant from the state of Coahuila-Texas. Beale portrayed Los Moras Creek as a lush valley with rich topsoil; the Rio Grande, he claimed, could even be navigated by steamboats, making it ideal for cotton development. But the land was sandy, and steamboats had never reached the creek. The small collection of settlers stayed a year and gave up in the following spring, 1836.

Two families, one headed by John Horn and the other by a Mr. Harris, joined with eleven single men for the trip out in April 1836. The group traveled peaceably east into the Nueces River valley, a stream that had flowing water only during spring. While much of the upcountry bordering it was barren, the banks were covered with mesquite, and livestock were let loose to gorge on the pods. Wildflowers were blooming. Mrs. Horn and Mrs. Harris, distracted by the beauty of the day, prepared some food as the men in the party wandered off to hunt in the brush. All were unaware that they were being watched.

Suddenly mounted Indians appeared, coming up the valley. Some rode mules, looking oddly unthreatening with their legs dangling down nearly to the ground. Some men in the Horn party thought they had to be Mexicans. Little did they know that other Indians were hidden among the mesquite trees, armed and waiting. As the Anglo men tried to discern the intent of the approaching group, a torrent of arrows and gunfire hit them, killing and wounding the thirteen men within a few minutes. A few Anglo men fought back, but most were so stunned they offered little resistance.

The attack on the Horn party presaged a series of assaults by Plains Indians that continued throughout the summer. Often striking from ambush, the Indians gave little quarter. They consistently killed the men and carried off women and children. The latter were almost always ransomed. Upon returning to the East, they set about trying to restore their lives by writing narratives of their suffering, which generally sold well. The captivity narratives (and the violence they depicted) became a common genre of literature. These books, along with oral accounts spread and exaggerated by word of mouth, did much to shape the emerging opinion of Texans regarding Indians.

The survivors often witnessed and later recorded horrid events that sent shivers up the spines of frontier settlers. A young Mrs. Horn, clutching her children, could only watch as the Indians mutilated the men, carving them up with knives, and scalped her husband and the others. Blood spattered everywhere and on everyone; sometimes the men were still living as the Indians leaped on them. Mrs. Horn offered a description of the scalping process in her memoir: the Indians "made an

incision round his head, stood upon his shoulders and tore it [the scalp] from him."
When the skin let go from the skull it popped.[1]

The attack on the Horn and Harris families occurred well beyond the boundaries
of what had been Austin's colony. It might have gone unnoticed were it not for the
fact that during the summer of 1836, several similar assaults occurred. The most
noteworthy—an oral rendition of which every Texan came to know—came in June
at Parker's Fort on the Navasota River, where Caddos, Wichitas, and Comanches
overran the small collections of settlers. The Indians killed five men and took five
women and children captive. This time every Texan heard the horrid news. To them,
Parker's Fort was an important outpost and the Parker family, which suffered from
the attack, was exceedingly well known.

The attack on Parker's Fort had revenge writ large. The fort had become a center
for Texas Ranger activity in 1835, even serving as a base for rangers who were
organized in its vicinity. The fort's owner, Silas Parker, had been appointed by the
General Council to organize the defense of northern Texas. But the previous year,
the rangers had burned to the ground at least two Indian villages north of the fort,
killing a number of Wichitas. The Indians likely had planned the assault for some
time. They too used deception to gain access.

Rachel Plummer, pregnant at the time, left an account of the ordeal that matches
in astonishing detail the narrative of Mrs. Horn. The large Indian party came,
according to Plummer, under a "white flag." Silas Parker went out to talk with them
and was quickly dispatched. In the melee that followed, four other Texans met their
death, killed at close range with lances and hatchets. Others, at work in the fields,
escaped by hiding in the woods. The war party was more concerned with pillaging than
killing. Once inside the fort, the attackers ransacked it and took what was usable.

Inside the fort the Indians encountered Granny Parker, willowy and spry though
still in her seventies. After wounding her with a lance, the Indians stripped her of
clothing, "with the exception of her undergarments," and left. The scalps of old men
or women were not honorable, and the spunky old lady, her hair intact, recovered
from her wounds. While subsequent Texas historians reported that poor granny was
raped, no evidence suggests that such an attack occurred.[2] Her clothing was taken
simply because of its value, as Indian women cherished woven dresses more than
deerhide skirts.[3]

Rachel Plummer, Elizabeth Kellogg, and the children Cynthia Ann Parker,
John Parker, and James Pratt were taken into captivity. They were tied on horses and
forced to ride for hours to escape the vicinity of the fort. They all were badly treated,
being whipped and deprived of food and water, but again, no evidence suggests
rape even after the party reached Indian villages. Soon their treatment improved,
and the women were ransomed. While everyone in Texas knew of the attack at the
fort, the deed became even more infamous when *A Narrative of the Capture and Subsequent Sufferings of Mrs. Rachel Plummer, during a Captivity of Twenty-one Months* was

published in 1844. A ghostwriter obviously helped make the language more ghastly, as James Parker, the author of record, was hardly literate.[4]

As violence with Indians escalated, attitudes within the Texas settlements hardened. Especially on the upper Brazos and Navasota rivers, rangers—some of them just returning from the battle of San Jacinto—quickly went into action. These hardy parties of men pushed the Texas frontier northward and westward, launching campaigns into the San Gabriel River valley, then northward, up the Brazos River, and finally, into the Trinity River valley.

Lieutenant William Hill, who had been part of Moore's and Burleson's companies, which had started the war with the Wichitas in 1835, did much to wrest the San Gabriel from Indians. Seeking revenge for the attack on Parker's Fort, Hill's ranger company surprised a Comanche camp on the San Gabriel River during the summer of 1836 and killed many Indians. George Erath's ranger company followed this assault by launching a winter campaign, hitting another Comanche village in early January 1837. Erath knew that the Indian towns were vulnerable during the winter, a time when campaigning was difficult for all concerned. His men were able to get within twenty feet of a Comanche town when dawn struck, and they opened fire at point-blank range. The rangers killed dozens of Indians, ten just in the first volley.[5]

The Texas onslaught continued into the spring, as the companies who left to campaign in the west became larger and more determined. Hill, Erath, Moore, and Coleman (all successful leaders) had consistently returned from their campaigns with hundreds of horses and hides, which were turned into considerable cash. With this in mind, Lieutenant John Vanthuysen's ranger company of over fifty men headed west into the San Gabriel valley. This party too sought an Indian village and plunder.

This time, however, the rangers ran into a well-armed party of 150 Wichitas, Caddos, and Comanches. About 50 Delawares, not interested in fighting for either side, watched from the sidelines as the two armed groups engaged each other. Amid gestures from both sides that included mooning, howling, brief speeches, and challenges to individual combat, the two forces finally collided, violently. The spectacle included a daring charge by the Indians in which some sixty men were left dead on the field. Vanthuysen's force lost ten men and had many wounded, but they held their ground.[6]

In most major conflicts, such as the one fought by Vanthuysen's men, the superior weaponry of the Texans made a difference. Kentucky long rifles were simply more effective than trade muskets and bows and arrows. In addition, Texans carried a pistol or sometimes two in their belts. Weaponry likely proved the difference when twenty-three surveyors under Walter P. Lane were assailed by perhaps three hundred Wichitas and Kickapoos as they worked well north of the settlements—some twenty miles northeast of the old Waco town—in 1838. Lane's gang fought off the Indians for a time, killing thirty or forty, but they lost sixteen of their own men in the desperate clash.[7]

To protect themselves in their settlements, the Texans also built substantial block-houses that could be defended by a few well-armed men. Fort Milam, located roughly thirty miles south of the abandoned Waco village, near present-day Marlin, was the first fort constructed near the central Brazos River. It represented a substantial leap northward. The fort had attracted both rangers and settlers by the summer of 1836. From within its protected walls many ranger campaigns were launched, one of which did battle with the largest congregation of Indians that Texans had faced to that date. Both sides knew that the Texans had come to force the Plains tribes from their bison-hunting lands west of the Brazos River.

The rangers at Fort Milam were organized by Captain John Bird, an aggressive leader who had no fear of Indians. Bird launched several expeditions into the west, literally chasing Indians from their lands and even, at times, overrunning bison-hunting camps to seize the meat. But on one occasion in the late spring of 1839, his forty-five-man patrol charged pell-mell into a small Indian force, dispatching several, only to discover hundreds of Indians on the hills before them. Retreating rapidly to a ravine, the rangers prepared for a desperate struggle.

A Comanche chief, "mounted on a beautiful horse and wearing on his head a buffalo skin cap," quickly organized his minions. The huge force of warriors soon rode down on Bird and his men, screaming and howling and firing muskets and arrows. After the Texans managed to beat them off twice, the chief called for an all-out charge. "They advanced with impetuosity to the very brink of the ditch," as one ranger recalled. But "dozens of them fell within twenty or thirty feet of our rifles—almost every shot killed or wounded an Indian." In a final, desperate act, the chief himself rode down on the party, leading two dozen men. A bullet blew him from his saddle; the attacking Comanches then gave up. Bird and several other Texans lay dead in the ravine, for the captain had taken an arrow in the chest, an arrow shot from the unbelievable distance of two hundred yards.[8]

With every move westward and northward, Texas Rangers, settlers, and surveyors became bolder. The surveyors often worked under the protection of groups of rangers, often thirty men in a party. Virtually no restraints were placed on the surveyors, since during the period of the early republic, the legislature allowed for the creation of land offices at the county level, gave land scrip to men who fought in the revolution, and sold land at ridiculously low prices. The legislature also adopted the policy of granting large sections of land to colonizers, much like Mexico had done. The easy access to land produced a rapidly advancing westward movement that permitted Texans to invade Indian lands at an unprecedented rate.

While the advance of surveyors and settlers up the Brazos, Navasota, and San Gabriel rivers was well under way, other Texans looked with greedy eyes upon much of the land north and west of Bastrop, in the vicinity of what would become Austin and Georgetown. Speculators were quick to praise this new land, which had been the home of the Penateka Comanches for a century; the prairies and valleys were thought to have dark, rich soil, and the streams had cascading crystal-clear water. Now and then, bison appeared in numbers, and Anglo parties hunted them. This land in the Colorado River valley and along the southern tributaries of the San Gabriel River was often every bit a promised land.

John Webster, a relatively new arrival to Texas, knew the value of such land. He and some friends had purchased a large slice drained by the headwaters of the San Gabriel River valley, some fifty miles north of Bastrop. Webster, in his sixty-fifth year, had a young wife named Dolly, two young children, and an African American slave. He intended to build a blockhouse and open the land. He had convinced others to join him in making a settlement; these twelve companions were mostly young men.

But Webster, unlike Horn and Harris, knew the risks involved. Rangers had on several occasions clashed with Indians in the region. Webster also had lived near Bastrop for two years and had heard the stories of what had happened at Parker's Fort and likely to the Horns. The members of Webster's party, then, were all well mounted, well armed, and cautious. With two wagons of provisions, Webster's group left Bastrop in September 1839, two months after Bird's desperate stand against Comanches. They reached the headwaters of the San Gabriel River valley a week or two later but found signs of many Indians—indeed, hundreds. After considerable discussion, the party, though not terribly frightened, decided to return. On the morning of October 1, sixteen Comanche Indians appeared at their rear.[9]

Most of the armed men wheeled and charged—these were not timid English settlers like the Horns who wanted to talk first. The ox-drawn wagons were coaxed toward a small stream that offered brush as protection. Confident of having driven off the Indians, the men returned triumphant. As they glanced back, however, covering their rear, the tall grass and brush along the riverbank came alive. A hundred Comanche warriors let fly a torrent of arrows; smooth-bore musket balls fired from at least fifty or sixty guns splintered the wagons and pierced the horses and men as they quickly dismounted. The sixteen mounted warriors had been only a decoy.

The thirteen Anglo men, some wounded, finally regrouped and desperately fought back. Their long rifles were effective, but here and there, fighting in the open, they eventually fell, wounded, dying, and dead. With the defenders' numbers depleted by half, the Comanche horsemen charged down on them, whooping and hollering, letting fly arrows and bullets and lances. Dolly Webster huddled under a wagon clutching her two young children when the Indians came back again to overwhelm the wounded and desperate men. The battle had lasted less than an hour.

Dolly later remembered the last scenes of battle, which revealed wounded men, a few with arms broken by bullets, swinging empty guns against mounted Indians with lances. While all thirteen of the men died, they killed at least eighteen Comanches. The victorious Indians then mutilated and scalped the dead men. Only the heads of a bald Mr. Stilwell and a white-haired John Webster survived unscathed. A chief of the party prevented the scalping of Webster, saying in Spanish, "*Blanco, blanco.*"

The Indians pillaged the wagons, taking watches, clothing, mirrors, and anything that they considered valuable. Then they turned their attentions on Mrs. Webster, whom they tried to disrobe. But a burly chief with considerable authority stopped the young men. As in the case of Granny Parker, the warriors wanted the clothing for their own women and were not contemplating sexual assault. Mrs. Webster and her two children were accordingly tied onto horses and led into captivity.

The Comanche attack on this party was well planned. The Webster party had been seen days before by Comanche scouts, who had an observation post on Pilot Knob, a 180-foot rise that separates the headwaters of the San Gabriel from the Colorado River. The Penateka and their scouts had tracked the party, waiting for the wagons to enter the ambush. Once the Texans were in the killing zone, they had little chance. Comanche war parties were professional and lethal. The leaders of the raid had no difficulty in attracting young men to join them, for the Comanches had come to hate the Anglo-Texans, seeing them as invaders and murderers of women and children. Comanches viewed themselves as human beings; they killed mostly men and took women and children as captives.

Comanches came to equate the surveyor's chain and the settler's wagon with the loss of hunting grounds. The thousands of Anglo-American settlers who swarmed into Texas after 1836 came with those very items. They rode in wagons pulled by oxen, and they marked the land; they eagerly explored the river valleys and built farms and ranches. The best land was in those valleys—the same valleys that bison herds needed for survival—especially along the Brazos and Colorado rivers and their smaller tributaries, just beyond the San Antonio–Nacogdoches road. In many cases, given the Indians' long-held practice of wildfire to drive the bison during their hunts, the new settlers seldom had trees to clear. That this land belonged to the Comanche and Wichita Indians seemed ludicrous to the Anglo-Texans; the hero Houston had determined who owned Texas on the battlefield at San Jacinto, or so the argument went.

Nevertheless, in the camps of the mobile Comanches (to the west and north of San Antonio) and even in the towns of the Wichitas (which were then well up the Brazos and Trinity rivers), talk of war with Texans occurred constantly in the mid- to late 1830s. Raids along the Santa Fe Trail became almost commonplace, since most commercial freighters avoided Comanche, Kiowa, and Wichita villages by this time as they carried their goods to Santa Fe. Good relations existed between the Plains tribes and Coffee, Chouteau, and a few other traders, but these men had culti- vated these relationships and often had even married into the various bands. They occasionally had artificial blood ties that offered protection. The freighters were foreign, not related by any process of adoption, and they, like the Anglo-Texans, had invaded Comanche lands.

The growing animosity between Anglos and Indians along the Santa Fe Trail and the fighting between Wichitas, Comanches, and Anglo-Texans created a spiraling conflict that was often based on the need for revenge, on both sides. When settler houses were destroyed, rangers went looking for Indian villages, since they seldom if ever caught up with the actual raiding parties. They scalped Indians and took prisoners only when they thought that the captives could be sold at a profit. A number of young Indian women and children were sold into slavery after the attack on the Wichitas in 1835, for example, and this had occurred in the past.[10]

Tribal societies, by contrast, had men whose honor required that they avenge the death of relatives, including virtually anyone from within the extended family group or even the residence band. Comanche leaders often listened to Wichita elders who spoke of the evil of Texans around campfires late at night. And when Comanches lost warriors, as they did when they attacked the Webster party, there were always young men who wished to avenge the loss of their relatives. Comanches, then, quickly became entangled in this web of conflict, which for them was a family affair.

Further confusing matters, the immigrant Indians—Cherokees, Delawares, Shawnees, Seminoles, Choctaws, Creeks—constantly entered Comanche towns. Some worked for men like Coffee; they often had embraced the frontier economy, wearing clothing from the East and speaking some English as well as Indian languages. While they may have been less incendiary, other immigrants entered Plains Indian camps, smoked with elders, and created fictive kinship bonds, particularly by taking Comanche or even Mexican wives. Some of these men related their bitter experiences back East, of being thrown off their lands by the U.S. government. Others explained how the surveying parties worked, how they marked the land for settlers. Plains Indian politics became increasingly anti-Texan and anti-American.

Comanche war parties, then, had multiple reasons for going to war. The 150 men who attacked the Webster party had three or four nights to organize before they sprang their trap. The war party came together much as all war parties did; a war chief of some note announced to all who would listen the existence of the Webster party on Comanche land. His rationale may have been revenge or even booty; perhaps even immigrant Indians had noted the purpose of the Anglo-Texans—to survey and settle the upper San Gabriel River valley and deprive Comanches of even more hunting ground. When sufficient men came forward to form a party, the chief then designated the next day as one of celebration. In the morning, the warriors donned their finest regalia—feathered headdresses, bedded vests and shields, lances and bows and arrows, and war paint—and paraded through the town. The old men and the women and children watched, all the while pounding drums, blowing whistles, and shaking pebble-filled gourds.[11]

Once the parade reached the center of town, the old men brought the celebration to a fever pitch by chanting of their many past war deeds and shaking the poles that carried the scalps that they had claimed. Such trophies were the marks of success in Comanche society. They also assured the young men that if they came back successfully with scalps, the unmarried girls in camp would be ready for them—they would receive wives.[12] Success in war enabled Comanche men to marry, at least once. A few Comanche men had six or seven wives owing to their military prowess.

Brought to a fever pitch, young warriors one after another entered the circle and pledged themselves to be brave—or not to come back alive. As the day passed in feasting and celebration, a huge bonfire was set off in the center of the village, where only the men gathered by evening. Women and children were kept away. More glorious deeds were recounted, but this time, usually the voices of the war party leaders explained how the raid would transpire. The members of the party then took many different pledges, one of which obligated them to remain separate from women from then on; the smell, the presence, and the powers of women would distract the warriors and sap them of their strength.

This pledge of celibacy before and during the making of war was common with Indians in North America. The Pueblo peoples would separate themselves from women for several days before going on a hunt or a raid—they believed that the smell coming from women during copulation could be detected by enemies or animals. The same taboos existed among the immigrant Indians, such as the Choctaw, Cherokee, and Creek, who had nothing to do (sexually or otherwise) with even their wives for three or four days before going to war.[13]

Taboos against sexual relationships or even contact with women existed in other contexts as well. Comanche men, in particular, had nothing to do with women during menstruation, which was literally viewed as polluting the society. Women commonly separated themselves from their husbands and families for days on end during this time. Anything touched by the woman before she left the tepee had to be avoided or washed with the utmost care to prevent a bad hunt or death on a raid.[14] These were strong taboos, and both Comanche and Wichita warriors lived by them.

This taboo extended to women captured on raids, white or otherwise, even though such women were considered to be future wives by the successful raiders. All Comanche raiding parties generally took three to five women with them to serve as cooks and take care of the horses. When captive women were brought into a raiding camp, they were turned over to these women, who promptly set out to "season" them. They were quickly taught to gather firewood or scrape bison hides, even before the party reached the main village. Most often, the warriors in the party never spoke to captured women, avoiding them entirely. The only contact made with any frequency came in tying them up. It was very bad for a warrior to lie with a women during such a crucial time.

While the women were quite safe then from sexual assault—and the captivity narratives demonstrate this—the raiding party would observe the time-honored ritual that Comanches had practiced for over a century. Mrs. Horn and Mrs. Harris, for example, were dressed in Indian garb (their dresses had been taken from them), put in a ring, and danced around before they reached the main Comanche camp. The center pole picked for the ceremony had painted figures of both women on it. Once the ceremony was under way, the women were forced to use a stick to beat the scalps of their loved ones. This symbolically represented their eventual incorporation into a Comanche family. Mrs. Harris received a "mother" who was at times brutal, but Mrs. Horn was given to a kind woman of Mexican heritage who treated her as a daughter.[15]

Mrs. Webster had a more colorful description of this process of incorporation. She called it "the fandango party." The Indians ushered her and her children into "a large ring encircled by Indians," where they underwent "the ceremony of being made a Comanche, which was to join them for a few moments in the dance." If the captives refused, they "were beaten severely." Mrs. Webster was given more and more freedom in camp. She eventually left late one night, made her way back to San Antonio, and was united with her two sons. She became the toast of the town, even being introduced to the president of the Texas Republic, by then Mirabeau Lamar. Crowds gathered around her to hear her story, which became more frightening with each retelling. The issue of rape, which discreet and honorable Anglos did not discuss, never came up; Anglo men simply assumed that it had happened.[16]

At first, Mrs. Horn (like most women who fell under Indian control) feared the "fate worse than death." In reality, while the treatment she suffered through was severe—beatings with whips were common, especially when domestic chores were poorly performed—almost all the punishment was orchestrated by senior Comanche women, not men. This was also true with Rachel Plummer, who noted that "two Comanche women stuck me several times with a leather whip . . . I suppose it was to make me stop crying."[17] And when captive women stood up to or even fought with the senior women who controlled them, they were given a degree of respect in camp and, accordingly, more privileges.

Once near the headwaters of the Colorado River, the Comanches joined other Indian parties that had captives. Mrs. Webster noted two young women named Lockhart and Pierce, four children named Putnam, and a young man named Lyons, who had been with the Comanches for some time. From Matilda Lockhart, Webster learned to obey the senior Comanche woman who had charge of her and to perform various household tasks. The more willing she was to perform these functions, the less punishment she received.[18] She soon blended into everyday life, doing the sort of domestic chores that contributed to the economy of a tribal society.

As Webster traveled with the Comanches, she grew familiar with their loosely associated allies. At one point, after she managed briefly to run away, a party of Caddos, African American slaves, and Tejanos recaptured her. They fed her and her children but seemed reluctant to take her to safety. One of the Tejanos was Manuel Flores, a noted Mexican collaborator and spy. The African American slaves were not overtly happy, as some of them had been moved to Bowles's Cherokee village by their master, who wished to avoid giving them up for debt. They were then under the charge of the immigrant Indians, and they wished to return home. This group, when eventually in contact with the Comanches, returned Webster and her children to her original captors.

Mrs. Webster saw several trading brigades come and go in the large Comanche camp she was in. Some forty-five "traders"—the majority being immigrant Indians—headed by an American arrived at one point, and just a few days later came some sixty-five more. The last group, mostly Shawnees, Delawares, and Cherokees, was tied to Coffee.[19] Webster seemed convinced that Coffee had tried to purchase her, without success. Perhaps by design, Anglo traders seemed reluctant to bargain for captives, given the obvious implications; they were exchanging arms for horses with the same people who were taking captives in Texas, and buying the captives back simply led to more captives being taken.

Coffee certainly knew how difficult life as a captive in a Comanche camp could be. And he, much like other males, may have thought that once among the Indians, a white woman would be dishonored by rape and could not return to Anglo civilization. Some captives were killed for resisting; a very few even faced death after failed war parties returned, having lost members. A mourning warrior was likely to strike out at any Texan, woman or not.

The murder of Mrs. Harris's three-month-old child, however, attests to a certain level of cruelty that Texans could never understand. Because of the long route home—from the Nueces River to New Mexico—the Indians knew the baby would never survive. He might also cry at an inopportune moment and give the party away. Mrs. Harris's baby was thrown in the air and allowed to bounce until dead. To compound the mother's anguish, the corpse was tied by the neck to the mule that she rode. Rachel Plummer, to her distress, faced a similar circumstance. She gave birth, had the baby taken from her, and had to watch as it was dragged to its death.[20]

The savagery of such treatment was seldom lost on Texans. But the logic of it, from the Indian standpoint, is reasonable when considering the nature of Plains tribal societies. Indians too lost children; perhaps only one in two Indian babies lived to the age of three. With infant mortality extremely high, the loss of many of their own likely diminished the value of Anglo babies to the Indians. It likely even led to an acceptance of the notion that life began when a child could talk (rather than cry) and walk. Such children had economic value; they could pick berries or carry water. Infants took labor to keep alive.

A few captives saw the human side of Plains Indians. Mrs. Horn's narrative reveals a woman who came to have grudging respect for Comanches despite what they did to her family. She praised their cleanliness and the way in which people worked together. She even seemed less than despondent about her sons, who, unlike Mrs. Webster's children, remained with the Indians when she was ransomed. They had been adopted and cared for. As for herself, Mrs. Horn concluded her narrative by discussing that which was of "the most sacred importance to a captive female"—that her worst "fears were in no part realized." In other words, she was never raped or forced into an unwanted marriage.[21]

One or two dozen other Anglo-Texan women endured captivity among the Indians. Some left brief accounts, but most said nothing once they were returned to their homes through ransom. Elizabeth Kellogg perhaps suffered the least, being ransomed for $150 in goods by Delaware Indians and returned to Nacogdoches in 1838. But Mrs. Webster came to realize that the process of ransom was complicated; some Indian families became attached to their captives, especially children, and refused to give them up. Webster decided to depart her captor's camp when she learned that they intended to ransom the six or eight captives they had, one at a time, over a long period of time.[22] She and her children simply walked away from camp one night and traveled for days without food before reaching San Antonio.

When adult women were returned home, they generally appeared in Indian dress and somewhat weathered by their ordeal. A few had scars from whippings, but most had been well fed, which was crucial for their ransom. Nevertheless, it was hardly surprising that local, male reporters of the age and turn-of-the-century historians alike quietly mused that such women had been "treated in a manner too shameful to be related."[23] The growing Victorian mores of the age made it difficult, if not impossible, to address such an issue openly. And so the real truth remained unaddressed.

The captivity narratives show yet another side of the story. Trade fairs of the sort Webster witnessed led inevitably to assaults on Mexico. Large war parties were seen returning with horses and captives in abundance. Ironically, the Horn and Harris women were captured as a result of a massive raid near Matamoros in April 1836. Composed of Wichitas and Comanches, the party of several hundred men took mostly horses and mules, killing anyone who resisted. Yet another group of Plains raiders hit Laredo in June and leisurely moved up and down the Rio Grande, selecting stock from the various ranchos. The raids were similar to those of the early 1820s, when Mexican *peones* and *vecinos* either cooperated with the Indians or faced death. Northern Mexico was helpless to defend itself, for Santa Anna had taken all the troops available into Texas.

The situation deteriorated further the next year. In February 1837, five hundred Comanches descended upon Camargo and Reynosa. They left over nine hundred carcasses of livestock, mostly cattle, since the ponderous animals were too slow to move north and had replaced bison herds. Comanches in similarly large numbers slaughtered another hundred head of cattle outside Matamoros the next month. And in July, the Comanches mounted a thousand-man raid, taking mules and horses from the Rio Grande ranches and committing depredations in several of the river towns. One report suggested that ten Cherokees, fighting for Mexico, perished while defending the area; another, appearing in the *Mercurio de Matamoros,* claimed that Indians and *colonos* (Texas revolutionaries) had joined together outside of San Antonio to assault northern Mexico.[24]

Mexican officials blamed Texans for the trouble. As proof, they described the actions of Juan Seguín, now a hated rebel. The Texas government had ordered Seguín to secure San Antonio in June 1836, but according to Mexican officials, he had used Indians and Texans to sack the town. Those same Indians then proceeded on to the Rio Grande, or so the story went.[25] In reality, Seguín had only demanded that Tejanos move cattle and horse herds east and north, out of the clutches of centralist raiders, who were posed to reinvade Texas. Some Tejanos refused and departed for Mexico, carrying the news of Seguín's supposed high-handedness.

Not surprisingly, Mexicans soon blamed Indians for becoming the pawns and allies of Texans, while Texans concluded during the revolution that those same Indians were the allies of Mexico.[26] The news brought by Dolly Webster that Manuel Flores was in the camps of the Plains tribes only confirmed what Texans had long since concluded—that Mexico was in league with the Indians. Yet neither claim had any foundation in fact. Comanche and Wichita war parties had long since made distinctions between Anglo-Texans and Mexicans, especially after Anglo-Texans began invading their hunting grounds in the months after Santa Anna's defeat.

With charges and countercharges flying this way and that and Texans and Indians becoming increasingly convinced of each other's savagery, any attempt to separate the combatants faced many obstacles. Indian war parties came from many different camps, even at least four very different tribes—southern Comanches (Penateka), northern Comanches (Yamparica), Wichitas, and Caddos. More confusing, Texas Ranger companies operated almost completely on their own from small settlements on the frontier that had little contact with more populous East Texas. The rangers attacked and burned at will, giving no mercy. They, much like their Comanche opponents, inflicted revenge upon Indians who they believed had killed innocent settlers and violated the honor of their womenfolk.

The new Texas government, faced with an angry Mexico in the south, could ill afford a two-front war. Nor was such a tangled web of conflict necessary, since there was plenty of land for everyone. But Texans wanted the river valleys, and they pushed up the bottomlands with determination. Newly arriving settlers searched for that perfect valley, with rich soil and plenty of water. They moved into regions far in advance of more complete Anglo settlement and government, leaving large sections of upcountry unoccupied. Texas needed to bring the rush into the west under control.

This could be accomplished with proper legislation, much as the U.S. government, under the Constitution, had taken over western land development and Indian affairs in 1789. Initially, the Texas government needed to rein in surveyors and land speculators. Then the republic had to consolidate military authority—especially the paramilitary ranger units—under a single command. Finally, Texas had to create a land policy that recognized Indian rights to the west if Indians and Texans were to be separated; this meant convincing the new republic's legislature to ratify the Cherokee treaty.

To make Texans consider such restrictive policies would not be easy. Many men elected to the new legislature of the republic that came together in the fall of 1836 had diametrically opposite ideas. What is more, creating a fair and peaceful Indian policy would have had to be accomplished during a period of escalating war, with violence bred of hatred, revenge, and expanding brutality. While the culture of violence that had settled into Texas was not inevitable, it certainly was deep-rooted.

Juan Seguín. Portrait by Jefferson
Wright, 1838. Courtesy Texas State
Library and Archives Commission.

Stephen F. Austin. Courtesy Texas
State Library and Archives
Commission.

Thomas Jefferson Rusk. Courtesy
Texas State Library and Archives
Commission.

Sam Houston. Rose Collection
no. 114. Courtesy Western History
Collections, University of Oklahoma
Libraries.

Antonio López de Santa Anna.
Rose Collection no. 107. Courtesy
Western History Collections,
University of Oklahoma Libraries.

Mirabeau B. Lamar. Courtesy Texas
State Library and Archives
Commission.

David G. Burnet. Courtesy Texas State Library and Archives Commission.

Edward Burleson. Courtesy Texas State Library and Archives Commission.

Indian council at San Antonio, Texas, 1850s. Note the involvement of U.S. Army officers. Rose Collection no. 183. Courtesy Western History Collections, University of Oklahoma Libraries.

Chief Bowles, Cherokee leader. Drawn by William A. Berry from descriptions. Courtesy Texas State Library and Archives Commission.

Black Beaver. Courtesy National Anthropological Archives, Washington, D.C.

George Washington, Caddo chief. Soule Collection no. 22. Courtesy Western History Collections, University of Oklahoma Libraries.

Caddo village. Courtesy National Anthropological Archives, Washington, D.C.

Kickapoo man, photo taken at Anadarko, Indian Territory, 1888. Rose Collection no. 1019. Courtesy Western History Collections, University of Oklahoma Libraries.

Going to Town, a painting of a two-wheeled Tejano oxcart called a *carreta.* Copy of a painting by Gentilz. Rose Collection no. 309. Courtesy Western History Collections, University of Oklahoma Libraries.

A Tejano *jacal* (brush house or hut). Rose Collection no. 315. Courtesy Western History Collections, University of Oklahoma Libraries.

10

SAM HOUSTON, THE LEGISLATURE, AND A FAILED INDIAN POLICY

As the news of the Texas victory over Mexico roared across America, glasses were raised in honor of "Houston, the hero of San Jacinto." Nashville, Tennessee, erupted in celebration; whiskey flowed in the streets to a greater degree even than when Jackson had thumped the British at New Orleans. Eliza Allen, who had spurned Houston so unexpectedly, suddenly sought reconciliation—an offer the glib and no-longer-forlorn Houston ignored. In the fall of 1836, Houston was elected president of the republic with a complete mandate: some 5,119 votes to a mere 586 for the ill Stephen Austin. Houston assumed office in late October as the first duly elected president of the Texas Republic.

The new president of Texas was nothing but optimistic. Vast amounts of empty land existed in Texas that could be used to finance government and could be allotted to "good" Indians who would help defend the republic in the continued war with Mexico. Santa Anna had agreed to Texas independence to save his skin, but Mexican centralists had not. Fortunately, a vast expanse of mostly treeless and waterless land lay between San Antonio and the Rio Grande, acting as a buffer to give Texas time to react to any invasion. The borders separating Indians and Texans, by contrast, were completely undefined. Correcting this would be a fundamental challenge for the new president.

Over Christmas, Houston surveyed his realm. It was in disarray, lacking law and order and basic institutions of government. Most communities acted under the southern creed; duels were the remedy of the day. A volunteer army remained in the field, and more men were arriving at the coastal ports ready for a fight. Unfortunately, most lacked even shoes, let alone arms and provisions. Two officers fought over command. One was the braggart Felix Huston; the other, Albert Sidney Johnston, who had had military training at West Point. This distinction perturbed the maniacal Huston, and he challenged Johnston to a duel, fired early, and wounded Johnston in the buttocks. Most of the officers and men, including even the embarrassed and wounded Johnston, wanted to invade Mexico, but Houston had a different plan for Texas.[1]

Even as Houston sought ways to dismantle the Texas militia, he turned his attention increasingly to Indian affairs. Indeed, they consumed the two years of his first administration. The thousands of armed and angry warriors in the north and west posed a greater threat to the republic than did Mexico. Houston wanted desperately to make friends, reestablish trade relations, and negotiate alliances. Such an Indian policy would allow Texas to prosper. But first, Houston knew, the vagabond men in Texas, the undisciplined Texas army, and the paramilitary Texas Rangers had to be brought under control.

Fortunately, Burnet, despite his shortcomings as ad-interim president, had made a start by enlisting the aid of Indian trader Alexander Le Grand during the summer of 1836. Le Grand had agreed to carry the news of Texas independence and the new republic's desire for peace to the Plains tribes, and he had acted swiftly. He had purchased presents in New Orleans and by fall was headed up the Arkansas River into Indian Territory.[2]

As Le Grand passed through Fort Gibson, leisurely coaxing his boats along the Arkansas River, he collected information from the various immigrant Indians who had been on the plains. The news was not good. The Plains tribes now distrusted almost everyone. Le Grand entered what he called the "Big Prairie" of western Indian Territory in February 1837, at a time of scarcity. Here he encountered some starving Wichitas, whose village the Pawnees had recently overrun. He left presents, which the desperate Indians appreciated, and pushed on.

Farther south, Le Grand found a Waco village on the north bank of the Red River whose inhabitants were also suffering. They had been involved in fighting the Pawnees as well and were in a bad mood. "From a great tribe," Le Grand noted, "they had been reduced to a handful." The stubborn Wacos would hear nothing of peace with Texas: they despised all Anglo-Texans. In exchange for presents, they did help Le Grand find the main Comanche town in the vicinity, a village under the leadership of Chief Chicorny.

Chicorny graciously received the presents that Le Grand had brought. Comanche etiquette required that strangers bearing gifts always be allowed to talk. After Le Grand had made his purpose known, however, the chief was blunt and to the point. "So long as he [Chicorny] continued to observe the gradual approach of the Whites and their habitations to the hunting grounds of the Comanches," Chicorny said, he would believe what the immigrant Indians had told him: that Texans would deprive his people of "their country." The Comanches had made up their mind; peace with either Texas or Mexico was impossible. Seeing the impasse, Le Grand's reports to President Houston became pessimistic and warned of war.[3]

Houston challenged this information, coming as it did from a Burnet appointee. The new president questioned Le Grand's honesty and even his expense account. But other evidence pointed to the same conclusion. U.S. Army officers at Coffee's Fort expected war and urged General Matthew Arbuckle to seek reinforcements for Indian Territory. Severe clashes had occurred between the Osage and Delaware Indians. The Comanches, meanwhile, had attacked a hunting band of Delawares and Shawnees. The Pawnees were at war with the Wichitas, and even the Kiowas and Comanches were feuding with the Cheyennes and Arapahos. The U.S. treaty of 1835 was disintegrating.

Even more squabbling occurred in the newly constituted Creek Nation, where the McIntoshes and Benjamin Hawkins continued to conspire. One of the leading Creek chiefs, Opothleyaholo, had become "much disaffected" and was considering moving to Texas. Houston knew Opothleyaholo well; the new president had likely been the one who had put the thoughts of Texas into Opothleyaholo's head. If not Houston, it was certainly his friend Hawkins, who continued to work at settling Indians in Texas.[4] Once Houston became president of Texas, however, the scheme had a political cost, and Houston had to distance himself from Hawkins and ignore Opothleyaholo.

Fortunately, American agents and army officers continued to work at pacifying the Plains tribes, much as Houston had hoped. During the early spring of 1837, several of Pierre Chouteau's traders visited various Comanche camps. Chicorny seemed the most rebellious, openly speaking of destroying any Americans or immigrant Indians who appeared on the plains. He had come to realize that the treaty of 1835 had granted immigrant Indians the right to hunt on the plains; this provision Chicorny rejected outright. The bison were declining on the southern plains, and his people depended almost entirely on the animal for their traditional way of life.

The Comanches, who had ruled the southern plains without challenge for many decades, suddenly realized the importance of identifying their hunting grounds. When asked by Chouteau's men, they clearly outlined their claim. The Creek agent F. W. Armstrong was somewhat surprised at the news, reporting to Washington the Comanche claim and the problems that it posed. "The Creeks and Choctaws," he wrote, "own a large portion of the country . . . which the Comanches . . . have not only used as a hunting ground, but considered as their right and privilege to occupy." Much of this land was actually east of the Wichita Mountains, where Dodge had first met the Comanches in 1834.[5] And these hunting grounds extended southward into Texas, including much of the central Colorado and Brazos river valleys.

Chouteau's men further learned that a party of Mexicans recently had introduced arms and munitions, using the goods to obtain council with the Comanches. The Mexicans advised the Indians that "the whites, if successful in the war now waging between Mexico and Texas, will [take] . . . the country now inhabited by the different [Comanche and Wichita] tribes." Lamenting the obvious failure of the 1835 peace treaty, Chouteau saw two Plains camps emerging: one somewhat friendly, at least willing to listen to Americans, and the majority "inviterably [sic] hostile" to Texans and even Americans.[6]

The new U.S. Secretary of War Joel Poinsett was shocked to hear this news. In April 1837, he again hired Chouteau—one of the most respected traders on the plains—to go among the tribes and see, in particular, the hostile chief Chicorny. Poinsett's blunt and legalistic approach would do little good. Chouteau was to inform Chicorny that his Comanches possessed only the "occupant title" to land onto which the Creek and Choctaw Indians were moving. Chicorny would have been amused had he heard the speech. When Chouteau looked for the Comanches in October, they had disappeared. Likely they knew their friend Chouteau's purpose and wished not to offend him with a rejection of his words.[7]

Meanwhile, President Houston began organizing his own western Indian policy. His plans were spun from his many years of experience with various tribes along the middle border. Having been involved in the Indian trade, he knew how important commerce was to all the tribes. It could be used to attract allies and make friends. If Anglo-Texans could not directly approach Comanches, then intermediaries with goods purchased by Texas would have to suffice. His old friends the Cherokees were the most logical choice; as president, he could protect their land claim and in turn use them to bring peace to the land.

He unveiled these plans to William Goyens, whom he hired to talk with Bowles in January 1837. Goyens had been involved in negotiations and trade with Indians since he had first appeared at Nacogdoches in 1820. A mulatto who married a white woman, Goyens was always forced to defend his property and freedom (at one point he was forced back into slavery) in the courts of Louisiana and Texas. But he hired and paid the best attorneys, including Thomas Jefferson Rusk. Despite these troubles, Goyens helped authorities track escaped slaves, doing the bidding of those in power, and developed a friendship with Houston. Above all, Houston trusted Goyens with some of the most important business of the young republic.[8]

Houston issued Goyens a passport (likely one of the first granted by the new nation) in January 1837 so that he might legally go among the Cherokees and Comanches. Once at Chief Bowles's village well north of Nacogdoches, Goyens found the old chief eager to assist him—the chief undoubtedly viewed Houston's election as a good sign, since Houston had consistently promised the immigrant Indians land. Indeed, Bowles, now past eighty in age, had learned that some of his "Cherokee brothers" were in Chicorny's Comanche village. He agreed to make the trip to the plains for Goyens, leaving on January 20 with ten of his young men.[9] Many Texans distrusted Bowles, however. Rumors soon mushroomed in the Texas communities that Bowles was conspiring with the Plains tribes to destroy Texas![10]

Bowles remained in Chicorny's village for fifteen days, watching as no less than three war parties returned from the south with captives and livestock. After several talks, Bowles found Chicorny to be quite obstinate: "he could not make peas [*sic*] with the Americans nor the Mexicans, the Americans becaus [*sic*] they were . . . killing his Buffalo and that they would starve him." From Mexico, the chief said, "I git [*sic*] . . . horses and mules and sell them to Coffee."[11] Le Grand, Chouteau, and then Bowles had discovered exactly the same sentiments: Texas expansion into the west was a serious source of contention, as was the hunting of various immigrant Indians. The Comanche political economy was heavily connected to protecting hunting grounds, raiding, stealing horses and mules, and ransoming hostages.

Houston, who likely distrusted Bowles to some degree, sought other channels. He commissioned Colonel Henry W. Karnes, who had taken over command of what mounted troops existed at San Antonio, to carry peace messages to the Comanches. Karnes was expected to be able to make use of several Tejanos, including Ruíz, one of the most prominent citizens of San Antonio. The goal was to coax the chiefs back to San Antonio, where they had made peace many times in the past. The place had always been an open city where Comanches and others gathered to discuss diplomacy.

Karnes was capable but more prone to fight than talk. He had organized practically the only company of mounted Anglo troops during the revolution—the others had been Tejano. Karnes's men had provided valuable service as spies at San Jacinto. But Karnes, like Gaines, was a blusterer. He returned Houston's order with a request for two hundred armed and mounted men, not exactly the right formula for making peace. In fact, Karnes, who could have made contact with the Comanches through a number of San Antonio emissaries, never undertook Houston's peace commission at all. Instead, he organized eight different volunteer ranger companies that were sent into the upper Colorado River valley to search for Comanche villages.[12] Mrs. Webster, while still in the Comanche camp, overheard the elders talk of Karnes's troops, and the Indians seemed familiar with Karnes's name.[13]

Similar problems dogged Houston in regard to peace initiatives aimed at the eastern Caddos. Texans bitterly complained of Caddo depredations, mostly on livestock. U.S. Army colonel James Many at Fort Jesup, called upon to investigate, consistently found no evidence to support the allegations. Houston, however, seemed convinced of Caddo duplicity, and he selected commissioners to deal with the Caddos sternly. He even instructed his representatives in Washington to demand that U.S. troops under Many prevent "such raids" (although the United States had yet to officially recognize Texas).[14] Because of the lack of evidence of depredations, Many bristled over Houston's efforts.

But as Houston wrote letters cajoling Many, Texan complaints in northern Texas mounted. Many Anglo-Texans, returning to their farms after the victory over Mexico, discovered missing livestock and household goods and blamed the losses on Indians, while newcomers who flocked into the new republic simply wanted the Caddos removed so that land could be opened up to them. Settlers slowly settled on land claimed by Cherokees, Shawnees, and Caddos, forced the Indians from their fields, and even removed some from houses, often at the point of a gun.[15] These new arrivals put incredible pressure on the lands and hunting resources of immigrant Indians in East Texas, most of whom had a mixed economy of farming, hunting, and trading.

Some Texas land quickly fell under the control of land speculators. They garnered political support from men like Texas senator Isaac Burton, who—along with Mirabeau B. Lamar, vice president of Texas—opposed Houston's policy of Indian negotiation because of the possible interference it might have with western land sales. Burton helped write the first Texas land bill, passed in 1837, which created positions for surveyors and opened local land offices. Houston vetoed the bill, fully aware that it was intended to push settlement into the west, but the legislature passed it overwhelmingly over his opposition.

Speculators purchased government land scrip, often from former soldiers who had no interest in farming, and claimed other titles through the local boards of land commissioners, which they often controlled. Burton, for example, helped select the first land commissioner in Nacogdoches County—one Warren Ferris, a close friend. Senator Burton worked closely with other Texans associated with land speculation near Nacogdoches, including the old empresarios Frost Thorn and Burnet, as well as Adolphus Sterne, Henry Raguet, Robert Irion, and even General Rusk.[16] Houston himself was at best a "reformed" land speculator. At least he had stopped supporting Hawkins's Creek schemes.

While the notion of negotiation and compromise seemed reasonable to the president, many new settlers viewed the situation differently. Thievery and occasional Indian raids only confirmed the rumor-driven beliefs—begun during the revolution—that all Indians were untrustworthy. The presence of Mexican agents among various Indian bands further incensed the evolving Anglo-Texan community. Unfortunately, it also led to the occasional persecution of loyal Tejanos, whose homes were invaded and whose stock was occasionally pilfered.

By spring of 1837, some Tejano leaders, including Vicente Córdova (the militia captain who had protected Texan property during the revolution), had left Nacogdoches to live with the Kichai and Anadarko Indians well to the north and west. These actions came partly as a result of Anglo-Texan efforts to disenfranchise Tejano voters in and about Nacogdoches. Some Anglos argued that these individuals had failed to support the revolution, a charge that had a ring of truth even though the Tejanos had banded together to protect property. Unfortunately, other Mexican agents and Tejanos, numbering perhaps a hundred, soon joined Córdova. The group included Eusebío Cortinas and other well-known Nacogdoches citizens.[17]

Lieutenant Bonnell at Fort Jesup, an objective observer, had learned that Córdova and Cortinas often secretly communed with other Tejanos at Córdova's old house, some nine miles north of Nacogdoches. They also used the house of Nathaniel Norris, another sympathizer who lived eighteen miles north of town. While they apparently had committed no crimes—some evidence, likely biased, implicated Córdova in horse thievery—they seemed determined to prepare the Indians for use when a Mexican army advanced on Texas.[18] This sort of polarization, occurring near Nacogdoches, was also happening in central Texas, where suspicions regarding the loyalty of Tejanos persisted.

Some members of the Tejano community tried to defuse the situation. Francisco Ruíz of San Antonio, serving in the Texas legislature, had offered a bill in which the government would give assurances that seemingly disloyal Tejanos would be allowed to return to their homes "without fear and molestation." But the full legislature rejected the bill even though Houston supported it. More and more Tejanos lost land and property to the new mass of Anglo-Texans who were taking charge of the local governments and local land offices. Men like Córdova, watching the process unfold near Nacogdoches, quickly sensed that the new Anglo majority would do little to protect the rights of the Tejano minority, some of whom had lived on their land for over a decade but had no real title to it.[19]

Not all Tejanos suffered Córdova's fate, however, which explains Ruíz's and Seguín's continued support of the Texan government. At San Antonio some semblance of order finally emerged in which Tejanos elected a Tejano mayor and enforced local law. To prevent the further loss of property, the Tejano elite frequently offered their daughters in marriage to incoming Anglo-Texans, who accordingly inherited estates they were then able to protect in the courts. The Navarros, Sotos, Garzas, Zambranos, Seguíns, Veramendis, and Yturris all accommodated themselves to the new Texan regime in this fashion.[20] Even so, more and more Anglos moved into San Antonio, and the Tejano population, once dominant, soon became a minority. Such was also the case in many communities just north of the Nueces River.[21] Tejanos were assimilated or marginalized, and a few grew restive. Houston's new government seemed helpless to protect the majority of Tejanos in Texas.

All of these rumors of Tejano and Indian conspiracy wreaked havoc on Houston's policies. At times, the president even found that his closest friends—including Thomas Jefferson Rusk and Robert Irion—were abandoning him on the issue of negotiating with Indians. General Rusk, secretary of war in Burnet's interim government, had supported Houston at his darkest hour, when Burnet was goading him to action in the days before San Jacinto. And Irion, Houston's secretary of state and later a senator, was Houston's neighbor from Nacogdoches. Irion had patiently watched as Houston had courted Anna Raguet, the most eligible young woman in town, and when she rejected the president, Houston graciously encouraged Irion, who eventually married her. While Irion faithfully served Houston for nearly a year, in the spring of 1837 he left the executive branch to serve in the senate, which gave him more independence to speak.

Both Rusk and Irion soon began to push for a more aggressive Indian policy, one akin to that supported by Burton and Burnet. "The Caddos ought to be exterminated,"

Rusk privately wrote to Irion in May 1837, "and I am not so sure about the Cherokees."[22] Irion soon introduced a bill in the Texas legislature that called for a military expedition against the "vagabond tribes" supposedly committing depredations north of Nacogdoches—the bands that had taken in Córdova. Yet Irion expected Houston to derail the effort. "The President seems averse to the policy . . . & whether this measure will meet his approbation I think is doubtful."[23] As expected, Houston derailed the effort, opting instead to organize 120 "gun men" who, along with some Indian allies, would patrol the northern approaches.[24]

As he lost support in the legislature, Houston tried to separate baby and bathwater; certain Indians deserved the support of the government, others, severe punishment. To him, the hostiles included "murderous hordes of wild Indians" on the plains. In contrast, Cherokees, Shawnees, Biloxis, Kickapoos, Coushattas, and Choctaws the president saw as useful allies.[25] Houston pressed again and again for negotiation, especially with the "good" Indians. Given the growing indebtedness of the republic and the unwillingness of the U.S. Congress to support military actions, this seemed the only logical action. Irion and Rusk both realized that only the commander-in-chief, Houston, could launch campaigns.[26] Neither man wished to challenge their old friend, but both were increasingly upset with Houston's pacifism.

The two committees on Indian affairs in the house and senate did issue several reports by the fall of 1837 that followed Houston's lead by placing Indians in categories. The small tribes to the south—Tonkawas, Lipan Apaches, and Karankawas—had either moved below the Nueces River or had signed various peace agreements.[27] They had few if any solid claims to land, or so the Texas Congress thought. Those people living to the east and south of Nacogdoches—Alabamas, Coushattas, and Biloxi Indians—seemed to have "very limited if any pretensions to territory." And Indians along the Red River corridor, including the Kickapoos, Shawnees, Delawares, and Potawatomis, also had "but slight pretensions to soil." All these groups were represented as being relatively friendly hunters who would eventually move on.[28] But the committee took a different tone when discussing Indians who wished to protect land claims.

The tribes with noteworthy claims included the Indians living well west and north of Nacogdoches in the upper Trinity, Neches, and Sabine river valleys. This group included especially Wichitas and Caddos, the majority of the Caddos considered to be "united with the hostile tribes that dwell there." All were "thought to be the greatest rogues and the most treacherous on our frontier."[29] However, the threat they posed to Texas primarily derived from their relationship with the Cherokee Nation, or so many legislators thought. For over a decade, the Cherokees had spoken on the behalf of many small Texas Indian bands at the same time they pushed for land claims on behalf of other immigrant Indians.

The senate committee—chaired by the sometimes ranger and rising politician Edward Burleson—determined what to do with these Indians in its final report in

October 1837. After "the most mature reflection," the committee chair concluded, the Cherokees possessed only "the *Prima-facia* right of occupancy," rather than having any "vested right" in the land. Houston's treaty of 1836 constituted only "false promises," since the land in question had been granted to David Burnet and Burnet's colony "was filled or nearly so prior to the Declaration."[30] But Burleson finalized the report with a conciliatory message; trade houses should be built and the Indians offered goods and presents. The only war that Burleson openly advocated, at least that fall, was with the Comanches, who had challenged land speculators on the upper Colorado River—as it happened, in Burleson's home district.[31]

Houston could do little with his congress thereafter. Led by Burton and Burleson, with occasional support from Irion and Rusk, the Texas legislature increasingly opposed recognizing Indian claims to land anywhere.[32] Despite some lingering confidence, the president's hope of convincing the senate to implement the Cherokee treaty was fading, and without the treaty, the cornerstone of a peace agreement in Texas crumbled. While the hero of San Jacinto would continue to push for negotiation into the spring and summer of 1838, he failed to hold back the rush to war that soon engulfed Texas.[33]

In retrospect, the likes of Irion and Rusk were only absorbing the views of their constituents. Many new arrivals in Texas, as well as longer-term settlers, had come to expect the removal of Indians. The Indians were long gone from the U.S. South by 1838, with over 100,000 having been removed to Indian Territory. This process of removal opened vast new lands to Anglo settlement. And the raids and counter-raids that expanded in Texas in the late 1830s only fed the advocates of war. How could peace even be offered to Indians who abused women and children?

Worse, the seeming inevitability of Indian war prompted the reorganization of the military by the Texas legislature. Crucial to this reorganization was Burleson's ability to convince Rusk and other Houston supporters to bypass the president. Burleson's legislation passed the congress in the spring of 1838 over Houston's veto. The bill gave the Texas Congress the authority to name the commanding general of the militia. Burleson's committee on Indian affairs declared that an emergency existed: the committee concluded that Houston's "conciliatory and friendly character had failed to produce the desired results" of peace. The congress then created three divisions of troops, placing these men directly under "General" Rusk, who resigned his senate seat to take command. This stab in the back must have hurt Houston, who had always counted Rusk a close friend.

The troops had yet to be raised, and there was some concern whether they could be, since the treasury lacked the funds to pay them. Nevertheless, their mission increasingly became clear; in a tabled resolution, Burleson's committee designated the creation of a line running one hundred miles west of the most exposed settlements. Indians—including all East Texas tribes, such as Cherokees, Delawares, Shawnees, Caddos, Choctaws, and others—were to be removed from the regions east of this line.[34] The Texas Congress, then, had turned the tables on Houston, moving from a policy of negotiation to removal, and should the Indians resist, an army was being raised to wipe these tribes from the land.

In response, President Houston chastised the legislature in a series of messages. Instead of attributing the problems to the Indians, he blamed land surveyors, especially those working in the Colorado, Navasota, Brazos, and Trinity valleys. These men would soon reach the San Saba Valley and even, he sarcastically muttered, the "Great Salt Lake" of Utah, if Texas failed to rein them in.[35] In a second message, Houston mused over why so many Anglo-Texans coveted Cherokee lands. Could it be, he speculated, that "their snug cabins, their well cultivated fields and their lowing herds excite the speculators?" Finally, Houston attacked the defense bill, which effectively relieved him of command of the yet-to-be-raised federal militia. Similar ranger units, he pointed out, had abandoned their posts recently on the Brazos River to attack a peaceful Indian village and steal horses. Militia or rangers, often impossible to control, Houston argued, simply invited war.[36]

As the banter went on, settlers, surveyors, and rangers dictated the unfolding of events as much as did the Texas Congress. A ranger unit from Bonham quickly moved beyond the Cross Timbers, building Fort Inglish near where the prairie town of Dallas would soon emerge. In central Texas, Navasota had been laid out, and settlers moved upriver beyond Parker's old fort. Even more significant, speculators had pushed well up the Colorado River; one of the most prominent was Congressman Burleson, who preached hatred of the Comanches while coveting their lands and livestock herds.

Burleson, using his connections in government, speculated heavily in the lands of the upper Colorado River valley. He surveyed and opened the town of Waterloo in the spring of 1838. While not successful, Waterloo existed in the same locale as what would become Austin, Texas, the next year. George W. Bonnell, who visited Waterloo in July, found a small garrison—called, ironically, Fort Houston (different from the ranger fort of the same name on the Navasota River)—three miles below. One noticeable family, headed by a man named Barton, "ran a narrow chance of being scalped," Bonnell concluded, "but [he] carries a good rifle." Bonnell saw men fitting out expeditions to survey the Llano and San Saba river valleys, much as President Houston had feared.[37]

Despite the obvious invasion of Comanche hunting grounds by Burleson and others, Houston continued to push for negotiation, instructing his secretary of war, Barnard Bee, to try to reach the Comanches. Ignoring many of the more militant soldiers who were then connected to Burleson and Rusk, Bee ordered General Albert Sidney Johnston to pick several trustworthy men to travel west and take counsel with any bands they could find. Houston perhaps vainly hoped that Johnston, who had remained above the squabbles in the Texas Congress, might embrace negotiation.

General Johnston carried out the order. He convinced Joseph Baker and Horatio A. Allsbury to lead the expedition. The party traveled west for many days before reaching the Pedernales River, where they found a large Comanche camp and were treated as ambassadors—Comanche hospitality always prevailed, even during times of war. Invited to council, seventeen Comanche chiefs sat quietly in the lodge, smoking and eyeing their guests. The head chief, one Tsawakana, slowly gathered his wits and, using a Mexican captive as interpreter, got to the point. Having come to hate the Anglo-Texans, he had never negotiated with them before. He asked Baker and Allsbury to state their business truthfully.

The delegation answered that they came to promote peace. They wished that Comanche leaders would follow them to San Antonio and trade with them. This would afford the Comanches "a market for their horses, mules, etc." Tsawakana listened patiently, but he shifted the discussion. Shawnee traders, then in the Comanche camp, had warned them that Mexico had fought the recent revolution with Texas over the issue of Indian rights to land. The Texans, the Shawnees insisted, coveted Comanche land along the Colorado River. Indeed, they were occupying it as the discussions were under way.

Given these realities, Tsawakana made several immediate demands. He insisted "strenuously" that in any negotiation, the "lands north of the Guadaloupe [*sic*] Mountains [the Hill Country north and west of San Antonio] should be secured to them by treaty." When asked to define this region, the chief indicated that roughly the northern boundary of Bastrop County (some twenty miles east of what would later become Austin) constituted the actual line and that Comanches would "kill all surveyors" found within their claim. Such a view explains the attack on the Webster party and others who had breached this line. The Texans, surprised at Tsawakana's composure, had no answer, offering excuses instead. Four days later, the commissioners handed out presents and left.[38]

On hearing of this contact, both General Johnston and Colonel Karnes, the military officials at San Antonio, demanded instructions from Houston and Bee. The commissioners had invited the Comanches to San Antonio, and it was assumed that they would appear in April 1838. Secretary Bee, conferring with Houston and aware that the Texas legislature would fail to ratify any treaty that granted land to Indians—especially lands then being pursued by speculators such as Burleson—finally offered the officers the following guidelines: "say to them that they will continue to hunt [on their lands], whence they have done." If Texans appeared "with passports," the Comanches should treat them kindly, "as our people will do should the Comanches come into our settlements."[39] Such a solution was asinine, but it was the only recourse for Houston.

A similar muddled state of affairs, which existed in East Texas, soon distracted Houston from the Comanches. The president had selected yet another agent, Jefferson Wright, to assist Goyens with the Cherokees. In their first council, Goyens and Wright found Cherokee leaders to be visibly upset. Bowles and Big Mush had been told nothing about the actions of the Texas legislature and fully expected Wright and Goyens to show up with land titles—Houston had guaranteed as much a year before. "All were afraid the delay was some plot to deceive them again," Wright wrote to Houston on June 17, 1838. "Mush said it looked like [Houston was] making fools of them all." In an obvious reference to Houston's familial responsibilities, Big Mush could only add that "he and his friends feel ashamed and hurt."[40]

Wright assured them that a boundary for their land would be marked. While this assurance helped, suddenly other Indians who had been forcefully removed from land in the lower Trinity River valley fled onto Cherokee lands. Over three hundred Coushattas, poor and destitute, had camped near Bowles's town, eating literally everything in sight. Other Caddos, Ionis, and Kichais, being pressured by the settlers at Fort Inglish, fled south as well from near Red River, all complaining of Anglo-Texans and relating fear of ranger attacks. Bowles informed Wright and Goyens that he would take in all the refugees, provided Bowles received a deed for his land.[41]

While Bowles's suggestion seemed harmless, the thought of more Indians listening to the old chief suddenly worried Houston. And rumors of a Mexican/Tejano/Cherokee conspiracy were rampant. President Houston, believing the reports that Delawares and Cherokees had visited Matamoros that summer and that war was possible, warned General Rusk to prepare for military action in East Texas.[42] Houston, by the summer of 1838, seemed to be moving toward a compromise with his political opponents—he especially appeared willing to destroy the Caddos.

A spark soon ignited this powder keg when a frustrated Vicente Córdova, joined by many of the Nacogdoches Tejanos, began a revolt. The Tejanos were upset by the failure of Texas to protect their property and maintain their political voice. Córdova, who had traveled to Matamoros, had received a commission from General Filisola to raise "the Indians as auxiliaries to the National army." Manuel Flores, a Mexican agent who worked for Filisola, was to bring the Indians into the conspiracy.[43]

The news of a "Mexican revolt" reached President Houston while he was visiting Nacogdoches on August 6. The Tejano force had congregated on the south side of the Angelina River, some thirty miles below Nacogdoches, where it had joined a large band of Kickapoo Indians as well as some displaced Alabamas and Coushattas. While the number of Tejano rebels is difficult to ascertain—one exaggerated report put the number at 250—many leading citizens of Nacogdoches were involved, including Córdova, his brother, Telesforo Córdova, Nathaniel Norris, Guillermo Cruz, and Juan Galán. When later questioned by Anglo-Texans, Cruz said that "they had been [treated as] dogs long enough."[44]

The involvement of the highly respected Galán and Norris led Houston to understand the seriousness of the situation. But the president also surely saw the local nature of the revolt—the rebels were all from Nacogdoches and had been shabbily treated. Despite his growing disagreements with congress and the organization of a militia, Houston ordered General Rusk to call out as many troops as possible. Over the course of several days, Houston and Rusk fielded a force of seven hundred men near Nacogdoches and called out others in the north. The entire Texas army eventually totaled nearly three thousand men.[45] The Tejano revolt—Córdova perhaps had forty Tejanos and two hundred Indians, only some of whom might fight—was doomed to failure almost as quickly as it revealed itself.

To contain the rebellion, Houston opened communications with the Cherokees, who so far had remained neutral, and with Colonel Many at Fort Jesup. Houston's appeal to the colonel, written likely at the point of exhaustion, bordered on hysteria. Indians from the United States had joined "rebellious and traitorous Mexicans," the president wrote, with the intent of destroying Texas. Under the often cited treaty of 1831, Houston claimed that Many had a duty to render "immediate assistance" by sending U.S. troops into Nacogdoches. Houston then asked for two "six pounders," preferably on wheels. "The Indians embodied with the Mexicans," the president solemnly promised the colonel, "are tribes from the United States and some within the last three years."[46]

Turning to the Cherokees, Houston pressured Big Mush. The trouble, he argued, was between Tejanos and Anglo-Texans. Houston then assured Bowles—despite his belief that the old chief was in the thick of the conspiracy—that Houston had ordered the boundary line for Bowles's land run even though the men entrusted with the act were too frightened at that point to accomplish the task. Finally, despite the actions of the Texas Senate, the president claimed to his friend Bowles that he would never abandon the 1836 treaty: "I will never lie to that treaty while I live, and it must stand as long as good men live and water runs!"[47]

Just who received the larger lie, Colonel Many or Bowles, is open to debate. Many did know the situation well and had no intention of acting rashly. But Bowles had put faith in Houston; his trip to the Comanches clearly proved that. Whether he had learned by this time that the Texas legislature would not grant his people land is uncertain; however, Bowles suddenly did come to see through his "friend" Houston. Likely he listened to Córdova in desperation.

Rusk's army reached the Angelina River on August 12, 1838, and his spies found the Tejano camp abandoned. Some forty Tejanos—this number coming from Rusk— had moved west to the Neches River. While Rusk had demonstrated rashness in the past, at this point he moved cautiously, being somewhat uncertain of the situation, since Mexican troops might be involved, although there were no signs of them. When Rusk discovered that the Tejano force had camped within a mile of Bowles's Cherokee town, he expected a major fight, if not war.

At this point, both Rusk and Houston sent a barrage of letters to Big Mush and Bowles. They pointedly assured the chiefs that troops from the United States were coming from Fort Jesup and that war would mean utter disaster for the Indians. Wright, Goyens, and Joseph Durst, another Nacogdoches friend of Houston's, were enlisted to carry in the correspondence, along with the retired Mexican Indian agent Peter Bean.[48] The situation reached a crisis on the evening of August 14, when Rusk lambasted Houston. He wanted orders to attack and feared he was "being embarrassed" by the continued negotiations. Rusk's honor was at stake. Houston, he said, must come to deal with Bowles and Big Mush or "I shall march up there with my whole force and not wait to talk much with a set of internal scoundels [*sic*] who have meditated the death of women and children."[49]

With Rusk poised to pounce on the Cherokee town, Goyens and Durst finally convinced Chief Big Mush and nine other Cherokees to visit General Rusk on the morning of August 15. Bowles, however, was absent, and Rusk's men remained at the ready. The Indians informed Rusk that the Tejanos had fled westward, making a battle unnecessary.[50] Houston's diplomacy, while filled with lies and distortions, had won the day. Yet all sides concerned came away from the crisis with a sense that the issues remained unsettled.

Bowles had frantically negotiated with Córdova during the affair, but it remained unclear whether the Cherokee leader wanted war or peace. Houston eventually praised Rusk, but the friendship between the two men was severely strained. Rusk thereafter became more militant and determined to exterminate Indians. While Houston attempted to preserve Tejano property and coaxed some involved in the rebellion back home, many Tejanos ignored his proclamation. They no longer trusted Houston or their Anglo Nacogdoches neighbors thereafter. On August 18, Houston called for the army under Rusk to retreat from Cherokee lands. This Rusk reluctantly did.[51]

Sam Houston realized that a major war had been averted. The president also learned a day or two later that the republic could expect no help from the U.S. government. Colonel Many had refused all requests for troops, artillery, and ammunition. While the colonel forwarded these requests to the War Department, he added in his report that the Indians supposedly harassing Texas had been "residents in that place much longer than three fourths of the present [Anglo-Texan] inhabitants." Most had been "settled in that country long before the Independence of Texas was thought of."[52] Many's sympathies rested with the Cherokees and Tejanos, not the Anglos.

Many had ordered Lieutenant William S. Harney, a young, rising U.S. officer, into Nacogdoches at the height of the trouble. Harney, who later gained a reputation as an Indian fighter during the plains wars, reported that the whole affair was of a "domestic nature"; a few horses had been stolen or retaken by a handful of Tejanos—Anglo-Texans later termed this a "raid" conducted by Telesforo Córdova. When armed Anglos went after the Tejanos, a fight ensued. The Tejanos had fled to the Indians for help, and General Rusk called out the army. The struggle thus had nothing to do with Indians from the United States.[53]

Anglo-Texans, not surprisingly, had a different view, and the naysayers even included Houston. Speaking for the president, Barnard Bee called it "Córdova's rebellion" and proclaimed that it involved a massive conspiracy of Tejanos and Indians. Nine Indian tribes—many from the United States—supposedly had joined the Tejanos, who were expecting a Mexican army. The Tejano citizens near Nacogdoches had simply struck too early, taking horses before the time to act had been reached. This view justified expelling most Tejanos from northern Texas. Some forty Tejano men stood trial for treason, although only one was convicted and he was later released. Many Tejano families, however, lost everything; some fled to Louisiana.[54]

The Córdova rebellion brought upheaval to all of northern Texas, including the settlements south of the Red River in the Bois d'Arc, near Fort Inglish, and along the Sabine River valley. The rebellion gave Houston the chance to punish the Caddos, who he felt "deserve chastisement." He ordered militia general Thomas H. Dyer to organize ranger companies and scour the countryside on August 11.[55] Dyer sent several companies to attack Caddo and Wichita villages lying west of the settlements, near the three forks of the Trinity River. One of the first expeditions, consisting of ninety men, was commanded by Captain Robert Sloan; they departed Fort Inglish in mid-August.

As was typical of rangers, the men joined for two reasons: the excitement of an Indian fight broke the monotony of the frontier, and overrunning an Indian village resulted in plunder. Sloan's mounted men, recruited mostly in the saloons of the Bois d'Arc valley, left for the west (as one later reported) "all in high glee under the influence of strong drink." After a mere three days, the party found an unidentified Indian camp. "The Indians were soon dispatched," ranger John P. Simpson later recalled, "and the scalps taken from their heads." One ranger was wounded and one horse killed. When a wounded Indian man was found nearby in the brush, Captain John Hart instantly dispatched him and took his scalp, still not knowing or caring about who he was killing. With a few trophies and abundant plunder, the victorious and by this time sober rangers headed back to Bois d'Arc.[56]

Upon its return, the Sloan party met a local Tejano named Alexander Peñeda, riding a sturdy mule and displaying expensive pistols and a double-barreled shotgun. His fine dress caused quite a sensation, and soon the party forced Peñeda to tell the company that the clothes and guns had come from a Mexican officer that he had killed just south of Fort Inglish. When subsequently examining the dead Mexican, A. G. Wright from Bois d'Arc found a journal and a collection of letters that identified the man as Pedro Julian Miracle, an officer in the Mexican army. The journal, written in pencil, was hardly legible, but Wright deciphered enough to determine that Miracle intended to raise all the Indians of the Red River valley, even those in Indian Territory, against the Texans. Wright copied the journal and passed it on to General Arbuckle at Fort Gibson. Its publication in the *Arkansas Gazette* a few days later caused a stir, as did a copy that the Texas Department of State sent to the U.S. government in Washington.[57]

Miracle had left Matamoros in May with thirty-two Mexican soldiers, over a dozen vecinos, and twenty Cherokees and Caddos. Only Miracle and the Indians proceeded northward, however, reaching the Kickapoo village near the Trinity River in early July. While Miracle tried to speak with the various Indian leaders, frustration filled the pages of his diary, as he lacked interpreters and mostly failed to get his message across. At times, he was even abandoned for many days, his so-called Indian allies leaving him at an isolated house most of the time.

Finally on July 20, Córdova and a group of Nacogdoches Tejanos arrived, and a council that Miracle attended was convened at Chief Bowles's house. During the meeting, according to Miracle, the Cherokee leader agreed to fight with the Mexican army, a decision that surprised the increasingly disgruntled Miracle. At that point Miracle left, visiting some Caddos on the upper Trinity River just as the Córdova revolt prematurely began. These Caddos treated him politely but seemed uninterested in the Mexican plot. Miracle's journal, with the exception of the brief meeting with Bowles, strongly suggests that his efforts to drum up Indian support had fallen on deaf ears.[58]

But Anglo-Texans interpreted the situation differently. Wright concluded that all the Trinity River Indians had joined with Mexico, for Miracle had given them presents of powder and guns. "Hostilities have commenced and war dances were [being] held over scalps of Texians," he wrote to the U.S. Army colonel J. G. Voss at Fort Towson.[59] The rumor mill worked well into the fall. George Bonnell, writing in his journal in September while along the Angelina River, reflected the mood of Anglo-Texans. "Much excitement" existed "on account of the movement of certain Mexican citizens to overturn the government." He joined the militia units that Rusk and Dyer kept in the field, both men being convinced that a Mexican army existed just over the southern horizon.[60]

Houston thought the escalation unnecessary. There was no evidence of a Mexican army anywhere above the Nueces River. But rumors were powerful in Texas, and few channels of objective communication existed. Rusk flatly rebuked the president, defending his saber-rattling actions, "with dire deference to your [Houston's] opinion."[61]

Certainly on the issue of land and expansion, Houston's opinions did differ somewhat from those of most Anglo-Texans. He especially urged General Rusk to "run the line" (that is, survey the boundary of the Cherokee grant).[62] But the president's argument, outlined in a letter to yet another newly recruited agent, Charles Sims, displayed a backpedaling attitude that once again brought into question any sincere belief that it would help the Cherokee. He said to Sims, "If the Indians have no right [to land], making a line will give them none!" But the line would satisfy them and prevent war, he thought. "I tell you once and for all, all people in other countries will be slow to assist Nacogdoches in an Indian war *for land*."[63]

Ever the politician, Houston openly blamed certain Indians and Tejanos for the conspiracy while at the same time speaking out for boundaries and negotiation. With Colonel Many, in late August, he even used the race card, hoping to fan southerners' fears: "*Low* Frenchmen"—a reference no doubt to the trade families who had settled with the Caddos—were engaged with the Tejanos and "Negroes and Indians," ready to pounce on the Anglo-Texan settlements. "They are men who never look at the destiny of their race. In this they are different from all the Anglos."[64] Houston then went a step further. Should the Indians and Tejanos triumph, Houston lamented to Many, "the Mexicans, with their abolition policy, and united with the Indians, will invite the slaves of the south to revolt!"[65]

President Houston believed that the Indians most compliant in the conspiracy were Caddos and Kickapoos. Some reports confirmed growing discontent among the Kickapoos, who had moved their women and children high up the Trinity River. By mid-September, some Wichitas joined them. Then, on October 1, a large party of Indians and Tejanos descended upon several farms and stripped them of food, although they killed no one. Major L. H. Mabbitt, at Fort Houston on the Navasota, located the raiding party some fifty miles southwest of Nacogdoches and sent out a scout of fifty rangers, who broke and ran when discovered by the Kickapoos and Tejanos. A few days later, Indians and Tejanos attacked nineteen surveyors. The surveyors stood their ground, but several perished in the engagement.[66] In all, some two dozen Anglo-Texans had lost their lives to the upper Trinity River Indians and Córdova's men.

Frustrated and downright angry, General Rusk set out on October 14, 1838, to drive the marauders out of the central Trinity valley. With a force of 220 men, he marched on the Kickapoo village, found the Indians and Tejanos, and defeated them in a frontal assault on the morning of October 16. The Indians and Tejanos had eleven dead, including one Cherokee, two Tejanos, and the remainder, Caddos and Coushattas. But many more, perhaps two dozen (one report put the number at twenty-six), died in the Indian camps afterwards. Rusk had eleven men wounded, all of whom lived. The battle of the Kickapoo village, the most ferocious to that point, put East Texas in a state of war.[67]

After his success at the Kickapoo village, Rusk took total command of all troops in Texas. He ordered Brigadier General Mosely Baker and his force to march up the Trinity River, "destroying, on your route, the villages of all Indians." The tenor of his advice left little ambiguity: "Guard your camps well *at night*; and, when you fight, exterminate."[68] As Rusk put in motion forces north and west of Nacogdoches, he also organized men from the rapidly growing regions near the Sabine River. Stirring the pot even more, the U.S. government had finally delivered on promises to provide the Caddos with annuities, among them arms and munitions. This news caused a sensation in northeastern Texas. Joining Dyer's command, Rusk marched on the eastern Caddos in late November.[69]

Rusk and Dyer finally cornered the eastern Caddos near their town at Caddo Lake, along the Louisiana border. While a brief exchange of gunfire occurred, the Indians soon fled to the protection of their U.S. Indian agent, Charles Seawall, at

Shreveport, Louisiana. Rusk, with two hundred militia, followed in hot pursuit, crossing the border into the United States and demanding the surrender of the Indians. While a tense moment ensued, in which the Caddo agent called upon the U.S. military at Fort Jesup for help, cooler heads prevailed and generals, Indians, and agents reached an agreement. The 120 Caddo men surrendered the locks of their new weapons to the agent. Rusk, acting for Texas, agreed to feed the Caddo in the future.[70]

Unbelievably, Rusk's invasion of the United States hardly caused a stir in Washington. It somehow seemed justifiable under the 1831 treaty. Texas officials wrote a flurry of letters in which copies of the Miracle journal were enclosed, using it as proof that Mexican agents had recruited the Caddos. These were, in the view of Anglo-Texans, U.S. Indians conspiring to overthrow the republic.[71] Moreover, the activity had bypassed President Houston, who had lost control of the militia and war strategy to Rusk. All Houston could do was try, in the last few weeks of his administration, to carve out a boundary for the Cherokees and their allies, a boundary that he knew would never be respected by his congress.

Throughout September and October, the president went through nearly a half-dozen surveyors in his efforts to get the line run demarcating Cherokee lands. Some feared the Indians, while others opposed the project. Finally, in early November, Colonel Andrew Horton reported to the president that the line had been run, carved out of the woods and creeks that formed the high country between the upper Sabine and the Neches River.[72] This last-ditch effort to pacify the Cherokees and prevent war was soon challenged in the Texas legislature. Within days, the house of representatives passed a resolution condemning the act and demanding that the president explain what authority he used in carrying it out. Then it passed other resolutions giving General Rusk "full and entire approbation" for his conduct.[73]

The outgoing president defended himself on November 19, 1838, in a long letter addressed to the Texas Congress. He noted that the 1832 convention at San Felipe had "recognized" the Cherokees' rights to land and that again in 1835, representatives of the newly forming country had given sanction to land for the Indians. The treaty of 1836 had clarified that a surveyed line was to be run and that such a line was necessary. Then the president asked: should the legislature not compel "those few seditious speculators to render obedience to the laws," or was the congress going to sit idly by and watch as the entire northern part of Texas erupted in Indian war?[74] By this time, Houston knew the answers to his rhetoric; law and order had been replaced by militant generals and out-of-control Texas Rangers.

As the Texas constitution had determined, in November an election had been held to select a new president for the republic. While pro-Houston supporters had tried to find a candidate sympathetic to the president's views—in a curious twist the two men whom they approached, Peter W. Grayson and James W. Collinsworth, both committed suicide prior to the election—the job fell to Vice President Mirabeau B.

Lamar, almost by default. As some indication of the future land and military policies of Texas, the people selected David G. Burnet as the new vice president. Both Lamar and Burnet despised Houston and his policy of conciliation with Indians.

With Lamar's election, Houston quietly left Texas for the East. He wished to visit family and leave his troubles in Texas behind. And he was courting again, this time with more success. But Houston was very much aware that Indian war was on the horizon in Texas and that his policies had been rejected.

11

LAMAR, HIS GENERALS, AND ETHNIC CLEANSING

Mirabeau B. Lamar migrated to Texas from Georgia in the months just preceding the revolution. Lamar's views mirrored those of most southern men; he believed that the Anglo race should inherit the earth because they cultivated it and that Indians lacked sovereignty because of their "savagery."[1] The new president defended southern honor and believed in the glories of southern culture. He had proved his mettle at the battle of San Jacinto; yet Lamar brooded afterwards because he felt that Houston had slighted his heroic contribution. The two men never drew pistols, but they openly despised one another.

During September through November 1838, the months prior to Lamar's inauguration, military conditions in Texas deteriorated. Small raiding parties hit the northern settlements. The raids were conducted by Caddos, Wichitas, and a few defiant followers of Córdova, all of whom had recently been attacked by rangers. In the south, Comanches clashed with surveyors and settlers along the Colorado River and north and south of it. The violence only whetted Lamar's appetite for war. He had believed from the start that all Indians, regardless of circumstance, should be driven from Texas. Indeed, Lamar adopted a policy of ethnic cleansing almost from the first day he came into office.

The republic, however, was young and broke. Lamar needed money and allies in the Texas Congress, and he worried about the influence of Houston, who was still immensely popular. By the time of his inauguration, Lamar had discussed the situation with General Rusk, who had other concerns. Rusk fretted over the inactivity of the government and the malaise of the population. Settlers increasingly refused to serve in his militia; when Rusk ordered three hundred men to form a company near Nacogdoches in mid-November, only forty-five volunteered. The general requested that as one of his first acts as president, Lamar should ask the congress to organize a regularly paid frontier army of five hundred men.[2]

Rusk also encouraged Lamar to demand once again that the United States remove its Indians. If the United States remained "faithless enough," the general averred, then "we must await a more auspicious moment than the present to exterminate them [the Indians]." The word "extermination" was consistently creeping into the vocabulary of Texas officials. Rusk's use of it clearly bolstered Lamar; the president had discovered a warm political ally in General Rusk, who had many friends in the Texas Congress and seemingly hated Indians. Other former "Houstonites" would listen to Rusk because he had done much to stabilize the army. The time seemed right for a more aggressive Indian policy.[3]

The job of convincing the U.S. government to act fell to ambassador Anson Jones, a man who could spin a good tale. Jones's protest to U.S. Secretary of State John Forsyth categorically stated that Indians from the United States—notably "Caddos, Kickapoos, Choctaws, Coushattas, Cherokees, Tawakonies, and a few from several other tribes"—had congregated on the upper Trinity River and had begun a war with Texas. Jones feared that since the "hostile combination extends to a portion of some of those tribes now residing upon the borders of the United States" (that is, in Indian Territory), the Texas Indians would receive reinforcements from their relatives north of the Red River. Under the terms of the much-quoted treaty of 1831, the ambassador concluded, the United States had an obligation to help Texas defend itself.[4]

The U.S. government saw this rhetoric for what it was—exaggerations and outright lies fine-tuned to get the United States involved in Texas. By this time, U.S. Army officers were constantly monitoring the situation on the Louisiana–Indian Territory border. Colonel J. G. Voss, who had temporarily replaced Colonel Many at Fort Jesup, received information daily. Some letters came from Texas settlers demanding that U.S. troops come to their rescue. The colonel ignored them. Mostly he followed Many's practice of sending in his own reconnaissance to learn the truth. Voss knew that some horses were disappearing and that occasionally a settler's cabin had been attacked. But when queried by Washington in the late fall of 1838, Voss was able to say with certainty that "no Indian war" existed in Texas.[5] He, like Many, came to view Anglo-Texans as sniveling complainers who moved onto Indian lands, started conflicts, and then ran to the U.S. government for relief.

Many U.S. politicians, immersed in the slavery debate, considered Texas by this time to be a political liability. Helping the new republic would lead to the expansion of slavery (something even President Jackson had strenuously avoided), which might in turn destroy the Democratic Party. The constant appeals for military aid from Burnet and then Houston had soured U.S. Army officers—with the exception of General Gaines. Most of those stationed in Louisiana and Indian Territory simply did not believe Texas officials anymore.

Lamar turned instead to constructing his own militia, as Rusk had suggested. One of his first acts as president was to push through another militia bill, this one calling for some 840 troops to be assigned to eight different locales, from the Nueces to the Red River. As Rusk had suggested, all troops would receive $16 per month and be given a $30 signing bonus. Even these modest payments soon plunged the fragile republic into debt.[6]

President Lamar justified the military buildup in his first address to congress on December 21. His message avoided any specific discussion of the causes for the Córdova revolt or the battle at the Kickapoo village. But he did briefly touch on land speculation, suggesting that if such an action "has been pushed by any of our citizens beyond the boundaries of prudence," it was to be "regretted." But he stated that Indians had no legal claim to Texas and thus no "just cause of complaint." The Indians (or, as he termed them, the "wild cannibals of the woods") had started the war by committing a series of massacres "with the ferocity of tigers and hyenas." Texas had to retaliate, he continued, by carrying "an exterminating war upon their warriors, which will admit of no compromise and have no termination except in their total extinction."[7]

Realistically, Lamar could list few instances in which the "tigers and hyenas" had killed Anglo-Texans on lands that originally had been part of empresario-controlled colonies. Both the assault on Parker's Fort and the destruction of the Webster party had occurred well outside of the settlements. And rangers had always retaliated. Time and again, Indians had been pushed off their land by surveyors and land speculators. Often the Indians had not even fought back. This had been true of the Shawnees in the north, the Alabamas and Coushattas along the Trinity River, and even, to some extent, the Kickapoos.[8]

Depredations, when they did occur, usually involved Comanches, Wichitas, and Caddos or even renegade elements that did not belong to any specific tribal society. One attack on a Texas farm near Bonham supposedly involved "twelve Indians" who assaulted the Kitchen family. The attackers were driven off and lost one man. The slain "warrior" when examined, "was found to be a wooly-headed negro."[9] Another complaint sent to President Lamar came from Franklin, Texas, located along the frontier just east of the Brazos. The citizens petitioned that Indians had made "some 20 widows" in town. In fact, the occurrence referred to was the attack on Walter P. Lane's surveying party, which had encroached on Indian lands. Friendly Indians had warned the surveyors to leave, and they had refused. Most of these casualties occurred near the falls of the Brazos River, eighty miles northwest of Franklin, well within Comanche-Wichita hunting grounds.

While it is uncertain whether Lamar, or even Houston, could have stopped such surveying activity, the Texas Congress could have established boundaries (such as those in the United States) separating Indians and Anglo-Texans. But rather than attempt this solution, Lamar's government encouraged surveys; he even endorsed the efforts of his congress to order the capital of the new republic moved to the locale of Waterloo on the upper Colorado River in 1839. The new site—well within the recognized hunting grounds of the southern Comanches—would soon be called Austin, and its very location reinforced a policy of rapid westward expansion.[10]

If this legitimized expansionism were not provocative enough, Lamar ordered his new militia into the field. With the promise of pay, some four hundred militiamen joined Rusk by Christmas. They intended to march against the Caddo and Wichita towns that were then on the upper Trinity River. The Indians, learning of the expedition (likely from Tejano allies), moved farther west into the Brazos valley. A Texas spy company soon found them; the towns held forty Tejanos, including Vicente Córdova, and nearly seven hundred Caddo, Wichita, Kickapoo, Biloxi, Coushatta, and Shawnee warriors, some of whom frequently left for the plains to trade. The intelligence came too late for Rusk, however, who had lingered in the central Trinity valley, burning abandoned Indian towns. All had been deserted, the general reported on January 9, "and evidently with precipitation." Rusk's delighted men pilfered bison skins, blankets, and even broken guns.[11]

Other mounted ranger volunteers organized themselves independently of General Rusk. Colonel Jacob Snively, with fifty men, occupied the Saline District just west of the Cherokee towns. Ironically, some fifty-four Cherokees joined him, followers of Big Mush who either believed that Houston's line would be respected or hoped to keep an eye on Snively. Cherokees were clearly divided over how to deal with Anglo-Texans by this time. From Nacogdoches appeared another handful of men, mostly Tejanos under the command of Louis Santos, suggesting that Houston's amnesty of the Tejanos involved in the Córdova revolt had also done some good. Snively's mixed command illustrates the confused sense of loyalties that existed in East Texas as late as the spring of 1839. Nevertheless, his small force dissolved a few weeks later without engaging anyone.[12]

Some Texans wondered if Lamar and Rusk had not overestimated the threat. In March, the Houston *Telegraph* printed several letters suggesting that the number of hostile Indians along the Trinity was actually quite small, perhaps only four hundred, exclusive of the Comanches. Such speculation brought into question Lamar's need for a federal militia.[13] Not everyone in Texas was as convinced as Lamar and Rusk of the need to exterminate Indians or to pay soldiers to do it.

An event unfolding just north of the new town of Austin, however, soon provided Lamar with an excuse to implement ethnic cleansing. In February 1839, as Anglo-Texans began to settle in the area known as Austin and Barton Springs, a handful of Lipan Apaches brought news that a large Comanche camp existed in the San Saba River valley. The extent to which the Comanches might or might not have been involved in raids seemed unimportant. The Tennessean John H. Moore, by now a veteran Indian fighter, gathered his La Grange rangers, a few other volunteers from Bastrop, and a dozen Lipan Apaches. The party numbered eighty men.

Frontiersmen eagerly joined Moore, who held no rank in the Texas army and promised no pay. These men were activated by the excitement of campaigning, but they also hated Indians and moreover were desirous of the possibility for plunder. Many had come to Texas hoping to join filibustering campaigns against Mexico. Although Houston had disbanded the army they had hoped to join, Moore offered them a second chance. Few, if any, had vocations, and they had little money with which to buy land. In addition, Indian villages were far softer targets than Mexican towns; Matamoros, for example, had Mexican troops protecting it.

Riding hard, Moore's force reached the Comanche camp on the San Saba at sunrise on February 14, 1839. The weather was bitter cold, and the Indians were snug in their tepees, asleep. Moore quickly attacked before the women and children could escape. John Wesley Wilbarger gave a vivid account of what happened next: "the wildest scene of confusion ensued—warriors yelling, women screaming, and children crying—all running hither and thither." Henderson Yoakum took pleasure in recounting the surprise of the Indians: the rangers "opened the doors of the wigwams . . . slaughtering the enemy in their beds." The ground turned red with blood as the killing continued. Some sixty to eighty Indians fell in the first salvo.[14]

Catching the Indians completely by surprise, Moore and his men had an immediate advantage. But the rangers soon saw the tide turn, and they retreated to a position of strength, from which they managed to hold off more than three hundred bitterly determined Comanche warriors, some of whom likely came from other villages upriver. At ten in the morning, a Comanche woman appeared and inquired whether the Texans had captives to exchange—the Comanches held five Texas captives (children, supposedly) taken in earlier raids. Unfortunately, the Lipan Apaches—and most likely the rangers—had fought without quarter and had killed what prisoners they might have taken. No deal could be reached; after having lost well over a hundred people, with many more to perish later of their wounds, the Comanches withdrew, leaving what was left of the burning town to the Texans.[15]

The massacre on the San Saba enraged the Comanches. Indian raiding parties assailed the Anglo settlements thereafter, overrunning farms located near Bastrop and Austin and killing nearly a dozen settlers. The Coleman family near Well's Prairie, the Morgan family at the falls of the Brazos, and others all suffered from the reprisals. Relatives of Senator Edward Burleson near Bastrop were even under siege, and he abandoned his senatorial seat to rush home. Lamar had asked Burleson to organize the bulk of the new army authorized by congress, and Burleson put together a regiment as quickly as possible. But many men still refused to sign up for lengthy periods of time—short-term, unpaid, ranger volunteers remained the most effective force the republic could muster.

One such unit of fifty men fell under the command of Burleson's brother, Jacob. A large Comanche force caught this ranger company in the open just north of Bastrop and nearly annihilated it in a desperate fight that went on for hours. Jacob Burleson died of wounds just days before his brother, Senator Burleson, came to the relief of his family.[16] The Comanches were not going to give up the central Colorado valley without a fight.

The next month, several units of Lamar's militia encountered yet another armed force of sixty-odd men. The Texans soon learned that this group included Vicente Córdova. The Tejano revolutionary had been at the new Brazos River Caddo and Wichita towns but was returning to Mexico. A two-day running fight ensued, during which the Texans killed nearly two dozen of Córdova's men (many of them Tejanos from Nacogdoches), who had been caught in the open. Córdova suffered serious wounds but escaped. Not long after, Senator Burleson returned to the senate, where he thundered that the party constituted evidence of the collusion between Mexican agents and the eastern Indians. In truth, even Burleson knew that only six Indians were with Córdova, but he neglected to mention this fact.[17]

As the central Colorado River valley became a battleground, riders raced into Austin on May 16 telling of another surveying party under assault. Burleson dispatched several patrols, one of which found the offending attackers only ten miles from town. Young Lieutenant James Rice charged pell-mell into the group of roughly twenty or thirty Indians and Tejanos. While Rice's men killed only three—the others abandoned everything and fled—the lieutenant soon identified one of the dead as Manuel Flores, Córdova's lieutenant. The captured baggage contained substantial amounts of munitions loaded on a large number of pack mules. While the munitions went to the Texas government as contraband, Rice's troops, in typical ranger fashion, divided the spoils of war, which included 114 horses and mules. Indeed, in what became ranger fashion, they fought over them![18]

As the rangers rifled through the party's belongings, they found papers in the possession of Flores. He recently had been in Matamoros conferring with General Vicente Filisola, as well as General Valentín Canalizo, who replaced the former in mid-February. Filisola's letters revealed that Flores had been charged to recruit Tejano and Indian allies.[19] Such commissions were routinely issued, but Canalizo's letters went much further, outlining a strategy for an upcoming northern campaign. Canalizo ordered Flores to inform all the northern Indians that Mexico would soon launch an army to recapture Texas. Meanwhile, Flores was to foster the "feelings which the faithful Mexicans" had always held for Indians and to "induce the friendly tribes . . . to aid in fulfilling the instructions which are sent to them."[20]

Both Córdova and Flores had found relief in the camps of so-called hostile Indians, which were mostly high up the Brazos River by this time. That such men would court these Indians could hardly surprise anyone. Nonetheless, the letters again pointed to Mexican/Indian collusion, and despite the mounting criticism of the cost of Lamar's militia, the president decided to use the letters as a justification for expanding the war.

Shifting the blame northward by noting that Cherokees had sided with Mexico as well, Lamar wrote to Chief Bowles on May 26, 1839, to demand that the Cherokees leave Texas immediately.[21] Lamar claimed that Anglo-Texans had achieved sovereignty over the lands because of "many rightful and glorious achievements." While Lamar lamented the possibility of war, violence could be avoided only if the Indians left. To keep the Shawnees neutral, Lamar simultaneously assured them that they would not be molested.[22] He then called upon Generals Rusk and Burleson to make their forces ready to attack the Cherokee towns.[23]

Fearing Houston's opposition, several prominent citizens wrote to the former president hoping to silence him. General Rusk sternly warned Houston of the "crisis" on June 9, assuring Houston that a "movement" would be made against the Cherokees and that Texas politicians needed to maintain a united front, "whatever opinions may be entertained in relation to the policy of this step."[24] A friend of Houston's in Nacogdoches, D. S. Kaufman, sent a similar epistle in which he argued that Flores had implicated the Cherokees and that "all the citizens of Nacogdoches" supported military action. The policy was "no longer open to discussion," Kaufman wrote, implying injury to Houston's political future or perhaps even his physical self should he oppose the effort.[25]

Yet President Lamar still contemplated the possibility that he could avoid war through the peaceful removal of the Indians. Despite his rhetoric, ethnic cleansing did not require extermination—only removal, preferably through threats instead of action. Burnet, Johnston, Rusk, Burton, and James S. Mayfield (all committed to policies of either expulsion or extermination) agreed to approach the Cherokees and ask them to leave.[26]

Once the "peace" commission reached the main Cherokee town between the headwaters of the Sabine and Neches rivers, however, Chief Bowles rather than Big Mush greeted them. This was a bad sign, for it meant that the majority of the Cherokees would not go. Bowles bluntly told the Texans that his men would fight. Big Mush, the peace chief, had obviously been set aside. But Bowles, now in his eighty-fourth year, lamented the decision. He favored evacuating the Cherokee towns, but he felt a moral responsibility to fight alongside his young men.

On the morning of July 16, 1839, Generals Rusk and Burleson, each at a head of a regiment of more than two hundred men, moved on the Cherokees. The troops had been hastily recruited. Some were armed with long rifles, others with shotguns. Floppy hats and homespun were the uniform of the day: the Texas army could not afford braids, brocade shirts, or brass buttons. Reaching the main town, the troops found it evacuated. Moving west, they discovered the main Cherokee force entrenched in a nearby ravine along the Neches River. The ground was heavy with brush and trees; it might have provided an opportunity for ambush. Texas skirmishers prevented this, however, dooming the chances of a Cherokee victory.

The Cherokees likely had only 150 men—some of whom were only boys—who elected to stay and fight. Many of the warriors had abandoned Texas with Big Mush. Though outnumbered by Rusk's and Burleson's militia nearly three to one, they stood and fought. As the Texan buglers sounded the charge, the militia went in with fixed bayonets. Several volleys later, dense smoke allowed the Texans to quickly envelop the ravine. But they took casualties, as the large balls fired from the .50-caliber trade muskets of the Indians tore off arms and even legs. The Texans had 40 wounded men down and half a dozen dead after carrying the field.

Cherokee losses mounted as well, especially under the fire of the long rifles of the Tennesseans in the Texas army. Eighteen Cherokees were dead in the ravine, and nearly a hundred were wounded. Bowles, still tall and picturesque in his old age, refused to leave the camp in the ravine. Wearing a brightly colored coat and hat and carrying a special cane, all items that Houston had given him, he urged his men on until he too took a ball. Wounded, he sat down in front of a cooking fire. A Texas soldier approached him from the side, put a pistol to his temple, and blew his brains out. Left on the battlefield for the wild animals, Bowles's bones could be observed bleaching in the sun along the Neches River some twenty years later.[27]

Over the next few days, the Texas army surveyed the countryside, crossing over into the headwaters of the Sabine River to the east. Along their march, they found several abandoned Indian towns (three of which had been occupied mostly by Cherokees), complete with granaries and fields. The soldiers "burnt the houses and cut down the corn." Anything of value was collected as booty. One town, only recently abandoned, held "oxen, tools, peltries and other plunder."[28] The most marketable items, such as cattle, horses, and even bags of corn, were sold in Nacogdoches to the highest bidder.[29]

With the Cherokees routed, the generals of the Texas army turned to the Shawnees. Lamar's promise soon proved valueless. General Rusk told the assembled Shawnee leaders that they too would have to vacate Texas. Seeing the troops, Chief Green Grass agreed, saying that he had "hoped to find peace here" but was "still surrounded by trouble." As the Shawnees gave up their gun locks and packed their belongings, Rusk handed out over $3,000 in silver. The general promised more in the form of goods. Some sixty-three Shawnee families then departed for Indian Territory.[30]

As the largely peaceful immigrant Indian bands were forced from East Texas, they left a vacuum that renegades and marauders soon filled, often organizing into larger parties north of the Red River and descending upon the Texas settlements to kill and plunder.[31] What remained of Bowles's Cherokees split into several groups. The majority fled to Indian Territory, where General Arbuckle—outraged by the behavior of the Texas government—gave the refugees rations. When queried about Cherokee threats, Arbuckle huffed that there was not "the slightest reason to suppose" that they would harm anyone.[32] A second band fled west, hoping to escape to Mexico. Burleson, who had been named "Colonel Commandant," found this group on Christmas Day and attacked with nearly two hundred men. The outnumbered Cherokees had little chance; Bowles's son John perished, along with many others.[33]

In the aftermath of the "Cherokee War," Texans debated Lamar's policies. The new congress met in the fall of 1839. Sam Houston, who had returned to represent San Augustine, attacked Lamar. Houston's indignation increased considerably when General Burleson handed him the coat and cane that the ex-president had given as a present to Chief Bowles. Houston fumed over the removal of the capital to Austin, which was patently unsafe. But the ex-president reserved his greatest tirades for the land speculators—including Burleson and Burnet, who had promptly claimed the Cherokee lands under Burnet's old empresario grant.[34]

Lamar, not to be outdone, defended his policies on November 12. The Cherokees, he said, had been guilty of "the most horrid atrocities" and had refused to leave peacefully when asked by the government. "In my opinion," he went on, "the proper policy to be pursued toward the barbarian race is absolute expulsion from the country." While such rhetoric had been used by other politicians and military officers in the United States at certain times in the past, never had it come from a chief executive and never had military expulsion become state policy.

Lamar, however, went on to mark the clear distinctions that existed between U.S. Indian policy and that of Texas. The alternative to his views, he noted—the type of "humane policy" adopted by the U.S. government in Washington—"has generally resulted in injury to whites, without any adequate benefit to the savages." While Lamar would have been hard-pressed to explain how his policies benefited Indians, especially farmers like the Cherokee, he was certain of one thing: whites and Indians "cannot dwell in harmony together. Nature forbids it!"[35]

Despite the bombast, Anglo-Texans other than Houston questioned Lamar's policies. The fear of Indian trouble in the east had receded considerably since independence. The few Caddos of East Texas—the only notable tribe remaining northeast of Nacogdoches—had become pitiful outcasts, a mere three hundred people living in huts on the outskirts of Shreveport, Louisiana. The very thought of such Indians being a threat to Texas was absurd.[36]

Critics of Lamar also pointed to the massive expenditures—soon reaching millions of dollars—that the president had spent on his various campaigns and to the growing lawlessness in the republic. While northern Texas mostly had been cleansed of Indians, bands of robbers roamed in and about San Antonio, traveling eastward to the gulf coast. Consisting mostly of Anglo-Americans, these robbers occasionally marshaled twenty to thirty men and attacked ranches and farms, killing and stealing. In some areas of the new republic, law and order had broken down.

The Tejano ranchers who lived in and about Goliad probably suffered the most. Anglos looked down upon them, questioning their loyalty to the republic as well as their qualities as men. In the few years after the revolution, forty of forty-nine Tejano ranches near Goliad had fallen into Anglo hands—nearly one million acres. Sheriff's auctions, tax liens, and outright gangsterism proved effective for depriving Tejanos of their land. Even when Tejanos sustained themselves against Anglos, gangs rustled their cattle and sheep to the point where the Tejanos had to leave. One gang, according to an observer, openly proclaimed its intention to kill Tejano ranchers and "make a clean turn" of their cattle.[37] The estimated three hundred men of this gang made their work look like that of Indians, a trick that more renegades soon began to utilize.[38]

With lawlessness on the rise and Lamar's Indian war looking more and more like a land grab, Houston went on the attack. On the floor of the legislature, he first defended the Cherokees, pointing to the fact that evidence of their duplicity was nonexistent. But Houston did not dwell on the past—removing Indians from East Texas had been popular. Instead, he argued that the Cherokees had been given land by the Mexican state of Coahuila-Texas; as a result, the republic (not David Burnet) now owned the land. More important, since Lamar had incurred a huge debt in prosecuting the Indian war, selling the Cherokee lands would help pay off the republic's loans. Many congressmen—with the obvious exception of Burleson, Burton, and Burnet—agreed and supported Houston's Cherokee Land Bill.[39]

Ironically, to accept Houston's argument, the Texas Congress had to acquiesce to Indian ownership of Texas land. In language taken from old English law, the senate committee on Indian affairs finally declared that the Cherokees had held "a possessory right" to East Texas land for sixteen years. While the committee never conceded that the Cherokees had owned the land—the bill used the phrase "reserved for"— both houses of the legislature passed Houston's Cherokee bill on January 25, 1840. A month later, a commissioner was sent to East Texas to open a land office on the site of "Bowles's old village," forty miles northwest of Nacogdoches.[40]

Hardly noticed during the legislative hiatus of that fall was the entrance of three Comanches into San Antonio asking for peace. They handed over a small white boy, identified ultimately as John Horn, of the Horn and Harris party. Mrs. Horn, having been ransomed the year before, was living in Missouri. Colonel Karnes received the Comanches and listened to their story on January 10, 1840. The three Comanches claimed that their people had rejected various appeals made by other Indians and Mexicans to join a war on Texas. They offered to bring in a large contingent of their leaders to secure a new peace in twenty to thirty days. Karnes agreed but admonished them by saying that a lasting peace could be negotiated only when the Comanches gave up the Anglo captives that they held, estimated at thirteen.[41]

The Penateka Comanches likely had plenty of young men who opposed the notion of peace after the fighting of the previous summer. But peace to the Comanches meant securing a respite from fighting long enough to open up exchange, as had been the pattern during the earlier Mexican and Spanish regimes. San Antonio was the largest community within reasonable distance of the Comanche villages, and it possessed the manufactured items that they wanted. Moreover, as in the past, peace at San Antonio did not necessarily mean peace all across Texas.

Karnes, having little experience at Indian diplomacy, sent messengers to Lamar asking that commissioners be sent to negotiate. He further suggested that a regiment be sent to impress the Indians; if the Comanches showed up without the Anglo captives, Karnes suggested that the Indian delegation be held as hostages. Never before had the republic's predecessors, Mexico and Spain, attempted such a scheme. San Antonio had historically been an open city where Comanches came and went under a banner of neutrality. Delegations had been received peacefully—much like the Comanches had received Texans the year before—for over seventy years. These were unwritten but fully understood rules of diplomacy, at least for Indians.

Secretary of War Johnston knew little of this history. He ordered Lieutenant Colonel William S. Fisher to pull together three companies of troops from Burleson's regiment, which had been disbanded before the holidays, and send them south to support Karnes. Johnston then selected General Hugh McLeod and Colonel W. G. Cooke to serve as "peace" commissioners. Both men disliked Indians and could not patiently participate in a debate with Indians. Adding to the potential for conflict, Johnston heeded Karnes's advice; Fisher had orders to seize the Comanche chiefs if they failed to bring in the thirteen Anglo captives.[42]

True to their word, a large Comanche delegation approached San Antonio on March 19, 1840. They obviously came in peace, since the delegation of sixty-five people included thirty-five women and children—the women in characteristic fashion came to exchange their wares for goods. Of the thirty men, twelve held leadership positions. Texas authorities directed these leaders to the local jail, which had a council chamber. The eighteen young Comanche warriors dispersed into the streets. Some watched a dozen or so Indian children play ball, to the amusement of San Antonians, while still others took shelter in a nearby building.

Once in council, the smoking took less time than usual—the Indian chiefs wanted to get down to business. They presented Miss Matilda Lockhart to the Texas authorities. "We have brought the only one we have," Chief Mukawarrah said, following the statement with a query translated as, "How do you like the answer?"

The Texas leaders sat quietly at first. By this time, Miss Lockhart, apparently unaware of Mrs. Webster's escape with her two children, had revealed that other captives—including two or three children—still remained at the Comanche camp. But even Lockhart had no knowledge of the ten others that the Texans had hoped to get back. Cooke and Fisher readied the troops; McLeod then ordered the interpreter to tell the chiefs that they were now prisoners, to be held as hostages until the Comanches turned over the other captives. Suddenly silent, the interpreter (a Tejano who knew Comanches) slowly moved toward the door, aware that it would be an unacceptable breach of Comanche honor to agree to captivity. As he prepared hastily to depart, he translated the message.

When the chiefs heard the news, all hell erupted. Some chiefs ran to the door, while others attacked well-armed soldiers with bare hands or knives. A frantic Colonel Fisher gave the order to fire, and the troops let off a volley at point-blank range, killing many Indians and two unlucky Texans. The carnage in the small room was unbelievable—guns exploding, bayonets finding their mark, and knives ripping flesh in fierce fighting. When the dust settled, the twelve Comanche leaders all lay dead on the floor, as blood oozed out the doorway. The council room had become a death chamber.

Outside, chaos reigned as Texans and Indians, both enjoying the sunny civility of the occasion, ran for cover. The two Texas companies shot down many of the young Comanche men, some while they tried to go to the aid of their chiefs. A few warriors barricaded themselves in a stone storehouse but were soon killed. Another handful managed to cross the river that ran through town, only to perish on the other side. When the carnage ended, thirty-five Comanches lay dead, including five women and children. Seven or eight Texans had lost their lives as well, some to friendly fire. The remaining thirty Indian women and children were quickly incarcerated in the jail.[43]

In the weeks that followed, Texas newspapers exonerated those responsible for the massacre. In particular they pointed to the Comanche abuse of captives—the Webster woman who arrived at San Antonio in the aftermath had supposedly received treatment, as one editor put it, "too painful and too horrid to bear description."[44] This, of course, was not true; Mrs. Webster attested to the fact that she had been kindly treated. What the newspapers failed to report was that the council house massacre, rather than being a rash reaction of menfolk seriously afflicted by the mistreatment of Anglo women, was a major diplomatic and military blunder. The Texans had miscalculated Indian resolve. They had failed to understand that Comanches would rather die than surrender and face the ridicule of their people.[45]

While Texans had hoped that the meeting with the Comanches in San Antonio would produce a lasting peace, in reality the council house massacre (most often identified in Texas history as the "Council House Fight") only expanded the conflict. Critics of Lamar and his generals soon noted the opprobrium that the action engendered in the press in the United States and even in Europe over the fact that men coming in peace with their families had been shot down in cold blood.[46]

There can be no doubt that the council house massacre became a seminal event in Comanche history thereafter. The Texans had left too many witnesses: women and children who returned to their people to tell and retell the story. The Comanche people would take nearly a decade to get over the loss; the event would be brought up again and again as attempts were made to negotiate a settlement between these people and the Texas government. In fact, the term "Texan" became anathema in Plains Indian camps. Warfare was honorable to Indians, but so was negotiation. The leaders of the San Antonio party had waved the banners of peace before coming into the city, had been admitted to a peace council, and had been shot down. It was unforgivable.

Texans not only thought otherwise but came to see the event in a positive light. They had sent one of the Comanche women back to camp with word that if the captives were brought in, the Comanche women and children being housed in the Alamo would be exchanged for them. In April, a Comanche party brought in nine children, two of whom were Anglo—likely the only ones who remained among them. The Texans released nine Comanches in return. Another exchange, involving seven Mexican children, occurred in May. This time the Texans gave up only two Comanches, since the majority of the returned captives were from Mexico.[47] It was the last peaceful exchange that ever occurred, because the rest of the Comanche women and children escaped one night and made their way back to their people.

Naturally, the Lamar administration scoffed at those who criticized the actions of Texas troops at San Antonio. Rumors giving different versions of the event even spread; one suggested that the Texans had been surprised by the Indians and had used "rocks, axes, and anything they could get hold of" to defend themselves.[48] Lamar, viewing the event as a major victory over the Comanches, turned by summer to organizing military expeditions into the trans-Nueces region. Finding the treasury completely devoid of money, however, and being unable to pay the promised salaries to militiamen, he turned instead to voluntary troops—rangers—and ordered Colonel Karnes to organize them.[49]

This situation at first seemed innocuous. The months of June and July 1840 passed without much discussion of the shift back to ranger forces—or much action. The lack of comment occurred partly because Houston, Lamar's nemesis, was in Alabama, courting again. This time Houston found a wife, Margaret Lea. The former president and his new bride arrived in Galveston just as the dull, hot days of summer came to an end. Houston's return brought two eruptions. The former president soon lambasted Lamar; there was, Houston said, corruption in Lamar's government. The criticism was nearly drowned out, however, by the violence and mayhem that suddenly struck the Texas settlements.

12

THE INDIANS' LAST STAND
IN CENTRAL TEXAS

The Penateka Comanches mourned their dead through the late spring months of 1840. Thirty men killed on one afternoon was a terrible blow. Wailing started in the camps as soon as the news arrived, with women and children howling and screaming, bending to their knees, and throwing dirt on themselves. Quickly the wives, children, and brothers of the slain chiefs and warriors sharpened their knives and cut gashes along their arms and legs, not penetrating the muscle but letting the blood flow. Soon tears and blood became intermixed, matting the hair of the mourners. All was done publicly, because the louder the crying, the more honor was granted to the lost man.

In between the wails, the women slashed their clothing and cut their hair short to symbolize their loss of status; they were now widows in a society that cherished marriage. Arranged marriage occurred only after a man had proven himself in war, and thus married men and women had more status. But life had to go on. The surviving relatives broke up the dead men's tent and all that he owned in yet another symbolic gesture. They wished never to hear the man's name again or to remember him by seeing his property. Even his horses, the most valued of Comanche possessions, were given away.[1]

Comanche honor dictated that these men, lost through despicable guile, be avenged. Literally as the band mourned, packed its tents, and prepared to move, the crier went through the town informing people of the disaster at San Antonio. But the loss had been so great for the Penateka that they desired nothing more than to effect a heavy blow on Texans. Such a course of action, they hoped, might wrest central Texas from the growing clutches of the Anglos. For this they needed help from other relatives, farther north and west. By May 1840 they had turned north looking for allies.

Word spread quickly through the Comanche nation of the council house massacre, of the treachery of the Texans. As the Penatekas hunted along the headwaters of the

Red, Canadian, and Arkansas rivers that summer, they made contact with the various Yamparica bands, the most populous of the Comanches. Even as the Penatekas approached New Mexico, an eerie quiet settled over San Antonio and Austin. Anglo-Texans expected revenge raids. In May they prepared for raiding parties; by June and July, many Anglos doubted that the vengeance would come. The Comanches, having lost a significant number of leaders, had simply disappeared.[2]

Perhaps, thought a few of the more optimistic Anglo-Texans, the Comanches had given up. Such a conclusion was vastly premature. Many Comanche leaders did recognize their limitations in combat, however. Lances, bows and arrows, and a few muskets had worked well against poorly armed Mexicans; they were less effective against the Anglo-Texans, as the Comanches had learned when they overran the Webster party in 1839. Only one-third of their warriors had firearms, and the ambushed party, firing Kentucky long rifles, had killed nearly two dozen warriors.

Firearms were difficult for the Comanches to acquire. Chouteau had brought a few short muskets in the mid-1830s. His trade house near Fort Holmes on the Canadian River had been a busy place. But Chouteau died in 1838, and his post was closed the next year.[3] The depression of the late 1830s had even driven Holland Coffee back into Texas; even though Mrs. Webster had talked with Coffee while with the Comanches in 1839, he was serving in the republic's legislature by 1840. These were not good years for the Indian trade, as the economy had collapsed.

The best option for acquiring weapons was Bent's Fort, built on the upper Arkansas River in the early 1830s by William and Charles Bent. Both the Comanches and their Kiowa allies knew of Bent's Fort, where Mexicans from New Mexico often encountered Americans using the Santa Fe Trail. But the Bent brothers had created strong fictive kinship bonds with the Cheyenne and Arapaho Indians, who were avowed enemies of the Comanches. This made it difficult for the Comanches to even approach the fort. Extreme situations required unusual actions, however. Sometime that summer the Comanches did the unthinkable; they invited their old enemies to a peace council.[4]

This Indian gathering—which rivaled Sitting Bull's massive encampment at the Little Big Horn in 1876—quickly became a curiosity to the Americans living inside the thick adobe walls at Bent's Fort nearby. George Bent, whose father ran the post, left a marvelous description. The mostly Comanche and Kiowa delegation approached the Cheyennes and Arapahos on foot, carrying the scalps of forty-two "Bow-string Cheyennes," which they humbly offered as a present. Cheyenne leaders shuddered at the sight and asked that such "gifts" be removed and buried—Indians, who did not know each other well, also occasionally struggled at diplomacy. Despite the initial gaffe, peace talks finally convened.

The leaders of the two groups came together under a large arbor, as was common. They sat and smoked, and sat and smoked, without much conversation, for two solid days. Bad feelings still held between the two groups; smoking was the only remedy, as it required the telling of truth, the baring of one's soul. Indian leaders from both sides wanted to judge the sincerity of their opposites.

When the sizing-up had finally ended, the Comanches, Kiowas, Cheyennes, and Arapahos conducted ceremonies that led to fictive kinship adoption. They exchanged presents and created familial bonds. Not long thereafter, the Comanches and Kiowas asked their newly made relatives for guns, as well as blankets and kettles. They, in turn, offered the Cheyennes and Arapahos large numbers of horses. One young Kiowa man bent on displaying his generosity gave three hundred ponies—pride in the ability to give was an Indian virtue. The treaty marked the beginning of a lasting alliance of southern Plains Indians that came as a direct result of the events in San Antonio.

After days of feasting and smoking, the former combatants moved up to Bent's Fort, and the Cheyennes introduced their new relatives, the Comanches and Kiowas, to the Bents. Thereafter, the fort, as well as two other establishments built along the Arkansas River by the Bents (one became known as Adobe Walls), became a source of munitions and supplies. That fall, the Bents took out a license at St. Louis to trade with the Comanches, Kiowas, and Plains Apaches, making the exchanges legal. The Comanches, meanwhile, broke camp to return south, carrying along some guns and munitions that they hoped would prove adequate for the fight against the Anglo-Texans that was sure to follow.[5]

Some Texans assumed that the war with the Plains tribes was over, but this speculation diminished considerably in early August when a Comanche and Kiowa war party numbering at least seven hundred Indians worked its way through the dense thickets and trails that made up the hill country to the west of Austin. Having considerable knowledge of the country, the huge party escaped detection until it reached Gonzales, Texas, eighty miles east of San Antonio. The size of this party and its mobility made it nearly invulnerable.

The mass of Indians rode east. On the morning of August 6, the coastal town of Victoria, Texas, a shipping point established near the mouth of the Guadalupe River, awoke to a distant mirage of horsemen, the line of attackers a quarter of a mile wide, kicking dust and coming on hard. In front were the chiefs in full regalia, the feathers of their headdresses bobbing in the breeze. The sight struck terror in the hearts of the citizens, who ran for cover and for weapons. But the Indians skirted to the left and right, collecting nearly 1,500 valuable animals that were grazing within site of town. Fortunately for the several hundred Victorians, some of whom were Tejanos, the Indians spent most of the afternoon organizing the new herds in plain view of the town.

Hurriedly, the townspeople, collecting themselves, built barricades of wagons and crates and whatever might stop a charge. They watched as bonfires burned that night a mile or so off, in the open country outside of town. The Indians were dancing and building up their courage. The drums would stop occasionally so seasoned warriors could tell stories of their bravery in battle, offering examples for the younger, untested men. As the sun rose, the Comanches charged the town but faced merciless gunfire from well-protected positions. Miraculously, the alerted Victorians, reinforced by outlying settlers, drove the Comanches and Kiowas back. The Texans lost a mere nine men, a surprisingly small figure given the level of combat.[6]

During the remainder of the day, the Indian army marched south and east in an open plain. The warriors found and killed an occasional settler and captured two women.[7] On August 8, they reached the small coastal town of Linnville, established a decade earlier along LaVaca Bay. Linnville sported a customs house, many warehouses, and several dozen frame houses, but as one traveler noted, it also was "the headquarters of a party of robbers," likely the same men who had been marauding in southern Texas for some time. The steamer *Mustang,* fresh from New Orleans, sat at anchor in the bay, preparing to unload its goods.

Fortunately for the residents of the town, the approach to Linnville was treeless, surrounded by prairie in three directions. As the Indian force in full battle array rode ever nearer, the townspeople could see the Comanches, still two miles out and kicking up dust, riding down on the community, which was much smaller than Victoria. Rushing to boats or swimming desperately out to the steamer, the people in town made it out alive. The attackers took out their frustrations on the buildings of Linnville. Parties of warriors set houses on fire and destroyed property. But the warehouses became the most tempting targets. Bolts of cloth were tied to the tails of horses, black top hats replaced feathers, and many a mounted warrior pranced about town holding an umbrella over his head.[8]

After burning Linnville, the party turned northwest, hoping to carry their plunder safely into the hill country. The Anglo-Texans, slowly recovering from the shock, gathered volunteers throughout the interior, coming together from Victoria, Gonzales, Bastrop, and Austin. Many of the same men who had precipitated the Indian war responded, including Burleson and Felix Huston. Near Bastrop, two hundred troops assembled and selected Huston to lead them. They expected to meet the Indian force along Plum Creek, an exit route with good water for stock. Almost immediately news arrived that the Indians were five miles below and coming fast. While the Indians vastly outnumbered the Texans, the raid had netted at least two thousand horses and mules, and many of the Indians, overburdened with loot from the Linnville warehouses, hung back to protect the stolen and heavily laden stock.

As the Comanches came into sight, General Huston ordered his force of roughly two hundred men to dismount and await an expected charge. Instead, the Indians flanked the Texas troops by moving southward and westward. The ranger forces, annoyed at the incompetence and caution of Huston, remounted and pursued. The Comanches—with slow, loaded-down animals—were forced to make a stand near Casa Blanca, where a grove of trees protected them. "They lined the timber and almost literally covered the prairie," one of the rangers later reported. "Decked in all the gaudy trumpery and trimmings which usually constitute a Comanche's warlike attire," the Indians stood their ground. Out front were the chiefs, sporting "huge helmets of buffalo or elk-horns—armed with glistening shields with bow and quivers, with guns and lances and mounted on fleet chargers."[9]

The rangers, carrying long rifles and possibly a few newly introduced Colt revolvers, were better armed. They also fought as units, dividing themselves into two columns and charging the flanks of the Indians. The Comanches soon yielded. A running fight across the Texas hills ensued for over an hour, the Texans seemingly gaining the upper hand but never overrunning the main body of Indians. Ultimately, the Indian force reached a boggy area near present-day San Marcos. Here the Comanches broke up, with small bands collecting what they could and fleeing west into the hills. They had left a path of destruction that ever after was called the "Great Comanche Raid."

The Texas forces, while hardly victorious, celebrated the event as the "Victory at Plum Creek." The rangers recovered one female captive but found the murdered body of another. Roughly thirteen settlers and African American slaves were killed. Hundreds of mules and horses, some still packing goods, fell into the hands of Huston's troops, but the Indians nevertheless carried off the majority of what they had taken in their raiding.

In the hours that followed—somewhat euphoric, as the adrenalin from the fight subsided—General Huston first claimed that his men had dispatched forty Comanches. The numbers escalated as the Texans compared stories. Soon, the casualty figure was sixty, and finally eighty.[10] In reality, the Comanches had carried off the majority of their wounded and dead, so these figures are nothing but inflated estimates. Hamilton P. Bee, no fan of Huston, later quietly reported to the secretary of war: "I heard more men say there were 13 killed than 25. . . . Gen. Huston of course makes it out a second Waterloo."[11]

The Plum Creek fight hardly compared with Napoleon's downfall. It did reveal the vulnerability of Texas settlement patterns, something that would continue into the 1840s and 1850s. Anglo-Texans built their communities along the river valleys, and their scattered and isolated ranches were perfect targets for Comanche raids.

In the aftermath of Plum Creek, cries came from many quarters to squelch the "Indian Menace" once and for all. The *Austin City Gazette* called upon General Huston to raise sixteen hundred men and launch "a war of extermination" against the Plains tribes.[12] The blustering Huston completely agreed, reporting anxiously to the Texas Congress in late September that a recent patrol had discovered a large trail of Comanches. "What should be the only policy pursued towards our savage Indians," he cried out in print, "is utter extermination."[13] Secretary of War Archer immediately appealed to the congress for funds. Unfortunately, Lamar had nothing in the treasury.

Archer's polemics reached new levels as he stated that "it has been most justly remarked by a distinguished patriot of our country, 'that humanity to them [Indians] would be cruelty to ourselves.'"[14]

It remained for the volunteer rangers to carry extermination to the Indians. This was business for Colonel John Moore, who agreed with the animated Huston and quietly organized his volunteer rangers, who now uttered words of revenge. Moore waited several months, collecting information on the whereabouts of the Comanches. Moore had cultivated the Lipan Apaches still in Texas, a handful of Indians who often worked as spies and scouts. Chief Castro, their leader, agreed to join Moore with some seventeen others. The Lipan Apaches, like their ranger brethren, rode for booty and revenge. They mostly were at war with the Comanches.

Moore, who (unlike Huston) seldom publicized his exploits or even reported them to government officials, recruited his men from the saloons and settlements in and about Austin and Bastrop. The Austin papers helped by revealing his plan to invade Comanche land. The men who joined Moore knew his vindictive spirit and his willingness to engage the Indians, even many hundred at a time. They also knew his reputation for successfully bringing back goods and livestock, which paid handsomely for the venture. This was a critical attraction, for the republic's offer to pay salaries to militia troops was as hollow as was its treasury.

Under terms, then, that guaranteed nothing other than hardship and possible plunder, Moore and his men headed up the Brazos River in early October. They chose their time to ride knowing that Indians in villages never expected a winter attack. Turning west at the old Waco town along the central Brazos, they passed through the Lampasas River valley and finally struck the Colorado way out on the plains.[15] Then a fierce norther—a snowstorm driven by high winds—descended upon them. Moore refused to turn back, even after one ranger died of exposure. Suddenly, on the night of October 23, the Lipan scouts returned, having found a large Comanche village nestled along the south bank of the Colorado. Moore's rangers quietly stashed their supplies and moved undetected to within two hundred yards of the encampment. Just as dawn broke, the ninety Texans and the seventeen Lipan Apaches fell on the village and tore it apart.

The Comanche village sat at the foot of a bluff, making it ideal for a winter location but difficult (indeed, impossible) to escape from. As the Comanches came out of their tepees, many were gunned down at point-blank range, the rangers firing their rifles first and then turning to pistols, mostly single-shot weapons that worked well at close range. According to Moore, "the bodies of [Indian] men, women and children were to be seen on every hand wounded, dying and dead." The carnage even expanded to the banks of the river, where unarmed Indians tried to swim across. Moore ordered his cavalry to shoot them in the back.

In roughly twenty minutes, Moore's troops killed 140 Comanches, taking 35 captives, mostly small children. But the total numbers may have been twice that, since many had perished in the cold waters of the Colorado as they tried to swim to safety. Further, the rangers then burned everything in the camp, including tepees and food. Starvation faced the survivors. As an indication of the extent of the slaughter, Moore had but two wounded rangers, both of whom recovered. Moore's actions constituted a massacre of the highest order. To pay the rangers, Moore collected more than five hundred horses—worth easily $15,000, or $150 per man (nearly a year's wages)—and many bundles of pelts and food, which he later sold to the highest bidders in Austin.[16] Anglo-Texans in Austin saluted Moore's returning rangers, as the expedition exemplified the "war of extermination" that Lamar had hoped to unleash upon the west.

Seeing the potential for payoffs that could exceed $100 per man, excited volunteer rangers sprang into action all across Texas come the spring of 1841. Moore demonstrated on several occasions that rangers risked little when attacking Indian villages; very few instances occurred during which rangers died in the actions, and the poorly armed Indians had to protect their families, making them vulnerable. A ranger could make more in one good raid than a rancher or a cotton planter would pay in a year for labor.

George M. Dolson scrambled to put the next command of rangers into the field. Dolson, using Indian scouts, marched his charges up the Colorado River in late March 1841 and found yet another unsuspecting Comanche village. Dolson boasted later that as he attacked, "nothing could stop the impetuosity of my men," and he watched as "the Indians broke in every direction." Shooting, looting, and burning followed, as usual. While this Comanche camp was much smaller than the one that Moore had assaulted—Indian casualties numbered only a few dozen—yet another southern Comanche band had in the process lost all their food, their shelter, and many animals.[17]

Dolson's success encouraged two more ranger expeditions to leave Austin in late May 1941, bound for glory and plunder. Although they encountered only a few scattered parties of Comanches, more ranger units followed in July and August. Captain John C. Hays, slowly acquiring fame as a Texas Indian fighter, led one unit well into the headwaters of the Llano and Frio rivers. In early August, Hays's Lipan Apache spies found a Comanche village. Being somewhat prepared this time, Comanche warriors sent off their women and children, and the rangers took several hours to carry the camp. Somewhat indignant over this state of affairs, since they had managed to take only a few scalps, the rangers had to settle for a mere five hundred horses, which they trailed back to San Antonio.[18]

The war expanded to northern Texas as well that spring. Ranger companies, flushed with the hope of duplicating Moore's success, formed up in Franklin, Texas, where Eli Chandler commanded a party of rangers, and near Fort Inglish just south of Red River. As Chandler's men charged into what was described as a "full" town along the upper Trinity River, the Indians fled, "abandoning every vestige of their property." Again, plunder seemed to be as important as scalps; Chandler carefully documented the collection of "9 mules, 23 head of horses, some powder, lead, axes, peltry," all worth some $3,000.[19]

By summer, ranger patrols had become so lawless that they cared little whom they attacked. In early June, Colonel Thomas Smith's ranger force shot up a camp along the upper Navasota River, a locale that was close to Anglo settlements. After killing five men, Smith belatedly determined that they must have been "some northern tribe," since they were "dressed like Americans."[20] The carnage continued into the summer as volunteers formed under General E. H. Tarrant in late May 1841. Tarrant wanted to find the large Indian village that many sources had placed somewhere along the several branches of the Trinity. Rangers realized that this encampment, filled with Wichitas, Cherokees, Shawnees, Kickapoos, and Caddos, would contain considerable plunder.

Tarrant first searched the main branches of the Trinity but found only the remains of what had once been prosperous Indian communities—likely the villages that Rusk had burned. Moving south, the party of roughly a hundred rangers crossed and recrossed various forks of the Trinity, scouring the rolling prairies. But they found little indication that a large Indian community existed anywhere in the region. Like Moore, however, Tarrant refused to give up. He turned west, searching the southwestern branches of the Trinity River, and then south, stumbling onto a small town along a pristine creek that likely flowed into the Brazos.

Just below present-day Fort Worth, Texas, this community looked as though it could easily be taken. Tarrant ordered his men quickly to come on line, and the troops charged headlong into the town, overrunning it "in an instant." The rangers offered little quarter. Indians, surprised and bewildered, fled in every direction, "scarcely having time to leave their lodges before we were in the village; several were shot in attempting to make their escape." Most were unarmed and shot in the back. While discussions had occurred among the rangers relative to the appropriateness of killing unarmed Indians, Tarrant's men generally held to the views plainly stated in the official report: "It was not the wish of General Tarrant to take any prisoners."[21]

The mounted troopers pressed on, and as the Indians fled down the creek, other towns came into view. Tarrant had uncovered a complex of communities. Most of the men were busy in the west hunting bison, the women were tending their fields, and some children were playing among the grass lodges and tepees. The few men who remained, mostly old and infirm, rushed to their weapons. The rangers by this time had exhausted their horses and pursued on foot. "From this time, there was no distinction of villages, but one continued village," the official report concluded. As the firing became more intense, the attackers paid less attention to Indian women and children (whom "we suffered to escape if they wished") and concentrated on the men, regardless of age, "who neither asked, gave, or received any quarter."

Soon, Tarrant (somewhat like Custer in a later age) recognized that he had taken on more than his force could handle. The complex housed many different bands; it was indeed the center of activity for the so-called hostile Indians that Córdova and Flores had sought refuge among. The many tribes represented there included Caddos, Wichitas, and a host of immigrant Indians. In all, Tarrant counted 225 lodges, but others existed beyond the view of the rangers; the entire community held perhaps as many as ten thousand people.

Tarrant was amazed at the sophistication of the residents. In one town, the rangers found a complete blacksmith shop. In others, "all manner of farming utensils of the best quality, except ploughs," were discovered in and near the fields. But seeing the Indian opposition finally get organized—and knowing that his men were more inclined to plunder than fight—Tarrant ordered a retreat. As Tarrant's rangers headed home, the sounds of clanking brass kettles revealed a column of horses and mules loaded with axes, metal hoes, buffalo robes, firearms, and even two "ladies saddles." The general counted a dozen Indians killed in the first town, but his troops shot many more as they ran ahead of him. The rangers had one casualty.[22]

At least one Indian account of this action has survived. One of the towns—probably one of the last ones attacked—contained mostly Caddos of the Anadarko band. They had as chief the young, charismatic José Maria, an Indian leader who would make a substantial mark in Texas history. Born at Nacogdoches about 1800, José Maria received his name from a Spanish missionary even though he did not adopt the faith. During Tarrant's onslaught, José Maria rallied his men and halted the attack.

While parading in front of his warriors, the Caddo leader took a ball in his chest, but it came from a nearly spent cartridge and, rather miraculously, bounced off a bone. Refusing to even dismount, José Maria rallied his people to defend their community, an action that seemingly turned the tide of the battle. Acts such as this were what determined Indian leadership, and José Maria's stature rose accordingly; after that day his bravery was never questioned.[23]

Texas Rangers made one last effort to eradicate José Maria and his kind in late July. George B. Erath took command of at least a hundred men from Robertson and Milam counties for one last campaign before winter set in. A few other adventurers joined him, including the still relatively unseasoned, flamboyant Felix Huston, who seemed always to be looking for a fight. Heading west, the expedition found several evacuated towns but no occupied ones. Skirmishes followed with a few Cherokees and Kickapoos, but as the first week of August came and went, the party failed to find José Maria's town or any others.

Erath's relative failure confirmed the success of General Tarrant in making José Maria and members of the other nearby immigrant bands realize the vulnerability of their towns. All these people had fled farther west because they knew that the rangers would return.[24] While Captain Erath ultimately returned home without a scalp or even a bison hide to his credit, he had fulfilled the general policy of the Texas Republic. Fear of attack had led the Indians to abandon central Texas, which was the principal goal of ethnic cleansing.

The dozen ranger expeditions of 1839–1841 were credited as having been immensely successful. President Lamar confirmed the ultimate goal in his October 1841 orders to Captain Hays, some of the last that he would issue as president: "It is the desire of the government," Lamar wrote, utilizing the language of ethnic cleansing, "to have the entire western country cleared of the enemy."[25] Ethnic cleansing had become state policy. A gracious nation paid high tribute to the actions of the rangers, and a gracious president lauded them for carrying out what he perceived as his just policy. While the legislature of the Texas Republic had not passed laws or decrees sanctioning such behavior, it had failed to do so simply because it lacked the resources to promote wholesale ethnic cleansing. The majority of members certainly approved of the ranger initiatives.

By 1842, so few Indians could be found in the central valleys of the Colorado, Brazos, and Trinity rivers of central Texas that ranger units could no longer be compensated for their efforts with plunder, although the thousands of dollars' worth of livestock and goods stolen from Indians is one of the most lucrative examples of looting in the history of the American frontier. Furthermore, the "cleansing" had opened fertile valleys for Texas towns such as Dallas, Waco, and Fredricksburg, all of which would appear shortly thereafter.

The legacy of Lamar's war would carry Texas into new decades of violence; the lessons learned by the rangers, the glories of their "victories," the fireside stories told of them, and the trophies—human scalps especially—that they brought back only solidified the Texas creed, further entrenching their hatred for people of color. The only circumstances that prevented the utter destruction of more Plains Indian bands was the retreat of these people farther into the interior and the fact that the growing scarcity of available targets of opportunity brought a temporary hiatus to ranger campaigns as President Lamar left office in October 1841.

For the Comanches, Kiowas, Wichitas, Caddos, and the few immigrant bands that had joined them, the efforts to seek revenge for the council house massacre had led to disaster. These people had had little idea of how vulnerable they were in their towns or of how efficient ranger companies could be when using Indian scouts to find them and surprise them. Many a surviving villager had fled west in fear and humiliation and sorrow, driven onward by the wails of women and children along the bloody, tear-filled trail that led away from their homeland.

13

THE FAILURE OF
WELL-INTENDED EFFORTS

Sam Houston had battled his way back into Texas politics by the summer of 1841. The former president had broken with Rusk, and he seldom spoke with his old friends at Nacogdoches. He took the expulsion of the Cherokees personally. He knew whom to blame: Lamar and his government seemed totally out of control, with rangers marauding this way and that. In the pursuit of military victories Lamar had bankrupted the country. He had printed promissory notes by the bushel, and by 1841 the notes were worth a mere three cents on the dollar. The Texas Republic had exhausted itself in clearing central Texas of Indians. Many Texans, particularly those in the west, applauded this policy; others were no longer sure that it had been good policy.

The critics of Lamar's policy were mostly men and women who lived in eastern counties and saw the need to consolidate control over what land the government claimed. This was a touchy question: where was the boundary of West Texas? The town of Austin was still in an unprotected area, as were the regions of the central Brazos, the old Indian community of Waco, and the falls of the river. Jonathan Bird had constructed Bird's Fort (near present-day Dallas) in the fall of 1841, and a general migration into that region of fertile prairie had occurred, but the fort had been abandoned when in August the land was granted to W. P. Peters as a colony, one of the last acts of President Lamar. The southern boundary was another matter. More aggressive politicians argued for the Rio Grande, while in reality there was little law and order south of San Antonio and virtually none in the Nueces River valley.

But what Texas had conquered was a good land. The valleys of the Colorado, Brazos, and Trinity rivers had flooded regularly, leaving alluvial soil for miles on either side. Occasional groves of post oaks, other hardwoods, and pine crept into these valleys, but the trees had to compete with woody brush such as mesquite. Mesquite had never been a problem in pre-Spanish Texas, as birds could not transport the heavy pods out of the arroyos where they thrived. Cattle and horses, introduced by Europeans, ate the pods, however, and the seeds often survived in their dung, spreading the plant quickly. The loss of an Indian population in the valleys also played a role, as the Native peoples had used fire to control brush. By 1841, the republic had nearly secured the best agricultural land in Texas (given the farming technology at the time). Much of the land west of settlement would be useful mostly for ranching.

Many Texans realized that the Indians had been driven far west of these conquered regions, and they considered the advantages of consolidating this new Texas. The people of San Augustine had seemingly demonstrated that sentiment in 1840, when they elected Houston—a politician who had promoted negotiation—to the senate in absentia. Houston had agreed to serve even though he was distracted by his new wife, one Margaret Lea of Alabama, a young women of twenty-one. Houston's lack of concentration may have been a godsend, for it kept him generally out of the fray. Lamar's policy of ethnic cleansing had led to a fit of greed. The most dramatic demonstration of his ambition came during the summer, when the outgoing president launched what he hoped would be his most important legacy—the invasion of New Mexico.[1]

Lamar was convinced that New Mexicans would welcome Texans and that he could extend the border of the republic westward a thousand miles. It seemed like a grand idea. Setting out in June 1841, this celebrated folly attracted 270 heavily armed adventurers, commanded by Colonel Hugh McLeod, of council house massacre fame. Still showing support for the Texas cause—or at least its capitalistic component— a leading Tejano citizen of San Antonio, José Antonio Navarro, joined the party. Unfortunately, the expedition became lost near Palo Duro Canyon, suffered terribly from a lack of water, and soon fought with Comanches. Some turned back, while the majority eventually surrendered to Mexicans well east of Santa Fe.

Rumors regarding the disaster took time to surface in Texas. Very little was known of the fate of McLeod and his men during the last few months of Lamar's administration. The prisoners, chained together with leg irons, had to endure a virtual death march south into Chihuahua and then east to the coast. Rumors of the vicious treatment of the prisoners, who languished in the dungeon of Perote at Vera Cruz, slowly spread through the republic after Christmas. They posed serious problems for the newly elected president, Sam Houston, who came into office in December 1841.[2]

Houston's return was not appreciated by all. The western districts, poorly populated and still harassed by Indians, wanted Burnet, Houston's opponent. The election had been a grudge match to say the least. Burnet charged Houston with drunkenness, which was hardly a lie. But Houston struck back, laying out Burnet's land deals and his overspending of the republic's money while vice president.[3] Burnet demanded satisfaction, claiming that his honor was at stake. This time Houston, who had to prove nothing regarding his honor, laughed off the challenge. In the end, Houston won because Texas desperately needed a change. It had to consolidate its boundaries and make peace with the western tribes. Drunkard or not, Houston would try to achieve those ends. The more populated eastern districts supported him almost two to one.

For Houston, the first year back in office proved more than frustrating. During the last days of the previous administration, Lamar had entertained a curious offer from General Mariano Arista, the Mexican commander at Matamoros, who had suggested an armistice with Texas so that he might campaign against the hated Comanches. Lamar had dabbled with this proposal, not saying no, but then Mexican leaders learned of the presidential order for a campaign against New Mexico. This outraged the Mexicans. General Santa Anna, back in power, ordered a brief nuisance raid on San Antonio; seven hundred mostly mounted Mexican troops under General Rafael Vásquez seized the town for several days in early March 1842. They carried a number of San Antonians back to Mexico—an insult if nothing else.

The raid caused panic among some Texans and righteous indignation among others. The "War Hawks" in the Texas Congress forced Houston to act. The president ordered General Alexander Somervell, a short stub of a man, to command the assembling volunteers at San Antonio. Men of all kinds came pouring into town, some shoeless, most horseless, some seeking adventure, and others of the criminal sort, wishing only to sack Mexican towns and villages. As Houston had hoped, Somervell acted indecisively. Soon, considerable looting of Tejano stores in San Antonio, coupled with out-and-out insubordination, broke up the volunteers before they could march on Mexico and start a major war.[4]

Even with this singular failure and the fact that the Texas debt stood at $7,000,000, warmongering in Texas became an obsession. The Texas Congress—without money or much sanity but angered by the mistreatment of McLeod and his men, who were by then rotting in Vera Cruz—called for the annexation of northern Mexico and, in late June, passed a bill (over Houston's veto) calling up one-third of the country's young men for military service. The congress agreed to sell ten million acres of public land to finance the conquest of Mexico.[5]

Houston could hardly ignore his congress, especially after the Mexican general Adrian Woll and fourteen hundred troops again captured San Antonio in September. Houston once again summoned Somervell to organize and lead the volunteers but hoped that the Texas general would remain north of the Nueces River. But as the army grew to 750 men, even Somervell realized that he would have to act. His volunteers had taken on an identity of their own; had he refused to march, the troops would have left him.

The voluntary force that turned south on November 25 put even some ranger units to shame for its ugly element. A few of the men were legitimate farmers or ranchers, but most were not. A number had just arrived in Texas. As one put it, he wanted to experience "that unextinguishable love of chivalric immortal fame" that came with campaigning. A few of the officers, such as Captain William S. Fisher (prominent in destroying the Cherokees), had led troops in several early battles. Anyone who agreed to serve with Fisher would, he said, be rewarded by "the richness of the land and the fatness thereof." Then there was Ewen Cameron, known as the "Attila" of Texas, a huge man who ran a large gang of horse thieves out of Goliad. What made Cameron unusual was that among the three hundred to four hundred criminals in his party, he stuck out. The gangs saw the Somervell expedition as a chance to expand their stealing operations.[6]

The placid Somervell had little chance of controlling this mob. But with his men swept up in the war hysteria, he had to either lead the army south or watch it leave on its own. Crossing the Nueces this time, the Texas volunteers pushed south to Laredo. Along the way, mutiny and threats of violence were as common as carried-out orders; tempers flared, and challenges were common. Marching into town on December 8, the army was greeted by the alcalde of Laredo. Most of the local men had fled, taking what property they could (especially horses, mules, and cattle); women and children danced in the streets, trying to show appreciation for the desperate-looking "liberators." Somervell placed the Texas flag in the town square and ordered his army to camp in a nearby ravine.

Early that evening and into the next morning, small groups of Texans left camp, most without orders, and returned to Laredo. Their numbers soon approached two hundred. They looted the commissary stores first but found little in them. Then they turned to the remaining townsfolk, almost all women. They used logs to break down doors of private residences, herded the occupants out, and forced them to turn over all their valuables. Many of the Mexican women were disrobed, some in public. Others were attacked inside residences. None of the official Anglo documents mention rape, but many women were abused. Thomas Jefferson Green, one of the most flagrant violators, was overheard on several occasions saying: "Rake them down, boys; rake them down."[7]

Some troops, disgusted with this activity, left for home. Others helped Somervell confiscate at least part of the loot; most of it was clothing, stacked to the height of a good-sized house. Many of the garments were women's dresses and underwear, of the sort "that our blushing muses forbids us to catalogue," recorded one embarrassed soldier.[8] A number of looters heard of Somervell's ambush and hid their take in the bushes. All the general could do was try to find a fight for the troops to move them away from Laredo.

The army was slowly breaking up as a result of the disorder and looting. The 500 who remained followed Somervell south to Guerrero, where more pillaging occurred. Here a mutiny erupted in which 189 men followed Fisher, Cameron, and Green into the Mexican town of Mier. These were the most desperate of men, led by the most depraved officers. They ignored Somervell when he tried to stop their depredations. Fortunately, General Pedro de Ampudia ended the rapine and violence by forcing the Texans to surrender after a vicious fight in the center of town that began on the morning of Christmas Day and lasted into the afternoon hours. After the forces briefly escaped and were recaptured, Santa Anna ordered a peculiar but perhaps appropriate "trial"; the 170-odd prisoners were ordered to select beans from a pot. The 17 who drew a black bean were promptly shot.[9]

The Mexican invasions of San Antonio in 1842 and the Mier fiasco, which continued into the spring of 1843, nearly paralyzed Texas. Many Texans in the western districts blamed Houston, who seemingly abandoned the Mier captives. The congress too seemed outraged, directly challenging the president's authority. Yet as eastern and central Texas became more settled, Houston found political support among an increasing number of Texans who wanted stability. With support emerging among these constituents, the president tried to demilitarize the south and rebuild his policy of negotiation, often as his unruly congress did whatever it could to promote war. Houston's efforts to convert the hearts and minds of Texans started with his inaugural address in December 1841.

In this speech, Houston avoided criticizing individuals, but he did ask the congress pointedly if all the money spent to exterminate Indians had made Texas more secure. "The hope of obtaining peace by means of war," Houston said, "has, hitherto, proved utterly fallacious." The new president proposed building trading posts where his agents could create reciprocal commercial relationships with Indian leaders.[10] In the days following, Houston vetoed several bills, one of which would have authorized the payment of salaries to "minute men" (volunteer rangers). Such units, he informed the congress, "signally failed to achieve the object" of protection.[11] Rangers caused more trouble than they were worth. Lamar's "policy of 'extermination' by war," Houston concluded, had failed.[12]

Throughout the summer of 1842, Houston stuck with this theme: Lamar's policy of extermination had failed. The president—without any authority from the congress—even issued "licenses" to trade with the Indians; three went to Ethan Stroud, Abel Warren, and Thomas S. Torrey, all supporters of Houston's policy.[13] These traders hired some members of the immigrant tribes to work for them, including Delaware Jim and the Shawnee Jim Shaw. Mixed-bloods with some knowledge of the geopolitics of the region, these men acted as agents for Texas. Houston hoped they could begin a dialogue that would lead to peace. The first opportunity came when several small refugee bands of Texas Indians (who were then living in Indian Territory) agreed to listen.[14]

U.S. agents in Indian Territory helped arrange the meetings that followed between Texas authorities and the Texas refugee Indians, since fears persisted that various bands in Indian Territory might readily join Vásquez or Woll. U.S. dragoons also marched up the Washita River, and the officers warned the most disgruntled Indians that interference in the conflict between Texas and Mexico would bring retaliation. Just the same, while some agreed to listen, not all did. The hothead Seminole Wild Cat (or, as he was known in the Muskogee language, Coacoochee) had just reached Indian

Territory after surrendering to none other than Lieutenant William Tecumseh Sherman in Florida in November 1841. Wild Cat was a young, dynamic Indian leader. While at council with officers of the U.S. Army, he had once proclaimed, "I would rather be killed by white men in Florida than die in Arkansas." While Wild Cat had avoided Arkansas, he also refused "to participate in the smoking" with Texans, even though he had never been in Texas.[15]

Despite Wild Cat's intransigence, talks did occur as Texan James Logan met some Wichita leaders in early June 1842.[16] Two months later, commissioners Stroud, Joseph Durst, and Leonard Williams met Caddo leaders and some Cherokees, Kickapoos, and Biloxi Indians near Holland Coffee's old trading post on the Red River. The Texans hired the Cherokee mixed-blood Jesse Chisholm to bring in Comanche leaders, but to Chisholm's chagrin, they refused.[17] While the talks helped, when the commissioners invited ninety rangers from Fannin County, Texas to accompany them, both Indians and the U.S. agents balked. By fall, Indian agents F. W. Armstrong and A. M. M. Upshaw discouraged Texans of any sort from crossing the Red River.[18]

Houston seemed encouraged by his Indian policy. He wrote to the indomitable John H. Moore demanding that the colonel send any Comanche prisoners taken during Lamar's war to the western trading houses that were being constructed, to be returned to their people. Unfortunately, many Indian women captives, especially younger ones, had been sold by rangers into servitude in Texas homes. They would be difficult to recover.

Then Houston penned conciliatory letters to various chiefs whom he knew personally, in particular Big Mush and Linney. He stressed that "bad men"—meaning Lamar—had caused all the trouble. The "chiefs whose council was wicked" were all gone, and the Indians once again could return to Texas.

A policy emerged from these meager beginnings. Houston believed that Caddos and Wichitas as well as immigrant Delawares, Shawnees, and Cherokees would make excellent buffers to protect the frontier from Comanches—hardly a new idea. The president personally pledged to ship a hundred Mackinaw blankets to the old Waco village to be used as presents to attract various leaders and their people back into Texas.[19] Houston understood reciprocity. He would reinforce the leadership capabilities of the Indian chiefs, who could redistribute the presents and create obligations among their young people. This, in turn, would give them influence over the warriors of their bands. Yet the difficult question of where these Indians would live had not been addressed.

Another issue that concerned Houston was depredations, by both Indians and Anglos. In a long letter to his commissioners he stressed that raiding had to be outlawed on both sides. He proposed the creation of a line separating the combatants, with a system of passports to govern travel. Obviously, ranger attacks had to be stopped. Houston concluded: "Any White man trying to raise a raiding party without the permission of the President was to be charged with a felony." If local courts would not try the man, the president would court-martial the offenders.[20]

No provisions of this sort existed in Texas law. The republic's legislature already had reservations regarding Houston's policies; that it would agree to the court-martial of rangers seemed farfetched. When the president went before his congress in December, however, he pressed these very points. "If individuals assume the right of projecting campaigns," Houston argued, "they are liable not only to thwart the designs of government but by a diversion of a portion of its means bring on disaster." The legislature must establish civil rule "for the purpose of suppressing insurrectionary acts." The policy of his predecessor Lamar, Houston continued—which had settled upon the "Extermination of all Indians within our boundaries"—had produced a culture of violence. For every attack by rangers, Texas could expect Indian retaliation. The cycle must be broken; a boundary line would secure the peaceful development of Texas. In effect, Houston wanted law and order.[21]

Members of the legislature responded to the president in January 1843. The congress accepted Houston's trading houses, realizing that they would prove helpful in collecting information about the state of affairs in the west. Nevertheless, the Texas Congress wholly disagreed with the president on military policy. It passed yet another militia law, appropriating $20,000 for defense. This one called for the recruitment of six companies of rangers, each of fifty-six men. Growing weary, Houston rejected the militia measure.[22] He wanted peace, not offensive Indian war.

The U.S. government tried to help by sending Pierce Mason Butler to Texas. Butler, as a young military officer, had demonstrated considerable leadership during several campaigns in the first Seminole war in 1836. Two years later, he was elected governor of South Carolina, and then he was rewarded again by being selected as Cherokee Indian agent in the West. Ambitious, courageous—while severely wounded at the battle of Churubusco in 1847 he continued to lead his troops—Butler was forty-five years of age when he reached the council grounds along Tawakoni Creek (just south of the old Waco village) in mid-February. Confident that solutions existed, he unfortunately found only a handful of Indians in attendance.

The largest group included twenty Delaware and Shawnee families, relatives of Delaware Jim and Jim Shaw, whom Houston had already "converted" to the cause. Their families had a request; they asked for permission to settle in the Brazos River valley. Needing these intermediaries, Houston granted them a spot on Bosque River, a nearby western tributary of the Brazos that was heavily wooded and untouched by Anglo settlement. Pleased with the answer, Jesse Chisholm, Louis Sanchez, Jim Shaw, and Delaware Jim then organized trading/diplomatic parties that visited the western tribes. Everywhere, they found opposition.

Houston nevertheless persevered. He appointed George W. Terrell the new commissioner of Indian affairs and sent him into the west. Terrell was an old friend, having served as Houston's attorney general during Houston's brief tenure as governor of Tennessee in 1828. Terrell could be trusted to spend as little as possible and keep his mouth shut. Upon Terrell's arrival at Tawakoni Creek, he found a discouraging situation: "There is great distrust on the part of all the Indians towards our people."[23]

A desperate Houston ordered Terrell to negotiate with whoever appeared. The president had become convinced that he could end the fighting along the western edge of settlement to the betterment of everyone. Nearly half a dozen councils followed, starting in the spring of 1843 and lasting into the fall of 1844, when Houston's term as president expired. Houston supported these negotiations with money that had been appropriated by the Texas Congress for defense.

The first discussions began innocently at the Tawakoni Creek council house that had been built near the old Waco town. Sitting down mostly with the Delaware and Shawnee interpreters and their relatives—about thirty in all—Terrell negotiated the Treaty of Tawakoni Creek on March 28, 1843. Following Houston's lead, Terrell encouraged these men to convince other Indians to return to Texas. The agenda even included discussion of a line separating Indian lands from those belonging to Anglo-Texans, but given the poor turnout, the drawing of such a line was impossible. Linney signed the treaty for the Shawnee even though he had no intention of returning to Texas. His Shawnees had had enough of Texas and Texans; he had come mostly for the presents. At least one new convert did step forward: José Maria, the Anadarko chief, also signed, representing most western Caddos.[24]

Although several Indians followed Terrell back to Washington, Texas (which was temporarily the capital after the Mexican invasions), where they met with Houston, the entire effort had accomplished very little.[25] Butler wryly wrote to U.S. officials that "but few Indians" had attended the council. The Texans had picked a horrible time of year, characterized by cold weather and rain. Worse, Tawakoni Creek was now too far down the Brazos River because the rangers had pushed the village Indians nearly two hundred miles beyond the old Waco town. Butler concluded that the United States had an obligation to "exercise a control" over the Plains tribes. He started planning his own council to be held on the Red River in November. Butler laid the groundwork by courting the same Delaware, Shawnee, Cherokee, and Caddo leaders who had been at Tawakoni Creek.[26]

Butler had high hopes. But after making friends with the Waco leader Acaquash— the only Waco who had attended the March discussions—the U.S. Cherokee agent had learned that Texans had driven these people from their old village on the central Brazos some fifteen years before. Acaquash seemed pessimistic: "he feared that the Tomahawk, if buried, would soon be ploughed up again." Jim Shaw and Jesse Chisholm confirmed this attitude. Wichitas hated Texans. They even believed some Choctaw Indians who had told them that Houston's blankets (which had been distributed as presents) had been infected with smallpox. But the Comanches proved the most obdurate. "The bones of their brothers that had been massacred at San Antonio," they told Jim Shaw, "had appeared in the Road and obstructed their passage." They would not attend any council with Texans![27]

If this information discouraged Houston, he failed to show it. He continued to create a Texas Indian bureau, hiring Joseph C. Eldridge to act as superintendent under Terrell and sending him into the far west. Upon reaching the council ground near the old Waco town, Eldridge spent considerable time talking with the Delawares and Shawnees living nearby. John Conner, Jim Shaw, and Jim Second Eye were all acquainted with the Plains Indians and, for a price, would lead the new superintendent to them. After recruiting Thomas J. Torrey, who was active in the Indian trade and had opened a store near the council house in late May 1843, Eldridge agreed to his guides' terms and with a well-stocked commissary headed up the Brazos River.

Pushing north, Eldridge and Torrey had productive conversations with José Maria, who had just moved his village to the upper Trinity River, just west of Bird's old fort. The two Texans then spoke with Acaquash, who convinced them to travel even farther west to the Wichita and Comanche villages, a dangerous mission. Not sure how they would be received, the small delegation left for the plains on June 3.[28]

Terrell had returned several Wichita prisoners to their people some months before, and Eldridge and Torrey hoped that this gesture of good faith would be reciprocated. Acaquash soon joined the group, which helped even more; he directed them to the main Wichita community of sixty to seventy houses. Before reaching the community, the Texans passed through "about one hundred acres of corn, beans, melons, and pumpkins" in the bottomland of the Trinity River.

The town seemed surprisingly quiet as the party approached—too quiet, in fact. Suddenly, as Eldridge related, "in a few minutes our ears were greeted with the most terrific screaming and yelling together with the noise of drums and fifes." The noise was coming from the tree-and-brush-lined riverbank, where most of the people had hidden. At a signal, the aging Wichita chief Kechikaroqua, at the head of 150 warriors, lurched out of the woods. The Wichitas rode "in circles around us at the full speed of their horses, beating their drums and blowing their thrill whistles or fifes." This, as it turned out, was a greeting, but not a common one. The Wichitas wished to show the Texans what they could have done.

In council, Eldridge and Torrey discovered that Kechikaroqua spoke for all the farming communities nearby. Leaders of the Waco, Tawakoni, and smaller Kichai and Anadarko villages all listened attentively to his address. Kechikaroqua declared that "the ground upon which you sit is my ground, the water of which you drank is my water, and the meat of which you have eaten was mine." While Kechikaroqua said he could have annihilated the Texans many years before and killed the delegation that sat before him, he had not. But the "white man became strong, then he killed my people, [and] took our land." Kechikaroqua expressed joy over learning that Houston wanted them to move back to Texas. The chief then asked for powder and lead balls, something the Texans could hardly refuse. The Texans then asked for assistance in reaching the Comanches, who were some 250 miles farther to the west.[29]

The delegation left for the Comanche villages on July 5, passing more Wichita and Kichai towns along the Cache Creek of Red River. They departed with some trepidation; rumors suggested that a Comanche party had just returned from Matamoros, where they supposedly had made peace with the Mexicans—and worse, they had brought back smallpox, which, as Eldridge noted, "carried them off by the hundreds." This was definitely not safe ground for a small party of Texans. Well out on the plains, the Texans finally found the Comanche village of Pahayuco, a major chief. But the chief was gone; the second chief promptly seized the men and placed them in his lodge.

Eldridge and Torrey decided to look around a bit before Pahayuco returned. The camp of several hundred tepees was entirely different from the Wichita town, being spread over half a mile of open prairie. A small creek nearby provided water for the huge horse herd and the people. When Eldridge started walking toward the other end of camp, however, the second chief stopped him; "it was not good," he said and made a scalping motion with his finger. Some Comanches were in mourning and had separated themselves from Pahayuco's lodge group; others seemed friendly, even thronging into the Anglo camp. Conner and Shaw, who had led them to the Comanches, were not happy, though; some Kickapoos and Cheyennes, the latter likely working for the Bents, had recently been in camp and had exchanged goods for many serviceable mules and hides.

When Pahayuco finally arrived, the parlaying got under way—or at least, so Eldridge assumed. Pahayuco greeted the Texans but said nothing at first. He lay on a robe and was fussed over by his three wives. They took off his hunting shirt, his leggings, and his moccasins. He then went off to council with a group of warriors, a meeting to which the Texans were not invited; it went on into the late evening hours. A good hundred yards from the discussions, Eldridge could see that many of the warriors were "excited and violent in their gesticulations and manners." The Texans learned that the warriors were relatives of those slain at San Antonio, and they wanted to kill the Texas delegation.

Acaquash rose to the defense of the Texas party, arguing that the chief in command in 1840 was not Houston, who now wanted peace. The debate was not yet resolved when the sun came up, and the discussions continued. The situation worsened when a delegation of Wichitas appeared, informing the Comanches that their people were sick, doubtless with smallpox, and they blamed the Texans. Finally, by midafternoon, Pahayuco made his intentions known. He was a powerful man, standing above six feet tall, a bit portly but commanding. Eldridge had liked him from the start, describing him as having a "pleasing expression of countenance" and being "full of good humor and joviality." Fortunately, Eldridge had been right; Pahayuco ruled that the Texans should live and agreed to listen to them the next day.

Once in council, the elders and the chief sat quietly while the Texans, using Shaw and Conner to interpret, assured the Comanches that Houston could be trusted and that the notorious bad men of Texas were gone. To show good faith, Eldridge also returned two Comanche children who had been taken by Moore in 1840. A grandfather came forward and embraced his granddaughter "with flowing tears." While this helped break the ice, few Comanches—especially the young men—believed the Texans. Pahayuco even refused to travel east when asked for future councils.

The chief, defiantly hospitable as was always the case with Comanches, clearly wanted more time to judge the sincerity of the now, supposedly, good Texans. In a display of considerable political importance, he even refused to smoke with Eldridge and Torrey when the council began. But Pahayuco did allow one concession; he brought forward the "Alamo Council Pipe," which obviously had not been with the delegation massacred at San Antonio in 1840. This special pipe had been used at San Antonio, likely for many decades, in the negotiation process. To the Indians it likely possessed considerable powers that forced the speakers to tell the truth. Although Pahayuco brought the pipe forward, he stayed on the periphery of the council chamber, allowing the elders to smoke it with the Texans.[30]

Finally, after all the formalities, Pahayuco spoke. He indicated that he would be willing to make a treaty with Texas, but that it would take some time. Of utmost importance was the need to speak with the leaders of the other Penateka bands; "all the chiefs of my several bands must be present that there may be no lies spoken on my side," Pahayuco said. Meanwhile, he agreed to take Eldridge's words to the other Penateka leaders and see what they thought. The entire tribe would winter on the Clear Fork of the Brazos, some 250 miles above the old Waco town—a safe distance from prowling rangers—and the Texans could send runners to the Comanches there.

Given the earlier threats by the Comanche warriors, Eldridge thought Pahayuco's speech a good one. There was division to be sure, since many younger warriors were still "burning with revenge for the wrongs done them at San Antonio." Others from other tribes—Wichitas, Caddos, and many different immigrant groups—also plotted to keep up the war. Yet Eldridge had faith in Pahayuco and in his "friendly disposition." However, the Texas delegation left with no answer to the question of to what extent this man's opinions would be accepted by others.

Upon their return to Bird's Fort, Eldridge, Torrey, and their Indian guides found a dozen more tribal leaders waiting to sign peace agreements with Texas. Houston, when made aware of this modest breakthrough, sent a conciliatory message. In council, Terrell had to admit that Texas "was yet poor" and that he had only modest gifts. But in exchange for signing a peace treaty, more goods would be delivered in the spring. With that, a few Caddos and Wichitas signed the document on September 29, 1843. References to a line were deleted; it was foolish to debate one without the Comanches present. But the chiefs in attendance hoped that a line eventually would be drawn.[31]

Though not entirely successful, the Texas peace commissioners had accomplished some good. Indian raiding declined appreciably during 1844, a condition confirmed by John Wilbarger, who could find no evidence of a single attack.[32] Smallpox may have been a contributing factor. As important was the curtailing of trade in arms and munitions in Indian Territory by the United States government as a consequence of the Mexican invasions of Texas. The poorly armed Comanches found it impossible to fight the better-armed Anglo-Texans. Given the extreme distance of Indian villages from Texas settlements, rangers stopped searching for their towns.

The only exception to the peace occurred when a small company of rangers out on patrol met a much larger force of Indians near Walker Creek, some sixty miles northwest of San Antonio on June 8, 1844. The Indians were in their hunting ground, but the line separating Indians and Texans had only been suggested, not agreed to. Major John C. (Jack) Hays, in command of the fifteen rangers, had taken on Samuel H. Walker, one of the Mier captives, who had recently been paroled from Perote prison in Mexico. After his release, Walker had visited the Colt firearms factory in New York and had obtained a quantity of five-shot Colt revolvers, which Hays's men carried with them. Others in Hays's party included Ben McCulloch, who would ride into ranger fame later, during the Civil War. It was a group of tough, well-armed men.

The sixty unsuspecting Indians had little idea of what they were about to face. Later evidence demonstrated that they were a combination of Yamparica Comanches, Kiowas, and even a few Shoshones, most of whom had never fought Texans before. Being unsure of themselves, the Indians withdrew, ascended a bluff, and dismounted. In Spanish they taunted the Texans and mooned the rangers by flinging up their breechcloths. Hays's men ducked into a ravine and dashed to the flank of the Indian party. When the rangers exited the brush, they faced the Indians head-on in an open plain.

Whether the hunting party wanted to fight or not is questionable. But in the face of the wild charge, they too raised their lances and shields and came screaming across the prairie. The rangers dropped several using rifles and then turned to pistols. The fighting was soon hand to hand; several Texans were wounded with lances. But the Indians paid dearly, gunned down as the Colts threw lead left and right into the much larger Indian party. The Texans had even brought extra loaded cylinders, which they were able to quickly change out during the fight. This allowed Hays's men to hold their ground despite being outnumbered four to one.

When the bewildered Comanches finally retreated, they left twenty-three dead warriors on the ground. A dozen or more others, severely wounded by the .36 caliber Colts, likely died later. Hays had one dead and four wounded, including the indomitable Walker, who had taken a lance in his shoulder.[33]

Houston quietly expressed concern over Hays's victory, which he assumed would disrupt the peace process that Houston had painstakingly crafted the fall before. But the tribal affiliation of the Indians involved soon became known; they were not Penateka Comanches. There would be no mourning in Pahayuco's towns this time. The discussion, begun in 1844, went on unabated into the next spring and summer at the Waco council house as Indians came and went.

The talks revealed the immense suspicions that Indians had of Texans. The competition that had developed between Butler, who worked for the United States, and Eldridge and Torrey of Texas also hurt the negotiations. Resources were at the heart of the conflict, as Butler had been paying the Delaware and Shawnee scouts well, more than the Texans could pay. So when Butler called for a meeting of all the Plains Indians to be held at Cache Creek in December 1843, a huge number of people came.[34] Unlike the Texas commissioners, Butler arrived with an escort of thirty disciplined U.S. dragoons and a large store of presents. Butler spent eighteen days feasting these Indians, and the Comanches present openly embraced him. While Butler also spoke of peace in the same fashion as the Texans, the Indians fully understood the differences between the diplomacy of Texas and that of the Great Father in Washington.[35]

Showing an interest in Indians that was unmatched by most Americans, Butler spent many hours collecting information on the Plains societies. His census data likely were the most accurate at the time. The Penateka Comanches (including the Hois band) numbered 400 lodges—a considerable decline from the 1780s, when the southern Comanche population had been five times that large. To the west, on the high plains, were the Quahadas, who had 200 lodges, and the Cuchanticas (or, as Butler identified them, "Cachetacahs"), who numbered 300 lodges. The northern bands of the Canadian and Arkansas rivers included the Yamparicas with 500 lodges, the Tenawas (or Tanimas) with 400 lodges, and the Naconis, who had 250 lodges. In all, Butler's numbers put Comanche populations at fifteen thousand. These tribes might form one single village in the spring, but most of the time they remained in smaller hunting bands, given the decline of bison.

The Wichitas and Caddos had likewise diminished since being driven west. Butler counted fifteen hundred people in the two main Wichita towns on the upper Trinity River. Another five hundred or six hundred lived in two Wichita communities near the Wichita Mountains more. José Maria's Caddos had moved to the upper Trinity River, while others stayed on the Brazos. Their relatives from Louisiana frequently migrated west to join them. In total, the Wichitas and Caddos likely could muster a thousand men, but their villages seldom worked together. Moreover, Lamar's war, disease, and drought had made it difficult for these people to feed themselves, given the locations of their communities.[36]

Butler understood that these western tribes were no match for Texas. He warned his superiors that sooner or later they would need help in merely surviving because the areas in which they lived were not as productive agriculturally as central Texas and, as one Comanche prophetically said, their "bows and arrows can no longer reach the buffalo."[37] Overhunting of these animals had occurred, and herds were declining. Bent's Fort had become a bison-hide factory where the skins were pressed, bundled, and shipped east to markets. And the peace of 1840 had resulted in Cheyennes and Arapahos coming into Comanche camps, where they competed with immigrant Indians for hides and horses.[38]

Back in Texas, Houston used the lull in fighting to stress the success of his policies to his congress. The changed atmosphere led a reluctant Texas legislature to ratify the Bird's Fort treaty of September 29, 1843. The vote gave a certain legitimacy to Houston's policy, despite the fact that the president failed to reveal that few Indian leaders of importance had signed it. The legislative actions reflected the obvious; Texas had entered a new period in its history, one marked by a growing population that lacked a frontier mentality. Indeed, some newcomers had never seen an Indian. The racial rhetoric that had justified Indian removal in the 1820s and 1830s had dissipated. And European immigrants, who had just begun to enter the hills northwest of San Antonio, had come to America to avoid war. They hoped to remain at peace with Indians.[39]

Nevertheless, various legislative committees were still controlled by hard-liners. Many still saw the need for an aggressive military policy, and members of the Texas Senate Committee on Indian Affairs vigorously chastised Houston for his failure to prepare for war. On the same day that the Bird's Fort treaty was ratified—February 3, 1844—the committee demanded to know what had happened to the $20,000 appropriated for "frontier defense" two years before. Had it been spent on presents for Indians, such as arms and munitions? "The Committee is constrained to believe that the scalps of your [Houston's] frontier people will prove a tribute to this suicidal policy!"

Understandably, the committee further thought it "slanderous" for Houston to call the council house affair of 1840 at San Antonio "a massacre." The valiant soldiers and commissioners at the council house had simply "repelled the assault from the faithless and perfidious Comanches," an act that most Texans believed to be both "honorable to the commissioners and to the country."[40]

But the most serious disagreement came over Houston's efforts to bring Indians back into the republic after Lamar had expelled them. The president, for his part, saw this as the key to his policy of negotiation. Houston had even built a permanent treaty house on Tawakoni Creek, stocked it with corn, and added an apartment for the chief executive to live in during treaty talks. By the spring of 1844, then, despite the president's successes, some Texas legislators were very critical of his policies just as Houston prepared to make a major effort at negotiating a lasting peace.

The breakthrough for the president seemingly came in April 1844, when a large collection of over five hundred Indians appeared at the Tawakoni Creek council house. Mostly Delawares, Shawnees, Wichitas, and Caddos, the group listened as new Texas commissioners J. C. Neill, Leonard H. Williams, Benjamin Sloat, and Thomas G. Western distributed goods and spoke of peace. Two prominent Indian speakers were St. Louis, a Delaware, and Bintah, a Caddo chief. They expressed an eagerness to return to their lands in Texas and to farm—they asked for hoes and seed.[41] Other speakers who said the same included Caddo chiefs Red Bear and José Maria and even Kechikaroqua, who spoke for the upper Trinity River Tawakoni Wichitas.

Given the location of these people on the upper Trinity and Red rivers, the commissioners proposed the establishment of a line to run from the old Waco town north to the Red River, splitting the upper and lower Cross Timbers. Such a line would pass just west of Bird's old fort, the westernmost Texas settlement. The commissioners assumed this position of the line would seem logical to Texans, because after a traveler broke through the western Cross Timbers, he passed the 98th Meridian and entered the Great Plains.

Acaquash innocently answered the query by raising the issue of whether Houston would attend the meeting. This shifted the debate away from the line. Some Wichitas still doubted the sincerity of the negotiators. "I am not satisfied," the cagey Kechikaroqua added; "I want to see Houston and hear him talk and talk with him myself." Unfortunately, individual bands trusted each other no more than they did Texans. Several Caddos charged Wichitas with stealing and raiding, and the blame shifting went back and forth. As the incriminations escalated, discussions of the line had to be suspended.[42]

Houston meanwhile realized that agreement with the sedentary Wichitas and Caddos was meaningless unless the southern Comanches also accepted the drawing of a line. He sent John Conner and Louis Sanchez to the Penateka camp on the upper Colorado River to feel them out on the proposal. While Pahayuco was hunting, the second chief Mopechucope, in discussions with Conner and Sanchez, spoke in favor of Houston's proposed boundary line. Mopechucope was apparently willing to give up the central Colorado valley (Austin and vicinity), a concession that was more than Houston had hoped for. The line designated by this Penateka leader ran from Comanche Peak on the Brazos southward to a point just below where the San Saba River entered the Colorado, nearly a hundred miles west of Austin.

The discussions, however, soon became muddled and dangerous as news arrived in the village of Hays's devastating victory over mostly Comanches at Walker Creek. Conner and Sanchez did not wait around to discover that the Comanches involved were not Penatekas.[43] When the identity of the Indians became known, everyone breathed a sigh of relief—especially Houston, who observed, "There will be some struggles from those tribes who have made peace with us, and [have young men who] seek to involve their nations in trouble and war." The "same spirit" existed among the Texans, Houston thought, with one example no doubt being Hays.[44]

Despite Hays's triumph—which quickly made him a hero in Texas—Comanche leaders agreed to attend a council at Tawakoni Creek that fall. Their only demand was that Houston attend. An assemblage of over a thousand Indians appeared in September. The president, whose reputation as a man of peace had preceded him, began his address with his stump reference to Lamar: "bad men" had taken his place, "murdered" the Comanche chiefs at San Antonio, and destroyed the Cherokees. Houston told his listeners that he wanted to end the fighting. "If our red brothers want to steal, there are more horses on the Rio Grande [Mexico] than in Texas," he slyly pointed out.

Channeling Plains Indians to attack Mexico had been a favorite scheme of Houston's ever since the first days of the revolution. But his proposal quickly turned to the boundary line that he wanted to establish with the southern Comanches. They had always used the Colorado and Nueces rivers as avenues into the Texas settlements; Houston proposed that they stay west of a line drawn from Comanche Peak (well above the Waco town on the Brazos River) to just below the mouth of the San Saba River, thence running south through the hills west of San Antonio. This line was far in advance of settlement, but it was the line that Mopechucope had supposedly proposed.

Buffalo Hump—a protégé of Penateka's—then rose to speak. Angrily, Buffalo Hump proposed a line "four days fast riding below the mouth" of the San Saba, much farther eastward than had been anticipated by the Texans. Thinking that perhaps Conner and Sanchez had exaggerated their success with Mopechucope or had misunderstood him, a surprised Houston objected; this would put Austin, Texas, within Comanche lands. Buffalo Hump remained adamant, insisting that Austin was on Comanche land. The president then referred to the benefits that a trade house would provide. But Buffalo Hump growled, "We do not want it." Comanche leaders, being well versed in boundary markings, demanded that Texas recognize their claim to the central Colorado River.[45] The two sides had reached an impasse.

Houston could do little else with the Comanches. Factions among them refused to accept the loss of the central Colorado River valley even though they had stopped raiding Texas. Others, however, seemed more than willing to comply. If a formal agreement could not be reached, Houston decided to establish the trade houses and try to force the line upon the Indians. This latter decision at least avoided the possibility of having a formal treaty with the Indians rejected in the legislature.

Three new trade houses did appear in 1845: one on the South Fork of the Trinity River, a second on the West Fork, and a third farther south on the upper Colorado River. They constituted a line of sorts separating Indians and Anglos and became small multicultural communities where "peace" became the sermon of the day and a brisk exchange occurred in items of every kind. The traders talked regularly with Comanche, Wichita, and Caddo chiefs, developing networks that provided accurate information.[46] They employed many of the Delaware and Shawnee men who lived nearby as interpreters.

Nevertheless, this trading-post line lacked official sanction, and it became impossible to enforce as many different people violated it—some Indians and some Texans. Jim Ned, Roasting Ear, and other Delawares constantly tested the patience of Texas Indian agents, slipping below the trade houses to shop in local Texas towns. At one point, Ned traveled all the way to Montgomery, in East Texas, on a commercial venture. Ned and other mixed-bloods like him disliked paying higher prices at river posts and searched for better markets in Texas towns.[47] They used their community at Bosque Creek to enter the Texas market economy.

Worse, the dynamic Houston, who by force of personality had brought some semblance of peace to Texas by 1845, would soon pass from the scene. In the fall 1844 election, Anson Jones replaced Houston as president of the Texas Republic. Jones had little experience or interest in Indian affairs. More significantly, that fall the United States had elected James K. Polk as president on a platform of Texas annexation. Spurred by the departing president, John Tyler, the U.S. Congress made an offer to Texas to join the union even before Polk reached the Oval Office. In the spring of 1845, the fidgety Jones initially balked. However, the vast majority of Texans wanted to enter the union, and a new state constitution was written the following summer.

The new constitution read similar to those of other southern states, but it left several issues unresolved. First, in a surprising turn of events, the United States allowed Texas to keep its public lands so that the state might pay off its huge debt. Texas would be the only state in the union added after the initial colonies to receive such a benefit. Unfortunately, this decision negated the application of the U.S. Intercourse Acts to Texas. These federal laws (first passed in 1790 and consolidated in a single bill in 1834) required U.S. citizens to be bonded before entering Indian land to trade. The Intercourse Acts also made provisions for Indian agents who implemented the laws. Such laws might have prevented some ranger groups from attacking Indian villages (and the revenge raids by Indians in return). Worse, without such laws, a delineation of Indian lands in Texas would not exist unless the state decided to enact a law on its own.

Texas, then, in 1845 sat at a crossroads. Houston had struggled to make friends with western Indians and to prevent more fighting with Mexico. Some modest success had occurred on both fronts. Certainly some of the most difficult men to control—Cameron and Green, for example—had been tamed at Mier. Cameron had drawn one of the black beans and had been shot.

But despite all his best intentions Houston had failed to solve the most important problem in Texas; he left office without a boundary. In addition, as he went off to the U.S. Senate to serve the new state of Texas, he left behind a legislature and a governor that, despite the recent entry of Texas into the union, had complete control over western lands and Indian affairs.

The state's troubles with Indians would not be solved with a few presents handed out to Indian chiefs or with the creation of a few trade houses; the many thousands of Indians who still lived in the west had no intention of giving up their land claims. The struggle for the promised land of Texas still had many scenes to be played. And it had one new actor: the U.S. government.

14

THE BOUNDARY LINE FIASCO

The nomination of James K. Polk, as the presidential candidate of the Democratic Party, came with a promise to annex Texas to the union. His victory in a close election in the fall of 1844 convinced the U.S. Congress to offer statehood to Texas. Celebrations broke out in every Texas community. Annexation would result in protection by the U.S. Army and an end to the Mexican threat of invasion, which in turn would encourage more migration into the new state.

Texas president Anson Jones ultimately called for a convention to meet in July, and a referendum followed in October. There was never any doubt about the vote; 4,174 voted in favor while only 267 opposed annexation. By February 19, 1846, the drama that was the Republic of Texas finally came to an end. At Austin, new state officials, including governor-elect J. Pinckney Henderson, took down the ensign of the republic and replaced it with the Stars and Stripes of the United States. Houston gathered up the old Lone Star flag as a souvenir.

Annexation brought a new era to Texas, but it was intertwined with that of the United States. Americans had been expanding into the West at an unprecedented rate by the 1840s, opening the Oregon Trail, which resulted in the settlement of Oregon and the casting of eyes upon California, a weakly defended province of Mexico. In the very summer that Texas voted on annexation, debate began in the United States over a new geopolitical philosophy called Manifest Destiny (the phrase coined by an eastern newspaper editor). This idea reinforced some aspects of the Texas creed—that it was the destiny of Anglos to dominate western lands, that Indians and Hispanics had little idea of what to do with the land they claimed, and that Americans were destined to advance into the West bringing democracy and Protestantism.

The westward glance of many in the United States included Texas. The new state grew more rapidly in population than any other region beyond the Mississippi

River, from 140,000 people in 1845 to 600,000 in 1860. Most settled in the eastern counties and turned to growing cotton. But the state had cheap land everywhere. Texas created a head right system, allowing anyone residing in the state prior to March 1, 1836, to receive 4,605 acres free. Likewise, a new preemption law made it even easier for settlers to claim land, develop it, and eventually purchase it.[1]

The land still occupied by Indians was another story, and there were thousands of acres of it. Directly after statehood, some sentiment existed for selling the state's public lands (those in the west) to the United States, the estimated price being $7 million—the approximate size of the republic's debt. After such a sale, some of the Texas legislators prophesied, the United States could implement its own Indian policy, which these congressmen assumed would lead to the gradual removal of all Indians.[2] But moving beyond simple debate in both the senate and the house was often very difficult; too many legislators were still heavily involved in land speculation to give up the west, and the state's colonization plan was fully under way.

The new Texas state legislature believed so completely in the need to rapidly settle Texas that it adopted a colonization scheme in 1841 that resulted in several massive grants to companies. W. S. Peters and Associates received roughly 16,000 square miles of land, bordered on the north by the Red River and extending south to include most of the vicinity of modern Dallas and Fort Worth. Frenchmen Henri Castro began settlement of a huge tract southwest of San Antonio after receiving his grant in 1843. Perhaps the largest parcel went to Henry F. Fisher and Burchard Miller, who promptly sold their grant west of Austin and San Antonio to a German colonization firm called the Adelsverein.

Given the speculative inclinations of many Texas legislators, the grants had several caveats. The republic (and later, the state) retained every other section of land within the grants. Obviously this land would be sold to finance state government. And any parcel of land already appropriated by a speculator—which often included the best land—was not available to the contractor. In general, the grants promoted the development of West Texas as rapidly as possible, leading to a general increase in land value across the west.

Very rapidly after 1845, settlers from the upper South descended upon the "Grand Prairie," as it was called, the section of land contained in the Peters Grant. The Grand Prairie bordered the western Cross Timbers, a strip of forest that ran north and south between Comanche Peak along the Brazos River (an elevation some sixty miles above the Waco town) to the Red River. The nature of this land slowed settlement somewhat, and after pushing through it, the settlers faced the Great Plains.

To the south, German settlers rushed into lands some sixty to seventy miles west of Austin. In 1846, they founded Fredericksburg, which became the center of a thriving community. Many Germans also moved into Castro's colony near Castroville, even though this colony was organized by French interests. Fredericksburg grew so rapidly that within a year it boasted eighteen stores and the famous

Nimitz Hotel. By 1860, some thirty thousand Germans had settled in Texas, many in and about Fredericksburg.[3]

This land designated for the colonies had exciting possibilities. The Grand Prairie had rich soil and many small oases of trees: tall post oaks, a few cottonwoods, and pines. This area would in the future support an extensive cotton culture, but most farmers who entered it in the late 1840s practiced near-subsistence agriculture. Only after the Civil War and the establishment of railroads were farmers able to get their crops to market. Much the same was true of the areas west of Austin, often called the "Hill Country." Created by the Balcones Escarpment, a geological fault zone, the region was dominated by rolling hills (often with trees) and an abundance of artesian wells (with pure water). While the Germans tried traditional farming, they found themselves adapting to a more mixed form of agriculture, which included stock raising.

The rapid development of central Texas, a region that had been in Indian hands just ten years before, put incredible pressure on western Native societies. Much of this new land, whether the Grand Prairie or the Balcones Escarpment, had been prime bison-hunting ground; it also held large numbers of wild horses, or mustangs (the word came from the Spanish *mesteños,* meaning "strays"). Mustangs were hardy animals, small for horses at about thirteen or fourteen hands high, but they could run like the wind and survive on natural grasses. The wild mustang herds of the Hill Country were part of Comanche lore, and many a young Indian fumed at the thought of giving up this land. But European and American settlement quickly led to the destruction of both wild game animals and wild horse herds.

The Plains Indian societies that watched this movement had dealt with Texans for over a decade by this time. Some of the tribes recognized the need for compromise to avoid a disastrous war. Comanches had suffered far greater casualties in the wars of the late 1830s than had Texans, who seemed to grow exponentially in numbers. U.S. Indian agents also counseled the Plains groups to remain at peace, as did some Delawares and Shawnees who worked at Houston's trade houses, which were then located in many of these rapidly developing areas. Many Plains chiefs realized that they could not effectively fight Texans, who could find them in their villages almost at will.

The numbers of strangers who entered Comanche and Wichita lands increased as the populations of the indigenous groups declined from disease. Comanche populations dipped to perhaps ten thousand by 1850, as epidemics seemed to invade their towns almost every year after 1844. The newcomers included groups that defied tribal affiliation—Texans and the other settlers called them "renegades," for lack of a better term. Along with the usual Shawnee and Delaware hunters, the newcomers took bison at will, and some Plains societies became more concerned about their activities than those of Texans.

Some of these renegade groups contained Indians or mixed bloods that had broken from their tribes in Indian Territory. They recruited a number of African

Americans—often former slaves of Choctaws, Cherokees, and even Seminoles. A few Irish immigrants sometimes joined these groups of mostly hunters. Many of these men had fought wars against the United States and had witnessed the ugly racist temperament of the nation that now claimed Texas as one of its states. They might have been interlopers to the Comanches, but they also made known their concern of American—and Texan—aggression.

Fortunately, Houston had opened a serious dialogue during the summer of 1844, albeit one that had failed to establish a clear boundary. With settlers pouring into Texas, his efforts took on a more urgent meaning. President Jones half-heartedly had tried to solidify the boundary line before leaving office in 1845. The new Indian superintendent Thomas G. Western had warned of the need to prevent Indians from crossing the line and visiting the settlements because such trips violated "existing treaties." Yet Texans seemed unwilling to support mercantile prohibitions. In some locales, whiskey shops suddenly planted themselves in advance of settlement and the proprietors claimed the right to sell to anyone; even the trade houses kept large quantities of alcohol, attracting Indians inside Houston's unmarked line.[4]

Superintendent Western persisted, however, and received some authority to control these groups in the spring of 1845. First, he ordered the Delawares to leave their town on Bosque Creek, where Houston had given them land. This led to the exodus of Jim Ned and others, west; most left under protest. The Bosque Creek community was too close to Anglo settlement; kegs of liquor were common in the town, and alcohol consumption caused trouble. Most of these Indians resettled near Wichita or Comanche towns and continued to trade, tapping into markets in Indian Territory.

A second effort to separate Indians and Texans came when another newly hired Texas agent, Robert Neighbors, went to work in the south. Neighbors had charisma, liked Indians, and would soon become the most celebrated Indian official in Texas. While he worked for the Texas state government from 1845 to 1847, he adopted the practice of virtually living with his charges. Gaining their confidence, Neighbors was able to convince the few remaining Tonkawas and Lipan Apaches to move west to the upper Guadalupe River. While the location was just south of Fredericksburg and was soon to be coveted by Texans, it was as far west as they would go, given their fear of attacks from Comanches.[5]

This "second" forced removal of the Delawares, Shawnees, Lipan Apaches, and Tonkawas involved only a few hundred people. But it came at a time when Plains societies were debating such issues as removal, boundary lines, and advancing Texas settlement. This debate frequently led to heated discussions and factionalism in Indian towns. Caddo chief José Maria wanted peace and believed that if he built a peaceful agricultural community, Texans would leave him alone. He soon told Texas agents that northern Wichitas opposed such a course and wanted to implicate his people in raiding and to draw his young men into war. Some Wichitas had openly threatened the Caddos if they did not move farther west and support a more anti-Texas stand.

The debate over the line and the expulsion of the Shawnees and Delawares, with whom they traded, also divided the southern Comanches. Some of the younger warriors saw the visits of Texas officials as meddlesome; Indian agents tried to search Indian camps for stolen horses and captives, and the Comanches had plenty of both—especially Mexican captive children. Most younger men refused to give up animals or captives taken in raids. Younger Comanches wanted their leaders to stop talking with Texans altogether and return to raiding. Thus, when Western called for a council with Indian leaders, to be held in September 1845, while José Maria and other friendly Indians appeared, both Buffalo Hump and Pahayuco ignored the summons. And when Texas agents rebuked the Wichitas for threatening José Maria's people, discussions nearly broke down.[6]

The factional disputes revealed an obvious dilemma; the more Texas officials counseled peace with Plains tribes, the more they tried to settle disputes and establish a line, the more settlers pushed west, which in turn alienated Indians. And while the Delawares and others made wonderful intermediaries, capable of finding the Comanches on the plains and arranging peace negotiations, they too seemingly had to be removed, and this alienated them. Texas agents thereafter worried that they might be poisoning the minds of the people they were supposed to help bring into council.

Worse, even the representatives of the United States that had successfully portrayed themselves as friends of the Plains tribes saw trouble coming. Conditions had changed dramatically in a short time. Butler had sent emissaries west in the fall of 1845 and had found the Comanches unwilling to come and talk even with him. Indeed, on one occasion Comanches nearly killed the "runners" sent with messages. Butler concluded that the Comanches and "their associates," despite what he had perceived as being very successful discussions the year before, were preparing for war.[7]

In hopes of preventing a conflict, now that Texas was finally a state in the union, Butler proposed that the United States take charge of Indian affairs in Texas. Officials at the Bureau of Indian Affairs agreed and selected Butler and M. G. Lewis to visit the Plains tribes the next year. As usual, the commissioners recruited delegations of Indians from the settled tribes in Indian Territory; they hoped these delegations would help demonstrate the benefits of signing treaties. They then informed officials in Texas of their hope to meet the Comanches on the upper Brazos River in May 1846. Runners entered Indian towns over the winter, telling leaders that if they came to Comanche Peak, on the upper Brazos, there would be many gifts.[8]

Butler put together a large pack train, which slowly entered the western prairie, crossing the Washita River on its way into the prairie country of West Texas. In a gesture indicative of his concern, he hired considerable numbers of Delawares, Shawnees, Cherokees, Kickapoos, and Choctaws—all men who had lived at one time or another on the edge of settlement and knew the west. They also could handle the oxen used to drive the train, which was packed with blankets, kettles, trinkets, and food.

While closing in on the Red River, Butler seemed pleased to learn that Pawnees had struck the Wichita town near the Wichita Mountains because this would make the Wichitas, who had been harassing the Caddos, more compliant.[9] Nevertheless, there was opposition to his efforts. "Renegades from the friendly tribes have attempted to excite the prejudice and distrust of the Prairie tribes against the United States," he wrote, "by representing us as having been sent among them to disseminate disease through the presents we were to give them."

These so-called renegades—people of mixed lineages and cultures—were much the same as those people whom Butler had employed. Several, but not all, believed that an "organized treaty" might exclude them from Plains Indian towns and trade, as well as plains hunting grounds. Along the headwaters of the Trinity River in January 1846, Butler met a number of such parties, some heading into the plains and others returning. Butler identified them initially as "Creeks, Choctaws, and Kickapoos," and he tried to convince a number to join the expedition. A few Kickapoos agreed.[10]

Besides these groups, the plains every year saw a mounting number of ethnically mixed hunting parties prey upon the diminishing herds of bison, elk, and deer. Some of these hunters traveled in small, almost harmless groups, and some were large, well-prepared, almost factorylike parties. The latter brought women with them (to clean hides) and set up camps where they could press and pack the prepared bison hides for shipment east. They used heavy wagons and oxen for transport. And they were heavily armed. Most had little good to say about either Texans or the U.S. authorities in Indian Territory.

The large hunting party of this sort that Butler encountered while in the vicinity of the Red River was not anxious to sit and parlay with the U.S. agent. The men were dressed in a variety of costumes, some sporting store-bought clothes and others in deerskin shirts and leggings. At first glance, Elijah Hicks, who had joined Butler, thought he recognized the men. "Met a caravan of Kickapoos, hunters, men, women & children, horses heavily loaded with peltrie," Hicks confided to his diary. They were obviously returning from a successful hunt.

But Hicks (a mixed-blood Cherokee), unlike Butler, was welcome in their camp, and he looked more closely. He counted three hundred people in total. And suddenly he realized that most were not Kickapoos. "This was a motley party," Hicks continued, "consisting of whites, Cherokees, Chickasaws, Seminoles, Spaniards, & Negroes."[11] In reality, it was not an Indian band at all but rather a collection of market-oriented bison hunters who simply looked like Indians at a glance but who came from varied ethnic backgrounds. Some might be viewed as social outcasts back in the more settled areas of Indian Territory. They came together primarily because of their rejection of tribal rule and because of a common interest in the plains hunt, one of the few occupations that paid. Above all, they were loyal to no one other than themselves.

Butler and Lewis wished to bring people of this sort into the peace process. But the "renegades" were a suspicious and wily lot, and they wanted little to do with

Americans or Texans—or peace, since peace and boundaries might restrict them from bison herds. Butler could do little other than let the bison hunters pass, unmolested.

Butler had hired the dependable Jesse Chisholm, Black Beaver, and a few other mixed-blood guides. While Chisholm and Black Beaver might do as the former South Carolina governor wanted, they could not vouch for the others in their own party, some of whom had long since given up doing the government's bidding. Some of the mixed-bloods in Butler's own party had very different agendas than Butler did. A few were downright hostile to the United States; they had come along only for the rations and the chance to trade. Some (including Wild Cat, the Seminole, who had joined Butler with some of his young men) were total newcomers to the region. John Guess, Sequoyah's son, even showed up. He came into camp along with Worm and several other Cherokees. They had been living in Mexico with the expatriate Cherokee community that had fled from Texas. Guess, being Bowles's son-in-law, hated Texans—and with good reason.[12]

Once they had set up their camp, Butler and Lewis sent the mixed-blood and Indian guides to call the Plains chiefs together into council. Hicks, Wild Cat, and a few others formed one guiding party. Once away from the Americans, various members of the group voiced their distrust for both Americans and Texans. Wild Cat, especially, regaled his fellow travelers with stories about the Seminole Indian war. He thought very little of the bravery of U.S. soldiers and believed that William Tecumseh Sherman, to whom he had surrendered, had made "fine promises" regarding the land of Indian Territory. Contrary to what Sherman and others had said, however, the land had little game and few bison. They had lied, and Wild Cat's people had nearly starved back in eastern Indian Territory.

Wild Cat, Guess, and perhaps even Black Beaver and Chisholm at times likely remained cynical regarding the objectives of the U.S. delegation. Wild Cat obviously had used the expedition as an opportunity to develop his own geographic knowledge of the region, for it was apparently his first trip west. In the following October, he led 650 Indians from Indian Territory—they came from many different tribes— south into Texas, crossing the Red River at Warren's trading post. Wild Cat hoped to hunt on the upper Colorado River and likely had set his sights on Mexico.[13]

Large numbers of Comanches, Wichitas, and Caddos met the caravan on the upper Brazos River. All knew that the Americans had brought plenty of food and presents. Their chiefs smoked, talked, and ate but failed to resolve the important issues separating the parties—the Texas boundary line controversy and the invasion of the plains by immigrant hunters. The main objective of the treaty increasingly became peace and the extension of the intercourse laws to the Texas plains—prohibition against raiding, the development of a licensing system for traders, the exchange of prisoners, and an end to the use of liquor.[14] The U.S. Senate ratified the agreement the next year.

Agent Robert Neighbors reached the council grounds to represent Texas. His role is uncertain, but he clearly informed Butler that the Texas state legislature would never agree to a line. As Butler and Lewis put it, "We were detered [*sic*] from making any proposition on this subject by the fear of bringing into collision the authorities of Texas and the Federal Government." But Butler and Lewis did openly discuss the line, which at least through oral agreement the Indians were sworn to uphold. For the Intercourse Acts to have any validity, some line obviously had to exist. Moreover, Indians could not thereafter allow traders into their camps without licenses, and they would be required to stay out of the areas of Texas settlement, including the Grand Prairie and the Hill Country.

Later evidence shows beyond doubt that while all the Comanches in attendance— and some thirty leaders signed the final accord—may not have fully understood the concept of the line, the Caddos and Wichitas certainly did. José Maria by this time understood lines and boundaries, and he wanted to make sure that his new town, located thirty miles below Comanche Peak, was on Indian land. It supposedly was. With this sort of understanding, part written and part verbal, dozens of Indian leaders signed—including the Comanches Pahayuco, Buffalo Hump, and Mopechucope and the Waco Acaquash, along with other Caddos and Wichitas.[15]

Butler and Lewis did add to the growing collection of information in the United States regarding the Plains tribes. They visited the new Wichita and Caddo towns that had recently been built on the upper Brazos River, most well above Comanche Peak, or northward on the Trinity River. Acaquash had gained considerable authority in these communities. The commissioners put the Brazos River Wichita populations at seven hundred people; other Wichitas remained along the Red River. The combined Caddos now counted fifteen hundred; most accepted the middle-aged José Maria as their spokesman.[16]

Indian concerns varied from tribe to tribe, but the more-agricultural tribes wished to live farther east in central Texas. Also, all of these Indians had come to fear smallpox, and they still suspected that Anglos might be responsible for the disease. The virus had lingered; many Wichitas sickened with it that fall of 1845. This less virulent epidemic likely had convinced the Caddos to abandon their town on the Trinity in 1845, returning once again to the Brazos River.

Butler also noted some cases of measles and whooping cough as well as "autumnal" or fall fever—very likely malaria. Still suffering the loss of housing and food from war, the Plains people continued on a downward demographic spiral.[17] Comanche bands were consolidating as a result, as many southern Penatekas moved northward to join northern bands. Wichitas and Caddos were doing the same, trying to preserve as much of their traditional village life as possible.

Yet the one resounding cry that Butler heard from everyone dealt with the decline of the bison, an animal that had once roamed in herds of tens of thousands from the Rio Grande northward into the central plains.[18] Drought and overhunting had decimated this critical resource; at times, the animals could not be found at all. But given the fact that herds did still exist, the hunting in the upper Brazos and Colorado river valleys was still better than in the region east of the Wichita Mountains, which many of the guides and mixed-bloods with Butler noticed.[19] Indeed, Wild Cat had concluded that his people and some Kickapoos could find bison only along the upper Colorado River.

The competition over plains resources only increased after the United States declared war on Mexico in April 1846. Traffic grew exponentially along the Santa Fe Trail; entirely new roads were opened into parts of New Mexico. Northern and western Comanches as well as Kiowas increased raiding activity on caravans all along the trail in 1846, almost simultaneously with Butler's negotiation at Comanche Peak. Indians killed more than sixty Americans, burned three hundred wagons, and took six thousand head of livestock during the fall of 1846. A severe drought, which was then in its second year, literally made the grass disappear along the Arkansas and Canadian rivers, forcing Indians to eat horses at times.[20]

In Texas, news of the war and the conflict along the trail frightened Governor Henderson. While he and most other officials welcomed the war with Mexico because it would likely solidify the southern boundary of the new state, it might also convince the Plains tribes that they could easily raid the newly forming, relatively unprotected settlements. Agent Neighbors, while with Butler at Comanche Peak, spent much of his time negating rumors then circulating that the lead elements of Colonel Zachary Taylor's army, the Second Dragoons, had been destroyed. In reality, the dragoons had successfully crossed the Brazos River the preceding August; the sight of 450 mounted troopers marching through Texas did much to dispel concerns of state officials and settlers alike.[21]

The U.S. Army quickly swept across the Southwest. The fall of New Mexico late that summer revived the goals of Lamar's failed Santa Fe expedition of 1841. The war also encouraged mobilization in Texas at a time when the state was poised to expand dramatically into the west. Governor Henderson initiated the call-up, convincing Brevet Colonel William S. Harney of the U.S. Army of the need to mount Texas Rangers. By fall, five ranger companies had formed—at Castroville, at San Antonio, at Little River, at Torrey's trading post on the Brazos, and on the upper Trinity River. The state anticipated that most of these troops would receive their salaries from the federal government and remain in the west to combat Indians. But General Taylor, who questioned the Indian threat, had different plans. He needed troops and materials for his campaigns in the south, and he ordered a halt to the mobilization.

Taylor's actions outraged Governor Henderson as well as the usually more moderate Sam Houston, who was then in the U.S. Senate. Both men lobbied feverishly in Washington, D.C., and their actions saved the companies. Thereafter, a pattern for ranger organization emerged that existed for the next thirty years. County officials, usually county judges, lobbied the governor for permission to organize a company, knowing that the congressmen and senators from Texas would, in turn, lobby the U.S. government for arms and salaries. Some of these rangers (including the company of John Hays) went off to fight in Mexico, but others (such as those of Captains Samuel Highsmith and Middleton Tate Johnson) stayed in Texas.

Buttressed by federal support, Texans became increasingly militant regarding the west, often organizing ranger companies at will. At times, the U.S. government refused to pay the men; when that happened, the rangers turned to plunder. The ranger companies formed in 1846 were sent up the various river valleys well in advance of settlement. They, in turn, encouraged Texans to move farther west, literally challenging the last vestiges of the boundary line that Houston had tried so hard to establish.[22]

Some of these settlers made efforts to get along with Indians. The newly arriving Germans first negotiated with the southern Comanches on their own, handing out considerable numbers of presents in 1846. They also benefited from another round of epidemics that almost paralyzed the Indians. After they had seized the best lands in the Pedernales River valley, however, their surveying parties moved farther west and south. Governor Henderson, despite realizing that the settlers' encroachment into Indian lands would lead to war, could not keep the surveyors from entering the region of the Llano and San Saba rivers.

Predictably, though, a war party finally struck the surveyors (killing four) in July 1847 and tried to drive out the settlers.[23] Agent Neighbors initially suspected the Penateka Comanches, but, suffering from smallpox, they had fled far to the north. The agent soon discovered that the attackers consisted of Indians from several bands, most being northern Comanches. Regardless, the surveying went on. Soon other settlers crossed into the Guadalupe and Medina river valleys, running out the Lipan Apaches. The Apaches had been given that land just two years before by Neighbors, and they retaliated.

Ranger "Big Foot" Wallace, who lived in the area at the time, described the troubles with the Lipan Apaches as being directly related to the settler occupations of the Medina River valley. The Lipan Apaches resisted and protested to the rangers for two days and then departed, vowing revenge. Small parties of Lipan Apaches returned and took a number of animals, although supposedly no one was killed. One of the mules driven off belonged to Big Foot. Wallace waited until the Indians assumed that they were safe—in the spring of 1848—and then he gathered together thirty rangers and stalked their new village. It was nestled in a rugged valley at the head of the Frio River, nearly on the edge of the Great Plains.

In this rugged country, ranger spies with Big Foot's group soon saw two boys driving a herd of horses toward what appeared to be a village. The Texans followed, integrated themselves with the horses, and hit the camp undetected. Most of the Lipan men were totally surprised, having hung their bows, arrows, and shields in the nearby trees. The rangers attacked on horseback at full gallop; most were armed with rifles rather than Colt revolvers. The scene soon became chaotic as the Lipans "were overrun and crushed . . . and soon scattered in wild flight." The only thing that saved a few Indians was the misfiring of several rifles; Wallace's flintlock, for example, failed to discharge several times, likely from the damp weather.

When the rangers regrouped, they collected well over a hundred horses and mules as booty, worth at least $3,000. Some ten Indians were dead on the ground; others, wounded and dying, had fled to the brush.[24] It mattered little that these same Lipan Apaches had played a crucial role in defeating Comanches during Lamar's war of extermination, acting as guides for Moore, or that most were unarmed. The only bit of compassion shown by the rangers was Wallace's rescue of a young Lipan girl whom he personally knew. But his actions, which both state and federal authorities either ignored or felt they could do nothing to prevent, became part of a pattern that repeated itself across Texas—the indiscriminate killing of Indians.

With tensions rising and the campaigns against Mexico scaling down in the north, the U.S. government hired Robert Neighbors as "special" federal agent for Texas, sending him west in 1847 with $7,000 worth of presents to placate Indians who had been removed west. Neighbors wrote, "On my arrival at the trading house of the Messr. Torrey, I found the whole frontier . . . in great alarm and all appeared apprehensive of an immediate attack." Jim Ned, the Delaware, had spent the winter trading with the Wichitas, encouraging them to steal horses in Texas and attack surveyors. Liplin and Black Cat, a shadowy Seminole and Shawnee, respectively, of a like nature, did the same.[25] The forced removal of the Shawnees and Delawares from Bosque Creek had turned many of these plains traders into enemies of Texas.

Over the winter of 1847–1848, Neighbors tried to assure the tribes that the United States wanted peace. He started negotiations with the group most likely to resist Texas expansion, the Penateka Comanches. After many days of discussions with several of their leaders, Neighbors found growing tribal factionalism. A few Penateka chiefs (often older ones with fewer followers) actually argued to chiefs of the Tenawas and Naconis (more northern Comanche bands) that they should leave Texas alone and stop attacking surveyors. Several Penateka leaders realized that they could no longer winter in safety in the upper Colorado River valley—a favorite haunt—if Texas Rangers were after them.

Neighbors learned that some northern Comanches felt obligated to listen to their southern brethren—Comanche etiquette always required listening. The northern Comanches even gave their southern relatives some horses to return to Texans. But listening was one thing; calling a halt to raiding was an entirely different issue. As one of the Penateka chiefs told Neighbors, "they [the northern Comanches] wanted to see how long before the old chiefs of the Penatekas would get tired of returning stolen horses!"[26] These "old chiefs" did not represent the majority of young warriors.

Those men who fit the category of "older chief" included Pahayuco and Neighbor's favorite, the pliable Mopechucope. After daylong political discussions, Neighbors would often retire to Mopechucope's tent, where a few select men and the agent would feast, smoke, and talk. As Neighbors put it, "I found them to be a very jovial set." The discussion invariably settled "on the usual themes among the Prairie bands. viz—'war and women.'" The closeness of Neighbors and these Indian leaders, as indicated by the jovial nature of their discussions, likely led to adoption, with Neighbors becoming fictive kin of the old man's.

But just two months later, even Mopechucope confronted Neighbors: "You told me that the troops [rangers] were placed there for our protection. . . . I think it is not so." The rangers had moved their camp farther up the Brazos River, and when Mopechucope applied to Captain Ben McCulloch for permission to hunt bison on the lands around the captain's new camp, McCulloch turned the Indians back.[27] The line was moving farther west.

The same apprehension existed among peaceful Caddos. When Neighbors spoke with José Maria, he discovered that Texans had driven the Caddo leader's people off their newly broken farmland thirty miles below Comanche Peak on the Brazos. The wily Seminole Wild Cat, who had a chance meeting with José Maria just afterward, had told him that Neighbors' presents represented payment for this land rather than simple kindly acts. Even the friendliest of Indians were confused and angry. Did the line exist for both sides or only the Indians? José Maria wanted to know.

Neighbors was outraged at this activity; it clearly challenged his authority as a federal agent, and it invalidated attempts to implement the Intercourse Acts. His report, with an obviously sarcastic tone, went directly to the commissioner of Indian affairs. "I deem it proper to notify the department," he wrote, "that the Indian country in Texas is *now open* to all persons who may choose to visit our state."[28] Even so, Texas newspapers continued to report "Indian depredations"—most being fabrications or horse thievery for which the perpetrators were never uncovered. These reports produced a growing restlessness among the ranger companies, who Neighbors believed at times sold liquor to Indians and openly planned assaults on Indian villages.[29]

In truth, the surge of western settlement had made honest attempts at creating a boundary line a fiasco, as the Texas legislature was determined to prevent one from forming. Settlers had long since overrun the Indian trade houses that had formed the first line in 1843; the houses were moved west only to be overrun again by 1846–1847. But given the large numbers of renegades on the plains who carried liquor and goods for trade, these houses had become somewhat irrelevant in terms of their role in separating Indians and Texans.

Neighbors, frustrated and angry, decided upon the only course of action that he thought possible. He ordered ranger captain Middleton Tate Johnson's company to forcibly remove settlers who had taken over the lands of the Caddo village below Comanche Peak. Neighbors hoped this would set an example and curb movement up the river. He assumed that he had the authority to order this action under the

Butler and Lewis treaty, which Congress had ratified in 1847. The treaty did justify implementing the Intercourse Acts, which the United States had used for years to keep whites off Indian land.

Johnson did his duty but faced opposition. One occupant, Eliphus Spencer, vigorously argued that a "temporary line" did not exist and that the Caddo had no rights to land. Spencer's wife was outraged at "being forced into a wagon by a parcel of rude men."[30] Spencer and others filed lawsuits and protested to the state legislature. The state courts acted quickly, siding with the Spencers against Neighbors.

The state legislature responded with an even more severe reproof, condemning the actions of both the governor and the agent. The Senate Committee on Indian Affairs argued that the state had lost no rights to its western land after annexation: "No Indian boundary line was ever recognized by the authorities of Texas." The committee demanded that the governor make a "bold assertion of our state rights" to the Bureau of Indian Affairs in Washington, D.C., and curtail the injurious actions of Indian agents such as Neighbors.[31]

Texas, then, even as a state, seemed incapable of policing itself. The government under the republic had failed to control expansion; the state was doing no better, with the legislature seemingly oblivious to the correlation between western settlement and Indian war. The Texas legislature also refused to enact and enforce the intercourse laws that U.S. authorities had reconfirmed with the Indians but were unable to implement given the lack of federal ownership of land. The only avenue that the state did successfully pursue, with considerable vigor, was the organization of ranger companies. And these paramilitary groups were getting restless.

The tensions and conflict that characterized the late 1840s also resulted from the increased fracturing of Indian communities. The loss of leadership from war and disease, the meddling of "renegades" in the west, and factionalism within tribes and bands made peace difficult to maintain. Despite these problems, though, the Plains tribes seemed ready to end their disputes with Texans. There was no question that those bands living closest to Texas settlement were peacefully disposed and would try to prevent their young men from raiding Texas settlements.

The only possible solution to the tension and the conflict was expanding the involvement of the U.S. government, but this would take more than one Indian agent—Neighbors. Fortunately, as Neighbors struggled to keep the contending parties separate, the U.S. Army was consolidating power in New Mexico and along the Rio Grande. Many Texans assumed that the federal army would soon deal with the "Indian menace" in Texas. Optimism abounded in the frontier communities of Texas in the spring of 1848, and thousands of new people flocked into the western counties.

These, then, were the issues confronting the U.S. government as it took charge of the Southwest in 1848. Houston, Butler, and Neighbors had readily illustrated the possibilities for a negotiated peace, despite the tendencies of some western Indians to oppose it. With a mighty federal army coming back from victory in Mexico, certainly the Texas problem could be solved. A solution, however, would require cooperation and compromise, traits that Texans and their legislature had been slow to embrace in the past. Moreover, these were traits that Texas Rangers had consistently rejected.

15

LINES, POLITICS, DEPREDATIONS, AND THE U.S. ARMY

The winter of 1847–1848 had been relatively peaceful in Texas. Come spring, everyone expected a new rush of settlement in the west. The Mexican War had ground to a halt; all the fighting in the north was over. Surveyors and settlers had begun once again pushing up the many river valleys of Texas, entering the Llano and the San Saba in the south and continuing to move up the Colorado, Brazos, and Trinity in the north-central part of the new state. Along the Brazos, they had nearly reached Comanche Peak.

Several companies of Texas Rangers protected the newcomers. One, under Captain Samuel Highsmith, was particularly high-strung, looking for action at almost every turn. It even campaigned over the winter, when Indians seldom attacked. Come spring, Highsmith was still busy hunting Indians, despite the peaceful times. Highsmith, a determined North Carolinian who had fought at Gonzales and San Jacinto, and even under John C. Hays in Mexico, had yet to do something valiant enough to lead to honor and political success. Both he and his men wanted action.[1]

Highsmith worked his mounted troop hard, scouring the valleys in advance of the surveyors. In early April 1848 his scouts reported Indians. They had stumbled onto a hunting party of twenty-six men and boys, who had camped to make dinner in a valley well south of the Brazos River. Most of the Wichita and Caddo Indians in the camp had hung up their arms as they lounged about the cooking fire. High-smith's troop crept to within a hundred yards and then charged the Indians, firing Colt revolvers at man and boy alike.

The startled Indians had little chance. Some jumped into the nearby stream and were shot in the back. Others reached the bank on the far side and tried to escape up the bluff, making easy targets. When the smoke cleared, Highsmith counted twenty-five dead Indians. His men gathered up the hides, meat, horses, and scalps and jubilantly rode back to San Antonio to be hailed as heroes by the townsfolk.

Not one ranger had suffered a scratch during the slaughter, and only one young Indian had escaped to tell the story. A disgusted Neighbors heard it from him. The agent termed Highsmith's actions simply another "massacre."[2] The Indians were from Keckikaroqua's village, which had been friendly since 1843. Keckikaroqua had signed the 1847 peace treaty; apparently he perished in the slaughter. The loss of men in his town forced the community to break up, and the remaining Wichitas in the town once again fled north.

Just why Highsmith destroyed these Indians is difficult to ascertain. He failed to leave a report and resigned sometime later, perhaps expecting to run for office. The chance never came, as Captain Highsmith died in San Antonio the next year during the influenza epidemic. Evidence of Indian depredations north of Fredericksburg that spring had been nonexistent. The only explanations for Highsmith's attack were plunder and fame.[3] A few days after the attack, a party of Indians from the Wichita town ambushed and killed three surveyors on the Trinity River in Peters's colony. The attack brought more Indian revenge and more ranger retaliation.

Lieutenant Thomas Smith's ranger company, assigned to the Brazos River, went into the field to subdue the killers of the surveyors. Finding an unoffending band of Wichita and Caddo hunters, Smith's men opened fire with Colt revolvers, murdering twenty-four in a few minutes. As in Highsmith's attack, not one ranger was even wounded. Killing Indians apparently had become "sport" once again in Texas. The lieutenant claimed that he tried to question the Indians before ordering his men to shoot, but his explanations lacked the ring of truth, especially given the actions of his command a few days later.

On their return to camp, Smith's rangers spotted a sixteen-year-old Caddo youth who, Neighbors later reported, "had given no offense—whatever." Twenty rangers gave chase and shot him down. They fired nearly a dozen times. Five bullets penetrated his body, and two shattered his skull. While poking at the corpse, they discovered that the boy had served them faithfully as a hunter for several months over the past winter.[4] He came from José Maria's peaceful Caddo town.

Despite the cholera and influenza that had hit the Indian towns, most chiefs informed Neighbors that their young men wanted revenge. After receiving Neighbors's report of the incidents, the War Department finally ordered an investigation. Captain E. Steen received the assignment. From Fort Washita he rode south with forty dragoons into the Trinity valley. Steen held no romantic illusions about Indian warfare, but he also was somewhat objective. He found no evidence of who had been responsible for killing the surveyors and, while diplomatic, concluded that Smith's and Highsmith's rangers were somewhat out of control: "These acts of violence on the part of the volunteers [rangers] upon that frontier without a full knowledge of the circumstances," Steen reported, "would seem too severe if not unauthorised."[5]

Neighbors met quickly with both José Maria and Acaquash about the incidents in late April and, upon finding the men anguished, offered presents. (It was the Indian way to cover death with presents.) These chiefs wanted to live peacefully but could hardly remain leaders of their bands without resolving the issue of the death of the boy. The agent asked for their patience and pledged that the terms of the 1847 treaty would be kept—that the men responsible would be tried in a court of law for their acts. Neighbors knew how impossible this would be, but it placated the two chiefs.

In a flurry of letters, Agent Neighbors, military officers such as Steen, and other Texas politicians called upon federal officials to send in the military and take over Indian affairs. The war in Mexico was over, and troops were available. The government could interpose itself between the Plains tribes and Texans, much as it had done on other frontiers.

Senator Houston kept abreast of the situation while in Washington. His political friend back in Texas, C. B. Fletcher, confirmed much of what Neighbors was reporting officially to the War Department. "The onset made upon the Indians by Captain Highsmith, the death of the Caddo boy, the difficulties growing out of the violation of the line agreed upon" had produced a critical situation, according to Fletcher. The rangers were primarily at fault; "they are brave, efficient, and active, but are too fond of fighting," Fletcher wrote. They had no regard whatsoever "for the rights of the Indians . . . they think that the death of an Indian is a fair offsett [*sic*] to the loss of a horse."[6]

U.S. troops in numbers were requested. They would, Neighbors and others of like mind hoped, garner respect from the local citizens and rein in the rangers. But as the Mexican War closed in 1848, the U.S. Army was exhausted and ill equipped for this new task: it now had a vast new empire to control, including California, New Mexico, the Great Basin, and the Pacific Northwest. The defense of Texas would take time to organize, and considerable strategy—given the thousand-mile area of settlement, which extended virtually from the Rio Grande to the Red River (see map on page 126).

What is more, Texas lacked many of the standard ethnic and geographic features of other frontiers. It held friendly Indians, hostile Indians, and a few that were in between, a Tejano population in the south that had come to distrust Texans, groups of renegades, and finally, the paramilitary rangers. All were fighters at times, and all answered to different authorities. No clear boundary existed that separated the various contesting groups. Roads for transportation were nearly nonexistent; even the many rivers remained navigable for only short times of the year. Merely supplying infantry troops would be a problem.

General Zachary Taylor, the hero of the northern campaigns during the Mexican War, received the initial order to occupy Texas. But he would be followed by a host of other generals who came and went in Texas in 1849 and 1850, all struggling to get a grip on the problem. In the early years of the army's presence, the constant change in command only exacerbated the difficulties.

While in Mexico, Taylor had reached a conclusion regarding the task at hand; the general had seen firsthand the brutality of Texas Ranger units that served under him. Taylor knew that they were part of the problem in Texas; Neighbors's reports made that clear enough.[7] Taylor had been especially appalled by ranger behavior at Reynosa, a Mexican border town where some Texans had been held prisoner after the Mier debacle in 1842—and where rangers had pillaged, murdered, and raped at will.

General Taylor could not countenance the settling of old scores; "I fear they [rangers] are and will continue to be too licentious to do much good," he wrote to the governor of Texas during the war.[8] He wanted to send them home but needed their scouting ability. Once the fighting subsided, Taylor issued "Special Order #149," which called for "the final discharge of the volunteers." The order did not mince words; "get the 'rangers,' so called, out of service," he wrote to the Texas state militia commander, Colonel P. Hansborough Bell.

The order came as a thunderclap to Bell and other state officials who not only supported the rangers but also realized that their own political futures rested, to some degree, on maintaining the volunteer companies in the field. The units were very popular in the western counties, being raised mostly by politicians—and, of course, some voted—and they were perceived as being necessary for defense, despite the infrequency of Indian depredations since 1844. Bell, a political appointee of the new Texas governor, George T. Woods, defiantly refused Taylor's order and promptly wrote to Washington, D.C., demanding protection for the most "exposed" positions in West Texas.

Bell got his reprieve when General David Twiggs replaced Taylor in July. Taylor, who was running for president against Polk, had been ordered east. He no longer would command troops as long as the Democrat Polk remained in office. (Taylor, of course, was elected president in November.) Twiggs, who hailed from the South, took a different view of the rangers, especially after his infantry began to disappear. Enlistments were ending, and he had little choice but to rely, at least temporarily, on the rangers along the line of settlement.[9] By doing so, he placated Governor Woods, who wanted the U.S. government to pay the rangers' salaries permanently.

While Twiggs tried to organize his command, law and order deteriorated, especially in southern Texas. Hundreds of "malicious white men," as Neighbors described them, roamed between Corpus Christi and the Rio Grande, committing depredations that newspapers occasionally blamed on Indians. Some, according to reports, were "followers of the army from Mexico" who had decided against going home. Some were mustered-out Texas Rangers. They had little, if any, respect for property, and most lingered in the small saloons along the western line of settlement that fall, out of work and uninterested in honest labor. While Twiggs, when assuming command, believed that his most serious problem was in the region of the upper Brazos River, he soon found that it was actually in the south of Texas.

Most of these vagabonds despised men like Neighbors, who sought some law and order and even protected Indians. The desperadoes were particularly rough on Tejanos; vecino herders and carters were poorly armed, making them easy prey. Anyone who challenged these renegade Anglos generally came out the loser. But Neighbors stood up to at least one group and reclaimed some horses that they had stolen from the Lipan Apaches. The renegades promptly circulated a petition identifying Neighbors as a "man of turbelent [*sic*] and violent disposition, without morrel [*sic*] virtue."[10] The petition, with its colorful language, was ignored by the Bureau of Indian Affairs.

News of the gold strike in California (which reached Texas by Christmas 1848) helped siphon off many of the troublemakers, but it produced other problems as wagon trains of Forty-Niners began to cross the state by February 1849. Many of the gold-seekers left from Fort Smith, Arkansas, to cross Indian Territory. Still others arrived that spring at Fredericksburg, Texas, hoping to make the trip via El Paso. Nothing resembling a road existed west of Fredericksburg, and Brevet Major General William Worth, who assumed command in Texas in spring 1849, ordered Neighbors to scout a road.

Neighbors relished the job, for it offered adventure and the opportunity to blaze a trail. He was accompanied by an odd collection of friends. John Harry, a Delaware, joined him, as did Joe Ellis and Tom Coshatte, both Shawnees. One Patrick Goin, a Choctaw, along with Jim Shaw, the most respected interpreter and tracker in West Texas, rounded out the group, along with several Texans from San Antonio. Comanches Mopechucope and Buffalo Hump initially agreed to go, since they knew the country, but then disaster nearly destroyed the expedition.

While Neighbors organized supplies in early February, Buffalo Hump returned to Fredericksburg, where he spoke with Major Gates. The major told him wild stories of roads and even railroads that would in the future extend over the very land they were to survey. Once aware of Neighbors's purpose, the Comanches withdrew, leaving the agent with oaths "full of asperity and bitterness of feeling." Both chiefs said they had compromised as far as they could; they would fight to "keep the settlements below the present line of posts."[11] Jim Shaw, ever aware of Comanche attitudes, recruited more armed men for the expedition.

General Worth's troops marched onto the Texas frontier just as Neighbors prepared to depart. The army constructed barracks at key points. Some twenty-eight companies were spread across the western plains of Texas. Even at half their projected strength, the number of soldiers in blue reached well over a thousand. General Worth and other commanders of these mostly infantry forces soon learned that they desperately needed transportation. The army promptly purchased mules for some of the troopers and mounted them.

In the north, one of the few dragoon regiments—the Second Dragoons, commanded by Colonel William Harney—advanced into the upper Trinity River valley, where they constructed Fort Graham in May. The garrison was located forty miles above the old Waco town on the Brazos. In the south, two hundred more dragoons camped near Fredericksburg and soon started construction on Fort Martin Scott.[12] Captain Robert W. Montgomery, the commander of the new post, talked with Comanche leaders and found them to be "sincerely disposed to be friendly." In reality, the southern Comanches had few other choices; epidemics had continued unabated, depleting their populations. Montgomery only feared trouble between the Indians and the nearby Germans, who traded in liquor.[13]

Other infantry companies joined the dragoons and built forts over the spring and summer of 1849. Major Ripley P. Arnold constructed Fort Worth on the west branch of the Trinity River, and other garrisons appeared at Austin, San Antonio, and the newly built Fort Gates, on the Leon River. Three infantry posts soon dotted the Rio Grande—at Brownsville, Camp Ringgold (opposite Camargo), and at Laredo. This military presence projected American influence into a region that had little law and order. Finally, the Third Infantry, under Brevet Major Jefferson Van Horne, reached El Paso in early August. Along the way, Van Horne started Fort Inge on the upper Nueces River and later built Fort Bliss, near El Paso.[14]

All of these garrisons, from Fort Worth to Fort Inge, formed a new line that was intended to separate Indians and Texans. The western Plains tribes—especially Caddos and Wichitas—had sought such a line for some time, and while they had no voice in its eventual construction, they welcomed its arrival, for they hoped it would hold back the advancing Anglo populations. With the troops almost in place in May 1849, General Worth issued Order No. 28, which forbade Indians from passing below the line. Worth then told Neighbors to meet with the Plains bands and inform them of the new boundary and its purpose.[15] A new era—a new, supposedly enforceable policy—seemed to have arrived in Texas.

The troops gave a sense of security to the Forty-Niners, whose numbers multiplied in Texas during the spring of 1849. Even so, after what Neighbors had learned, most travelers expected trouble. To everyone's surprise, however, all the goldseekers' trains went through without incident. The only trouble was an outbreak of cholera that struck suddenly, carrying off hundreds of people (including General Worth and many of his soldiers) in the towns that the travelers left behind.[16] Most Comanches stayed clear of the new towns, the pack trains, and the soldiers, which was perhaps a testimonial to the army threat but also to the Indians' terror of the deadly epidemic, which eventually hit their camps too.

Even when overlanders met parties of Indians, both sides generally interacted peacefully, at least at first. Benjamin Butler Harris, whose party stopped at Harney's dragoon camp on the Trinity River, expected trouble, especially after Colonel Harney—who later gained the nickname "Butcher" Harney for his massacre of Sioux Indians at Ash Hollow—gave "the sound advice to shoot at every Indian we saw."

But Harris's group, joined by many mustered-out ex-rangers, had a safe passage. The first "Indian" met by the party was Jim Shaw, who had just returned with Neighbors's party from the west. Harris described him as "finely proportioned, seven feet tall and sinewy and symmetrical, sporting a scalplock as defiant, fearless and triumphant as ever fluttered in a prairie breeze."

A few days later, Harris and his companions met yet another party of Indians. They were so friendly that he and his party joined them in a late-night dance, parading around the campfire, hollering and stomping. This party of fifteen Comanches was bound for Torrey's post on the Red River.[17] It seemed as though the efforts of Butler, Neighbors, and the threat posed by the U.S. Army had made the plains a more peaceful place, despite Buffalo Hump's threats.

Yet intelligence supplied to Neighbors suggested something different. The agent learned that a huge war party consisting of "Comanches, Lipans, Apaches, Wacos, Wichitas and renegades" had departed for Chihuahua, Mexico, a month before the overlanders had hit the western trails. The Indians had crossed the Rio Grande in January 1849 just below Presidio del Norte, "being joined at that point by a few renegade Mexicans and Americans." Such a group operated under somewhat different prerogatives of warfare, plundering items of all sorts tradable in the increasingly diverse plains market. In addition, they lacked the restraints of Comanche war parties, which at least had taboos against rape. They promised to make West Texas a more violent place, and they brought havoc and death to Mexico.

The raiders overran a number of Mexican towns and ranches. The Harris overland party met one small group returning from a raid in March 1849. Several young Mexican boys were herding horses for the raiding party. When spoken to in Spanish, one boy of ten related that "his and the other youths' families including entire settlements and villages had been slaughtered by the Indians and that they (the boys) were spared to be retained as slaves and herders." The Indians in the party confirmed much of what was said by displaying the scalps of many men and women.[18] Increasingly, the renegade Mexicans and Americans, united with younger Indian warriors who refused to listen to their chiefs, were plundering Mexico.

The renegades who operated along the Rio Grande had also become active in the lucrative market in Apache scalps. This scalp market had been activated by Mexican authorities who began to advertise rewards for Apache scalps in the 1830s. Two Americans, Benjamin Leaton and James Kirker, were the most successful participants, heading large gangs of renegades that had hunted Apaches for money, mainly in Chihuahua. A number of Shawnees and Delawares had joined them, finding scalp hunting to offer more excitement and rewards than the Indian trade on the plains.

Leaton, who had recently left Kirker, had opened a post near Presidio del Norte. Here he supported a congregation of very tough men. They continued to work in the scalp trade, collecting one hundred pesos (a peso was worth roughly a dollar) for an Apache man's scalp, fifty for a woman's, and twenty-five for a child's.[19] Then, in the spring of 1849, Leaton notified Major Van Horne that a Major Michael Chevallie and John Glanton had organized more than one hundred armed men to raid into Chihuahua, stealing for the most part but also hunting Apaches for money.[20] Chevallie and Glanton had been ranger captains under Taylor in Mexico; their violent, murdering rampages had done much to call into question their usefulness. Ironically, an irate

Leaton wanted the army to stop Chevallie and Glanton and their gang, which was a rather cynical request given Leaton's past.

While the figures vary, Major Van Horne reported that the governor of Chihuahua had offered Chevallie and Glanton $150 for an Apache scalp and $200 for a captive (this information was perhaps provided by Leaton); inflation had seemingly occurred in the postwar period. Van Horne realized that Leaton had encouraged some Apaches to work for him, probably raiding on occasion into southern Texas. One specific aspect of Leaton's protest to the U.S. military authorities stemmed from the fact that one night the followers of Chevallie and Glanton had crossed back into Texas and attacked the "peaceful" Apache camp, scalping many of their victims. Leaton really wanted the army to build a post at Presidio del Norte to protect him and his robbers.[21]

As Major Van Horne tried to sort out the muddled situation in the Rio Grande valley, Agent Neighbors received orders to proceed to Washington, D.C. Seeing an opportunity, Neighbors wrote a number of letters to officials there, arguing that Indians needed titles to land and that the military line, established by the posts, had to be made permanent. The Caddos and Wichitas especially, pushed west on several occasions, wanted to know where they should plant crops and build towns. And the Plains tribes, despite their recent loss of hunting grounds, had to be convinced that what they still possessed would remain in their possession: Buffalo Hump had made this very clear.

Neighbors discovered, however, that his trip had little if anything to do with government policy. Once he was in Washington, the new Whig administration under Taylor curtly notified him to prepare his accounts; John H. Rollins, a man who had never lived in Texas, had been given the job. While Neighbors pondered the system of government patronage that saw fit to replace him, Rollins inherited an agency without funds or any semblance of an Indian policy. Worse, he became agent just as the cholera that had proved deadly in Texas communities finally swept through the southern Comanche towns, killing three hundred people, including Neighbors's friend Mopechucope.[22]

The epidemic did lessen conflict with the rapidly expanding German populations in the Texas Hill Country. Yet it also devastated the very Indian bands and leaders who were most likely to embrace peace. Angry over the loss of relatives—Indians by this time knew where such disease came from—and upset over the constant attacks launched by Texans upon Indians without cause, as well as disturbed by the growing activity along the new El Paso and Santa Fe trails, small Indian raiding parties from more-northern Comanche towns turned on Texas late that summer. The first raid of any consequence occurred near Brownsville, where a small force drove off horses and mules. News of the attack, the first of its kind in some time, originated from a citizens' committee. Petitioning Governor Wood, the committee reported that the Indians practiced "the usual and well-known characteristics of blood, rapine & plunder."[23]

The petition made good newspaper copy—where casualties were overblown—and soon Governor Wood demanded of General George M. Brooke, Worth's replacement, that new ranger units be organized. Brooke, who had served with distinction in Mexico, refused, noting that the federal government had continued to employ over one hundred rangers; besides, sufficient army troops were then in service in Texas to control the situation. Brooke, like Taylor, saw rangers as troublemakers.

To the general's surprise, Governor Wood ignored him and ordered the organization of three new companies. The governor then wrote directly to the War Department in Washington to authorize the rangers' enlistment. Justifying his decision, Wood referred to the "frequent depredations of the savages and the state of alarm."[24]

Brooke was baffled. "No Indian forays have been made for some time previous to my arrival, notwithstanding the constant reports in the newspapers of the state of murder and plunder," he wrote to Washington in July. The reports of depredations, the general insisted, "proceed from very interested motives, such as that additional troops may be called out, bringing money into the country." Worse, some Texans occasionally launched raids against Indian camps. One such ranger group was disarmed in July by Major Lewis G. Arnold in country theoretically allocated to Indians, on the upper Trinity River.[25] Arnold, yet another veteran of the Mexican campaigns (and a future Civil War general), suspected that the target of these rangers was the peaceful Caddos. More rangers simply meant more trouble.

Even so, Texas politicians applied pressure in Washington for more ranger companies. Many Texas editors, politically Democrats who naturally wished to embarrass Taylor's new Whig administration, increasingly criticized the army for providing insufficient protection. The growing outcry in the Texas press may have been, as Brooke believed, directed at forcing the army to build and occupy more forts, which in turn became markets for new settlers in the Grand Prairie or the Hill Country. But it also introduced a touchy issue that generals wished to avoid; it severely questioned the ability of the mostly infantry troops of the army to protect a state with a vast, unsettled interior. This criticism had some validity.

Because of the politics and economics of the situation but also because Brooke despised Indians (who were, in his mind, savages), he eventually agreed to equip new ranger units. He even suggested that the War Department provide "percussion rifle and pistol, holster, and munitions."[26] A pattern soon emerged in which cries of depredations in the Texas newspapers, whether vaguely accurate or not, led to pressure on the army and on politicians in Texas and Washington, resulting in the general acquiescence of the federal government to pay and equip ranger units even when the military thought they were not needed.

But Brooke fully expected the army to be able to halt the small incursions and the renegade activity that had occurred thus far in the south of Texas. He debated the strategy of how to accomplish the task with General Harney in late August 1849. Brooke argued that the line of forts had been formed haphazardly, with some being occupied mostly by infantry and others by dragoons. In the process, eight infantry companies had been left in the rear, at "interior" posts. The general decided to integrate infantry and dragoon units, moving one infantry company to every army post on the line, from Fort Inge to Fort Worth. This would free the mounted troops to pursue the handful of raiders—whoever they might be—that had suddenly appeared that summer.[27] These actions did not pacify Texans.

The Texas state senate Committee on Indian Affairs took up the issue of Indian defense that fall. It too had received the petition from Brownsville. Beginning on November 15, 1849, several resolutions were passed. Senator David Gage, the author of one such document, wondered why the U.S. government had not instituted the immediate removal of all Texas Indians after statehood; he argued that Indians had "no right of the soil" and were "intruders." More inflammatory memorials followed in December, and by January 1850 the state legislature had worked itself into a frenzy. Hearing that the War Department was questioning the need for rangers and refusing to pay them, despite Brooke's acquiescence, various senators waved the "bloody shirt," decrying the inhumanity of the ferocious Indian.

Not surprisingly, an old but fiery Senator Edward Burleson took the stage to lambast the government and the army on this account. "Men," he lamented, had been "butchered before their wives and children, and they inhumanely violated, and either massacred, or taken into a cheerless and hopeless captivity." Burleson claimed that over one hundred Texans had been killed just during the spring and summer of 1849. A month later, the number of casualties reported by the Texas Senate reached a more exact figure: 171 killed, 7 wounded, and 25 captured.[28] Although the source of such figures is unclear, Texas newspapers had no difficulty believing them. The newspaper editors led the charge against the supposedly hapless federal army.

These charges were totally without merit. In a land where communication occurred by word of mouth, editors printed one story after another despite the lack of verification (even had they wanted to find the truth). Not surprisingly, the number of depredations and casualties jumped in number from month to month as editors read and reread their own copy. When the Catholic cleric Father Emanuel Domenech later published the memoirs of his travels through Texas for the year 1849, he concluded that "more than two hundred persons, to my knowledge, were scalped in the west of Texas" during that year.[29] Governor Wood, who had to have been aware of the fictitious nature of the information, used these numbers in official reports—or complaints—to Washington, telling the secretary of war in December that "150 persons" had been killed.[30]

Army officers then in the field had an entirely different story, one that General Brooke believed. Lieutenant Colonel D. S. Miles, gathering information relative to the situation at Fort Brown, near Brownsville, indicated that one Don Tamora had been killed and his wife and two daughters carried into captivity that summer. Miles knew of no other depredations. A second raid netted some horses, but it was difficult to determine from where, much less who the perpetrators were. Neighbors, who had returned from Washington, assumed those responsible were running with Santa Anna, a Comanche who had put together a large band of Indians, "and renegades." They had crossed into Mexico in January near Eagle Pass. On further investigation, army officers and Neighbors concluded that some of the victims reported in the papers had to be Mexican carters. But when investigated, even these rumors of attacks turned out to be utter fabrications.[31]

Other evidence demonstrated that virtually all the Indians, with the exception of Santa Anna's Comanches, were peaceful. The Penateka Comanches spent most of the month of June determining who would replace Mopechucope as chief; they decided upon Buffalo Hump, who, although upset about American encroachment in February, soon became resolved to accept the new military line of forts. Indeed, Buffalo Hump visited most of the forts along the line and talked with the officers in command.

Buffalo Hump particularly impressed Captain William Steele, who commanded the fort near Fredericksburg. Steele found the chief to be friendly and reasonable and had a long conversation with him. "They had been to war with Texas . . . and they had gained nothing by it," Steele noted that the chief had told him. Now that Texas was joined to the United States, "a war would lead to the destruction of their nation," he said. To Steele's knowledge, the Penatekas had not been involved in any raids whatsoever.

Lieutenant Frank Hamilton, at Fort Graham, completely agreed: Buffalo Hump and the other chiefs were dedicated to peace. Indeed, the entire region from the Red River southward into Fredericksburg and on into San Antonio had suffered no depredations in a long while. Even José Maria had forgiven the rangers, accepting $500 in goods for the death of the Caddo boy. Hamilton lambasted the Houston *Morning Star* for its incredibly inaccurate reports of conditions in the west of Texas; one article even reported that a dragoon force had been overrun by Indians. Texas newspapers had moved beyond the point of exaggeration to a new level of incredible misinformation.[32]

General Brooke agreed that the situation along the Rio Grande was tenuous, primarily because of the actions of Chevallie, Glanton, Leaton, and the rest. Some of the fighting in the trans-Nueces region (between the Nueces River and the Rio Grande), as the general and the Texas population well knew, involved these former Americans and Texas Rangers, some newly arriving Forty-Niners, and Tejanos. But Brooke failed to find evidence that Indians had killed even a dozen people north of the Rio Grande. Seeing the violence as "domestic" in nature and not therefore a concern for the army, Brooke asked the new Texas governor, P. Hansborough Bell, to use the rangers on the Nueces River. They seemed like the most appropriate state force to employ against "renegades."

When Brooke's request became public, within days, political friends of the governor wrote to recommend various supporters as ranger "commanders." Reputations as Indian fighters (crucial for success in local Texas politics) led to judgeships and election to the state legislature. Moreover, the right to raise ranger companies came with salaries—money to hire unemployed men who would later support ranger "captains" at the voting both. Ex-Governor Wood had been a ranger, and so had Bell. Indeed, most Texas politicians—with the notable exception of Houston—had been rangers. It had become a duty, a part of the Texas creed, to fight Indians.

While General Brooke seemed content to let state officials solve the troubles in the trans-Nueces region, controlling the Indian situation was another matter. Both the general and Indian Bureau officials were aware of the large force that Santa Anna had supposedly led into Mexico. Brooke proposed making one grand strike against Santa Anna's raiders, sending General Harney at the head of those dragoons then posted in West Texas.[33] New to Indian warfare, especially warfare on the plains, Brooke assumed that the guilty parties could easily be differentiated from others such as Buffalo Hump and his people and that the "hostiles" would stand and fight. As the general planned his campaign, the situation changed from serious to critical in the spring of 1850.

The trans-Nueces region erupted into a series of small skirmishes between renegades, Indians, rangers, and soldiers. Increasingly young army officers and ranger captains alike reported clashes in the region, especially between January and October 1850. The War Department files show that nearly twenty skirmishes occurred over these months—or two a month—mostly along the Nueces River. Frequently, both army officers and ranger captains failed to identify the raiders, but they nonetheless mostly supposed that Indians made up the parties.

The only real success against these raiders came in one deadly clash when ranger captain John S. Ford surprised an Indian party, supposedly killing eight—the fact that Indians constituted this party brought many to conclude that such people had been responsible for all the trouble. In all, that spring and summer nearly two dozen raiders were killed, as well as eight soldiers and rangers. Casualties among civilians remained low; one unverifiable report listed seven killed and two girls being carried into captivity.[34]

Unfortunately, Texas newspapers painted a different picture. When the Texas legislature met in late August 1850, the Senate Committee on Indian Affairs reported that some 71 Texans (down notably from Burleson's 171 of the previous fall, 1849) had died and that thousands of horses and mules had been carried off. As in the previous year, army reports failed to confirm any estimate that approached these numbers. In a strange but revealing comment, even the Committee on Indian Affairs recognized that the army was questioning its numbers: "We are grieved to know that our remonstrances and petitions have received from the Government of the United States the most insulting incredulity."[35] Texas and the U.S. Army and Indian Bureau were increasingly at odds over the numbers; even moderately objective observers failed to agree on the issue.

Most Indian agents and army officers who worked either in Indian Territory or in Texas vigorously contested the Texas position. Neighbors's replacement, Agent Rollins—who was not from Texas—quickly concluded that Texans caused most of the trouble. Referring to Texas Rangers and renegades, he wrote to a friend in 1850, "There is a large class of people here who prefer the wild and indolent life of the volunteer to any other condition." They had one desire, he said, and that was "to fight and exterminate the Indians," a belief strongly ingrained in the "minds of the people of Texas." This "frontier" creed led to a culture of violence in which "hatred of the Indians [has] been cultivated both by the newspapers and interested individuals."[36] It had obviously reached a point at which killing Indians, even friendly ones, was praiseworthy.

Federal officials often agreed with Rollins's assessment, especially since this Texas creed prevented the establishment of a workable Indian policy. Whig Secretary of War George Crawford—who had selected Rollins to replace Neighbors—sarcastically responded to the repeated call for more rangers by diplomatically blaming the "incursions" on the "undefined condition of the enjoyment of the Indians to lands." While Texas was "extending her laws without any recognition of the occupant right of the Indians," the secretary continued, "it must be apparent that the latter [Indians] must either recede, or be annihilated."[37] Texas refused to consider such criticism, coming as it did from a northern Whig.

Realizing that a military expedition was being planned, the rather inactive Agent Rollins finally traveled west to inspect his dominion in the spring of 1850. Near the Colorado River he met a few surviving Lipan Apaches—those who had avoided "Big Foot" Wallace a few years before. Rollins also met for the first time the new Comanche chief Ketumsee, who led a band of the Penatekas. While Rollins described Ketumsee as a "distinguished and daring" man, the agent's comments reveal his inexperience. Ketumsee was quite elderly and had never surfaced in councils previously. While Rollins had no way of knowing this, the chief had inherited his position after the cholera had carried off other, more prominent Penateka chiefs.

As Rollins continued with his discussions, he seemed oblivious to yet another important fact: Ketumsee's emergence signaled a division within the southern Comanche band. Rollins knew nothing of Pahayuco, the leading chief, who with his protégé Buffalo Hump had moved increasingly northward into the upper Red and Canadian rivers. Ketumsee, trying to maintain the Comanche presence in the south, negotiated on behalf of a faction of his tribe—about seventy older people and children—but his efforts soon made many enemies in the groups that split from him. Worse, Ketumsee and his following, in Rollins's words, "lived in a state of destitution." Seeking food, Ketumsee agreed to every demand made by the agent, which gave Rollins false hopes.

Nor were all of the agent's encounters successful. Rollins found Wild Cat and some two hundred Seminoles and Kickapoos—"twenty to twenty-five Negroes" being particularly conspicuous in the group—defiantly hunting in southwestern

Texas. When the agent demanded that they leave, the wily chief simply replied: "'Maj. Neighbors' often told us the same thing, and we have never been hurt, and maybe so you lie?"[38] Wild Cat likely was involved in helping slaves (who feared being re-enslaved) escape to Mexico by crossing the Rio Grande that spring. The migration of these African Americans to Mexico led to the creation of a black community west of Piedras Negras; this community became a haven for escaped slaves during the 1850s, with growing numbers coming from Texas. Rollins could do little to control Wild Cat; after all, his people were armed to the teeth.[39]

Dragoons under Brevet Colonel Samuel Cooper ultimately followed Rollins into Indian lands with the hope of punishing marauders such as Wild Cat; at the very least, the colonel hoped to track the resettlement of the Caddos and Wichitas, who after being forced to leave the area below Comanche Peak had built new towns well above it. Cooper found them in several locales. José Maria's Caddos had towns on either side of the river about thirty miles above the peak, and others could be found thirty miles farther up. "I found these people perfectly peaceful," the colonel reported. "They were tilling the earth, raising corn and vegetables extensively and their crops appear in a fine state."[40] Despite this seemingly idyllic condition, just a few days before, a party of Texas Rangers had crossed into Indian Territory and struck a hunting camp of Caddos, killing an undetermined number, leading to some trepidation at the Caddo towns.[41]

Both Cooper and Agent Rollins heard very little about western or northern Comanches, who remained, for the most part, on the high plains. By fall the news that trickled in regarding these groups was all bad. The first evidence came from New Mexico, where a small party of *comancheros* (New Mexican traders, mostly Indian) stumbled onto a package of letters and papers attached to a wooden pole on a trail leading into Santa Fe. The letters included Houston's speech to the Comanches, dated May 4, 1843; Eldridge's treaty of later that year; an Anson Jones letter regarding peace, dated July 14, 1845; and a "talk" from Agent Butler as well as his treaty of 1846. These documents had to have come from Buffalo Hump and Pahayuco, who apparently were becoming more dissatisfied with the advance of the U.S. Army and Texas settlers into their territory.

The meaning seemed obvious—all agreements of the past, whether partially kept or otherwise, had been discarded by the northern Comanche chiefs. Pahayuco, whose son apparently had been killed while raiding, was the most distraught.[42] Throughout the fall, Rollins unsuccessfully sent out runners, hoping to meet with Pahayuco, but to no avail. Experienced traders were abandoning their trading posts on the upper Red River for the security of the east. Even so, a handful of Comanches, Wichitas, and Caddos met Rollins on the upper San Saba in December 1850. They smoked, the agent handed out presents, and everyone signed yet another treaty. Buffalo Hump attended, but he remained sullen and, as Rollins put it, "is a politician and intriguer." General Brooke saw the effort as worthwhile but called it "incomplete."

More and more, Brooke, like Rollins, hoped that feeding the Comanches might allow some control over them. Once settled on land, the general thought, necessary schools and agricultural implements would lead to "civilization."[43] Some encouraging information came in the form of demographics—Comanche populations were falling. Captain Randolph B. Marcy, at the new Fort Washita in Indian Territory, noted this trend over the winter of 1850–1851. Epidemics were the major culprit, yet, as the captain said, "the northern and middle Comanches" had also suffered from reversal in war, "several of their members having been killed." Sometimes the conflict was with other Indians, especially with Pawnees and Osages, and some losses occurred in Mexico.

Marcy also noted a rather peculiar geopolitical view that most northern Comanches leaders held in 1850. The chiefs regarded the Texans living north and east of the Colorado River as friends—perhaps because of Houston's efforts—but remained "at war" with those southwest of the river, which included Tejanos and Mexicans. They distrusted Texans from San Antonio (the council house massacre remained fresh in their minds) and Austin—places where rangers congregated.[44] But they also feared those regions, an attitude that obviously helped the struggling German settlements. The early historical argument that these Germans developed better relations with Indians than did Anglo-Texans must be tempered by the realization that the Comanches had lost many warriors to rangers and soldiers in the hills north and west of San Antonio.[45]

Fighting in the south continued to lure a few Indians into the conflict. Rangers clashed with a small party of Comanches on the Aransas River on January 4, 1851. Young Lieutenant Edward Burleson, the senator's son, surprised fourteen Comanches a few miles south of the Nueces on the 30th. His charge with eight men ended in a hand-to-hand struggle that left only one Texan standing without wounds; four Indians and one Texan died. Just a day later, Lieutenant Andrew J. Walker ambushed fifteen men—likely Comanches—near Fort McIntosh, the renamed garrison near Laredo, Texas. Nearly all the rangers received wounds, and four later died. The army speculated on the ethnic makeup of these marauding groups, but the northern Comanches had warned of their intention to attack this region.

Similar small assaults, often conducted by only five or ten men, continued into June along the Nueces River. Unlike the Comanches of old, the raiders no longer came in large parties of a hundred or more; more important, the reports suggest that major chiefs (the kind who wore distinctive headdresses and gaudy dress) seldom led the parties. The raiders, failing to challenge the army or ranger units, utilized a hit-and-run strategy, taking horses and mules. Even more surprising, they often walked into the settlements, leaving no trail, and rode out stolen livestock.[46]

Governor Bell insisted in letters to the army and Indian agents that these small raiding parties had killed many Texans. In response, Rollins and other army officers contradicted the governor; Rollins could list only one citizen killed near Aransas Bay during the winter and spring of 1850 and 1851, and a boy and two girls carried off.[47]

The constant attacks by the press and Governor Bell's almost belligerent battering of General Brooke, however, was taking its toll on federal officials. Brooke seemed at times ready to concede that the army may have been wrong. He especially criticized Rollins's December treaty with Ketumsee—an agreement signed by a small band of seventy Indians that General Brooke had never even sent to Washington—in which the Comanches supposedly had agreed to give up their captives. The agreement had placated no one, and worse, as Brooke concluded to the governor, "The Indians had not complied with a single article of their [its] stipulations."[48]

Accordingly, sure of the need to act, General Brooke finalized his orders for a western campaign. He commanded his dragoons, under Colonel William Harney, to take the field against the Indians and to "punish them severely," to "destroy their villages and other property, [and] to take their cattle, horses and mules." Finally, "when positive murder can be proved against any Indian or Indians, they should be put to death on the spot."[49] While attending to preparations, however, General Brooke died at San Antonio on March 9, 1851. This mattered little; under Harney, Companies A, B, C, and G of the Second Dragoons would invade the west and force compliance with the treaty of December 10, 1850.[50] A successful campaign would hopefully satisfy the Texas press and the state's governor.

As the troops mustered, Agent Rollins rather innocently wrote a letter to Governor Bell confessing that he knew of only one Anglo captive in Indian hands. The initial report of two girls being taken near Aransas Bay, Rollins reported, was false. The state legislature had claimed that dozens of captives existed in Indian camps in both 1849 and 1850, he wrote, and asked whether the governor had a list of other possible captives. Moreover, the only confirmed death attributed to Indians had been the young German boy. Rollins asked for the names of other Texans who had been killed recently by Indians (in particular, by which Indians, and where).[51]

The pompous and demanding Bell evaded the issue. In fact, Bell possessed nothing resembling a list. Nor did any legislator have one. Yet Bell assured Rollins that many depredations had occurred. The western tribes needed to be punished, Bell declared; how could an Indian agent question such a need?[52]

Fortunately for the southern Plains tribes, Colonel Harney took command of all Texas troops after Brooke's death. While the colonel was hardly soft on Indians, he was forced to assign the undertaking of the campaign to Lieutenant Colonel William Hardee. A West Point graduate and Alabama plantation owner, Hardee was a fine officer. Later commanding a corps at Shiloh, Perryville, and Murfreesboro, he showed a steady resolve. Hardee, like many regular army officers, even came to like Indians, more so than complaining Texans.[53]

Hardee took command of two hundred dragoons on the Llano River in late May 1851 and quickly moved west into the San Saba country. Soon his guides found the camps of the Lipan Apaches and Ketumsee's southern Comanches. Hardee easily could have proclaimed these Indians guilty and attacked the undefended villages—

in essence, adopting the strategy of the Texas Rangers. But because the camps were occupied mostly by women, children, and old men, Hardee rejected the easy victory. Instead, on May 28, Rollins and the colonel spoke with the handful of Comanches, initially demanding of Ketumsee that he turn over all captives and identify Indians involved in raiding.

Ketumsee openly cooperated, allowing Hardee to search his entire camp, which produced no captives. Hardee seemed less than surprised when he found nothing to incriminate Ketumsee's band. The old chief volunteered that the Lipan Apaches camped nearby possessed seventeen Mexicans, whom they promptly surrendered. The colonel then collared the second chief of the southern Comanches, the more vigorous Cariwah, who led the dragoon column northward to the Clear Fork of the Brazos River, where more Comanches, including Buffalo Hump, were believed to live. There, Cariwah said, he would point out any bad Indians.

Primed for a confrontation, the dragoons marched north, reaching the Brazos River in a few days. To Hardee's dismay, the Plains Indians had long since moved north. Only a few friendly Caddos and Wichitas lived nearby on the river. This first major expedition of mounted U.S. troops into the wilds of West Texas saw little action. Hardee could only report to Harney that if Comanches were committing depredations, the evidence for such activity was difficult to find. In addition, to raid Texas settlements, Comanches would have to travel hundreds of miles. Hardee thus seemed to suggest that the Indians were innocent.[54]

Nevertheless, Hardee's expedition provided a rationale for the army to wrest control of the upper Brazos and Red rivers from the northern Comanches, who used the valleys as a refuge during the harsh winter months. General William G. Belknap had begun that attempt a few months before, exploring the junction of the Clear Fork and Brazos rivers, locating a spot for a military post. Following Hardee's and Belknap's recommendations, the army began construction on what would become Fort Belknap in late July 1851.[55]

Fort Belknap became one of the most important military garrisons in the west, surviving the Civil War and ultimately being abandoned in 1876. Its location some eighty miles north and west of Comanche Peak, placed it nearly on the edge of the plains. It soon attracted a settlement, and many wagon trains headed west from Fort Smith, Arkansas, used it as jumping-off point for the trek across the Great Plains. But it was a thorn in the side of the Plains Indians because it invaded what was clearly their ground.

Simultaneously, Colonel Harney ordered troops to advance fifty miles northwest of Fort Martin Scott to construct Fort Mason. Nearly on the upper San Saba, this garrison controlled the heart of the old southern Comanche domain. Thus, the army, in attempting to pacify the west, had advanced the unmarked Texas settlement line some fifty miles west in the spring of 1851 alone. The so-called line, negotiated and defined with Indians on several occasions in the 1840s and then reaffirmed in 1846 and 1847, had been moved once again.

The army's move came as a result of new information. Colonel Hardee reported that the Comanche populations had fallen to three thousand people (of whom only three hundred were warriors) after the epidemics of the previous two years. Such figures were less than half of the real numbers. But these estimates supported the growing suspicion that the western tribes no longer possessed the manpower capable of overrunning posts located well in advance of settlement, which made the division of commands feasible. Harney concluded in his report to Washington that the army's mission should be to prevent small raids rather than prepare for clashes with large Indian forces.[56]

All the evidence, what little did exist, supported Harney. The brief skirmishes on the Nueces River in the spring of 1851 had been with small groups. Lieutenant Richard J. Dodge, patrolling out of Fort Martin Scott, discovered a trail in the San Saba valley of twelve Indians, trailing a dozen horses, in March 1851. They were found, attacked, and most either killed or wounded. A few days later, Dodge's tracker, one Don Pedro Espinosa, found another trail of three Indians, this time on foot. More and more, the army was discovering that a handful of Indians or renegades would walk into the settlements, steel horses, and ride out. Most, however, completely avoided settlers, who would give the alarm. These tactics were making the army's job more difficult.[57]

Other army officers agreed. Captain Marcy, who left Belknap's command while on the upper Brazos to explore the plains during the spring and summer of 1851, spent many hours counseling with Comanche leaders and came to believe that even renegades could be subdued with presents of food. "I am decidedly of the opinion," he wrote upon returning, "that the wisest and most economical policy that can be adopted towards the Comanches is a conciliatory one." Increasingly, Hardee, Harney, and Marcy saw the role of the army as a police force; Marcy concluded that trouble in Texas was almost always caused by a "certain class of people upon the border"—Texans and renegades who lacked employment, raided Indian towns for profit, stole horses from settlers, or just simply hunted in the west. More dispersed army garrisons, while perhaps poorly manned, would stop such people.[58]

Yet the army's move onto the edge of the southern plains disturbed some Indians. Captain Henry H. Sibley, who commanded dragoons on the Brazos River, found the Wichitas and Caddos sullen and upset over the presence of Fort Belknap. They disliked having a garrison "above them" on the river and especially found fault with General Belknap. The general gave them a stern lecture and threatened to destroy their villages if he traced any stolen livestock to their towns. U.S. Indian agents, including the newly appointed Jesse Stemm and John A. Rogers (Rollins had died that summer), found similar concerns while being introduced to various tribal leaders. Ketumsee especially was angry that his people had been pushed from place to place. If the president of the United States would authorize the creation of a "line, and set apart a section," the chief said, then his people could farm and live in peace.[59]

Colonel Harney presented these suggestions to Governor Bell that summer. Hardee's expedition had demonstrated that no real Indian threat existed, other than very small raiding groups that wished to avoid detection. These raids could be stopped if Texas would agree to a permanent line, which the army would enforce. The land west of the line, with the proper federal legislation, might also fall under the province of the Intercourse Acts. It had taken the army three years to arrive at the same conclusion that former agent Neighbors had reached in 1846 (and Houston, some years earlier than that). Anticipating a positive response from the governor, Harney issued Special Order no. 34, warning against "the nefarious system of intercourse with the Indians" that was typically undertaken by western traders. The purchasing of mules and horses west of the line was thereafter outlawed by military decree.[60]

Several officials, including former agents Neighbors and Rollins, had argued for such an order for some time. In an interesting assessment, Rollins believed that the line should begin at roughly the 100th Meridian, extend southward to the Concho River, and turn west to the mountains. This boundary, he believed, would cut the Comanches off from Mexico, since the Indians would not be allowed south of the El Paso road. But he, like Harney, had learned much of Texas politics during his short stay. Rollins did not believe that the state would accept this obvious solution. Too many speculators in "unlocated land certificates" lobbied the legislature against such a line, and Rollins believed that Governor Bell was in league with these profiteers. In addition, being of the "War Party," Bell did not want peace.[61]

But Bell felt obligated to answer Harney, and after careful consideration, he did so on May 5. The governor applauded Harney's action. The federal intercourse laws, in his words, "contain most wholesome provisions," if "they can be made legally applicable." There was, however, a question of jurisdiction. Since the Intercourse Acts of 1834 legally defined "Indian Country" and Bell's definition of this statute put Texas outside of the law's protection, nothing could be done "until the formal consent of the state" had been obtained. What is more, Bell concluded, "the known treachery and double dealing of the red men, though unseduced by corrupt dealers [traders], would still lead him to abduct persons and property." It was the "lazy nomadic habits of the tribes" that led to horse and mule theft, according to Bell; the presence of good or bad traders had little to do with it.[62]

The impasse was obvious. The federal laws might be good legislation, but the army's job was thought to be solely to protect Texas from Indians—not to separate the two contending groups. Serious questions existed as to whether the Intercourse Acts could ever be applied to Texas. The federal government, Governor Bell believed, should implement complete removal. Bell was convinced that Indian depredations continued to be the problem; the army, he argued, should stick to its own business and leave the sovereignty of Texas—"her right to full and complete jurisdiction over every portion of territory within her present limits"—alone.

To a certain degree, the army had fulfilled its mission. The military forts had limited depredations to the Nueces valley; there, nuisance raids continued, but troopers and rangers often caught the groups responsible. It was almost impossible to point to a single settler's cabin that had been overrun between 1849 and 1851. And army officers took no responsibility for the general mess that existed in the trans–Nueces River region.

But for all the success of the garrisoned forces, army officers seemed oblivious to the fact that the arbitrary placement of forts (and thus the westward intrusion of the boundary line) had angered many Indians and had split them into factions, some advocating peace and some planning war. In addition, the Rio Grande valley remained a hotbed of intrigue and conflict. As Texans entered the new (supposedly secure) ranchland opened by the line of forts, the cry of "Indian depredations," so frequently used to lure readers to Texas newspapers in the past, would once again raise its ugly head.

16

GENERAL PERSIFOR SMITH
AND THE SALVATION OF TEXAS

Brevet Major General Persifor S. Smith, another veteran of Mexico, took command
in Texas in October 1851. Smith's organizational skills and bravery made up for his
lack of formal military training. Steady and self-assured, Smith had been at the front
of the line at the battle of Monterrey and later commanded the assault on the Mexican military cadets at Chapultepec in Mexico City. General Winfield Scott called
him "cool" and "unembarrassed," a thoughtful general rather than a loud one, who
often revealed the value of his Princeton education.[1]

Smith, more than any other general, made his mark in Texas. Unlike Brooke and
Harney, he never engaged in bombastic racial rhetoric, and he recognized immediately
the complex nature of the Texas population. Rather than fight with Texas Rangers,
he tried to use them in areas of southern Texas where they might do some good—
of course, Tejanos likely disagreed with such a conclusion. His demeanor led to better
relations with Texas state officials and less acrimony. But most of all, General Smith
developed a plan for Texas that actually worked, to some degree.[2] Smith's plan brought
peace to Texas by 1853, which in turn convinced the Texas state legislature to finally
allocate land, in the form of reservations, to Plains Indians. Fundamentally, Smith
helped bring Texas to the point of nearly ending its defiant policy of ethnic cleansing.

General Smith readily agreed with Hardee that starving Indians had to be fed.
Feeding Indians was increasingly being done on northern plains reservations with the
hopes that these people would give up the bison hunt. Nevertheless, Smith still believed
that the army would face continued hit-and-run raids and that while a serious threat
no longer existed to military forts in the west, army resources in Texas could be better
utilized. After surveying his command—especially the placement of forts and troops—
he contrived a new strategy, designed to be more cost-efficient and using infantry more
effectively; the War Department, seeing the genius of the plan, quickly sanctioned it.

Smith first concluded that "the single line of defense—the only one hitherto practicable with the number of troops here—is very defective." He wanted a double line. In a troop deployment contrary to the conventional logic of the time, Smith ordered the infantry to the most advanced posts, including the newly developed Fort Belknap (on the upper Brazos) and Fort Mason (on the headwaters of the Llano River). To this advanced line were added six new infantry posts: Fort Chadbourne (on the headwaters of the Colorado River); Fort McKavett (at the head of the San Saba River); Fort Phantom Hill (near the head of the Clear Fork River); Fort Terrett (on the north fork of the Llano River); Fort Clark (on the headwaters of the Nueces River); and Fort Ewell (on the central Nueces River).

These new garrisons often possessed only a company of troops, and infantry at that. Nevertheless, Smith theorized that if infantry occupied the very few sources for water that raiding parties needed for their escape, the raiders could be ambushed at these water holes on their return from the settlements. And since livestock often perished on the high plains, it made more sense to keep mounted troops near the settlements at forts such as Graham and Martin Scott, where the animals of the garrison had access to grain.

The second element of the plan was less defined by the general when he took over command, but it emerged piecemeal in 1852 and 1853. Army officers at the far western posts had constant contact with Indians. They spoke with chiefs on a regular basis, giving them presents and counseling peace. Smith's strategy sacrificed the immediacy and speed of the mounted dragoons for the slower but more sustained benefit of public relations. However, it also employed the classic hammer-and-anvil tactic, as the searching dragoons might drive raiders into an infantry ambush at an isolated waterhole. Even Smith's officers came to enjoy their contact with Indian leaders; of course, this was often their only source of amusement, given the isolation of the posts.[3]

Smith's plan, brilliant as it was, took a toll on troops. Captain D. M. Frost of the Eighth Infantry, who helped build Fort Ewell, gave a detailed account of the wear and tear on the soldiers in the many letters that he sent home to his wife. Only twenty men defended the fort, while the others constantly patrolled on foot. "The whole rifle regiment at the present moment are wandering over these desert plains," he wrote in September 1852. Frost had just returned from an eighty-mile hike and had orders to conduct another. Tired feet and worn-out boots did more to muster soldiers out of the army than did fear of Indian attack.

Making matters worse, Frost and his men faced a constant barrage of outrageous criticism in the Texas press. "The newspapers abuse all the regular troops like pickpockets," Frost complained to his wife. The constant stories regarding depredations and the ineffectiveness of the infantry were untrue, despite the claim of one editor that such soldiers in West Texas were "as much out of place as a sawmill on the ocean." By December 1852, Frost categorically declared that he had not seen or heard of an Indian anywhere for months and that there had been no credible reports of stolen stock. The captain's letters turned again and again to the sterility of the land surrounding Fort Ewell and to castigating the complaining Texans who often visited him.[4]

Smith's plan, despite the sore feet it inflicted, offered further advantages in terms of information. Once the army began patrolling the headwaters of the San Saba, Colorado, Clear Fork, and Brazos rivers, depriving raiders of these regions, Smith realized that many tribes were having difficulty just surviving. The dwindling of bison herds and the drought, particularly the dry years of 1845–1848, had deprived many Plains Indians of traditional food sources. Smith theorized that perhaps former raiders might be convinced to join the small, friendly band led by Ketumsee, settle on a reserve, and be fed. Agent Neighbors had begun a program of feeding these Indians briefly in 1849, but Rollins had lacked the energy to continue it. Smith saw the value of supplying them with food and tried to reinstate this practice at the various forts.

Former Texas Ranger George Howard, a newly hired "special agent," also received orders from the Indian Bureau to cooperate. Howard eventually expanded the program beyond Ketumsee's Comanches when he realized that the Caddos and Wichitas, situated in six villages above Comanche Peak, also had suffered over the winter of 1851–1852. Several cavalry officers from Fort Graham had visited these towns, reporting the appearance of promising crops but little available food. One old Caddo woman reportedly dropped her hoe as the officers approached her "and by an unmistakable sawing motion with her hand across her stomach, [she] manifest[ed] the cravings of hunger." To assist Howard, army troops gave the Indians what extra meat and bread they could spare until the crops matured.[5]

The army's assistance came at a crucial time—it would have been difficult for Howard to move food so far west during the winter—but the soldiers' close proximity did foreordain a problem. As Howard and his assistant, Jesse Stemm, learned in conversations with José Maria, the chief knew that the fort would soon attract Texas settlers, who would invade fields and attempt to drive off the Indians. By 1852, the Caddo villages had reached the western limit for riverine agriculture. José Maria's people would not be able to farm above the mouth of the Clear Fork, their next location, should they have to move west.[6] Howard and Stemm were brought to realize that the existing approach to provisioning the Wichitas and Caddos was temporary. Permanent locations had to be agreed upon for the construction of Indian villages, their attending fields, and even government warehouses.

Ketumsee's Comanches suffered as much as, if not more than, the Caddos and Wichitas. Howard had received $10,000 from the Bureau of Indian Affairs to feed them, and Stemm went through East Texas communities buying up corn and beef over the winter. Much of this food—including 16,543 pounds of beef—reached Fort Graham in February and was distributed to the Indians. For well over a month, Ketumsee's Comanches stayed near the fort, ate government rations, and received presents. Other small bands, including Buffalo Hump's and Sanaco's, cautiously joined

Ketumsee's people. Agents and army officers alike confidently assumed that it would be an easy matter to co-opt all the Plains bands in this fashion.[7]

Ketumsee felt obligated to match such kindness with reciprocal gifts. He did so in June, using the opportunity to lobby Agent Howard with a long oration on the condition and concerns of his people. "The hunting grounds in which we and our fathers have been for so many generations accustomed to roam undisturbed," Ketumsee said, "are now fast passing away." The country around them, "where until a short time [ago], the white man has never been seen, is now dotted over with the tents of soldiers." Ketumsee openly asked Howard for land for his Comanches and a boundary line that would keep Texans at bay. After the oratory, Ketumsee handed over twenty-seven Mexican captives, who were returned to their homes.[8] In Comanche culture, such a gift literally demanded action on the part of the receiver.

Not everyone applauded Ketumsee's actions. At Fort Mason, Brevet Major Hamilton W. Merrill spent many hours talking with the chief. Merrill learned that Ketumsee's appeasement of U.S. officials was causing factional disputes, in particular with Pahayuco's and Buffalo Hump's people. Indeed, fifty of these Indians had been down from the north in mid-March hoping to chastise Ketumsee. Outraged over his repatriation of Mexican captives, they threatened the chief; his actions reflected upon the legitimacy of raiding Mexico.

Whether the northerners were jealous of the food distribution or of Ketumsee's increased coziness with Americans mystified Merrill. But Merrill could see that a tug-of-war was going on for the hearts and minds of the southern Comanches; he was less certain of Ketumsee's ability to prevail. The major could only pledge to protect the old Comanche chief. "I have watched and known him intimately for over two years," Major Merrill concluded. "I believe him to be a true man."[9]

Merrill was not alone in his praise of Comanche leaders. Captain Arthur Tracy Lee, commanding at Fort McKavett, had daily contact with Buffalo Hump, Yellow Wolf, Ketumsee, and Sanaco—all southern Comanches. "I have upon all occasions found them to be friendly & well disposed towards the whites," he wrote on May 15, 1852, "provided they were supplied with food necessary to sustain life." Lee noted that the new western posts had created some excitement among them, but he was certain that if the government would set aside land for them, their concerns would dissipate. Lee, Merrill, Howard, and even General Smith openly defended these Comanche leaders' honesty and sincerity. Dealing with the Comanche leaders directly, they saw the Indians in a much different light than did Texans, who were frequently stirred up by rumors and fearmongering. They even believed that a time would come when Indians and Texans could live side by side on the plains in peace.

Captain Lee also confirmed much of what Marcy and others had said about the predicament of the Penatekas. Game had disappeared to such an extent that these southern Comanches would starve if the government failed to feed them. The lack of game had also fractured them, for they had broken up into four or five small groups, each with its own individual leaders. Despite Buffalo Hump's elevation to the position of "chief," then, he likely only commanded a small number of the Penatekas. If they did turn to raiding to feed themselves, it would be increasingly difficult to hold anyone accountable. But the cost of feeding them was so "trifling," as Lee put it, that the provisioning constituted good policy.[10] Unfortunately, Howard's efforts proved too modest, and some Comanches starved that fall. The government needed a better-funded system of supply.[11]

Ironically, as Plains leaders endorsed peace in exchange for food, violence erupted again in the south of Texas. Smith caused part of the problem during the summer of 1852 when he ordered the three ranger companies serving along the Nueces River mustered out because of a lack of Indians for them to fight. Leaving service reluctantly, many rangers refused to turn over their government-issued Colt revolvers, and many turned to Mexico, serving as mercenaries for various revolutionary groups.

Smith's assessment of the turmoil showed that more and more rangers and other renegades frequented the Rio Grande border towns, hiring their guns to whoever paid the most. Even town leaders supported the violence. "A large part of the population in the towns," the general wrote, "looked forward to disturbances there as being likely to cause large public expenditures." The army's presence in Brownsville, Laredo, and Eagle Pass offered payrolls and supply contracts; the more troops, the more federal expenditure. Smith even suspected a civil conspiracy of sorts, stating that "the press, public meetings, and inferior civil officers joined in everything that could aid in producing the event, or embarrass and obstruct those engaged in preventing it."[12]

Smith's assessment of the rangers, the ex-volunteers, and the nature of the ethnic milieu in southern Texas was not an isolated view. Some areas—although not all—in the trans-Nueces region had fallen under the control of lawless sorts, who, though they might be in the minority, dominated the border towns. While some simply took what they wanted, others took over the courthouses and slowly dispossessed surrounding Tejanos of their land. The abbé Emanuel Domenech, who visited the region in the early 1850s, was aghast at the violence of the Anglo-Texans: "The greater part of the Kentucky Americans," as he called them, "simply install" themselves on the land and defend their claim with Colt revolvers.

The lawlessness was mostly caused by violent ruffians unaffiliated with any tribal society. "The Americans of the Texian frontier," Domenech continued, "are . . . the very scum of society—bankrupts, escaped criminals, old volunteers, who . . . came into the country protected by nothing that could be called a judicial authority." In the Nueces and Rio Grande valleys, they committed murder with impunity—such killings, the abbé noted, had become "very common." Domenech suspected that many of the killings along the Rio Grande that were often blamed on Indians or Mexicans were in fact the work of gangs of Texans. There is no doubt that at least some of the reports in Texas newspapers of depredations and killings stemmed from this violence.[13]

Frederick Law Olmsted, who entered southern Texas about the same time, offered similar observations. While at Goliad, the traveler from New England surveyed the old Spanish mission, noting in his account that "the Americans had destroyed it." They commonly used Catholic church sanctuaries as stables. Olmstead found that although Tejanos had once "owned all the land" in and about Goliad, Texans had taken it without any "pay." Local Tejanos who still remained on their ranchos possessed a few flocks of rather scrawny sheep—Olmsted thought the animals so worthless that they seemed incapable of growing hair on their underbellies—and took jobs of the lowest order. "Mexicans were regarded in a somewhat unchristian tone," Olmstead mused, "not as heretics or heathens . . . but rather as vermin, to be exterminated."[14]

Tejano marginalization increased as well in the Rio Grande border towns after the Mexican War. Brownsville quickly filled with Anglo commercialists who soon dominated life. Domenech, who traveled through the city, described the local Tejano citizenry as living a life of "apathy [and] listlessness, carried to amiability." A good many Tejanos simply lived as *barilleros* (water carriers). They literally moved drinking water on a daily basis from the Rio Grande into the heart of Brownsville, where they sold it. They reminded Domenech of the *lazzaroni* of Naples—the bare-foot, bare-breasted laborers who worked in simple cotton drawers. A few rancheros lived in the countryside and occasionally came into town to buy and sell their wares. A handful even owned large ranches with considerable herds.[15]

The poverty of the majority of the Tejanos, along with their lack of education, contributed to their meager status. Many of the peones still in southern Texas had been marginalized by the previous rulers—the Tejano elite and the Mexican aristocracy. Confusing matters further, some rancheros had moved back into the trans-Nueces region after the Texas Revolution, acquiring new land titles from the Mexican state of Tamaulipas. Texas claimed this region even though it failed to administer it until after the Mexican War. While a Texas state commission, headed by William H. Bourland and James B. Miller, met from 1850 to 1852 in an attempt to sort out land titles, the endeavor created considerable suspicion. The best that can be said of the commission is that it confirmed title to several hundred Tejano claims.[16]

General Smith fully grasped the volatile nature of the situation in the south, a problem that his army could not solve and one that he, personally, wished to avoid. But at nearly the same time as the general claimed victory over the Indians, revolutionary violence and even slave hunting escalated south of the Rio Grande. The problem originated during the summer of 1851, when former Texas Rangers—including John "Rip" Ford, who had been forcefully retired from law enforcement, and "Captain" Warren Adams—combined to invade Mexico and retake the former slaves who were living with Wild Cat's Seminoles. Governor Bell endorsed the plan, although he offered no official assistance. Adams, who led the first attack, soon found stiff resistance to his "nigger hunting," and he withdrew. But the rewards, given the fact that male slaves often sold for $2,500, led to more efforts.[17]

The attempts of Texans to retake former slaves soon paled in comparison to the fighting that erupted over control of the state governments of Nuevo León and Tamaulipas. The struggle was part of the continuing debate between so-called liberals, who wanted more unrestrained markets in northern Mexico, and centralists, who did not. Wild Cat's Seminoles, some Kickapoos who had joined them, and a number of Texan volunteers—curious allies to say the least—joined in the struggle, which soon involved sizeable armies. Many Anglos were involved, smuggling being their principal occupation; others sought plunder.[18] As the fighting intensified, raiders crossed the Rio Grande and attacked isolated ranches. Francis P. Parker, a local official from Brownsville, wrote Governor Bell in May that "murders and robbery by large parties from the other side [Mexico], are almost of daily occurrence."[19] It was unsafe to travel outside of town.

General Smith hoped that these "local matters" would solve themselves. He focused instead on the tensions on the northern plains. Northern Comanches, while angry at Ketumsee, especially detested the invasion of the plains by the U.S. Army and the occupation of headwaters of various rivers that had been used in supporting raiding expeditions into Mexico. The key blocking positions were Forts Belknap, Phantom Hill, Chadbourne, McKavett, and Terrett. The forts made it virtually impossible for large raiding parties to descend into Texas without being spotted and harassed by the army.

Some concern existed that the parties would simply travel farther to the west, entering New Mexico. Reports even suggested that the northern Indians had entertained comanchero traders, who promoted an alliance in which the two groups agreed to drive the Americans from New Mexico.[20] The first inkling that the rumor might contain some truth came when news flashed across both Texas and Indian Territory that the army expedition under command of Captain Randolph B. Marcy had been destroyed while mapping the upper Red River.

Marcy, Captain George McClellan—whose Civil War exploits made him famous—and half a dozen Delawares, including Jim Ned and Black Beaver, had left Fort Washita in April 1852 for their second expedition into the west. They joined up with a company of dragoons at Fort Belknap, bringing the command's strength to seventy men. With the Delawares as guides, Marcy worried little about the safety of the group, but given the growing concerns regarding the northern Comanches—after their virtual declaration of war—the possibility of annihilation was real.

On July 7, a Kiowa rode into Fort Arbuckle in Indian Territory and reported the destruction of the command. The news spread like wildfire. The report by Captain J. G. Stevens at the fort is typical: "I do not believe there is a probability of a doubt but what *every man in the command* has been killed by the Comanches."[21]

Riders racing eastward spread the news of the disaster, and newspapers embellished the reports to attract readers. Soon nothing short of Indian war existed all across the plains, or so it seemed. Texans, turning on General Smith, took a told-you-so attitude and called for the extermination of all Indians in the west. The War Department in Washington used the crisis to ask Congress for more money for defense, and the federal legislature, fearing political backlash, quickly complied. The Marcy family said goodbye to their beloved family member and martyred army officer with an elaborate New York City funeral—without a casket, of course—complete with the attendance of Marcy's more famous relative, Governor William L. Marcy of New York.[22]

Texas braced for an Indian onslaught like no other all across the western settlements, as farmers "forted up" and brought in their animals. In late July, dozens of requests reached Governor Bell's desk asking for commissions to form ranger units. R. N. Goode of Waco sounded the main theme in writing that "the news is quite prevalent . . . that the Indians have killed a large number of soldiers and officers." Goode recommended the raising of at least four companies—he, of course, volunteered to form one.[23] James W. Throckmorton, later to be a Civil War general as well as a Texas governor, wrote much the same from McKinney, Texas: "Accounts that can be relied upon are coming in every day of the manifestations of the hostile intentions of some of the wild tribes." Marcy, it was assumed, "had been cut off by the Comanches."

In what at times appeared to be a political conundrum, Governor Bell was threatened with demands from his political "friends." Louis T. Wigfall (later a U.S. senator) stated that "a better company than the one that will go from this county [Harrison] will not be mustered into service." Wigfall followed by warning Bell, "Harrison county has some claims on you"—one would assume he meant a political claim.[24] As testimonials grew—most of them fabricated—regarding the number of Texans killed, Bell finally succumbed on August 2. James Gillette, who was then adjutant general of the state militia, organized four new ranger units even though the federal government had not authorized salaries.

Several of these units went immediately into action. In late September, while patrolling twenty miles southeast of Laredo, Captain Owen Shaw's company fell upon nineteen people, reported to be Indians, who had just crossed the Rio Grande. The ethnicity of the group was never fully determined. Shaw's men charged, killing nine outright and severely wounding others. The party, armed with a few rifles and bows and arrows, was driving a handful of horses (which Shaw and his men confiscated). No evidence connected this group to depredations. Even the now-determined U.S. Army, which sent out more patrols in September and October, found nothing: no Indians, and no one committing depredations.[25]

The startling appearance of the quietly amused Captain Marcy at Fort Arbuckle in late July did much to defuse the situation. His party, leisurely mapping the tributaries of the Red and Canadian rivers, had crossed the plains without so much as firing a shot in anger. Captain Henry Sibley, at Fort Graham, Texas—perhaps a bit nervous a few weeks before but increasingly condescending about Texans after Marcy's return—broke the news regarding Marcy, belittling the governor's frantic call to arms. "Not a half-dozen horses have been stolen by Indians" within forty miles of the post, he wrote. "On the contrary, several have been captured from droves of mustangs."[26]

General Smith joined the chorus of told-you-soers after hearing of Marcy's safe return. "I have no intelligence of any murder or robbery by Indians within any part of that frontier," he gleefully reported to a frustrated governor Bell, "and the only stolen animals I have heard of, are some taken from the outer posts, beyond all the settlements." The various Indian agents likewise reported only one disturbance, and that by a group of Delawares who had received liquor near New Braunfels and scared several citizens. Given the circumstances, Smith refused Bell's offer of rangers, and in late September the secretary of war declined to pay for them. The secretary noted General Smith's assertion that the claims of depredations—and thus, the governor's justification—had been "entirely unfounded."[27]

Meanwhile, in typical fashion, rumors caused more trouble than any act of an Indian band. Perhaps the most devastating was one carried into San Antonio by a Tejano in the late fall of 1852. In an excited fashion, the Tejano announced to Colonel Harney that a group of Lipan Apaches had attacked a ranch forty miles south of town, wounded several people, and carried off dozens of horses. The Indian party supposedly cried out to the rancheros nearby that they were "Lipans," belonging to the band of "Manuel." Such a declaration should have been viewed suspiciously; Indians did not announce their identity in such a fashion.

Indian agent Howard, knowing Manuel's Lipan band, could hardly believe the news. He knew, as did the army, that groups consisting of renegade Mexicans and Americans frequently crossed the Rio Grande to steal. Howard noted often in his correspondence that they "dressed in the Indian garb" and were responsible for most of the "reported Indian outrages." The Lipan Manuel and his people, numbering perhaps two hundred, Howard soon discovered, at the time of the attack were actually visiting Fort Mason, some two hundred miles to the northwest. This news failed to reach Colonel Harney, who still sought Indian blood. The colonel immediately ordered his troops to "attack the tribe" and "to exterminate, if possible, every man in it, and make prisoners of the women and children."[28]

Brevet Lieutenant Colonel Philip St. George Cooke, a competent officer new to command in Texas, carried out the order. Cooke had served in various western territories for nearly a decade but lacked Harney's desire to exterminate Indians. On January 12, 1853, he found the peaceful Lipans in their village near the head of the Guadalupe River. They seemed innocent. As Cooke considered negotiation, the suddenly suspicious villagers broke and ran. Cooke's dragoons went in pursuit, catching the band in the open. The troops charged into them, killing several. The soldiers took eighteen women and children prisoners and rounded up 150 horses. Just before leaving, they "burned a large quantity of their [the Lipans'] abandoned property."[29]

Once the military learned of its mistake, rectifying the damage became impossible. Colonel Harney made a half-hearted move to return the captured stock, but as Indian subagent Horace Capron pointed out, the attack had "scattered the tribe," and many Lipans had died of wounds after the assault. These people had been "stripped of their horses and mules, their clothing & Wampum," Capron protested, and "their camp [had been] burned." Even the presents "lately distributed among them by their Indian agents, and their blankets . . . [had been] taken from them as trophies of war." With the survivors of the small band destitute and "loose upon the border" in inclement weather, Capron thought it would be difficult to regain their trust.[30]

Ironically, the attack on the Lipan village, which was soon recognized as a clear mistake, had some redeeming value. It finally put pressure on the Texas legislature to address, once and for all, the Indian boundary issue. Harney's defense of the attack on the Lipans rested on the simple fact that he lacked any sense of where Indian land began and where it ended. How could the army police a vast western frontier while not knowing who was a friend and who was a foe? More important was the fact that rumor after rumor of Indian war had turned out to be false. The governor's call to arms had not been necessary, Harney's attack could not be justified, and the whole frontier problem seemed to hinge on the saber rattling of Texans. Smith and a battery of army officers and Indian agents argued that the troubles would end with a boundary and proscribed Indian reservations.

Some progress had been made on this issue during the 1851–1852 legislative session, as a bill had empowered the governor to negotiate a deal with the United States. The federal government would be allowed to purchase land for the Indians from the state. But Governor Bell, who opposed any Indian occupation, did little to implement the idea. In addition, the legislation did not indicate what land was available, the extent of it, and how it would be managed.

The election of Franklin Pierce as president and his appointment of an aggressive secretary of war, Jefferson Davis, made the issue a priority in the spring of 1853. Davis pressured the state to identify land and give it to the federal government rather than wait on a land sale. The state legislature ultimately agreed, despite Bell's foot-dragging, with two important stipulations. Texas would give land for Indian reservations if, first, the federal government agreed to the removal of all Indians who were not native to the state, and second, if the federal government agreed to return the land to the state once the reservations were not needed.[31]

Part of the problem was solved when many Wichitas, who were then living near Fort Belknap on the Brazos River, fled north in April 1853. Hungry as usual in the spring, they had killed five cows for food. Fearing retaliation from the soldiers, they quietly left, leaving mostly Caddos, Tonkawas, and Comanches, who were certainly Native Texans, as well as a few hundred Delawares, Shawnees, and Quapaws, who were not.[32] The U.S. Congress appropriated $15,000 for the removal of the latter peoples, and Agents Howard and Capron assembled a number of them near forts Graham and Croghan in April. The immigrant Indians grudgingly moved back into Indian Territory, some for the third time.

While Capron and Howard claimed that the resettled Indians numbered three hundred, the total was in fact much smaller. Robert Neighbors, who once again received an appointment as Indian agent for Texas under the incoming Democratic administration, believed that only eighty had actually made the journey. Regardless, these people had been forced out of Texas before and likely would return. A few joined the ultimate survivor, Jim Ned, who had a village on the Red River. Although the army convinced Ned to relocate to the north bank, thus fulfilling the desires of the Texas legislature, the sometime trader Ned moved about the plains at will, fearing no one. Neighbors saw the "removal" as a huge waste; Howard and Capron had spent $12,000 of the fund in the effort.[33]

After the army and agents had fulfilled their parts, it was time for the legislature to act. Secretary of War Davis wrote Governor Bell a long letter on the issue of Indian affairs on September 19, 1853. Davis, a military hero severely wounded in the Mexican War, knew the West and Texas. He spoke and wrote with authority. "Much of the difficulty [with Indians] could, in my judgement, be obviated by the Government of Texas," Davis wrote. "While the Indians have no territory of their own, they have virtually the right to roam where they will, and the military force can only interpose when they assume the character of an enemy." The solution, Davis felt, was confinement to a reservation with clearly defined boundaries, where the military could watch them.[34]

Davis, probably as much as any other Washington politician, was responsible for the emerging reservation policy that would become prominent on the high plains after the Civil War. The idea of reservation confinement, especially of so-called hostile Indians, was very new to the federal government. It had yet to be implemented anywhere with much success, although reserves for more militant Indians were being set aside on the northern plains. But Davis would make the reservations places for experimentation in assimilation: agricultural and educational programs designed to convince the tribal people to adopt an Anglo-American lifestyle.

Davis's letter seemingly had an immediate affect. Governor Bell asked that the legislature draft a law in early November that would specifically outline the amount of land to be provided for reservations and just where to confine the remaining Indians. On February 6, 1854, the legislation finally emerged and was signed by the new governor, E. M. Pease, who (although he had campaigned on a platform of Indian removal) saw a need for the measure. The law provided twelve leagues of land in West Texas for the settlement. Most officials assumed that the upper Brazos River would be an ideal locale.[35]

The legislation had limitations—for example, it never provided for large, roomy reservations such as those forming elsewhere on the plains—yet it did give the U.S. government a chance to settle the Plains people and introduce farming and grazing. And since the so-called Indian war in Texas had virtually ended, Agent Neighbors seemed optimistic about the plan. To give Neighbors even more authority, Davis named him the new "supervising agent" for Texas Indian affairs.

Somewhat of a self-righteous man—attacking Howard and Rollins for their removal efforts was typical of him—Robert Neighbors experienced considerable success at Indian diplomacy in the early history of the state. His success came partly from his political astuteness; he had served in the Texas army during the period of the republic as a quartermaster, had been a ranger under Jack Hays, and had been elected to the state legislature in 1852. Neighbors had helped write the bill that led to the appropriation of land for the Indians. Although inclined to drink, Neighbors despised slackers, such as Rollins, and often spent months traveling from Indian band to band, almost preferring the Indian camp to home. And Neighbors was essentially the last chance for the Texas Plains tribes; he, unlike most other Texans, was committed to helping them acquire some sovereignty over their land.

The new Texas law was certainly a watershed for the state and its people. Its bounties even spread to the small population of Alabama-Coushatta Indians, who still lived in separate but closely allied bands on the north edge of the Big Thicket in East Texas. The state legislature appropriated sufficient money for them to purchase 1,280 acres of land, upon which they established a reservation.[36] The Alabama-Coushattas were so isolated that most Texans were likely unaware of their existence.

The degree to which these efforts indicate a change of attitude in Texas is clouded by subsequent events. But the rhetoric of extermination was subsiding in the press—such language, after all, was indicative of a frontier mentality, a formative stage in state development that more-established regions of the state now rejected. Such an attitude seemed inappropriate for still other reasons; most Indians had left Texas by 1854 or lived high out on the Panhandle. These bands, Texans assumed, would soon disappear as a result of their natural decline. Ethnic cleansing as state policy, then, briefly subsided by late. General Smith's plan was certainly an important factor; Texans felt increasingly safe in their homes.

Bell's insistence upon organizing rangers during the Marcy scare and the subsequent rejection of them by the federal government also took the wind out of the ranger movement. Some Texans began to see rangers for what they really were—an embarrassment and a threat to law and order. Concomitantly, the army became more trusted. Much of the credit for this change in attitude came from the actions of the officers in command at the most exposed posts. They constantly spoke with Indians and prevented raids. With the exception of Harney, most were steady and fair, and few if any looked for conflict with Indians. Instead, they fed hungry bands and tried to maintain friendly relations.

But the newly adopted idea of building a reservation system still had to be implemented. Neighbors had to select a location that possessed suitable amounts of water and find competent employees who would help teach farming and ranching.

His goal was to create stable agricultural communities. Such a task remained somewhat daunting—transportation of food alone would prove arduous without good roads. But Neighbors, despite his faults, possessed boundless energy and a Houstonian temperament. He was convinced that Indians and Texans could live side by side in this land that possessed great promise.

The reserves unfortunately would be exposed to the Plains Indians of northern Texas, since the lands offered were south and west of Fort Belknap. The troops at the fort (and those at Fort Phantom Hill, some seventy miles southwest of Fort Belknap) would supposedly bring security to the region. Hopes were high that the violence in Texas had run its course. Many Texans must have wondered whether this could possibly be true. At least the Texas legislature had endorsed a plan that showed some promise.

17

RESERVATIONS OR CONCENTRATION CAMPS?

General Smith had brought a modicum of peace to Texas by dismantling the Texas Rangers and by supplying a workable strategy for the defense of West Texas. In part, his success was contingent upon the growing support of the War Department. By 1853, the Texas garrisons had expanded to a whopping 3,294 soldiers, the largest military presence in one region of the United States since the War of 1812.[1] This concentration of American might should have ended the culture of violence that had plagued Texas for so many years. General Smith felt confident that it would. Little did he know that within a year, troubled times would reappear and ethnic conflict would escalate once again. Texas seemed destined to be a violent place.

A series of interconnected events helps explain why Texas, which seemingly had such a bright future, slowly slid into near anarchy once again. It was not that the reservations, which were perceived as the solution in 1853, failed. But once they were established, state and national political officials, army officers, and even Indian agents, such as Neighbors, completely stopped discussion of the land needs of northern Comanches, Kiowas, or such Indians as the Lipans and Tonkawas, all of whom had a claim to either western Indian Territory, Texas, or northern Mexico. The creation of the reservations buttressed the argument that the rest of Texas— much of it barren, drought-stricken plains, good, it seemed at the time, only for ranching—should be ethnically cleansed of Indians.

Some of these other Indians, unlike the southern Comanches, did at times act in concert with renegades, former African American slaves, and Mexicans in northern Mexico. This only increased the turmoil that already existed in southern Texas, a derivative of the early conflicts between Anglo-Texans and Tejanos. Many of the unsettled Indians and their renegade cohorts, such as the Lipan Apaches, had good reason for seeking revenge in Texas. As claims of depredations grew in the south—

this time legitimate ones—General Smith fundamentally ignored them. He defined the role of the army as mostly protecting the frontier from organized tribal societies rather than renegades.

The violence in the south might have been isolated and contained were it not for the expanded militancy of the northern Comanches. Drought and overhunting had brought serious decline to the bison herds of the southern plains and even affected those along the upper Red and Arkansas rivers by 1855. Some Comanches faced near-starvation and turned to eating their horses during the winter, a clear sign of desperation. They blamed other tribes that invaded their hunting grounds, as well as Americans and Texans. Several of these bands debated the notion of joining the southern Comanches on their new reserves, where food was handed out, but they remained unwilling to give up their freedom.

A second factor promoting lawlessness was the reassignment of army troops to other locales in the West, something that the northern Plains Indians watched with interest. The country in quick succession faced two major crises in the form of "Bleeding Kansas" in 1855 and then the Mormon War of 1857. The turmoil in Texas suddenly lay within a national context. The U.S. Army was not prepared to engage in three conflicts at once. At this crucial time, troop strength in Texas fell by a thousand men to 2,351, most of them infantry.[2]

This put the western settlements of Texas—which had expanded during the early 1850s—in jeopardy, or so Texans thought. It also threatened the reservations along the upper Brazos River and its tributary, the Clear Fork. With the withdrawal of federal troops, Texans screamed for the reorganization of rangers, and mostly they got their wish. The new generation of rangers and captains in the late 1850s was little different from its predecessors. They often rode for plunder and glory, and they frequently created more problems than they solved.

After 1855, a new clique of army officers came to Texas as well, and at times they were little better than the rangers. They had more weapons at hand, particularly when the First and Second United States Cavalry arrived in the region. But their officers generally rejected the subtle and measured responses that had been the hallmark of infantry commanders in the early 1850s. Both military officers and ranger captains came to see the reserves as concentration camps rather than communities that fostered "civilization." As such, the very existence of the reserves offered both groups the excuse to kill any Indian found outside the perimeters of either reserve, and they did so on many occasions. After 1855, neither rangers nor army officers considered the fact that they might be invading Indian lands by their offensive actions. The creation of the reserves had ended the debate over what constituted "Indian country."

Nevertheless, during the spring of 1854, optimism continued as Texas basked in what appeared to be a lasting settlement of its so-called Indian problem. Neighbors and his agents were everywhere, planning and exploring, working on details for the new Indian sanctuaries. The reserve Indians cooperated fully, as Caddo and Wichita leaders offered advice on possible sites and helped explore them. Good farmland was scarce in the regions beyond the 98th Meridian, where the prairies turned gradually into the plains and the land was dry.

Hearing of Neighbors's appointment and of the new boundaries that would be drawn, a small contingent of Wacos and Wichitas, under the friendly Acaquash, moved back to the Brazos. A hundred or so Delawares led by John Conner and Jim Ned joined them, Indians whom Neighbors had thought it foolish to remove the year before.[3] The men of these bands had been the guides and trailblazers that had allowed the army to map most of the plains. Neighbors saw them as assets rather than liabilities. Most even spoke some English and dressed in Anglo attire. They would serve as examples for the seemingly wild Indians who were expected off the plains.

Optimism and the emerging Indian sanctuaries notwithstanding, not all Texans had mellowed in their views regarding Indians or Tejanos. The slightest incident could and often did set Texans off. When aroused, they drew up petitions demanding protection, and they castigated any government officials who seemed reticent to support them. Just as the reserves were being organized, such a situation erupted when a report reached San Antonio on April 18, 1854, that an incident had occurred in which a settler family named Forrester had been attacked twenty miles northwest of town.

The assault on the isolated Forrester ranch had been brutal. Professing friendship, the perpetrators walked up to the family, and Mr. Forrester, standing in the doorway, agreed to get them food. But as he was distracted, one of the intruders shot him through the heart. They then proceeded to methodically murder his three young daughters, the oldest being fourteen. But the three so-called Indian perpetrators overlooked the mother, who hid. She later reached San Antonio. The surviving Forrester woman had little idea of the identity of the murderers; dazed and bewildered, she could only mutter that they must have been "savages."[4] The fact that Mr. Forrester seemed unalarmed by them, had lowered his guard, and had communicated with them, however, suggests that they appeared unthreatening: a mixed-race group of renegades if not Anglos.

The Forrester killings resembled many of the small actions that plagued Texas in the mid-1850s. Hundreds of such renegades wandered north and south along the thin line of ranch settlements. A few were honest laborers seeking work, others were rustlers looking for unguarded livestock, and a few were simply brutal murderers lacking any sense of right and wrong. But as Texans gathered in small groups in Austin, San Antonio, and other small towns, rumors escalated and brought cries for action. It had to be Indians, most argued; civilized men would not do such a thing.

The three men who committed the crime were never identified, but Texans commonly blamed entire tribes for the actions of unknowns, whether the guilty parties were connected to tribes or not. New England abolitionist Frederick Law Olmsted was in San Antonio at the time. Despite being a rational, highly educated man, he—

like everyone else—was quickly swept up in the rhetoric. The trail of the perpetrators, he reported, "had evident marks of Lipan origin"—as if a New Englander would know! Frontier murders became the order of the day, Olmsted confidently surmised, with the renegade Lipans supposedly taking "more than a hundred lives by the most horrid means."[5] Such numbers—a hundred lives—was typical of the rumored exaggerations.

Olmsted's assertions seemed more viable the next month when Indians identi-fied once again as Lipans swooped down on a train of fifteen wagons not far from Fort Ewell, killing five men and "cutting the mules out of the harnesses." Most of the Tejano muleskinners ran, leaving the attackers to their plunder. A group of men who were clearly renegades struck again in November, overrunning a ranch on the Medina River. This time, the attackers killed a man named Williams and took his wife and two small children prisoner. They released the captives a few days later, Agent Howard reported, "after one of them ravished the mother." Had this been a tribal war party it would have held the women and children for adoption or ransom. Renegades, however, lived on the fringe of Anglo settlements and could not ransom captives.

The army sent mounted troops after these groups but seldom caught up with them. After the attack on the Forrester family, a patrol supposedly discovered the group's trail; Agent Howard, some mounted infantry from Fort Inge, and Chief Castro of the Lipan Apaches—who pleaded the innocence of his people—went in pursuit. Unfortunately, some men with the party soon cast a suspicious eye on poor Castro, who had always been loyal and friendly. In fear for his life, he abruptly fled to Mexico, leaving the others to assume what they would.

With Texans concluding that Lipans constituted the guilty party in all these events, Apaches thereafter received little quarter. In early October 1854, an army patrol surprised the inhabitants of sixty lodges of Lipan and Mescalero Apaches east of El Paso, four to five hundred miles from the Medina River. The troops pitched into the camp and killed seven men outright, wounding "many" others. After carrying the town, the troops burned everything usable.[6] Although allies of Texas in the early 1840s and peaceful throughout much of the early 1850s, the Lipans had become a marginalized people in a few short months and were cleansed from southern Texas. Their leaders had but little choice but to flee to Mexico and plot revenge.

The Lipan Apaches found a number of allies in Mexico. One was the Seminole Indian Wild Cat. General Smith had hired spies to collect information on Wild Cat and others who lived near him. They concluded that he was in league with the Lipans as well as with Kickapoos and even many former African American slaves. By 1852, the Mexican state of Coahuila had given the Seminoles, who numbered several hun-dred people, land near El Nacimiento, on the Sabinas River. A contingent of former slaves who lived nearby followed a man named Gopher John. Two bands of Kickapoos lived in the vicinity, including what army officers suggested may have been as many as five hundred warriors. These Indians and former slaves constituted a formidable force.[7]

It was within the context of this growing consolidation of forces in the north and the south, and the removal of federal troops, that Neighbors tried to organize the Texas reservations. He had high hopes for success, even though most government officials thought the effort an experiment. The word seemed appropriate given the fact that the U.S. government had had little success in confining big-game hunters, such as the Comanches, to reserves.[8] But Neighbors was certain of the loyalty and support of the Caddos, Wichitas, Delawares, and Shawnees.

Major Marcy, a friend of Neighbors, joined him in selecting the land needed. The state had provided some twelve leagues, but only eight were chosen, measuring roughly 17,712 acres. Suitable land was found just south of Fort Belknap for the Wichitas and Caddos (the Brazos River Reservation), and a second plot along the Clear Fork of the river was surveyed for the Comanches (the Clear Fork Reservation). Neighbors started coaxing the Indians to move to their new homes in the late fall of 1854.

While Neighbors expected to house some 3,500 Indians on the reserves, far fewer actually showed. Ketumsee's band, numbering 177 people, quickly came. Demographically, the group was missing many of its young men, some of whom had likely joined the northern Comanches; others probably just stayed away, leery of reservation life. A second small group, numbering 72, joined Ketumsee's people in March 1855. They brought news that the northern bands and the Kiowas planned to break up the reservations; the existence of the reserves had produced a divisive debate in many Comanche lodges.[9]

The Caddos and Wichitas, being successful farmers, readily settled into the bottom-lands of the Brazos reserve. The easternmost Caddo village, located on the north bank of the Brazos, held 160 people. Another, built a mile and a half to the west, contained 137 under the leadership of José Maria. Five miles farther up the river, a Wichita town quickly emerged, with nearly 200 people. Other smaller communities of Delawares, Shawnees, and Tonkawas soon joined these main towns. When another 239 Tonkawas were added in May, the Brazos reservation had nearly 750 Indians; it would grow slowly to more than a thousand.[10]

The Brazos reserve Indians maintained ties with their relatives living in Indian Territory. At Fort Arbuckle, Lieutenant Francis N. Page counted another 735 Wichitas, all living northwest of the garrison in 1854. Military officers often pitied them, since they received almost nothing from the government and at times were destitute. The location of their villages also proved problematic. Comanches and Kiowas, who sometimes suffered for food, often took advantage of the Wichitas, showing up especially at harvest time. Pawnees from Kansas were even worse, occasionally raiding Wichita towns, especially when most of the men were hunting bison.[11]

Military officers at Fort Arbuckle tried to glean information about the northern Comanches and Kiowas. The largest of the Comanche bands—Yamparicas and Naconis—supposedly numbered five to six thousand in total. A few smaller bands, those called Tenawas and Quahadas, contained five hundred people each. A similar number of Penatekas and Hois, or southern Comanches, had joined the northern Indians. The officers at Fort Arbuckle knew little about their leaders—Pahayuco, Buffalo Hump, and Sanaco were the only chiefs who consistently negotiated with U.S. officials. Allied with the northern Comanches, the Kiowas stayed mostly along the Canadian and Arkansas rivers. They numbered two thousand, under chiefs Satanka and Tohansen.

Above all, the northern Plains tribes distrusted Texans. The sting of the council house massacre still resonated even after fifteen years.[12] But their leaders had also learned that fighting rangers or even government troops was dangerous. Official army reports of clashes with Indians suggest that tribal leaders had taken some efforts to prevent Comanche young men from attacking Texas. While 1850 had been a bad year for raids, both 1851 and 1852 had been relatively peaceful, and in 1853 and 1854, what trouble had occurred had been with the Lipan Apaches in the south, not with Comanches. These official reports mostly ignored newspaper reports of raids.[13] The seemingly peaceful situation had been one of the justifications used by the army to move troops north, first to Kansas.

Military concerns regarding hostilities with Indians along the Oregon Trail mounted dramatically when tensions between army troops and Indians erupted into conflict in August 1854. A foolish young lieutenant, John L. Grattan, tried to rescue a Mormon cow from some hungry Lakota Sioux. In the fight that ensued near Fort Laramie, the Lakotas killed Grattan and twenty of his men. Within months, Colonels Philip St. George Cooke and William Harney were both patrolling the Oregon Trail with dragoons that had been stationed in Texas.[14]

The Second Dragoons were the major force that was reassigned. These troops came mostly from Fort Croghan, northwest of Austin, and Fort Mason, near Fredericksburg, both of which were abandoned by 1855. While the army worried little about the impact of the redeployment, it fundamentally took the hammer out of General Smith's hammer-and-anvil strategy.[15]

The depletion of troops soon caught the eye of Texans, and in late 1854 many petitioned Governor Pease, complaining of the lack of protection along the western fringe of settlement. There had been no attacks of importance since the clash with the Lipans, but that mattered little. Texans wanted the federal government to employ rangers because livestock was supposedly disappearing in McLennan, Bosque, and Coryell counties, newly opened ranching regions just west of the Brazos River and not far from the bustling new town of Waco, which had been platted just five years before. These locations were in the vicinity of where the Second Dragoons had been patrolling.

Similar petitions came from Starr, Webb, and Nueces counties, north and east of Laredo (in the notorious trans-Nueces region).[16] In late July, a citizens' committee—including the future reconstruction governor, Edmund J. Davis—met with General

Smith demanding more rangers to fill the shoes of the departing army regulars. Smith refused, saying there had been few depredations, the exception being the attack on the Forresters.[17]

Such outcries invariably brought Governor Pease into the fray. Pease lobbied General Smith relentlessly. Organizing rangers was always good politics—so many political supporters could be rewarded with jobs. Ultimately, like previous governors, Pease acted on his own. The many "murders and outrages that have been committed by the Indians," he said, compelled him to order into the field six ranger companies, or so he wrote to the U.S. secretary of war on September 23, 1854. He requested federal funds to pay the rangers' salaries. The threat, as the governor saw it, came in the form of northern Comanches and renegades who came into the state from Mexico. Since controlling these marauders constituted a federal responsibility, Pease believed that Washington should pay Texans to do it.[18]

Even before an answer arrived from the East, Pease had deployed a number of ranger companies. Captains John G. Walker, William Henry, and Charles E. Travis occupied Fredericksburg, Texas, in early November, replacing the departed dragoons. Captains Jiles S. Boggess, William Fitzhugh, and Patrick H. Royer took up positions along the Brazos River valley, northwest of Waco.[19] But the handful of robberies— if in fact they had occurred—stopped as quickly as they had begun. The rangers moved this way and that but saw no action. One company captain, fearing that his chance for glory had passed, demanded that the governor recommission him and his men for six more months. He simply could not return to civilian life without doing something to earn the title of ranger captain.[20]

The rangers' failure to find a fight did not end matters. John S. Ford, one of the best-known rangers in Texas, entertained an offer to reorganize several companies and launch a filibustering expedition against Cuba. Ford's was hardly a novel idea. The island had been the target of other invasion attempts by Americans. The "Ostend Manifesto," published in every newspaper in the United States late that fall, revealed that even high-level Democrats in the Franklin Pierce administration advocated such an expedition. Hugh McLeod, of Santa Fe Expedition fame, headed the Cuba scheme, which was hardly a surprise to anyone.[21]

Captain Henry's company, by contrast, saw fit to filibuster in Texas. After patrolling along the Nueces River for several months without seeing a hostile Indian, he led his men into the small German Catholic community of D'Hanis, one of Henri Castro's colonies, located just south of Castroville. The town had become quite prosperous. Indeed, Olmsted had visited it the year before and had been surprised by the table fare, which consisted of "venison, wheat-bread, eggs, milk, butter, cheese, and crisp salad." He also mentioned an "odd little church" and a priest who ministered to the families. Henry's men had less appreciation of Catholics or their church, and once in town, they looted everything of value. Henry himself led the charge into D'Hanis while intoxicated.[22]

The swirl of activity that fall—much of which fizzled, especially ranger efforts—nevertheless convinced General Smith that the army should do something, even if it was unnecessary. The general ordered a campaign against the Comanches in late January 1855 despite his diminished strength and lack of guilty targets. He picked Captain William J. Newton, new to command in Texas, to lead what dragoons were available—a mere three hundred men. Newton formed up his troops at Fort Chadbourne.

Smith's adjutant general put the orders in plain language to Captain Newton, instructing him "to *search out and attack all parties or bands,* to which *depredations* can be traced, whether these be notoriously attributable to the whole band, or only chargeable apparently to a few individuals."[23] Rangers had commonly endorsed guilt by association; to them, an Indian was an Indian. But the army generally had been more prescriptive.

As the troops slowly assembled, a rumor suddenly reached Agent Neighbors—perhaps it was sent deliberately—that Newton intended to attack the friendly Comanches newly settled on the Clear Fork Reservation. Smith and Newton both agreed—without any evidence—that the Comanches must have pilfered the stock from the regions west of Waco. Fortunately, Captain E. Steen, commanding at Fort Belknap, visited both Ketumsee's and Sanaco's camps and found no stolen animals. His report placated Captain Newton, who turned his attentions elsewhere. Nevertheless, rumors of an attack spread through the Indian reserves like wildfire. Many Comanches fled, including Sanaco's band. Newton's troops scouted all the way to the Red River, but the Indians fled before him and avoided his dragoons.[24]

Neighbors fumed over General Smith's provocative move. "It is certainly strange," he lamented, "that one Department of government should employ agents to make Peace, select lands for permanent settlement, and another should assemble troops . . . to make war on the same Indians." Naturally, the Texas newspapers enjoyed the federal quarrel, charging the army with "stampeding" the friendly Indians and failing to punish them at the same time. Seeing Neighbors's criticism as slander, Smith defended himself by saying that the troops had yet to move when the Comanches fled.

In further reports of the incident, Smith both denied culpability and defended his order to chastise the reservation Comanches. "Sanaco and Buffalo Hump have sent detachments down to the settlements near Fredericksburg where they are reported to be killing cattle and men," he charged. Neighbors was nearly apoplectic at such a charge—to his knowledge, no one had been killed, animal or otherwise. The upshot of the event was to create a serious breach between the army and the Indian agents, a division that only widened thereafter.[25]

General Smith's "evidence" came in talking with his infantry officers at Fort Chadbourne and from the newspapers. He stubbornly remained convinced that the livestock theft west of Waco had been committed by southern, rather than northern, Comanches. Nevertheless, the increasingly frustrated general just as quickly lambasted the same newspapers he cited: "The repetition of stories of depredations committed in the beginning of the winter [1854], published in papers some distance off and copied again as new outrages," Smith reported to Washington, "has multiplied apparently the number of incursions & amount of losses." He described the majority of the depredations to the War Department as hungry Indians killing a few cattle "for food." If true, these were hardly events that warranted an all-out attack on the reservation Indians.[26]

General Smith found the situation even more confusing when officers in his own command gave him contradictory evidence. While information gathered at Fort Chadbourne had implicated the southern Comanches, a month after the event, Major Steen at Fort Belknap clearly implicated the northern Comanches. All that Steen and the general could agree on was the role played by the Texas newspapers. There were "many false and exaggerated newspaper statements of killing and stealing on this frontier," Major Steen noted in agreeing with the general. Steen especially identified the *Texas State Times,* published at Galveston, which had blamed all the troubles along the upper Brazos—problems grossly overstated—on Major Steen, no less![27]

As the acrimony grew, Neighbors and his assistant Hill added fuel by openly declaring that the southern Comanches had nothing to do with any of the robberies, a claim that they were hard-pressed to prove. Captain Newton, Hill matter-of-factly declared, had felt it his duty "to chastise in a summary manner" whatever Indians he met but "particularly the southern Comanches." The agents' attack on the army continued into August and September 1855 as stock losses suddenly increased, a few animals even disappearing from the new reservations. Just who was to blame is impossible to determine. The perpetrators—likely rustlers—were, however, unwittingly bringing down the wrath of the agents, the army, and Texans on the reserve Indians.

Neighbors ultimately compromised regarding the problem. He began describing the raiders as some thirty "Comanches" who had broken off from their tribes. Part of the problem was the fact that Neighbors and his fellow agents had portrayed Ketumsee as a legitimate Comanche leader who could control his people. As was learned later, a handful of Comanches were coming and going through the Clear Fork reserve, and Ketumsee had no control over them. With livestock losses mounting, Neighbors sheepishly asked Major Gabriel René Paul, at Fort Belknap, for help in defending reservation stock. The major, no doubt sensing his commanding officer's wrath, refused.[28]

Having little choice, Neighbors ordered Shapely P. Ross, a former ranger and the new agent at the Brazos Agency, to recruit friendly Caddos, Wichitas, and Delawares to patrol north of the reservations. These Indian "rangers" soon tracked a raiding party that had just stolen some horses. After reaching the Red River, the patrol fell in with ten Yamparica Comanches, who informed Ross's party that Naconi Comanches had just passed after having killed a man on the Clear Fork of the Brazos. Realizing that the Yamparicas were headed toward the Texas settlements, Ross's men crept into their camp at night, killed several, and brought back the Yamparica chief's shield, which had a number of scalps attached to it.

Agent Neighbors proudly forwarded Ross's report—and the shield—to the army, with the obvious implication that his reserve Indians were now doing the job of the army. Major Paul, hoping to fend off embarrassment, condemned the action. Indians killing other Indians of questionable intent would only start a war, he averred.[29] The army's growing jealousy and general lack of cooperation made the reserves even more vulnerable. Neighbors accordingly asked the governor for state troops for protection. He had once been a ranger himself and obviously assumed that he could control the men sent to help protect the reserves.

Governor Pease was more than willing to comply, as Neighbors's endorsement could be used in Washington to get pay for the ranger companies whose organization he had ordered several months before. Given the problems all across Texas, the ranger companies were split into two groups, one to patrol the Nueces River valley and the other to guard against invasion from the north. They were ready to campaign by late August.

The largest troop (over a hundred men) came under the command of John H. Callahan, who was given orders to defend southern Texas, the region where the most trouble existed. His men were to check the Nueces valley and move south to the Rio Grande, where Apache raids were anticipated. In an interesting admission, he interpreted his mission in a letter to his second in command, young Lieutenant Edward Burleson, Jr., who commanded a company. The rangers, he said, while perhaps being paid by the federal government, would also be rewarded "in the property" that they took from Indians.[30]

Callahan, intent on plunder, had somewhat different motives than the governor. He saw a virtual windfall in the recapture of former slaves in Mexico—prime field hands in Texas sold for $2,500 each. On October 4 he ordered his troop to cross the Rio Grande just above present-day Eagle Pass. He hoped to surprise the Lipan and Seminole villages and retake the former slaves in them. Many Lipans, reportedly allied with the local Mexicans, had formed a large village in the vicinity of San Fernando, some thirty miles southwest of Piedras Negras, the border town across from Eagle Pass. But when Callahan's company reached a point eight miles from the town, the rangers met stiff opposition from some seven hundred Mexicans and Lipans. A skirmish ensued, in which the Texans quickly retreated and requested help from the U.S. infantry troops stationed across the river at Fort Duncan.

The commanding officer, Captain Sidney Burbank, felt obligated to comply. To support the ranger retreat, he quickly moved several cannon to the river, only to find that his move bolstered Callahan's determination to stay. The Texans next moved into nearby Piedras Negras—a poor Mexican community filled mostly with vecinos— and sent runners into San Antonio, calling for reinforcements. Meanwhile, most of Callahan's men strip-searched as many Mexican women as possible, taking mostly jewelry and clothing.

Just as the Texans seemed safe, however, Seminoles and Kickapoos under Wild Cat joined the Mexicans and Lipans, making Callahan's situation hopeless a second time. The ranger captain set Piedras Negras afire and asked Burbank to cover his retreat. Outraged, Burbank refused. Instead, he forced Callahan and his rangers, who had made hundreds of poor Mexicans homeless, to discard their arms and the plunder they had taken from the town and swim the river.[31]

In the aftermath of the disaster, Callahan claimed to have killed eighty Mexicans and Indians. In Austin, Governor Pease jubilantly proclaimed the action as heroic and justified. Callahan momentarily reaped a host of praise, but General Smith, after corresponding with Captain Burbank, discovered that the rangers had killed a mere four Mexicans and had lost five of their own men. Moreover, in escaping from Piedras Negras and crossing the river, they had even thrown away their pistols, some of which were army issue.[32]

If anything, Callahan's invasion only emboldened the Lipans, who needed little encouragement to attack Texas. However, within days of the engagement, hundreds— indeed, thousands—of Texans poured into San Antonio, forming up with the expectation of joining Callahan and striking the Indians in northern Mexico. Suddenly the border counties and much of southern and western Texas were in a state of anarchy; the increase in the number of depredations by raiders presumed to be Indian had provided "an excuse," as General Smith put it, for privately organized "ranger" bands to launch marauding raids into the Nueces and Rio Grande valleys and Mexico itself, persecuting mostly Tejanos.[33]

As Governor Pease heard the news of the battle at Piedras Negras, more rumors floated into Austin, giving vague details of Indian depredations all along the frontier. Perhaps hoping to deflect criticism from the debacle at Piedras Negras, Pease declared Texas to be under a "state of siege" and ordered the mobilization of all able-bodied men. He advised Neighbors, who had already asked for state assistance, to call out the "frontier settlers," telling the agent that he would try to convince the legislature to pay these men for their duty.[34]

As the whole state prepared for action, the small rustling raids stopped. By Christmas 1855, reports of depredations ceased. Ranger unit after unit searched in vain; the energetic Burleson could find no Indian raiders, even in the Nueces valley. In February 1856, many of the companies called to arms the previous October for three months' duty asked to be paid. Governor Pease, using available funds, paid each recruit just over half of what had been promised. Most of the rangers took what they could get and went home.[35]

Much of the hysteria had been self-induced by Texans, who, along with their governor, had fashioned a crisis. The most serious raids had been on livestock herds that roamed the vast unfenced western prairies beyond most settlements. These animals were almost impossible to protect. And the government could only speculate on who the raiders actually were—perhaps a handful of Indians connected to the northern tribes, or the discontented Lipans and a few of their Seminole and Kickapoo friends, or possibly organized gangs of renegades, some of whom were likely from Indian Territory, Mexico, or (even more likely) Texas.[36]

The panic of 1855 had done little, however, to disrupt progress on the Texas Indian reservations. After the Indians had been settled, Agent Ross hired men to help open farms and construct buildings for storing goods and food. The Indians' agricultural abilities amazed many visitors, who had questioned whether anything could be grown so far west. More than four hundred acres of land had been broken at the Brazos reserve by October. The only real trouble, besides the loss of a few horses to theft, had been smallpox, which had killed twenty-four Wichitas.

The relief from raiding allowed Neighbors to organize a legal system of rules, at least on the Brazos River reserve with the Caddos, Wichitas, and others. Indians were not allowed to leave the reserve without the agent's approval, and the government pledged to expel anyone who violated the law. Ross soon found other Wichitas moving south from Indian Territory, hoping to live on the reserve.[37] Over winter, the Caddos and Wichitas built houses—most in the Wichita style, a circular house made from grass—and constructed corrals for oxen.

The state legislature aided the reservation effort by endorsing legislation that (for the first time in Texas) put into effect some of the federal intercourse laws, thus banning liquor sales within ten miles of reservation boundaries. The state's willingness to enforce such laws was an entirely different matter. Indeed, both reserves were often awash in alcohol, to the point that brawls affected day-to-day operations. Agent Ross condemned the men who sold the alcohol as "low caste whites," but some of the sellers were army officers of low morals who seemed to enjoy watching an Indian community erupt in violence. Liquor also allowed for the exploitation of Native women by soldiers who had few other outlets for sexual frustrations.[38]

The success that the Caddos and Wichitas experienced at the Brazos Agency eluded the Comanches at Clear Fork. Reasons for the failure fell partly on the shoulders of the Comanches, who had said that they would try farming but never took to plowing. Comanche men were warriors and hunters, not farmers. Instead, Comanche leaders more or less ordered four or five Mexican Comanches, men who had elected not to become warriors, to take up the plow. A number of these Mexican men had been with the tribe for more than a decade, and they often stayed behind in camp with the women when the men went hunting. But they too had little experience at plowing.

The new agent assigned to develop the reserve, John R. Baylor, also bore some of the responsibility for failures. Baylor came from a prominent Texas family and at first seemed interested in his job. But being a scoundrel at heart, he had a deep-seated belief in the Texas creed. He had even evaded a murder charge connected to a challenge of his honor in Indian Territory in the late 1840s. Baylor left the reservation over the winter of 1855–1856 on two separate occasions to attend to personal business—he too was building a ranch. The agricultural effort suffered the first year as well because Clear Fork, farther west than the Brazos reserve, frequently experienced drought.[39]

Droughts had hit the prairies and plains of western Indian Territory and Texas on numerous occasions. They often came in cycles of five to ten years. But some lasted longer, the longest cycle likely being 1805–1821. Blowing dust and hot winds descended upon the region again in 1855, and for the next three years, there was little rain. According to tree-ring data, 1855 was the fourth-driest year on record for the upper Red River since 1690, the first year for which data exist. But 1857 and 1859 were nearly as bad. Both in 1855 and in 1856, crops at the reserves looked good in the spring, only to wither and die by summer. About all that the Indians harvested was some green corn and a few melons. Despite all the hard work and the rhetoric about farming, the Indians on the reserves survived on government-issued rations.[40]

Drought combined to create other serious problems. Brackish water in the Clear Fork began causing illness among the Comanches by summer 1856. Eight had died, probably from cholera, and many were lying sick in their tents. Fortunately, the virus was a mild one. The plague of grasshoppers that descended upon both reserves that summer was anything but mild. Neighbors, who replanted corn three times in the spring of 1856, ultimately gave up, noting, "The light of the sun was partially obscured by the immense numbers of those insects."[41]

The setback only hardened those elements in Ketumsee's band that remained restless and unappreciative of reservation life. Too many times Texas Rangers had hit their towns, killing indiscriminately. Many remained skittish. Making matters worse, considerable factionalism existed among the southern Comanches. Ketumsee (the older, more conservative leader) had been an advocate of peace, while Sanaco and Buffalo Hump remained sympathetic with the younger men, who occasionally tested their manhood in raids.

Just such an attack, believed to have been the work of Buffalo Hump's followers, occurred in October, when many horses disappeared from the Brazos Agency. The raiders likely needed mounts to replace those suffering and dying from the drought. Baylor finally asked for army troops to subdue Ketumsee's northern opponents. This time, Captain Paul agreed, and troops started construction of Camp Cooper, an unstockaded army tent community located ten miles from the Comanche agency.[42]

In January 1856, with Sanaco and some two hundred of his followers visiting the agency, the army upped the stakes. To replace the slow, relatively harmless infantry that had built Camp Cooper, a new unit arrived, part of four companies of the newly formed Second Cavalry under Major Hardee. Upon horses of matching color, each company paraded in the open in front of the Comanches. A day later, many of Sanaco's people quietly slipped away.

The appearance of the Second Cavalry on the Texas frontier marked a new era in the history of the West. The Second and its sister regiment, the First Cavalry, were meant to replace the slow-moving mounted infantry, or dragoons. The cavalrymen were trained and supplied to fight from horses, with their clothing, saddles, camp equipment, and so forth adapted to facilitate this mission. Secretary of War Jefferson

Davis personally designed and built these regiments. A student of the West, Davis wanted a mobile force that could hunt the Plains Indians in their backyard. The cavalry, then, constituted a striking force. While elements of the Second were assigned to Texas in 1856, the First eventually went to Forts Washita and Arbuckle in western Indian Territory.[43]

The ranks of the regiment of the Second Cavalry would fill with a remarkable collection of men. General Albert Sidney Johnston—Felix Huston's old dueling opponent—formed the troop and selected as his second in command Colonel Robert E. Lee. Junior officers included George H. Thomas, Earl Van Dorn, Edmund Kirby Smith, George Stoneman, John Bell Hood, Nathan G. Evans, Richard W. Johnson, Kenner Garrard, Charles E. Fields, and the veteran William G. Hardee. Nearly all of these men would gain experience in fighting Indians in Texas or Indian Territory, and all would later make a mark in the Civil War. (Indeed, seven would become Confederate generals and five, Union generals.)

But the troop would never really settle in Texas. "Bleeding Kansas" in 1855 and the Mormon War two years later kept the command on the move. Many of the officers were in Texas for only brief periods; they never came to fully understand the Indians or the Texas situation. Hardee, who had served in the state before, was an exception. He received the first opportunity to launch the fame of the regiment when Johnston ordered him to move four companies of the Second Cavalry to the Comanche reserve in early 1856.[44]

Hardee, who knew both Ketumsee and Sanaco, tried to convince these chiefs that the troops meant to protect them. The Comanche rank and file were not so sure. Hardee looked less threatening by March when a mysterious disease, called "the blind staggers," struck down his cavalry mounts. Undeterred, Davis soon ordered Colonel Robert E. Lee and fresh companies of the Second to relieve Hardee. Unlike Hardee, who preached friendship, Lee saw Camp Cooper as a staging area for campaigning against Plains Comanches, much along the lines of what Davis had designed the Second Cavalry to do.[45] Lee, also unlike Hardee, never appreciated Indians.

After Lee attended the obligatory council with Comanche leaders in April 1856, he reached several conclusions. Lee found Ketumsee to be a reasonable man, but Lee thought the overall effort to "humanize" Ketumsee's people was "uphill work." He wrote, "Their paint and ornaments make them *more hideous* than nature made them, & the whole race is extremely uninteresting."[46] While Ketumsee's band seemed friendly, Lee knew that over a thousand southern Comanches still remained with Sanaco and Buffalo Hump in the Red and Canadian river valleys, riding with the other, more imposing, northern Comanches. Lee saw his mission as one of destroying them, for they were, of course, off their reservation.

Lee's chance for action improved markedly when the army implemented a new directive, calling upon its cavalry to attack any Indians found beyond the reservation limits, even a few miles.[47] General Johnston believed that the role of the Second

Cavalry was to strike, not sit in tents watching peaceful Indians. Yet the new policy had its drawbacks. Most Indian agents depended to a small degree on bison hunting to supplement the harvests of their charges, especially after drought destroyed much of the anticipated food supply at both agencies. The Indians had to leave the reserves to chase these animals.

Lee was unsympathetic with the argument. He also was unappreciative of the work being done by the agents. He intended to enforce the new order at all costs. A party of Sanaco's Comanches fell victim to the new policy on May 24 when Lee's troopers caught them off the reservation and attacked. Several were killed in the skirmish.[48]

Then on June 7, some two dozen of Sanaco's people appeared at Fort Chad-bourne. The commander, Captain Seth Eastman of the Eighth Infantry, following Johnson's directive, promptly ordered their arrest. This had never happened at a military post in the past. Indians had always been able to come in peace, the women trading goods while the talking went on. Comanches loathed surrender, and a scuffle ensued in which seven Indians were killed. Many others suffered severe wounds, and several died while trying to get back to the reservation.

Both General Johnston and Neighbors applauded Eastman's actions, considering it a good lesson for the Indians. But when the survivors reached the Comanche reserve, Agent Baylor discovered the truth; while Eastman had reported nothing about the gender of the group, the seven dead were all unarmed women. Eastman's men had even captured one old woman who was supposedly clubbed to death while in the guardhouse.[49] This aggressive policy, increasingly implemented by a new collection of army officers who had little understanding of Texas or its Indians, had led to two vicious assaults that only unsettled the already tense frontier. The U.S. Army increasingly took its cue from the Texas Rangers; attack first and offer no mercy.

An uproar ensued at the Comanche reserve after the Eastman killings. Under-standably, the army might surprise a small party of raiders intent on taking horses. Chiefs like Ketumsee felt that such warriors deserved what they got. Killing peaceful women on a trading venture was unexplainable. Baylor noted the Comanche response: the attack had "caused by far the biggest *crying* yet" as the Indians lamented the loss of their relatives.[50] The killings, Baylor thought, would make it difficult to attract any more Comanches into the Clear Fork reserve.

Nevertheless, some northern Comanches appeared in early May, ostensibly to observe reservation conditions. They were rather sullen and suspicious, but Lee, unlike Eastman, had honored their flags of truce and Baylor counseled with them. The agent counted over a hundred people in the group and initially assumed that Buffalo Hump led them. To Baylor's surprise, the party included the famous Kot-chateka Comanche chief Iron Jacket—Baylor called him Iron Side—known for the Spanish metal armor plate that he often wore. Closely allied with the Naconi Comanches, the Kotchatekas had sent large war parties on occasion into Mexico. When inquiring about other leaders, Baylor learned that Pahayuco, the old Penateka chief, was still alive and living with the Naconis.

While little was known of the Kotchateka Comanches, Iron Jacket's reputation as a famous warrior was unquestioned. His visit seemed peculiar, though (since these Indians had seldom had anything to do with Texans), until Baylor described the people with him: "The condition of the Indians who have just arrived is wretched," the agent wrote. "They are destitute of everything and most of them came in on foot in a half starving condition." The drought had been devastating for them.

Bison herds had been declining for nearly two centuries. The decline had begun after 1650, when the herds receded northward from the Rio Grande. By 1800, they seldom visited the Colorado River, and by 1856, only occasional herds ventured south of the Red River. Continued hunting might have been a cause, but more likely, the drought conditions had taken a toll. The herds had to travel extreme distances to find grass and water, which affected their reproduction and killed off their young. These climatic conditions were similar to those of 1885–1888, when between 20 percent and 80 percent of the cattle on the plains—the lower figure admittedly more typical for Texas ranches rather than those in Montana—were killed from a combination of summer drought and winter blizzards.[51]

Captain Marcy, who had helped Neighbors lay out the Brazos agencies, went on a scout up the Red River in January 1855, retracing his trip of five years earlier. An astute judge, Marcy felt that the bison had "entirely abandoned" the lands south of the Red. The Indians had found "that the facilities for sustaining life" were "exceedingly precarious," he observed. Most ate their mules and horses over the winter. However, even Comanche livestock herds had declined to dangerously low levels. The Indians recognized these alarming trends; they would soon all starve.[52]

The condition of the Kotchatekas obviously offered the government a golden opportunity to settle these Indians on the reservation. After feeding the Indians, Baylor talked to them about moving to the reserve. They politely considered the option—rejecting it outright after eating the food of the Americans was contrary to Comanche social etiquette. Many in the group remained leery of Lee's cavalry, nearby at Camp Cooper. The majority of the band had stayed well north of the reservation, and the delegation, sent to check the situation, soon left to join them.

Shortly thereafter, as Baylor had suspected, the Comanche flirtation with reservation life was seriously tempered by news of the incident at Fort Chadbourne. Even though the Kotchatekas were not related to the women killed at the fort, the comparison with the council house massacre was obvious. Baylor quickly sent runners to explain the circumstances. He even issued "passports" of safety, arguing that the army would never attack them if they carried the paper.

Unfortunately, in a display reflective of this man's character, Baylor suggested to Lee that it would be a good time for the cavalry to strike these Indians. They were on foot and off the reservation, and, according to Baylor, they would soon steal more horses.[53]

Despite Baylor's failure to lure in Iron Jacket, the emerging Indian policy for Texas seemed to please almost everyone in a position of authority. The presumption that the northern Comanches would willingly enter the reservation despite being threatened by cavalry troops seemed logical to Baylor, given their suffering condition. Even Neighbors came to believe that army campaigns into the northern Comanche haunts would help force the Indians onto the reserves.

The army increasingly embraced the new policy for entirely different reasons: it was simplistic, and it offered the opportunity to showcase the new cavalry commands. No longer would there be any need to maintain a six-hundred-mile line of forts, stretching from Red River to the Rio Grande. Indians off the reservations could be presumed hostile and could be killed, even in their northern villages. In the course of a year and a half, U.S. officials seemingly had abandoned any suggestion that Comanches and Kiowas had claims to West Texas—the idea completely disappeared. They were to move to the Clear Fork or be killed.

This hardening of positions by agents, army officers, and Washington bureaucrats doomed the reservation civilization scheme almost before it celebrated its first year. The key to the success of the program was not the friendly Caddos and Wichitas, who adjusted rapidly to their new farmlands, but the Comanches, who had to be convinced that life on the Texas reservation was better than roaming across the increasingly barren, bison-deficient plains.

The vast majority of Comanches, however, remained well to the north. Most of them were northern Indians who had never lived with the Penatekas. Many of the best-known chiefs, including Pahayuco and even Buffalo Hump, had abandoned their southern relatives. This had led to the restructuring of bands, with smaller bands joining larger ones and southern Indians joining together with those from the north. This process of ethnogenesis was necessary because of population decline and economy. Larger bands could send out more hunters and find the elusive remaining bison herds.

Just as the Comanches reorganized themselves, the army adopted new tactics to deal with them. Some army officers wished to implement "total war" against these recalcitrant Indians, and some Texans in particular increasingly saw war as the only solution; in such a war distinguishing between Indians became practically impossible. This conclusion brought the final marginalization of the Plains tribes. The northern tribes soon were declared outlaws even in their far-off homelands along the upper Red, Canadian, and Arkansas rivers—lands that Texans had never even visited. But by U.S. law, these lands of the Panhandle region were part of Texas.

Moreover, the policy presumed that a state of conflict already existed, when in fact this was mainly a fiction. The rumor mill, the exaggeration of depredations, and the racist mentality of many Texans had brought even the army to accept the basic premise that the Plains tribes must either surrender or be exterminated. State officials contributed to the problem by failing to bring lawlessness in the Nueces River valley under control. This kept the issue of depredations on the front page of every newspaper in the state, almost on a daily basis.

Alternatives seemed beyond possibility by 1856. Violence had become ingrained in Texas, especially in the southern counties; it was firmly fixed to such an extent that most people—governors, rangers, and citizens—even saw it in an opportunistic fashion. Governors used such problems to employ rangers, adding to their patronage; rangers found employment or plunder; and settlers sold produce and fodder to army posts. Violence, especially against ethnic groups, had become economically institutionalized in Texas.

Above all, the army seemed anxious to test the concept of reservation confinement and total war—to unleash the new cavalry regiments. While officers such as Lee and Johnston avoided using such words as "extermination" in their correspondence, they quickly saw the advantages of the tactics used by the Texas Rangers—they would attack Indians in their villages and force Indian men to stand and defend their families. In an ironic twist, the founding of the two small reservations in Texas, which was supposedly beneficial to the Plains tribes, had provided the justification for declaring all-out war on them.

The prosecutors of this final war had but one goal: to cleanse from Texas those Indians who would not remain obediently confined to Indian Territory. The showdown, a product of the culture of violence that had existed in Texas since the 1820s, began in earnest in June 1856, when the cavalry took the field.

A ranger company, late 1850s or early 1860s. Rose Collection no. 1405. Courtesy Western History Collections, University of Oklahoma Libraries.

John Coffee Hays, ranger captain, veteran of the Plum Creek fight (1840), Enchanted Rock engagement (1841), and Bandera Pass fight (1842). Rose Collection no. 1406. Courtesy Western History Collections, University of Oklahoma Libraries.

John Salmon Ford, ranger captain who led the initial assaults on the Comanche villages on the Canadian River in the late 1850s. Rose Collection no. 1152. Courtesy Western History Collections, University of Oklahoma Libraries.

John R. Baylor, ranger captain, Confederate general, and leader of the opposition to the Indian reservation movement in Texas. Courtesy Baylor University Library, Waco, Texas.

Howeah (Gap-in-the-Woods), Yamparica Comanche leader who signed the Treaty of Medicine Lodge Creek in 1867 but remained adamant in defending the Comanche homeland. Soule Collection no. 29. Courtesy Western History Collections, University of Oklahoma Libraries.

Horseback, the key Naconi Comanche leader who signed the Treaty of Medicine Lodge Creek in 1867 and later helped arrange the surrender of the last Comanche groups in 1874–1875. Soule Collection no. 30. Courtesy Western History Collections, University of Oklahoma Libraries.

Mowway (Shaking Hand), the major Kotchateka Comanche leader who was one of the last men to surrender to the U.S. Army in 1875. Soule Collection no. 32. Courtesy Western History Collections, University of Oklahoma Libraries.

Young Buffalo Hump, son of the Penateka Comanche chief who tried to negotiate a peaceful resolution to the troubles on the southern plains. Courtesy National Anthropological Archives, Washington, D.C.

Mowway's camp. Courtesy National Anthropological Archives, Washington, D.C.

Comanche family portrait. W. S. Campbell Collection no. 196. Courtesy Western History Collections, University of Oklahoma Libraries.

18

THE PLAN

The die had been cast in Texas by the summer of 1856. The Texas reservations had been integrated into a new plan. They had become points of concentration, places Indians would be forced onto and then fed and clothed. Everyone—army officers, Indian agents, and politicians—agreed that such a policy made any other Indian or renegade caught outside the reserves a "hostile," subject to immediate attack. Army officials, such as General Albert Sidney Johnston, praised the idea, and so did Agent Neighbors. Unlike General Smith's strategy, the plan was offensive, not defensive. To a large measure, it originated with the birth of the United States Cavalry, mobile troops that would do the punishing.

Unfortunately, General Johnston and other officials in the state failed to realize that the new policy hinged on cooperation at several levels. Much like the lands to the west that the cavalry vowed to control, the new reserves had to be policed. Indian agents and army officials needed to work together to accomplish this. Both reservations constituted relatively large areas that held upwards of two thousand Indians. In addition, the Comanches remained unsettled; the northern brothers of the Penatekas were often willing to share government-issued food, but they refused to give up their freedom and become reservation Indians. This problem would solve itself, General Johnston thought, as soon as the Plains tribes were defeated.

A second level of assistance had to come from state officials. The governor's office had constantly meddled in army-Indian affairs, often doing more harm than good. As settlers moved into the region around the reservations (as they had begun to do by 1856), state officials needed to maintain civilian law and order. This included keeping away unsavory individuals such as whiskey peddlers and rustlers. Likewise, the state had to control the paramilitary rangers. The best solution was simply not to organize ranger units. This was difficult to do when citizens petitioned for them and newspapers clamored for action. Politicians in Texas often had been as responsible for violence as the civilians and Indians who committed the acts.

In reality, had a modest level of cooperation among all these groups—the army, the Indian Bureau, the state, and West Texas settlers—occurred, the policy might have succeeded. Instead, Texas entered yet another period of political confusion, as state officials bickered with army officers over the right course of action and individuals representing both of these groups entered into an acrimonious shouting match with officials of the Bureau of Indian Affairs. Adding to the confusion, civil unrest and horse thievery escalated. Texas, with all its land and all its promise, continued to reap nothing but violence from its long-term policy of ethnic cleansing. A chorus of protest and outcries for the dismantling of the reservations was soon the result.

But such a regression in the plans of the War Department and Bureau of Indian Affairs was far from the mind of General Johnston, who commanded the Second Cavalry in May 1856. Johnston confidently ordered a gifted officer, Colonel Robert E. Lee, to mount the first expedition designed to cleanse the plains west of the reserves of Indians. Lee had won three brevet ranks for bravery while serving in both theaters of the Mexican War. Hardened and determined, Lee had few of the qualms demonstrated by former army officers in Texas, regarding who was guilty of what. He would get the job done.

Colonel Johnston's orders to Lee were clear. There was to be little quarter in dealing with the Indians. The Comanches' "continued rejection of the privilege of settling on the Reservation under the protection of the government," Johnston said, "will be considered sufficient evidence of their unfriendliness."[1] Lee was to search for them and destroy them!

By 1856 the Second Cavalry had become the darling of the War Department. Lee mounted four companies, nearly two hundred men. Each company sported distinctive uniforms and equipment: blue flannel shirts with yellow piping; a light, short blue jacket; a floppy "Jeff Davis" hat, some with ostrich feathers; and a light, serviceable saddle. For weapons, most of the men had been issued the new breech-loading carbine, short with a detachable stock. Nearly all went into battle with the new six-shot Colt revolver—the weapon of choice for mounted troops since the Mexican War.[2]

Lee and his command left Camp Cooper with considerable fanfare and headed west. Like the rangers, Lee used Indian scouts; his were under the leadership of the towering, nearly seven-foot-tall Shawnee Jim Shaw, from the Brazos reserve. The scouts looked for horse trails in the Double Mountains near the headwaters of the Brazos River. Finding none, the troop turned north and entered the Texas Panhandle. Lee hoped to find Indian villages, especially those of Sanaco's and Buffalo Hump's Penatekas and even perhaps Iron Jacket's Kotchatekas, who, it was believed, had been responsible for recent depredations.

Finally, after three weeks in the saddle, Lee's force reached the Red River valley. A smaller command under Major Earl Van Dorn then broke from Lee's companies and moved to the advance. Van Dorn refused to give up until he found Indians. He took Jim Shaw and several Caddo and Delaware scouts with him. This group eventually discovered one small Comanche hunting camp, which Van Dorn's men tore into, killing four Indians. It was a shallow victory. Lee never closed with the Comanches, who likely had been told of his coming. Scouts soon determined that their main towns were another five hundred miles to the northwest, along the Arkansas River. Lee's dog-tired men, dirty and thirsty, were forced to walk back to the Brazos River. Their beautifully matched horses had had little to eat for weeks; all the grass was gone from the plains.[3]

Lee covered 1,600 miles in the first concerted effort of the U.S. Cavalry to demonstrate that it could campaign on the barren southern high plains in force. "The country had been fired in many places," Lee wrote to his wife. In some locales, it was "still burning and abandoned." The plains seemed at times like hell on earth. Worse, water was often difficult to find and forage for horses almost impossible to provide. Lee quickly grasped that it would be far better to campaign during the winter, when the severely hot weather would not be a factor. Lee consoled himself by reporting that he had forced several small raiding parties to retire and that the larger ones, far to the north, now knew that the army had an offensive weapon to use against them.[4]

Although the first testing of the policy had occurred in the northwest, the army soon expanded the idea to southern Texas. Since the Lipan Apaches had not been given a reservation, they too had been declared outlaws everywhere. Accordingly, when mounted infantry from Fort Clark stumbled onto a small Lipan camp along the Rio Grande during the summer of 1856, the troops attacked and killed a dozen Indians. No attempt was made to negotiate or even find out who they were, and Colonel Johnston acclaimed this action a success. "No hope will be held out to them of a respite from the pursuit and hostilities of the troops," he declared, "except upon the condition of placing themselves under the care of the Government." But to what reservation were they to go? They had none.[5]

This contradiction troubled some officers, including the commanding officer at Fort Clark, Lieutenant Colonel John B. Magruder. A handful of Lipan Apache women and children had been turned over to him, and no one in the army seemed to know what to do with them. Moreover, there seemed to be no contingency for Indians who might surrender. Johnston lacked a good answer to Magruder's inquiry regarding the prisoners, but he did offer a modest compromise. Indians then in captivity and those who surrendered in the future, he ordered Magruder, "need not be regarded as prisoners, nor made to feel that they are under forcible restraint." They were to be fed and observed closely. If they ran, "they were to be pursued with the utmost vigor."[6]

Colonel Johnston strongly believed that these new military policies had made a difference, as peace had seemingly settled over much of Texas by late summer. He failed to understand the severity of the drought, however, and how it had interfered with raiding. The disappearance of grass prevented long-distance movement of horses. Some bands, such as the Kotchatekas, had to eat their horses and mules. Another sign of the troubled times on the plains was the fact that most of the Indians remained throughout the winter on the upper Arkansas River, a stream that produced willows and cottonwoods, the bark of which kept horses from dying.[7]

Colonel Johnston's reports settled into a routine that resembled those of General Smith. The army, he assumed, was winning the war against the Indians. He even continued the well-used army custom of dismissing newspaper accounts in Texas. "The number of Indians composing the different [raiding] parties and of the persons said to have been killed, is," he noted, "as is usually the case, exaggerated."[8] Lee's cavalry, Johnston believed, had completed its mission by policing the plains and forcing the hostiles into far-off, northern river valleys.

The only tensions that surfaced come fall erupted between the cavalry troops at Camp Cooper and the two hundred to three hundred reservation Indians who found the troops troublesome. In most cases, soldiers were at fault, for even in the elite Second Cavalry, drunkenness was common and the whip had to be used to discipline enlisted men. Moreover, most of the recruits were a rough lot from the alleys of St. Louis or Cincinnati. Soldiers at Camp Cooper and Fort Belknap, for example, became active buyers of horses and mules from the reserve Indians, occasionally bartering with liquor. At one point, a drunken cavalryman from Lee's command fell from his horse while bartering and killed himself. The troopers blamed the Indians; in what must have been an embarrassing moment for Lee, several soldiers dressed as Indians attempted to assassinate an officer, hoping to blame the incident upon the reservation Comanches.[9]

Along with the army, the growing population of settlers near the reservations also proved problematic. With the relative peace, more and more Texans moved up the Colorado and Brazos rivers. Most were stock raisers, some of whom found the land barren and dry and left not long after arriving. The prolonged drought had affected Texans as much as Indians. Other "settlers" were really whiskey peddlers, and a few were rustlers. In 1856, the advance of Texan settlers convinced state officials to organize Young County, which included both Fort Belknap and the Brazos Indian Reservation, as well as Palo Pinto, Jack, Erath, and Wise counties, all nearly contiguous with the upper Brazos River. Along with organization came surveyors, the lead elements of land speculators.

Alongside the ranch settlements, dozens of whiskey shops sprang up that summer. It took little time for the shopkeepers' commodity to fall into Indian hands. At one point, Agent Baylor raided a shop that he identified as being "within the extended reservation" (the ten-mile limit within which the state had banned liquor sales near the reserves). The owner of the place had "on a dozen occasions sold to Indians," Baylor reported; "Every time Indians go or come by there they get drunk." Baylor smashed the stock of ten barrels. The peddler sued in court, forcing Neighbors to spend money to defend his agent.[10]

The situation at the Brazos reserve was somewhat similar. In 1857, Neighbors opened a school at the Brazos reserve and hired Zachariah Ellis Coombes to run it. Attendance varied, with anywhere from five to fifty students coming and going. Jim Shaw, when not campaigning with the army, faithfully served as interpreter for Coombes until Shaw's untimely death from a fall in late 1858. Acaquash came thereafter in his place, encouraging the Indian students to learn to read and write. Coombes made modest progress with his students, however, and was hindered by the liquor problem, as his "peculiarly private" diary reveals.[11]

Coombes's diary shows both the possibilities for the reserve and the problems associated with living in a mixed-ethnic community where cultural differences and moral complexities existed on many levels. Married and almost puritanical, the young Coombes possessed standards of piousness that often bordered on the extreme. Eventually, he got crossways with Neighbors, which might explain some of the more negative entries in his detailed "private" account of life on the Brazos reserve.

According to Coombes, the vast majority of the employees at the agency (perhaps a dozen men) were drunkards and gamblers. "In fact, it can scarcely be doubted that had these men never been employed here," he wrote in his usual condescending manner, "the interest and welfare of the Indians would have been promoted." Perhaps this view was extreme—since considerable progress had been made in building Indian houses and even plowing land—but Coombes's reflections upon the difficulty of hiring good men in an area on the edge of settlement are valid.

Beyond these problems, Coombes felt that some employees at the agency occasionally pilfered goods from the warehouses, and in his opinion "a more corrupt and dishonest set" of men could not be found.[12] Government service, especially work for the Indian Bureau, was seen by westerners as an opportunity for graft. In a region where land was cheap and easily attained, and gold was being discovered in many locales across the West, it was difficult to find upright men who would labor for a few hundred dollars a year. Those who did take the jobs expected other rewards.

Coombes's indictment of the reservation community for its overuse of alcohol was likely a truism (and indeed, in the mid-nineteenth century, most of the United States could easily face the same charge). Alcohol was undoubtedly safer to drink than some of the water, especially during the summer droughts, when West Texas streams became stagnant and brackish. But if Coombes is to be believed, the inhabitants of the Brazos and Clear Fork reservations wasted away in dissipation. And the drinking started at the top. Coombes said that such men as Agent Ross and the head sutler, George Barnard, were often inebriated. The only exception seems to have been Baylor, who did not partake. Neighbors joined in and made no effort to rein in his employees, whether farmers, agents, freighters, or whoever. The liquor easily reached the Indian villages, where drunkenness became common.

Besides the occasional paralyzation of the reserves from alcohol, a licentiousness existed that could not help but affect Indian families. "There are continually among the Indians a most degraded set of libertines," Coombes wrote of the government employees, "who make it their boast that there is not nor has been an Indian female on this Reserve with whom they have not had . . . illicet [sic] intercourse." The debauchery became so severe that laborers on the reserves even invaded the quarters of the fifteen-, sixteen-, and seventeen-year-old Indian female students at night. "Matronly Indian women," as Coombes described them, tried their best to run the laborers out. Worse, agents, including Neighbors, seemed to partake, at least occasionally. As Coombes delicately wrote of Neighbors: "From pretty good circumstantial evidence, he done something towards civilizing a certain Lipan Squaw today."[13] Coombes feared that Neighbors's next conquest was to be one of Coombes's seventeen-year-old students.

Despite the occasional debauchery, the upper Brazos River had also attracted a growing population of Texans who wished earnestly to see the reservation succeed. Coombes on several occasions noted the visits of Texan neighbors who came to see his efforts in school and praise his success. Many of the new citizens of Young County—thirty-five, to be exact—signed a petition lauding the congregation of the Indians on the reservations and noting the able leadership of Neighbors. Most of the praise was legitimate. Some frontier families came to see that the Delaware, Caddo, and Wichita Indians were honest, friendly, and productive—good neighbors. José Maria was often a houseguest among the nearby Anglo settlements; he played with their children, giving them horseback rides, and became a favorite on several Texas ranches.[14]

Nevertheless, some of the nearby settlers had a reason for contributing such commentary. The agents, with a considerable budget, purchased foodstuff and stock from them, generally enhancing the local economy. As long as peace existed and all were allowed to prosper, the agency Indians and the nearby settlers seemed to get along. Several changes, however, led eventually to calls for the removal of all Indians and the dismissal of the agents who supported them. This abrupt turnabout was directly related to the political climate in Texas. State officials turned against the reservations in 1857, and the Bureau of Indian Affairs dismissed Agent Baylor, who thereafter sought retribution through the encouragement of ranger violence.

Despite Neighbors's political acumen—he wrote well and often published pro-reservation pieces in the local papers—the Texas political climate was always volatile. The state legislature and the governor had supported the civilization scheme in 1853–1856, but this changed in 1857, as Neighbors and the agencies became part of a fierce battle over political turf. Neighbors had obvious ties to the now-aging Senator Houston, who openly supported the civilization plan. But given Houston's outspoken nature, and perhaps because of his opposition to the Kansas-Nebraska

Act of 1854, Houston was first turned out of his seat in the U.S. Senate and then, shortly thereafter, defeated by Harden Runnels in a run for the Texas governorship in 1857. That was a serious political defeat for Houston, yet it was equally a statement of the fickle nature of state politics immediately before the Civil War; Houston would return to win the governorship just two years later.

Runnels, a radical Democrat, offered little if any support for Neighbors's civilization plan. The agent fully expected to be turned out of office when, in the spring of 1857, he was called to Washington to clarify his accounts. But in a surprise move, the commissioner of Indian affairs removed Agent Baylor instead. The dismissal of Baylor, who would soon raise a large following in northwestern Texas and gain tenuous support within the Texas Democratic Party, hurt Neighbors, whose political support began to wane.

The son of John Walker Baylor (his father had commanded Washington's Life Guards at the battle of Germantown), John R. Baylor had two other brothers heavily involved in Texas politics. And their uncle, Robert Emmett Bledsoe Baylor, was a Texas judge, member of the supreme court, and licensed Baptist minister. In 1845, the elder Baylor provided land and money for the founding of Baylor University, Texas's first college.[15] The Baylor family was not to be trifled with.

To what degree Neighbors had caused Baylor's removal is not known. While Neighbors had been critical of Baylor the year before for Baylor's extended absences, the supervising agent's censure had been mild. Perhaps Neighbors had said something privately regarding Baylor's behavior while in Washington. In any event, rightly or wrongly, Baylor obviously came to blame Neighbors for his dismissal.

There was speculation after Baylor left office that his accounts were not in order. Said his sister in a letter to a friend: "Dismissed for stealing indeed!" Likely, Baylor had purchased cattle to feed Ketumsee's Comanches and some of the livestock had ended up on his new ranch. At any rate, after being supportive of the "civilization scheme" while a government employee, Baylor soon became its most outspoken opponent.[16] And in northwestern Texas, people listened to him.

Neighbors faced further uncertainty when the commissioner of Indian affairs opened the Wichita Agency in the summer of 1857. This agency was designed to shelter the northern Wichitas and Caddos, a thousand of whom had settled on the Brazos reserve. Some hope existed that Comanches and Kiowas might also settle on these lands in southwestern Indian Territory, something that Neighbors had frequently advocated. Unfortunately, the commissioner attached the new agency to the Southern (which included mostly Indian Territory), rather than the Texas, Superintendency. The decision struck hard at Neighbors's vanity.

Neighbors had little way of knowing that the commissioner's decision had more to do with the negotiations the government had undertaken with the Choctaw and Chickasaw Indian Nations. The Choctaws and Chickasaws had stipulated that the so-called Texas Indians would not be allowed to settle in the new district; the lands were to be used only by Indians from Indian Territory. The Choctaws and Chickasaws remembered too well the problems associated with the forced removal of Indians from Texas as a result of the Cherokee War of 1839.

When word of the new agency reached Texas in June, several Texas politicians immediately called for removal of the Clear Fork Comanches to the new reserve. Comanches supposedly had little need for a Texas agency when they could be confined to Indian Territory, and this had always been one of the Texas legislature's goals. When Neighbors learned that he would not have supervision of the new agency, he too wrote to the commissioner (whether out of anger or frustration) suggesting removal of the Clear Fork Comanches.[17] And if the Comanches were moved out of Texas, what of the Caddos, Delawares, Wichitas, and Tonkawas? Some members of the Texas legislature wanted them gone also.

While Neighbors's political friends—especially Houston—lobbied in hopes of reversing the commissioner's decision regarding control of the new agency, problems escalated when the military, for a second time, began removing troops from Texas. The Mormons in Utah increasingly resisted the imposition of federal judges, and in the spring of 1857, the War Department ordered the Second Cavalry (along with Colonel Lee and General Johnston) to join the army forces destined to subdue the rebellious Mormons. After Johnston and the best troops in the army headed to Wyoming and Utah, sixty-seven-year-old Brevet Major General David Twiggs took command in Texas.

Twiggs had served bravely in the war with Mexico, but he was a political general who wished to make no waves. He would be the senior commander in Texas when the Civil War broke out and would have the honor, or dishonor, of surrendering the Texas Military Department to the Confederacy in May 1861. This action earned him a dishonorable discharge from the Union army. Twiggs was well beyond the age of commanding any army when he reached Texas in 1857.[18] Worse, during his tenure of command, nearly half of the Texas frontier forts in the state were abandoned.

Under a new general order (no. 13), the number of horses for Twiggs's command was restricted to sixty, primarily because of the great demand for cavalry in the Utah campaign. While the general had the remnants of thirty-one companies at his disposal—just over two thousand men—the lack of cavalry and capable officers seriously limited the army's ability to maintain the peace in Texas.[19] The Lipan and Mescalero Apaches had concluded a year or two before that the army and Texas had declared war on them. They had patiently waited for the opportunity to inflict revenge upon Texas and perhaps sensed that the time was ripe when they saw forts being abandoned and troops leaving. Small parties of Apaches began crossing the Rio Grande that summer. The raiding occurred mostly along the Nueces River but also extended westward to include the Laredo and El Paso roads.

One of the first Apache assaults was on a small wagon train during the summer of 1857. The slow-moving train was traveling the Laredo road, some sixty miles south of San Antonio. The victims included several civilians; a woman and four children were carried off into captivity. Twiggs used the incident to demand more troops from Washington: "This affair is another evidence of the utter impossibility with the present force, of giving security to the inhabitants."[20]

Twiggs's concerns doubled when reports of a vicious battle reached him. An army patrol of seventeen infantrymen from Fort Mason had spent several weeks in early April scouting the rough chaparral country that lay around the headwaters of Devil's River, a tributary of the Rio Grande. Under the command of young Lieutenant J. B. Wood, the exhausted footsoldiers suddenly came face to face with an apparently peaceable party of men. Woods could not determine if the group consisted of Indians, renegades, or even Americans, and he waited cautiously for some indication of their intent.

Woods lowered his guard after one of the men waved a white cloth, a sign of peace. But as the soldiers approached, the man threw down the flag, and about thirty others jumped from the brush and attacked the infantry. Outnumbered and almost overwhelmed, Woods's men went for their six-shooters. In what the lieutenant described as a hand-to-hand melee, his men killed nine attackers at almost point-blank range and wounded a dozen more. Two of the lieutenants' men lay dead—the fifteen surviving infantrymen were all wounded in one fashion or another, some seriously. Woods ultimately identified the men as Lipans and some Mescalero allies. They were clearly getting bolder and less frightened of the army.[21]

The next month, August 1857, the Rio Grande frontier erupted after four attacks on patrols sent out from Fort Lancaster, a new post located at a ford of the Pecos River on the road to El Paso. When a reinforced mail party tried to ride through to the newly created Fort Davis, farther west along the El Paso road, Lipans and Mescaleros cut them off. A relief column of infantry almost succumbed to the Indians when it too fell under attack.[22] The army, sure of itself in 1855 and determined to adopt an offensive strategy in Texas, quickly found its undermanned military posts indefensible.

Making matters worse, civilian conflict escalated throughout the lower Nueces valley and then spread into towns north of it—in particular, Karnes City and Goliad. Problems there had little to do with Indians; Anglo-Texans were attacking Tejanos, stealing from them, and killing them. Some three major assaults and many minor ones occurred over the course of two months. The first report of this activity arrived at the governor's office in mid-September. It had been sent by Isaiah A. Paschal, a member of the state legislature. Paschal minced no words in declaring that "an attack was last night made on a train of Mexican carts, fifty five miles below this place [San Antonio]." Paschal noted that some thirty armed Texans "disguised as Indians" had made the assault. Casualties in the first assault had been light, since robbery had been the primary motive. But the "Indians" seemed to be expanding their ranks with new recruits.[23]

Anglo-Texans in the area were evenly split over the violence, with some supporting it and others condemning it. "I regard these men [the Texans] as *public enemies*, as *outlaws*—*Comanches*—as devils incarnate—as insurrectionists," wrote A. J. Mieux, a trusted friend of the governor's from the region. By contrast, Texans "of wealth" in Karnes City and Goliad, towns that supported the attackers, had "taken sides with the murderers," Mieux concluded. Local law enforcement officials were helpless to stop the attacks, either intimidated by the Texan renegades or involved in the attacks themselves.[24]

As the villains ran wild across southern Texas, newspapers took turns at printing distorted information. Some justified the raids by arguing that Tejanos had aided slaves in escaping into Mexico (where some four thousand former slaves were being harbored). Other Texans declared that Tejanos ran with renegades. Towns such as Seguin and Gonzales issued proclamations demanding that all Tejanos leave the region. In reality, as law and order broke down, the so-called cart war, as newspapers dubbed the conflict, broke out because a number of Texans saw an opportunity to once again blame Indians for pillaging and murder and then use such an excuse to attack Tejanos. The army was helpless to stop the carnage.[25]

A labor dispute between Tejano and Anglo carters may have launched the violence. The latter were angry over a special army contract for moving supplies in which Tejano cart drivers had underbid their Anglo counterparts. The renegades who joined in the attacks soon failed to discriminate, however, murdering Anglo as well as Tejano carters. The problem became an international incident when Mexico lodged a protest with Secretary of State Lewis Cass, who in turn demanded of Texas state officials that they end the violence. Rangers under Captain George H. Nelson helped stop the attacks, and the army began sending escorts with its supply trains. Texas renegades went mostly unpunished, although conservative reports put the number who died at their hands at seventy.[26]

Although the problems in the south seemed disconnected from events near the Indian reservations, trouble quickly spread northward. By the fall of 1857, the hot weather had finally moderated and rain appeared once again on the plains. The northern Comanches set out to augment their once large herds of horses and mules now that grass would again sustain their livestock. Not surprisingly, Neighbors learned in early October that some 450 northern Comanches had invaded Mexico. "If they are successful on that side of the river, they may not pay Texas a visit on their return," General Twiggs concluded. "If not, they certainly will."[27] With violence all across Texas, Twiggs prepared himself for an ugly winter. Twiggs soon faced the daunting task of checking the actions of the Comanches, Texans, Lipans, and renegade gangs then operating in the south.

Twiggs and Neighbors both placed some hope for stopping the Comanches on the efforts being made to organize the new Wichita Agency in Indian Territory. The new agent there, A. H. McKissick, met many of the western tribes in early October.

He hoped to consolidate his charges, much as had occurred in Texas. He had little trouble with the Wichitas, who during the drought had been forced to abandon their towns. He found 1,200 living some sixty miles west of Fort Arbuckle. Along the Canadian River was a village of 300 others, leaving only 360 Caddos, who had yet to settle into a community.

McKissick knew little about the 2,500 Shawnees, Delawares, and Kickapoos who still roamed west of the Wichita Mountains. They too had turned to hunting to survive during the drought years. Rumors suggested that a large Kickapoo party, learning of better grass on the southern plains, was headed to Texas to hunt. With most of the U.S. troops bound for Utah, the agent lacked a military force with which to turn back the Kickapoo hunters.

McKissick possessed even less influence with the Comanches and Kiowas. Some six hundred of them were camped in the upper Canadian River valley, near the 100th Meridian. McKissick did meet them, although he failed to identify their leaders—the agent was terribly inexperienced. These Comanches expressed a willingness to settle on the Leased District, but they talked openly of their hatred for Texans and their need to continue raiding in the south. The raids were necessary to sustain their economy, and they knew it.

The Comanches also noted the serious decline in bison herds. Most recently, the numbers of bison had fallen to the point where hunters could not find their prey for weeks on end. This made raiding an even more important part of the Comanche economy. Horses and mules could be eaten, and captives brought back from Mexico or Texas could be exchanged for food. A goodly quantity of food was being brought onto the plains from New Mexico by a growing number of so-called comancheros. The traders carried mostly corn tortillas in their two-wheeled carts and took back livestock—increasingly, cattle rustled from Texas ranches—along with any kind of marketable item, even clothing, in return.[28]

Within a month or two of McKissick's trip west, Neighbors acquired a more accurate description of what had transpired at the council. In a smug fashion, representative of his overall disappointment at losing control over the Wichita Agency, Neighbors informed Washington in November that Iron Jacket had spoken with McKissick. The chief had not been happy; he had demanded that the agent "pay him $100 in silver" and pay another $100 to each of his men. Such a verbal exchange is reflective of yet another change then occurring in the Plains Indian economy; to comanchero traders, silver was as acceptable as horses or mules. If paid off, Iron Jacket agreed to move to the west side of the Wichita Mountains or to the outskirts of the Leased District.

While Iron Jacket at least agreed to a council, Neighbors learned that the Naconi and Kotchateka Comanches were downright belligerent toward McKissick. The chiefs of both bands informed the Wichita agent of their intention to "exterminate the white settlements" in Texas soon, but McKissick failed to relate this information to Washington. When McKissick learned that the War Department had no intention of building a military fort in or near the Wichita Mountains to protect him and his agency, because of its remoteness, he retired to the east. Soon thereafter he left his new post for less dangerous work.[29]

At least some of these northern Comanches launched raids that fall of 1857, probably on their return from Mexico. A small party first struck the Penateka Comanche reserve, taking a half-dozen horses on October 26. Another, much larger group reportedly took some 180 horses from the ranch of Isaac Mullins on the Clear Fork a week later. Another 150 head of horses disappeared from Comel and Erath counties. By early December, as the claims of depredations hit the newspapers, even Neighbors had to admit that rustling was severely affecting the newly opened ranches along the upper Brazos River.[30] The Comanches seemed to be rebuilding their livestock herds at the expense of Texans.

Agent Shapely Ross had the best sources of information regarding these raiders, as he daily conferred with the friendly Indians of the Brazos reserve, who were constantly hunting and scouting north of the reserves near the Red River. Jim Pockmark, one of Ross's scouts, had recently discovered a large group of Kickapoos—likely the ones McKissick had learned of—hunting in the upper Brazos River valley, fifty miles northwest of Fort Belknap. Pockmark suspected that this Kickapoo party was guilty of some of the depredations, although he lacked proof. Quickly informing Major G. R. Paul, the infantry officer commanding at Fort Belknap, of the Kickapoo camp, Neighbors asked that troops force them to leave.

Major Paul had only a handful of men, and there were three hundred Kickapoos, all of them well armed. Neighbors realized the seriousness of the request, warning Paul in his letter that it would be "imprudent to attack them without thorough preparation." The warning was well advised, for much later (during the last year of the Civil War), these same Kickapoos would decimate a Texas Ranger company reinforced by Confederate troops. Paul lacked an appreciation for Neighbors's vast knowledge of Indians, however, and he viewed the warning as meddling, declining even to investigate the report.

In hopes of rectifying the situation, Neighbors wrote a long letter to Samuel A. Maverick, a friend in Austin who served in the state legislature. Unfortunately stretching the truth, Neighbors openly proclaimed that Kickapoos, not Comanches, had stolen the livestock from the Texas ranches along the upper Brazos.[31] Getting wind of the debate, Governor Runnels, then demanded that the army investigate. General Twiggs ordered Major Paul to send out a patrol on December 23. Neighbors had politicized the issue and embarrassed the army.

Paul's subsequent report, inaccurate and untruthful, concluded that there had never been a large Kickapoo camp anywhere near the fort. The only Indians in the upper Brazos were twelve Kickapoos who had joined with a few "white men" to hunt. They were a threat to no one and not responsible for horse thievery.[32] Worse,

Paul's ridicule of Neighbors prompted other army officers to do the same, defending the army against the Indian Bureau; Paul's actions began a feud between the agents and officers that only expanded in the months to follow.

Captain George Stoneman, who had just arrived at Camp Cooper with a company of the Second Cavalry, sided completely with Paul. Stoneman, who would later command a corps for the Union in the Civil War and eventually became governor of California, despised anyone who said positive things about Indians—any Indians. The captain soon clashed with Agent Matthew Leeper, who had replaced Baylor at Clear Fork; Stoneman invaded the reserve, forced the Indians from their tents, and ordered several enlisted officers to count Comanche heads. His purpose was to show that many of the so-called peaceful Comanches were actually off the reserve, supposedly committing depredations.

Stoneman reportedly found only 112 Indians on the reservation. Later, he would admit to 263. "The above numbers are the result of a careful and accurate count, not of sticks [a system of counting done by Indians], but of the Indians themselves," the captain matter-of-factly reported to Twiggs. Agent Leeper was outraged. He quickly wrote to Neighbors complaining of the invasion and the numbers that Stoneman had reported—the fewer the number, it would seem, the more the Indians were hostile. Leeper swore that all the Comanches were accounted for, numbering over three hundred. Acrimonious charges flew back and forth between Stoneman and Leeper, forcing Neighbors to demand that the captain be removed from his command, which further alienated the agent from army officers.[33] The fighting disturbed Twiggs from his usual slumber, but he lacked the courage to stop it. He left Stoneman in command of his troop.

The upshot of the whole affair was that a growing collection of people—both army officers and civilians—thought that the southern Comanches on the reservation were heavily involved in depredations. Organized opposition to Neighbors grew from this assertion, with a large group following the lead of the former discredited agent John R. Baylor. The crowd organized by Baylor first surfaced on December 13, 1857, when thirty-five citizens from Williamson County and another similar group from Lampasas County sent petitions to the governor asking for the removal of Neighbors. People from Young County, the location of the reserves, seemed not to have supported the petition. Both groups, in suspiciously identical language, argued that only women and children remained on the Comanche reservation. The Indian men, they alleged, supported themselves by stealing horses and killing citizens.[34]

Neighbors responded in a long letter published in the Austin-based *Texas Sentinel*. He complained of Baylor and Mullins, who were behind the removal effort, charging that both men had refused to help the agents and the army track the men responsible for the horse thievery, even though it was supposedly their horses that had been taken. Neighbors congratulated himself by noting that many citizens along the upper Brazos had refused to sign the petitions; they saw the reserve Indians as friendly and loyal.

Finally, the agent returned to his basic argument: Kickapoos had been responsible, and if Comanches were involved, they were from camps along the upper Arkansas or Canadian River.[35]

Just after Christmas, General Twiggs weighed in with a report to Washington. The best information he possessed suggested that some six hundred head of horses had been stolen and six to eight men killed, although he was vague on where these men had died. He apparently was taking the information from the newspapers. Twiggs had ordered another investigation by someone other than Stoneman or Paul. With his depleted command, however, he could do nothing more than send a young officer, Captain Nathan George Evans, to confer with the other officers and survey the situation around the reservations.[36]

As expected, Evans listened carefully to his fellow officers, who openly vilified the Indian agents. Captain Stoneman averred that he could not trust Agent Leeper, and since Stoneman was charged with maintaining order on the Comanche reserve, he had to count the Indians there occasionally. Major Paul reinforced Stoneman, criticizing the agents, Neighbors, and the entire civilization program. He called Neighbors's reports regarding the Kickapoos "entirely fabulous." Indeed, he argued, "Not much reliance can be placed on statements founded on such vague and unreliable authority" as the Delawares and Shawnees.[37] Of course, Paul had never campaigned (which virtually required using Delaware and Shawnee scouts from the reserves), and he knew nothing of the reliability of the information coming from them.

Paul's and Stoneman's statements suggest a conspiracy that hatched from a deep-seated hatred for Indians and very likely from economic motives as well. In what would soon become a tangled web of intrigue, Stoneman, Paul, and Evans came to indirectly support Baylor and his group. All of these men, with the possible exception of Stoneman, had interests in opening livestock ranches along the upper Brazos River. Paul and Captain Newton C. Givens had already bought land and built ranch houses. The inevitable removal of Comanche reserve Indians to Indian Territory would open to ranching 30,000 acres of the best-watered lands on the upper Clear Fork. Getting rid of the Brazos reserve would open a like quantity of range.[38]

When Evans offered his final report to Twiggs, it too brought into question the loyalty of the reservation Indians. First, Evans absolved the Kickapoos, who, he noted, had always been friendly to Texans. He also asserted that the northern Comanches used the reservations as a place of refuge during raids. According to Evans, those Indians had "many facilities afforded [them] by their relatives on the reservation"; in particular, they hid stolen horses in the rugged chaparral country away from the river.[39]

Evans believed that other information might be gained by sending a cavalry patrol to talk with the settlers. He ordered Captain Givens to undertake this trip in early February. Givens had already established his "Stone Ranch" near Camp Cooper (the name, while innocent enough, may suggest that Stoneman was a silent partner, as he was the only officer at Fort Belknap or Camp Cooper who was not openly involved in ranching). Givens dutifully visited most of the settlers in the Colorado and Guadalupe River valleys. After his return, Givens set the blame almost entirely upon the southern Comanches. He reported that Texans had actually seen Indians moving livestock onto the reserve and concluded that "the greater portion by far [of the depredations] was committed by the Texas reserve Indians—and that of the two reserves, the upper or Comanche reserve was responsible for most."[40]

After making such outrageous accusations regarding the Indians, Givens then turned to the agents. He attacked them openly, questioning the truthfulness of their reports. Leeper, he charged, failed to support the army's decree regarding roving bands; Leeper had let twenty to thirty Comanches leave the reserve at a time. Then Givens revealed his true spirit, claiming that the Indians were "born and bred to the profession of horse stealing." Givens knew of "no baptismal regeneration through which they have passed to relieve them from their old habits."[41] Givens, Paul, Stoneman, and Evans all contrasted markedly with the likes of Hardee and Marcy. They detested Indians and, just like Texans, speculated in western lands.

With mounting criticism, even the agents began to waver in their support of the reserve Indians. Leeper confided to Neighbors on December 31 that perhaps some of the southern Comanches had assisted their northern relatives. And Neighbors changed his argument as well, finally concluding that the Kickapoos had been responsible for several murders but that northern Comanches had stolen the large herds of horses. Neighbors even estimated the losses in livestock at $4,510 in a memo to the commissioner of Indian affairs, Charles Mix.[42]

With an increasing fear that the reserves would be broken up, Neighbors wrote to General Twiggs on January 18, 1858, calling upon the army to campaign against the northern Indians, "until they are reduced to proper subjection or exterminated."[43] These were tough words from an Indian agent who had spent considerable time in Comanche tepees talking of "women and horses," as he had once put it. His comments reflected the pressure that Texas culture exerted even on reasonable men. Put simply, most Texans of the time adhered to a creed regarding issues of skin color and race—it was difficult if not impossible to reject race baiting. Increasingly, Robert Neighbors's honor became inextricably tied to saving the reservations—and in his mind that required the cleansing of the Texas panhandle of northern Comanches. Such had come to be the story of Texas.

Twiggs, politician that he was, stayed above the debate initiated by his junior officers, at least in his general correspondence. However, he did move several cavalry units back to Fort Belknap. And he recruited Texas volunteers to serve as rangers for three to six months; he asked Governor Runnels for ten companies of seventy men each. The army provided rifles and "horseman pistols," and the state authorized $75,000 for salaries. By Christmas, John H. Conner, Neill Robinson, Thomas K.

Carmack, Thomas C. Frost, G. H. Nelson, and John S. Ford had received the welcome news to organize their men. They were to assist the depleted army garrisons in bringing order to the Nueces and Brazos river valleys.[44]

With all these rangers in the field, both Governor Runnels and General Twiggs expected the excitement generated on the upper Brazos River to subside. They were wrong. While the ranger units did practically nothing—only Conner's men found and clashed with a small party of Indians—they continued to spread misinformation regarding the role of reservation Indians in the depredations. Lieutenant Frost's letter to the governor in January typified the reports. Indian raiders, he believed, generally followed a path directly to the reservations. "I would state from a number of conspiring evidences, it is almost proved that if the Indians on the reservations are not the aggressors they are unquestionably concerned in the numerous and recent atrocities."[45] Frost never listed any atrocities, however—there was hardly any evidence that a single Texan on the Brazos had been killed by Indians.

Seeing an opportunity to add to their complaints, Givens and Paul launched yet another round of petitions. They became enamored with proving the southern Comanches at fault, in the hopes of driving them from Texas. This time, their petitions went not only to the governor of the state and various newspapers, but also to the secretary of the interior, the direct boss of the commissioner of Indian affairs. They ridiculed Neighbors for his attempt to blame the Kickapoos and lambasted the civilization program by identifying it as essentially a "beef feeding" program.[46] Owing to the drought, there was some truth to the statement.

As complaints mounted, the frontier citizenry soon split into factions. Some settlers who initially had praised the civilization effort seemed suddenly to shift their allegiance, influenced no doubt by the rhetoric of the army officers, Baylor, and the local newspapers. By Christmas 1857, only a minority of Texans still believed that the reservations had created a safer environment. A few others determined that the Brazos River reserve had done much to limit raiding, but they believed Baylor, Stoneman, and Paul were right in condemning the southern Comanches at Clear Creek. As one rancher said years later, Baylor "was a man highly respected."[47]

Despite the withering criticism, Neighbors defended the Indian program. In Austin in February 1858, he told anyone who would listen that the reservation Indians were not responsible for the depredations. He branded the attacks of the army officers and Baylor as "libelous." But he also noted that it might be impossible for the agents to "stem the tide of public opinion" that some men on the frontier had created "from selfish motives"—an obvious reference to the ranching potential of Indian lands. He complained of Paul and Givens, asserting that those officers "have greatly increased the excitement against the reserve Indians" and accusing them of wishing to break up the reservations.[48] Finally, in late February 1858, General Twiggs called for a special meeting to convene in Washington to discuss the Texas situation. He requested that Neighbors attend.[49]

As both the soldier, Twiggs, and the agent, Neighbors, prepared to depart for the East, good news appeared in the newspapers. President James Buchanan had reached an agreement with Brigham Young and the Mormons. A formal pardon was issued to the Mormons on April 6; the war was over, releasing thousands of troops, including General Johnston and the Second Cavalry. Perhaps Texas (and its reservation Indians) could be saved from annihilation, but the cost increasingly seemed to include the utter destruction of the northern tribes. Neighbors had grown to accept such a proposition; the army, especially the cavalry, welcomed it.

Being a Texan, Neighbors likely recognized that his trip east that spring consti-tuted the last chance for his Indian charges. Thousands of new settlers had streamed into Texas despite the dry weather of the late 1850s. The state's population exceeded half a million people. The Hill Country west of Austin was filled with Germans bent on doing some farming but also turning to livestock raising. The entire upper Trinity River had been staked out, as well as much of the land along the upper Brazos. In this blur of land speculation and development, any thought of respecting the sover-eignty of Indians, of recognizing that Comanches had a claim to West Texas, was lost to the creeping sound of wagon wheels headed west.

The population increases had brought considerable change to Texas and how people in the state viewed the so-called Indian problem. Just years before, the army had tried to implement a line of forts designed to separate Texans and Indians and defend settled ground. By 1858 this strategy had been abandoned; Texans were moving into the country northwest of Fort Belknap and were entering the high plains and the desert southwest. They would soon want even the desolate Panhandle, the last haunt of the nonreservation Comanches. Most simply wanted the "Indian problem" to go away. Most of them expected the federal government to do for Texas what it had done in the South—remove all Indians.

Somewhat like Andrew Jackson and Sam Houston before him, Neighbors faced a dilemma. He knew that total removal was unfair to the majority of reservation Indians, who lived in peace: Texas was their birthright. But as he traveled to Washing-ton, he also feared that the government would give the Texas Indians very little attention. The Mormon trouble had ended, to be sure, but talk of Civil War was everywhere. The Kansas question had been replaced by the Dred Scott court deci-sion, which resonated nationally. Everywhere, Americans talked of slavery and war. Would officials listen to a western Indian agent bent on helping a small population of Texas Indians?

19

ANARCHY AND "TOTAL WAR"

A few pioneer wagons still headed into West Texas during the summer of 1858, but an abrupt change soon became obvious. For the first time, almost as many settlers returned east as stayed. A similar regression occurred south of the Nueces River. Surveying and improvements on land, so common to Texas in the preceding thirty years, suddenly halted that summer. Settlement in western Texas had stagnated, perhaps even receded, a condition that continued into the Civil War years. While the drought of the previous year had been a factor, a second reason for the decline was the growing anarchy in the western counties.

Texas newspaper editors took turns blaming the federal and state governments for the lawlessness that contributed to the state's stagnation in 1858. The two branches of government seemed more interested in blaming each other than in cooperating to end the violence. But the newspapers failed to point out that many West Texas ranchers had expanded beyond the 98th Meridian, where water was scarce and livestock herds were difficult to defend. Making matters worse, most of the stock on these ranches—in a prebarbwire age—ran wild; just counting them to determine how many might be missing was problematic.[1]

As a further complication, who was doing the "depredating" (the term used by a few newspapers) seemed an unsolvable question. Renegade bands—sometimes Anglos dressed like Indians—had became so active that it was impossible for honest men to determine who was robbing whom. While suspicion regarding Anglo participation grew throughout 1857 and 1858, the certainty of such participation did not surface until Edward Burleson leaked to the papers that certain men, including Baylor, were using arrows to kill livestock so that the attacks would be blamed on Indians. The *Dallas Herald* printed the story on July 25, 1858.[2] The information hardly warranted attention, for by this time Indian war had already broken out.

Some—but not all—northern Comanche bands were also guilty of depredations. They would send in small groups of six to twelve men who mostly rustled livestock. On occasion, Neighbors's Brazos reserve Indians were able to identify the bands from which the raiders came. Regardless of the minor level of participation on the part of Indians, most Texans blamed them for the entire problem. Guilt was ultimately even attached to the people of the peaceful Brazos River reserves.

However, the state of Texas had matured by the late 1850s, with most of the population existing in eastern counties rather than isolated western communities. People in these eastern sections had moved to Texas from the Old South—Alabama, Mississippi, and Georgia. They had opened cotton lands and brought in slaves, and they wanted stability. Rather than fret about Indian depredations, they often discussed political issues such as slavery, the price of cotton, and (more frequently after 1858) possible secession from the federal union. It was not that Indian issues in the far west were inconsequential, just that cotton plantation farmers had less in common with western ranchers.

By the late 1850s, the voters in these more populous counties had seldom, if ever, even seen an Indian. Many adhered to the same creed as the rangers, and Texas Rangers were heroes to them, but they frequently supported senators and congressmen who refused to support legislation authorizing payment for rangers, which these eastern citizens deemed "pork barrel." While many Texans among the western settlements may have turned against Neighbors's Indian civilization program by spring 1858, this no longer meant that the state would finance a ranger assault on the reserves or even on the northern Indians.

Neighbors understood this political transformation as much as anyone. He realized that state authorities might still defend the reserves; the agent had friends in Austin who believed in the "experiment." Neighbors also had remained friends with some army officers despite his differences with Stoneman, Paul, and Givens. Thus, there were good men in both the state and the army who might still help Neighbors protect his charges. They simply needed to come forward, and soon, to save the reserves. And the reserves, with nearly two hundred well-armed and friendly Indian scouts, Neighbors believed, were what protected Texas from an onslaught by the northern Comanches.[3]

As the supervising agent prepared to depart for Washington to attend the meetings scheduled by General Twiggs, he only hoped that the reserves could hold out, although his subordinate Leeper seemed increasingly pessimistic of this possibility. The reports from Clear Fork Agency revealed that army officers stationed there had little intention of doing their duty. By the summer of 1858, even General Twiggs had joined in the land speculation. He ordered Captain Evans to move his troops from Camp Cooper to lands recently purchased from Captain Givens, where a new post was to be built. Neighbors and other nearby ranchers quickly figured out the scheme. Neighbors, while in Washington, roundly protested, and even Texas ranchers complained. To Governor Runnels, one wrote that "the troops . . . were to afford us protection, but from general observation I find out that they are a drunken parcel of rowdies."[4] Twiggs gave in and returned the small infantry force to Camp Cooper.

Seeing little help from the army, the agents turned to their other choice—state ranger captain John S. Ford. Ford had gained a reputation for being an aggressive yet responsible ranger. Nevertheless, because of the condemnation of the reserve Indians by the Texas press, he arrived in northwestern Texas with preconceived views of Indian depredations. He expected to catch reservation Indians red-handed stealing stock, and he immediately sent out patrols north and west of Fort Belknap.

Ford scouted the countryside for two weeks with his rangers, searching arroyos for trails and talking with various ranchers. But he failed to track any parties into the reserve. All that he could report to Governor Runnels with certainty was the impact of the horse stealing in 1858: "The sense of insecurity has paralyzed business almost entirely." Ford, like so many other Texans, blamed the Comanches at Clear Fork and offered in a letter to the governor to campaign against them. Indeed, he planned to run the few remaining Penateka Comanches out of Texas, because (despite his failure to implicate them) Ford was sure that they had been accomplices in the raiding.[5] If that course of action meant breaking up both reservations, so be it.

Despite Runnels's delayed response, Ford, his lieutenant Allison Nelson, John R. Baylor, and several of Baylor's associates met at Baylor's ranch on April 14 to consider plans for such an assault. Ford quickly recommended sending out "parties of reconnaissance" to determine whether a reservation Indian could be caught depredating. "If a trail can be traced from the point where a depredation has been done to the Comanche Reserve," he pointed out during the meeting, "then there can be no longer any doubt as to their [the southern Comanches'] complicity."

At this point, Lieutenant Nelson openly approached the captain and stated that "that thing can be arranged." Rather astonishingly, so many Texans had taken to the act of "Indian dressing" to cover up crimes that the idea had wide approval within the group. Baylor, when agent, had acquired Comanche bows and arrows, and Nelson proposed to have rangers go out that night and kill cattle and hogs in the nearby settlement. The rangers would then leave a clear trail into the reservation.[6]

To everyone's surprise, Ford hesitated. Despite his condemnation of the Indians, he had always acted with authority and under the law. Gathering support from other officers (including young Edward Burleson, Jr., who would later reveal the incident) and having not yet received sanction from Governor Runnels, Ford decided to order more patrols. He seemed convinced that real evidence—rather than manufactured depredations—would eventually appear.

For a solid week, the rangers scouted and probed the mesquite shelters along the various creeks and main branches of the Brazos, looking for clues both above and below the Clear Fork reserve. But trails simply did not exist. Becoming less convinced of the complicity of the southern Comanches, Ford visited Agent Ross at the Brazos reserve. Ross assured him that the trouble was with the northern Comanches, not their southern relatives living in peace on the reserves, and that his Indians would assist the rangers in punishing the perpetrators.

After considerable soul searching, Ford wrote to Governor Runnels that he believed Ross rather than Baylor and Baylor's ranger cohorts. Ross had even proposed that he and Ford launch a large expedition northward. The agent intended to recruit over a hundred Brazos Agency Indians to join the rangers. Combining with Ford's force of over a hundred men, the two groups would constitute a formidable army. Ross assured Ford that his Indian scouts could find the main northern Comanche camps and surprise the warriors within. An excited Ford wrote to Governor Runnels on April 26 that Ross had fulfilled his promise for support and that the Brazos agent had even entrusted Ford with his son, Lawrence Sullivan Ross, as the man picked to lead the Indian auxiliaries.

Ford agreed and then sought reinforcements from Baylor and others in the Weatherford area. Surprisingly, the seemingly militant Baylor refused to go along but instead recruited twenty-three rangers for "his own" company. He even demanded that the governor recognize the force.[7] However, Runnels balked at this irregularity. Ford had experience at Indian fighting; Baylor did not.

As Ford sharpened his plan, he spent several days surveying the Brazos River reserve. What he saw astonished him. The Caddos, Wichitas, and others there, he noted to Runnels, "had cut loose from the wild Indians . . . they say they wish to become Americans." Of the 1,100 people on the Brazos reserve, most had adopted white dress and had promising crops as a result of the rain that had finally fallen in 1858. "I should view any combination of circumstances which tended towards the breaking up of this reserve, as a serious misfortune to the state of Texas," Ford wrote to Runnels. The civilization program, so vilified by Baylor and others, was working, a rather astonished Ford concluded.

More significantly, Ford sensed the earnestness of his new Indian allies. Ross's charges manifested a "war spirit." They had few scruples about punishing the northern bands, which had carried off some of their livestock. Ford watched as they conducted several evening war dances, recruiting young men for the expedition.[8] With high spirits and hopes for success, the rangers and Indians departed for the north. They possessed the element of surprise because most northern Indians no longer feared the U.S. Army—Lee's expedition had been the most threatening, and it had accomplished little. The strongholds of the northern Comanches were also far distant from Texas and had never been invaded.

Riding northward for nearly two weeks, Ford's rangers and Ross's Indians ultimately reached the Canadian River valley, more than two hundred miles north of the agencies. Early on the morning of May 12, a contingent of Tonkawa scouts stumbled upon a small Comanche hunting camp of five lodges and killed several people. A few Indians escaped to alert the much larger village hidden a few miles away, along the north bank of the sparsely tree-lined Canadian. Following closely, Ross's Indians hit the town about 10:00 A.M. They dashed through the shallow water and rode between the lodges and the river, shooting from their horses.

Ford's men came in soon after, moving straight through the camp, firing their six-shooters at close range. Comanche men, taken unawares, were trying to protect their families, gather their arms, and mount their horses. A few fled north to where Lieutenant Nelson awaited them. Warriors fell everywhere as several prominent Comanche chiefs tried to make a stand. The most gallant was Iron Jacket, whose village was being torn apart. He had always said that his Spanish armor would make him invincible.

At the head of several dozen warriors, Iron Jacket bravely attacked Ross's Indian allies, riding straight at them. As one animated chronicler put it, the chief charged them dressed "in gorgeous array—clad in a coat of mail. . . . The sharp crack of five or six rifles brought his horse to the ground, and in a few moments, the chief fell riddled with balls." A Shawnee named Doss and the Caddo Jim Pockmark claimed the victory. Nearly every warrior who followed Iron Jacket fell in the futile charge.

By noon, the shooting had subsided, but then suddenly other Comanches appeared. This new, ever-increasing force swarmed about the hills to the north. Another village existed four miles upriver, and its chiefs frantically tried to consolidate the hundreds of warriors to save the first town. One of the leaders was the noted Peta Nocona.

Captain Ford, reveling in literary license, described the fluid combat. "A scene was now enacted beggaring description," he started. It reminded him of "the rude and chivalrous days of Knight-errantry. Shields and Lances, and bows, and head dresses—prancing steeds and many minutias [sic] were not wanting to complete the resemblance." Ross's Indians and the Comanches taunted each other "with every species of insult," some consisting of anatomical displays—mooning back and forth amid shouts, gestures, and horse parades. While a few individual contests occurred, neither side attacked.

Hearing of yet another Comanche force to the east, Ford and his Indian allies slowly retired. Rather than burn the village of seventy or so lodges, Ross's Indian allies argued that it should be left intact, as they refused to make war on women and children. Indeed, only a few noncombatants had been killed, with a dozen or so women and children having been taken prisoner. Ford agreed, inspecting the well-made bison-skin tepees before he departed, with their hair turned inside for warmth, and noting the dozen hides that graced the floors of each lodge. Ford and Ross counted seventy-six Comanche men dead on the ground; many more were wounded. The casualties among the Texans and the Brazos Indians were light, with two killed and three wounded, a testament to their better arms and the surprise of the assault.[9]

As Ford's rangers and Ross's Indians marched homeward, Neighbors settled into a hotel in Washington, D.C. Although he had failed to obtain sanction for the visit from the commissioner of Indian affairs—Twiggs had invited him, not the bureau—he would spend a month with government officials, working on the many problems that plagued West Texas and his agencies. Unfortunately, the charges of Paul, Givens,

Evans, Stoneman, and others had reached Washington—Twiggs had denied the agent access to the letters while in San Antonio—and Neighbors spent most of his time defending himself. He did convince the commissioner to undertake a formal investigation, hoping that it might alleviate the constant rumors regarding the agencies and their occupants.

Such a concession seemed a defeat. In many ways, the army had been vindicated. Not so much as one reprimand was sent out to the officers in charge at Camp Cooper or Fort Belknap. Back in Texas in mid-June without any promises of assistance, Neighbors put the best face on the trip. He announced to the newspapers that a tribunal would soon convene. He expected that it would reveal the "cruel slander" that had characterized the attacks of some army officers and John R. Baylor on the agents and the civilization program.[10]

The forces opposing the reservations quickly launched a counteroffensive. Lieutenant Nelson, back from the Canadian River where he had fought alongside Ford, wrote directly to President James Buchanan, charging Neighbors with "gross abuse of power." The Indians Neighbors supposedly controlled were, according to Nelson, killing citizens and stealing livestock. Nelson charged that some twenty-five citizens had been killed by Indians recently. Where such a claim came from is impossible to determine, as it was completely unsupported by the facts.[11]

The regular army and the agents continued to keep track of depredations. These reports reveal that while livestock had been disappearing, very few Texans had been killed. General Twiggs put the total number of deaths for 1857 at "6–8 people," but he had no idea who had killed them. Comanches apparently killed a rancher in late January 1858 while he tended his stock. The worst attack came in Jack County in late April, when two families, the Masons and Camerons, lost seven adults killed.

Subsequent evidence demonstrated that one of the attackers had "light hair" and spoke English. To a child left behind, he said he was a "Kickapoo," but two weeks later, an Anglo-Texan was arrested—he was a nearby settler named Bill Willis. Governor Runnels gave Captain Ford authority to call out as many men as he needed to find the other culprits. But even convicting Willis proved futile. He was later lynched after being caught with stolen horses, but the men who rode with him were never found. Despite the fact that Indians had killed possibly just one man during the entire spring and summer of 1858, ranchers continued to abandon the west.[12]

Baylor naturally came to the support of Nelson's charges. He called for citizens to write petitions; upon failing to get much of a response, he wrote them himself. He also tried to incite testimony against the agent, encouraging local citizens to speak out. In one such letter, Baylor revealed that he hoped to expel Neighbors and replace him with Nelson, who would make a better agent. The citizens of the upper Brazos, he coyly pointed out, "should *hang together and unite.*"[13]

But Neighbors also had political allies. Sam Houston helped immeasurably. Houston first recommended that former governor Pease, increasingly an advocate of the civilization program, be appointed to investigate the charges made by the army officers and those sent on to the president by Nelson. After Pease was found to be unavailable—probably because the job did not suit his political taste—Thomas J. Hawkins from Lexington, Kentucky, agreed to conduct the investigation. Hawkins would at least be objective, although because he was not a Texan his recommendations would carry little weight.

Hawkins informed Neighbors that he would be at Camp Cooper by late September 1858, and he wanted the agent there to cross-examine witnesses. General Twiggs even cooperated, granting leave to Captain Givens so that he might testify. Hawkins published letters in the local press, announcing the dates and times for citizens to come forward with evidence. When he was finally at Camp Cooper, however, only three Anglo-Texans appeared. Their testimony, as Hawkins reported, was "confined to vague and rather indefinite accusations as to the horse-stealing and cow-killing propensities of Indians in general." There was no decisive evidence of any Texan having been killed by Indians in the twelve previous months. Givens, Nelson, Evans, Stoneman, and Baylor all refused to meet with Hawkins or to give statements even on paper.[14]

Although Hawkins's report exonerated the agents and the Indians, he still saw many problems. The northern Comanches and Kickapoos seemed determined to cause trouble for the Texas Indians, and Anglo-Texans had tried to build ranches all along the river, both above and below the agencies. The pressures of settlement would likely cause more trouble in the future. Hawkins believed that the Comanches, especially, should be moved north to Indian Territory. Despite Hawkins's overall endorsement of the civilization program, he felt that the Brazos reserve Indians would be better off in Indian Territory as well.[15]

One final observation by Commissioner Hawkins dealt with the northern Comanches. He had heard, no doubt through the Brazos River Indians, that the Ford raid had infuriated the northern bands. The various agents assigned to Indian Territory confirmed this conclusion through discussions with Wichita leaders. Buffalo Hump and the nephew of the recently deceased Pahayuco, both Penateka Comanches, had organized seven or eight bands on the Canadian River into a coalition devoted to destroying Texas. They had drawn many Yamparica Comanches into the pact.

Buffalo Hump and his fellow chiefs had even approached the Wichitas and Caddos in Indian Territory, seeking more allies. The Wichitas and Caddos in general had long since given up war. They now walked a tightrope, balancing themselves between the Americans and the western Plains tribes. Probably making the situation more difficult was the fact that Fort Arbuckle, to the east of the Wichita Mountains, had been completely abandoned in 1857 because of the manpower needs of the Mormon War. When U.S. agents met with Wichitas, those Indians expressed a fear that the Comanche coalition might mistake them for American allies.[16]

Despite Hawkins's report, rustling increased throughout the late summer. Reports of raids on horse herds often included the suggestion that "renegades" had joined the Comanches, a very unlikely combination. Large numbers of single men lived in pockets along the Texas frontier, some simple gamblers working the various saloons, others cowboys working at a ranch for a short time and then moving on. Reports occasionally noted that the thieves spoke openly to each other "in good English." There seemed to be no doubt that other Anglo-Texans or former Kansas Jayhawkers who had moved into Indian Territory were taking Nelson's advice; they dressed as Indians and rustled livestock.

Despite the implications of other Texans in killings such as that of the Cameron and Mason families, many Texans continued to blame Indians for their troubles. And a few raids did occur, which only solidified the effect of newspaper reports. A small party from Ketumsee's village, then living with Buffalo Hump, had lingered around Givens's ranch, selecting the horses that they wanted in late July. While they killed no one—indeed, they avoided settlers, the majority of whom were heavily armed and lethal—two members of the party stopped to visit relatives at the Clear Fork Indian reserve. When Ketumsee told them to leave, they refused. Making matters worse, their relatives on the reserve protected them in standard Comanche fashion. Blood and kinship ties were always more important in Indian camps than were political arrangements.

Ketumsee went immediately to Agent Leeper with the news. His actions suggest that this sort of quandary had seldom happened in the past. Leeper called upon the new military commander, young Lieutenant Cornelius Van Camp, a pliable man who had replaced the obstreperous Evans two months before. Van Camp quickly marched his twenty-one men to the house containing the two northern Indians. All that everyone wanted was for the Indians to leave. Ketumsee stepped to the side of Van Camp, hoping to avoid bloodshed. But the Comanches inside refused to surrender, and with the backing of some seventy of their relatives, they defied Van Camp's demands that they vacate the reserve.

At this point, Lieutenant Van Camp prepared to storm the house with his men. Just as the order was about to be carried out, a sergeant informed Van Camp that the soldiers had turned in their ammunition the day before in preparation for being moved back east. The two squads of men had a grand total of one bullet! In abject horror, Lieutenant Van Camp retreated, claiming in at least one report to superiors that he had negotiated a "compromise" in which the Indians were allowed to leave.[17]

The Van Camp incident embarrassed everyone. As Neighbors put it in his report to the governor, "General Twiggs is greatly annoyed to think that a company of U.S. troops should go into a fight with only one round of ammunition." Twiggs actually began court-martial proceedings against Van Camp, a serious step for the cautious, political-minded Twiggs.[18]

The incident occurred as the state government was also in disarray over the western problems. Governor Runnels had been lobbying heavily for more military assistance from both the federal and the state government. But the state legislature, dominated by men from eastern and central Texas, had refused to hire more rangers. Newspaper editors, exasperated with the army, railed increasingly against the governor. Suddenly, everyone lamented the fact that Captain Ford and his men had been mustered out in August for lack of funds, several days before Van Camp's debacle at the Comanche reservation.[19]

The events at the agency as well as the constant complaints by state officials finally brought some response from the War Department, which agreed to reassign some troops to Texas in September. Twiggs had been pleading for help for months because he realized that Ford's success against the Comanches, when contrasted with Van Camp's incompetence, had made the army look ineffective and foolish. Twiggs had requested four companies of the Second Cavalry that were returning from Utah. He still believed that a viable striking force in Texas would solve the rustling problems. These troops would "follow up the Comanches to the residence of their families" and destroy them.[20]

Twiggs finally got his wish when Major Earl Van Dorn and elements of the Second Cavalry reached Fort Belknap. Van Dorn, who had served earlier under Lee and had campaigned on the plains, was an experienced, determined officer who believed in using Indian scouts and in the doctrine of total war. Van Dorn eagerly anticipated implementing Twiggs's order. Army honor was now at stake.[21] He collected the most reliable Delaware, Shawnee, Caddo, and Tonkawa scouts at the Brazos Agency and prepared to campaign over the winter, dressing his men warmly and organizing supply trains.

Meanwhile, the arrival of Van Dorn allowed Twiggs to resolve a second issue. He asked the War Department to investigate the affair at the Comanche reservation and arrest any Indians who were implicated in defying Lieutenant Van Camp. In September, the order went out to Neighbors, requesting him to seize the Indians implicated "at all hazard." Twiggs believed that some punishment of the men involved was necessary. "I am deeply mortified at the occurrence at the Comanche Reserve," he wrote to the War Department. "To parade for a fight, and on the eve of the commencing to find the command without ammunition, is distressing." If it were his decision, Twiggs continued, "I would order a force there and take them all prisoners, or shoot them if they resisted."[22] Texas had a way of bringing senior military officers to a point of exasperation.

But Neighbors had a much different view. He wrote to Twiggs that the Indians involved had returned the next day, pleading that the northern Comanches would have destroyed them had they allowed the army to take the two men. Neighbors insisted that to punish these Indians at this point would be counterproductive. In addition, it was Neighbors and not the army who had authority within the confines of the reserves. Twiggs, unconvinced, was terribly upset; privately Neighbors informed the commissioner of Indian affairs that the general "swears that he [Twiggs] will never send any more [military] protection to the reserve."[23]

As the wrangling went on, Van Dorn marched north with a command of 225, most of them veterans of the Utah War. But a large force of Brazos River Indians also joined the army, again under the command of Sul Ross. Establishing a base camp on September 29 at Otter Creek (a small tributary of the Canadian River), the Delaware, Shawnee, Caddo, and Tonkawa spies—led mostly by the noted Tonkawa Placido—soon learned of a large Comanche camp, located just a few miles from the main Wichita town near the Wichita Mountains. The Comanches were doing their usual exchanging of bison meat, hides, and horses for Wichita corn, beans, and dried pumpkin.

Van Dorn quickly mounted his force and rode the ninety miles eastward, entering the Leased District, a region set aside for future Plains Indian reserves by the 1855 treaty. Just as the sun appeared on the morning of October 1, Van Dorn's troops hit the sleeping Comanche town of 120 lodges. Mostly Buffalo Hump's Penatekas, the few men in camp had done little to prepare for battle. Some were out hunting, unaware of the fate that beset their people.

Most of the killing was accomplished by the army troops as their Indian allies drove off the substantial pony herd. While Van Dorn lost a mere three men—including the disgraced Van Camp, who was seeking to redeem his honor—the troopers killed fifty-nine Comanches during the initial assault. Many wounded Indians fled into the hills that surrounded the camp. Troopers pursued them, killing a dozen or so. While Van Dorn prided himself on having shot only two women, everything in the camp was burned and those who escaped were entirely destitute. The fierce Van Dorn proudly reported to his superiors that "nothing was left to mark the site of their camp, but the ashes and the dead."[24]

While the army had destroyed part of Buffalo Hump's band, what Van Dorn and the other officers involved did not know was that on the morning of the attack, Buffalo Hump and many of his men were talking with Elias Rector, superintendent of Indian affairs in Indian Territory at nearby Fort Arbuckle. Rector had asked them in to negotiate. Colonel William H. Emory, the new commanding officer of the First Cavalry Regiment, which had just been assigned to Fort Arbuckle, had joined in the discussions. The massacre of Buffalo Hump's people—given the wide disparity in the numbers of dead on both sides, it is difficult to call it a battle—brought an abrupt end to the parlay.

Rector, upon hearing the news, condemned the assault. He had hoped to settle these very Indians on the new reservations in Indian Territory. Eastern newspaper editors heard his side of the story first, which understandably pointed to the duplicity of government policy. Reporters also had overheard one of the chiefs of the unsuspecting Wichita town nearby complain that after the battle Van Dorn's men had "commenced killing our dogs and chickens, they also took some of our brass kettles and broke them up." Van Dorn's provisions had apparently been insufficient for such a large force; his troops ate the chickens and anything else they could steal. An anonymous letter soon appeared in the *Washington Intelligencer* that condemned Van Dorn, his thieving troops, and the army attack.

But Twiggs would have none of it, calling such commentary "slanderous." He blamed Emory (who, being a close friend of Secretary of War Jefferson Davis, frankly cared little about Twiggs's assessment). Van Dorn protested vigorously. "What they say," he wrote to a friend, "is of very little importance to me as I long since ceased to take notice of anything that regards Indians except to try and destroy as many of them as I can." Emory, in hopes of making amends, sent food to the Wichitas. In a letter to Twiggs, he later denied being the source of the information in the newspapers. Twiggs, for his part, stood behind his junior officer. In his final report to Washington, he wrote, "It will be difficult to prove in this state that the Comanches were ever not in a hostile attitude."[25]

Twiggs's views obviously represented those of many Texans. However, many Anglo-Texans had given up on the army. Many of the concerns regarding Indian affairs were soon debated—certainly by 1858—within the context of the evolving secession movement in the South. If the federal army could not protect civilians, then why should states like Texas remain in the union? Asked more and more often, it was a question that Twiggs, a southern sympathizer, could not answer.[26]

This politics of frontier protection interested Baylor, who had immense political ambitions. Taking his cue from former Texans who had fought Indians and used their success to achieve high office, he ultimately decided that the best way to reach his goals was to organize the effort to drive all Indians out of the state. It only required convincing a large number of West Texans to join him in what amounted to ethnic cleansing.

To bring in the recruits, Baylor launched a newspaper campaign in 1858. His constant rhetoric supporting genocide appeared in many papers—but especially his own, which he called *The Whiteman*. Racist and filled with inflammatory charges, it provided a rallying post for every Indian-hater in Texas. Baylor contributed an endless supply of letters. His campaign became so vitriolic that even members of his own family, prominent in both Texas and Louisiana, began to question the saneness of it.

Baylor's main goal was to destroy the reservations. He spoke out against the Brazos Valley farmer Indians as strongly as the Comanches at Clear Fork. One letter (dated April 15, 1858), for example, claimed that while the depredations in the west were generally confined to "killing cattle and stealing horses," most citizens believed that the reserve Indians were definitely responsible.

Baylor's twisting of facts (if not blatant lies) was so constant throughout the summer and fall of 1858 that many citizens of West Texas came to believe him. A recent attack, Baylor argued, had been made by "Indians . . . dressed in new Hickory shirts and blankets," similar to those distributed on both reserves, and an arrow taken from a dead man "was feathered with *chicken feathers.*"[27] The reference to the chicken feathers could mean only one thing; Baylor was building a case against the Brazos reserve, for everyone knew that the Comanches did not keep chickens, whereas Wichitas and Caddos did.

By fall, most of Baylor's efforts were oriented toward organizing groups and writing petitions aimed at breaking up the reservations. He called many public meetings in the frontier communities of Weatherford, Jacksboro, and Gainesville, where he dominated the discussions. With petitions already written, Baylor convinced—indeed, some evidence suggests that he bullied—individuals to sign them. He then dispatched delegations to see the governor. Many of these petitions included the names of individuals who later claimed to Neighbors and others that they had never signed them.

Nevertheless, some of the more recognized citizens of West Texas did sign the petitions. One was George Erath, an early ranger in Moore's company, who hated Indians and made his living as a surveyor. Erath founded the towns of Caldwell and Waco, and he served in the Texas Senate. As prominent citizens of this sort joined Baylor, less prominent ones had more difficulty speaking out against the growing crowd. Most increasingly felt intimated by Baylor and his gang. What made the situation even more frightening was the fact that Baylor, Erath, Givens, Nelson, and others also had attracted a considerable number of renegades and ne'er-do-wells, men who saw opportunity in turmoil. The number of these men soon reached several hundred.

As the power of the group grew—it took the form of vigilantes rather than renegades, since it operated in the open—West Texas fell into a state of anarchy. Had it been the only region of the state to do so, Runnels and army officers might have restored law and order. But vigilantism appeared in other parts of Texas as well, especially across the south and in the Rio Grande valley, as the debate over slavery—and the attendant suspicions regarding the actions of Tejanos—secession, and the fear of slave insurrection reached a crescendo.

Often, the violence was clothed with the respectability of local law enforcement. It could, for example, be initiated by a local sheriff who formed a posse to deal with issues extralegally. At other times, it emerged from within the community, building upon the violence that came with lynching, especially of blacks.[28] In the west, former rangers often mustered the mobs; such men had little trouble finding others to follow them, for many new faces appeared in the West Texas towns of Weatherford, Jacksboro, Stephenville, Waco, and Fort Belknap over the summer of 1858. The older settlers feared the new arrivals, who were heavily armed and often looking for trouble. Some of these new arrivals had emigrated from "Bleeding Kansas."

Those from Kansas came from a territory that had been in a state of chaos since 1854. Some of these men had fought in proslavery vigilante groups, had fled into Indian Territory or Missouri when law and order was restored in 1857, and had moved on into Texas. They thrived in an atmosphere of thievery and pillaging, especially when such acts could be disguised by espousing a certain political doctrine.[29] Most pillaged livestock herds, but some even invaded houses. A ready market existed for whatever they stole, especially animals taken from the north of Texas, and they had a ready scapegoat—the Indian. Given the thievery, the mob atmosphere, and the ethnic difference, all that was needed was a spark to ignite a great conflict.

The spark was kindled in October 1858 when Sheriff Joseph R. King of Young County charged a young Comanche living on the Clear Fork reserve with shooting a citizen. King quickly organized a large posse of Baylor's ne'er-do-wells and rode to the reserve. Neighbors and Agent Leeper, both of whom were at the agency, took six soldiers and rode out to meet the mob. The parties met, and a war of words ensued. Neighbors contended that the reserve was federal property, thus outside the jurisdiction of any local sheriff. Faced with defying the army, the sheriff and his men eventually withdrew. But this would be the start of many such encounters; the reserves were no longer safe from such invading groups.[30]

With growing threats of invasion, Governor Runnels authorized Captain Ford to re-form his ranger company in early November, despite not being granted authority by the legislature to do so. Lawlessness was increasing everywhere in the northwest. But Runnels, who was up for re-election the next year, firmly cautioned Ford against campaigning against the Indians. Some in the state, particularly in East Texas, opposed the sort of bloodshed that led to Indian war. Some questioned whether Ford's and Van Dorn's attacks on Comanche villages had not done more harm than good.[31]

Ford's troop did little good. Just after Christmas, a vigilante group of Texans found a small hunting camp of friendly Caddos and Wichitas just off the Brazos reserve. They crept up on the sleeping Indians and fired openly into the tents. While the attackers were too timorous to rush the few survivors to steal what goods and livestock were to be found, their actions illustrate the degree to which law and order had disappeared.

There was no possible way to justify the attack on these Indians, who numbered only seventeen, mostly women and children. They had been in the camp for several weeks hunting deer. Indeed, Texas settlers living nearby had made friendly contact with them. The whereabouts of the group was common knowledge. The attackers, coming from Erath and Palo Pinto counties to the south, had simply set out to kill Indians, knowing that such an act would never be prosecuted and that many of their friends would applaud such violence. In all, they murdered four men and three women and wounded many others, including all the children. One young girl had her thumb shot off.

Within days, the entire makeup of the party was known. Most were proud to be a part of the massacre and had boasted about their actions in the nearby towns. An enraged Neighbors asked for an indictment and the arrest of the leaders: Peter Garland, Daniel Thornton, W. E. Motherel, W. W. McNeill, R. Duprey, W. J. F. Lowder, and John R. Waller.[32]

Neighbors's demands, however, were quickly challenged, even by politicians who should have seen the growing chaos. Erath, who served in the state senate, justified the actions of the mob: "Hostile Indians were making continual incursions, and the population," he wrote to Runnels, "suspicioned [sic] those Indians." Senator Erath informed the governor that more than two hundred men had formed to protect the killers; to instruct Ford to seize them for trial would lead to an all-out war. Erath proposed that he meet with the reserve Indians and arrange a payoff.

Erath's plan to buy off the trouble turned Neighbors's stomach. Neighbors quickly asked District Judge Nicholas Battle for an arrest warrant. Battle, of Waco, courageously complied and ordered Captain Ford to seize the killers. But Ford declined, stating that he would only assist the county sheriff—and the sheriff of Erath County sided with the mob.[33] At this juncture, Neighbors asked Runnels for martial law to be imposed.

As northwestern Texas slid into anarchy, General Twiggs amazingly made one last effort to bring war to the northern Indians. He believed that once the army conquered these people, the problems with vigilantes like Baylor and Nelson would somehow go away. He even asked for Van Dorn's troop, which had been reassigned after the debacle at Buffalo Hump's village. The War Department, although it must have had serious reservations, agreed.

Twiggs then reshuffled his entire command, moving more troops to the areas of settlement where unrest existed. The infantry at Fort Brown (outside of Brownsville) moved to Fort Duncan near Eagle Pass. Fort McIntosh, near Laredo, was also abandoned, its troops being moved to the desolate location of the new Camp Hudson, seventy miles northwest of Eagle Pass. These troops were supposed to rein in the Lipan Apaches. Other older forts, such as McKavett and Mason, were also shut down, their men mostly sent back to Camp Cooper, on the Clear Fork. Twiggs obviously had decided to re-engage the Indians, hoping to replicate General Smith's success of the early 1850s.[34]

Twiggs's actions left much of the southern frontier open at a crucial time. Yet the general seemed confident that his gamble would pay off, despite the skeptics in Washington. There "is not, nor ever has been, any danger of the Mexicans crossing on our side of the river to plunder," he wrote to the War Department in late March 1859. A quick outcry from Texans along the Rio Grande did little to change his mind. A petition from Brownsville depicted a horrible situation, stating that "the highways are literally thronged with bands of armed soldiers and highwaymen . . . who propose a system of plunder and robbery." Twiggs shrugged off the protests, perhaps with good reason: "At every post that has been abandoned in Texas an outcry has raised, and plenty of Indian signs seen!"[35]

Governor Runnels, who was rapidly losing support in the state, saw little benefit from these actions. He wanted more rangers and asked the War Department to pay for them. The federal government, he argued, was obligated to protect Texas. Yet at the same time, Runnels refused Neighbors's call for martial law and instead through various memorials tried to convince the vigilantes and renegades near Weatherford to stand down. The governor explained to them that Neighbors had asked Washington officials to remove the Texas Indians permanently to Indian Territory.

The most important of the vigilantes, John Baylor, openly rejected the governor's plea. Through his newspaper, he argued that if the reserve Indians were allowed to leave peaceably, they would simply return to plunder. Baylor, Nelson, and others called upon Texans everywhere to join their cause and massacre the reserve Indians immediately, before they got away. By Christmas 1858, Baylor had an army of 350 ruffians. Agent Ross suspected that another 500 might eventually join.[36]

While Baylor made preparations to strike the reserves, newly promoted Colonel Van Dorn fulfilled Twiggs's expectations, moving against the northern Indians. Recruiting forty-odd Caddo, Delaware, and Wichita scouts—some of the best men on the reserve—the colonel marched north out of the reservation. The party was expected to stay out for months.

Whether the Indian scouts knew at the time that this would leave the Brazos Indians unprotected is uncertain. Only a handful of Indian boys and older men remained on the reservation. Seeing the possibilities that this created for Baylor and his thugs, both Neighbors and Runnels pleaded with General Twiggs for help. Although some troops were on the Comanche reservation, the agents wanted cavalry sent to the Brazos River reserve. Unbelievably, even though Indians from the reserve were assisting his troops in the field, Twiggs refused. In a letter of March 23, 1859, he declared the trouble to be "purely a civil matter with which he [Twiggs] has nothing to do."[37]

Later, Twiggs had second thoughts. The massacre of friendly Indians while he commanded Texas would not have looked good on his record. He decided to turn the issue over to Colonel M. L. Johnston, an artillery officer who commanded Fort Belknap. Johnston, more concerned by Baylor than Twiggs appeared to be, ordered the only troops available in northwestern Texas to the reserve—one company under Captain Joseph B. Plummer, with one piece of field artillery. Ironically, one of Plummer's junior officers was Lieutenant William E. Burnet. Lieutenant Burnet was the son of David G. Burnet (the ad interim president of the Texas Republic), who decades before, had done his share to blame Indians for raiding.

Young Burnet was a fine officer, honest and decent and lacking in the general racial bigotry of the day. He even appreciated Indians and their culture. By contrast, "The Whites," William wrote his father, "without any proof that these Indians have done wrong, and with many well-known facts showing that they have done much good . . . have determined to exterminate them." This, young Burnet would not countenance. He quickly organized what reserve Indians still remained for defense. The best strategy was to bring them all into the agency, where they could be protected by the artillery and soldiers available. But even Lieutenant Burnet believed that fewer than a hundred Indians and soldiers could not hold out against three hundred determined Texans.[38] He expected a massacre!

The precautions soon proved necessary. On March 28, 1859, Baylor ordered his motley army to the edge of the reserve and sent in scouts. Yet he did not attack—perhaps he feared the artillery. Mostly, parties of his men pillaged the abandoned Indian homes, in typical ranger fashion, "taking all they could get, right or wrong," as Burnet put it.[39] Then confusion broke out in the ranks as Lieutenant Nelson joined

Baylor. He had been expected to bring in several hundred more men but had managed to recruit only thirty-five. Baylor reconsidered his plans and delayed the attack.

The crisis further abated when a letter arrived from Commissioner of Indian Affairs Charles Mix, approving Neighbors's recommendation to remove the Texas Indians. Neighbors had the letter published in the local press. While some editors praised the decision and lambasted the Indians, at least one—W. L. Thomas, from the *McKinney Messenger*—exhibited moral scruples: "The forcible expulsion of the Reserve Indians from the homes provided for them by the fostering care of Government would be an act of violence unsanctioned by any existing principle of law."[40] Unfortunately, few principles of law remained in West Texas.

Meanwhile, as the Brazos Indians huddled in fear for their lives, Major Van Dorn found his prey on May 13 just north of the Cimarron River. He charged at dawn, leaving forty-nine Comanche men dead and "unavoidably" killing eight women. The troops then burned yet another Comanche town. Jim Pockmark, who was with Ford, tried to obscure the trail to the town and prevent what was becoming consistently a disgusting slaughter of Indians by the army.[41] But the cavalry was becoming what Jefferson Davis had wanted: units that hunted Indians on the plains and attacked them in their villages.

Indian losses in the three attacks on northern Comanche towns likely approached three hundred dead and twice as many wounded. Some of those with wounds would not survive, given the state of medical care at the time. The number of Texans killed by Indians—certainly less than a dozen in the three or four years previous to Van Dorn's raids—paled by comparison. The new cavalry tactics seemed to be paying off. But there was no certainty that Van Dorn's actions would bring an end to violence in Texas and Indian Territory, as Twiggs hoped.

Certainly Neighbors, Ross, and young Lieutenant Burnet did not think it would. As Van Dorn rampaged through another Comanche town, Neighbors and his cohorts faced a vicious mob that was bent on their destruction. And it was a mob that had long since abandoned respect for any law and order, even that of the U.S. Army. As the Brazos and Clear Fork Indians—mostly old men, women, and children—awaited their fate, they must have wondered why they had ever agreed to let their young men join Van Dorn.

20

THE FINAL EXODUS

In early April 1859, Agent Ross began collecting what property could be taken on the exodus north. Wagons, saddles, farming equipment all had to be gathered. Fearing attack, the Brazos River Indians huddled in makeshift shelters near the agency, eating what beef had been in storage. Many refused to help the agent, as they expected no quarter at the hands of the rangers. Ross's main concern was livestock. The Indians owned several thousand head of horses and cattle, which had to be corralled. This task proved difficult because of the closeness of Baylor and his vigilante rangers.

Despite the commitment to removal, Baylor, Nelson, and the others reorganized their efforts to overrun the agency. There could be little motive to their efforts other than plunder and killing; the agency Indians had few material goods but did possess blankets, kettles, and axes, which brought a good price on the Texas frontier. The fact that such items had been issued to the Indians by the government made little difference to the vigilantes. George Erath and a few of the governor's other confidants began to openly question Baylor's motives. Erath warned Governor Runnels that the men following Baylor intended "not to allow any of the Indians now on the Brazos Reserve to be removed to the North." The supposed rangers, according to Erath, had a permanent solution: "Kill them indiscriminately."[1]

Erath and other Texans along the upper Brazos still supported the rangers, but a few increasingly recognized that the actions of this three-hundred-man mob had intimidated county officials to such an extent that local law and order had vanished. Judicial officials in Young County feared to meet and mostly abandoned the county offices in Fort Belknap. The grand jury in Palo Pinto County even offered indictments against Indians rather than those Anglo-Texan ruffians who had recently murdered reserve Natives. The fictitious charges bordered on the absurd; one levied against the aged Caddo chief José Maria claimed that he had stolen a mule.

Neighbors assumed that Governor Runnels supported the rangers under Baylor because the governor had failed to halt the descent into anarchy or to offer any protection to federal government officials. "Every county . . . is raising and arming a band of lawless men who term themselves Rangers," Neighbors wrote to Commissioner Mix, stating that the vigilantes had the avowed intention of "murdering every Indian they met." And then Neighbors, tired and anguished by political affairs in his state, added a prophetic postscript: "I fully believe . . . that they would also murder the agents if they had an opportunity." In this, he would soon be proved correct.[2]

In an attempt at respectability, Baylor renamed his army the "Jacksboro Rangers," in honor of the town that had mostly fostered his efforts. As a few more recruits trickled in, Baylor finally ordered the lead elements of his "rangers" to take up positions near the agency in early May. Patrick Murphy, a particularly obnoxious fellow already well known for horse thievery, led the scout forward. A few miles from the agency, Murphy viciously intercepted and killed an Indian mail rider carrying federal mail from Fort Arbuckle to Neighbors. Murphy's group then pursued five other Indians whom they also tried to kill.

The five men, realizing their precarious position, raced their horses headlong toward the protection of the agency. Fortunately, Murphy's mob became distracted by plunder. Several of the rangers broke from the attack to gather up six ponies, some blankets, and two dropped guns.[3] Murphy, meanwhile, was scalping the mail rider, who lay sprawled on the road. Trophy in hand, Murphy retreated back to Baylor, who, leading the larger group, used the grisly affair to motivate his force. In a strong voice that rose above the mob, Baylor openly pledged to "exterminate the Indians" rather than let them move, "so as to prevent . . . further depredations."[4]

Neighbors had assumed that once the order to remove was made public, Baylor's force would dissolve. This logical thinking proved to be untrue; the agent was no longer dealing with rational men. A day after the killing of the mail rider, Neighbors made one last effort to face down the growing mob. He convinced a U.S. marshal to attempt to arrest Murphy and his fellow murderers, who had ridden into Jacksboro to boast of their deed. A mob quickly assembled in Jacksboro and nearly cut off the marshal from the twenty U.S. soldiers under Lieutenant Burnet and the ninety armed Indians who supported him. While no shots were fired, the Indians and the army made a hasty retreat.[5]

To justify their defiance, the leaders of the Jacksboro rangers wrote a manifesto that was published in many of the leading Texas newspapers a day later. The language was the work of J. A. Hamner, Baylor's business partner in his racist newspaper, *The Whiteman*. The message of the manifesto was clear: "We regard the killing of Indians of whatever tribe to be morally right and that we will resist to the last extremity the infliction of any legal punishment on the perpetrators."[6] The marginalization of Indians in Texas had reached its final stage; extermination rather than removal was now demanded.

Baylor and his people had even moved beyond state- and federal-sanctioned ethnic cleansing to advocate genocide.

Convinced that the Jacksboro rangers could overrun the agency, Baylor, Nelson, Murphy, and three hundred followers finally launched their anticipated assault on the agency headquarters on May 23. The massive mob, spurred on with liquid courage, took up a position one mile below the main buildings. There, Baylor met Captain Plummer and a company of army infantry. Plummer later described the meeting: "He [Baylor] had come to assail the citizen Indians, but should the troops fire upon his men during the fight, he would attack them also." Baylor then warned Plummer that the "civil authority" was fully behind the rangers and that if any troopers killed any of his men, they would be prosecuted and executed by the state of Texas. Plummer, struggling to control himself, admitted that he knew little of "civil law" but stated that the army would defend the agency, its federal property, and its Indians.

As Plummer and Burnet stared Baylor down, the mob's intent became brutally obvious. Baylor's men managed to capture an old Indian man and an old woman, both about eighty, who had wandered away from the protection of the agency buildings. They killed the woman but tied a rope around the man's neck, hung him up, scalped him, and left him to die on the rope. In response, some fifty or sixty enraged reserve Indians, led by old José Maria and Jim Pockmark (who had just returned from Van Dorn's raid), ferociously attacked the ranger forces. Outnumbered at least six to one, the Indians had only surprise to work with, but this they used to advantage, hitting the drunken trespassers with bullets and blood-curdling yells. Young Lieutenant Burnet and several troopers rode into battle with the Indians at Plummer's order.[7]

To Captain Plummer's astonishment, Baylor and his force of three hundred turned and ran, pell-mell, to the south. Most had more of a stomach for killing defenseless old men and women than for assailing the seasoned veterans of many army campaigns. After the running retreat, Baylor's force took over the ranch of William Marlin, located just outside the reserve boundary. Marlin had supported the Indians, working occasionally in the Indian trade with George Barnard. Here the two sides, Indians and Anglos, dug in and fought throughout the afternoon.

At one point, Jim Pockmark rode forward and demanded that Baylor come out and meet him "in single combat." Baylor hid in the ranch house, refusing to take on Pockmark, who had a reputation for being a ferocious fighter. Captain Plummer and Agent Ross, watching the affair from a distance, could hardly believe their eyes. As Lieutenant Burnet, a Texan by birth, later put it, "There was never a more cowardly thing done, by any set of men, to run from less than fifty Indians, when they numbered nearly three hundred."

Baylor's force finally withdrew under cover of night. Mrs. Marlin, who had remained at her ranch during the fighting and had no appreciation for Baylor, later said that the Texans were "badly scared"; some were praying, and at least one tried to hide under the floor. Various proclamations from the Baylor crowd soon followed, defending the actions of the renegade rangers and giving exaggerated casualty figures. Plummer reported that five Indians had been wounded and that two Texans had apparently died, with many more severely wounded. When news of the action reached Major George Thomas at Fort Belknap, he could only report that "all civil authority [in northwestern Texas] seems to be at an end." He made preparations to remove the Indians and asked for cavalry.[8]

The persistent agent Neighbors still hoped to indict the leaders of the Jacksboro rangers. But most citizens refused to testify, and Governor Runnels had no intention of arresting Baylor. Instead, Runnels organized a state commission to negotiate a peace and issue pardons. His commission consisted of mostly pro-Baylor people— Senator George Erath, M. M. Smith, Richard Coke, J. M. Steiner, and John Henry Brown. None of them would find fault with Baylor or his rangers.

Besides Erath, two other men on the commission went on to have distinguished careers. Coke, who later served as a Texas Ranger, used his reputation as a killer of Indians to gain public office, serving as governor and U.S. senator. But Brown likely had a more substantial impact. Also a ranger, he worked diligently as a newspaper editor, later served in the Texas legislature, and finally wrote his two-volume History of Texas. Brown's monumental study, which virtually deified the founding fathers of Texas (as well as the Texas Rangers), became the foundation for much early Texas history, being read—and believed—by many Texans.[9]

Neighbors trusted none of these men. The Texas Indian Commission finally visited the agency during the summer, but Neighbors ordered the commissioners to leave immediately.[10] In a later report, the commission concluded that reserve Indians had been responsible for the depredations in Texas, which was clearly an outrageous lie.[11]

The commission continued to meddle in frontier affairs, but from a distance. Brown even organized a ranger company of more than a hundred men to watch the Indians as they prepared to leave. His real purpose seemed to be to prevent the reserve Indians from rounding up the livestock that had scattered during the conflict with Baylor. Unfortunately, Captain Plummer's infantry could not protect the Indians in their efforts to find lost horses and cattle. Most of the animals were left behind, several hundred head ultimately being sold in the towns of Jacksboro and Weatherford.[12]

With Twiggs's blessing—a massacre of Indians right under the noses of the troops at Fort Belknap would not look good on any military record—the army finally prepared to march at the head of the Indian caravan. The Indian exodus out of Texas began in late July 1859. Agent Leeper started first, putting some 380 Comanches on the trail northward. They had been harassed by a dozen or so of Brown's rangers before departure, but the sniping of a few malcontents failed to escalate into serious warfare. Neighbors and Ross joined the Comanches with a party of 1,056 Indians (Caddos, Wichitas, Shawnees, Delawares, and Tonkawas) from the Brazos Agency. Captain Plummer, now with four companies of troops, provided protection. All guarded the date of departure to keep Brown and his rangers from ambushing them.

The whole train moved quickly northward, crossing the Red River safely on August 8. As the last wagons forded the shallow stream, Neighbors wrote to his wife that the Indians had finally passed "out of the heathen land of Texas." Indeed, he continued, "if you want to hear a full description of our Exodus . . . read the Bible where the children of Israel crossed the Red Sea."[13]

The federal government had known of the removal for several months, but agents of the Southern Superintendency in Indian Territory were nevertheless ill prepared for the new arrivals. The Texas Indians were to be attached to the Wichita Agency under the direction of Samuel Blain. While this broke the terms of the 1855 lease, the removed Indians would act as a buffer, protecting the eastern immigrant tribes from the northern Comanches. Unfortunately, Blain's situation was nearly as desperate as Neighbors's had been; Blain was attacked by Comanches and Kiowas, who blamed Wichitas and Caddos for the army assaults on their villages. The removal had brought the most active scouts and army fighters literally under the nose of the western tribes. Blain had yet to establish a permanent agency and seemed reluctant to do so until the army committed to building a post west or north of the Wichita Mountains to protect it.

Blain had found land northeast of the Wichita Mountains for such an agency. It ultimately took shape well up the Washita River on lands that had prospects for farming and were far enough from Texas to provide safety from Texas Rangers, who had in the past crossed the Red River into Indian Territory to attack Indians. The army designated lands just below the agency for the construction of Fort Cobb (located just west of present-day Anadarko, Oklahoma), which was opened that fall. As Neighbors departed for Texas, he felt relieved that the Texas tribes had acquired a good country and that they would be protected.[14]

Meanwhile, back in Texas, General Twiggs seemed pleased with the results. The Indians were being removed, and he had not heard of any depredations along the northwestern frontier for several months.[15] This lull broke in late September when Tejano rancher Juan Nepomuceno Cortina collected a hundred supporters and invaded the unprotected town of Brownsville, thus starting a border war in the region that Twiggs had considered safe from a Mexican invasion.

Cortina had feuded with the local marshal, who had mistreated several rancheros, including one of Cortina's ranch hands. During the assault on Brownsville, which occurred early in the morning hours of September 28, 1859, Cortina stormed the jail, killed the jailor, shot and killed at least two other Anglo-Texans, and awakened the populace by threatening to return. As he left, Cortina issued a proclamation to his fellow Tejanos: "Many of you have been robbed of your property, incarcerated, chased, murdered, and hunted like wild beasts" by Anglo-Texans. Cortina called upon all Tejanos to unite and fight.[16]

Cortina soon amassed a force estimated at six hundred men—many coming to his cause from south of the Rio Grande. Twiggs had few options at hand to quell the outbreak, and he must have suspected that some reports, particularly those suggesting mass murder, were exaggerated. He ordered the immediate reoccupation of Forts Brown and McIntosh, and he proposed to launch a campaign up the Rio Grande to protect American interests.[17]

The situation worsened by early November. Cortina, preparing to take the city, moved his force to within twelve miles of Brownsville. Texans barricaded the town and pleaded for help. Surprisingly, some loyal Tejanos responded, as did a small troop of Mexican infantry from nearby Matamoros that volunteered to assist the town. These Tejanos and Mexicans had been partners of Texans in a smuggling trade that existed across southern Texas. But Cortina soon routed the international force, took its two cannon, and could have overrun Brownsville had he wished to do so. In the chaos that followed, ranches up and down the Rio Grande were looted and burned. Warehouses that had been used to support an expanding coastal trade were seized and pillaged.

Hordes of freebooters—several hundred of them being ruffians from the vicinity of Victoria, Texas—joined in the looting. For a time, everything of value in the south appeared to have been lost. On November 12, General Twiggs was forced to report to his superiors, "Brownsville Burnt, one hundred Americans murdered." Twiggs, now seventy years old, asked to be relieved of his command: "*I am not able to take the field,*" he lamented. The army, finally cognizant of the seriousness of the rebellion—and its violent secondary surge of looting—ordered troops from as far away as Fort Leavenworth, Kansas, to prepare to move south to Texas.

But as had been the case many times in the past, the rumors of Brownsville's demise proved to have been exaggerated. On the same day that Twiggs reported the supposed disaster, infantry troops and Texas Rangers entered Brownsville. These forces, buttressed by seven more companies of army infantry and cavalry, fell under the command of Major Samuel P. Heintzelman, who slowly organized the reconquest of the Rio Grande valley. The major moved cautiously up the river on December 14 and captured Rio Grande City thirteen days later. There, Cortina made a stand. The Tejano revolutionary was roundly defeated, leaving sixty dead on the battlefield as he fled across the river.[18]

Major Heintzelman thereafter surveyed the damage of the so-called Cortina War and offered an interesting assessment. "The lower order of Mexicans hate Americans," he noted, "and the educated classes are not always exempt from this feeling." But Cortina seemed intent on seeking revenge against certain individuals; he was "a desperate, contrary fellow," in Heintzelman's opinion, who never had the support of many of his fellow Mexicans and Tejanos. Indeed, many of the Tejanos feared him more than they did their Anglo neighbors.

Cortina's War, in other words, was not a Mexican or a Tejano rebellion. It was a tragic affair bred of racial hatred, distrust, and lawlessness of the sort that the culture of violence in Texas consistently bred. But that hatred had resulted in the burning of ranches and the rustling of cattle and sheep as far upriver as Laredo. Hardly a ranch between the Nueces River and the Rio Grande remained undamaged, according to Major Heintzelman.[19]

Heintzelman's assessment reaffirmed the one central theme that had been consistent throughout Texas history: since before the creation of the Texas Republic, many Anglo-Texans had worked to marginalize people of color. Anglos viewed Indian removal as a vindication of their right to absolute sovereignty over the land. Tejanos, despite their deeds to land and their written language, were often judged by the same standard as were Indians. Put simply, the majority of Anglo-Texans, many of whom played major roles in local government, supported ethnic cleansing in one fashion or another. While some Indians and some Tejanos would on occasion be protected, by 1859 Texas had become a conquered land. The Texas creed, agreed to by a majority of the state's inhabitants, implied that the land belonged to Anglos and no others.

This was certainly the case in northwestern Texas, where Baylor and his followers came into ascendancy. Nevertheless, as Neighbors and others predicted, the breakup of the Texas reservations did little to end the rustling and violence that had become common along the West Texas frontier by the spring of 1858. Depredations actually increased after the Indians left a year later. More and more West Texas settlers departed for the east, continuing the exodus that had begun in 1858 and remained under way well into the Civil War.

Such a decline did little to sully the reputations of the men who had caused it. Many Texans would later look upon Baylor, Erath, Brown, and Nelson as heroes. Yet a few Texans held a different view. Lieutenant Burnet, in a letter to his father written on the eve of the Indian exodus, said this of the Jacksboro rangers: "If the world was picked over, I do not think there could be found a more vile and worthless set than the people who have squatted along this frontier and who the [news]papers style the 'Brave and injured Frontiersmen.'"[20]

In a final irony, the troubles of 1858 and 1859 produced such an uproar in the state that Sam Houston made a political comeback. He roundly defeated Runnels in a run for the governorship that fall. Runnels's handling of the frontier situation in the south as well as along the Brazos River had led to his downfall politically. Houston even carried some western counties. Nevertheless, in his inaugural address, Houston promised to equip more Texas Rangers for defense—following through on a campaign promise to end the violence—despite his historic disdain for such units.[21] Although a sometime friend of the Indian, Houston was the consummate political survivor.

With the Indians gone from the Brazos River, conditions worsened over the winter, just as the Indian agents had predicted. Small Indian raiding parties, seeking revenge, killed a few people and took livestock. Governor Houston, while somewhat less prone to exaggerate than past administrations had been, compiled a list of fifty-one Texans killed, in both the north and the south, and some 1,800 head of livestock missing by March 1860. Houston resorted to doing what nearly every governor preceding him had done: he jotted down depredation claims from newspapers. The deterioration along the frontier was real, however, as during the summer of 1860, the last inhabitants of the town of Fort Belknap packed their wagons and left. As many ranchers had feared, the breakup of the reserves had made the situation unlivable.[22]

This result was little consolation to the Indians who had called Texas home for centuries or to the Tejanos who had lost ranches and sheep herds in the south. For the Indians, the insult must have been galling; they had assisted Anglo-Texans in defending their sovereignty and on many occasions had chased off marauders along the frontier. All they left behind were a series of names that identify the towns and counties of the state—Waco, Tawakoni, Comanche, Wichita, and Cherokee—and the bones of their Texas ancestors.

A number of Texans realized that the farmer Indians on the Brazos reserve had been more of a barrier to northern Comanche penetration than a threat to the Texas settlements. Neighbors, his fellow agents, and the dozen or so agency personnel who had accomplished the removal took solace in this fact as they left their Indian friends at the Wichita Agency. Some of these employees, especially Neighbors, had known José Maria, Acaquash, Jim Pockmark, Placido, and Ketumsee for nearly twenty years. It was, then, a melancholy group of agents and government employees that began a return trip to Texas on September 2, 1859.

The trip south took only a few days, but some of Neighbors's men feared what would happen when they reached Texas. This foreboding suddenly became reality when a party of renegades jumped them near the Red River. In the brief shootout, which occurred at night, the attackers severely wounded Agent Leeper. He survived and later served as the new Wichita agent in Indian Territory, but the event unnerved everyone. Upon reaching Texas, moreover, the party expected to face Baylor's rangers—a frightening prospect given the fact that the army had orders to move northward. Some of Baylor's men had pledged to shoot the agents at first sight.

Fortunately, Neighbors, Ross, and Leeper had a good relationship with Captain Joseph Plummer. Plummer offered to detach a dozen or so infantrymen to protect the group; Neighbors respectfully declined. The ex-supervising agent had lived in Texas since the 1830s, and he was correct in his belief that many legitimate frontier Texans had supported his efforts. As the party approached the vicinity of the virtually deserted town of Fort Belknap, the group learned the good news that Brown and his rangers had disbanded.

Given the quiet, Neighbors confidently entered the town on the morning of September 14. He finished working up his official reports in the office of the Young County clerk of court, William Burkett. He penned a letter or two to his wife (who was then in Austin) and friends and entered the deserted main street. Neighbors was soon confronted by Patrick Murphy, whom he had never met but knew by reputation. Murphy (whom Neighbors wanted to indict for murder) distracted the agent while his son-in-law, Edward Cornett, placed a shotgun at Neighbors's back and pulled the trigger. Neighbors fell forward, landing face down in the middle of the dusty street. He died a few minutes later, unattended by anyone. The few respectable Texans in town so feared Murphy and his gang that Neighbors's body was left in the street until after dark.[23]

The death of Robert Neighbors symbolically ended an era in Texas history. While the U.S. Army continued to occupy several Texas posts until the Civil War broke out, Neighbors was the last official of the Bureau of Indian Affairs to work in the state. Texas had successfully rid itself of nearly its entire Native Indian population—the only exception being the several hundred Alabamas and Coushattas who still held a small parcel of land in the dense woods of East Texas and the northern Comanches who clung to the Panhandle. Almost all the others, literally dozens of tribes, indigenous and immigrant alike, had been forcefully driven from this promised land, Texas.

The final exodus of friendly Indians from Texas left a muddled state of affairs. Baylor and his men had intimidated local county governments so much that they ceased to function. The majority of Baylor's followers were, for the most part, criminals rather than frontiersmen. The exodus, then, led only to more violence and more anarchy, which continued for years to come—a clear indication of how insignificant the Indian contribution had been to the culture of violence in the state.

21

INDIANS AND THE CIVIL WAR

Optimists in Texas hoped that the removal of the reserve Indians somehow would end the rustling and violence that had afflicted their state for many years. But the counties west of Waco and Fort Worth and those south of the Nueces River remained violent places for more than a decade to come. Many Texans continued to blame Indians and, after March 1861, the Civil War, although both figured only minimally in the continued disorder.

Some Texas leaders recognized the problems associated with the breakdown of law and order, but they were less aware of the impact of the continued dry weather. Drought returned to the plains with a vengeance. The land south and west of San Antonio became cracked and dry, and the hot winds blew dust. Every year between 1860 and 1865, rainfall was well below normal in the upper Red and Nueces river valleys. Both 1860 and 1862 were terrible years, and 1864 was not much better, with rainfalls at levels close to the record drought year of 1855. These dry summers were followed by howling blizzards over the winter months. The weather destroyed crops, killed cattle and horses, and made it difficult for people in West Texas to survive.[1]

Those Texans who chose to stay often turned to occupations other than ranching. Some rustled horses, mules, and even cattle. Organized rings emerged in West Texas counties that openly committed these crimes. The newspapers often blamed Indians for the depredations, but the Plains tribes were so decimated by the drought that few could mount raids into Texas. When the nation slid into civil war, thousands of men fled west to avoid the fighting (and by 1862, conscription in the more settled parts of Texas). West Texas became a hotbed of discontented people, some trying without much luck to protect their property, others defending either the Union or the Confederacy, and finally, others simply using the chaos to steal and plunder.

The argument that rustling rings and drought caused much of the destruction in West Texas runs counter to traditional Texas history. The old story suggests that by 1863, many ranchers were "forting-up" to defend themselves against hordes of Comanches. Officials released exaggerated accounts of raids and kidnappings, leading some historians to conclude that as many as four hundred Texans were either carried off or killed by Indians during the war. In reality, the number is closer to forty.[2] What is more, the mythical nature of such casualty reports—that is, the Indians' role in them—was disguised by the complete breakdown of law and order in Texas as a direct result of the region's continued acceptance of the culture of violence. In other words, while a few minor Indian raids occurred—as well as one large one in 1864— it is fundamentally a myth that Indians overran the frontier areas of northwestern Texas between 1860 and 1865.

John R. Baylor and his supporters (more than any Indians) certainly contributed to the chaos. Baylor played a prominent role in the deterioration of West Texas.[3] Adding insult to injury, in early October the Baylor crowd began a newspaper campaign suggesting that Neighbors, Ross, and storekeeper Charles Barnard (an old friend of Houston's) had headed up a ring of horse thieves that was responsible for much of the trouble. The reserve Indians worked for them, or so the story went, and were "notoriously, criminally and unpardonably at fault." Such "news" was reprinted across the land.[4]

The attempted smokescreen, although it made good copy, failed to disguise reality—several organized rings of horse thieves had infested the region. They were responsible for many of the depredations attributed to the Comanches and reserve Indians. After the Civil War broke out in March 1861, the thieves often disguised their work by acting as volunteer rangers. Along with Union loyalists and many so-called bush-men, who generally refused Confederate service and lived in the west to avoid conscription, the renegades did immeasurable damage to Texas.

The notion that gangs of bush-men and horse thieves had infested Texas increasingly became a theme in the reports Neighbors wrote just before his death. He identified the main culprits as "about 50 horse thieves and notorious desperadoes."[5] Lieutenant Burnet agreed that the raids were the work of "a band of horse thieves who charge their acts on the Indians," and he thought they were connected to Baylor.[6] Certainly the party that attacked Neighbors and Ross as they returned to Texas in early September included renegades. One of Neighbors's party thought that he recognized one of the "Indian" raiders. When the corpse was rolled over and a rag was applied to the dead man's face, the dark color on his skin suddenly came off, and the man had short red hair.[7]

Murphy and his son-in-law, Cornett, both Baylor's men, were heavily involved. After killing Neighbors, Cornett fled north into Choctaw lands. In a weak attempt to justify the murder of Neighbors, Murphy reported that Cornett's wife had been kidnapped by reserve Indians.[8] This turned out to be a lie, and it might seem trivial except for a letter that surfaced in late December 1859 implicating Murphy in rustling. Signed only with the initials "D.L.M.," the letter originated from Caddo Creek, an isolated place on the boundary between Arkansas and Indian Territory, near the Ouachita Mountains. Addressed to "Dear Chum," it was carried west by a man named Page, who had a score to settle with someone at Camp Cooper. Page suffered the worst in his confrontation, and the letter soon fell into the hands of the new governor, Sam Houston, in Austin.[9]

The author of the infamous letter gave a fairly clear picture of how the ring operated, implicating Baylor. Several members had been Kansas renegades who had fled into Texas to avoid the law. One, a man named Williams, was described as having "acted badly . . . in Kansas." The ring was close-knit, and the author of the letter regretted Murphy's attempt to exonerate the killing of Neighbors by putting forward such a feeble explanation as the kidnapping of his wife. D.L.M. worried about Murphy, who "has too much mistaken pride," meaning that Murphy thought he could get away with nearly anything, including murder.

The letter's main purpose, however, was to assure the men working closely with D.L.M. that the last "drove of horses from Belknap" got through to Kansas. This theft likely included some 125 horses stolen from the reserve and other ranches nearby on February 24, 1859. Captain Ford investigated the robbery. Although he observed that the rustlers had ridden "shod" horses and that the arrows used "were not Comanche," Ford concluded that Indians had committed the crime.[10] D.L.M., who heard this, mused over the fact that the rustlers had "so completely fixed the affair on the Indians."[11]

This particular ring included individuals who were prominent Texas citizens. Among them was "Our *friend near* Camp Cooper," who had conveniently burned "his stable" to implicate the Indians. This was likely Lieutenant Givens, who had done everything possible to place blame on the reserve Indians. The letter made it clear that Baylor worked with the rustlers. D.L.M. wrote of him: "Tell our friend of the *Whiteman* [Baylor's newspaper] . . . to keep up the Indian excitement as it must be kept up until spring." The weather had turned cold, the drought was getting worse, and moving stock had to be postponed for better grass to appear.

Baylor did seem to have a role in directing ranger traffic so that the ring might more easily escape to Indian Territory with stock. Baylor had lobbied extensively for command of a ranger company, raising the men himself. Baylor's partner in this effort was Lieutenant Nelson, who had at one point tried to convince Ford of the need to plant evidence of Indian raiding in the settlements.[12] D.L.M. wanted to know about Baylor's success or failure, because the raising of the ranger regiment was "of all importance to us." If successful, the ring would "instruct him [Baylor] where we are likely to pass that he may know in what quarter to scout with his rangers."[13]

Both high-ranking government officials and some well-connected citizens from the upper Brazos continued to discuss the existence of the ring into 1860 and 1861. Agent Blain wrote to Houston that the property taken in Texas "is sold in Kansas," those responsible for taking it being "white skoundrels [*sic*] who plunder upon the credit of the Indians."[14] Several ranchers from Belknap even sent along a petition to Houston in March 1860, identifying those (such as Murphy and Cornett) who were part of the "D.L.M. Letter" crowd. Houston knew this to be true. The cry against the Indians, Houston wrote to a close friend, originated through "the prejudices of evil and designing persons, who keep up the cry to enable them the better to carry on their schemes of robbery and plunder."[15]

As notorious as it was, the ring thrived into the Civil War years and beyond. By the early 1870s, it was rustling horses in both Texas and Indian Territory, sending the livestock east to market. It finally faced law and order when it rustled a herd of 120 horses from near Fort Cobb and one member, a man named Jackson, was captured. He gave up the names of the leaders—Dick McCarty, alias "DLM," and John Hazelwood—and even offered details as to how they made their disguises using real bison hair. Once aware of how the ring operated, an army patrol caught up with the main group in December 1873 and captured eight, killed four, and severely wounded four. The rustlers proved to be "counterfeit white men in Indian disguise," and the ring by then numbered about a hundred men.[16]

Despite the considerable amount of evidence available in 1860, Houston failed to rein in the ring. He was frantically trying to defuse the growing secession movement and even joined the new Constitutional Union Party to do so. Incredibly, in 1860 the governor hoped to start trouble with Mexico, necessitating the involvement of the very rangers implicated in the ring. Houston seemed convinced that this would temporarily distract the gathering forces for secession in Texas and the South. A nationalistic war to conquer Mexico was better than a civil war between the states. Accordingly, Houston buried D.L.M.'s letter in his archives and turned to raising ranger units, fulfilling a pledge that he had made in his inaugural address.

Houston studiously avoided giving command of rangers to Baylor (who would receive a command only after the Civil War broke out and Houston was forced from office). The governor did organize over three hundred rangers and sent them west in the spring of 1860. Lawrence Sullivan Ross led one detachment, as did young Edward Burleson, William Dalrymple, and Middleton Tate Johnson, all men untainted by Baylor. As they scouted well west and north of the former reserves, on a barren plain that had little grass, they found virtually nothing to indicate that Indians were raiding Texas.[17]

Yet depredations continued. One of the worst attacks occurred in February 1860, when a party of renegades stole some four hundred horses, killed seven people in Erath County, and carried off two girls belonging to the Lemley family. They raped the girls repeatedly and after a few days abandoned them, naked but alive. When Captain Johnson spoke with the girls, he discovered that the men in the party understood English and were not Plains Indians. However, many Texans concluded that the perpetrators were former reserve Indians, and a public outcry for revenge soon reached Governor Houston. Petitions demanding action were even sent to President James Buchanan.[18]

Houston, elected because of Runnels's failure to stabilize the frontier, concluded that the northern tribes had to be punished regardless of their guilt.[19] He even asked the secretary of war, John B. Floyd, to provide three thousand Colt revolvers, two thousand percussion rifles, and one thousand Sharps rifles for the use of the ranger units that Houston had already organized. While the demands were preposterous— the army hardly had ammunition for its troops, as the Van Camp episode had demonstrated—the War Department recognized the serious nature of the situation and tried to organize its own campaigns against the Indians that summer.[20]

In an attempt to catch the perpetrators of the Lemley outrages, Captain Johnson crossed the Red River, reaching the vicinity of Fort Cobb by June 1860. The situation at the Wichita Agency was desperate because the drought had destroyed all the crops and the agent (who was absent without permission) had distributed little food.[21] Johnson's men searched diligently for evidence that implicated the reserve Indians in the Lemley rapes. They entered Wichita houses looking for clothing taken from the girls, and they spent nearly two months examining Indian horse herds. They even scouted one hundred miles up the Canadian River. They found nothing.[22]

Other evidence somewhat exonerated the northern Comanches. The highly knowledgeable William Bent, of Bent's Fort, reported that most of the Comanches, particularly those under Buffalo Hump, had remained on the upper Arkansas River throughout the winter of 1859–1860. Bent noted, "Buffalo Hump stated to me frequently that he was friendly disposed towards the United States and would never again raise his arm against any of the people." According to Bent, the second Van Dorn raid and the coaxing of government officials in Indian Territory had had an impact on Buffalo Hump. "The rest of the tribe [Comanches] were in the immediate vicinity," Bent reported, "where they had been since the month of November [1859]." A year later, Bent reported much the same: "The whole Comanche tribe"—which he put at nine thousand people—were near Bent's Fort and peaceful.[23]

Houston still believed that it was politically necessary to punish someone for the Lemley murders and rapes. He decided to use his rangers, paying for a campaign out of state funds. Houston authorized Sul Ross to lead the venture, with forty rangers, eighty-three volunteers, and a contingent of twenty-one enlisted men of the Second Cavalry, who although lacking an officer joined the expedition.[24] The party rode west in mid-December 1860, an ideal time to catch Comanches in camp.

It was a tough winter on the plains, and snowstorms had driven some Comanche bands well south out of the Arkansas River region. A few had followed the diminished bison herds into more sheltered valleys in the southern Panhandle of Texas, such as the Pease River, a small tributary of the Red River. There, in mid-December, Ross's spies found a Comanche hunting camp nestled in the bank of Mule Creek. The place was busy, for a new day had just arrived and the women of the camp were breaking down the lodges in preparation for leaving. Ross, seeing the confusion and distraction that came with the packing, placed his men on line and charged. The slaughter went on into the morning; the number of dead was never reported—most likely because most were women.

In fairness, the extreme cold weather made it difficult to determine the sex of an individual, since both men and women wore heavy buffalo-robe coats with hoods. However, most of the women were unarmed, and women often fled with children in hand. Many were shot in the back, a fact that Ross readily attested in his report. As even more obvious evidence that this was a brutal massacre, Ross's force had no casualties, not even a wounded man. He had attacked a hunting camp filled with unarmed women and children while the men were away chasing bison. There was no Indian resistance.

Captain Ross's actions, which he explained in detail in his memoir, were typical of the engagement. While pursuing a horse with two riders, Ross fired indiscriminately and shot in the back a young woman. She fell to the ground, dead. The rider, wounded in the arm, likewise tumbled off the horse. Confused and expecting death, the rider clung to a small tree with his good arm. Ross's black servant executed the man with a shotgun. Upon looking him over, the servant thought he had killed the chief Peta Nocona. The identity seemed plausible after another woman, who was about to be killed by the rangers, revealed her blond hair. She turned out to be Cynthia Ann Parker, Peta Nocona's wife. She was the last surviving captive of the 1836 Parker Fort raid.

The rangers could not communicate with Cynthia Ann, for during her twenty-four years of captivity she had mostly forgotten the English language. Everyone on the frontier knew of her existence, though, as traders had tried to ransom her on several occasions. Her husband was nearly as celebrated. Ross quickly exploited the situation. In his reports, Peta Nocona became more fearsome with time, being described much later by Ross as a "giant Indian, bearing himself with dignity" to the end. The fact that a wounded man clinging to a tree was executed by a black slave would do little to enhance a ranger's reputation for bravery.

Ross's fame rested to some degree on his success at killing Comanches on Mule Creek, which (being a worthwhile credential in nineteenth-century Texas politics) later helped put Ross in the governor's chair. But the claims were bogus. The hunting camp contained several Mexican men who worked with the women, men who had elected not to become hunters and warriors. Years later, the Parker family revealed that the man killed by the Ross party was only "No-bah," a Mexican who was trying to escape. Peta Nocona died three years after the raid during an epidemic.[25]

Ross's destruction of a camp full of women and children was the last ranger victory before the outbreak of the Civil War. While hailed in Texas, it came at a time when the South was preparing to leave the Union and form the Confederate States of America. Just a few months later, Houston was forced from office because of his unwillingness to lead his state into the upcoming conflict. And Ross, Johnson, Burleson, and many other Texas Rangers soon joined state troops assigned to protect Texas from encroachment from either Indians or Unionists.

These Texas Rangers looked nervously upon the 2,800 Union soldiers who remained in Texas. President Abraham Lincoln, however, wished to avoid war and ordered Union troops in Texas and Indian Territory to evacuate their posts. Most did, including the cavalry at Camp Cooper, which marched out on February 23, 1861, the day Texas joined the Confederacy. The U.S. forces at Forts Duncan, Chadbourne, Phantom Hill, McKavett, Inge, Stockton, and Davis then surrendered under a flag of truce, which guaranteed their right to return north. General Van Dorn, who took command of Texas Confederate troops, soon violated this truce and incarcerated the Union garrisons.

Governor Edward Clark, who succeeded Houston, faced the task of defending Texas during the war. Surprisingly, Clark believed that Texas had no obligation to fight in the East. Instead, he asked the Confederacy to replace the 2,800 soldiers who had been removed. Upon being rebuffed, he created Texas "reserve" regiments, consisting of men who would defend their "neighborhoods." William G. Webb, charged with organizing Confederate regiments, soon discovered that many Texas men used the reserve units as a "shelter," as he put it, and were "disinclined to enter active service." Most reservists, Webb thought, were "young, unmarried men," the sort who should join the Confederate Army.[26] The precedents set by Clark—making it difficult for the Confederacy to raise troops in Texas—continued under other governors. Texas, accordingly, sent only a handful of regiments to fight in the battles in the East.

Webb did finally organize several regiments that fell under the immediate command of Brigadier General Ben McCulloch, who was ordered to secure most of southern Indian Territory and the Red River valley. He did so by the spring of 1862. But the fighting tore up the region, pitting Creeks against Creeks, Cherokees against Cherokees, and Choctaws against Choctaws. The Indian nations that a mere thirty years before had been forced from the South saw their houses and crops destroyed, their horses and cattle stolen, and their people divided.

After Francis Lubbock was elected governor in Texas in the fall of 1861, he concentrated on forming "Frontier Regiments." Lubbock took the advice of Colonel Henry McCulloch, who argued that Texas needed at least fifteen thousand soldiers to defend itself, and mostly refused to allow these recruits to leave the state. Ten regiments did help defend Arkansas. A larger force was sent south to battle the Union invasion of first Galveston and then, by 1863, Brownsville. Only four hundred to six hundred men of the Frontier Regiments occupied strategic locations along the northwestern frontier of Texas.[27] Lubbock fretted over this thin line of defense because it invited Indian invasion. However, few Indians tested the mettle of these "soldiers," and they sat for months in camp.

Some of these men were clearly renegades who had been involved in horse stealing before the war. Many Texans along the frontier feared them more than Indians. DeWitt Clinton Peters, writing from Fort Davis in March 1861, described the lot who took over the garrison as "undisciplined" and "inferior" to the Union soldiers who had been there. Another Texas rancher near Fort Clark noted that the replacements were "the hardest looking crowd that ever you saw." He predicted that they would soon get tired of service and that the "Indians will run rough shod over this country."[28]

For a variety of reasons, such a prediction never materialized. Texas authorities took quick action in the spring of 1861 to occupy Indian Territory. After the Union departure, Colonel McCulloch's troops moved into Forts Arbuckle and Cobb. Soon thereafter an official representative of the Confederacy, Albert Pike, arrived to negotiate a peace treaty with the Indians. Pike knew the Comanches from years past, and he had sixty-four Creek and Seminole troops with him, in Confederate uniforms. Penateka Comanche leaders, as well as a few of their western relatives—the majority remained on the upper Canadian River—and chiefs of the Caddos, Wichitas, and Tonkawas all signed.[29]

The treaty pledged Indian loyalty to the Confederacy. The Indians could hunt in the west, but Pike demanded that they stop stealing horses, an act deemed by the treaty "disgraceful." The Confederacy also agreed to give the Indians annuities, providing cattle, hogs, corn, and farm equipment for each band, which they needed because of the drought. Pike also distributed rations and organized a supply depot near Sherman, Texas, placing it under the control of Charles B. Johnson, a very energetic contractor. Indian agent Matthew Leeper was to distribute the food, which consisted of beef, sugar, salt, and coffee, on a weekly basis.

This Confederate annuity distribution system survived throughout the war; in the early years of the conflict it worked better than the one it had replaced. The food that it provided became vitally important, given the depletion of bison herds and massive suffering of horse herds as a result of the drought. Comanche women, even those from the more western bands, came into Fort Cobb to collect beef and other commodities. Johnson's job became more difficult as the war went on. Nevertheless, his efforts helped keep many of the more hostile western Indians, who came into the agency each week, from raiding Texas. By Christmas 1861, the Confederacy was feeding two to three thousand Indians a week at Fort Cobb.[30]

Many Texans fumed over this treaty and its annuity provisions; they felt that the Indians should have been attacked, not fed. Some Texas military leaders also despised Pike, an Arkansas meddler, and expected an Indian invasion. Perhaps even more interesting, the old Indian trader George Barnard had grave reservations regarding the legitimacy of the treaty. He suspected that many of the chiefs who had signed it had failed to grasp that Texas was a part of the Confederacy. Barnard was certain that most of the Comanches and Kiowas had no intention of paying any attention to the treaty.[31]

The Indian war that Texans expected seemed in the making when a patrol of ten men led by Major Edward Burleson Jr. (stationed at Camp Cooper) was nearly overwhelmed by Indians on August 2, 1861. The outgunned patrol dug in on a wind-swept prairie well west of the post and fought off the mounted attackers; nearly every one of the soldiers suffered a wound.[32] Burleson ordered five companies—some 230 troopers—into the saddle to follow the marauders, who by mid-August had reached the Washita River. The Confederate force then moved up the Canadian, looking for a fight.

But to Burleson's dismay, the small groups of Indians that he encountered had "Confederate passports" from Pike. The leaders of the large Comanche and Kiowa villages had been alerted to his movements and had fled. Burleson could only snarl over the Pike intrusion, concluding that "for the frontier of Texas to sufer [sic] as they have . . . and the red devils to go unpunished is to me too much to believe!"[33] Burleson's subordinate officers did learn from Buffalo Hump (who seemed earnestly to want peace) that several factions of his people still wanted revenge in Texas for Van Dorn's attacks. One chief named Oquim, who had lost two sons in recent engagements, was trying to raise a party over the winter.[34]

The Wichitas, Caddos, Shawnees, and Delawares near Fort Cobb feared these Comanches because they had assisted the U.S. Army in 1858 and 1859. Most welcomed Confederate protection. A number had "good cabins" near Fort Cobb and did not wish to leave. Nevertheless, Burleson's invasion frightened them because he had not acted in accord with Pike's promises. In late November, Jim Ned fled north with several hundred others. All of them moved to the vicinity of Fort Larned in central Kansas. As Burleson's command returned to a temporary base along the Red River and to Camp Cooper, Agent Leeper increasingly feared for his life.[35] Fort Cobb was vulnerable even though the Indians seemed to be leaving Texas alone.

Union Army officials in Kansas knew of the virtual civil war that had raged in eastern Indian Territory during the summer and fall of 1861, but Lincoln's new government took its time selecting agents and superintendents to help the many refugees who streamed out of that troubled land. Agent A. G. Boone, grandson to Daniel, finally arrived at Fort Wise (later called Fort Lyon) in southeastern Colorado in October 1861. He found five thousand hungry Comanches and Kiowas, who rather proudly displayed their copy of the Pike treaty. Vindicating Barnard's pessimistic assessment, some of the Comanche chiefs were "astonished" to learn that Pike had not negotiated for the "Great Father" in Washington, D.C.[36]

Extreme cold weather and disease struck the camps of Indian refugees in Kansas as well as those in southeastern Colorado over the winter of 1861–1862. In March, Boone visited a huge Comanche and Kiowa village twelve miles below Fort Wise where "a large number"—perhaps running into the hundreds—had died of smallpox. These people had very little food, as they had not found bison for weeks. The epidemic would continue into 1862 and 1863 (eventually resulting in the death of Cynthia Ann Parker's husband, Peta Nocona), and it spread eastward to the refugees, the majority of whom had settled in the Neosho Valley, east of Fort Larned. Two hundred and forty died from virus in March 1861 alone, and many more were sick with pneumonia and would soon die. Unbelievably, the weather had been so cold that over one hundred limbs had had to be amputated because of frostbite. Conditions were, as one government official put it, "beyond description."[37]

The effects of the cold winter weather cycle were exacerbated by the opposite in the summers. Extremely dry and hot weather hit the plains with a suffocating stillness as the Civil War wore on. The drought and the storms were much worse—according to tree-ring data—than the drought and storms of the 1920s and 1930s, when one-third to one-half of the beef cattle on the plains had to be sold or destroyed. It is quite possible that bison herds declined by better than half during the Civil War years alone.[38]

The drought devastated the Indian economy. Pony herds suffered and died off, and many of the rivers of the plains were crusted over with mud. Trade with New Mexicans, who had often brought corn tortillas into Indian lands, became virtually impossible because of the inability to move carts long distances. But even if a few comanchero traders got through, the Plains tribes possessed few buffalo robes to exchange. The droughts undoubtedly forced some bands to seek food by raiding government supply trains, particularly those supplying troops in Colorado and New Mexico, or by begging for it.

The Union finally purchased rations and annuity goods for both the refugee Indians in Kansas and the Comanches and Kiowas in June 1862. Samuel G. Colley, who replaced Boone that summer as the upper Arkansas River agent, distributed $20,000 in food and clothing, an act that made the Plains tribes "highly delighted." The Kansas refugee Indians were so pleased that the Union was able to recruit 1,500 Creeks, Seminoles, Caddos, Wichitas, Shawnees, Delawares, and Kickapoos into the First Indian Brigade of the Union Army.[39]

Just who gave the orders is unclear, but this Indian force marched on Fort Cobb, striking the poorly defended agency on the night of October 23. While Agent Leeper had tried to organize several dozen Comanches and Caddos to defend the agency, he had returned to Texas at this crucial time, leaving the agency in the hands of an assistant, Horace Jones. The Indians nearby, under José Maria and Buffalo Hump, did nothing, as the Union Indian brigade burned the buildings and killed three of the agency personnel.

While losses in terms of food, goods, and men were minor, the success of the attack was a serious blow to Confederate Indian policy in western Indian Territory. Several hundred more Indians at the agency, including José Maria, moved north with the retreating victors. But before departing, they sought the camp of the Tonkawas, whose leader, Placido, had become a loyal Confederate. Finding their target some seventy miles south of Fort Cobb, near present-day Anadarko, Oklahoma, they overran the camp and killed a number of people there. While reports in Texas suggested that the entire tribe had been exterminated and that Leeper had been killed, both rumors were false. Governor Lubbock, however, in the aftermath, hurried to reorganize and rebuild the Frontier Regiments, since most of the men had been mustered out given the lack of an Indian threat.[40]

In the months that followed the Fort Cobb attack, Texas and Confederate authorities had increasing difficulty in maintaining contact with the western tribes. The cold weather, continued epidemics over the winter of 1862–1863, and the drought conditions of the summer kept the Indians from traveling far. Johnson and Leeper shifted their annuity handouts to Fort Arbuckle, near Anadarko, where some 166 Tonkawas and twelve Comanche families camped. Several companies of Chickasaw and Seminole troops were brought in to provide protection at the fort. Texas officers recruited a few scouts from among the Tonkawas, but the state mostly refused to feed them and they roamed along the Red River corridor, both hungry and angry.[41] As Texans had less and less information about what was happening in Indian Territory and the west, reports of raids mounted. Two attacks supposedly occurred in February 1863 in which horses and cattle were stolen and four ranchers killed.[42]

All spring Governor Lubbock fretted over the growing threat. He lobbied the Texas legislature for more money to meet the emergency, but it authorized only $800,000, hardly enough to pay and supply the six hundred men of the newly mustered-in Frontier Regiment over the winter. Lubbock then argued with Brigadier General John B. Magruder, commander of the Confederate Department of Texas, demanding that a Confederate regiment be sent into northwestern Texas. Magruder, for his part, wished to incorporate state troops into the Confederate Army and deploy them in the East. He saw little threat from the Indians.

With funds running out and virtually no Indians to blame for raiding, Lubbock finally relented and turned the force over to Magruder (thus placing the burden of paying the men on the Confederacy) after getting the general's solemn word that the troops would not be sent out of the state. Despite this concession, in September, Governor Lubbock ordered the state's conscription officer, John S. Ford, to exempt from service any man who had joined a frontier militia, or ranger, company.[43] While this violated the Confederate Constitution, which Texas had sworn to uphold, it was never challenged. When General E. Kirby Smith desperately needed troops to defend against the Union invasion of Louisiana and Arkansas in the spring of 1864, many Texas men claimed to be fighting Indians.[44]

Texans were able to avoid conscription because they exaggerated the level of Indian raiding in the 1860s. Rumors of Indian war and the belief that Indians would descend upon the frontier and massacre everyone made a powerful impression on citizens and politicians alike. During the war, it kept young men at home and away from the killing fields in the East. Accordingly, the governors of Texas continued to report Indian assaults even though most of the losses suffered in the west by this time constituted horse and cattle rustling. Many if not all of these robberies were perpetrated by white men who lived in the region.

A prominent renegade remained "Colonel" John R. Baylor, who commanded Texas Rangers and even was elected to the Confederate Congress in 1863. Baylor had participated in the Texas invasion of New Mexico the year before, but he fled the region after Confederate troops suffered a stinging defeat near Glorieta Pass, southeast of Santa Fe. As New Mexico fell to Union forces, Baylor returned to Weatherford, Texas, where he assumed command of a ranger unit that was involved in rustling, much as it had done before the war. By the summer of 1863, Baylor's men, according to one citizen, openly "robbed stores" in town and took whatever horses they pleased, even from prominent northwestern Texas ranchers. Baylor even hanged two men without trial and threatened to do the same to several others who challenged him.[45]

Lubbock could hardly use such a justification—of Anglo anarchism and vigilantism—to argue against sending men to the eastern front. He blamed the Indians instead, using reports as well as letters from friends and rangers to justify his action. John R. Rushing, from Weatherford, provided just such an epistle on August 12, 1863: "The country is absolutely full of Indians. . . . They are doing Great Mischief. Consternation pervades the entire frontier which is constantly receding." Rushing could not offer an example of an Indian raid; nor did he provide the name of a settler who had been killed, providing only vague references to women being carried off and men being scalped as they herded their stock.[46]

Despite lacking any confirmation or even a report from a ranger regiment that had recently fought Indians, two weeks later, Governor Lubbock reported the Texas situation to General E. Kirby Smith as being desperate. "The Indians on our frontier are becoming daily more bold and troublesome," he wrote. "Many men have been killed. Some of the women and children killed are families of soldiers in confederate service." Again, Lubbock offered no particulars. When refusing to turn the second reorganized Frontier Regiment over to the Confederacy, Lubbock concluded that the withdrawal "would cause the present frontier to be entirely abandoned, thereby bringing the frontier line only nearer the more densely settled country."[47]

Lubbock, like most Texans, presumed that Union officers were recruiting Indians to attack the Texas frontier. With the exception of the 1862 raid on Fort Cobb, which a low-level official at Fort Larned apparently had encouraged, this was not the case. By the summer of 1863, Agent J. W. Coffin had called the various refugee bands together near Fort Larned and extracted an agreement. They would be fed in exchange for ending "all jayhawking expeditions into Indian Territory." The Delaware Jim Ned was charged with enforcing the decree. Coffin's reasons were simple: most of the livestock taken belonged to Indians who were Union sympathizers.[48]

If Lubbock had his counterpart in the north, it was Governor John Evans of Colorado Territory. Evans had little interest in using Indians against Texas, but he too reported rumors of Indian depredations as fact. Evans arrived at his post in Denver during the summer of 1863. The Cheyennes and Arapahos had signed the Treaty of Fort Wise in 1861—very likely without knowing its terms—in which they gave up their claim to prime bison-hunting lands between the Platte and Arkansas rivers. In exchange, they received the Sand Creek Indian Reserve, a ninety-mile-wide stretch of poorly watered land lying just north of the fort. They were not happy with the deal. They had yet to receive annuities to help ward off the effects of the drought, and most resisted the government's attempts to force them onto the new reserve, as Evans promptly discovered.[49]

Worse, the Colorado gold rush of 1859 had led to frequent freighting across the plains. The trains pounded the grass as they slowly moved up the Oregon Trail, as well as over the Smokey Hill Trail, the southern route across the plains into Denver. Monthly supply trains also were directed into New Mexico after 1862, leaving northeastern Kansas with food and ammunition for the Union Army. Suffering from the drought, Kiowas began stopping the trains and demanding food in return for passage across the land. By the winter of 1863–1864, Comanches, Cheyennes, and Arapahos had joined the Kiowas.

As Indian discontent bubbled over in western Kansas, anarchy ruled in the region from Fort Belknap south to the Rio Grande. Major George B. Erath, commanding rangers in northwestern Texas, found the "neglect of duty and frequent disobedience of orders" so common among rangers and regular troops by April 1864 that he called for the organization of a "Provost Guard." Erath's counterpart near Fort Duncan (north of Fredericksburg), General J. D. McAdoo, warned a month later that "the Indians seemed to be the least talked of, the least thought of, and the least dreaded of all." The country, he lamented, "was infested with a great number of renegades, bushwhackers, and deserters."[50]

Some were German Unionists who had been conscripted and were deserting in droves. Texas Rangers had arrested several dozen and incarcerated them in the Fredericksburg jail. On May 25, sixty men stormed the jail, killed or wounded five rangers, and released the incarcerated deserters. Texans loyal to the Confederacy termed these men "Jayhawkers" and, as one group of petitioners noted, believed they "infested our frontier, burning houses and murdering the good citizens." Whether Unionists or Confederates—and both were heavily involved—thousands of such lawless men infested West Texas by 1864. Some four hundred were believed to work out of the towns of Mier and Laredo, in the south.[51]

Upon recovering somewhat from the effects of smallpox and drought, a Comanche war party finally joined in the carnage in October 1864; this was the first sizeable Indian raid of the Civil War. The party struck at Elm Creek, in Young County. Two pitched battles ensued. Many settlers had "forted-up" at Fort Murrah, a few miles northwest of Fort Belknap. A large party of Indians descended upon this stockade, but the defenders held out, reinforced by a dozen or so Texas Rangers who had been driven from the field by the overwhelming force of Indians. Seven settlers were killed, and another seven women and children were carried off. In an unheard-of display, the Indians took several thousand head of cattle, presumably to eat.[52] The raid brought near-hysteria to an already reeling Texas frontier community.

Similar attacks by Indians occurred in southern Kansas and Colorado in 1864, as the drought was finally lifting, allowing horses to travel easily. Kiowas stole 170 head of cattle from a government contractor along the Smokey Hill Trail in April; some four hundred Cheyennes attacked another train in June but were driven off. These Indians were hungry, angry, and vengeful after the terrible losses from epidemics. Other crucial attacks came in July and August, and dozens of trains were hit; estimates—likely exaggerated—placed the number of Americans killed at fifty. Among the victims were a rancher named Hungate, his wife, and his two small children, who were killed southeast of Denver. The treatment of their bodies, scalped and mutilated supposedly by Arapahos, prompted shouts for revenge from shocked Colorado citizens.[53]

In late August, Evans declared the situation "desperate." Rather than negotiate with or even feed the hungry Native people, he decided on a course of war. He demanded that troops destined for the East be kept in Colorado, and he turned over command of the Colorado militia regiment, the largest force in the region, to Colonel John Chivington, a man of considerable military experience, but one with an extreme hatred for Indians.[54]

The Union Army, meanwhile, had attempted to create a "friendly haven" for the Cheyennes and Arapahos who wished peace at Sand Creek. While Agent Colley doubted that the Indians would occupy the reserve, Chief Black Kettle indicated in July that many of his people wanted peace and would move to the spot, especially if they received some food.[55] Major Edward Wynkoop also spoke with Black Kettle in early September. He later led Black Kettle and others into Denver, where they met Evans and agreed to build a winter village along Sand Creek. By November, that village had over a hundred lodges—some seven hundred people.[56]

This turn of events angered Evans, who had lobbied Union military officers for more troops, claiming that an Indian war was in the offing. A treaty, even with a segment of the Cheyennes and Arapahos, "might embarrass the military operations against the hostile Indians," he wrote to Colley. However, Evans encouraged the agent to locate the peaceful Indians on Sand Creek, and then he asked for a leave to return to Washington, D.C. Meanwhile, both the Colorado Volunteers under Chivington and troops under General James J. Carleton in New Mexico were readying for winter campaigns against Plains Indians—indeed, almost any Indians.[57] Carleton ordered Colonel Kit Carson to take the field with four hundred men on November 6. They intended to punish the Kiowas and Comanches for attacking their supply trains.

After marching across the plains, covered with two feet of snow, Carson's Ute scouts located large villages on the South Canadian River on November 24. His forces quickly overran a camp of 170 Kiowa lodges, burning the tepees and killing a number of Indians. On the hills nearby, several thousand head of cattle were seen grazing, some undoubtedly taken from Elm Creek. Most Kiowas, however, fled east, the old chief Tohausen carrying the cry for help to the much larger Comanche towns nearby. They rallied quickly, descending in three directions upon Carson and nearly cutting off this wily frontier scout, who had been in many a tight place.

At this point, Carson's mountain howitzers went into action, spitting grapeshot into the attacking Comanches. Many of their horses bolted, allowing Carson's men to reach the protection of the abandoned trading post called Adobe Walls. Once the Comanches and Kiowas realized that their women and children were safe, they sniped away at Carson but let him escape. Carson knew that had the Indians not let him go, he and his entire command would have been annihilated.[58]

Meanwhile, Chivington's regiment, seven hundred strong, left Denver on the same morning that Carson hit the Kiowas. The Colorado militia, reinforced by over a hundred men from Fort Lyon, found the Cheyennes and Arapahos just where they were supposed to be, in a village on Sand Creek. On November 29, Chivington's troops unlimbered its artillery and charged the village with cavalry.

The Indians, including the peaceful Cheyenne chief Black Kettle, met Chivington's charging troopers with white flags. Black Kettle had trusted the Union and was flying a U.S. flag as well as a white flag of peace on a lodge pole, presuming troopers would never fire upon their own flag! Most of the Colorado militia, bloodthirsty and committed to taking no prisoners, took no notice but shot down men, women, and children as they ran for cover. Two hundred peaceful Indians perished; the majority of the bodies were carved up by Colorado soldiers seeking souvenirs among the mangled dead in the aftermath. Trophies, which were later attached to the walls of the opera house in downtown Denver, included the private parts of Indian women.[59] Black Kettle somehow escaped the carnage and fled east with three hundred or four hundred people, many wounded, some of whom died days later in the cold and heavy snow.

These attacks on winter villages brought incredible hardships to the people who survived them. Some four hundred lodges alone had been destroyed, housing that kept Indians from freezing over the winter. Comanche, Kiowa, Cheyenne, and Arapaho leaders all feared more attacks similar to Chivington's massacre. Some leaders wanted revenge; others wanted peace. A delegation of ninety-five leaders met the new Kiowa agent J. H. Leavenworth on February 19, 1865, pledging to halt all attacks on freighting trains. Leavenworth, parroting a growing sentiment in America, believed that he could end the fighting, "if I can so control the military as to prevent them from committing outrages on these Indians."[60]

Authorities in Texas knew nothing of these negotiations or of the status of Carson's and Chivington's campaigns. They expected the worst to come in the spring of 1865. By this time, Brigadier General J. W. Throckmorton recognized that the Frontier Regiment had mostly disappeared. No more than a few dozen men had fended off the attack at Elm Creek a few months before. He worked with the new governor, Pendleton Murrah, to reorganize the regiment, adding Confederate forces at one point. He hoped to launch an offensive campaign into the north to stop the rustling of Texas beef cattle and horses.[61]

Throckmorton's hopes seemed dashed, however, when shocking news reached Austin. A combined force of 370 Confederate and Frontier Regiment troops, under the command of Captain Henry Fossett, had received news of a large Indian party camped west of San Angelo. Without preparation or even the formation of ranks, Fossett pitched into these Indians on January 8, 1865, gunning down a man and two children who came out waving white flags. The disordered Confederate/ranger assault was soon met with a massive counterfire from a hundred new Enfield rifles. The Confederates had attacked a camp of 1,400 peaceful, but extremely well-armed, Kickapoos on their way to Mexico.

The Kickapoo gunfire killed fifteen Texans instantly, turning back the first wave of cavalry. Another twenty or so men died in attempting to capture the Kickapoo horse herd. Over sixty Texans had been wounded. Captain Fossett and another officer apparently showed the "white feather" and led a retreat that became a rout. Some officers tried to stop the disordered mass, but it was no use. The Kickapoo held the field at the end of the day and traveled on to Mexico, where they joined Lipan Apaches and Seminole Indians. They had lost eleven people, including the woman who was first shot down and a child.[62]

The "cowardice," as Throckmorton termed it, displayed at the so-called Battle of Dove Creek was symptomatic of a larger problem. Texas was exhausted, law and order had vanished on the frontier, and capable men refused to volunteer for service. The state could not even procure firearms; Fossett's men had attacked the well-armed Kickapoos with mostly shotguns and squirrel rifles.[63]

Perhaps ironically, the Plains tribes had suffered as much as, if not more than, the Texas settlers who so feared them. The culprit was not fighting but drought and disease. Comanche populations had fallen from some 9,000 people (as reported by the Bent brothers) in 1860 to 5,000 by 1865. The Yamparicas were the most numerous, with 1,800 people; followed by the Quahadas, at 1,000; the Cuchanticas, at 700; and the Naconis and Penatekas, at 600 each. Smallpox, cholera, starvation, and finally the losses and displacement caused by the Union campaigns of November 1864 had been devastating.[64] Bison herds, the very means of subsistence for the Comanches, failed to appear in their usual places.

U.S. agents found a similar situation among the refugee Indians who slowly began moving back to Fort Cobb in the fall of 1865. The combined Caddo and Wichita population hardly reached a thousand people, while their Shawnee and Delaware neighbors numbered under 600. The smallpox epidemic of the winter of 1864–1865 had, as their agent indicated, "proved fatal in many cases." And little remained for them back at Fort Cobb, the snug cabins that they had built in 1859 having been totally destroyed.[65]

Many Indian leaders begged for peace by the summer of 1865, and Agent Leavenworth worked to convince government authorities of the sincerity of their words. In addition, an outcry had erupted back East over the Chivington massacre. As a congressional investigation got under way, Senator James R. Doolittle of Wisconsin was selected to head a high-level commission to restore peace in the West. He worked closely with Leavenworth, who had enlisted old Jesse Chisholm, the part-Cherokee stalwart of the plains, to bring in Indian leaders. The commission even had the power to force the army to suspend campaigns into the upper Arkansas and Canadian rivers. On August 15, the first treaty of peace was signed near the mouth of the Little Arkansas River (present-day Wichita, Kansas). A formal agreement was concluded on October 10.[66]

Given the collapse of the Confederacy, the diminished position of the Indians, and the need to reorganize Indian Territory, federal officials had a free hand. Agent Leavenworth, in particular, wanted to right past wrongs. He pointed out to General John B. Sanborn of the treaty commission that Chivington's attack had both angered the Plains tribes and made them more cautious of Americans in general: "An angel from heaven could not induce them [the Plains tribes] to believe but what another Chivington massacre was intended." Tribal leaders realized that they were completely vulnerable in their villages, especially during winter. They came to the treaty table that fall with the intention of making peace; their key demands included preserving their right to hunting grounds and keeping the likes of Chivington and Carson, and the U.S. Army in general, off those lands.[67]

The treaties of 1865 actually favored the Plains tribes, demonstrating the federal willingness to attempt a new solution. The one negotiated with the Cheyennes and Arapahos created a new reserve for them between the Arkansas and Canadian rivers and allowed bison hunting north of the Arkansas in Kansas. The obvious weakness of the treaty was its attempt to create buffer zones around the main-traveled freighting routes into Colorado and New Mexico, an idea that proved impracticable.[68]

The treaty with the Comanches and Kiowas was even more liberal in allocating land. It gave the tribes West Texas, including a boundary that started at the northeastern corner of New Mexico, ran south along that territory's eastern border to its southeastern corner, turned "northeastwardly" to cut across West Texas, reaching the Red River near the 100th Meridian before turning due north to the Cimarron River and finally west to the starting point. Buffalo Hump, shrewd with years and astute when it came to recognizing boundaries, readily encouraged other Comanche leaders to sign.[69] It was literally the first time in history that Texans or Americans had recognized the Comanche claim to a homeland.

U.S. negotiators understood that they were giving West Texas land, owned by the state, to American Indians. General William S. Harney, who had served in Texas before the war, was one of the commissioners. What Sanborn, Harney, Leavenworth, and the other commissioners seemed to sense was that if there ever was to be peace in the West, the southern Plains tribes would have to be given the bison-hunting lands that belonged to them. State officials in Texas knew nothing of these events. Governor Murrah and other high-ranking officials had fled to Mexico after the war and had no representatives at the negotiating table.

In a final irony, the Civil War with all its destruction offered one last chance for peace between Indians and Texans. The 1865 treaty provided that the property rights of Texas Indians be respected and that ethnic cleansing end. Nevertheless, the war had also perpetuated many of the myths and problems that had existed since the 1820s. Rumors of terrible Indian raids had been used to justify a Texas military presence on the frontier, when in reality, frontier violence was most frequently home-grown, as it had been for decades. And Texas would certainly gain its feet once again and protest the 1865 treaty. With the exceptions of three small reservations—two of which had since been destroyed—Texas had historically denied Indians the right to land.

Peace seemed in the offing, then, as the postwar Southwest was slowly put back together. This tenuous peace was agreed to, however, only because all sides were exhausted and tired of fighting. Union military officials were more concerned with occupying the South than with fighting a guerrilla war against Indians on what they perceived as unoccupied plains. Moreover, the violence that Texas had endorsed as a part of patriotic nation building had brought about a state of inner civil war—manifested by killing, raping, and stealing of unprecedented proportion. Texas needed to reinstate law and order within the confines of its own state, which took time, energy, and resources.

Unfortunately for all, the exhaustion of war would last only so long, and the 1865 treaty was not a final settlement. Texans had fought for decades to prevent the very concession that the treaty provided. The U.S. government would soon reappear and begin to renegotiate. The Plains Indians—and even the few ragtag bands of northern Mexico, now reinforced by the heavily armed Kickapoos—had yet to make their final stand for what they still believed was their promised land. Many were prepared to do so despite their suffering during the Civil War. They too had honor and pride, and a way of life to protect.

22

THE FINAL ETHNIC CLEANSING
OF TEXAS

Buffalo Hump was unique among Comanche or Kiowa leaders. He more than others understood what had happened in 1865—a boundary had finally been determined, giving his people northwestern Texas. This land included the headwaters of the Brazos, Red, and Canadian rivers—the Panhandle and much of the land south of it—land still capable of feeding many of the diminished number of Plains Indians who had survived the Civil War droughts and epidemics. This land would allow the Comanches and Kiowas (and even their northern neighbors and allies the Cheyennes and Arapahos) to maintain their ways of life. It offered a permanent homeland, a chance for regeneration.

Such a concession could not have come at a better time for the Plains tribes, who had suffered terribly during the late 1850s and early 1860s. Not only that, other factors allowed these Indians to recover and make one last effort to hold this land and preserve their lifestyle. Texans, who had consistently wished to exterminate them, had been humbled by the war, and the federal government, too, had little stomach for more fighting. While the U.S. Army moved into Texas, it occupied only a few strategic places, ignoring much of the western ranch country. Finally, and perhaps most importantly, returning rains helped foster a revived economy in the Southwest: the surviving Indians were rapidly able to participate in it.

The economy of the Plains Indians had always been tied to bison and livestock: hides and meat and horse and mule exchange. Catastrophic droughts had depleted all animal herds, but the bison also had been overhunted since the 1830s, when the immigrant Indians had begun to enter the plains in numbers. This overhunting had begun just after another periodic drought, that of 1805–1821, had diminished the herds in West Texas. The overhunting expanded in the 1860s as American and New Mexican hunters entered the contest for the remaining animals. Even the army got in the act as soldiers occasionally slaughtered bison. Hundreds of thousands were killed by these new plains hunters between 1865 and 1880, by which time the animal had virtually disappeared.[1]

The slaughter spelled doom for the Plains tribes unless they could transform their economy. Thousands of Americans had flocked into Colorado in 1859, and thousands more invaded New Mexico and other regions of the West after the Civil War. These people needed horses, mules, and even cattle, which they consumed in large numbers. Many such animals lay on the periphery of this new Comanche homeland—especially cattle, which mostly ran wild, even those on Texas ranches. The Plains tribes could, and after 1865 increasingly did, supplement their diets with corn tortillas from New Mexico, carried in by comanchero traders. And beef cattle, whether taken from Texas or given to the Indians by the government, became almost as important as bison. What is more, hardly any self-respecting Comanche family could go without coffee, sugar, and American tobacco by the late 1860s. This changing diet and economy required raiding.[2]

Three unique circumstances (compliant governments in Washington and Austin, a wetter climate, and a dramatically expanding plains market) enabled the northern Indians to recover. The recovery led to a growing militancy, a willingness to raid into Texas and Mexico and even northward to the Smokey Hill River. Such raids by Comanches, and increasingly by Kiowas, were justified by the usual rationales—revenge, the need to prove manhood, and honor. And as Buffalo Hump was sure to add, the need to protect the new Comanche homeland.

The federal government made little effort to regulate the expanding plains market. Troops were mustered out after the war in such numbers that several key western forts could not be occupied, including Forts Cobb and Arbuckle in Indian Territory and Fort Zarah in Kansas. Nearly fifty thousand Union troops were in Texas in June 1865, but their numbers fell quickly thereafter; most of the remaining soldiers were posted along the Rio Grande, since the United States wished to convince the French army, which had invaded Mexico, to leave.

A military commission organized by General Philip Sheridan studied the Texas situation in 1866 and selected newly constructed Fort Concho as a central headquarters. The Fourth Cavalry and several infantry regiments arrived the next spring and fanned out across the state, deploying troops to Forts Belknap, Richardson, and Griffin in northwestern Texas and McKavett, Davis, and Stockton in the southwest. But their numbers remained small in comparison to the 2,800 troops that had occupied the frontier in 1860. U.S. Army commanders, including Sheridan, rightly concluded that Texans had exaggerated the Indian threat during the war years, and he saw no reason to assume that conditions had changed. Sheridan ignored the rising cries of Texans who wanted more troops in the west after 1865.[3]

The U.S. Army also prevented Texans from raising their own troops, despite the efforts of Governor J. W. Throckmorton, who was elected under the first reconstruction government in August 1866. After Congress passed the March 1867 Reconstruction Act, which called for the dismantling of state governments and the creation of military districts across the South, Throckmorton was removed from office. General Charles Griffin replaced him with Elisha M. Pease, an appointed governor. The general's attitude regarding Indian depredations mostly mirrored that of Sheridan; during the summer of 1867 he wrote to Pease that "there are twenty persons, or more, killed in the settlements by the residents of Texas, not Indians, where there is one killed by savages." Griffin refused to employ rangers or to give them rations or arms.[4]

Under such circumstances, the plains livestock trade flourished. William Bent, an astute trader still working out of Bent's Fort, had consistently reported to U.S. officials that little raiding had occurred during the war, but by 1866 that state of affairs had changed markedly. "Large amounts of [Texas] stock," Bent observed, were suddenly passing into New Mexico and Colorado. The animals were being moved by both Mexicans and Americans. A Dutchman staying at his fort had just purchased some sixty head of cattle from the Kiowas. Such a market only encouraged the Indians "to go and get more."[5]

Americans as well as comancheros had entered the livestock business on the plains. In May 1866, Agent Leavenworth of the Kiowa Agency was asked to investigate the rumors of an expanding cattle trade, with most of the animals being stolen from Texas. He thought the reports "exaggerated" and placed the blame on "Mexicans," who "supplied [the Indians] with ammunition, cloth—" mostly items of little value. Two years later, however, after being removed from office, Leavenworth set up a shop "dispensing fire-water and Colt pistols" to the Indians west of Fort Cobb, according to Captain George T. Robinson of the Tenth Cavalry. Several reports later indicated that Leavenworth had been at the center of much of the traffic in livestock.[6]

Many different livestock trading firms had moved into Indian Territory. A company owned by two men identified simply as Davis and Lewellen brought in large quantities of whiskey to use in their trade. They employed a number of men who went out to the Indian camps. Yet another whiskey peddler of note was young William Mathewson, known as "Buffalo Bill" (not to be confused with Buffalo Bill Cody). Major W. A. Elderkin, at Fort Cobb, described Mathewson as "a notorious rascal" who "should have been hung" a long time before.[7] Major Elderkin and other officers tried to convince the Indians to run such men out of their camps, but with little success.[8]

In 1872, U.S. troops patrolling out of Texas ultimately captured six comancheros from a party of over fifty. The officer in command learned that the comancheros had well-established rendezvous points with the western Comanches: the first was near the headwaters of the Clear Fork of the Brazos River, and the second, at the head of the Red River. American merchants in New Mexico provided many of the goods for these trade fairs and disposed of the animals that were brought back. Increasingly, in the late 1860s, these goods included the most up-to-date arms, such as Colt revolvers.[9] Indian warriors quickly took to the Colts, which they had seldom been able to acquire before.

With expanding markets and grass for ponies, Comanche and Kiowa raiding parties became more active. A series of raids erupted; these continued into the 1870s and ended only after the army finally defeated the Plains tribes in what was called the Red River wars. While the conduct of some raiders remained similar to that of earlier raids, other war parties in the 1860s and 1870s exhibited considerably more brutality. The increased violence may be explained by the fact that sometimes comancheros joined the raids, while at other times, the raiding parties were mixtures of warriors from various bands that included some renegades, some of whom were livestock dealers. In either case, the traditional Indian mechanisms that previously had limited violence mostly to men at times became inoperable.

Just how an Indian raiding party acted often depended upon its leaders. Many older leaders, including Peta Nocona, had died in the epidemics of the 1860s, and their absence opened opportunities for younger men, like Peta Nocona's half-Texan son, Quanah. These young warriors wished to gain status. Chiefs and the young men who followed them also became angry over the government's fickle annuity policies, which allowed Indian agents to stop food distribution without any warning to bands considered hostile.[10]

Indian agents had constant contact with the various Comanche and Kiowa chiefs after 1865, and they came to know which Indian leaders were for peace and which opposed it. Their sources even provided them knowledge as to the number of Texans killed and the number of captives taken by raiding parties. The Comanche Yamparica chief Ten Bears, who replaced Buffalo Hump (who had died in the spring of 1867), was considered a leading advocate of peace. The Penateka chief Asahabit was another. The raiding groups included Horseback's Naconi band; two bands of Quahadas led by Paracoom and Mowway; two Yamparica bands under Cheevers and Homeah; and a growing number of Kiowas, often led by Big Bow, Kicking Bird, or Satanta.[11]

While Horseback remained somewhat friendly to the agents, his brother often convinced a number of young men to follow him into Texas. About thirty-five of Horseback's Naconis descended upon Wise and Jack counties in northwestern Texas in the spring of 1866, committing a number of depredations and finally overrunning the Babb family farm. They killed Mrs. Babb and carried off two children and a governess. That summer and fall, four other Texas men and one woman were killed by raiding parties from identifiable Comanche and Kiowa bands, and ten children were taken into captivity.[12] These were definitely brutal raids, not carried out with the help or under the direction of renegades. The fact that women and children were taken was a key indication of who had committed the acts.

The attack on the Babb family caused considerable anguish near Decatur and Jacksboro, Texas. But as in the past, the captive children were treated amazingly well. Dot Babb, a fourteen-year-old boy, came to like Comanche life to such an extent that he debated over leaving it when the army paid the equivalent of $230 for his ransom two years later. His sister, Bianca Babb, age eleven, later remembered her "Indian family" of thirty-five people with fondness—"everyday seemed to be a holiday," she later wrote. "Children came to play with me and tried to make me welcome into their kind of life." Her only noted scare came when she went to fetch water and passed in front of the "warrior's tent." She was severely reprimanded and told to stay away from the men. Warrior taboos against having contact with females while planning a raid or conducting one still existed within Horseback's Naconi camp.[13]

Nevertheless, the growing tendency of government officials to ransom captives, such as the Babb children, had a negative impact. On at least one occasion, captive white women were abused. It happened when Kiowas Satanta and Stumbling Bear attacked the Box farm near Gainsville, Texas, on September 2, 1866. They killed the man of the house—"his head was skinned, his stomach cut open," according to one account.[14] The Kiowas then carried into captivity the man's wife and his three children, two of whom were daughters, aged seventeen and thirteen. Weeks later, Satanta and Stumbling Bear readily met army officers in Kansas and sold them the girls. But when the girls were collected, the eldest claimed (in the words of an army officer) that "she had been abused as a mistress by one or more of them." Secretary of the Interior O. H. Browning, upon hearing the account of what had happened to the Box girls, halted all annuity distributions.[15]

Although such a statement was weak on details and somewhat inconsistent—the army officer was unsure of whether one Kiowa man or several had abused the girl, which suggests that he was drawing conclusions on his own—it implied gang rape. The girls' brief account of their captivity suggests that they were neither adopted into families, like the Babb children, nor protected from abuse. They were simply taken captive so that the Kiowas could acquire sugar, coffee, guns, and ammunition with the anticipated ransom. More violent attacks occurred in Texas in 1867 and in 1868, one of the worst years on record. Sixteen women and children were taken that year, and eight men killed. An editorial in the *Dallas Herald* agreed with a position taken by the *San Antonio Herald*—the Indians, the papers said, "should be exterminated."[16]

The editorials did little, however, to arouse concern within army ranks in Texas. A gang of outlaws numbering hundreds of men had closed down the Laredo–San Antonio road. The gang had killed dozens of men (many of them Tejanos) and threatened to overrun small communities in southern Texas. If that were not enough, a few Kickapoos and Lipan Apaches had crossed the Rio Grande and attacked ranches in the Nueces River valley. General Griffin, who commanded U.S. forces in Texas, was more concerned with the Texas thugs, one group of which he identified as the Taylor gang. Texas had a host of troubles after the war, and Indians remained a rather minor concern, at least for the U.S. Army.[17]

Army officers in Kansas seemed more prone to act. Major General Winfield S. Hancock, one of the heroes of Gettysburg, had been assigned the job of keeping the wagon trails open to Colorado and New Mexico. The Kiowas especially needed taming for their attack on the Box family and their "barbarous treatment" of the girls, Hancock concluded. By mid-April, his force had marched well up the Pawnee Fork of the Arkansas River and found a large village of Cheyennes, Arapahos, and Sioux. While Hancock offered them peace, the men, women, and children in the camp fled at night. The next morning, Hancock burned the village.[18]

Hancock's actions reinforced the belief among the Plains tribes that the army, much like Texans, meant to exterminate them. As well, it created a serious rift between the military and the Bureau of Indian Affairs that would widen in the years to come. Agent Leavenworth was livid—as well he should have been, for the destruction of the village certainly disrupted his trade in horses, mules, and cattle! Leavenworth reported that the expedition had done "a great deal of harm" and that the military was involved in "mistakes or mismanagement" of considerable proportions. When Leavenworth confronted General of the Army William Tecumseh Sherman at Fort Leavenworth on May 22, the general shrugged him off, declaring that all Indian matters were in Hancock's capable hands.[19]

Leavenworth, despite his weakness for whiskey and his commercial ambitions, had friends in Washington—he was the son of General Henry Leavenworth, for whom the famous fort in Kansas was named. Leavenworth traveled east to meet with the secretaries of war and the interior, and he convinced many officials of the need to once again negotiate with the Plains tribes. Coincidentally, that same spring of 1867, the Senate commission under the charge of Senator James R. Doolittle issued its final report.

The Doolittle Commission report pushed for the creation of a new policy, a "peace policy" based upon Christian principles. The report levied many serious charges of corruption and mismanagement on the Indian Bureau, and it castigated the large number of "lawless whites" who caused trouble in Indian lands. It concluded that the Plains tribes were rapidly declining, as were the bison, their main means of support, and that they needed to adopt agriculture. The report recommended removing the Plains tribes to reservations, where they could be confined and given farm equipment, cattle, and educational instruction. Many eastern congressmen agreed—with often vehement protests from their western counterparts—and in June, Congress created the Indian Peace Commission, which headed west to negotiate the treaties necessary to implement the reforms.[20]

The peace commission fell under the control of several intensely religious civilians. Commissioner of Indian Affairs Nathaniel G. Taylor, a part-time preacher, headed the group, which included Indian reformer Samuel F. Tappan, Senator John B. Henderson (who had sponsored the legislation), and General John B. Sanborn (who was then practicing law in Washington). The president also appointed General Sherman, Major General Alfred H. Terry, and General William S. Harney, the latter perhaps the most experienced with western affairs. The commission convened at Medicine Lodge Creek, a tributary of the Arkansas River, and a number of Comanche and

Kiowa chiefs signed the new treaty offered them on October 21. In it, they surrendered West Texas in exchange for a reservation in Indian Territory.[21]

Tribal leaders who signed this agreement had little idea that they were giving up vast amounts of land. Buffalo Hump, who knew the boundary debate, had died and was replaced by Ten Bears, who increasingly lived near Fort Cobb and had become a pawn of the U.S. government. Other Comanche signatories included Toshewa (better known as Silver Brooch), Horseback, and Iron Mountain, men who had become close to Agent Leavenworth. The Yamparica and Quahada bands were poorly represented, if at all. Homeah, Cheevers, Mowway, and Paracoom all failed to attend. Kiowa chiefs signing the agreement included Satank, Satanta, and Stumbling Bear, while Big Bow and Kicking Bird avoided the ceremony.[22] Representation among the Cheyennes and Arapahos, who were offered a similar treaty with a similar reserve in northwestern Indian Territory, was nearly as limited as that of the Comanches.[23]

Regardless of the validity of the agreements, the Bureau of Indian Affairs was totally unprepared to implement the treaty. Some Comanche and Kiowa bands starved over the winter, and in the spring, Leavenworth expected at least 2,000 Kiowas and 3,100 Comanches to invade the new reserve begging for food. This left some 2,000 Comanches, who the agent felt would not come in at all.[24]

The agent's pleadings seemed justified when crowds of sullen Indians did appear, forcing him to buy food from traders. On no less than three occasions, Leavenworth then requested army protection. The Indians demanded food and threatened bureau officials. General Sheridan found Leavenworth's requests increasingly irritating, and they ultimately led to the agent's dismissal in September 1868.[25] The situation deteriorated thereafter, as the summer 1868 raids into Texas seemed to indicate. Hoping to halt the carnage, Secretary Browning withheld food annuities once again. This mattered little, however, as General Sheridan had commandeered all the wagons in Kansas to move supplies for an upcoming winter campaign against the very Indians that the Bureau of Indian Affairs had failed to feed.[26]

General Sheridan brought together elements of the Seventh Cavalry and the Ninth Kansas Volunteer Cavalry to mount his winter strike. Sheridan had adopted the strategy of the Texas Rangers, recognizing that the Indians would be easy targets in their winter villages. Sheridan gave command of the striking force to the newly reinstated Lieutenant Colonel George Armstrong Custer, who arrived at Fort Dodge in November. Custer had performed with reckless and brilliant abandon during the Civil War, and Sheridan expected the same of him on the plains. On November 23, Custer departed Fort Supply (Sheridan's base along the upper Canadian River) at the head of the Seventh Cavalry. Despite heavy snow, the regimental band led the column, playing "Garry Owen," Custer's newly adopted fighting song.[27]

Just three days later, Custer's troops hit an Indian village of fifty-one lodges nestled along the bank of the Washita River, just inside the border of Indian Territory. He divided his command into three forces for the attack—much like he would later do at the Little Big Horn in Montana. Custer later confessed that his troops, who killed Indians at will, had no intention of saving anyone over eight years of age. When the killing had stopped, 103 Indians lay dead, including the peaceful chief Black Kettle, who had survived Chivington's massacre in Colorado four years before; some 53 others, including some women, were taken prisoner. Custer's men then collected and shot 875 ponies, which was a new "total war" strategy.[28]

Receiving word of larger Comanche and Kiowa villages to the east, Custer retreated northward. He departed quickly, perhaps assuming that a patrol of nineteen men under the command of Major Joel H. Elliott would later join him. Elliott, meanwhile, had scouted to the east; his command was overwhelmed and killed by warriors from other villages on the Washita. Sheridan's initial elation over the campaign turned to confoundment when he learned of Custer's abandonment of Elliott.[29] Custer's actions certainly caused resentment among the surviving officers of the Seventh Cavalry.

Even worse, Custer's attack looked somewhat like another Chivington massacre. The peace movement had gained momentum in Congress and the country. Samuel Tappan, who had negotiated the Medicine Lodge Treaty of 1867, thought the strike an open violation of the treaty. These actions put the army on the defensive, and even General Ulysses S. Grant, who was elected president in November 1868, endorsed a "peace policy" for the plains after watching the criticism unfold; he would later endorse vigorous campaigns against the same Indians.[30]

President Grant implemented the new policy by the summer of 1869, hiring a number of Quakers to serve in the Indian Bureau. It was assumed that Quakers were honest and compassionate, and it was hoped that they would convert the Indians to their pacifistic doctrine. Among these Indian Bureau Quakers were Enoch Hoag, who took over the Central Superintendency; Brinton Darlington, who became the Cheyenne/Arapaho agent; and Lawrie Tatum, who assumed control at the Kiowa/ Comanche agency. These men hoped first to confine the Plains tribes to their reservations and then teach the Indians farming and Christianity.[31]

Tatum seemed duly optimistic during the first year of his service in the West. He made friends with a number of Comanche and Kiowa leaders, including Ten Bears, Horseback, Homeah, and Kicking Bird. Thereafter, these leaders often brought in stolen horses, mules, cattle, and even captives. A few Comanches even tried farming near the new agency that had been selected for them near Fort Sill, in southwestern Indian Territory. But upwards of two thousand Quahadas, Yamparicas, and Naconis remained on the high plains, and the Kiowas showed no interest in farming even though they stayed closer to Forts Cobb and Sill.[32]

Those Indians who remained on the plains had grievances. The Kiowa chief Lone Wolf, who opposed the peace policy to the end, noted on many occasions the failure of the government to provide the promised annuities. There were not "enough rations," he said, "especially of coffee and sugar . . . very little annuity goods & no ammu-nition." At one point in September 1870, Lone Wolf and most of the Kiowas bolted from a council when it was obvious that Tatum had too little sugar to satisfy them. Tatum then withheld rations altogether, punishing them. Three months later, Tatum could not understand why the Kiowas had organized raiders who went into Texas.[33] The Quaker agent lacked an understanding of the plains economy and the role of raiding in it.

The second problem faced by the peace-policy advocates involved the age-old issue of boundaries. Most Kiowa and Comanche chiefs misunderstood the fine print in the 1867 treaty. Agent Tatum quickly discovered this in a July 1870 council at Fort Sill, when a number of rather friendly chiefs demanded ammunition for hunting bison and insisted that "the boundary line of all reservations [be] eradicated." The Quahada chiefs, who continued to ignore invitations to come in and negotiate, told Lone Wolf to relay the same message. Texans, the chiefs had told him, "had stolen their country & they [the Comanches] would get some of it back."[34]

The impasse with the Indians that Tatum reported in the fall of 1870 had actually been brewing for several years. Raids in the south had increased, and many younger Comanche and Kiowa chiefs had been trying to unite all the Plains tribes in war against both Texas and the United States. Representatives of all the Plains tribes had attended a large Medicine Dance in May where those chiefs who advocated war made their case. Only Ten Bears, Horseback, Toshewa, and Asahabit argued against it.

Those leaders who favored war dominated the discussions. The Cheyenne chiefs, the Kiowas Satank and Big Bow, and the vast majority of Quahada and Yamparica chiefs, such as Mowway, Iron Mountain, and Paracoom, all demanded war to the end. The interpreter at Fort Sill, Horace Jones, received a complete report on the event. "The actions of the government in making reservation lines, and trying to compel [the Indians] to remain on them," as well as the failure of Tatum to issue ammunition, Jones felt, were the primary causes for the growing rebellion. Young men speaking in the council had branded the older "peace" chiefs, such as Ten Bears, "Old women and cowards."[35]

This polarization among Comanche and Kiowa leaders and the growing mili-tancy of those living in the Texas Panhandle came at a time when the state of Texas was able to force the federal government to rethink its policies. Colonel Benjamin H. Gierson, commanding the Tenth Cavalry at Fort Sill, continued to parrot the army line—that there had been few depredations in Texas, "exaggerated newspaper and other reports to the contrary."[36] But by 1870 Texas politicians had finally "redeemed" their state—as they put it—from U.S. Army occupation, and they demanded a new army assessment. Edmund J. Davis, a Republican, had been elected governor, and the Republican Grant administration wanted to support him as much as possible. When Davis organized seven new ranger companies during the summer and implied that the army had failed to protect the state, the secretary of war ordered an investigation.

Davis had a valid argument. Depredations were increasing. Several of the companies Davis had created clashed with small raiding parties that fall. Some of the raiders had crossed the Rio Grande from Mexico and included Kickapoos and Lipan Apaches. Others were made up of western Comanches and Kiowas. The largest action came near Fort Inge, where Captain H. J. Richarz's troop engaged seventy Comanches in December 1870. The fighting was intense, and Richarz lost several men, including his son. A dozen Indians died, or so the rangers claimed.[37]

Amid growing complaints from Governor Davis, General Sherman elected to look into the situation himself. He arrived at Fort Richardson on the evening of May 18, 1871, only to hear of an attack by a hundred Indians on a freighter's train ten miles west of the fort, along the very road over which he had passed just a few hours before. Sherman did not know it at the time, but the Indians had considered attacking his party, in which case they probably would have killed the general of the U.S. Army.

The supply train teamsters, who had been surrounded, put up a stout fight, killing or mortally wounding seven Indians even after being ambushed. But after seven mule drivers were killed, the five survivors abandoned the train to the Indians and fled. Once Sherman had heard the details, he quickly ordered Colonel Ranald S. Mackenzie to the scene, where the colonel found one of the teamsters chained to a wagon wheel, his body roasted. It was a gruesome sight, seldom if ever before seen in Indian warfare on the plains. Sherman was outraged.[38]

The general ordered Mackenzie to give pursuit while Sherman headed north to Fort Sill. Mackenzie's force never found the perpetrators, but when Sherman arrived at the fort, he discovered that their identity was known. The Kiowa Satanta had bragged of the act to both Agent Tatum and Colonel Grierson. He lightheartedly mused that his people had lost the same number of men, killed and wounded, and that the attack should be considered a draw. An embarrassed Tatum, not prone to condemn anyone, nevertheless quickly notified the Indian Bureau that he intended to have the men responsible arrested.

Sherman had no intention of asking permission to act. Upon hearing Tatum's story, he arrested Satanta, Satank, and Big Tree, all of whom were implicated in the murders. Big Bow, more guilty than the others, was tipped off and fled. The seizure of these men prompted a riot; the Kiowas under Lone Wolf, who was the son of Satanta, even feinted an attack on the garrison. Sherman probably would have arrested others of the party, had he had the chance. Fearing the army, the Kiowas fled in every direction.

Colonel Mackenzie mounted the three unrepentant and chained Kiowa men on wagons and headed to Texas for trial. En route, Satank grabbed a rifle from one of the guards and was shot dead. But even the trial of the two remaining Kiowa raiders was appreciated in Jacksboro, Texas. Satanta and Big Tree faced a tough jury. Both were sentenced immediately to death. The Quaker Tatum, troubled by the decision, interceded. He argued that to hold the two chiefs as hostages might bring the Kiowa tribe in line. Governor Davis reluctantly agreed, and the chiefs were incarcerated at the Huntsville, Texas, penitentiary.[39]

The incident had embarrassed General Sherman. From that point on, he sought ways to destroy the southern Plains tribes, peace policy or not. Yet the army had to tread softly. The treaty of 1867 made the Indians the wards of the Indian Bureau. Colonel Grierson told Agent Tatum privately that he doubted that the military would be allowed to campaign against the tribes, despite Sherman's anger.[40] Certainly, the military had no jurisdiction on the reservation. But this limitation did not stop Sherman, who ordered Colonel Mackenzie and his cavalry to scout the lands west of Indian Territory that fall. In one engagement, Quahadas nearly overran part of his forces and stampeded many of the cavalry's horses.[41]

Mounting evidence suggested that Tatum could not settle the Indians on their reserve. Tatum became particularly discouraged when news arrived in June 1872 of the killing of yet another Texas settler family, named Lee, along the Clear Fork of the Brazos River. Troops from Fort Griffin confirmed the slaughter of the parents and their young daughter; two teenage daughters and a boy had been carried off. The Kiowa White Horse, who had lost a son in the wagon train fight, had led the attack.[42]

While Tatum scurried to ransom the girls, he also had several long and telling conversations with Major George Schofield at Fort Sill. Tatum admitted that the Kiowas were out of control and that the Quahadas and many Naconis simply ignored him. Tatum then took these complaints to the Indian Bureau, which responded in typical fashion; it sent a commission to study the situation in July. But Tatum had already decided that army action was necessary. This Quaker, an "advocate of peaceful measures," Schofield reported to army officials, "is now satisfied that there is no good in these Indians, unless it is whipped into them." Even the bureau's commission, which stayed in western Indian Territory throughout August, did not challenge Secretary of the Interior Columbus Delano's decision to wash his hands of the situation and to turn it over to the secretary of war.[43]

A determined General Sherman gladly accepted the responsibility, ordering Mackenzie to boots and saddles in the spring of 1872. This time, Mackenzie established a base on the Double Mountain branch of the Brazos with ample supplies to subsist a large force. With 284 officers and men, and fresh horses, Mackenzie's force approached the North Fork of the Red by late September. There, it struck a large village of 262 lodges. The Indians had some forewarning, and only 24 warriors were killed. The troops took 124 women and children captive and burned all the lodges. The captive Indians became hostages, much like the two Kiowas at Huntsville.

Mackenzie had attacked Mowway's Quahada camp, which had been involved in raiding. But most of the leaders and the vast majority of the warriors had escaped— most were likely hunting. The troopers also captured some three thousand ponies, but Mackenzie seemed uncertain what to do with them. The Quahadas, still full of fight, stampeded and recovered the animals during the night. Thereafter, Mackenzie's

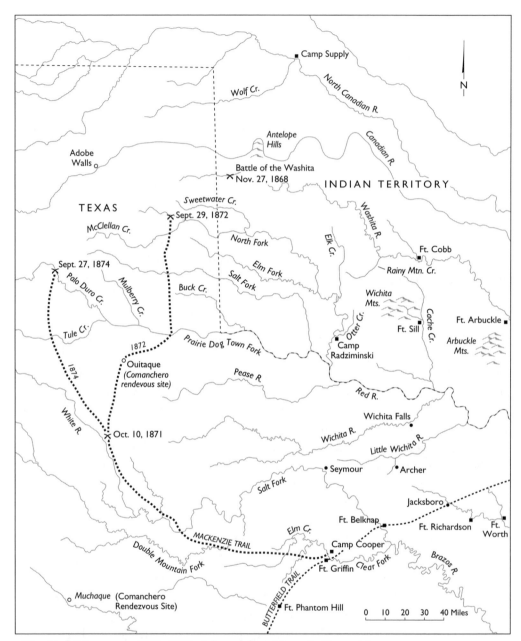

The Red River wars, 1871–1875. Adapted from Nye, *Carbine and Lance*.

standing orders were to shoot captured animals on the spot, much like Custer had done at the Washita.[44]

The attack had a sobering impact on the Plains tribe. The army had demonstrated that it could find the Indians wherever they hid. Over Christmas 1872, the two leading Quahada chiefs, Mowway and Paracoom, visited with Tatum and expressed an interest in peace. They marveled somewhat at fifty new houses under construction on the reservation, most of which were to be occupied by Toshewa's peaceful band. This left Tatum, whose term as agent would end that spring of 1873, more optimistic. He even helped negotiate the release of the 124 Quahada hostages and, despite horrendous opposition from Texas, arranged a pardon for Satanta and Big Tree.[45]

The army did march the Comanche hostages from Fort Concho in Texas to Fort Sill in June, but Lone Wolf grew angry waiting for the return of his father, Satanta. He joined other relatives holding nightly vigils, reminding Agent J. M. Haworth, who had replaced Tatum, that the government had promised to release the Kiowa leaders. Governor Davis, meanwhile, had rethought the pardons. It was simply political suicide—especially for a Republican in a Democratic state—to agree to a release. When Davis finally turned the men over in early September, he did so with a stipulation: the Kiowa chiefs were to be held in the guardhouse at Fort Sill until the northern Indians had surrendered their ponies and weapons.[46] The demand was a new wrinkle for the peace policy, but an effective deterrent.

Reports of small raiding parties along the Texas frontier filtered into Fort Sill as the bickering over Satanta's and Big Tree's release continued. Some of the villains were likely Texas renegades, but others, including some Indians, had crossed over from Mexico to steal cattle and horses. Colonel Mackenzie struck a blow at the latter in May when he led his cavalry into Mexico, in defiance of international protocol, with orders to "annihilate" the Lipans and Kickapoos. His initial charge on a Lipan camp killed nineteen; many more were wounded and died later. Several of the dead were women and children. Forty prisoners were taken to be used as hostages.[47]

Haworth, like Tatum, came to believe that most of the Kiowas and Comanches wanted peace as Christmas 1873 approached.[48] But he just as quickly discovered the implacable sentiment of the Indians regarding their lands in Texas. At one council, even the friendly chiefs continued to argue that "they had rights in Texas" and that they had been "forcibly driven" from that land. They even claimed that when "Samuel Houston was, as they regarded it, owner of Texas," he "drew an imaginary line," in which the land on one side "he gave to them and their children forever."[49] The Comanche leaders were well aware of their rights, and the Texas policy of absolute ethnic cleansing remained as the major roadblock to peace.

U.S. Army officers in the past had often sympathized with that argument; Sherman, Sheridan, and Mackenzie, however, did not. Even agents and superintendents in the Indian Bureau had come to view the Texas Panhandle as a refuge for hostile Indians who had to be destroyed or driven onto reservations. Quakers Haworth and Enoch Hoag at times had difficulty accepting that argument, for they generally opposed the use of the military against these Indians. But over the winter even their objections ceased, and the decision was made to stop all annuities and force the raiding groups to come in and be disarmed and dismounted.[50]

On the plains, this ultimatum was received with considerable derision. Yet it came at a time of unbelievable stress. Often hungry (and angry) warriors who had been refused annuities looked elsewhere for help. One possible solution was to save the bison herds that were being systematically slaughtered by gangs of white hunters. In June, Big Bow and Kicking Bird came into Fort Sill to complain vociferously of this practice. The bison was "their money," they tried to explain to Haworth. The animals were being killed at a rate of several thousand a month, for only the hides.[51]

A solution seemingly came in the form of a visionary Quahada named Eschiti, who through sleight of hand convinced many Comanches and Kiowas that he could vomit bullets sufficient to kill all the intruding hunters.[52] Eschiti's power rose during the May Medicine Dance; some of the peaceful chiefs even feared him. Shortly thereafter, Eschiti led more than three hundred warriors against a group of twenty-eight bison hunters at Adobe Walls, the crumbling old trading post that the Anglos used to store their hides. The Comanche, Kiowa, and Cheyenne force struck at daybreak, convinced of a swift victory. A few hunters had risen early, however, and saved their comrades. About a dozen Indians died in the first assault, but many more were mortally wounded, as the hunters were heavily armed. The hunters held out against determined Indian charges.[53]

The failed attack at Adobe Walls seemed to foreordain the end for the militant Indians who remained on the plains. The bison were disappearing rapidly, and there was little the Indians could do about it. The Bureau of Indian Affairs would no longer issue rations to anyone who refused to surrender and remain on the reserve. Once the Plains bands were settled on the reservations, the agents counted heads and set up annuity rolls to make certain who was where. Most of the Kiowas had surrendered by late September; only some Naconis and Quahadas remained at large— some four hundred men and parts of their families.[54] By fall, the army proposed to deal with them once and for all.

Troops marched west from Fort Sill in late August. General Nelson Miles's cavalry force drew first blood, breaking up a large village along the South Fork of the Red River on September 1, killing seventeen. Colonel Mackenzie then dealt a death blow when he discovered a series of five connected Indian camps at the bottom of Palo Duro Canyon, south of present-day Amarillo, on September 28. While his men had difficulty finding their way down to the canyon floor, and most of the Indians fled, he took almost the entire herd of two thousand ponies. The next day, Mackenzie ordered every animal shot.[55]

By October, small groups of Plains Indians were coming into Fort Sill and Fort Cobb in increasing numbers. Those who had ponies or arms surrendered them in exchange for food. The parade of Indians entering the agencies continued into the spring of 1875. The only key leaders who remained out were a few Quahadas: Mowway, Wild Horse, and Quanah, the son of Cynthia Ann Parker. They finally surrendered in April and May 1875. Little did they know that President Grant had ordered that the leaders of the surrendered groups—some 126 Indians—be incarcerated at Fort Marion, Florida. Several, including Lone Wolf, died there.[56]

These surrenders brought to a close the Red River wars. Even the Rio Grande frontier became a calmer place after 1875. Only a few stubborn holdouts remained, and these were often unknown to the army. On May 9, Captain Jonathan B. Jones of the Texas Rangers ran into one such party of seven Indians in Lost Valley in Jack County. The fight extended over many miles, and five of the marauders were killed. The Indians were well armed with shotguns and pistols. They fought to the death. Upon examining the bodies, Captain Jones was flabbergasted to see that "one of those killed was a squaw." She had "handled her sixshooter quite as dextrously as the bucks," Jones wrote in his report of the action. Another was a "half-breed," who before dying spoke some "broken English." Even more curious, "he was quite fair, having curly auburn hair."[57]

Perhaps it was fitting that one of the last serious raids into Texas had among its combatants a pistol-wielding Indian woman and a man with auburn hair, who was likely a renegade rather than a member of any tribal society. Much of Texas history is filled with such people. Their presence complicates the standard, simplistic version of this conflict, which has dominated the pages of old history books. Such enigmatic people—whose ranks include the many immigrant eastern tribes and their many different bands, the gangs of Texas renegade rustlers, and the fiery Texas Ranger companies that pillaged for a living—often had more to do with determining Texas history than did governmental legislatures, federal armies, or recognized tribal leaders.

Whatever their story or their motive, they made Texas history something that all Texans revel in even today—a history unto its own, unique and more violent than any of the other states that Texas joined in 1845, or that joined later. And what of the young adventurers, cotton farmers, land speculators, and hardworking Anglo and Tejano settlers who tried and at times succeeded in making a peaceful life in Texas? Theirs is a different story, one that is untold here but is found elsewhere. There can be no doubt, however, that the most dramatic aspect of Texas history in the first fifty years of its Anglo development is the story of its frontier. Here, people fought over the land, and too many lawless people—Anglos, Tejanos, Indians, and renegades—dreamed of empire and chose violence as a way of obtaining it.

Unlike other regions of the West, Texas was slow to turn its attention to building schools and working legal systems—the elements that lead to a stable society. The western Anglo settlements of Texas remained in a continual state of flux as people came and went through many decades; this instability bred violence. Texas never seemed capable of implementing laws that might control this violence. Even the Texas legislature, under the Republic and during early statehood, did little to help establish orderly rule. The state government instead used rangers, often disorderly men themselves, to implement law and order and adopted a policy of ethnic cleansing.

While the rangers obviously were a minority, the majority Anglo population worshipped them as heroes, elected them time and again to public office, and supported the policy of ethnic cleansing that embroiled the state in violence well into the 1870s. Tragically, when it came to Tejanos, violent outbreaks against those long-time citizens continued at times well into the next century. This violence, or the fear of it, was the tool used to cleanse Texas of unwanted ethnic groups. The job mostly had been completed by 1875, when the last militant Indians surrendered in Indian Territory.

The racial prejudices of nineteenth-century Texans, who came predominantly from the slaveholding South and feared both slave conspiracy and slave revolt, led them to expect people of other races to conspire against them. Such a worldview distorted Texas history: Indians, brutal and bloodthirsty, were always at fault, and Texas Rangers were saviors, brave and righteous in their actions. In this Anglo-Texan scheme, Tejanos were often viewed as agents of Mexico, perhaps good for herding horses and sheep or for moving goods in carts, but for little else.

Such a historical interpretation—written by the first two generations of Texas historians—is mythology. Some will undoubtedly claim that ranger brutality came in response to Indian depredations and murders—that the Indian was simply intractable. Others will suggest that Tejanos had weak titles to land or sold it willingly. But is this true? While some bands or even tribes embraced war at certain times, an accommodation along the lines of the "false peace" was always possible, and at times, many Indian bands went well beyond that, acting as allies and supporters of Anglo-Texans in hopes of acquiring land titles. Many Indian leaders called for boundary lines that would have separated the two peoples and prevented war even during the Red River wars of the 1870s. And Tejanos, for their part, tried to work side by side with Texans in building a new nation.

Texans, then, had many opportunities to end the violence. Had Texans supported Houston's policies in the 1830s and 1840s, the problem might have been solved. And had law and order been established in southern Texas, Tejano populations might have prospered early. Later, had frontier ranchers and rangers supported the reservation system, violence might have been curtailed well before the Civil War. And during the council at Fort Cobb in 1861, conducted by Confederate officials, a boundary could have been established. It was an ideal time to grant Comanches and Kiowas their lands.

Texans never agreed to accept the existence of western Plains Indians in the state under any circumstances. It was this denial, this refusal to accept ethnic diversity— seemingly inevitable given the Southern code—that condemned Texas to a history of violence and instability. Once started, once viewed as heroic and honorable, such violence was difficult to bring under control—it became simply the price of what Texans perceived as "civilization."

Roughly thirty-five thousand Indians called Texas home in 1835; this population was larger than that of the Anglo inhabitants when the revolution broke out. Some eighteen thousand Mexicans and Tejanos lived along the southern fringes of the region—if the lands in and about El Paso and the lower Rio Grande are included.

Only a few thousand Indians remained in the Panhandle by 1875, when they made their last stand. And many Tejanos fled or were displaced from homes and jobs during the 1850s and 1860s. The surviving Indians reemerged in Indian Territory or in Mexico and attempted to rebuild their lives. Some Tejanos managed to hang on in the south of Texas; they later rebuilt their populations through immigration and reemerged in the twentieth century as an increasingly successful people.

The historic existence in Texas of these people will always live on in John Wayne films and the distorted history created by Anglo founding fathers such as John Henry Brown. But let us remember that the conqueror first tells the tale of his success. In its retelling, heroism and myth soon dominate. But the truth's reemergence is always in the offing.

J. W. Throckmorton, former Confederate general, elected governor of Texas in 1865, later removed by U.S. authorities. Rose Collection no. 122. Courtesy Western History Collections, University of Oklahoma Libraries.

Edmund J. Davis, elected Republican governor of Texas under Reconstruction in 1870. Davis tried to bring order to the state, but he received little cooperation given his connections with Reconstructionists. Rose Collection no. 123. Courtesy Western History Collections, University of Oklahoma Libraries.

General Henry E. McCulloch, Texas ranger and commander of the northwestern district of Texas, 1862–1865. Rose Collection no. 1223. Courtesy Western History Collections, University of Oklahoma Libraries.

Colonel Ranald S. Mackenzie, commanding officer of the Fourth U.S. Cavalry, leveled the final blow against the Plains Comanches at Palo Duro Canyon in late 1874. Rose Collection no. 1178. Courtesy Western History Collections, University of Oklahoma Libraries.

Toshewa (Silver Brooch), a Penateka Comanche chief who had been forced from Texas in 1859. He later led the peace movement at Fort Sill in Indian Territory. Soule Collection no. 40. Courtesy Western History Collections, University of Oklahoma Libraries.

Asahabit (Birch Chief), a strong Comanche advocate of peace in the 1870s. Soule Collection no. 8. Courtesy Western History Collections, University of Oklahoma Libraries.

Quanah Parker, a young Naconi Comanche leader who became increasingly influential on the reservation after his surrender in 1875. Rose Collection no. 935. Courtesy Western History Collections, University of Oklahoma Libraries.

Kicking Bird, a Kiowa chief who worked well with Indian agents on the reservation in the 1860s and 1870s. Soule Collection no. 41. Courtesy Western History Collections, University of Oklahoma Libraries.

Satank (Sitting Bear), a Kiowa chief who was shot and killed while attempting to escape in 1871. The army was moving him to Texas for trial. Soule Collection no. 44. Courtesy Western History Collections, University of Oklahoma Libraries.

Satanta (White Bear), a Kiowa chief arrested and condemned to death for murdering five teamsters in 1871. He later jumped to his death from a window while incarcerated at the Texas State Prison in Huntsville. Rose Collection no. 1090. Courtesy Western History Collections, University of Oklahoma Libraries.

Satanta's youngest daughter, a Kiowa woman who likely had cut her hair, mourning over the death of her father in Texas. Soule Collection no. 58. Courtesy Western History Collections, University of Oklahoma Libraries.

Big Bow, a Kiowa leader who escaped prosecution for the murder of the teamsters in 1871. He later became an important reservation chief. Soule Collection no. 43. Courtesy Western History Collections, University of Oklahoma Libraries.

Lone Wolf, one of the last Kiowa leaders to surrender in 1875. He was considered so dangerous by the army that he was kept in chains until finally transferred to prison in Florida, where he died. Rose Collection no. 1091. Courtesy Western History Collections, University of Oklahoma Libraries.

Sitting-in-the-Saddle, Lone Wolf's son, later became a reservation leader. Soule Collection no. 64. Courtesy Western History Collections, University of Oklahoma Libraries.

Wappah, Marnme, and Qnamothkee, Comanche women taken captive during the plains wars. Soule Collection no. 37. Courtesy Western History Collections, University of Oklahoma Libraries.

Agent Lawrie Tatum with five ransomed Mexican captive boys. Courtesy National Anthropological Archives, Washington, D.C.

NOTES

INTRODUCTION

1. The agricultural value of the Texas river valleys has been noted by many observers and scholars. "The relief, soils, and natural resources of these rolling prairies," Robin W. Doughty claims, "provided the ideal setting for hard-working immigrants to carve out a 'garden,' in the watersheds of the Brazos, Colorado and Guadalupe Rivers." See Doughty, *Wildlife and Man in Texas: Environmental Change and Conservation* (College Station: Texas A and M University Press, 1983), 3–22, quotation on page 14.

2. To those readers who believe that "presentist" arguments are unfair, I would suggest that as an explanatory model, ethnic cleansing sheds much useful light. And it is well understood. For further reading, see Norman M. Naimark, *Fires of Hatred: Ethnic Cleansing in Twentieth-Century Europe* (Cambridge, Mass.: Harvard University Press, 2001), and George J. Andreopoulos, *Genocide: Conceptual and Historical Dimensions* (Philadelphia: University of Pennsylvania Press, 1994).

3. John Wesley Wilbarger, *Indian Depredations in Texas. Reliable Accounts of Battles, Wars, Adventures, Forays, Murders, Massacres, etc., etc., Together with Biographical Sketches of Many of the Most Noted Indian Fighters and Frontiersmen of Texas* (Austin: Hutchins Printing, 1889), and John Henry Brown, *A History of Texas from 1685 to 1892,* 2 vols. (St. Louis: L. E. Daniell, 1893).

4. See Wilbarger, *Depredations in Texas,* 144–145, 184.

5. See John Henry Brown, *History of Texas*; E. C. Barker, *The Life of Stephen F. Austin* (Nashville and Dallas: Cokesbury, 1925); R. N. Richardson, *The Frontier of North West Texas, 1846–1876* (Glendale, Calif.: Arthur H. Clark, 1963); and Walter Prescott Webb, *The Texas Rangers: A Century of Frontier Defense* (Boston: Houghton Mifflin, 1935). Perhaps Richardson's best-known work is his textbook, first issued in 1943: Rupert N. Richardson, Ernest Wallace, and Adrian Anderson, *Texas: The Lone Star State* (Englewood Cliffs, N.J.: Prentice Hall, 1988).

6. Some of the newer revisionist tribal histories include Dianna Everett, *The Texas Cherokees: A People between Two Fires, 1819–1840* (Norman: University of Oklahoma Press, 1990); Morris W. Foster, *Being Comanche: A Social History of an American Indian Community* (Tucson: University of Arizona Press, 1991); David LaVere, *The Caddo Chiefdoms: Caddo Economics and Politics, 700–1835* (Lincoln: University of Nebraska Press, 1998); Paul H. Carlson, *The Plains Indians*

(College Station: Texas A and M University Press, 1998); Kelly F. Himmel, *The Conquest of the Karankawas and the Tonkawas, 1821–1859* (College Station: Texas A and M University Press, 1999).

7. See Gregg Cantrell, *Stephen F. Austin, Empresario of Texas* (New Haven: Yale University Press, 1999), and James L. Haley, *Sam Houston* (Norman: University of Oklahoma Press, 2002).

8. For the quotation, see Andrés Tijerina, *Tejanos and Texas under the Mexican Flag, 1821–1836* (College Station: Texas A and M University Press, 1994), 113. See also Arnoldo De León, *The Tejano Community, 1836–1900* (Albuquerque: University of New Mexico Press, 1982); David Montejano, *Anglos and Mexicans in the Making of Texas, 1836–1986* (Austin: University of Texas Press, 1987); Armando C. Alonzo, *Tejano Legacy: Rancheros and Settlers in South Texas, 1734–1900* (Albuquerque: University of New Mexico Press, 1998); Paul D. Lack, *The Texas Revolutionary Experience: A Political and Social History, 1835–1836* (College Station: Texas A and M University Press, 1992). An excellent study of early San Antonio, during its prime in the eighteenth century, is Jesús F. de la Teja, *San Antonio de Bexar: A Community on New Spain's Northern Frontier* (Albuquerque: University of New Mexico Press, 1995).

9. Jesús F. de la Teja, "The Colonization and Independence of Texas: A Tejano Perspective," in *Myths, Misdeeds, and Misunderstandings: The Roots of Conflict in U.S.-Mexican Relations,* ed. Jaime E. Rodríguez O. and Kathryn Vincent (Wilmington, Del.: Scholarly Resources, 1997), 80. In a standard textbook recently revised and reprinted and used in both public schools and college classrooms, the term "Tejanos" does not even appear in the index. See Richardson, Wallace, and Anderson, *Texas.*

10. See Robert M. Utley, *Lone Star Justice: The First Century of the Texas Rangers* (New York: Oxford University Press, 2002). Quotation is on page 17.

11. Utley, *Lone Star Justice,* 23. Utley relies far too heavily on printed sources, and many are nineteenth-century ranger memoirs. Despite Utley's early work in military history, he has failed to consult crucial collections of military documents on Texas in the National Archives. These include, for example, the Records of the United States Army Continental Commands (RG 393), including the records of the Sixth Military Department, 1832–1853, and the Western Division and Department, 1820–1854, both massive collections that have substantial information on Texas, the Texas Indian wars, and Texas Rangers. American military officers had a much different view of Texas Rangers than that offered by the historian Utley.

12. Utley, *Lone Star Justice,* xi.

13. Walter L. Buenger and Robert A. Calvert, "The Shelf Life of Truth in Texas," in Walter L. Buenger and Robert A. Calvert, eds., *Texas Through Time: Evolving Interpretations* (College Station: Texas A and M University Press, 1991), ix–xxxv.

14. Randolph B. Campbell, *Gone to Texas: A History of the Lone Star State* (New York: Oxford University Press, 2003), quotations on pages 113 and 205. See also pages 189–206.

15. T. R. Fehrenbach, *Lone Star: A History of Texas and the Texans* (New York: Macmillan, 1968). Fehrenbach's book had gone through three printings by 1974 and continued to be reprinted. Regarding Indian claims to land, Fehrenbach first quotes Theodore Roosevelt, who said that to confirm the Indian's rights to land would require setting aside a vast continent "as a game preserve for squalid savages." Southerners who moved to Texas had considerable experience with Indians, Fehrenbach continues, developing a "sense of being a chosen people" and thereby coming to despise Indians. Tejanos (or, in Fehrenbach's parlance, Mexicans) were a new experience for Texans, "but the quirks of Mexican warfare—the parleys, the guile, and the frequent treacheries—were quickly learned." All quotations are from pages 446–448. Unfortunately, Fehrenbach also wrote about Indians. See his *Comanches: The Destruction of a People* (New York: Alfred A. Knopf, 1974).

16. James Axtell, while certainly not part of this "new school," comments on the issue of genocide, suggesting Texas as an example, in *Beyond 1492: Encounters in Colonial North America* (New York: Oxford University Press, 1992), 243–263. New England, the subject of Axtell's work, had its fair share of "war crimes" committed against Indians.

17. See, for example, David Stannard, *American Holocaust: Columbus and the Conquest of the New World* (New York: Oxford University Press, 1992), particularly section 2, "Pestilence and Genocide," pages 57–147. Yet another proponent of this school is Russell Thornton, *American Indian Holocaust and Survival: A Population History since 1492* (Norman: University of Oklahoma Press, 1987), pages xv–xvi, and 127.

CHAPTER 1. AT THE DAWN OF THE AMERICAN INVASION

1. Ross's unidentified journal is in the William Trimble Papers, Ohio Historical Society, Columbus. It is entitled "Exploration of Texas." The author of the piece is identified in Thomas Gales to the secretary of war, August 16, 1815, National Archives Record Group (hereafter referred to as NARG) 75, Letters Received (hereafter cited as LR), Secretary of War Papers Relating to Indian Affairs, Correspondence of the Bureau of Indian Affairs.

2. Such a statement may seem controversial to some. The size of Comanche horse herds came up a few years back at an Ethnohistory Conference attended by John Ewers, the noted expert on Plains Indians. Ewers categorically believed that Comanche herds were usually twice the size of those found farther north. Much of Ewers's information came from his editing of Jean Louis Berlandier, *The Indians of Texas in 1830* (Washington, D.C.: Smithsonian Institution, 1969).

3. Most of the discussion that follows regarding the southern plains political economy comes from my own work. See Gary Clayton Anderson, *The Indian Southwest, 1580–1830: Ethnogenesis and Reinvention* (Norman: University of Oklahoma Press, 1999), 179–265.

4. The argument that peace broke out in the late 1780s and lasted into 1810 is also discussed in James F. Brooks, *Captives and Cousins: Slavery, Kinship, and Community in the Southwest Borderlands* (Chapel Hill: University of North Carolina Press, 2002).

5. See Alonzo, *Tejano Legacy,* 36–49.

6. Cordero to the Commandant General, March 31, 1807, Bexar Archives (hereafter referred to as BA), Eugene C. Barker Library, University of Texas, Austin. For a discussion of the "false peace," see Anderson, *Indian Southwest,* 251–265.

7. Determining Comanche populations is excruciatingly difficult. Contemporaries such as Berlandier put their numbers in 1828 at 10,000–12,000, comparable to Zebulon Montgomery Pike's estimate in 1806 of 1,020 lodges. Major William Trimble, the commanding officer at Fort Jesup, Louisiana, in 1816 and Governor Antonio Mendoza at San Antonio in 1822 both gave figures that suggest populations of well over 50,000. More reasonable estimates include those of Pierre Chouteau, who put the number at 4,500 warriors, and Agent Robert Neighbors, who specified 4,000 warriors and 20,000 people in 1849. But Pierce Butler, a special agent to the Comanches who spent considerable time with them, wrote that the Comanches were "Supposed to number about fifty thousand souls and to be able to bring into the field ten thousand effective warriors." Of course, populations fluctuated, given factors such as disease in-marriage, and adoption. For the debate, see Berlandier, *Indians of Texas,* 114; Pierce M. Butler, "Report, April 29, 1843," Butler Papers, Huntington Library, San Marino, California; Ernest Wallace and E. Adamson Hoebel, *The Comanches: Lords of the South Plains* (Norman: University of Oklahoma Press, 1952), 25–32; Anderson, *Indian Southwest,* 211–229 and 335–336n.6.

8. Comanche band names are problematic. Other names that I have not listed in the text can be found in primary documents. But the preponderance of sources support the ones discussed, with some observers dividing the so-called northern Comanches into "middle" and "northern" divisions. Spellings are also problematic. "Penateka," for example, is spelled at least twenty different ways in Hodge alone, but the most common—including the spelling used by Hodge—is "Pena-teka." See Frederick Webb Hodge, ed., *Handbook of North American Indians North of Mexico,* 2 vols. (Washington, D.C.: Government Printing Office, 1910), 2:224.

9. Early Caddo history has been the subject of two recent studies. See Timothy K. Perttula, *"The Caddo Nation": Archaeological and Ethnohistorical Perspectives* (Austin: University of Texas Press, 1992), and LaVere, *Caddo Chiefdoms.*

10. For an analysis of Wichita society and economy, see Anderson, *Indian Southwest,* chapters 7 and 8.

11. Anderson, *Indian Southwest,* 218–226.

12. Berlandier, *Indians of Texas,* 112. Lundy reported that many immigrant Indians flocked into Nacogdoches to trade when he visited the town in July 1832. See Lundy Journal, July 1832, Ohio Historical Society, Columbus.

13. Some scholars believe that Bowles was the son of William Agustus Bowles, an early English trader, but more likely he belonged to the clan that the Englishman married into. For information on Bowles's lineage, see J. Leitch Wright Jr., *William Agustus Bowles: Director General of the Creek Nation* (Athens: University of Georgia Press, 1967), 172, 177n.30; Albert Woldert, "The Last of the Cherokees in Texas and the Life and Death of Chief Bowles," *Chronicles of Oklahoma* 1 (January 1921): 179–226; Dorman Winfrey, "Chief Bowles of the Texas Cherokee," *Chronicles of Oklahoma* 32 (Spring 1954): 29–41. The supposition that Chief Bowles was the son of William Agustus Bowles comes from Wright, who concluded that the son was born some-time after William Agustus Bowles reached Creek lands in about 1780. Such a chronology is impossible, however, since Chief Bowles of the Texas Cherokees was born in the 1750s.

14. Berlandier, *Indians of Texas,* 142. The Delaware and Shawnee villages built on the Red River during the summer of 1818 contained roughly 500 people by fall. By 1823, the commu-nities were located along the Sulphur Fork of the Red River on lands claimed by Louisiana. The Shawnee town had merely fifty families in 1823. The next year, the agent at Red River Agency reported a total of 160 adults in both towns. See John Fowler to Thomas L. McKenney, July 4 and August 29, 1818, NARG 75, LR, Sulphur Fork Factory; G. Gray to secretary of war, Feb-ruary 28, 1824, *The Territorial Papers of the United States,* 28 vols., ed. Clarence E. Carter and John P. Bloom (Washington, D.C.: Government Printing Office, 1934–{#}), 19:611–612; "List of Indian Tribes belonging to Red River Indian Agency, Sulphur Fork," 1824, NARG 75, LR, Red River Agency.

15. James F. Brooks has suggested that across the Southwest, captivity generally led to slavery. This was likely the case in New Mexico, where Brooks found one case study in which 68 percent of 272 captives became slaves. Most of the remainder likely suffered a similar fate. But Comanche society was nonagricultural, extremely mobile, and warlike, and was thus open to social mobility. Captivity was more of a temporary state. See Brooks, *Captives and Cousins,* 236.

16. Don Felix Trudeau revealed the commercial content of the expedition and noted that it consisted of Ross, Gutiérrez de Lara, sixteen or seventeen Spaniards, and eleven Americans. See his testimony dated 1816, "Blue Transcripts," Nacogdoches Archives (hereafter referred to as NA), Texas State Library (hereafter referred to as TSL), Austin.

17. David G. Burnet, who later became the ad-interim president of Anglo Texas, was in the thick of this burgeoning trade, even though he later claimed to have traveled to the Comanches

only to recover his health. See Mary Whatley Clarke, *David G. Burnet* (Austin and New York: Pemberton Press, 1969), 15–20; Ernest Wallace, ed., "David G. Burnet's Letters Describing the Comanche Indians," *West Texas Historical Association Year Book* 30 (October 1954): 115–140. Reports on Spanish "renegades" are found in Francisco Adam to Mariano Varela, January 17, 1816, Joaquín de Arredondo to Ignacio Peréz, September 17, 1816, and Peréz to Arredondo, October 14, 1816, BA; Manual Rivera report, October 8, 1819, Spanish Archives of New Mexico (hereafter SANM), State of New Mexico Records Center, Santa Fe.

18. "Statement of News Gathered on the Frontier," March 15, 1821, "Blue Transcripts," NA.

19. Trimble to John C. Calhoun, March 2 and August 7, 1818, Trimble Papers.

20. Jacob Fowler, *The Journal of Jacob Fowler, Narrating an Adventure from Arkansas through the Indian Territory, Oklahoma, Kansas, Colorado, and New Mexico, to the Sources of the Rio Grande del Norte, 1821–1822,* ed. Elliott Coues (New York: Francis P. Harper, 1898), 6–72. Harlin M. Fuller and LeRoy Hafen, *The Journal of Captain John R. Bell: Official Journalist for the Stephen H. Long Expedition to the Rocky Mountains, 1820* (Glendale, Calif.: Arthur H. Clark, 1973), 180–200.

21. For primary sources, see "Bent's Fort," 1824–1826, a manuscript written by George Bird Grinnell, in the Grinnell Papers, Southwest Museum, Los Angeles. The mapping of the Santa Fe Trail was begun by George C. Sibley in 1826. Many of his journals and letters are found in the Merideth M. Marmaduke Papers, Western Historical Manuscript Collection, University of Missouri, Columbia.

22. J. P. Cabanné to Pierre Chouteau, November 8, 1824, Chouteau Papers, Missouri Historical Society, St. Louis.

23. The development of the fur trade in New Mexico can be followed through the correspondence of Cabanné, William B. Astor, John G. Stevenson, and E. St. Vrain and others in the Chouteau Papers, Missouri Historical Society, St. Louis. See also David J. Weber, *The Taos Trappers: The Fur Trade in the Far Southwest, 1540–1846* (Norman: University of Oklahoma Press, 1971).

Chapter 2. The Texas Creed in a Tejano and Indian Land

1. See the description of Nacogdoches in the Benjamin Lundy Journal, 1832, Ohio Historical Society, Columbus.

2. For Rio Grande populations, see Alonzo, *Tejano Legacy*, 41–45. Jesús F. de la Teja and John Wheat assess the demographics of San Antonio in "Bexar: Profile of a Tejano Community, 1820–1832," *Southwestern Historical Quarterly* 89 (July 1985): 7–34.

3. See Tijerina, *Tejanos and Texas,* chapter entitled "The Emergence of Tejano Politics," 113–135; Jesús F. de la Teja, ed., *A Revolution Remembered: The Memoirs and Selected Correspondence of Juan N. Seguín* (Austin: State House Press, 1991), 13–28; Stephen L. Hardin, "Efficient in the Cause," in *Tejano Journey, 1770–1850,* ed. Gerald E. Poyo (Austin: University of Texas Press, 1996), 51; Cantrell, *Stephen F. Austin,* 193.

4. Montejano, *Anglos and Mexicans in the Making of Texas,* 16–36; Tijerina, *Tejanos and Texas,* 139–144; Galen D. Greaser and Jesús F. de la Teja, "Quieting Title to Spanish and Mexican Land Grants in the Trans-Nueces: The Bourland and Miller Commission, 1850–1852," *Southwestern Historical Quarterly* 95 (April 1992): 445–464.

5. See Francis Paul Prucha, *The Great Father: The United States Government and the American Indian,* 2 vols. (Lincoln: University of Nebraska Press, 1984), in particular chapters 2 and 3.

6. Thomas Jefferson, *Notes on the State of Virginia* (New York: H. W. Derby, 1861; reprint, New York: Harper and Row, 1964), 57–60.

7. A recent discussion of Jeffersonian philosophy is in Anthony F. C. Wallace, *Jefferson and the Indians: The Tragic Fate of the First Americans* (Cambridge, Mass.: Harvard University Press, 1999). Jefferson masked his rhetoric in moral tones, whether in dealing with Indians or foreign countries, and he quickly endorsed policies that led to the creation of a homogeneous "white" society. Whenever anyone threatened Jefferson's dream of American empire, Rousseauian logic went out the window. In other words, much of what Jefferson wrote in his *Notes on the State of Virginia* was intended for a European audience to offset the unjust criticism of the United States rendered by the comte de Buffon, Georges Louis Leclerc, in *Histoire Naturelle, Générale et Particuliére* (Paris: Imprimerie Royale, 1774–1789).

8. Cass's criticism of Cooper is discussed in Roy Harvey Pearce, *Savagism and Civilization: A Study of the Indian and the American Mind* (Baltimore: Johns Hopkins University Press, 1953), 109–211.

9. See Roy Harvey Pearce, "The Significance of the Captivity Narrative," *American Literature* 19 (1947): 1–20.

10. The Boone theme is explored in detail in Richard Slotkin, *Regeneration through Violence: The Mythology of the American Frontier, 1600–1860* (Middletown, Conn.: Wesleyan University Press, 1973), 268–284.

11. Richardson, Wallace, and Anderson, *Texas,* 182–185; James Oakes, *The Ruling Race: A History of American Slavery* (New York: Vintage Books, 1983), 79.

12. Oakes, *The Ruling Race,* 61–65.

13. Richardson, Wallace, and Anderson, *Texas,* 181.

14. Oakes, *The Ruling Race,* 22–24.

15. Oakes, *The Ruling Race,* 22–24.

16. The term "cultural hegemony," developed by Antonio Gramsci, an early-twentieth-century Italian Marxist, has been used to characterize this southern mentality. Gramsci argued that dominant elite groups maintained power by winning the "spontaneous" support of subordinates to a common set of values. More recently, James Scott and others have generally rejected the argument, pointing to the "hidden transcripts," as Scott puts it, of the subordinates and the frequent factionalism that exists among the elites. But Scott concedes that in the Antebellum South the idea perhaps has some merit, given the attempted paternalism of the planter class and the acquiescence of the subordinates to it. Historian Eugene Genovese has also used the idea successfully in describing the "agreement," of sorts, that defined both the master's and the slave's role. See Quinton Hoare and Geoggrey Nowell Smith, *Selections from the Prison Notebooks of Antonio Gramsci* (New York: International Publications, 1971); James C. Scott, *Domination and the Arts of Resistance: Hidden Transcripts* (New Haven: Yale University Press, 1990); Eugene Genovese, *Roll, Jordan, Roll: The World the Slaves Made* (New York: Pantheon Books, 1974). Yet another interesting attempt to apply Gramsci's concept is T. J. Jackson Lears, *No Place of Grace: Antimodernism and the Transformation of American Culture, 1880–1920* (New York: Pantheon, 1981).

17. The best discussion of Southern honor is still Bertram Wyatt-Brown's collection of work, including *Southern Honor: Ethics and Behavior in the Old South* (New York: Oxford University Press, 1982); *Honor and Violence in the Old South* (New York: Oxford University Press, 1986); and *The Shaping of Southern Culture: Honor, Grace, and War, 1760s–1890s* (Chapel Hill: University of North Carolina Press, 2001). Historian Grady McWhiney draws on Wyatt-Brown's work in developing his argument regarding southern attitudes toward fighting the Civil War. See McWhiney and Perry D. Jamieson, *Attack and Die: Civil War Military Tactics and the Southern Heritage* (Tuscaloosa: University of Alabama Press, 1982); McWhiney, *Cracker Culture: Celtic Ways in the Old South* (Tuscaloosa: University of Alabama Press, 1988); and McWhiney, "Ethnic Roots of Southern

Violence," in *A Master's Due: Essays in Honor of David Herbert Donald,* ed. William J. Cooper Jr., Michael F. Holt, and John McCardell (Baton Rouge: Louisiana State University Press, 1985), 116 and 117.

18. For a discussion of Jeffersonianism and the Indian, see Bernard W. Sheehan, *Seeds of Extinction: Jeffersonian Philanthropy and the American Indian* (New York: W. W. Norton, 1974).

19. See Wallace, *Jefferson and the Indians.*

CHAPTER 3. MEXICAN POLITICS AND THE STRUGGLE TO SETTLE EARLY TEXAS

1. There are many descriptions of the Hidalgo Revolt. See, for example, Lesley Byrd Simpson, *Many Mexicos* (Berkeley: University of California Press, 1964), 185–195.

2. See Donald E. Chipman, *Spanish Texas, 1519–1821* (Austin: University of Texas Press, 1992), 216–241.

3. Julia Kathryn Garrett, *Seven Flags over Texas: A Story of the Last Years of Spain in Texas* (Austin: Pemberton Press Reprint, 1969), 84–177; Richard W. Gronet, "The United States and the Invasion of Texas," *Americas* 25 (January 1969): 281–306; "José Bernardo Maximiliano Gutiérrez de Lara," in *The Handbook of Texas,* 2 vols., ed. Walter Prescott Webb and H. Bailey Carroll (Austin: Texas State Historical Association, 1952), 1:749–750.

4. See testimony taken by don Felix Trudeau from Captain Lafitte of Bayou Pierre, 1816, and "Interrogatory" of Captain Antonio Aguirre, February 4, 1817, "Blue Transcripts," NA. The *ayuntamiento* (city council) at San Antonio reported in 1821 that the only chance for Texas was to open trade with the United States, "where goods are cheap and the price of horses (of which there are a great number in this province) is high." Sugar could no longer be purchased in the town, basic food was extremely scarce, and tradesmen, such as shoemakers, had retreated south sometime before. See report on "Conditions in Texas," 1821, NA. A Spanish patrol entered Nacogdoches in the fall 1820 and found no one. See Gregorio Pérez diary, February 7, 1821, BA. On Bean's extraordinary life see Bennett Lay, *The Lives of Ellis P. Bean* (Austin: University of Texas Press, 1960). Bean generally signed his name Peter Ellis Bean, rather than using his given name of Ellis Peter Bean. See Anderson, *Indian Southwest,* 186 and 195; David J. Weber, *The Mexican Frontier, 1821–1846: The American Southwest under Mexico* (Albuquerque: University of New Mexico Press, 1982), 9–10.

5. Report of Mendoza and José Angel, May 1, 1821, R. B. Blake Papers, Eugene Barker Library, University of Texas Library, Austin.

6. For biographies of the Austins, see Barker, *Life of Stephen F. Austin,* and Cantrell, *Stephen F. Austin.*

7. Cantrell, *Stephen F. Austin,* 80–103.

8. Reuben McKitrick, *The Public Land System of Texas, 1823–1910,* Bulletin of the University of Wisconsin No. 905 (Madison, 1918), 30; Thomas Lloyd Miller, *The Public Lands of Texas, 1590–1970* (Norman: University of Oklahoma Press, 1971), 15–16.

9. Richardson, Wallace, and Anderson, *Texas,* 64.

10. Miller, *Public Lands of Texas,* 16–17.

11. Ibid., 17.

12. Ibid., 17–21.

13. Martínez to don Gaspar López, December 1, 1821, Fomento-Colonización, Archivo General de la Nación (hereafter referred to as AGN), transcripts in BL.

14. López to Iturbide, December 28, 1821, Fomento-Colonización transcripts, BL. The source of information on Nacogdoches was likely Santiago Dil, who later reported on the growing

Anglo presence in the city and their role in the illegal horse and mule trade. See Dil to Trespalacios, August 22, 1822, BA.

15. Austin to James E. B. Austin, March 23, 1822, *The Austin Papers,* ed. Eugene C. Barker (Washington, D.C.: American Historical Association, 1919–1928), vol. 2, 487. Cantrell notes that Austin did not speak Spanish when he arrived in Texas in July 1821 but took a "fanatical" approach to quickly learning it. Undoubtedly, Austin could communicate in the language to some degree when he met Comanches in southern Texas the next year. See Cantrell, *Stephen F. Austin,* 115–116.

16. Rafael Gonzáles to Juan de Castañeda, June 5, 1824, BA.

17. Martínez to alcalde of Bexar, December 21, 1821, Lopéz to Martínez, January 11, May 6 and 18, 1822, and José Encarnacion Vásquez to Martínez, June 27, 1822, BA.

18. Trespalacios to Lopéz, December 11, 1822, BA.

19. Lopéz to Trespalacios, February 7, 1823, Castañeda to José Antonio Saucedo, June 23, 1824, and Mateo Ahumada to Gutiérrez de Lara, August 17, 1825, BA. James Gaines, who ran a ferry over the Trinity River, makes several interesting comments regarding the tendency of early settlers in Austin's colony to also trade with western Indians. See Gaines to Austin, June 18, 1824, *Austin Papers,* vol. 2, 834–835.

20. Juan Ignacio Blanco to Antonio Elozúa, December 1, 1824, and report of José Ignacio Calindo and other "*cudadanos,*" January 1, 1825, BA.

21. Juan José de Eleguezábal to Elozúa, February 27, 1825, BA. Interestingly, the Baron de Bastrop reported to Stephen Austin that this Comanche party had "committed excesses against some poor women who were alone at a distant ranch," a detail the original report neglected to mention. See Bastrop to Austin, March 19, 1825, *Austin Papers,* vol. 2, 1058.

22. Elozúa to Gomez Pedraza, August 9, 1825, and Elozúa to Rafael Gonzáles, August 10, 1825, BA.

23. José Ibarra's deposition, November 16, 1825, Cayetano Andrado to Elozúa, November 16, 1825, and Andrado to Elozúa, November 20, 1825, BA. The term *fresada* could also be *frezada,* meaning "blanket." But most New Mexican *comanchero* traders who went to Comanche camps (according to Rafael Chacon, who was heavily involved in the trade in the 1840s and 1850s) carried either corn tortillas, wheat bread, or "piloncillos" (brown sugar). See Chacon, *Legacy of Honor: The Life of Rafael Chacon, a Nineteenth Century New Mexican,* ed. Jacqueline Dorgan Meketa (Albuquerque: University of New Mexico Press, 1982), 95–107; see also Fowler, *Journal of Jacob Fowler,* 71–72.

24. Tijerina quotation in Juan Martín de Veramendi to José Antonio Saucedo, September 1, 1825, BA. See also Andrado to Elozúa, December 16, 1825, BA.

25. Juan José Llanos to Elozúa, July 27, 1825, Ahumada to Elozúa, August 7, 1825, Ahumada to Gutiérrez de Lara, August 17, 1825, and Ahumada to Austin, August 19, 1825, BA; Bastrop to Viesca, August 19, 1825, *Austin Papers,* vol. 2, 957–959.

26. This view again differs from that in Brooks, *Captives and Cousins,* primarily because Brooks focuses on New Mexico, where slavery was more prominent.

27. Bastrop to Viesca, August 19, 1825, *Austin Papers,* vol. 2, 957–959.

28. Tijerina, *Tejanos and Texas,* 79–80. The leaders of these Tejano "flying companies" have seldom been identified in most Anglo history of the period. They included Carlos de la Garza at Victoria, Mariano Rodriguez at San Antonio, and, of course, Juan N. Seguín, Salvador Flores, and Vicente Córdova, the latter responsible for the revolt at Nacogdoches.

29. See Miller to the secretary of war, May 1822 and September 27, 1822, Colonel Matthew Arbuckle to the acting adjutant general, September 30, 1822, and August 2 and September 3,

1823, Robert Crittenden to John C. Calhoun, September 28, 1823, and Arbuckle to General Edmund P. Gaines, December 3 and 4, 1823, in Carter and Bloom, *Territorial Papers,* 19:437–440, 460–461, 462–463, 536, 545–546, 546–550, 570–571, 572–574; Gaines to the secretary of war, July 20, 1826, and John Jolly to Edward W. DuVal, December 4, 1826, in Carter and Bloom, *Territorial Papers,* 20:272–275 and 318–319; Pierre Chouteau to Major Robert Graham, February 24, 1824, NARG 75, LR, Osage Agency; Graham to William Clark, May 29, 1826, Chouteau to Clark, June 10, 1826, and Clark to James Barbour, June 11, 1826, NARG 75, LR, St. Louis Superintendency; *Arkansas Gazette,* February 19, 1822, and May 25, August 29, and November 29, 1826.

30. The best information on Fields is found in Richard Drinnon, *White Savage: The Case of John Dunn Hunter* (New York: Schocken Books, 1972), 183. See also Everett, *Texas Cherokees,* 132n.4 and LaVere, *The Caddo Chiefdoms,* 85–86.

31. Richard Fields to Martínez, February 1, 1822, BA.

32. Fields reached Saltillo in November 1822 and went on to meet with the emperor of Mexico, Agustín de Iturbide, that winter. Agreement between Trespalacios and Fields, November 8, 1822, NA; Trespalacios to Iturbide, November 8, 1822, and López to Trespalacios, December 14, 1822, BA.

33. Draft of Luciano Garcia's letter to Felipe de la Garza, July 22, 1823, and Fields to Saucedo, March 6, 1824, BA. See also Ernest William Winkler, "The Cherokee Indians in Texas," *Texas State Historical Association Quarterly* 7 (October 1903): 98–106.

34. Fields to Saucedo, March 6, 1824, and J. Norton's petition, October 25, 1824, BA; Juan Norton to alcalde of San Antonio, October 29, 1824, Gaspar Flores to Governor Rafael Gonzáles, October 30, 1824, and Gonzáles to minister of state and relations, March 29, 1825, Fomento-Colonización transcripts, BL; George Gray to secretary of war, April 1824, in Carter and Bloom, *Territorial Papers,* 19:664–665.

35. Tijerina, *Tejanos and Texas,* 87.

36. Austin's address to colonists, August 5, 1823, *Austin Papers,* vol. 2, 678. Austin reported the organization of these men to Luciano Garcia, the ad-interim governor of Texas. He indicated that Indians had stolen stock from several herds and killed one herd boy, thus necessitating the actions. He asked Garcia to pay wages to the sergeant and ten men whom he had commissioned. See Austin to Garcia, August 11, 1823, BA.

37. For the original accounts, see William B. DeWees, *Letters From an Early Settler of Texas* (Cincinnati: Hull, 1853), 37–40, and Jesse Burnam, "Reminiscences of Capt. Jesse Burnam," *Texas Historical Association Quarterly* 5 (1901): 12–18. See also Himmel, *Conquest of the Karankawas,* 48–49, and Anderson, *Indian Southwest,* 40. The official report (sent by John Tumlinson to Trespalacios, February 26, 1823, BA) lists only eight dead in the village and many wounded Indians, who undoubtedly died later. The conflict over hunting is documented in a variety of places, including Amos Rawls to Austin, June 13, 1824, in *Austin Papers,* vol. 2, 830–831, and Austin to the military commander of Texas, April 24, 1824, "Blue Transcripts," NA.

38. See Burnam, "Reminiscences of Captain Jesse Burnam," 15.

39. C. Dyer affidavit and other affidavits in *Austin Papers,* vol. 2, 1319–1321.

40. Austin to Saucedo, September 22, 1824, BA; Austin to alcalde at San Felipe, May 25, 1824, Austin to authorities at La Bahía, November 1, 1824, Thomas B. Bell to Austin, October 3, 1824, Saucedo to Austin, July 19, 1825, and Austin to Ahumada, September 25, 1825, *Austin Papers,* vol. 2, 803, 930, 1198, 1153, and 1220. Cantrell argues that Austin actually would have preferred to have peace with the Karankawa Indians, but obviously he also wanted their land. See Cantrell, *Stephen F. Austin,* 136–138.

41. The exact date of the attack is unclear. See Recollections of Capt. Gibson Kuykendall, James and William Kuykendall Papers, Ralf W. Steen Library, Stephen F. Austin State University, Nacogdoches, Texas; Judge Thomas M. Duke, "Reminiscences of Early Texas: A Collection from the Austin Papers," *Texas Historical Association Quarterly* 5 (July 1901): 250; Himmel, *Conquest of the Karankawas,* 51. Mexican negotiation began in the fall of 1826. See Ahumada to commandant of La Bahía, October 9, 1826, and Rafael Manchola to Ahumada, October 10, 1826, BA.

42. Austin to Josiah H. Bell, August 6, 1823, *Austin Papers,* vol. 2, 682.

43. Cummins to Austin, March 13, 1824, *Austin Papers,* vol. 2, 755. See also Thomas M. Duke statement, 1823–1824, Kuykendall Papers.

44. Duke to Austin, June 1824, *Austin Papers,* vol. 2, 842–843.

45. One of the most interesting rumors came in the form of a discussion that was supposedly initiated by a Canadian, or "Englishman," who sought, along with a Spaniard, to stir up trouble. See Declaration of a Cherokee Indian, May 2, 1826, NA; Juan Martín de Veramendi to José Antonio Saucedo, September 1, 1825, Mateo Ahumada to Antonio Elozúa, September 4 and November 13, 1825, Austin to Saucedo, September 8, 1825, Rafael Gonzáles to Ahumada, September 10, 1825, Gonzáles to Saucedo, September 22 and November 1, 1825, Ahumada to Saucedo, November 10, 1825, and Saucedo to Ahumada, November 11, 1825, BA; Austin to Saucedo, September 8, 1825, Austin to Ahumada, September 8 and 10, 1825, Referendum on Indian Relations (Austin), September 28, 1825, John G. Purnell to Fields, October 4, 1825, and F. Durcy to François Grappé, November 10, 1825, *Austin Papers,* vol. 2, 1194, 1196–1197, 1097–1098, 1208, 1220–1221, 1231–1232.

46. For Arciniega's instructions, see Ahumada to Austin, February 1, 1826, Lucas de Palacio to comisario particular at Bexar, February 6, 1826, and Ahumada to commandant general, February 17, 1826, BA.

47. Fields to Saucedo, March 20, 1826, Herbert Eugene Bolton Papers, Bancroft Library, University of California, Berkeley. For Arciniega see Saucedo's and Ahumada's responses, in Saucedo to Ahumada, April 13, 1826, and Ahumada to Gutiérrez de Lara, April 15, 1826, BA.

48. Ahumada to Austin, April 10, 1826, BA; Austin to Ahumada April 10, 1826, *Austin Papers,* vol. 2, 1300–1303. At this time, the only real evidence of possible Wichita raiding against the new Anglo settlements came in April when seventeen Tawakonis were surprised by militia troops along the lower Colorado River. Eight Tawakonis were killed and others wounded. They had ropes with them. One report suggested that the party was in search of Tonkawas, their enemies, and may have meant no harm to the Anglos. See Austin to commanding general, April 6, 1826, *Austin Papers,* vol. 2, 1304.

49. Austin to Fields, April 24, 1826, *Austin Papers,* vol. 2, 1307–1309.

50. Austin to Ahumada, May 8, 1826, Austin to Cherokee chiefs, May 8, 1826, Austin to Ross and Buckner, May 13, 1826, and Ahumada to Austin, May 18, 1826, *Austin Papers,* vol. 2, 1323–1325, 1332–1333, 1316–1317. Ahumada's force never materialized, probably because Bernardo Gutiérrez de Lara had embezzled a large sum of money earmarked for its supply. See James E. B. Austin to Austin, August 22, 1826, *Austin Papers,* vol. 2, 1430.

51. Austin to Ahumada, May 18, 1826, *Austin Papers,* vol. 2, 1338–1340.

52. Austin to Saucedo, June 6, 1826, and Ahumada to Gutiérrez de Lara, July 23, 1826, BA; recollections of Captain Gibson Kuykendall, May 22–23, 1826, Kuykendall Papers; Austin to Ahumada, June 16 and July 31, 1826, and Saucedo to Austin, June 29, 1826, *Austin Papers,* vol. 2, 1359–1360, 1395, 1364. Tijerina argues another side of the debate over militia organization. The governor of the state of Coahuila-Texas in 1828–1829 was at times perturbed over Austin's failure to keep an active militia in the field. See Tijerina, *Tejanos and Texas,* 88–89.

53. Juan José Llanos to Ahumada, February 18, 1826, Ahumada to Gutiérrez de Lara, March 16, 1826, Ahumada to Elozúa, April 2 and November 12, 1826, Saucedo to Ahumada, April 5, 1826, Tomás de Oquillas to Elozúa, October 14, 1826, Elozúa to Anastacio Bustamante, November 1 and 27, 1826, Vicente Arreola to Elozúa, December 8 and 13, 1826, Ahumada to Bustamante, December 10, 1826, BA; Saucedo to alcalde at Nacogdoches, June 26 and November 7, 1826, and Austin to Saucedo, August 14, 1826, NA; Austin to Saucedo, July 17, 1826, *Austin Papers,* vol. 2, 1374.

CHAPTER 4. THE MUDDLE OF EARLY MEXICAN FEDERALISM

1. The first serious discussion of the growing Indian and Anglo presence in Texas is found in a commission report filed in 1823. See report of Francisco Rojo and Alexandro Treviño, May 26, 1823, "Blue Transcripts," NA.

2. See Vito Alessio Robles, *Coahuila y Texas: Desde la consumación de la independencia hasta el tratado de paz de Guadalupe Hidalgo,* 2 vols. (Mexico City: Editorial Porrúa, 1979), 1:214–220.

3. Fields to Saucedo, March 20, 1826, Bolton Papers; Saucedo to Ahumada, April 13, 1826, BA.

4. Fields to Saucedo, March 20, 1826, Bolton Papers; Saucedo to Ahumada, April 13, 1826, and Ahumada to Gutiérrez de Lara, April 15, 1826, BA; Graham to William Clark, May 29, 1826, NARG 75, LR, St. Louis Superintendency. See also Everett, *Texas Cherokees,* 33–37.

5. Ahumada to Antonio Elozúa, April 2 and November 12, 1826, Saucedo to Ahumada, April 5, 1826, Vincente Arreola to Elozúa, December 13, 1826, Elozúa to Anastacio Bustamante, November 1 and 26, 1826, and Ahumada to Bustamante, December 10, 1826, BA; Austin to Saucedo, August 14, 1826, NA; Austin to Saucedo, July 17, 1826, and Fields to Austin, August 27, 1826, *Austin Papers,* vol. 2, 1374 and 1440.

6. See James E. B. Austin to Austin, August 22, 1826, *Austin Papers,* vol. 2, 1430. Gutiérrez de Lara had reported in February that he was purchasing 1,000 horses in Coahuila for the mounted army that he intended to use against "las familias de los Indios Comanches." See Gutiérrez de Lara to Saucedo, February 2, 1826, BA.

7. Fields to Norris, May 24 and August 26, 1826, Gutiérrez de Lara to commandant general, June 1, 1826, and Saucedo to Alcalde Norris, November 16, 1826, NA; James Kerr to Austin, August 23, 1826, and Norris to Austin, October 3, 1826, *Austin Papers,* vol. 2, 1435 and 1470.

8. See Drinnon, *White Savage,* 3–13, 37–57, 178–197. For Hunter's memoir, see John Dunn Hunter, *Memoirs of a Captivity among the Indians of North America,* ed. Richard Drinnon (New York: Schocken Books, 1973). Mexican officials had considerable knowledge of Hunter and his purpose and basically ignored his appeals in behalf of Fields. See Saucedo to Victor Blanco, January 9, 1827, Saltillo Archives transcripts, BL; Elozúa to Gutiérrez de Lara, August 20, 1826, and Samuel Norris to Erasmo Seguín, August 22, 1826, BA; James Kerr to Austin, August 23, 1826, and Fields to Austin, August 27, 1826, *Austin Papers,* vol. 2, 1435, 1440; Norris report, August 22, 1826, and September 5, 1826, Blake Papers; Bean to alcalde of Nacogdoches, June 28, 1826, Fields to Norris, August 26, 1826, and Austin to Saucedo, August 28, 1826, NA. Hayden Edwards provides the best insight into Hunter's role in his letter to George Gray, May 17, 1827, NARG 75, LR, Red River Agency.

9. Saucedo's request may also have been influenced by Austin, who feared that Comanches would overrun his colony by the fall of 1826. From a military standpoint, Austin argued, "100 Cherokee warriors are decidedly superior to 500 Comanches." Austin to Saucedo, September 11, 1826, *Austin Papers,* vol. 2, 1452. On slavery, see Barker, *Life of Stephen F. Austin,* 204–206.

10. Sepulveda to Saucedo, November 13 and 28, 1826, and Sepulveda, Anastasio de la Serda, and Eduardo Arriola to Saucedo, December 3, 1826, Blake Papers; Saucedo to Ahumada, December 10, 1826, BA; "A Bloody Christmas Eve," Newspaper Clippings file, December 26, 1826, Halton-Meisenheimer Papers, Ralph W. Steen Library, Stephen F. Austin State University, Nacogdoches, Texas; Bean to Saucedo, December 31, 1826, NA. The Fredonia Revolt is dealt with in a variety of secondary studies. See Edmund M. Parsons, "The Fredonian Rebellion," *Texana* 21 (Spring 1967): 11–52; Everett, *Texas Cherokees,* 25–41; Lay, *Lives of Ellis P. Bean,* 120–130.

11. Several copies of the December 21, 1826, "Declaration" issued by Edwards and Fields have survived. See them in Blake Papers and Saltillo Archives transcripts, BL.

12. Bean to Austin, December 25, 1826, and Edwards to Green DeWitt, December 25, 1826, Saltillo Archives transcripts, BL; "A Bloody Christmas Eve," December 26, 1826, Newspaper Clippings File, Halton-Meisenheimer Papers. There is some evidence that Austin's militia commanders, discontented over the inability of Mexico and Austin to protect the frontier, inadvertently encouraged Edwards by writing him that Saucedo and Austin could bring together only some 30 soldiers. See Bean to Saucedo, December 31, 1826, NA. Austin and Bean both worked feverishly to divide the rebels. Bean wrote to Fields that, in reality, Hunter's failure in Mexico City had occurred because he "lacked credentials" and that the Cherokees would eventually get land. Austin sent emissaries to the Cherokees, who were offered amnesty by the Mexican government and once again were promised land. See Austin to Saucedo, January 2, 1827, Saltillo Archives transcripts, BL; Bean to Fields, January 4, 1827, Blake Papers; Austin to Cherokee chiefs, January 4, 1827, and James Kerr to Austin, January 27, 1827, *Austin Papers,* vol. 2, 1592–1593, 1591–1592.

13. Quotation in Cantrell, *Stephen F. Austin,* 185.

14. Bean to Ahumada, February 7, 1827, Blake Papers; Ahumada to Bustamante, February 13, 1827, Ahumada to Austin and Francisco Rojo, February 16, 1827, and Ahumada to Bustamante, March 11, 1827, BA. The infighting between Bowles and Fields eventually produced a split in the Texas Cherokees as some of the Indians loyal to Fields later fled back to Indian Territory. See Alexander Cummings to Matthew Arbuckle, March 4, 1827, in Carter and Bloom, *Territorial Papers,* 20:413–414. Mariano Sánchez reported that most of the Caddos and Kickapoos wanted nothing to do with Fields or Edwards. The Caddo "captain" at Nacogdoches had spurned Fields in council, telling him "with a finger [pointing at Fields], that he [Fields] was blind, and that the Americans [including Edwards] always have fought with them." See Patricio de Torres to Bexar postmaster, January 14, 1827, BA. The slavery compromise is complicated; see Tijerina, *Tejanos and Texas,* 111–115.

15. Alessio Robles, *Coahuila y Texas,* 1:222.

16. Bean to Ahumada, February 25, 1827, Martin de Leon to Saucedo, March 11, 1827, Ahumada to Bustamante, March 11, 1827, Patricio de Torres to postmaster at Bexar, March 20, 1827, Ruíz to Ahumada, April 14 and May 14, 1827, José Candido de Arcos to Elozúa, April 16, 1827, Bustamante to Candido de Arcos, April 19, 1827, and Lucas de Papaccio to comisario particular, April 30, 1827, BA; Bustamante to Ahumada, April 27, 1827, NA.

17. Ruíz to Austin, May 28 and June 2, 1827, and Bean to Austin, June 3, 1827, *Austin Papers,* vol. 2, 1627, 1653, and 1656; Ruíz to Ahumada, June 3, 1827, and Patricio de Torres to Erasmo Seguín, June 13, 1827, BA.

18. A large party of Comanches had negotiated a similar treaty at Chihuahua in October 1826. See Treaty with Comanches, October 18, 1826, SANM.

19. Bustamante to Austin, June 19, 1827, *Austin Papers,* vol. 2, 1660; Bustamante to Elozúa, June 18 and July 27, 1827, and Peace Treaty, July 31, 1827, BA.

20. Bustamante to Elozúa, July 27, 1827, BA. Manuel Barrera from San Antonio followed up this treaty with another council in the Wichita towns in October. See Barrera's talks with Miguel Menchaca, Quirue, Aniseria, Ontecuia, Pashata, and El Bicho, October 5, 1827, BA.

21. Ayuntamiento to Elozúa, September 27, 1827, diary of events at Laredo, October 14, 1827, Bustamante to Elozúa, October 5, 1827, Vicente Arreola to Elozúa, October 14, 1827, Tomás de Oquillas to Elozúa, November 26, 1827, and Bustamante to Saucedo, December 23, 1827, BA.

22. See ayuntamiento to Elozúa, September 27, 1827, Bustamante to Elozúa, October 5, 1827, and José Antonio Rodriguez to Elozúa, October 13, 1827, BA.

23. Mariano Cosió to Ahumada, June 26, 1827, BA; Ahumada to commandant general of the interior states, July 10, 1827, Fomento-Colonización transcripts, BL.

24. For discussions of immigrant Indian populations see Dana Dickson to Henry Clay, July 1, 1827, Dispatches from Consuls in Texas, 1825–1844, Eugene C. Barker Library, Austin; Austin to Francisco Madero, November 11, 1827, *Austin Papers,* vol. 2, 1721–1722; *Arkansas Gazette,* January 15, 1828. Edwards's report on Fredonia is in Edwards to George Gray, May 27, 1827, in Carter and Bloom, *Territorial Papers,* 20:482–483.

25. Actually, Kickapoo fears regarding Durst turned out to be valid, since he quickly forwarded a report of the council to Americans at Natchitoches. See John Sibley to Edmund P. Gaines, June 26, 1827, in Carter and Bloom, *Territorial Papers,* 20:494–495; Cosió to Ahumada, July 10, 1827, and Bustamante to secretario de guerra, August 9, 1827, Fomento-Colonización transcripts, BL; Bustamante to Ahumada, July 11, 1827, and Piedras to Elozúa, December 28, 1827, BA.

26. G. Prorain to the secretary in charge of Ministry of Foreign Relations, August 3, 1827, Fomento-Colonización transcripts, BL.

27. Mateo Ahumada to the commandant general of the Interior States of the East, July 10, 1827, Fomento-Colonización transcripts, BL.

28. Austin to Madero, November 11, 1827, *Austin Papers,* vol. 1, 1721–1722. Austin had received letters from other colonists reflecting the same views, particularly concerning the hostility of the Shawnees. See, for example, Hugh B. Johnston to Austin, November 9, 1829, *Austin Papers,* vol. 2, 283–284.

29. Gray to secretary of war, June 13, 1827, in Carter and Bloom, *Territorial Papers,* 20:479–481.

30. Petition of inhabitants of Pecan Point, March 22, 1828, Major S. G. W. Pearson to Governor George Izard, March 22, 1828, Izard to Rector, April 7, 1828, and Rector to Izard, May 8, 1828, NARG 75, LR, Arkansas Superintendency; certificate of Jesse Shelton, summer 1828, in Carter and Bloom, *Territorial Papers,* 20:788; *Arkansas Gazette,* April 16 and May 7, 1828.

31. Hyde to adjutant general, November 17, 1828, in Carter and Bloom, *Territorial Papers,* 20:784–785. Emphasis in original.

CHAPTER 5. CENTRALISTS AND THE STRUGGLE FOR TEXAS LAND

1. Jack Jackson and John Wheat have recently translated and edited Mier y Terán's 1828 journal. See Jackson and Wheat, ed. and trans., *Texas by Terán* (Austin: University of Texas Press, 2000). Other copies of this journal are in the Yale University Library and the Herbert Eugene Bolton Papers in the Bancroft Library. See, for example, report of Mier y Terán to the minister of foreign affairs, June 9, 1828, Guerra y Marina, Barker transcripts, BL (also in Bolton Papers, Bancroft Library). For a discussion of centralism and federalism, see Michael P. Costeloe, *The*

Central Republic in Mexico, 1835–1846: Hombres de Bien *in the Age of Santa Anna* (New York: Cambridge University Press, 1993).

2. "Noticias sobre la frontera de Méjico copias de diario de viage que necesitan correcciones. Año de 1828," May 26–June 3, 1828, Guerra y Marina, Barker transcripts, BL; Bean to Mier y Terán, July 11, 1828, Guerra y Marina, Barker transcripts, BL; Berlandier, *Indians of Texas,* 11–13.

3. Mier y Terán, "Noticias sobre la frontera de Mejico copias de diario de viage que necesitan correcciones. Año de 1828." Guerra y Marina, Barker transcripts, BL.

4. Mier y Terán to the president, June 9, 1828, Guerra y Marina, Barker transcripts, BL. On the Cherokee town, see José Maria Sanchez, "A Trip to Texas 1828," *Southwestern Historical Quarterly* 29 (April 1926): 286. While Diana Everett has identified Bowles as the political or peace chief of the Texas Cherokees, both primary and secondary sources clearly dispute this. And Bowles would later lead the defense of his village during the 1839 Cherokee war. Jackson and Wheat have listed the many sources that identify Bowles as a war leader. See Jackson and Wheat, *Texas by Terán,* 237–238n.159; Everett, *Texas Cherokees,* 26.

5. Mier y Terán to the president, June 9, 1828, Guerra y Marina, Barker transcripts, BL.

6. Mier y Terán to the president, July 7, 1828, Guerra y Marina, Barker transcripts, BL.

7. Mier y Terán to Victoria, June 30, 1828, in Alleine Howren, "The Causes and Origins of the Decree of April 6, 1830," *Southwestern Historical Quarterly* 16 (April 1916): 395–398.

8. Piedras to the commanding officer at Saltillo, June 8 and 26, 1828, NA.

9. Bean to Mier y Terán, July 11, 1828, Guerra y Marina, Barker transcripts, BL. Another description of this council is found in Sanchez, "A Trip to Texas, 1828," 286–287.

10. Bean to Mier y Terán, July 11, 1828, Guerra y Marina, Barker transcripts, BL.

11. Elozúa to military chief of Nuevo León, January 16, 1829, Elozúa to Bustamante, January 19, 1829, Nicasio Sánchez to Elozúa, March 15, 1829, and Bustamante to Elozúa, April 18, 1829, BA.

12. Green DeWitt to Austin, March 3, 1829, and DeWitt to Ramón Músquiz, May 8, 1829, *Austin Papers,* vol. 2, 175, 215–216.

13. Bustamante to Austin, March 23, 1829, *Austin Papers,* vol. 2, 194–195; Elozúa to Bustamante, April 11, 1829, BA.

14. Ruíz's report is enclosed with Elozúa to Felipe de la Garza, June 2, 1829, BA. See also Ruíz to Elozúa, May 23, 1829, BA.

15. Músquiz to Austin, May 28, 1829, and Austin to Elozúa, July 29, 1829, *Austin Papers,* vol. 2, 219, 242–243; Bean to Elozúa, June 9, 1829, BA; Felipe de Garza to Elozúa, June 20, 1929, NA.

16. Ruíz diary of events at San Antonio, July 16, 1829, and treaty of peace with Wacos and Tawakonies, August 22, 1829, BA.

17. Memoir, 1829, Kuykendall Papers.

18. Músquiz to Elozúa, January 12, 1830, Músquiz to José Maria Viesca, February 14, 1830, Elozúa to Mier y Terán, March 6, 1830, and Bean to Elozúa, March 6, 1830, BA.

19. Bean to Elozúa, June 22, 1830, and Ruíz to Elozúa, August 1, 1830, BA; (Elozúa) to commandant general and inspector of the internal states (Mier y Terán), June 28, 1830, Guerra y Marina, Barker transcripts, BL. An interesting account of the battle, recorded in 1842, is found in John Henry Brown, *Indian Wars and Pioneers of Texas* (Austin: L. E. Daniell, 1897), 13–14.

20. Elozúa to Mier y Terán, September 14, 1830, Elozúa report, September 21, 1830, Nicasio Sánchez to Elozúa, September 19, 1830, Gaspar López to Músquiz, September 19, 1830, Mier y Terán to Elozúa, September 24, 1830, Ruíz to Elozúa, August 6, 1831, José Dionisio Palomo to comisario of Bexar, November 14, 1831, BA; memoir, Kuykendall Papers.

21. Músquiz to ayuntamiento of Bexar, August 8, 1831, NA; José Maria Viesca to Músquiz, February 5, 1831, José Manuel Barberena to Alozúa, August 21, 1831, Ignacio Rodríguez to Elozúa, August 24, 1831, Mier y Terán to Elozúa, October 4, 1831, José Maria Garcia to Elozúa, October 22, 1831, José Dionisio Palomo to comisario of Bexar, November 14, 1831, Manuel la Fuente to Elozúa, November 24, 1831, and Elozúa to José Mariano Guerra, December 31, 1831, BA.

22. Smallpox first appeared in Matamoros and Goliad in January 1831, spreading to the eastern Caddos by spring. See Músquiz to José Maria Viesca, January 31, 1831, Ruíz to Elozúa, June 11, 1831, and Manuel de los Santos Coy to Músquiz, July 5, 1831, BA; D. W. Smith to Martin Van Buren, February 6, 1831, Matamoros Consul Records, microfilm, BL.

23. Howren, "The Causes and Origins of the Decree of April 6, 1830," 406–413.

24. Mier y Terán to secretario de relaciones, interior y exterior, September 12, 1830, Fomento-Colonización transcripts, BL; Frost Thorn to Austin, October 29, 1830, and Mier y Terán to Austin, February 5, 1831, *Austin Papers,* vol. 2, 524 and 576–577; Músquiz to the alcalde of Nacogdoches, April 12, 1831, NA. For a biography of the controversial commander at Anahuac, see Margaret Swett Henson, *Juan Davis Bradburn: A Reappraisal of the Mexican Commander of Anahuac* (College Station: Texas A and M University Press, 1982).

25. Barker, *Life of Stephen F. Austin,* 262–265.

26. Ibid., 97–98.

27. Secretario de relaciones to excellency senior, March 5, 1830, and Victor Blanco to excellency senior governor (at Saltillo), June 5, 1830, Guerra y Marina, Barker transcripts, BL; State of Coahuila-Texas, land records, July 24, 1830, Saltillo Archives transcripts, BL; Peter E. Bean to Governor Pope, August 10, 1830, in Carter and Bloom, *Territorial Papers,* 21:264–265; J. M. Guerra, list of land grants, September 30, 1830, and Mier y Terán to José de los Piedras, December 22, 1830, Bolton Papers. James Milam visited at least one of the several Shawnee towns that had been given land by Mier y Terán. He found "30 or 40 cabbins [*sic*]" located on a peninsula making irrigation feasible. See James Milam diary, December 29, 1830, Bancroft Library.

28. Mier y Terán to José de los Piedras, December 22, 1830, Bolton Papers. Mier y Terán also agreed to give land to some 227 Coushatta people and 370 Alabamas living in the Big Thicket of eastern Texas. Francisco Madero, the land commissioner for the region, highly recommended them. See José Maria de Letona to commandant general of Eastern Provinces, June 25, 1831, and Mier y Terán to secretario de relaciones, interior y exterior, Fomento–Colonización transcripts, BL.

29. On the refusal of the Mexican government to grant the Creek Indians land, see Juan Maria Viesca to minister of state and relations, April 19, 1830, secretario de relaciones to Mier y Terán, June 16, 1830, Mier y Terán to secretario de relaciones, July 29, 1830, Piedras to Mier y Terán, August 2, 1830, and Mier y Terán to secretario de relaciones, September 2 and November 15, 1830, Fomento-Colonización transcripts, BL; Piedras to commandant general, December 20, 1830, BA; Mier y Terán to secretario del despacho de relaciones, June 6, 1830, Bolton Papers; Jehiel Brooks to secretary of war, August 16 and September 17, 1830, and January 17, 1831, NARG 75, LR, Caddo Agency; James Bowie to political chief at Bexar, December 10, 1831, NA.

30. José Maria Letona to Músquiz, March 22, 1832, and Músquiz to Letona, April 22, 1832, in Dorman H. Winfrey and James M. Day, eds., *The Indian Papers of Texas and the Southwest, 1825–1916,* 5 vols. (Austin: Pemberton Press, 1966), 1:4 and 14–15; Lieutenant Colonel don José Maria Dias Noriega to governor of state of Coahuila-Texas, April 26, 1832, Saltillo Archives transcripts, BL. At the same time that such orders were being issued, the state legislature of

Coahuila-Texas allowed David G. Burnet and José Vehlein three more years to prove up their *empresario* grants. See José Maria de Letona certificate, April 28, 1832, NA; Elozúa to José Mariano Guerra, May 30, 1832, BA. Elozúa dates the extension April 27, 1832, but the certificate shows that it was authorized by the state a day later.

31. Músquiz to Letona, January 30, 1832, Ruíz to Elozúa, February 4, 1832, Manuel Fuente to Elozúa, February 9, 1832, José Antonio de la Garza to Letona, February 11, 1832, report of Trinidad Coy, February 11, 1832, and Elozúa to Mier y Terán, February 28, 1832, BA.

32. Piedras to Elozúa, May 21 and June 18, 1832, Elozúa to Piedras, June 4, 1832, Elozúa to Músquiz, June 4, 1832, ayuntamiento to Músquiz, July 4, 1832, and Juan Hernández to Elozúa, July 13, 1832, BA.

33. The treaty was finally signed by both countries on January 12, 1828. A copy is printed in Hunter Miller, ed., *Treaties and Other International Acts of the United States of America* (Washington, D.C.: Government Printing Office, 1933), 405–411. The treaty endorsed a boundary separating the two countries that essentially followed the same line as that of 1819, starting at the mouth of the Sabine River and running north to where it intercepts the 32nd degree latitude, thence to the Red River and up the Red to the 100th degree longitude. The treaty also considered Indian depredations along the Santa Fe Trail; President Jackson requested a thorough investigation of the issue. Several reports regarding the Indian "menace" are contained in secretary of war to the president, February 8, 1832, Senate Document 90, 22nd Cong., 1st sess., ser. 213.

34. The full text of the treaty and later protocols are in Miller, ed., *Treaties*, 599–644.

35. Miller, ed., *Treaties*, 622–623.

36. For this period see Costeloe, *Central Republic in Mexico*; Weber, *Mexican Frontier*, 242–272. The best description of Mier y Terán's last days is found in Jackson and Wheat, *Texas by Terán*, 186–187.

37. Lundy Journal, June–July 1832, Ohio Historical Society, Columbus.

38. Lundy Journal, July 2–6, 1832.

39. M. K. Wisehart, *Sam Houston: American Giant* (Washington, D.C.: Robert B. Luce, 1962), 103–105.

40. Many biographies of Houston have been written. See Wisehart, *Sam Houston*; Llerena B. Friend, *Sam Houston: The Great Designer* (Austin: University of Texas Press, 1954); Randolph B. Campbell, *Sam Houston and the American Southwest* (New York: HarperCollins, 1993); and Haley, *Sam Houston*. The most useful literary effort is Marquis James, *The Raven: A Biography of Sam Houston* (Indianapolis: Bobbs-Merrill, 1929).

CHAPTER 6. THE AMERICANIZATION OF TEXAS

1. John A. Wharton to Houston, June 2, 1832, and Houston to James Prentiss, June 9 and August 18, 1832, Houston Papers, BL.

2. The best discussion of Houston's tenure in Indian Territory is found in Brad Agnew, *Fort Gibson: Terminal on the Trails of Tears* (Norman: University of Oklahoma Press, 1980), 77–88. For other accounts see Jack Gregory and Renard Strickland, *Sam Houston and the Cherokee, 1829–1833* (Austin: University of Texas Press, 1967); Frank Foreman, "Some New Lights on Houston's Life among the Cherokee Indians," *Chronicles of Oklahoma* 9 (June 1931): 139–157; Mary Whatley Clarke, *Chief Bowles and the Texas Cherokees* (Norman: University of Oklahoma Press, 1971).

3. A good description of the event is found in Robert L. Jones and Pauline H. Jones, "Houston's Politics and the Cherokee," *Chronicles of Oklahoma* 46 (Winter 1968–1969): 418–432.

4. Tijerina has an excellent discussion of how many Tejanos bought into this capitalistic strategy, calling the group the "Coahuiltejano" capitalists. See Tijerina, *Tejanos and Texas,* 113–136.

5. Ruíz to Elozúa, August 1 and 15, 1832, James W. Bullak to Elozúa, August 15, 1832, and Elozúa to Ruíz, August 15, 1832, BA.

6. See, for example, Elozúa to José Antonio de la Garza, August 29, 1832, Manuel de Dios diary, September 2, 1832, Manuel de Sáenz diary, September 7, 1832, Elozúa to commandant at Matamoros, September 10, 1832, Elozúa to Ignacio de Mora, September 15, 1832, Antonio López to Elozúa, September 19, 1832, Agustin del Moral to Elozúa, September 20, 1832, Juan José Hernandez to José Antonio de la Garza, September 22, 1832, José Andrés de Sobrevilla to Elozúa, September 29, 1832, and Elozúa to commandant general of Coahuila-Texas, November 3, 1832, BA.

7. Músquiz letters, unaddressed, September 22 and November 19, 1832, BA.

8. Elozúa to Juan Martin de Veramendi, February 8, 1833, Manuel Barragán's diary, February 14, 1833, case against citizens from Taos for aiding Comanches, April 6, 1833, Alejandro Treviño to Elozúa, March 27, 1833, and Vicente Filisola to Elozúa, May 27, 1833, BA; military commander of Coahuila-Texas (Barragán) to minister of war, February 20, 1833, "White Transcripts," NA.

9. A good description of Fort Terán and Bean's role in building it is in the online *Handbook of Texas* http://www.tsha.utexas.edu/handbook/online/.

10. Bean to Lewis Cass, February 24, 1833, "White Transcripts," NA. See also Bean to Jehiel Brooks, February 25, 1833, NARG 75, LR, Caddo Agency.

11. For the military situation in Indian Territory, see Agnew, *Fort Gibson,* 29–33. While Fort Jesup in Louisiana initially had been garrisoned with four companies of troops, that number had decreased to 127 men by 1825. See J. Fair Hardin, "Fort Jesup—Fort Selden—Camp Sabine—Camp Salubrity: Four Forgotten Frontier Army Posts in Western Louisiana," part 1, *Louisiana Historical Quarterly* 16 (January 1933): 14–15. For the inability of these troops to control trade and feuding, see Francis Paul Prucha, *American Indian Policy in the Formative Years: The Indian Trade and Intercourse Acts, 1790–1834* (Lincoln: University of Nebraska Press, 1962), 169–178.

12. Brooks to Elbert Herring, April 4, 1833, Brooks to Leavenworth, April 6, 1833, Brooks to Herring, April 9, 1833, Leavenworth to Brooks, May 2, 1833, and Brooks to Bean, May 15, 1833, NARG 75, LR, Caddo Agency.

13. Armstrong to Lewis Cass, April 13 and 20, 1832, and September 26, 1832, NARG 75, LR, Choctaw Agency West.

14. Arbuckle to adjutant general, July 25, 1832, in Carter and Bloom, *Territorial Papers,* 21:523–525.

15. For descriptions of the commission and the negotiations, see Arrell Morgan Gibson, *The American Indian: Prehistory to the Present* (Lexington, Mass.: D. C. Heath, 1980), 314–315; David LaVere, *Contrary Neighbors: Southern Plains and Removed Indians in Indian Territory* (Norman: University of Oklahoma Press, 2000), 72–90. See also Ellsworth to Herring, December 11, 1833, NARG 75, LR, Western Superintendency; William Clark to Lewis Cass, June 18, 1832, NARG 75, LR, St. Louis Superintendency. Clark's figure of 72 Comanche dead conflicts with a report of 77 in the *Arkansas Gazette,* June 20, 1832.

16. See, for example, White Hair's Band, Little Osage's Band, and Clairmont's Band to Andrew Jackson, May 17, 1832, NARG 75, LR, Osage Agency; *Arkansas Gazette,* August 14, 1833.

17. Ellsworth to Herring, December 11, 1833, S. C. Stambaugh to Lewis Cass, December 22, 1832, and Stokes to Cass, August 15, October 27 and November 26, 1833, NARG 75, LR, Western Superintendency.

18. Houston's sojourn with the Cherokees in Indian Territory is the subject of Gregory and Strickland, *Sam Houston and the Cherokee.*

19. Houston to Ellsworth, December 1, 1832, Houston Papers, BL.

20. For Houston's interest in land, see Houston to James Prentiss, June 1 and 9 and August 18, 1832, and John W. Wharton to Houston, June 2, 1832, Houston Papers, BL.

21. Houston to Indian commissioners, February 13, 1833, Houston to Henry Raguet, February 13, 1833, and Houston to Prentiss, March 28, 1834, Houston Papers, BL. Houston was also encouraged to get involved in a scheme to buy land for the migrating Chickasaws. See A. C. Allen to Houston, February 28, 1834, A. J. Houston Papers, TSL.

22. See W. B. Morrison, "A Journey across Oklahoma, Ninety Years Ago," *Chronicles of Oklahoma* 4 (December 1926): 333–337.

23. Pike to Cass, March 16, 1833, NARG 75, LR, Western Superintendency. Another copy is found in the Chouteau Papers.

24. *Arkansas Gazette,* June 12, 1833; General Leavenworth to Brooks, May 11, 1834, NARG 75, LR, Caddo Agency. See Carolyn Thomas Forman, "Colonel James B. Many: Commandant at Fort Gibson, Fort Towson, and Fort Smith," *Chronicles of Oklahoma* 19 (June 1941): 119–128.

25. De la Teja, "Colonization and Independence of Texas," 923–993; Tijerina, *Tejanos and Texas,* 130; de la Teja, *A Revolution Remembered,* 19–23.

26. Barker, *Life of Stephen F. Austin,* 348–369.

27. Ibid., 370–375. While Farías ordered Austin's arrest, he had just the month before finally acquired an audience with General Santa Anna in which several agreements were reached, including a revocation of the April 1830 immigration law. On the epidemic, see Barker, *Life of Stephen F. Austin,* 395.

28. Biographer James Haley suspects that Houston stayed in Washington, Arkansas, because of a land scheme involving Benjamin Hawkins. Houston had told Hawkins that he expected to negotiate with Texas Indians on the upper Trinity River in June, and this corresponds with the march of the U.S. Army across Indian Territory that summer. More than likely, Houston was waiting to see what opportunities that army would create for filibustering in Texas. See Haley, *Sam Houston,* 102.

29. Colonel Leavenworth ordered Lieutenant William Eustis to carry the requests of the commission to Nacogdoches, Texas. Schermerhorn to Stokes, April 21, 1834, Stokes and Schermerhorn to Leavenworth, May 12 and 27, 1834, Brooks to Leavenworth, June 4, 1834, NARG 393, Correspondence and Reports Relating to Special Subjects, 1831–1851, LR, 2nd Military Department; Benjamin Hawkins to Samuel Stambaugh, May 26, 1834, NARG 75, LR, Western Superintendency; Agnew, *Fort Gibson,* 121–122.

30. Colonel Juan Nepomuceno Almonte to Stokes and Schermerhorn, June 18, 1834, NARG 393, LR, 2nd Military Department.

31. Carolyn Thomas Forman, "Nathan Boone: Trapper, Manufacturer, Surveyor, Militiaman, Legislator, Ranger, and Dragoon," *Chronicles of Oklahoma* 19 (December 1941): 322–247.

32. Good descriptions of the entire expedition are found in Agnew, *Fort Gibson,* 123–136, and LaVere, *Contrary Neighbors,* 72–90.

33. Quotation is from Carolyn Thomas Forman, "Black Beaver," *Chronicles of Oklahoma* 24 (Autumn 1946): 269–292. See also Stan Hoig, "Jesse Chisholm: Peace-maker, Trader, Forgotten Frontiersman," *Chronicles of Oklahoma* 66 (Winter 1988–89): 350–373.

34. The description of the disease is from Lieutenant Colonel Stephen Watts Kearny in his letter to Colonel R. Jones, July 22, 1834, NARG 393, LR, 2nd Military Department. Caddos

who reached the sick camp on the Washita River likely helped spread the cholera outbreak in Louisiana on their return.

35. "Journal of Col. Dodge's Expedition from Fort Gibson to the Pawnee Pict Village," August 26, 1834, *American State Papers: Military Affairs,* 5:375–376.

36. "Journal of Col. Dodge's Expedition," 376–377.

37. Ibid., 377.

38. Ibid., 381–382.

39. Arbuckle to R. Jones, February 1, 1835, NARG 393, Letters Sent (hereafter referred to as LS), 2nd Military Department.

40. Cass to Stokes, March 26, 1835, NARG 75, LR, Western Superintendency; Arbuckle to Major General Alexander McComb, NARG 393, LS, 2nd Military Department; Agnew, *Fort Gibson,* 143–144.

41. Captain John Stuart to Lieutenant W. Seawell, March 28, 1835, NARG 393, LR, Ft. Coffee; Arbuckle to Brigadier General R. Jones, April 3, 1835, NARG 75, LR, Western Superintendency.

42. For the quotations on Delaware depredations, see R. A. McCabe to Armstrong, April 5, 1835, NARG 75, LR, Creek Agency West. See also Armstrong to Elbert Herring, April 16, 1835, NARG 75, LR, Creek Agency West; Arbuckle to Jones, April 3, 1835, NARG 75, LR, Western Superintendency; Colonel Harold W. Jones, "Notes and Documents: The Diary of Assistant Surgeon Leonard McPhail on His Journey to the Southwest in 1835," *Chronicles of Oklahoma* 18 (September 1940): 281–292.

43. McCabe to Armstrong, April 9, 1835, Arbuckle to Cass, May 5, 1835, and Stokes, Arbuckle, and Armstrong to Cass, May 14, 1835, NARG 75, LR, Western Superintendency; Arbuckle to Jones, April 15, 1835, NARG 75, LR, Choctaw Agency West; Agnew, *Fort Gibson,* 144–145. The exact location of Camp Holm, also called Camp Mason, was on the left bank of the Canadian River, near present-day Asher, Oklahoma. See also Grant Foreman, "The Journal of the Proceedings at Our First Treaty with Wild Indians, 1835," *Chronicles of Oklahoma* 14 (December 1936): 393–413.

44. Colonel Henry Dodge, "Journal of a Detachment of Dragoons under the Command of Colonel Dodge, during the Summer of 1835," *American State Papers: Military Affairs,* 6:130–143. Hugh Evans left a journal account of this expedition. He noted the appearance of comanchero traders from New Mexico who had already started bringing whiskey among the Cheyenne and Arapaho Indians. While Dodge was negotiating with their leaders in Bent's Fort, Evans attended a "predicament" in which all the Indians—"men, women and children[—]were drunk." See Fred S. Perrine, ed., "Hugh Evan's Journal of Colonel Henry Dodge's Expedition to the Rocky Mountains in 1835," *Mississippi Valley Historical Review* 14 (September 1927): 211–212.

45. Mason to Arbuckle, July 8 and 12, 1835, NARG 393, LR, 2nd Military Department. See also Armstrong to Herring, June 18, 1835, NARG 75, LR, Western Superintendency; Arbuckle to Mason, June 22, 1835, and Seawell to Mason, July 8, 1835, NARG 393, LS, 2nd Military Department.

46. Mason to Seawell, July 17, 1835, NARG 393, LR, 2nd Military Department. See also his follow-up letter, Mason to Seawell, July 20 and 26, 1935, NARG 393, LR, 2nd Military Department.

47. Arbuckle to Mason, August 6, 1835, treaty articles with the Comanche, Wichita, Cherokee, Muscogee, Choctaw, Osage, Seneca and Quapaw Indians, August 24, 1835, and Arbuckle to Jones, September 13, 1835, NARG 393, LS, 2nd Military Department. A printed copy of the negotiation is found in Grant Foreman, "The Journal of the Proceedings at Our First Treaty with the Wild Indians, 1835," *Chronicles of Oklahoma* 14 (December 1936): 406–417. See also

Agnew, *Fort Gibson,* 146–150. For a more detailed discussion of the Stokes Commission and its work within Indian Territory, see LaVere, *Contrary Neighbors,* 72–90.

48. Arbuckle to Cass, September 15, 1835, NARG 75, LR, Western Superintendency.

49. See Mason to Seawell, July 26, 1835, NARG 393, LR, 2nd Military Department.

50. Mason to Seawell, July 24, 1835, NARG 393, LR, 2nd and 7th Military Departments. See also Stokes and Arbuckle to secretary of war, December 29, 1835, NARG 75, LR, Western Superintendency.

51. See William C. Davis, *Three Roads to the Alamo: The Lives and Fortunes of David Crockett, James Bowie, and William Barret Travis* (New York: HarperCollins, 1998), 426–427.

52. De la Teja, *A Revolution Remembered,* 20. For a sketch of the life of Seguín, see Webb and Carroll, eds., *Handbook of Texas,* 2:590.

53. On slavery see Alwyn Barr, *Black Texans: A History of African Americans in Texas, 1528–1995* (Austin: Jenkins Publishing, 1973; reprint, Norman: University of Oklahoma Press, 1996), 15–17; Randolph B. Campbell, *An Empire for Slavery: The Peculiar Institution in Texas, 1821–1865* (Baton Rouge: Louisiana State University Press, 1989), 10–34.

54. A. A. Parker, *Trip to the West and Texas. Comprising A Journey of Eight Thousand Miles, Through New-York, Michigan, Illinois, Missouri, Louisiana, and Texas, in the Autumn and Winter of 1834–1835. Interspersed with Anecdotes, Incidents and Observations. With a Brief Sketch of the Texian War* (Boston: Benjamin B. Mussey, 1836; reprint, Austin and New York: Pemberton Press, 1968), 149–152.

55. See Juan Nepomuceno Almonte, "Statistical Report on Texas," Carlos Castañeda, trans., *Southwestern Historical Quarterly* 28 (January 1925): 177–221.

56. Almonte to secretario de estado y del despo. de relaciones, interiores y exteriores, June 5, 1834, Fomento-Colonización transcripts, BL.

57. This petition was handed to state officials in Monclova by the Cherokee Chief Bowles during the summer of 1833, but since the Mexican political situation was in such turmoil, officials apparently implied that the grant would be made, while knowing full well that a different decision might be made. See petition of "Col. Boles, John Boles, Richard Justice, Piggion, Andrew Mabann, Eli Harlin," July 16, 1833, Saltillo Archives transcripts, BL; petition of Cherokee for land (same petitioners), July 16, 1833, Archivo de la Secretarios de Gobierno del Estado, BL; (Alejandro Treviño) to Peter E. Bean, October 24, 1833, BA.

58. On centralist versus state opinion regarding land grants, see don José Maria Diaz Noriega to the governor of the state of Coahuila-Texas, April 6, 1834, Archivo de la Secretario de Gobierno del Estado, AGN (transcripts, BL); Placido Benavides to Músquiz, June 12, 1834, BA.

59. Almonte to secretario de estado y del despo. de relaciones, interiores y exteriores, May 5, 1834, Fomento-Colonización transcripts, BL.

60. Almonte to governor of the state of Coahuila-Texas, June 16, 1834, Archivo de la Secretario de Gobierno del Estado, Fomento-Colonización transcripts, BL. The response of the Cherokees to Almonte's visit is found in yet another petition, attached to Almonte's report, dated August 25, 1834, probably prepared with some help from Bean. It indicates a degree of impatience with failed Mexican promises but strong support for the Mexican "Great Father the President" and a desire to obtain the "paper" that would finally grant them land. See petition, August 25, 1834, Almonte to governor of state of Coahuila-Texas, June 16, 1834, Archivo de la Secretario de Gobierno del Estado, Fomento-Colonización transcripts, BL. Almonte also provides population figures for the various bands, noting "more than ten thousand" for the Comanches and "two to three hundred men" for the Wichita. See Almonte, "Statistical Report on Texas," 195; Bean to Músquiz, June 16, 1834, BA.

61. See Tijerina, *Tejanos and Texas,* 134–135.

62. Almonte to secretario de relaciones, interiores y exteriores, June 16, 1834, BA; Almonte to Governor Juan José de Elguezabal, September 23, 1834, Almonte to secretario de relaciones, interiores y exteriores, December 10, 1834, and February 20, 1835, Fomento-Colonización transcripts, BL. Martín Perfecto de Cós, who assumed command of troops in San Antonio somewhat later, reported Almonte's fear of the Dodge negotiation to authorities in Mexico City. See Cós to the president of the republic, December 29, 1834, Fomento-Colonización transcripts, BL. Almonte's fears resulted in an exchange of letters with Anthony Butler, the U.S. ambassador, and a debate over the 1831 treaty. See Butler to José M. Gutierrez de Estrada, February 24, 1835, Fomento-Colonización transcripts, BL. See the treaty as Document #70, "Mexico: April 5, September 17, and December 17, 1831," in Miller, ed., *Treaties,* 599–640.

CHAPTER 7. THE TEXAS CREED AND THE CLOUDS OF WAR

1. Rueg to the alcalde of Nacogdoches, February 16, 1835, NA.

2. Ruíz to alcalde at Nacogdoches, February 20, March 8, and July 11 and 29, 1835, in Winfrey and Day, *Indian Papers of Texas,* 1:6–8; Radford Berry to Sheriff James Carter, March 6, 1835, Antonio Tenorio to military commander of Coahuila-Texas, April 9, 1835, and *State vs. Jeremiah Strode,* July 21, 1835, Blake Papers; Rueg to alcalde at Nacogdoches, April 14, 1835, and John Bodin to Rueg, April 16, 1835, NA; Forrest Daniell, "Texas Pioneer Surveyors and Indians," *Southwestern Historical Quarterly* 60 (April 1957): 501–506. Surveyors even invaded the lands of the Cherokee war chief Bowles in November. See George Pollett to Houston, November 10, 1835, A. J. Houston Papers.

3. The source for Hawkins's relationship with Houston is the unpublished "A History and Genealogy of Chief William McIntosh, Jr.," compiled by Harriet Turner (Porter) Corbin and edited by Carl C. Burdick. The author is indebted to Professor Michael Green at the University of North Carolina, who kindly provided a copy. The oral history notes much of interest, including Hawkins's service alongside Houston at the battle of San Jacinto and the fact that he was apparently killed in 1839 "for political reasons," likely a connection to his land schemes or perhaps because of his support of Houston's policy of giving land to the Cherokees.

4. Testimony of Manuel Moran with assistance of Miguel Cortinas and Juan Leon, February 12, 1835, NA; José María Tornel y Mendivil to secretario de relaciones, interiores y exteriores, enclosing letter of governor of Coahuila-Texas, April 9, 1835, Fomento-Colonización transcripts, BL. The plight of the entire McIntosh family is best followed in Michael D. Green, *The Politics of Indian Removal: Creek Government and Society in Crisis* (Lincoln: University of Nebraska Press, 1982), 95–97. Haley notes that Houston was conspiring with Hawkins in the fall of 1834, when the former governor lived in Washington, Arkansas. Haley also believes that Houston promoted the Creek migration to Texas as a way of starting war. When Hawkins's plan for the removal of eastern Indians to Texas backfired, however, Houston promptly disavowed it. See Haley, *Sam Houston,* 102, 106–107. Interestingly, while Haley is convinced that Houston acted with duplicity toward Hawkins, the oral history from the Hawkins family suggests a very close, and long, relationship. See Corbin, "History and Genealogy of Chief William McIntosh." An entirely different view of Houston's activities in 1834–1835 is expressed in Campbell, *Gone to Texas,* 132. Campbell argues that Houston "lived quietly" in Nacogdoches between 1833 and 1835 and tried to prevent war. Campbell is apparently unaware of Houston's scheming with Hawkins, the time he spent in Washington, Arkansas, or his trip to Washington, D.C.

5. Bean to Ugartechea, June 15, 1835, BA; Bean to the military commander at San Antonio, August 18, 1835, Blake Papers; John Forbes, Samuel Houston, Henry Raguet, D. A. Hoffman, S. R. Peck, William G. Logan, and George Pollitt to Jackson, September 11, 1835, Houston Papers, BL.

6. Juan Benito Camacho y Estrada to the political chief at Nacogdoches, March 2, 1835, NA; Domingo de Ugartechea to Cós, March 9, 1835, Angel Navarro to José Maria Falcoñ, March 23, 1835, Isidro Benavides to Angel Navarro, April 13, 1835, and Bean to Ugartechea, April 21, 1835, BA. By this time, Bean was more than willing to fill in the U.S. military regarding the various planned Indian campaigns. See "Chieftaincy of Police" (Nacogdoches) to the ayuntamiento, March 2, 1835, NARG 393, LR, 2nd Military Department; Arbuckle to Cass, May 19, 1835, NARG 75, LR, Western Superintendency.

7. Henry Rueg to political chief of Nacogdoches, May 18, 1835, NA; Bean to Ugartechea, April 21, 1835, Ugartechea to military commander at Nacogdoches, May 7, 1835, and Navarro to Ugartechea, June 1, 1835, BA. While Coffee's "wizardry" is never explained, a common trick of traders was to take a cup of brandy, set it ablaze, and threaten to do the same to the lakes and rivers, should the Indians fail to obey.

8. Cós to Ugartechea, May 26 and June 8, 1835, and Bean to Ugartechea, June 15, 1835, BA; Tornel to secretario de relaciones, interiores y exteriores, July 17, 1835, Fomento-Colonización transcripts, BL.

9. Second Lieutenant H. Swartmont to Colonel J. B. Many, June 12, 1835, NARG 393, LR, Ft. Jesup.

10. See Kuykendall Papers, and Joel R. Robinson Memoir, Ralf Steen Library, Stephen F. Austin State University, Nacogdoches. Brown offers the only evidence on the casualties. See Brown, *Indian Wars and Pioneers of Texas,* 26. See also Thomas M. Duke, "Reminiscences of Early Texas: A Collection from the Austin Papers," *Texas Historical Association Quarterly* 7 (July 1903): 29–64. Robertson's rangers may have been the first group to mount itself to reach an Indian village. Tijerina has argued that Anglo ranger squadrons copied Tejano *compañias volantes.* See Tijerina, *Tejanos and Texas,* 90–91.

11. The quotation is from John H. Jenkins and Kenneth Kesselus, *Edward Burleson: Texas Frontier Leader* (Austin: Jenkins Publishing, 1990), 29–32.

12. Jenkins and Kesselus, *Edward Burleson,* 32–33. A relatively accurate description of the campaign is also found in Brown, *Indian Wars and Pioneers of Texas,* 26.

13. Rueg to the political chief of the Department of Brazos, July 11, 1835, Blake Papers.

14. See Rueg to ayuntamiento at San Augustine, February 18, 1835, Blake Papers.

15. See Austin affidavit, November 24, 1835, in de la Teja, *A Revolution Remembered,* 135; Hardin, "Efficient in the Cause," 52–55. For an excellent general discussion of these events, see Lack, *Texas Revolutionary Experience.*

16. There is some question as to the size of Cós's army. Hardin gives it as just over 600 men; others have placed it at 1,200. See Stephen L. Hardin, *Texian Iliad: A Military History of the Texas Revolution* (Austin: University of Texas Press, 1994), 25; Richardson, Wallace, and Anderson, *Texas,* 101.

17. The "General Council" was preceded by a "Permanent Council," which lasted only three weeks in October. The Permanent Council had been organized hurriedly by the Committee of Public Safety in San Felipe de Austin, and it consisted of the committee and representatives of the other Anglo communities. See Richardson, Wallace, and Anderson, *Texas,* 103–104.

18. Forbes, Houston, Raguet, D. A. Hoffman, S. R. Peck, William G. Logan, and George Pollitt to Andrew Jackson, September 11, 1835, in Sam Houston, *The Writings of Sam Houston,*

ed. Amelia W. Williams and Eugene C. Barker, 8 vols. (Austin: University of Texas Press, 1938–1943), 1:299–301 (hereafter cited as Houston, *Writings*). This letter also appears in the *Niles Register,* November 7, 1835.

19. Document #70, "Mexico: April 5, September 17, and December 17, 1831," in Miller, ed., *Treaties,* 622–623; Bean to Jackson, September 11, 1835, Guerra y Marina, Barker transcripts, BL.

20. Journal of the Proceedings of the General Council, October 17, 1835, vol. 1, Records of the Secretary of State, TSL.

21. Jacob Garret to Houston, November 9, 1835, A. J. Houston Papers; Houston to Chief Bowles, November 22, 1835, in Houston, *Writings,* 3:7. Anna Muckleroy, in what is still the most complete discussion of Houston's promise, concluded that he had no right to make such a pledge since Mexico had not given the Cherokees land, thus negating any promises from the Americans. See Muckleroy, "The Indian Policy of the Republic of Texas," part 1, *Southwestern Historical Quarterly* 25 (April 1922): 251–252.

22. Pollitt to Houston, November 10, 1835, A. J. Houston Papers. Dianna Everett speculates that this marriage of Houston to one of Bowles's daughters may have occurred between 1809 and 1811, when Houston was living with Cherokees in Tennessee. It is more likely the case that the relationship occurred "in the Indian fashion," during the spring of 1833, when Houston was often near or in Nacogdoches. In a matrilineal Indian society such as the Cherokees, biological husbands were not very important in the general social scheme, since uncles and brothers generally played major roles in raising children. Houston could easily have taken Bowles's daughter as a wife, lived with her for a short time in 1833, and then left, without creating so much as a stir. See Everett, *Texas Cherokees,* 88–89, 145–146.

23. See "Done in Convention, San Felipe de Austin," November 13, 1835, and "Report," November 16, 1835, Journal of the Proceedings of the General Council, vol. 1, Records of the Secretary of State, TSL.

24. Smith recommendation, November 16, 1835, ibid. Houston also played a key role in assuring the Cherokees that surveyors would no longer bother them and that "so soon as possible, you will find commissioners sent to you to hold a treaty and fix your lines, that no bad men will go inside them without leave." See Houston to Chief Bowles, November 22, 1835, in Houston, *Writings,* 3:7–8.

25. Raguet to Houston, December 3, 1835, A. J. Houston Papers.

26. Instructions to Indian Commissioners Forbes, Cameron, and Houston, December 30, 1835, Administrative Documents of Texas, TSL. See also report of Committee on Land and Indian Affairs, December 17, 1835, Henry Smith to the president and members of the General Council, December 18, 1835, and "Resolution" of the General Council, December 22, 1835, Secretary of State Records, TSL.

27. Houston to Henry Smith, January 17, 1836, and James W. Robinson to Hugh Love, January 24, 1836, Secretary of State Records, TSL.

28. Houston to Bowles, February 5, 1836, Houston Papers, BL.

29. Copies of the treaty are in several locations. See "Treaty with the Cherokees," February 23, 1836, Administrative Documents of Texas, TSL; Cherokee treaty, February 23, 1836, Winfrey and Day, *Indian Papers of Texas,* 1:14–17.

30. Houston and Forbes report, February 29, 1836, Houston papers, BL. This report (dated March 4, 1836) is also in Houston, *Writings,* 1:356–358.

31. Hardin, "Efficient in the Cause," 62–64.

CHAPTER 8. REVOLUTION AND THE "RUMOR" OF INDIAN WAR

1. Published accounts of the fall of the Alamo are numerous. The most recent utilize the recently discovered diary of Colonel José Enrique de la Peña, which sheds considerable new light on the struggle. See Hardin, *Texian Iliad*, 127–149; Randy Roberts and James S. Olson, *The Line in the Sand: The Alamo in Blood and Memory* (New York: Free Press, 2001), 154–168.

2. The supposed execution of Crockett and his six companions is perhaps the most controversial aspect of the battle today. See Hardin, *Texas Iliad*, 149, or for another view, see Roberts and Olson, *Line in the Sand*, 167–168.

3. Hardin, "Efficient in the Cause," 58.

4. See Margaret Swett Henson, *Lorenzo de Zavala: The Pragmatic Idealist* (Fort Worth: Texas Christian University Press, 1996), 92–118.

5. James Gaines to Burnet, March 25, 1836, Records of the Ad-Interim Government, Secretary of State Records, LR, TSL; Clarke, *David G. Burnet*, 64–66; Houston, *Writings*, 2:102n.4.

6. Grant Wilson and John Fiske, *Appletons' Cyclopedia of American Biography*, 6 vols. (New York: D. Appleton, 1888), 2:571–573. The Gaines brothers were the sons of James Gaines, who had served in the North Carolina legislature. Edmund had joined the army at a young age, had fought Indians in Florida during the War of 1812, and became a southern cotton plantation owner. In 1839, Gaines married the infamous New Orleans heiress Myra Clark, the illegitimate daughter of Daniel Clark, a millionaire who recognized his infant daughter Myra. Despite the obvious stain on poor Myra's lineage—her mother was supposedly married to a Frenchman when she gave birth to Myra—Gaines and Clark were likely the richest couple in Louisiana after the marriage. Gaines would ultimately be forced into retirement from the army at the ripe age of sixty-nine for illegally raising volunteer units for the Mexican War; he hoped to capture Mexico City himself.

7. Secretary of war to Gaines, January 23, 1836, in Carter and Bloom, *Territorial Papers*, 21:1154–1156. See also Hardin, "Fort Jesup, Fort Seldon, Camp Sabine, Camp Salubrity," part 2, 283; Herring to Armstrong, January 25, 1836, NARG 75, LR, Western Superintendency.

8. Quotations in Houston to James Collingsworth, March 15, 1836, Houston Papers, BL; Houston to Collingsworth, March 7, 1836, A. J. Houston Papers; Houston to Collingsworth, March 17, 1836, and Houston to Rusk, March 23, 1836, Houston Papers, BL.

9. Burnet to Menard, March 19, 1836, in Winfrey and Day, *Indian Papers of Texas*, 1:17. See also Webb and Carroll, eds., *Handbook of Texas*, 2:170. Menard, a French Canadian, had marvelous credentials, being a fur trader who had lived with Indians, including the Shawnees, for many years.

10. See Green to president of the United States, March 11, 1836, in Hardin, "Fort Jesup, Fort Seldon, Camp Sabine, Camp Salubrity," part 2, 288. Houston had foolishly added to the rumor mill when he wrote to friends, suggesting that Juan Ibarbo, the son of the founder of Nacogdoches, had seen Santa Anna in the south and that Ibarbo intended to "*incite* the Indians" (emphasis in original). See Houston to Raguet, March 13, 1836, Houston Papers, BL.

11. See Committee of Public Safety at Nacogdoches report, March 19, 1836, and John J. Mason to Major Nelson, March 20, 1836, NARG 94, LR, Adjutant General's Office (hereafter referred to as AGO).

12. Mason to Gaines, April 1, 1836, NARG 94, LR, AGO.

13. Gaines to Cass, March 29, 1836, NARG 94, LR, AGO.

14. Gaines to governor of Louisiana and Mississippi, April 8, 1836, House Document 256, 24th Cong., 1st sess., 47–48.

15. Carson to Burnet, April 4, 1836, Executive Department Journals, TSL; Burnet to Henry Raguet, April 7, 1836, Secretary of State Records, TSL.

16. Jesse Benton, John L. Mason, Frost Thorn, and Henry Raguet to Burnet, April 6, 1836, Records of the Ad-Interim Government, Secretary of State Records, LR, TSL; Darrington to Burnet, April 10, 1836, A. J. Houston Papers.

17. Petition of Charles Sims, April 11, 1836, A. J. Houston Papers; testimony to Committee of Public Safety, Nacogdoches, April 11, 1836, Committee of Public Safety to Mason, April 11, 1836, testimony of Menard, April 11, 1836, and petition from committee to General Gaines, April 12, 1836, NARG 94, LR, AGO.

18. Statement of Miguel de Cortinas, April 12, 1836, NARG 94, LR, AGO; Hardin, "Fort Jesup, Fort Seldon, Camp Sabine, Camp Salubrity," part 2, 291–292.

19. Gaines to Arbuckle, April 12, 1836, NARG 393, LR, 2nd Military Department.

20. Mason to Gaines, April 13, 1836, NARG 94, LR, AGO.

21. Roberts and Olson argue for good treatment for both Dickinson and Joe. See *Line in the Sand,* 173.

22. Houston to Raguet, March 13, 1836, Houston Papers, BL.

23. Carson to Burnet, April 14, 1836, Executive Department Journals, TSL.

24. Ibid.; emphasis in original. Another copy of this letter is found in Records of the Ad-Interim Government, Secretary of State Records, TSL. It has the incorrect date of April 16, 1836.

25. Gaines to Cass, April 20, 1836, NARG 94, LR, AGO; emphasis in original. Francis Paul Prucha interprets this event differently, noting Gaines's call for troops but viewing him as a more circumspect commander. See Prucha, *The Sword of the Republic: The United States Army on the Frontier, 1783–1846* (London: Macmillan, 1969), 307–311.

26. Captain John Stuart to Acting Assistant Adjutant General Lieutenant William Seaville, February 10 and March 6, 1836, NARG 393, LR, Fort Coffee; Arbuckle to Brigadier General R. Jones, February 16 and May 24, 1836, NARG 393, LS, 2nd Military Department; Arbuckle to Jones, February 23, 1836, NARG 94, LR, AGO.

27. Chouteau to Stokes, April 19, 1836, and Chouteau report, April 25, 1836, NARG 75, LR, Western Superintendency; Stuart to Jones, June 7, 1836, NARG 393, LR, Ft. Coffee; Arbuckle to Jones, June 14, 1836, NARG 393, LS, 2nd Military Department.

28. Big Mush (written by G. C. Collins) to Committee of Vigilance and Public Safety, April 13, 1836, A. J. Houston Papers.

29. Irion to Cordova, April 14 and 15, 1836, Cordova to Irion, April 14, 1836, Irion to Houston, April 17, 1836, and Raguet to Houston, April 17, 1836, A. J. Houston Papers; Raguet to his wife, April 16, 1836, Henry Raguet Papers, BL.

30. James Gaines to Burnet, May 5, 1836, Executive Department Journals, TSL. Thomas Jefferson Rusk clearly confirms Burnet's complicity in the conspiracy by writing him on April 10 and reporting that several spies had been sent into the regions southwest and northwest of Houston's army camp on the Brazos River to look for Mexican troops. "I would place my head on the forfeit that there is no Mexican force in that direction." This evidence, which indicated the falseness of the reports that had reached General Gaines on the morning of April 14, was never forwarded to Carson or the Committee of Vigilance and Public Safety in Nacogdoches. See Rusk to Burnet, April 10, 1836, Records of the Ad-Interim Government, Secretary of State Records, LR, TSL.

31. Actually, Flores probably was trying to cause trouble since he had mortgaged his farm and then sold it. He was wanted for fraud in Louisiana. See the series of reports on Flores in Bonnell to Gaines, April 20 and June 4, 7, 14, and 16, 1836, NARG 94, LR, AGO.

32. Gaines to Secretary of War Cass, April 20, 1836, LR, AGO; General Alexander Macomb to Cass, April 25, 1836, in Hardin, "Fort Jesup, Fort Selden, Camp Sabine, Camp Salubrity," part 3, 448; Cass to Gaines, April 25, 1836, House Document 256, 24th Cong., 1st sess., 43–44; Cass to C. C. Cambeeleng, May 4, 1836, *American State Papers: Military Affairs* 6:412; Marilyn McAdams Sibley, "The Texas-Cherokee War of 1839," *East Texas Historical Journal* 3 (March 1965): 21; Eugene C. Barker, "United States and Mexico, 1835–1837," *Mississippi Valley Historical Review* 1 (June 1914): 1–30; *Arkansas Gazette,* May 3, 1836. Part of the reason for Cass's growing concern over the situation in Texas was a strong questioning of President Jackson's policies in the region by John Quincy Adams, who was then a member of Congress. See Cass to Gaines, May 12, 1836, in Hardin, "Fort Jesup, Fort Selden, Camp Sabine, Camp Salubrity," part 3, 446–448.

33. Hardin, "Efficient in the Cause," 59.

34. There are many descriptions of the battle of San Jacinto. For an overview see James W. Pohl and Stephen Hardin, "The Military History of the Texas Revolution: An Overview," *Southwestern Historical Quarterly* 89 (March 1986): 269–308. An analysis of the composition of the changing Texas army is Lack, *Texas Revolutionary Experience.* As one example of the Tejano participation, Tejano sergeant Antonio Menchaca ran headlong into the Mexican camp, stumbling onto a Mexican officer whom he recognized. As the man pleaded for his life, and with several Texans watching nearby, Menchaca screamed, "No, damn you . . . I'm no Mexican—I'm an American." Turning to the Texans, Menchaca ordered them to shoot the Mexican officer. And they did. Menchaca's quotation is from Hardin, "Efficient in the Cause," 60.

35. Petition of Caddo leaders, January 9, 1837, and John G. Green to E. M. Ripley, January 20, 1837, NARG 75, LR, Caddo Agency.

36. The attack on Parker's Fort, often later reported by Texas historians to be the work of Comanches, actually seems to have been planned by Caddos and Wichitas, the latter mainly Wacos and Kichais. Sterling C. Robertson, who had colonized parts of the Navasota valley, had heard that "Caddo Indians" were "foremost in the attack and were recognized." Robertson thought this evidence significant enough to convince General Gaines to send an army into Texas. See Sterling C. Robertson to Rusk, June 18, 1836, Rusk Papers, BL. The *Arkansas Gazette* of July 26, 1836, reported the attack, using as a source a letter from General Gaines. The general placed the responsibility almost entirely on the Caddos. The only firsthand account of the attack is Rachel Plummer, *The Rachel Plummer Narrative: A Stirring Narrative of Adventure, Hardship and Privation in the Early Days of Texas, Depicting Struggles with the Indians and Other Adventures* (n.p.: privately published, 1926; reprint, Austin: Jenkins Publishing, 1977), 5–6. So much was written about the attack in years to come that distortions and fabrications abound, especially regarding the rape of women at the fort. Plummer's account suggests only that the women were tied and beaten, a common treatment for newly taken captives.

37. Rusk to Gaines, June 10, 1836, Rusk Papers.

38. Armstrong to Herring, May 6 and 13, 1836, NARG 75, LR, Western Superintendency; Arbuckle to Gaines, May 8, 1836, and Arbuckle to Jones, May 17, 1836, NARG 94, LR, AGO.

39. Austin to Houston, with note by Houston to Gaines, July 4, 1836, in Houston, *Writings,* 4:22–23.

40. Captain J. Dean to Lieutenant Colonel J. H. Vose, May 10, 1836, and Assistant Adjutant General A. McCall to Lieutenant Colonel Vose, June 3, 1836, NARG 94, LR, AGO; Gaines to Arbuckle, June 3, 1836, NARG 393, LR, 2nd Military Department; Arbuckle to Vose, June 7, 1836, NARG 393, LS, 2nd Military Department.

41. Gaines to Houston, July 6, 1836, A. J. Houston Papers; Gaines to commander at Nacogdoches (Bonnell), July 10, 1836, NARG 393, LS, 2nd Military Department; Gaines to Arbuckle, August 10, 1836, NARG 393, LR, 2nd Military Department; Bonnell to Gaines, July 19 and August 9, 1836, Gaines to adjutant general, July 21, 1836, and Gaines to Brigadier General Henry Atkinson, August 9, 1836, NARG 94, LR, AGO.

42. Arbuckle to William Clark, June 12, 1836, NARG 393, LS, 2nd Military Department; Captain John Stuart to Lieutenant W. Seawell, June 12, 1836, NARG 393, LR, Fort Coffee; Armstrong to Herring, June 23, 1836, in Carter and Bloom, *Territorial Papers,* 21:1230–1231. Gaines and Arbuckle both had trouble convincing Arkansas officials to organize militia troops. See Arbuckle to Governor William S. Fulton of Arkansas, July 8, 1836, and Jones to Arbuckle, July 20, 1836, NARG 393, LR, 2nd Military Department; Arbuckle to Jones, September 5, 1836, NARG 94, LR, AGO.

43. Deposition of M. B. Menard, June 11, 1836, A. J. Houston Papers.

44. Rusk to the people of Texas, June 27, 1836, Houston Papers, BL. See also Rusk to Burnet, June 11, 1836, Rusk to Major John K. Allen, June 18, 1836, and Rusk to Gaines, June 18, 1836, Rusk Papers.

45. Anonymous to P. P. Rea, July 1, 1836, Executive Department Journals, TSL. This report, unsigned for obvious reasons, was soon confirmed, as the activity of the Indians was even reported in the local newspapers. See *Arkansas Gazette,* August 23, 1836. Urrea reported the incident to his superiors, indicating that he had told the Cherokees that the land on which they lived was still part of Mexico. See José María Tornel y Mendivil to secretario de relaciones, August 16, 1836, Fomento-Colonización transcripts, BL. The fascinating letter in the war department in Washington, D.C., indicates that the U.S. Army had employed two spies, identified as Travinia and Ruendes, in Matamoros. They also confirmed the visit of an Indian delegation during the summer of 1836. See A. Macomb to Arbuckle, May 4, 1838, NARG 393, LR, 2nd Military Department.

46. Houston to Raguet, July 4, 1836, Raguet Papers; Houston to Colonel N. Robbins, August 2, 1836, A. J. Houston Papers.

47. Deposition of Miguel Cortinas, July 10, 1836, Documents Relating to the Committee of Vigilance and Safety at Nacogdoches, BL. Gaines later sought proof of Cortinas's role in the Matamoros trip. It is confirmed in the affidavit of Juan Francisco Bosque, September 7, 1836, NARG 94, LR, AGO. See Lack's general description of Tejano neutrality during the revolution and the increasing ethnic friction thereafter. Paul D. Lack, "The Córdova Revolt," in *Tejano Journey, 1770–1850,* ed. Gerald E. Poyo (Austin: University of Texas Press, 1996), 90–95; Tijerina, *Tejanos and Texas,* 138.

48. Report of A. B. Menard, August 9, 1836, NARG 94, LR, AGO; Gaines to Arbuckle, August 10, 1836, NARG 393, LR, 2nd Military Department. These events provided Burnet with yet another opportunity to seek the intervention of the United States, writing the representatives of the Texas government in Washington, D.C., that the Cherokees and others were "thrown upon our territory by the peculiar *transplanting* policy of that Government [the United States]" (emphasis in original). Thus, under the terms of the 1831 treaty, the United States was responsible for the immigrant Indians. See Burnet to James Collinsworth and Peter W. Grayson, August 10, 1836, "Governor's Letterbook," Secretary of State Records, TSL.

49. Menard's numbers are likely very accurate. He listed 150 Alabamas and Coushattas, 60 Biloxis, 100 Choctaws, 120 Shawnees, 40 Anadarkos, 40 Delawares, 180 Kickapoos, 400 Caddos, and 140 Cherokees, for 1,230 warriors. See Menard census, July 21, 1836, NARG 75, LR, Western Superintendency.

50. See Webb and Carroll, eds., *Handbook of Texas,* 1:713–714.

51. Bowles to Houston, August 16, 1836, and Houston to Gaines, August 25, 1836, A. J. Houston Papers.

52. Houston to Whistler, August 17, 1836, A. J. Houston Papers.

53. Houston to citizens of Texas, August 29, 1836, Houston Papers, BL (emphasis in original); Houston to James Smith, September 8, 1836, and Houston to Daniel Parker, September 8, 1836, A. J. Houston Papers.

54. Houston to Gaines, August 29, 1836, A. J. Houston Papers.

55. Michael Costley, a ranger, had already scouted the Cherokee village by September 2 and found it peaceful. See Houston to Costley, September 1, 1836, in Houston, *Writings,* 4:23; Costley to Houston, September 2, 1836, A. J. Houston Papers.

56. Riley to Gaines, August 24, 1836, NARG 94, LR, AGO.

57. Houston to Gaines, September 12, 1836, A. J. Houston Papers; Arbuckle to Colonel Stephen Watts Kearney, October 5, 1836, and Arbuckle to Lieutenant George McGale, October 11, 1836, NARG 393, LS, 2nd Military Department; Whistler to Arbuckle, November 22, 1836, NARG 393, LR, 2nd Military Department.

58. Houston to Gaines, September 12, 1836, A. J. Houston Papers; *Arkansas Gazette,* November 22, 1836; special order to commanding general at Fort Jesup, December 5, 1836, NARG 393, LR, Ft. Jesup. Ironically, Arkansas did finally send some volunteers to the Red River frontier in December, long after their usefulness had passed. See Arbuckle to paymaster general, December 10, 1836, NARG 94, LR, AGO.

59. Houston to Captain Costley, September 16, 1836, Houston to Lenee, chief of the Shawnee, September 18, 1836, and Houston to captain of the Cherokee rangers, September 23, 1836, A. J. Houston Papers; Houston to Martin Lacey, September 17, 1836, and Colonel James Smith to Houston, October 5, 1836, Houston Papers, BL. The only near snag in the new policy was the attempt of Colonel Smith and his rangers to attack the Ioni village. See George W. Browning to Houston, September 16, 1836, A. J. Houston Papers.

60. William G. Cooke to Nathaniel Robbins, K. H. Douglas, and H. Millard, November 13, 1836, Douglas Estate Papers, BL; Houston to James Hall, August 23, 1836, and George W. Browning to Houston, November 15, 1836, A. J. Houston Papers.

61. Resolution of Representative Burton, October 20, 1836, *Proceedings of the House of Representatives, from the 3d of October to the 23d of December* (Columbia, Tex.: G. and T. H. Borden, 1836), 60–61.

62. Houston's inaugural address, October 22, 1836, *Proceedings of the House of Representatives,* 66. A copy of the address is also in Houston Papers, BL.

63. House resolution, November 8, 1836, *Proceedings of the House of Representatives,* 72–74.

64. House debate, November 12, 1836, *Proceedings of the House of Representatives,* 94–95. Burleson's support for Houston's policy is surprising, given what his own sympathetic biographers call "a long-held hatred of Cherokees." He probably opted for negotiation to allow time for the new republic to get established. Many families in his own county of Bastrop had not yet rebuilt their farms. Burleson did recommend all-out war against the Comanches who had recently killed his brother-in-law just above Bastrop. See Jenkins and Kesselus, *Edward Burleson,* 148–149.

65. Houston to the senate, December 20, 1836, Houston Papers, BL; Houston's appeal for the Cherokee treaty, December 20, 1836, in Earnest W. Winkler, ed., *Secret Journals of the Senate: Republic of Texas* (Austin: Austin Printing Company, 1911), 35–36.

66. See Philip Dimitt to Ira Ingram, December 13, 1836, Army Papers, RG 401, TSL; Felix Huston to the secretary of war, December 13, 1836, and Anthony Butler to Felix Huston, December 21, 1836, Notes from the Texan Legation in the United States, Consular Letters,

1836–1845, Microfilm, BL; Joseph Milton Nance, *After San Jacinto: The Texas-Mexican Frontier, 1836–1841* (Austin: University of Texas Press, 1963), 113.

Chapter 9. Indian Intransigence

1. E. House, *Narrative of the Captivity of Mrs. Horn, and Her Children, with Mrs. Harris, By the Camanche [sic] Indians, after they had Murdered Their Husbands and Traveling Companions; with a Brief Account of the Manners and customs of that Nation of Savages of Whom So Little is generally Known* (St. Louis: C. Keemle, 1839), 6–15. Historians continue to debate the nature of Indian captivity. James F. Brooks recently has argued that most frequently captivity led to slavery for the person involved and that women, when taken even by the Comanches, often suffered a similar fate. He cites, for example, anthropological data collected by E. Adamson Hoebel that suggests the existence of "chore wives" (Brooks would suggest that the term translates to "slaves") among the Comanches. I see no real evidence to support Hoebel's assertion other than the fact that women, like boys and girls, had to be "seasoned" to the tasks of curing hides and collecting food and firewood. Indian captivity was mostly a temporary state in Plains societies; if they stayed with the tribe, boys moved on to become warriors, and women became wives. The only exception seems to be a small number of Mexican boys who failed at becoming warriors and stayed with the women while the menfolk hunted or raided. Of course, I agree strongly with Brooks's assertion that selling captives—who then often became slaves—in the El Rescate of New Mexico was crucially important in the creation of the Comanche political economy, as I have argued in my earlier work. See Brooks, *Captives and Cousins,* 179–195; Wallace and Hoebel, *The Comanches,* 141.

2. On the issue of rape, Texans commonly believed that women automatically faced the "fate worse than death" when becoming captives or even before being killed on the battlefield. Due to the high drama that soon became common in Indian-Anglo warfare along the Texas frontier (and the many rumors that spread with it), historians also have generally concluded that rape automatically occurred. See, for example, the outrageously biased assessment of T. R. Fehrenbach, who describes in detail (without any reliable sources) the terrible rape of poor granny. Fehrenbach then proceeds to argue the following: "There was never to be a single case of a white woman being taken by Southern Plains Indians without rape." See Fehrenbach, *Lone Star,* 450.

3. The Parker attack is a very important symbolic event in Texas history for several reasons. The nine-year-old girl, Cynthia Ann Parker, later grew to maturity and married the war Comanche chief Peta Nocona and had a son named Quanah, who became a famous Comanche leader. When retaken, both Cynthia Ann and her younger brother found it impossible to return to Texas homes, preferring to live with Indians. The initial publication of Rachel Plummer's narrative is in James W. Parker, *Narrative of the Perilous Adventures, Miraculous Escapes and Sufferings of Rev. James W. Parker, during a Frontier Residence in Texas, of Fifteen Years. . . . To which is Appended a Narrative of the Capture and Subsequent Sufferings of Mrs. Rachael Plummer (His Daughter), During a Captivity of Twenty-one Months among the Cumanche [sic] Indians, with a Sketch of Their Manners, customs, Laws, etc.; with a Short Description of the Country over which She Traveled whilst with the Indians* (Louisville, Ky.: Morning Courier Office, 1844). See also Plummer's *Rachel Plummer Narrative.* The description of the lancing and disrobing of granny Parker comes from Wilbarger, who would have mentioned her rape had it occurred. See Wilbarger, *Depredations in Texas,* 307.

4. I have used the shortened title of Rachel Plummer's account here, which was given as a separate story in the 1844 account published by James W. Parker.

5. Wilbarger, *Depredations in Texas,* 222; Brown, *Indian Wars and Pioneers of Texas,* 46–47.

6. Wilbarger, *Depredations in Texas,* 192–193.

7. The best account of Lane's fight is in Brown, *Indian Wars and Pioneers of Texas,* 47–50.

8. Wilbarger, *Depredations in Texas,* 352–353, 361, 367. See also Brown, *Indian Wars and Pioneers of Texas,* 70–72.

9. Dr. Benjamin Dolbeare, *A Narrative of the Captivity and Suffering of Dolly Webster among the Camanche Indians in Texas: with an account of the massacre of John Webster and his party, as related by Mrs. Webster.* (Clarksburg, Va.: M'Granahgan and M'Carty, 1843; reprint, New Haven, Conn.: Yale University Press, 1986).

10. For the selling of the Indian women and children, see Wilbarger, *Depredations in Texas,* 218.

11. The best description of Comanches preparing for war comes from Jean Louis Berlandier, who witnessed the process. See his *Indians of Texas,* 72–75.

12. To what extent this happened is debatable. Much evidence suggests that Comanche young men were often deprived of wives and that older, successful warriors took many of the eligible mates. This produced a competition for women that led to raiding and the taking of captives. The competition argument can be followed in Gerald Betty, *Comanche Society: Before the Reservation* (College Station: Texas A and M University Press, 2002), 134–137.

13. See Ramón A. Gutiérrez, *When Jesus Came, the Corn Mothers Went Away: Marriage, Sexuality, and Power in New Mexico, 1500–1846* (Stanford, Calif.: Stanford University Press, 1991), 77. James Adair, who published an account of the eastern Indians in 1775, had this to say about abstinence and raiding: "The Indians will not cohabit with women while they are out at war; they religiously abstain from every kind of intercourse even with their own wives, for the space of three days and nights before they go to war, and so after they return home, because they are to sanctify themselves." See *Adair's History of the American Indians: Edited under the Auspices of the National Society of the Colonial Dames of America, in Tennessee* (New York: Promontory Press, 1930; reprint of 1775 edition), 171.

14. House, *Narrative of the Captivity of Mrs. Horn,* 59–60. Another excellent discussion of this avoidance process is found in Theda Purdue, *Cherokee Women* (Lincoln: University of Nebraska Press, 1998), 29–35.

15. House, *Narrative of the Captivity of Mrs. Horn,* 22–26.

16. Anthropologist E. Adamson Hoebel, who did fieldwork among the Comanches in the 1930s and 1940s, found that once adopted, captive women were protected by either a "blood covenant" or the fact that they were the property of another man and woman. Hoebel found few (if any) incidents of captives being raped. See Wallace and Hoebel, *The Comanches,* 240–242. For another look at Comanche captivity, see Michael L. Tate, "Comanche Captives: People between Two Worlds," *Chronicles of Oklahoma* 72 (Fall 1994): 228–263.

17. Plummer, *Rachel Plummer's Narrative,* 6.

18. Dolbeare, *Dolly Webster,* 10–17.

19. Ibid., 12–25.

20. Plummer, *Rachel Plummer's Narrative,* 10.

21. House, *Narrative of the Captivity of Mrs. Horn,* 26–60.

22. Dolbeare, *Dolly Webster,* 25.

23. Hilory G. Bedford, *Texas Indian Troubles: The Most Thrilling Events in the History of Texas* (Benjamin, Tex.: Hargreaves, 1905), 28–31.

24. José Antonio Fernández to ayuntamiento de Matamoros, March 17, 1837, and Francisco Villaseñor to ayuntamiento of Matamoros, May 12, 1837, Matamoros Archives, BL; D. W. Smith to John Forsyth, August 4, 1837, Matamoros Consul Papers, BL; *Mercurio de Matamoros,* September 29, 1837, Núm. 152, Matamoros Archives, BL; D. M. Vigness, "Indian Raids on the Lower Rio Grande, 1836–1837," *Southwestern Historical Quarterly* 59 (July 1955): 18–21.

25. J. N. Molano to governor of the department, April 21 and June 1, 1836, Matamoros Archives, BL; Vicente Filisola to secretario del despacho de la guerra, June 7, 1836, José Urrea to secretario del despacho de la guerra, July 29, 1836, and José María Ortiz to secretario del despacho de la guerra, August 1, 1836, AGN, Guerra y Marina, Barker transcripts, BL.

26. San Antonio Tejanos suffered some pillaging during the summer of 1836. Colonel James Smith, who replaced Seguín, seems to have disobeyed orders from General Rusk to leave private property alone. Years later, Mexican officials would compile a massive documentary history of the Comanche raids, arguing that Texans had incited the Indians against them after 1836. See Paul D. Lack, "Occupied Texas: Bexar and Goliad, 1835–1836," in *Mexican Americans in Texas History,* ed. Cynthia Orozco Zamora and Rodolfo Rocha (Austin: Texas State Historical Society, 2000), 46–47.

Chapter 10. Sam Houston, the Legislature, and a Failed Indian Policy

1. Haley, *Sam Houston,* 164–183.

2. Rusk to Houston, July 2, 1836, Houston Papers, BL; Burnet to Le Grand, September 10, 1836, Le Grand Papers, TSL; Le Grand to Houston, December 4, 1836, A. J. Houston Papers; Burnet to J. Toby and brother, September 13, 1836, Records of the Ad-Interim Government, Secretary of State Records; Burnet to the senate, October 12, 1836, Messages and Proclamations of the Presidents, LS, Secretary of State Records; Le Grand to Burnet, November 7, 1836, Domestic Correspondence, Secretary of State Records.

3. Le Grand to Houston, April 26, 1837, A. J. Houston Papers. Questions were later raised by Houston relative to the disposition of the $1,200 that Burnet had given to Le Grand. Houston also questioned the information from Le Grand that suggested that Indian war was imminent. Le Grand responded by saying that such a war could be avoided "had my instructions authorized me to secure to them [Comanches] their hunting plains, which are valuable only to them and can never be inhabited by a civilized people." See Le Grand to Congress of the Republic, November 23, 1837, Le Grand Papers.

4. Arbuckle to Gaines, October 3, 1836, and Jones to Stuart, January 7, 1837, NARG 393, LR, 2nd Military Department; Arbuckle to Jones, November 6, 1836, NARG 94, LR, AGO; Stuart to Jones, November 25, 1836, NARG 393, LR, Ft. Coffee; *Arkansas Gazette,* February 23, 1837; Armstrong to A. L. Chouteau, February 13, 1837, and Armstrong to C. A. Harris, February 13, 1837, NARG 75, LR, Western Superintendency; A. J. Raines to Houston, March 18, 1837, A. J. Houston Papers; George Bent to George Bird Grinnell, April 25, 1918, Grinnell Papers. George Bent suggests that a major conflict over bison between the Kiowas and Cheyennes occurred just east of present-day Denver in 1837. See Bent to George Hyde, March 1905, Hyde Letters, Denver Public Library.

5. P. L. Chouteau to Armstrong, February 1, 1837, and Armstrong to Harris, February 13, 1837, NARG 75, LR, Western Superintendency; Chouteau to Armstrong, February 4, 1837, A. J. Houston Papers.

6. P. L. Chouteau to Armstrong, March 1, 1837, A. J. Houston Papers; Armstrong to Harris, April 20, 1837, P. L. Chouteau to Armstrong, May 22, 1837, and Armstrong to Harris, May 28, 1837, NARG 75, LR, Western Superintendency. Rachel Plummer, while still a captive, spoke to a follower of the hostile group: "One Indian . . . stated that he was a Beadie [Bidi—a small band incorporated by the Caddos] . . . that they were determined to make servants of the White people, and cursed me in the English language." See Parker, *Narrative,* 12.

7. Poinsett to Auguste P. Chouteau, April 7, 1837, Chouteau Papers; Armstrong to Harris, May 28, 1837, NARG 75, LR, Western Superintendency.

8. A brief description of Goyens, completed by the Nacogdoches historian R. B. Blake, is found in Webb and Carroll, eds., *Handbook of Texas,* 1:713.

9. Goyens to Houston, January 7 and 20, 1837, Bowles to Houston, January 14, 1837, and Houston to Bowles, January 23, 1837, A. J. Houston Papers.

10. Walker Reid to Houston, March 22, 1837, A. J. Houston Papers.

11. Quotation in P. E. Bean to Houston, May 6, 1837, A. J. Houston Papers. See also Walker Reid to Houston, May 3, 1837, and May [no day] 1837, A. H. Houston Papers.

12. Houston to Karnes, March 31, 1837, Army Papers, RG 401, TSL. Other copies of this letter are in A. J. Houston Papers, TSL, and the Houston Papers, BL.

13. Dolbeare, *Dolly Webster,* 13–21.

14. Houston to Colonel J. Snively, January 24, 1837, and Houston to Congress, May 17, 1837, Houston Papers, BL; petition of citizens from Cummings Creek, February 22, 1837, and Houston to Millard, March 6, 1837, A. J. Houston Papers; Colonel Many to Lieutenant A. Harris, February 25, 1837, NARG 393, LR, 2nd Military Department; J. Pinkney Henderson to William H. Wharton and Memucan Hunt, February 29, 1837, Notes from the Texan Legation in the United States, TSL; W. H. Secrest to Houston, March 1, 1837, in Winfrey and Day, *Indian Papers of Texas,* 1:20–21. Agent Brooks did in fact distribute some 50 rifles, 600 pounds of powder, and 1,800 pounds of lead to the Caddos. See Brooks to Harris, June 2, 1837, NARG 75, LR, Caddo Agency.

15. See the various reports, including especially Goyens to Houston, January 7 and 20, 1837; Bowles to Houston, January 14, 1837; Richard Sparks to Houston, February 4, 1837; Houston to Goyens, March 7, 1837; Rusk to Houston, March 11, 1837; Reid to Houston, March 22, 1837.

16. A. S. Thurston to Houston, April 17, 1837, and Rusk to Houston, May 8, 1837, A. J. Houston Papers. In the Kit Douglas Papers, there is considerable evidence that the economy of East Texas was booming by 1837 with growing pressures for more land to accommodate cotton production. Sufficient land existed in the region to settle a large number of people, but most cotton farmers quickly realized that the river valleys were much more suited to the crop, thus leading to a settlement pattern that left much of the prairie uplands alone. Suzanne Starling, *Land Is the Cry! Warren Angus Ferris, Pioneer Texas Surveyor and Founder of Dallas County* (Austin: Texas State Historical Association, 1998), 59–94.

17. Early Texas historian R. B. Blake, through research in the Nacogdoches Archives, concluded that Córdova had plotted with Mexico starting in the late summer of 1835. Other evidence fails to support this. Córdova's disenchantment stemmed almost entirely from the disenfranchisement of Tejanos and the robbery of their property in 1837. See Blake, "Cordova Revolution," in Webb and Carroll, eds., *Handbook of Texas,* 1:412–413; Lack, "The Córdova Revolt," 94–95; Tijerina, *Tejanos and Texas,* 138.

18. Bonnell to authorities at Nacogdoches, March 7, 1837, Rusk and Douglas to Houston, March 11, 1837, Goyens to Houston, March 22, 1837, Robert Irion to Houston, March 23, 1837, Redi to Houston, March 29, 1837, and John Dorr to Houston, April 15, 1837, A. J. Houston Papers. Vicente Filisola reports the appearance of Cortinas at Matamoros "with the Caddo Indians" who wished to "battle the enemy." See Filisola to ayuntamiento, June 25, 1837, Matamoros Archives, BL.

19. See Timothy M. Matovina, "Between Two Worlds," in *Tejano Journey, 1770–1850,* ed. Gerald E. Poyo (Austin: University of Texas Press, 1996), 77.

20. Montejano, *Anglos and Mexicans in the Making of Texas,* 36–37; Matovina, "Between Two Worlds," 80.

21. See Lack, "Córdova Revolt," 94–95.

22. Rusk to R. A. Irion, May 9, 1837, Irion Papers.

23. Irion to Raguet, May 12, 1837, Raguet Papers. Irion had been a recipient of one of the land grants handed out by state authorities in Saltillo in 1835. See Webb and Carroll, eds., *Handbook of Texas* 1:892.

24. Quotations in Houston to Rusk, June 7, 1837, Houston Papers, BL. See also Houston to James W. Parker, June 10, 1837, in Houston, *Writings,* 4:31–32; Houston to Rusk, June 16, 1837, and Houston to Bowles, July 3, 1837, Houston Papers, BL; Houston to Rusk, June 27, 1837, A. J. Houston Papers. Pressure from the public mounted substantially on the president to do something during the summer of 1837. James W. Parker, the father of one of the Parker captives, especially complained of inaction. See Parker to Houston, June 6, 1837, A. J. Houston Papers.

25. Houston to Rusk, June 7, 1837, Houston Papers, BL.

26. Bee to Sweitzer, August 24, 1837, and Bernard E. Bee, "Declaration," August 24, 1837, Henry W. Karnes Papers, TSL; Rusk and Douglas to Watkins, September 14, 1837, in Winfrey and Day, *Indian Papers of Texas,* 1:21–22.

27. Report of the Standing Committee, October 12, 1837, and treaty with the Tonkawa, November 22, 1837, in Winfrey and Day, *Indian Papers of Texas,* 1:22–28, 28–29.

28. Report of the Standing Committee, October 12, 1837, in Winfrey and Day, *Indian Papers of Texas,* 1:23–24.

29. Ibid.

30. Ibid., 1:25–26.

31. Report of Representative Burleson, November 1, 1837, and report, December 6, 1837, *Journal of the House of Representatives of the Republic of Texas: Called Session of September 25, 1837 and Regular Session, commencing November 6, 1837* (Houston: National Banner Office, Niles and Co., 1838).

32. Houston's annual message to congress, November 21, 1837, in Houston, *Writings,* 2:158–159.

33. On various treaties and the selection of Indian agents, see commission to Jefferson Wright (1838), James Powers to Houston, January 23, 1838, Thomas Western to Houston, March 4, 1838, Houston to Joseph Dillard, June 30, 1838, Houston to V. R. Palmer, June 30, 1838, Houston to Joseph Baker, June 30, 1838, and Houston to Karnes, June 30, 1838, A. J. Houston Papers; treaty with Lipan Apaches, January 8, 1838, and treaty with Tonkawa Indians, April 10, 1838, in Winfrey and Day, *Indian Papers of Texas,* 1:30–31, 46–48.

34. The May 1838 legislation, entitled "A Bill for the Defense of the Frontier," has never been found. For a discussion of the Texas militia, see Nance, *After San Jacinto,* 38–39. See also Sibley, "The Texas Cherokee War of 1839," 21–22; report of Indian Affairs Committee, April 24, 1838, *Journal of the House of Representatives of the Republic of Texas: Second Session, Adjourned Session* (Houston: Telegraph Office, 1838); Bee to senate and house, April 24, 1838, Bee Papers, BL. If a settlement line had been drawn in 1838, it would have stretched from Bonham in the north, directly south to Navasota (at the mouth of the Navasota River), and then west to the region just east of Austin before turning south and east and reaching San Antonio.

35. Houston to congress, May 4, 1838, in Houston, *Writings,* 2:214.

36. Houston to the senate, May 21, 1838, in Houston, *Writings,* 4:55–60; Houston to the house of representatives, May 25, 1838, Houston Papers, BL.

37. Memoir of John Simpson, 1838, Ralph Stern Library, Stephen F. Austin University, Nacogdoches, Texas; Lieutenant Colonel J. G. Vose to headquarters, April 6 and May 30, 1838,

NARG 393, LR, 2nd Military Department; Jenkins and Kesselus, *Edward Burleson,* 159–164. Jenkins and Kesselus have an excellent description of the early development of Austin. They rely upon the supposed anonymous journal published as "A Visit Up the Colorado River: Extracts from an Anonymous Diary," *[Houston] Telegraph and Texas Register,* May 1, 1839. The diary was likely that of George W. Bonnell, who visited the region in July 1838. A similar copy is "Bonnell's Observations," copied by W. J. Bollaert, 1838–1839, Bonnell Papers, Ayer Collection, Newberry Library, Chicago, Illinois.

38. The commissioners left rather hurriedly after a Comanche party returned from a raid, having lost one man to an Anglo settler's bullet. The presents were to appease the grief of the man's family. The final report is Joseph Baker and Horatio A. Allsbury to General Johnston, February 29, 1838, A. J. Houston Papers. Further information on the Comanche claim, in particular the reference to the northern boundary of Bastrop County, is found in Irion to Houston, March 12, 1838, Raguet Papers; Irion to Houston, March 14, 1838, A. J. Houston Papers. See also Bee to Johnston, February 24, 1838, Karnes Papers; Johnston to Bee, February 27, 1838, Houston Papers, BL.

39. Bee to Karnes, April 12, 1838, Karnes Papers. See also Kenny, Gastock, and V. P. Palmer to Houston, April 28, 1838, and V. P. Palmer to Houston, June 9, 1838, A. J. Houston Papers; treaty with Comanche Indians, May 29, 1838, in Winfrey and Day, *Indian Papers of Texas,* 1:50–52. V. P. Palmer returned to the Comanche village on the Colorado River in June, apparently to trade, and found the people to be friendly. Palmer had heard of twenty Cherokees, two Mexicans, and fifteen Delaware Indians who had just passed through the camp. The Cherokees and Mexicans were headed to Matamoros. See Palmer to Houston, June 18, 1838, A. J. Houston Papers.

40. It is unclear why Houston kept selecting various other Indian agents to assist Goyens with the Cherokees, other than perhaps the fact that Goyens, being black, might have needed such assistance in keeping peace between Texans and Indians. Wright's council with the Cherokee is in Wright to Houston, June 17, 1838, A. J. Houston Papers. See also Wright to Houston, May 29, 1838, Houston to Bowles, May 30, 1829, and Bowles to "My Brother" (Houston), June [no day] 1838, A. J. Houston Papers.

41. Wright to Houston, June 18 and 25, 1838, and Houston to Wright, June 23, 1838, A. J. Houston Papers.

42. Houston to Wright, June 23, 1838, A. J. Houston Papers.

43. Cordova to Manuel Flores, July 19, 1838, Notes from the Texan Legation in the United States, TSL. The letter is printed in Winfrey and Day, *Indian Papers of Texas,* 1:8. Lack notes that Telesforo Córdova had started the affair by organizing a Caddo raid in which fourteen horses were stolen. Texans later identified fourteen of the "principal revolted Mexicans at Nacogdoches," and the list included the name of Telesforo Córdova. See Lack, "Córdova Revolt," 89–109; list of "Revolted Mexicans," August 8, 1838, A. J. Houston Papers.

44. Quotation in Lack, "Córdova Revolt," 97.

45. Houston to Jóse María Norris, August 8, 1838, list of "Revolted Mexicans," August 8, 1838, Houston to Colonel McLeod, August 9, 1838, Houston to Rusk, August 10, 1838, Houston to Colonel S. S. Davis, August 10, 1838, and Houston to H. W. Augustin, August 10, 1838, A. J. Houston Papers.

46. Houston proclamation (sent to Many), August 9, 1838, NARG 393, "Correspondence between Colonel James B. Many and Sam Houston"; Houston to Many, August 11, 1838, A. J. Houston Papers. Colonel Many joined the army in 1798 and was a seasoned veteran when Houston tried to force his hand. The "Many and Houston Correspondence" in the National Archives reveals a classic example of Houston's attempts at political manipulation. Many, who

refused Houston's requests, died at New Orleans on February 23, 1852. See Forman, "Colonel James B. Many," 119–128.

47. Houston to Big Mush, August 10, 1838, Houston to Bowles, August 11, 1838, and Houston to George May, August 12, 1838, in Houston, *Writings,* 2:269–270, 273–274; Rusk to Houston, August 13, 1838, A. J. Houston Papers.

48. Rusk to Houston, August 11, 12, and 13, 1838 (four letters), August 14 (two letters), 1838, A. J. Houston Papers; Rusk to Bowles, August 13, 1838, Rusk Papers; Houston to McLeod, August 13, 1838, Sam Houston Papers, Gilcrease Library, Tulsa, Okla.

49. Rusk to Houston, August 14, 1838, A. J. Houston Papers. See also Rusk to Houston, August 14, 1838, Rusk Papers. These two letters, written on the evening of August 14, both demonstrate Rusk's impatience. The second may never have been sent. In it, Rusk wrote, "I wish this infernal question of war or peace with the Cherokees was settled. It embarrasses my operation greatly."

50. Houston to Bowles, August 14, 1838, in Houston, *Writings,* 2:277; Houston to secretary of war, August 14, 1838, Rusk to Houston, August 14 and 15, 1838, A. J. Houston Papers.

51. Houston to Rusk, August 15, 16, and 22, 1838, Elana (Shawnee chief) to Houston, August 15, 1838, Houston to Elana, August 16, 1838, F. H. Rankin to Houston, August 16, 1838, Houston "General Order," August 16, 1838, Bowles to Houston, August 17, 1838, Rusk to Houston, August 19, 1838, Bowles to Houston, August 20, 1838, A. Jordan to (Houston), August 21, 1838, A. J. Houston Papers; Rusk to Kickapoo Tribe, August 16, 1838, Rusk Papers; Houston "General Order," August 18, 1838, in Houston, *Writings,* 2:278.

52. Quotation in Many to R. Jones, August 16, 1838, NARG 393, "Houston and Many Correspondence." See also Many to Houston, August 14, 1838, NARG 393, "Houston and Many Correspondence"; Many to Houston, August 16, 1838, and Houston to Many, August 19, 1838, A. J. Houston Papers.

53. Lieutenant William S. Harney to Many, August 25, 1838, NARG 393, "Houston and Many Correspondence."

54. Bee to Ashbel Smith, August 26, 1838, Bee Papers. Houston issued a special order on September 1, 1838, calling for the return of all household goods, kitchen furniture, corn, poultry, and cattle taken from Mrs. Johanna Ybarbo, a direct descendent of Juan Ybarbo, one of the earliest founders of the town. A few days later, a report from Nacogdoches indicated that some two hundred head of cattle and thirty to forty head of horses had been collected from Tejanos and that their ripened crops would likely perish. See Houston, "General Order," September 1, 1838, Houston Papers, BL; John Roberts to Houston, September 7, 1838, A. J. Houston Papers. In a spirit of vindictiveness, a Texan jury convicted Antonio Menchaca of treason, even though he had not joined the rebellion and had acted as a mediator for Houston. He was later pardoned. See Lack, "Córdova Revolt," 106–108.

55. Quotation in Houston to Dyer, August 14, 1838, Sam Houston Papers, Gilcrease Library. See also Houston to Dyer and citizens of Red River, August 11, 1838, and Houston to Dyer, August 13, 1838, A. J. Houston Papers.

56. The Sloan attack on Caddos or Wichitas is typical of many ranger assaults in that the number of Indians killed is not reported. See memoir of John P. Simpson, 1838, Ralph Stern Library, Stephen F. Austin University, Nacogdoches, Texas; Wilbarger, *Depredations in Texas,* 427.

57. Copies of the Miracle journal appear in several places. The journal leaves little doubt that Mexican military agents were among the Indians. But most Indians contacted by Miracle seemed uninterested in his offers. A translation, done at Houston, is in Anson Jones to John Forsyth, December 31, 1838, in Senate Executive Document No. 14, 32nd Cong., 2nd sess., vol. 3, pp.

11–17. This document also contains correspondence between the United States and Texas regarding the Indians' situation. Wright's translation is found in A. G. Wright to Judge Doak, August 21, 1838, NARG 94, LR, AGO, and NARG 393, Correspondence and Reports Relating to Special Subjects, 1831–1851. In the last source, Wright asked Judge Doak to get the following information in the Arkansas paper: "There is at this time on the headwaters of the River Trinity and west of said River and on the Sabine River North and South various tribes of Indians and Mexican officers prepared for battle." See also Arbuckle to adjutant inspector general, September 4, 1838, NARG 94, LR, AGO; Anson Jones to John Forsyth, December 31, 1838, Notes from the Texas Legation, TSL; [Houston] Telegraph and Texas Register, October 27, 1838; memoir of John Simpson, 1838, Stern Library.

58. Miracle journal, Senate Executive Document No. 14, 32nd Cong., 2nd sess., vol. 3, ser. 660, pp. 15–20.

59. Wright to Voss, August 30, 1838, Sam Houston Papers, Gilcrease Museum; Armstrong to C. A. Harris, August 31, 1838, NARG 75, LR, Western Superintendency.

60. Quotations in "Bonnell's Observations," 1838–1839, Bonnell Papers.

61. Rusk to Houston, August 22, 1838, A. J. Houston Papers. Despite Rusk's efforts to raise troops, the general still felt the need to receive some sanction from Houston, writing him two days later that "I must with great deference urge upon you the consideration of the proposition [regarding troops] that I submitted to you." When Houston refused to act, Rusk addressed a proclamation to the "citizens of Fort Houston" in which he again addressed the issues of the militia. "I have three times since urged him [Houston] to do so [organize the militia] but as yet have received no answer. He alone is authorized to call out men [into service]." This last statement was untrue, since Congress had authorized the commanding general of the militia to organize troops, but Rusk likely still recognized the popularity of Houston and wished for his approval, at least in late August. In subsequent proclamations, Rusk simply "authorized" volunteers to form up. Quotation in Rusk to Houston, August 24, 1838, A. J. Houston Papers. See also Rusk to Houston, August 25, 1838, A. J. Houston Papers; Rusk to citizens of Houston County, October 1, 1838, Rusk Papers.

62. Charles Sims to Houston, August 25, 1838, Rusk Papers; Houston to Rusk, August 26, 27, and 29, 1838, A. J. Houston Papers.

63. Houston to Sims, August 26, 1838, A. J. Houston Papers.

64. Houston to Many, August 28, 1838, NARG 94, LR, AGO.

65. Houston to Many, August 28, 1838, NARG 393, "Houston and Many Correspondence." While Colonel Many clearly disagreed with Houston and his views regarding the west, General Gaines remained a staunch supporter. On September 20, Gaines wrote to the secretary of war and requested 10,000 mounted troops, to be used to protect Texas, a region that he called "an infant, Herculean Republic." Texans were "citizens of the same colour, speaking the same language . . . and separated only by an *unmarked line* which no human being of either civilized nation interested in the matter can designate" (emphasis in original). In what must have been terribly confusing to the War Department, reports reached Washington about the same time from both Agent Armstrong and General Arbuckle that completely refuted Gaines's request. After hearing of Gaines's call to arms, Armstrong wrote, "I can only report that the Indians are quiet, no organizations, no hostile movements, or even appearances of it can be seem!" See Gaines to secretary of war, September 20, 1838, NARG 393, LR, 2nd Military Department; Armstrong to Harris, September 28, 1838, and Arbuckle to R. Jones, September 25, 1838, NARG 75, LR, Western Superintendency.

66. Rusk to Houston, August 27 and October 4, 1838, McLeod to Rusk, September 9, 1838, Mabbitt to Rusk, October 1 and 3, 1838, J. W. Burton to Rusk, October 6, 1838, and

Sims to Houston and Durst, October [20], 1838, A. J. Houston Papers; R. M. Williamson to Houston, October 8, 1838, "Unpublished," Houston Papers, BL. The Kickapoos took no part in this attack and even gave assistance to the survivors. The attack was made by Caddos, Wichitas, and Mexicans. See Rusk to General K. H. Douglas, November 21, 1838, Douglas Estate Papers, in Starr Papers, BL.

67. Two reports of the event have survived. See John Durst to Colonel I. R. Lewis, October 24, 1838, C. C. Hill Papers, BL; McLeod to M. B. Lamar, October 22, 1838, in Mirabeau B. Lamar, *The Papers of Mirabeau B. Lamar* (hereafter referred to as *Lamar Papers*), ed. Charles A. Gulick Jr., Katherine Elliott, and Harriet Smither, 6 vols. (Austin: Von Boeckmann-Jones, 1921–1927), 2:265–267. McLeod reported that the Cherokee chief Bowles had reported the loss of an additional 24 Indians who died of their injuries. See McLeod to Houston, October 25, 1838, A. J. Houston Papers.

68. Rusk to Baker, October 26, 1838, A. J. Houston Papers.

69. U.S. agents generally failed to deliver to the Caddos much of what was promised to them in the 1835 treaty, making it necessary for them to find food wherever possible. President Houston complained to the U.S. military on several occasions regarding Caddo depredations, noting that they were Indians from the United States. Again, it would seem that Colonel Many at Fort Jesup ignored Houston's appeals. See T. G. H. Scott to Poinsett, August 29, 1838, NARG 75, LR, Caddo Agency; Houston to Many, August 27, 1838, NARG 393, "Many and Houston Correspondence"; Houston to Many, August 29, 1838, NARG 94, LR, AGO; Rusk to secretary of war, December 1, 1838, Army Papers, RG 401, TSL.

70. McLeod memoir, November 1838, Ashbel Smith Papers, BL; Charles A. Seawall to R. Garland, November 26, 1838, agreement between Texas and the Caddos, November 29, 1838, and T. G. H. Scott to Poinsett, December 25, 1838, NARG 75, Caddo Agency; agreement made by Rusk with the Caddos, November 29, 1838, and Rusk to secretary of war, December 1, 1838, Army Papers, RG 401, TSL.

71. See Anson Jones to John Forsyth, December 31, 1838, and March 10, 1839, and Rusk to Albert S. Johnston, February 25, 1839, Senate Executive Document No. 14, 32nd Cong., 2nd sess., vol. 3, ser. 660, pp. 11–24.

72. Houston to Rusk, August 26, 1838, Sims to Houston, September 8, 1838, Houston to Z. F. Worlay, September 30, 1838, and Houston to Horton, October 10, 1838, A. J. Houston Papers; Houston to Rusk, August 26, 1838, Rusk Papers; Houston to Sims, September 30, 1838, Army Papers, RG 401, TSL; Houston to Sims, September 30, 1838, and Houston to Rusk, October 10, 1838, in Houston, *Writings,* 2:284–285 and 288–289; Rusk to Raguet, October 30, 1838, Raguet Papers; Horton to Houston, November 10, 1838, *Journal of the House of Representatives of the Republic of Texas: Regular Session of the Third Session, November 5, 1838* (Houston: Intelligencer Office, S. Whiting, 1839).

73. Resolution of the House of Representatives, November 8 and 12, 1838, *Journal of the House.*

74. Houston to the Texas congress, November 19, 1838, in Houston, *Writings,* 2:299–304.

Chapter 11. Lamar, His Generals, and Ethnic Cleansing

1. For Lamar, see Stanley Siegel, *The Poet President of Texas: The Life of Mirabeau B. Lamar, President of Texas* (Austin: Jenkins Publishing, 1977), 9–13.

2. Aide McLeod to Lamar, November 16, 1838, and Rusk to Lamar, November 17, 1838, *Lamar Papers,* 2:293–294.

3. McLeod to Lamar, December 1, 1838, *Lamar Papers,* 2:308–310.

4. Jones to John Forsyth, November 26, 1838, NARG 75, LR, Western Superintendency. The secretary of war ordered General Arbuckle at Fort Gibson to reply to Jones. Arbuckle reported in April 1839 that no information existed supporting any of the allegations. Arbuckle did concede that if Mexicans and Indians in Texas started a war south of the Red River, some Indians from Indian Territory might join the fray. See Arbuckle to Jones, April 13, 1839, NARG 393, LS, 2nd Military Department.

5. See, for example, Lieutenant Colonel Daniel Montague to Lieutenant Voss, October 4, 1838, and Voss to headquarters, Fort Gibson, November 1, 1838, NARG 393, LR, 2nd Military Department.

6. Discussions of the militia legislation appear in Muckleroy, "Indian Policy of the Republic of Texas," part 3, 132–133; Nance, *After San Jacinto,* 85–86.

7. President Lamar's address is found in several places. See Lamar's First Message, December 21, 1838, *Lamar Papers,* 2:346–369; Lamar to congress, December 21, 1838, *Journal of the House of Representatives of the Republic of Texas, Regular Session of the Third Congress,* 18–19; Lamar to congress, December 21, 1838, Messages and Proclamations of the Presidents, LR, Secretary of State Records, TSL.

8. Typical of the lack of evidence was General Rusk's justification for his attack on the peaceful Caddos at Shreveport that fall. While three or four people had been killed in East Texas in the weeks before the assault on the Caddos, there was no evidence linking these deaths to the Indians. See statement of Elias Vansickle, January 23, 1839, and Rusk to Albert Sidney Johnston, February 25, 1839, Notes from the Texan Legation in the United States, TSL.

9. B. Lowe to Houston, December 6, 1838, and B. C. Walters to K. H. Douglas, December 14 and 20, 1838, Douglas Estate Papers, BL; memoir of John Simpson, 1839–1840, Stern Library. Wilbarger appears to have been wrong in asserting that Mr. Kitchens was killed. See Wilbarger, *Depredations in Texas,* 217.

10. Many of these men from Franklin likely died near the falls of the Brazos when 13 Texans were killed while surveying. See E. Melton circular letter, January 16, 1839, and petition of citizens of Franklin, Texas, February 6, 1838, *Lamar Papers,* 2:420, 436–437. In an interesting "sketch" of early Texas by the Frenchmen Frédéric Gaillardet, the author argues that Texans had already made enemies of many western tribes by expanding onto western lands. See Gaillardet, *Sketches of Early Texas and Louisiana,* trans. with introduction by James I. Shepherd III, (Austin: University of Texas Press, 1966), 54–57.

11. Captain S. E. Box to General K. H. Douglas, December 24, 1838, and Douglas to "Sir," December 30, 1838, Douglas Estate Papers, BL; McLeod to Lamar, December 20, 1838, and January 9, 1839, and Rusk to Lamar, January 9, 1839, *Lamar Papers,* 2:341–342, 405, 406.

12. Rusk to Douglas, January 1, 1839, and Snively to Douglas, January 13 and 14, 1839, Douglas Estate Papers, BL; Douglas to Snively, January 2, 1839, Army Papers, RG 401, TSL; Muckleroy, "Indian Policy of the Republic of Texas," part 3, 135–136. For the American view, see Vose to William Armstrong, January 3, 1839, Vose to assistant adjutant general, January 3, 1839, and G. P. Kingsbury to Vose, May 8, 1839, NARG 393, LR, 2nd Military Department; T. Hartley Crawford to Armstrong, February 19 and July 9, 1839, NARG 75, LR, Western Superintendency.

13. See reprinted letters from *Telegraph* in *The Daily Picayune,* March 19, 1839, in Bee Papers. Despite the criticism, Albert Sidney Johnston seemed to think that the policies of the Lamar administration were "everywhere sustained"—in particular, his efforts to build a militia. See Johnston to William Henry Dangerfield, April 12, 1839, Albert Sidney Johnston Papers, TSL; Johnston to Lamar, April 10, 1839, *Lamar Papers,* 2:522–523.

14. See Wilbarger, *Depredations in Texas,* 144–145; Henderson Yoakum, *History of Texas from the First Settlement in 1685 to Its Annexation to the United States in 1846,* 2 vols. (New York: Redfield, 1855), 2:261–262.

15. Moore to Johnston, March 10, 1839, in Winfrey and Day, *Indian Papers of Texas,* 1:57–59; Jenkins and Kesselus, *Burleson,* 180–181.

16. Lamar address, February 28, 1839, *Lamar Papers,* 2:474–475; Lamar proclamation, March 1839, Messages and Proclamations of the Presidents, LS, Secretary of State Records, TSL; Burleson to Johnston, March 2, 1839, A. J. Houston Papers; Yoakum, *History of Texas,* 2:262.

17. Jenkins and Kesselus have put together the best assessment of Burleson's role in the attack on Córdova's party. See Jenkins and Kesselus, *Burleson,* 186–189.

18. Burleson to Johnston, May 22, 1839, Army Papers, RG 401, TSL. Good descriptions of the engagement are in Jenkins and Kesselus, *Burleson,* 192–194. Alessio Robles puts the number of Mexicans and Indians in the party at 25. See Alessio Robles, *Coahuila y Texas,* 196–199. Nance has a wonderful discussion of the squabble that ensued after the Rice party met other rangers coming to assist them. The two different parties almost came to blows over the spoils. See Nance, *After San Jacinto,* 136–138.

19. Filisola to army of the north (Cordova and Flores), February 2, 1839, A. J. Houston Papers.

20. See Canalizo to don Manuel Flores, including "Instructions to the captains and chiefs of the friendly nations," February 27, 1839, Army Papers, RG 401, TSL; Spanish circular, signed by Canalizo, February 27, 1839, orders for Indians, February 27, 1839, Canalizo to Cordova, March 1, 1839, and Canalizo to Ensign Juan de la Garza, April 19, 1839, A. J. Houston Papers.

21. Lamar to Bowles and other head men, May 26, 1839, *Lamar Papers,* 2:590–594.

22. Lamar to Linnee and other chiefs and headmen of the Shawnee Indians, June 3, 1839, *Lamar Papers,* 3:11–12; Johnston to Douglas, May 30, 1839, Douglas Estate Papers, BL.

23. The order is reprinted in Winfrey and Day, *Indian Papers of Texas,* 1:61–62. Burnet instructed minister Richard G. Dunlap, in Washington, D.C., to inform the U.S. government of the intentions of Texas to expel the Indians on May 30. Any discussion regarding the rights of the Indians to land "can scarcely enter into your correspondence," he wrote. Burnet also sent copies of the Flores correspondence to Secretary of State John Forsyth. The secretary returned them without much comment on July 17. See Burnet to Dunlap, May 30, 1839, Forsyth to Dunlap, July 17, 1839, and J. R. Poinsett to Forsyth, July 18, 1839, A. J. Houston Papers; T. Hartley Crawford to William Armstrong, July 25, 1839, NARG 75, LR, Western Superintendency.

24. Rusk to Houston, June 9, 1839, Rusk Papers.

25. Kaufman to Houston, June 18, 1839, A. J. Houston Papers.

26. Lamar to Burnet, Johnston, Rusk, I. W. Burton, and James S. Mayfield, June 27, 1839, Messages and Proclamations of the Presidents, LS, Secretary of State Records, TSL.

27. The official account of the battle is "Extract from the Report of General K. N. Douglas to the Secy of War relative to the late Cherokee Campaign," 1839, Army Papers, RG 401, TSL. See also John H. Reagan, "The Expulsion of the Cherokee from East Texas," *Quarterly of the Texas State Historical Association* 1 (July 1897–April 1898): 38–46; Winfrey, "Chief Bowles of the Texas Cherokee," 29–41. Casualties are discussed in Douglas to Johnston, July 16, 1839, and Douglas to Lamar, July 17, 1839, *Lamar Papers,* 3:45–46, 46–47.

28. "Extract from the Report of Genl. K. N. Douglas to the Secy of War relative to the late Cherokee Campaign," 1839, Army Papers, RG 401, TSL.

29. Johnston, Rusk, and Mayfield to James Reily, August 1, 1839, Winfrey and Day, *Indian Papers of Texas,* 1:78; Douglas to Captain G. English, August 5, 1839, *Lamar Papers,* 3:54. The

commission selected to treat with the Cherokees had $25,000 on hand to give them for their improvements. After the battle, this money was returned to the Texas treasury. In another matter, a huge political misunderstanding quickly ensued after the battle, based on an incorrect report by General Douglas that suggested that Rusk's men had charged the camp and earned the victory. In actuality, Colonel Burleson and troops from southern Texas had done most of the fighting. Burleson was outraged by the report. See Jenkins and Kesselus, *Burleson,* 199–205.

30. Council with the Shawnee, August 1839, Rusk Papers; Rusk to Linney, Green Grass, and Pecan, September 3, 1839, and Mayfield and Rusk to Elina, Green Grass, Pecan, and Gibson, September 25, 1839, Washington Miller Papers, TSL; treaty with the Shawnees, August 2, 1839, in Winfrey and Day, *Indian Papers of Texas,* 1:80–81.

31. Burnet to Richard G. Dunlap, August 19, 1839, A. J. Houston Papers.

32. Quotations in Arbuckle to Jones, January 6, 1840, NARG 393, LS, 2nd Military Department. See also Arbuckle to Joseph Vann, May 22, 1840, ibid.; John Emberson to Johnston, October 25, 1839, A. J. Houston Papers.

33. Johnston to William Henry Dangerfield, December 31, 1839, Johnston Papers; Jenkins and Kesselus, *Burleson,* 218–219; Burleson to Johnston, December 26, 1839, in *Austin City Gazette,* January 1, 1840. Burleson took several prisoners in the engagement; they were sent back to Indian Territory. See Archer to Arbuckle, June 11, 1840, NARG 393, LR, 2nd Military Department.

34. Hotchkiss had been speculating in Texas lands since the early 1830s. See his argument in Hotchkiss to Lamar, December 5, 1838, *Lamar Papers,* 2:310–312.

35. Lamar's annual message to congress, November 12, 1839, *Lamar Papers,* 3:165–167.

36. See Crawford to Armstrong, October 2, 1839, NARG 75, LR, Western Superintendency; Armstrong to Crawford, November 27, 1839, and February 23, 1840, and H. G. Rind to Crawford, February 5, 1840, NARG 75, Caddo Agency.

37. Tijerina used the Goliad County records to show the number of Tejanos who had lost their land. See Tijerina, *Tejanos and Texas,* 158; De León, *Tejano Community,* 4–15.

38. J. Browne to Johnston, September 13, 1839, and H. S. Foote to Lamar, September 15, 1839, *Lamar Papers,* 3:106–107, 108–110.

39. Houston speech on behalf of the Cherokee Land Bill, December 1839, in Houston, *Writings,* 2:323–348; W. Brookfield to Lamar, January 6, 1840, *Lamar Papers,* 3:320–321; *Austin City Gazette,* January 22, 1840.

40. "Report" from Committee on Indian Affairs on the Cherokee Land Bill, January 22, 1840, and other documents in *Journals of the Fourth Congress of the Republic of Texas, 1839–1840, to Which Are Added the Relief Laws,* ed. Harriet Smither (Austin: Von Boechmann-Jones, 1931), 274–276, 291–293, and 302. Howland's commission is dated February 6, 1840 (in Houston Papers, BL).

41. Muckleroy, "Indian Policy of the Republic of Texas," part 3, 141; Bedford, *Texas Indian Troubles,* 36–39; Karnes to secretary of war, January 10, 1840, in Winfrey and Day, *Indian Papers of Texas,* 1:101–102. The Horn boy had nearly lost his ability to speak English after having been a captive for eighteen months. See *Austin City Gazette,* February 12, 1840.

42. Johnston to Fisher, January 30, 1840, in Winfrey and Day, *Indian Papers of Texas,* 1:105–106.

43. The official report of the council house fight is McLeod to Lamar, March 20, 1840, A. J. Houston Papers. It was reprinted in *Journals of the House of Representatives of the Republic of Texas: Fifth Congress, Appendix* (Austin: Gazette Office, 1841), 136–139, and also in *Austin City Gazette,* March 25, 1840. See also Bedford, *Texas Indian Troubles,* 36–39.

44. See *Houston Weekly Times,* April 9, 1840.

45. Ascertaining the events of Matilda Lockhart's capture is more complicated than doing so for Mrs. Webster, since Matilda failed to leave an account. Some sixty years after the event, Mary A. Maverick wrote an account, compiled from diaries and the notes that she had kept. She gives a frightful description of Matilda's condition: "Her head, arms and face were full of bruises, and sores, and her nose actually burnt off to the bone—all the fleshy end gone, and a great scab formed on the end of the bone. Both nostrils were wide open and denuded of flesh." While published in the 1890s, this description has been used by historians to claim that the massacre came about as a result of the justifiable rage of Texas men. Yet none of the Texas officials claimed this to be the case at the time; evidence of abuse is conspicuously missing in the primary documents. Maverick may have exaggerated Lockhart's condition because of the growing criticism of Texas in the American and European press. The most significant source on Matilda's condition is a brief statement made in a letter by her sister-in-law, Catherine Lockhart, who was in San Antonio. Catherine describes Matilda's release but says nothing of abuse. See Catherine Lockhart to her mother, Elizabeth Burton, April 9, 1840, Catherine Lockhart Papers, BL; Dolbeare, *Dolly Webster,* 10–25. For a different interpretation of this issue, see Donaly E. Brice, *The Great Comanche Raid: Boldest Indian Attack of the Texas Republic* (Austin: Eakin Press, 1987), 26–27.

46. *Austin City Gazette,* May 20, 1840.

47. Catherine Lockhart to her mother, April 9, 1840, Catherine Lockhart Papers; *Houston Weekly Gazette,* April 9, 1840; *Austin City Gazette,* May 6 and June 24, 1840.

48. Compare letter from Catherine Lockhart to her mother, April 9, 1840, Catherine Lockhart Papers with that of Hugh McLeod to Lamar, March 20, 1840, A. J. Houston Papers.

49. Lamar to Branch T. Archer, June 29, 1840, *Lamar Papers,* 3:322.

CHAPTER 12. THE INDIANS' LAST STAND IN CENTRAL TEXAS

1. The best description of early Comanche mourning is still Berlandier, *Indians of Texas,* 93–96.

2. After the council house massacre, the new secretary of war, Branch T. Archer, wanted to hire and equip more militia, but given the quiet, Lamar refused. See Lamar to Archer, June 29, 1840, *Lamar Papers,* 3:322; J. R. Cunningham to Captain Adam Clendenin, July 9, 1840, Army Papers, RG 401, TSL; William Banta and J. W. Caldwell, *Twenty-seven Years on the Texas Frontier; or fifty years in Texas* (Austin: Ben Jones, 1893), 1–3; *Austin City Gazette,* June 17 and 24 and July 8 and 15, 1840.

3. See Janet Lecompte, "Bent, St. Vrain & Co., among the Comanches and Kiowas," *Colorado Magazine of History* 44, no. 4 (Fall 1972): 273–293.

4. The council is described by William Bent to George Bird Grinnell. See Grinnell diary, November 8, 1901, Grinnell Papers. Grinnell later used the material in a manuscript entitled "Bent's Fort," also found in the Southwest Museum. A mention of the council appears in Lecompte, "Bent, St. Vrain & Co.," 273–293.

5. George Bent to George Hyde, February 15–17, 1905, Hyde Papers, Denver Public Library. See also Grinnell diary, November 8, 1901, and "Bent's Fort" manuscript, Grinnell Papers. To capitalize on their new trading partners, the Bents built a new post on the Canadian River, clearly in Comanche lands, in 1842. This was replaced by the post at Adobe Walls, constructed in 1845 and occupied for two years. See Lecompte, "Bent, St. Vrain & Co.," 281–282.

6. Brice, *Great Comanche Raid,* 27–48. For a firsthand account of the fighting at Victoria, see Elizabeth McAnulty Owens, "The Story of My Life," BL.

7. Besides the dead at Victoria, five other people (two of whom were women) were killed in the march on Linnville. See *[Austin] Texas Sentinel,* August 15, 1840.

8. Firsthand accounts of the destruction of Linnville include Gilbert Onderdonk, "Stories of Early Texas Life," BL; William H. Watts letter, *Austin City Gazette,* August 26, 1840. See also an account left by the founder of Linnville, John J. Linn, *Reminiscences of Fifty Years in Texas* (New York: Sadler, 1883). Linnville's reputation as a "nest" for robbers is reported by Falconer, diary entry for March 23, 1841, in Thomas Falconer, *Letters and Notes on the Texan Santa Fe Expedition,* ed. Frederick Webb Hodge (New York: Dauber and Pine, 1930), 202.

9. Quotation from "an observer from Gonzales," in *Austin City Gazette,* September 2, 1840.

10. This escalation in casualties is found in General Huston's successive reports to the Texas Congress. His report was influenced by General Burleson, who thought the number of Comanches killed was about 60. While some Texas historians have put the number of horses and mules recaptured at over 1,000, Huston gives a figure of 200, suggesting that the Indians got away with many. See Huston's report of the Battle of Plum Creek, August 12, 1840, with supplement, September 28, 1840, *Journals of the House: Fifth Congress, Appendix,* 141–143, 143–144. Another copy is Huston to Archer, August 15, 1840, A. J. Houston Papers. See other estimates of casualties in *[Austin] Texas Sentinel,* August 15, 1840; Jenkins and Kesselus, *Burleson,* 257–258. The best newspaper report of the action is *Austin City Gazette,* August 19, 1840.

11. Bee to Ashbel Smith, August 16, 1840, Bee Papers.

12. *Austin City Gazette,* September 2, 1840.

13. Huston to the speaker of the house of representatives, September 20, 1840, Army Papers, RG 401, TSL.

14. Report of Secretary Archer, September 30, 1840, *Journals of the House: Fifth Congress, Appendix,* 118–119; Lamar report, November 24, 1840, *Journals of the Senate of the Republic of Texas: Fifth Congress, First Session* (Houston: Telegraph Office, 1841), 39. Despite the lack of money, Huston went forward with plans to raise a force of 1,600 men, dividing his fictitious army into four divisions. See *Austin City Gazette,* September 30, 1840. Later in the fall, when conditions at San Antonio seemed precarious, Archer wrote Acting President Burnet that "not one dollar" existed in the treasury with which to purchase munitions. See Archer to Burnet, December 19, 1840, Army Papers, RG 401, TSL.

15. The complete report of the September scout up the Brazos River is in G. B. Erath to Felix Huston, September 8, 1840, Army Papers, RG 401, TSL; Jenkins and Kesselus, *Burleson,* 257. The Waco Indian town had been abandoned for many years, but a handful of Indians returned to it occasionally, mostly to camp. While Moore was launching his unauthorized expedition, Huston was talking with the newspapers. He planned to attack the Comanches in the winter, when they camped in the sheltered river valleys. All he needed was men and material, or so he said. See Huston statement, *[Austin] Texas Sentinel,* October 3, 1840. The Tonkawa leader Placido had joined several Texas ranger expeditions against the Comanches, for they were avowed enemies of the Tonkawas. He and a handful of his men were also at the battle of Plum Creek. See the recent history of these people: Himmel, *Conquest of the Karankawas and the Tonkawas.*

16. *[Austin] Texas Sentinel,* November 14, 1840. Moore's "official" report is in *[Houston] Telegraph and Texas Register,* November 18, 1840. Moore mentions several incidents in which Comanche women and children were spared, but he describes the battlefield as one littered with the bodies of men, women, and children. Yoakum, whose account was written in 1855, described the scene as follows: "As this was a war of extermination, the bodies of men, women and children were seen on every hand, dead, wounded and dying." Yoakum counted 48 dead in the village with 80 more bodies in the river. See Yoakum, *History of Texas,* 2:304–305. Despite the fact that Moore's ranger attack of that fall was the most crushing victory ever by a ranger unit, Utley gives it only two lines in his recent study, and he fails to mention casualties. He writes: "Moore

struck a Comanche village high on the Colorado River and all but wiped it out. As usual in surprise attacks on villages, men, women, and children fell victim to the deadly fire." See Utley, *Lone Star Justice,* 33.

17. *Austin City Gazette,* April 7, 1841.

18. Mark B. Lewis to Archer, June 2, 1841; Hays to Archer, July 1 and August 13, 1841, Army Papers, RG 401, TSL. Utley immortalizes Jack Hays in his study of the Texas rangers but uses Hays's fight of June 1844 with Comanches, never even mentioning this earlier encounter in which Hays also burned an Indian village. See Utley, *Lone Star Justice,* 10–12.

19. Chandler to Archer, May 26 and June 19, 1841, Army Papers, RG 401, TSL.

20. George M. Dotson to Archer, April 2, 1841, A. J. Houston Papers; the *Austin City Gazette* reported the encounter under the byline "Glorious News From the East." See April 7 and June 2, 1841; James Smith to P. S. Hollingsworth, June 13, 1841, Army Papers, RG 401, TSL.

21. The official report is William N. Porter to Archer, June 5, 1841, Army Papers, RG 401, TSL.

22. Another report is in *Austin City Gazette,* June 23, 1841. Eli Chandler later learned about this village from a Mexican captive and provided the government with an extensive description of it. See Chandler to Archer, June 19, 1841, Army Papers, RG 401, TSL, and a similar report in Chandler to secretary of war, June 19, 1841, *Journals of the Senate of the Republic of Texas: Sixth Congress* (Austin: S. Whiting, 1841), 421.

23. See Kenneth F. Neighbours, "José Maria: Anadarko Chief," *Chronicles of Oklahoma* 44 (Autumn 1966): 254–274.

24. A small party from this ranger expedition, led by Huston, actually crossed the river into Indian Territory, causing a minor incident. But Huston's men fortunately found no Indians. G. B. Erath to secretary of war, August 12, 1841, Army Papers, RG 401, TSL; James Wolf to Col. A. M. M. Upshaw, August 27, 1841, NARG 75, LR, Western Superintendency; Lamar to Burleson, September 1, 1841, Messages and Proclamations of the Presidents, LS, Secretary of State Records, TSL; *[Austin] Daily Bulletin,* December 15, 1841.

25. Lamar to Hays, October 2, 1841, Messages and Proclamations of the Presidents, LS, Secretary of State Records, TSL.

CHAPTER 13. THE FAILURE OF WELL-INTENDED EFFORTS

1. "Epílogo," Isidro Vizcaya Canales, ed., *La Invasión de los Indios Bárbaros al Noreste de Mexico en los Años de 1840 y 1841* (Monterey, Mexico: Instituto Tecnológico y de Estudias Superiores, 1968), 257.

2. W. C. Binkley, "New Mexico and the Santa Fe Expedition," *Southwestern Historical Quarterly* 27 (October 1923): 85–107.

3. The campaign is covered well in Haley, *Sam Houston,* 218–226.

4. The best analysis of the politics of the Mexican invasion is Sam W. Haynes, *Soldiers of Misfortune: The Somervell and Mier Expeditions* (Austin: University of Texas Press, 1990), 4–9. For the Mexican reaction, see Arista to his troops, April 13, 1841, Matamoros Archives, BL; Arista to the secretary of war, May 26, 1841, Francisco G. Conde to commandant of District of El Paso, June 20, 1841, Damasó Salasar to secretaria de la comandancia general, June 22, 1841, Conde to minister of war and marine, July 12, 1841, Bolton Papers (copies of originals in Archivo Histórico Militar de Defensa Nacional, Mexico City).

5. Haynes, *Soldiers of Misfortune,* 10–23.

6. Haynes does an excellent job of breaking down the various elements of the army in *Soldiers of Misfortune,* 42–45.

7. Green quotation is found in "Speech on Thomas Jefferson Green," August 1, 1854, *Writings of Houston,* 6:77–78.

8. Haynes, *Soldiers of Misfortune,* 54–55.

9. Ibid., 66–79.

10. Houston to congress, December 20, 1841, Messages and Proclamations of the President, LS, Secretary of State Records, TSL.

11. Houston later reported on January 12 that some $9,300 was due "Minutemen," over and above the $75,000 that the Texas Congress had already appropriated. Houston to house of representatives, January 2 and 6, 1842, and Houston to the senate, January 25, 1842, Messages and Proclamations of the President, LS, Secretary of State Records, TSL. On the militia bills, see Nance, *After San Jacinto,* 400–403.

12. Houston to the house of representatives, February 2, 1842, Messages and Proclamations of the President, LS, Secretary of State Records, TSL.

13. Houston to G. W. Adams, April 14, 1842, *Journals of the Sixth Congress of the Republic of Texas, 1841–1842* (n.p.: Capital Printing, 1845), 132–133. For the various appointments made during 1842, see Messages and Proclamations, LS, Secretary of State Records, TSL; Frank to Houston, May 12 and July 10, 1842, and Houston to Frank, September 26, 1842, A. J. Houston Papers.

14. L. Jordan to Houston, March 10, 1842, A. J. Fowler and L. Johnson to Houston, March 14, 1842, and William M. Crisp to Houston, March 17, 1842, A. J. Houston Papers.

15. Armstrong to Crawford, April 2 and 9 and May 24, 1842, Upshaw to Armstrong, April 6, 1842, and Armstrong to J. C. Spencer, May 1, 1842, NARG 75, LR, Western Superintendency; W. W. S. Bliss to James Logan, April 14, 1842, NARG 393, LS, 7th Military Department; Thomas Farrow Smith report, April 22, 1842, in Winfrey and Day, *Indian Papers of Texas,* 1:125–126. For Wild Cat's military career in Florida, see Edwin C. McReynolds, *The Seminoles* (Norman: University of Oklahoma Press, 1957), 200–226.

16. Logan to the president, June 1, 1842, A. J. Houston Papers.

17. Houston to the "Border Tribes," July 6, 1842, Messages and Proclamations, LS, Secretary of State Records, TSL; R. M. Jones to Red Bear, July 30, 1842, Army Papers, RG 401, TSL; Stroud, Durst, and Houston to Williams, August 1, 1842, and John Durst to Houston, August 4, 1842, A. J. Houston Papers; treaty with the Caddo, August 24, 1842, Houston Papers, BL.

18. Armstrong to Crawford, September 3, 1842, and Crawford to Armstrong, October 29 and December 15, 1842, NARG 75, LR, Western Superintendency; Stroud to Houston, September 14, 1842, A. J. Houston Papers (the date on this document has been incorrectly written as 1862 rather than 1842).

19. Houston to Moore, October 8, 1842, Houston to Red Bear, October 18, 1842, Houston to Frank, November 13, 1842, and Houston to Terrell, November 13, 1842, Messages and Proclamations, LS, Secretary of State Records, TSL: Houston to Terrell, October 21, 1842, Houston Papers, BL; Houston to Moore, January 10, 1843, A. J. Houston Papers.

20. Houston to Indian commissioners, October 9, 1842, Messages and Proclamations, LS, Secretary of State Records, TSL.

21. Houston to congress, December 1, 1842, *Journals of the House of Representatives of the Seventh Congress of the Republic of Texas, Convened at Washington, on the 14th Nov., 1842* (Washington, Tex.: Thomas Johnson, 1843), 16–28.

22. Houston to congress, January 14, 1843, *Journals of the House of Representatives of the Seventh Congress of the Republic of Texas,* 270. The trade houses are discussed in Joseph Carroll McConnell, *The West Texas Frontier, or a Descriptive History of Early Times in Western Texas* (Jacksboro, Tex.: Gazette Press, 1933), 39–41.

23. Quotation in Terrell to Houston, March 13, 1843, A. J. Houston Papers. For general information on organizing the council at Tawakoni Creek, see Houston to Warren, February 3, 1843, Houston Papers, BL; Joseph Durst to Houston, February 8, 1843, Terrell to Houston, February 10, 15, and 22 and March 11, 1843, Houston to Terrell, February 13 and March 11, 1843, and G. H. Hill to Houston, February 15 and 22, 1843, A. J. Houston Papers.

24. Houston to Terrell, March 20, 1843, Houston to chiefs of Wichitas, March 20, 1843, and Houston to Terrell, L. S. Black, and T. J. Smith, March 29, 1843, Messages and Proclamations, LS, Secretary of State Records, TSL; Terrell, L. S. Black, and Thomas Smith to Houston, March 24, 1843, A. J. Houston Papers; Minutes of Council at Tawakoni Creek, March 28–31, 1843, in Winfrey and Day, *Indian Papers of Texas,* 1:149–163; "Talk" of Pierce M. Butler to "Wild Indians," March 28, 1843, Butler Papers, Huntington Library.

25. Most of these men who met Houston asked for payment for their role in "bringing in" the Indians. Jesse Chisholm and Jim Shaw received $245 each, while others received lesser amounts. See Houston to J. C. Eldridge, April 17, 1843, Messages and Proclamations, LS, Secretary of State Records, TSL.

26. Butler to T. Hartley Crawford, April 29, 1843, Butler Papers, Huntington Library.

27. Butler "Report," April 29, 1843, Butler Papers, Huntington Library.

28. The best discussion of Superintendent Eldridge's efforts during the summer of 1843 is in Eldridge to Houston, December 8, 1843, Washington Miller Papers. See also Houston to Torrey, April 17, 1843, and Houston to Eldridge, May 4, 1843, Messages and Proclamations, LS, Secretary of State Records, TSL; Eldridge to Houston, June 2, 1843, Houston Papers, "Unpublished," BL; Eldridge to Houston, June 2, 1843, in Winfrey and Day, *Indian Papers of Texas,* 1:210–214.

29. Detailed (but different) reports of these councils are found in Eldridge to Houston, December 8, 1843, in Winfrey and Day, *Indian Papers of Texas,* 1:251–275, and in Eldridge to Houston, December 8, 1843, Washington Miller Papers.

30. Eldridge to Houston, December 8, 1843, Washington Miller Papers.

31. Terrell's talk to the Indians, September 25, 1843, A. J. Houston Papers.

32. Actually, Wilbarger missed an attack by Indians in Milam County, along the central Brazos River, that occurred on June 22. See Henry Kattenhorn to Thomas G. Western, June 22, 1844, A. J. Houston Papers.

33. Utley uses the Walker Creek fight as a way of introducing the Texas rangers in his first chapter, entitled "The Established." He gives short shrift to previous ranger fights with Indians, ignoring totally the northern campaigns of Erath and Tarrant (these men are not even in his index). As for Moore, the most successful Indian killer of all, Utley offers two sentences describing his 1839 attack on the San Saba and a simple paragraph describing his October 1840 slaughter of the Comanches on the Colorado River. While well over a hundred Indians perished, a number that is exceedingly significant given the fact that no rangers were killed, Utley gives no figure at all, concluding only that a few men, women, and children had died. Utley is correct in noting the significance of the Walker Creek fight in terms of the use of Colt pistols. See Utley, *Lone Star Justice,* 10–12, 19, 24, 33. On the makeup of the war party in 1844, see council ground notes, July 22, 1844, and Western to Houston, June 16, 1844, A. J. Houston Papers.

34. Butler to Crawford, December 15, 1843, Butler Papers, Huntington Library.

35. Butler, "Report on Negotiations at Cache Creek," January 31, 1844, Butler Papers, Huntington Library; Houston to Tah-sah-roque (Kechikaroqua), January 31, 1844, A. J. Houston Papers.

36. Butler actually collected demographic information for three years; his first census of the tribes is in Butler, "Report," January 31, 1844, Butler Papers, Huntington Library. A more

complete census for the Comanche people in particular is in Butler and M. D. Lewis to William Medill, August 8, 1846, NARG 75, Documents Relating to the Negotiation of Ratified and Unratified Treaties.

37. Butler, "Report," January 31, 1844, Butler Papers, Huntington Library.

38. The killing of bison by Indians and then Anglos is a debated issue that will not be resolved here. See Dan Flores, "Bison Ecology and Bison Diplomacy," *Journal of American History* 78 (1991–1992): 480–483, and Brooks, *Captives and Cousins*, 216–228.

39. Houston to the senate, January 9, 1844, and P. A. Porter to Houston, January 17, 1844, A. J. Houston Papers; Houston proclamation announcing Indian treaty, February 3, 1844, Records Relating to Indian Affairs, TSL. On the Germans, see Terry G. Jordan, *German Seed in Texas Soil: Immigrant Farmers in Nineteenth-Century Texas* (Austin: University of Texas Press, 1966).

40. Committee on Indian Affairs to the Speaker of the House, February 3, 1844, *Journals of the House of Representatives of the Eighth Congress of the Republic of Texas* (Houston: Cruger and Moore, 1844), 451–453.

41. Houston to John Torrey, February 15, 1844, and Houston to J. C. Neill and L. H. Williams, April 6, 1844, Messages and Proclamations, LS, Secretary of State Records, TSL; Sloat to Houston, April 7, 1844, L. Williams to Houston, April 7, 1844, Western to Houston, April 13 and 15, 1844, and G. W. Hill to Houston, April 26, 1844, A. J. Houston Papers, TSL; council minutes at Tehuacana (Tawakoni) Creek, April 27, 1844, and statement of Louis Sanchez, May 1844, in Winfrey and Day, *Indian Papers of Texas,* 2:19–21, 64–66.

42. Houston to Neill and Williams, May 1, 1844, Messages and Proclamations, LS, Secretary of State Records, TSL; council at Tawakoni Creek, May 13–15, 1844, Records Relating to Indian Affairs, TSL; council at Tawakoni Creek, May 13–15, 1844, in Winfrey and Day, *Indian Papers of Texas,* 2:31–56; Western to Houston, May 15, 1844, A. J. Houston Papers; Western to Sloat, June 6, 1844, in Winfrey and Day, *Indian Papers of Texas,* 2:69–70.

43. Henry Kattenhorn to Western, June 22, 1844, St. Louis to Houston, July 9, 1844, John Conner to Houston, July 9, 1844, Sloat to Houston, July 25, 1844, A. J. Houston Papers; F. L. to prefecto del distrito del norte, July 4, 1844, Matamoros Archives, BL; Richard Belt to John C. Calhoun, July 5, 1844, Matamoros Consul Records, BL; Western to Houston, July 27, 1844, Records Relating to Indian Affairs, TSL.

44. Houston to Western, July 29, 1844, Messages and Proclamations, LS, Secretary of State Records, TSL.

45. Western to J. F. Torrey, September 23, 1844, Records Relating to Indian Affairs, TSL; R. B. Mason to R. Jones, September 25, 1844, NARG 393, LR, 7th Military Department; Hill to Houston, October 3, 1844, and Captain Nathan Boone to Houston, October 14, 1844, A. J. Houston Papers; John Conner and Jim Shaw to Houston, October 2, 1844, and council minutes, October 7–9, 1844, in Winfrey and Day, *Indian Papers of Texas,* 2:103–119.

46. Western to Sloat, February 12 and April 2, 1845, and I. C. Spence to Western, September 9, 1845, in Winfrey and Day, *Indian Papers of Texas,* 2:199–200, 211–212, and 356–357; Western to Colonel S. H. Williams, April 2, 1845, and Western to Richard Fitzpatrick, May 5, 1845, Records Relating to Indian Affairs, TSL.

47. Western to Toasting Ear, a Delaware, January 26, 1845, Western to Sloat, February 28, 1845, and Western to Neighbors, March 2, 1845, Records Relating to Indian Affairs, TSL; Western to John F. Torrey, January 6, 1845, Western to Neighbors, March 2 and May 20, 1845, Williams to Western, August 16, 1845, and Neighbors to Western, September 15, 1845, in Winfrey and Day, *Indian Papers of Texas,* 2:161, 205–206, 252–253, 322, 361–362.

CHAPTER 14. THE BOUNDARY LINE FIASCO

1. The land policy of Texas is outlined in Richardson, Wallace, and Anderson, *Texas,* 144–149. See also Jordan, *German Seed in Texas Soil,* 40–50. The number of German settlers coming to Texas ranged in the thousands every year after 1844. The 1860 census figure of 20,000 German settlers living in Texas by the Civil War is probably too low.

2. The debate on public lands started in 1845 and continued into the 1850s. See David S. Kaufman, chairman, to K. L. Anderson, president of the senate, January 29, 1845, *Journals of the Senate of the Ninth Congress of the Republic of Texas* (Washington, Tex.: Miller and Cushney, 1845), 180–181, 186; A. J. Donelson to Eben'r Allen, June 13, 1845, *Journals of the Senate of the Extra Session, Ninth Congress of the Republic of Texas* (Washington, Tex.: Miller and Cushney, 1845), 30–33; V. S. Howard (chair), William T. Sadler, William L. Cazeneau, E. Mabry, J. S. Noble (Committee on Public Lands), report, March 1, 1846, *Journals of the House of Representatives of the State of Texas* (Clarksville, Tex.: Standard Office, 1848), 306; Thomas F. McKinney, chairman, report, March 24, 1846, *Journals of the Senate of the State of Texas, First Legislature* (Houston: Telegraph Office, 1848), 114–116; J. Pinckney Henderson to the senate, December 15, 1847, *Journals of the Senate of the State of Texas, Second Legislature* (Houston: Telegraph Office, 1848), 12.

3. A good discussion of settlement in West Texas in the late 1840s is still Jordan, *German Seed in Texas Soil,* 31–59.

4. Western to Toasting Ear, January 26, 1845, Western to Sloat, February 28, 1845, and Western to Neighbors, March 2, 1845, Records Relating to Indian Affairs, TSL; Western to John F. Torrey, January 6, 1845, Western to Neighbors, March 2 and May 20, 1845, Williams to Western, August 16, 1845, and Neighbors to Western, September 15, 1845, in Winfrey and Day, *Indian Papers of Texas,* 2:161, 205–206, 252–253, 322, 361–362.

5. Williams to Western, July 16, 1845, Western to Williams, July 24, 1845, and Western to Neighbors, February 12, 1846, in Winfrey and Day, *Indian Papers of Texas,* 2:290–292, 296–298.

6. Council with José Maria, January 10, 1845, Sloat report, July 12, 1845, Sloat to Western, August 18, 1845, Williams to Western, August 20, 1845, Western to Neill, E. Morehouse, and Thomas I. Smith, September 8, 1845, minutes of council, September–November 1845, in Winfrey and Day, *Indian Papers of Texas,* 2:162–164, 283–286, 325–326, 326–327, 353–355, 334–413; Western to Neighbors, April 9, 1845, Western to Sloat and Williams, April 9, 1845, Western to Williams, May 12, 1845, and Western to Sloat, May 12, 1845, Papers Relating to Indian Affairs, TSL.

7. Butler to Armstrong, May 12–21, 1845, James Logan to Armstrong, May 24, 1845, Armstrong to Crawford, June 8, 1845, and Crawford to Armstrong, July 3, 1845, NARG 75, LR, Western Superintendency.

8. Butler and M. G. Lewis to commissioner of Indian affairs, January 22, 1846, Pierce Mason Butler Papers, Library of Congress; Upshaw to Armstrong, March 31, 1846, NARG 75, LR, Western Superintendency.

9. Upshaw to Armstrong, March 31 and June 1, 1846, NARG 75, LR, Western Superintendency.

10. Butler and Lewis to commissioner of Indian affairs, January 22, 1826, Pierce Mason Butler Papers, Library of Congress.

11. Elijah Hicks, "The Journal of Elijah Hicks," *Chronicles of Oklahoma* 13 (March 1935): 72–73.

12. Hicks, "Journal of Elijah Hicks," 68–69; Brevet Major G. Andrews to Lieutenant F. F. Flint, December 4, 1846, NARG 393, LR, 7th Military Department; Butler and Lewis to

Medill, August 8, 1846, NARG 75, Documents Relative to the Negotiation of Ratified and Unratified Treaties.

13. Hicks, "Journal of Elijah Hicks," 75–76. An good description of Wild Cat's trip west is found in Susan A. Miller, *Coacoochee's Bones: A Seminole Saga* (Lawrence: University of Kansas Press, 2003), 98–103.

14. Treaty with Texas Indians, May 15, 1846 (filed at end of 1852), NARG 75, LR, Texas Agency.

15. Ibid.; treaty negotiation, M. G. Lewis to William Medill, July 13, 1846, NARG 75, Documents Relating to the Negotiation of Ratified and Unratified Treaties. A published copy of the treaty, which the U.S. Congress ratified in February 1847, is in Winfrey and Day, *Indian Papers of Texas,* 3:43–51.

16. Butler and Lewis to Medill, August 8, 1846, NARG 75, LR, Documents Relating to the Negotiation of Ratified and Unratified Treaties.

17. James W. Abert, *Through the Country of the Comanche Indians in the Fall of the Year 1845: The Journal of a U.S. Army Expedition Led by Lieutenant James W. Abert of the Topographical Engineers,* ed. John Galvin (San Francisco: John Howell Books, 1970), 17–18; W. H. Harvey to Medill, September 5, 1846, NARG 75, LR, St. Louis Superintendency; Neighbors to Medill, March 2, 1848, NARG 75, LR, Texas Agency.

18. The issue of the decline in herd size and distribution of bison, starting with the drying of the plains in the eighteenth and early nineteenth century, is covered in Anderson, *Indian Southwest,* 16, 59–60, 180–230.

19. The decline of bison populations is still a debated issue. Very likely, different causes for the decline can be found in different parts of the plains. For the Southwest, the most important factor in the first half of the nineteenth century seems to have been the severe drought of 1806–1821. For descriptions, see Abert, *Through the Country,* 12–13, 19, 90; Ralph P. Bieber, ed., "Journal of Marcellus Ball Edwards, 1846–1847," *Marching with the Army of the West, 1846–1848,* vol. 4 of The Southwest Historical Series (Glendale, Calif.: Arthur H. Clark, 1936), 130; Harvey to Medill, September 5, 1846, NARG 75, St. Louis Superintendency; Francois des Montaignes, *The Plains,* ed. Nancy Alpert Mower and Don Russell (Norman: University of Oklahoma Press, 1972), 32.

20. See Lecompte, "Bent, St. Vrain & Co." 289–290. In the years 1845, 1846, 1847, and 1848, rainfall in northern Texas was less than normal. While it is difficult to extrapolate the impact of such a climate onto the high plains, or the upper Red and Arkansas River valleys, other commentary seems to suggest the existence of drought. See David W. Stahle and Malcolm K. Cleaveland, "Texas Drought History Reconstructed and Analyzed from 1698 to 1980," *Journal of Climate* 1 (January 1988): 59–74.

21. Butler and Lewis to Medill, August 8, 1846, NARG 75, Documents Relating to the Negotiation of Ratified and Unratified Treaties; Western to Williams, August 13, 1845, in Winfrey and Day, *Indian Papers of Texas,* 2:318–319.

22. The reorganization of the rangers produced a long, tedious debate, mainly between state and federal officials. See Henderson to Brevet Colonel Harney, March 13 and May 3, 1946, Henderson to Captain R. A. Gillespie, March 13, 1846, Henderson to Butler, May 5, 1846, Henderson to Captain M. T. Smith, July 2 and 5, 1846, Albert Horton to Captain Shapley P. Ross, August 7, 1846, Horton to William B. Marcy, August 8 and October 20, 1846, Horton to S. Churchill, August 8, 1846, Horton to Captains Smith and Andrew Stapp, October 8, 1846, Henderson to President James K. Polk, November 23, 1846 (and postscript), Governors' Papers, TSL; Acting Governor Horton to Captain Smith, July 25, 1846, Major Frederick Faunt Le Roy

to Horton, July 29, 1846, Horton to Faunt Le Roy, July 31 and August 1, 1846, Horton to Captain John J. Grumbles, August 17, 1846, Horton to Smith, October 8, 1846, Horton to Polk, October 21, 1846, and G. T. Wood to Marcy, June 8, 1848, Correspondence and Proclamations of the Governors, Secretary of State Records, TSL.

23. Wilbarger lists the leader of this group as Captain Bartlett Sims and has the number of dead at three, with one severely wounded. He also gives 1846 as the year, which is incorrect. See Wilbarger, *Depredations in Texas,* 286.

24. Henderson to Major B. S. Beall, April 13, 1846, Horton proclamation, June 1, 1846, Henderson to Neighbors, January 15, 1846, and Henderson to Major A. W. Gaines, February 12, 1847, Governors' Papers, TSL; Henderson to Beall, April 24, 1846, Proclamations and Governor's Correspondence, Secretary of State Records, TSL; Neighbors to Medill, April 24 and August 5, 1847, Hays to Neighbors, July 13, 1847, and Henderson to Marcy, August 22, 1847, NARG 75, LR, Texas Agency. Phineas L. Slayton was with the surveyors and described the distribution of presents by the Germans. He also gave an excellent description of the countryside. See Slayton to Calvin Taylor, May 12, 1847, Taylor Papers, Louisiana State University Library Archives, Baton Rouge. Wallace's raid is recounted in John C. Duval, *The Adventures of Big-Foot Wallace, the Texas Ranger and Hunter* (Philadelphia: Claxton, Temsen, and Haffelfinger, 1871), 126–133.

25. Unlike some, Neighbors liked his job and remained honest. Yet he occasionally imbibed too much, and, like Houston, he had a weakness for Indian women. Brief liaisons with Indian women were possible because both men had access to presents that they distributed. On the positive side, Neighbors's philandering, much like that of Houston, created a more humane man, someone who tried to understand Indians. A sympathetic biography of Neighbors, which fails to mention the man's faults, is Kenneth F. Neighbours, *Robert Simpson Neighbors and the Texas Frontier, 1836–1859* (Waco: Texian Press, 1975). For an assessment of Neighbors's personality, complete with a critique of his vanity and promiscuity, see Z. E. Coombes, *The Diary of a Frontiersman, 1858–1859,* edited and privately printed by Barbara Neal Ledbetter. Coombes, the schoolteacher at the Brazos Indian agency, recorded several of Neighbors's relationships. Of more interest perhaps was the fact that Coombes had a twelve-year-old student named Samuel Houston in his class. Young Sam, a Caddo Indian, would have been born in 1845 or 1846, suggesting conception perhaps when Houston was negotiating with the Caddos in October 1844. See also Neighbors to Houston, December 3, 1846, and Neighbors to Medill, January 6, 1847, Robert S. Neighbors Papers, Library of Congress; Brevet Major G. Andrews to Lieutenant F. F. Flint, December 4, 1846, NARG 393, LR, 7th Military Department. Neighbors's appointment letter actually arrived in March 1847. See Neighbors to Medill, April 13, 1847, NARG 75, LR, Texas Agency.

26. Quotation in Neighbors to Medill, March 2, 1848, NARG 75, LR, Texas Agency. See also Neighbors to Medill, June 21, August 6, October 1, November 18, and December 13, 1847, and January 20 and March 2, 1848, Neighbors to Henderson, December 10, 1847, Henderson to Neighbors, December 10, 1847, and "Talk of the Tenish Chief, Pohocawaket, or Medicine Hunter," February 16, 1848, NARG 75, LR, Texas Agency.

27. Neighbors to Medill, March 2, 1848, NARG 75, LR, Texas Agency.

28. Ibid.; emphasis in original.

29. See Jesse Mercer and A. Locklin letters, May 8 and 15, 1847, NARG 75, LR, Texas Agency.

30. Captain Middleton Tate Johnson to Eliphus Spencer, January 4, 1848, and petition of Spencer, February 1, 1848, NARG 75, LR, Texas Agency.

31. Captain M. T. Johnson to Eliphus Spencer, January 4, 1848, and petition of Eliphus Spencer, February 1, 1848, NARG 75, LR, Texas Agency; Henry J. Jewett (chair), Edward

Burleson, James B. Wooten, D. Gage, and Edwd. Fitzgerald (report of Senate Committee on Indian Affairs), February 12, 1848, *Journals of the Senate of the State of Texas, Second Legislature,* 311–313.

CHAPTER 15. LINES, POLITICS, DEPREDATIONS, AND THE U.S. ARMY

1. Highsmith's political ambitions seem obvious, given his career. He had joined the army in 1835, continued in the service of various ranger companies after the revolution, and then accepted a position as sergeant-of-arms for the Texas House of Representatives in 1844–1845. He fought with Jack Hays in Mexico before raising his own ranger company in 1848. See Webb and Carroll, eds., *Handbook of Texas,* 1:809.

2. Neighbors was at a loss to explain the attack. It was "of course entirely unexpected as those Indians as far as my observations have extended remained perfectly quiet and friendly." See Neighbors to Medill, April 10 and 28, 1848, NARG 75, LR, Texas Agency. Maude Wallis Traylor, who left a short biography of Highsmith, incorrectly dates the attack as occurring in August 1847. See Traylor, "Captain Samuel Highsmith," *Frontier Times* 17 (April 1940): 291–302.

3. The ranger situation became confusing because many volunteer units were organized, some for the Mexican campaigns and some for home defense. Originally, five companies were stationed on the edge of Texas settlement. These companies were financed by the federal government for only six months. Others were organized as well, with the state government assuming that they too would be paid from Washington. Late in the fall, state officials appealed to renew the service of these companies for twelve months. By late fall of 1846, there was some question as to whether any of the home defense rangers would be paid by the federal government. This debate continued into the 1850s. Follow the early confusion in Henderson to Captain R. A. Gillespie, March 13, 1846, Henderson to William S. Harney, March 13, 1846, Henderson to Captain Thomas J. Smith, July 2, 1846, Andrew J. Horton to Smith, July 25, 1846, Horton to Captain Shapley P. Ross, August 7, 1846, Horton to Captains Smith and Andrew Stapp, October 8, 1846, Horton to William B. Marcy, August 8 and 20, 1846, Henderson to James K. Polk, November 23, 1846, Governors' Papers, TSL; chief executive to Smith, July 25, 1846, chief executive to Major Thomas Fauntleroy, July 31, 1846, chief executive to Captain John J. Grumbles, chief executive to Smith, October 8, 1846, and Horton to Polk, October 21, 1846, Correspondence and Proclamations of the Governors, TSL.

4. Neighbors eventually "covered" the boy's death with presents to the sum of $500. See agreement with the Caddo, September 13, 1848, Neighbors to Medill, September 14, 1848, A. M. M. Upshaw to Arbuckle, April 25, 1848, Neighbors to Medill, April 28, 1848, and C. E. Barnard to Neighbors, April 1848, NARG 75, LR, Texas Agency.

5. Captain E. Steen to Lieutenant E. B. Sacket, June 3, 1848, NARG 393, LR, 7th Military Department.

6. C. B. Fletcher to Houston, June 10, 1848, A. J. Houston Papers.

7. Jones to Taylor, June 6, 1848, NARG 75, LR, Texas Agency; Jones to Taylor, June 20 and 26, 1848, NARG 393, LR, Western Division and Department, 1830, 1848–1853; Taylor to adjutant general, July 13, 1848, NARG 94, LR, AGO.

8. General Taylor to Governor Wood, July 7, 1846, Governors' Papers, TSL. Utley again finds the behavior of the rangers at Reynosa to be somewhat "unrestrained by law or general morality" but otherwise acceptable. For certain, he argues, they "rarely took sexual liberties with the Mexican women." Utley does agree that General Taylor thoroughly despised them and wanted to send them home. See Utley, *Lone Star Justice,* 63, 78–79.

9. Bell to Captain George A. H. Blake, August 20, 1848, H. J. Wilson to Brevet Lieutenant Colonel W. W. S. Bliss, October 24, 1848, Twiggs to Bliss, October 25 and 28, 1848, NARG 393, LR, Western Division and Department, 1830, 1848–1853; Taylor to the Adjutant General's Office, October 23 and 30, 1848, NARG 393, LS, by Commanding General, Western Division and Department, 1848–1853; Twiggs to Bliss, November 4, 1848, NARG 94, LR, AGO.

10. Neighbors to Medill, November 7, 1848, Neighbors to J. T. Cochran, November 9, 1848, and petition, 1848, NARG 75, LR, Texas Agency; Neighbors to Houston, November 10, 1848, A. J. Houston Papers.

11. Neighbors to General Harney, June 4, 1849, NARG 393, LR, Western Division and Department, 1830, 1848–1853.

12. Brevet Major General W. J. Worth to assistant adjutant general, February 3, 1849, Harney to assistant adjutant general, May 8, 1849, Brevet Major General George M. Brooke to R. Jones, July 14, 1849, and Captain R. W. Montgomery to Worth, April 30, 1849, NARG 393, LR, Western Division and Department, 1830, 1848–1853; First Lieutenant F. Hamilton to R. Jones, June 30, 1849, NARG 95, LR, AGO. The dragoon troops on the Pedernales called their post Camp Chadbourne, not to be confused with the later fort of that name built well north of Fredericksburg in Coke County near the Colorado River.

13. Montgomery to Worth, April 30, 1849, NARG 393, LR, Western Division and Department, 1830, 1848–1853.

14. Van Horne to adjutant general, July 3, 1849, and Van Horne to George Deas, August 6, 1849, NARG 94, LR, AGO.

15. Order No. 28 declares that no Indians "were to pass within the line of military stations, towards the settlements. Any violators were to be treated as 'open enemies.'" See Order No. 28, May 25, 1849, NARG 75, LR, Texas Agency.

16. See Cornelius C. Cox, "Notes and Memoranda of an Overland Trip from Texas to California in the year 1849," and Robert Beeching, "Journal of a Trip from New York on the bark 'Norumbega' to Galveston and then overland through Texas, Mexico, Arizona and southern California to San Diego," 1849, both in the Huntington Library, San Marino, California. Beeching describes the German town of Fredericksburg as "built of logs & mud," with a population of 300 people.

17. Benjamin Butler Harris, "Account of Journey from Panola, Co., Texas," 1849, Huntington Library, San Marino, California. The journal was published as Harris, *The Gila Trail: The Texas Argonauts and the California Gold Rush,* ed. Richard H. Dillon (Norman: University of Oklahoma Press, 1960). The editor misidentifies Harney, believing the man to be a Colonel Harvey Mitchell, a Texan. Other overlanders left similar accounts describing what clearly was to them the "noble savage." Stanislaus Lasselle, for example, described a Kiowa whom he met along the Canadian River as having a face that was "painted all over with yellow clay." Lasselle continued, "Along his eyes was red paint. He had a buffalo robe, with pins from the back of his head reaching to the ground." His wrists revealed brass wire bracelets. But what most impressed Lasselle was his rifle; it was "covered over with white cow hide and at the muzzle of the gun was ten or twelve strings of white cow hide twisted which gave it the appearance of a pendant." Stanislaus Lasselle, "Diary of an Overland Journey . . . by way of Ft. Smith, Ark., to Santa Fe, N.M. and the Spanish Trail in 1849, Feb. 6–Aug. 21," Henry E. Huntington Library, San Marino, California.

18. Neighbors to Medill, June 18, 1849, NARG 75, LR, Texas Agency. The news that Comanches under their chief Santa Anna had left for Mexico is first reported in Neighbors to Medill, February 15, 1849, NARG 75, LR, Texas Agency.

19. See William Cochran McGraw, *Savage Scene: The Life and Times of Mountain Man James Kirker* (San Lorenzo, N.Mex.: High-Lonesome Books, 1972), 120–144.

20. Utley notes that Chevallie fought with both Ben McCulloch's and Mabry B. Gray's ranger companies in Mexico during the war. Chevallie's company was the last to be mustered out in 1848. Gray and Chevallie had been part of the Anglo "ravagers" who had attacked Tejano herders and carters in the trans-Nueces region before the war. See Utley, *Lone Star Justice*, 68–70, 78–79.

21. Forty-Niner Cornelius C. Cox, who reached El Paso in July, put the bounty as $200 for a scalp and $250 for a captive. He identified one of the leaders of the American raiding party as Major Chavalle. Many overlanders were tempted to give up the gold fields and hunt Apaches. Cox believed that a hundred had already done so. The business was supposedly begun by Kirker. Leaton was a member of this group, which had killed many Apaches. See Cox, "Notes and Memoranda of an Overland Trip"; Van Horne to Deas, August 6, 1849, and Leaton to Lieutenant Colonel J. M. Washington, February 20, 1849, NARG 94, AGO; Brevet Major J. M. Scott to Deas, November 17, 1849, NARG 393, LR, Western Division and Department, 1830, 1848–53; "Extract of a Letter from Bvt. Major E. B. Babbitt, October 15, 1849, Van Horne to Deas, November 8, 1849," and George W. Crawford to John Clayton, November 8, 1849, Governors' Papers, TSL. References to Leaton's relations to Kirker are found in McGraw, *Savage Scene*, 109–111.

22. Neighbors to Medill, February 15, 1847, Neighbors to Worth, March 7, 1849, Neighbors to Orlando Brown, October 9 and 18, 1849, L. H. Williams to Neighbors, October 9, 1849, Captain William Steele to Major George Deas, September 22, 1849, and Neighbors to Houston, November 30, 1849, NARG 75, LR, Texas Agency; Neighbors to Houston, October 16, 1849, A. J. Houston Papers; Van Horne to Deas, May 4, 1849, NARG 94, LR, AGO. The cholera epidemic reached well out onto the plains by late summer, striking the Kiowa, Cheyenne, Arapaho, Osage, and many other bands. William Bent's description of it near Bent's Fort suggests that half the Cheyenne tribe perished from it, or several thousand people. The ranger Big Foot Wallace indicated in his memoir that so many people died in San Antonio that one particular Sunday was called "Black Sunday." Many people fled into the hills, abandoning the town. See "Bent's Fort," 1849, a manuscript in the Grinnell Papers, and Duval, *Adventures of Big-Foot Wallace*, 134–135.

23. Petition of people at Brownsville, June 12, 1849, Governors' Papers, TSL.

24. Brooke to Wood, July 11, 1849, Governors' Papers, TSL; Brooke to Jones, June 21, 1849, NARG 393, LS, by Commanding Officer, Western Division and Department, 1830, 1848–1853; Wood to Deas, July 15, 1849, Proclamations and Correspondence of the Secretary of State and Governor, Secretary of State Records, TSL.

25. Brooke to Major General Winfield Scott, July 19, 1849, NARG 393, LR, Western Division and Department, 1830, 1848–1853; Deas to Wood, July 23, 1849, Governors' Papers, TSL.

26. Brooke to Jones, July 14, 1849, and Brooke to Wood, August 11, 1849, NARG 393, LR, Western Division and Department, 1830, 1848–1853; Deas to Wood, August 9, 1849, Order No. 53, August 11, 1849; Order No. 57, August 19, 1849, and Jones to Brooke, August 20, 1849, Governors' Papers, TSL.

27. Brooke to Harney, August 5, 1849, NARG 393, LR, Western Division and Department, 1830, 1848–1853.

28. David Gage, report in senate, November 12, 1849, report of the Committee on Indian Affairs, November 15, 1849, report of the Committee on Indian Affairs, December 1, 1849, report of Edward Burleson, December 29, 1849, and joint report of H. L. Kinney (chair, Senate Committee on Indian Affairs) and William H. Williams (chair, House Committee on Indian Affairs), *Journals of the Senate of the State of Texas, Third Session* (Austin: Gazette Office, 1849), 119–121,

131–132, 210–213, 327–328, and 428–439; report of the Committee on Indian Affairs, January 11, 1850, *Journals of the House of Representatives of the State of Texas. Third Session* (Austin: Gazette Office, 1849), 493–504. Governor Wood actually vetoed one of the resolutions that called for removal. See Wood on "Joint Resolution," December 4, 1849, NARG 75, LR, Texas Agency.

29. Ábbe Emmanuel Henri Dieudonné Domenech, *Missionary Adventures in Texas and Mexico: A Personal Narrative of Six Years' Sojourn in These Regions* (London: Longman, Brown, Green, Longmans, and Roberts, 1858), 73–74. Domenech also offers a story of the brutal killing of three Mexican men and a woman, the latter of whom had the scalp of one of her companions forced into her mouth. These were the sorts of commonly told stories that went with reported depredations.

30. Wood to G. W. Crawford, December 14, 1849, Secretary of State Records, Proclamations and Correspondence, TSL.

31. Lieutenant Colonel Miles to Lieutenant E. E. Flint, June 28, 1849, NARG 393, LR, 7th Military Department; General Brooke to Major General Winfield Scott, July 19, 1849, and Brevet Major J. M. Scott to Major George Deas, November 17, 1849, NARG 393, LR, Western Division and Department, 1830, 1848–1853; Neighbors to Medill, June 18, 1849, NARG 75, Texas Agency; George Deas to Captain John Lee, July 27, 1849, Governors' Papers.

32. Brevet Captain William Steele to Major Deas, September 22, 1849, NARG 75, LR, Texas Agency; Lieutenant Frank Hamilton to R. Jones, June 30, 1849, NARG 94, LR, AGO; Brevet Lieutenant Colonel D. S. Miles to Lieutenant E. E. Flint, August 26, 1849, NARG 393, LR, 7th Military District.

33. Brooke to Jones, January 3 and 31, 1850, and February 5, 1849, NARG 393, LR, Western Division and Department, 1830, 1848–1853; Brooke to Bell, January 10 and 30, 1850, Governors' Papers, TSL. Land speculator and state senator Henry L. Kinney lobbied both General Brooke and Governor Bell to organize more ranger units. When Brooke finally agreed, Kinney promptly wrote to the governor arguing that G. K. Lewis and Thomas Blackwell should "raise them." See Kinney to Bell, February 10, 1850, Governors' Papers, TSL.

34. The army reports are contained in the following documents: Brevet Lieutenant Colonel W. J. Hardee to Deas, March 3, 1850, Captain J. H. King to Deas, April 10, 1850, Lieutenant Charles G. Merchant to Hardee, May 20, 1850, John S. Ford to Deas, May 21, 1850, Brooke to Jones, June 2, 1850, Andrew J. Walker to Ford, June 19, 1850, Captain L. N. Plummer to Deas, June 30, 1850, Captain J. B. M. Brown to Deas, August 17, 1850, and Brevet Captain James Oakes to Hardee, August 17, 1850, NARG 393, LR, Western Division and Department, 1830, 1848–1853. See also J. D. Blair to Bell, January 12, 1815, petition of citizens of Leon, Lampasas, and Salada counties, January 12, 1850, W. W. Hudson to Captain Jonathan H. King, February 17, 1850, King to Deas, February 28, 1850, Brooke to Bell, March 6 and October 6 and 15, 1850, Governors' Papers, TSL.

35. Senate committee report of H. L. Kinney, Isaac Parker, Edward Burleson, A. M. Truit, and David Portis, August 30, 1850, *Journals of the Senate of the State of Texas. Extra Session—Third Legislature* (Austin: Gazette Office, 1850), 75–77.

36. Rollins to V. E. Howard, February 26, 1850, NARG 75, LR, Texas Agency.

37. Secretary of war to Wood, January 19, 1850, Governors' Papers, TSL.

38. Rollins to Brown, May 8, 1850, NARG 75, LR, Texas Agency. These Kickapoos and Seminoles had been assigned land near Piedras Negras in Mexico. In the following March, Colonel Juan Manuel Maldonado asked permission of the commanding officer at Fort Duncan, Lieutenant Colonel T. Morris, for them to travel north of the Rio Grande to hunt and trade. Morris agreed to let them enter Eagle Pass but only for trade. The Indians obviously had ignored

these restrictions, as Rollins saw them in May on the Llano River and Lieutenant J. T. Haile discovered them hunting deer on Chacon Creek on May 15. They had a large quantity of venison. The army was convinced that the Kickapoos and Seminoles worked in concert with the Comanches, giving them information, while Colonel Maldonado thought they were pursuing marauders when in Texas. See Morris to Colonel Juan Manuel Maldonado, March 24, 1851, Maldonado to Morris, March 29, 1851, and Haile report, May 15, 1851, NARG 393, LR, Western Division and Department, 1830, 1848–1853.

39. A number of Kickapoos were with Wild Cat. See Miller, *Coacoochee's Bones,* 122–123.

40. Brevet Colonel Samuel Cooper to commanding officer, June 24, 1850, NARG 75, LR, Texas Agency.

41. Brevet Lieutenant Colonel D. S. Miles to Lieutenant F. F. Flint, June 2, 1850, NARG 393, LR, 7th Military Department.

42. J. S. Calhoun to Brown, June 15, 1850, in James S. Calhoun, *The Official Correspondence of James S. Calhoun while Indian Agent at Santa Fe and Superintendent of Indian Affairs in New Mexico,* ed. Annie H. Abel (Washington, D.C.: Government Printing Office, 1915), 211–212; Andrew J. Walker to John S. Ford, June 19, 1850, NARG 393, LR, Western Division and Department, 1830, 1848–1853; H. G. Catlett to Dr. S. G Haney, September 14, 1850, Governors' Papers, TSL; Rollins to Luke Lea, September 15, 1850, NARG 75, LR, Texas Agency.

43. Brooke to Howard, December 26, 1850, NARG 75, LR, Texas Agency.

44. Marcy to F. N. Page, January 23, 1851, NARG 393, LR, 7th Military Department. Marcy's biographer, W. Eugene Hollon, notes the many excursions that Marcy made into the west and his overall general knowledge of Indians. See Hollon, *Beyond the Cross Timbers: The Travels of Randolph B. Marcy* (Norman: University of Oklahoma Press, 1955).

45. See Karl A. Hoerig, "The Relationship between German Immigrants and the Native Peoples of Western Texas," *Southwestern Historical Quarterly* 97 (January 1994): 423–452.

46. The reports of this activity are almost too numerous to mention. See, for example, Brooke to Jones, January 7, 1851, Burleson to Captain John Ford, January 30, 1851, Walker to Ford, January 31, 1851, Brooke to Jones, February 21, 1851, and Lieutenant Richard J. Dodge to Major P. Morrison, March 31, 1851, NARG 393, LR, Western Division and Department, 1830, 1848–1853; Brooke to Jones, February 15, 1851, NARG 94, LR, AGO. Brooke seemed convinced that the Indians attacked by Walker and Burleson had in their possession presents given to the Comanches by Rollins in December. See Colonel T. Staniford to Deas, January 28, 1851, NARG 393, LR, Western Division and Department, 1830, 1848–1853.

47. Rollins and Jesse Stemm to commissioner of Indian affairs, April 18, 1851, NARG 75, LR, Texas Agency; Rollins to Brooke, February 18, 1851, NARG 393, LR, Western Division and Department, 1830, 1848–1853.

48. Brooke to R. Jones, February 5, 1851, Governors' Papers, TSL.

49. Brooke to Jones, February 5, 1851, Governors' Papers, TSL; Brooke to Harney, February 7, 1851, NARG 393, LR, Western Division and Department, 1830, 1948–1853.

50. Rollins to Lea, March 4, 1851, NARG 75, LR, Texas Agency; Order No. 31, April 20, 1851, Governors' Papers, TSL; Order No. 34, April 21, 1851, NARG 94, LR, AGO.

51. Rollins and Stemm to Bell, April 15, 1851, NARG 393, LR, Western Division and Department, 1830, 1848–1853.

52. Bell to Rollins and Stemm, April 16, 1851, NARG 94, LR, AGO; Rollins to Lea, April 24, 1851, NARG 75, Texas Agency. While other Texans were supposedly captives of the Comanches, documented evidence of such children was difficult to obtain. The only report of substance was submitted to the governor by Johann Henrich Schneider, who had lost a ten-year-old

son to Indian captivity five years before. It was believed that Shawnees took him. See Schneider to Bell, June 1, 1851, Governors' Papers, TSL.

53. Wilson and Fiske, *Appletons' Cyclopaedia of American Biography,* 3:77.

54. Brevet Lieutenant Colonel William J. Hardee to Deas, May 28, June 2, and July 14, 1851, NARG 393, LR, Western Division and Department, 1830, 1848–1853. The 17 Mexicans were sent to Eagle Pass and handed over to Colonel Juan Manuel Maldonado. See Morris to Maldonado, June 22, 1851, NARG 75, LR, AGO. A party of Kiowas visited Fort Atkinson on the Arkansas River in September 1851. They supposedly held two "American" children and two "German" children, along with "a great number of Mexican men & women." These captives were not ransomed, as the Kiowas in general were described as being at war with the United States. See Lieutenant Henry Heth to Jones, September 4, 1851, NARG 75, LR, Texas Agency.

55. For a brief description of the early fort, see Barbara A. Neal Ledbetter, *Fort Belknap, Frontier Saga: Indians, Negroes and Anglo-Americans on the Texas Frontier* (Burnet, Tex.: Eakin Press, 1982), 39–45.

56. Harney to Jones, May 17, 1851, NARG 393, LR, Western Division and Department, 1830, 1848–1853.

57. General Brooke to R. Jones, February 21, 1851, and Lieutenant Richard J. Dodge to Major P. Morrison, March 31, 1851, NARG 393, LR, Western Division and Department, 1830, 1848–1853.

58. Harney to Jones, May 17, 1851, and Hardee to Deas, August 29, 1851, NARG 393, LR, Western Division and Department, 1830, 1848–1853; Captain C. S. Stevenson to AAG, July 20, 1851, Captain Randolph B. Marcy, "Memoir Accompanying Map of the Country between Fort Smith Ark. and Cona Ana, N. Mexico," November 25, 1851, NARG 94, LR, AGO.

59. Stemm to Luke Lea, November 1, 1851, Rogers to Lea, October 1, 1851, and council with Comanches, Lipans, and Mescaleros, October 26, 1851, NARG 75, LR, Texas Agency; Captain H. H. Sibley to Deas, July 23, 1851, and Brevet Brigadier General W. G. Belknap to Jones, October 1, 1851, NARG 94, LR, AGO.

60. Order #34, April 22, 1851, NARG 94, LR, AGO. The Federal Trade and Intercourse Act of 1834 had 30 sections, each section representing an individual law regarding relations with Indians. Some sections applied to federal lands in the West that were outside the province of any state. These lands were defined by Section One of the acts as "Indian country." But states refused to give up sovereignty to the federal government, and the legislation clearly defined which laws could be applied within a state, with only a few sections fitting this description. The 1834 law never completely settled the struggle of state versus federal jurisdiction, and Texas, which had not been a part of the union when the law was passed, claimed absolute jurisdiction over its land. See "Trade and Intercourse Act, June 30, 1834," in Francis Paul Prucha, ed., *Documents of United States Indian Policy* (Lincoln: University of Nebraska Press, 2000), 63–68.

61. Rollins to Luke Lea, March 20, 1851, NARG 75, Texas Agency.

62. Bell to Harney, May 5, 1851, NARG 94, LR, AGO.

Chapter 16. General Persifor Smith and the Salvation of Texas

1. Wilson and Fiske, *Appletons' Cyclopaedia of American Biography,* 5:583.

2. Historians have briefly assessed Smith's plan. Robert Utley states, "The plan looked good on paper, but as it worked out in practice the troops were too few, the Indians too cunning, and Texas too big for it to have much effect. The warriors now had several more places to avoid, but they still raided much as they had in the past." Utley fails to look at the army correspondence

in the National Archives that discusses the setting up of the plan and its impact over 1852 and 1853. This correspondence is in NARG 393, LR, Western Division and Department, 1830, 1848–1853; I use it as a primary source of information. Given Utley's incorrect conclusion regarding the Smith plan, other historians have followed him, including Robert Wooster, who briefly mentions Smith's plan, writing "even the new defensive lines failed to stem Indian attacks." Not surprisingly, this led Randolph B. Campbell to parrot Utley and Wooster. He concludes, "Texas frontiersmen readily saw the flaws in this plan and pointed out that only cavalry could locate highly mobile raiders." See Robert Utley, *Frontiersmen in Blue: The United States Army and the Indian, 1848–1865* (New York: Macmillan, 1967), 74–75; Robert Wooster, *Soldiers, Sutlers, and Settlers: Garrison Life on the Texas Frontier* (College Station: Texas A and M University Press, 1987), 8–11; Campbell, *Gone to Texas,* 197. If the line that Smith developed had failed so miserably, the Texas state legislature would never have granted Indian reservations to the Plains tribes in the fall of 1853.

3. Smith to Brevet Lieutenant Colonel W. W. J. Bliss, October 6 and November 3, 1851, and Lieutenant Colonel H. Brambridge to Deas, February 6, 1852, NARG 393, LR, Western Division and Department, 1830, 1848–1853; Smith to Bliss, October 21, 1851, and Smith to Don C. Buell, May 9, 1852, NARG 94, LR, AGO.

4. See the letters of Frost to his wife, dated August 29, September 29, October 21, November 22, and December 19, 1852, Kennett Family Papers, Missouri Historical Society, St. Louis. The editorial comment was typical for the Texas newspapers; the one in the text comes from the *Texas State Gazette* (Austin), January 12, 1850, and is cited in Wooster, *Soldiers, Sutlers, and Settlers,* 9.

5. Sibley to G. W. Hill, January 3, 1852, *Journals of the Senate of the State of Texas. Fourth Legislature* (Austin: State Gazette Office, 1852), 301–302; Howard to Lea, January 9, 1852, NARG 75, LR, Texas Agency.

6. Stemm to Lea, February 20, 1852, NARG 75, LR, Texas Agency.

7. Stemm to Sibley, February 18, 1852, Stemm to Lea, February 20 and April 16 and 21, 1852, Howard to Lea, February 27, 1852, Horace Capron to Lea, May 24, 1852, and return of articles purchased for Indians, June 30, 1852, NARG 75, LR, Texas Agency; Stemm to Bell, February 20, 1852, Governors' Papers, TSL.

8. Howard to Lea, June 1, 1852, and receipt for "captives," June 28, 1852, NARG 75, LR, Texas Agency.

9. Brevet Major Hamilton W. Merrill to Rogers, March 29, 1852, NARG 75, LR, Texas Agency.

10. Captain Arthur Tracy Lee to Howard, March 15, 1852, NARG 75, LR, Texas Agency. The government was also adopting a similar program in New Mexico Territory, particularly with Navajos and Utes. Agents there had been expending some $25,000 a year for food. See Lieutenant Colonel E. V. Sumner to Lea, May 26, 1852, Ritch Papers, Huntington Library, San Marino, California.

11. Capron to Howard, August 12, 1852, and Capron to Lea, September 30, 1852, NARG 75, LR, Texas Agency.

12. Smith to Jones, July 18, 1852, NARG 75, LR, AGO.

13. Ábbe Domenech, *Missionary Adventures,* 228, 240, and 259.

14. Frederick Law Olmsted, *A Journey Through Texas; or, a Saddle-trip on the Southwestern Frontier* (New York: Dixs, Edwards, 1857; reprint, Austin: University of Texas Press, 1978), 245, 258–259, 263–265.

15. Domenech, *Missionary Adventures,* 225–226; Montejano, *Anglos and Mexicans in the Making of Texas,* 31–32.

16.   Greaser and de la Teja, "Quieting Title to Spanish and Mexican Land Grants," 463–464. Armando C. Alonzo, who looked closely at the land situation in the trans-Nueces region, concluded that "sale of land made during the Mexican-American War appears ostensibly legitimate, but . . . such sales were often made under duress because Anglo newcomers challenged the Mexicans [and they] . . . sometimes went awry as a legal subterfuge turned out to be an actual deed." See Alonzo, *Tejano Legacy,* 148–149.

17.   See Miller, *Coacoochee's Bones,* 147–149.

18.   The problems in northeastern Mexico evolved from the growing role of Matamoros as a center of smuggling. Because of the profit involved, state and military officials in Tamaulipas opposed the liberal reforms of President Arista, and along with other conservatives, they forced his resignation in January 1853. This insurgency, led at times by José Maria Carvajal, brought the subsequent restoration of Santa Anna as president once again. See Justo Sierra, *The Political Evolution of the Mexican People,* trans. Charles Ramsdell (Austin: University of Texas Press, 1969), 248–264. The Seminoles and Kickapoos were living near the town of Musquiz when they joined in defending the Mexican government from the insurgency. They apparently participated in the battle for Saltillo, fought July 22–25. While the forces supported by the Indians lost, this did not affect the tenure of the Indians; the alcalde of the town of Musquiz noted that they had adapted well to the region in August 1852. "Reciden en esta villa se ocupan en sembrar maiz, frijos, en la hacienda del Nacimiento del Rio Sabinas, en las caza de venados y demas animales á que se dedican los basones, y los Mugeres introduciendo á este villa vanos, frustos del camp que venden ó cambian por viveros para la subsistencia de sus familias." See "Extractos y Copias el documentos existentes en el Archivo Documentos de la Comisíon Pesquisidora de la Frontera del Norte," August 1852, Archivo Relaciones Exteriores, Mexico City. An account of the battle is in Thomas Dirgan to William March, August 8, 1852, Matamoros Consul Records, TSL.

19.   Parker to Bell, May 18, 1852, Governors' Papers, TSL. See also affidavit of Thadoesus M. Rhodes, June 11, 1852, and Israel B. Bigelow to Bell, June 11, 1852, Governors' Papers, TSL; P. Nickels (sheriff) to Bell, June 15, 1852, and Harney to Deas, June 24, 1852, NARG 393, LR, Western Division and Department, 1830, 1848–1853. Kevin Mulroy has estimated the size of Wild Cat's community at 700, including his Kickapoo allies. John Horse, or Gopher John, led the African American contingent and frequently visited Eagle Pass. Americans there came to dislike him and saw this African contingent as a possible place of refuge for Texas slaves. See Kevin Mulroy, *Freedom on the Border: The Seminole Maroons in Florida, the Indian Territory, Coahuila, and Texas* (Lubbock: Texas Tech University Press, 1993), 54–89.

20.   The comanchero trade emerged in the early part of the nineteenth century, originating from the various small Mexican communities just east of the Rio Grande. Anton Chico, a small town southeast of Taos, was a center. The traders carried mostly corn products, made in the form of tortillas, and exchanged them with the Comanches for horses and some mules. An extensive number of permits for the trade show up in the Ritch Papers. See, in particular, account of fight between Jicarillas and Prairie Indians, March 13, 1852, request for trade license, March 23, 1852, James S. Calhoun to S. M. Baird, April 4, 1852, and John Greiner to Lea, July 31, 1852, Ritch Papers; Greiner to Lea, April 30, 1852, and July 31, 1852, NARG 75, LR, New Mexico Superintendency.

21.   Stevens to headquarters, July 9, 1852, NARG 94, LR, AGO (emphasis in original). A good discussion of the reporting of the supposed disaster is found in Hollon, *Beyond the Cross Timbers,* 129–153.

22.   Hollon, *Beyond the Cross Timbers,* 155–157.

23.   Goode to Bell, July 24, 1852, Governors' Papers, TSL.

24. Throckmorton to Bell, July 30, 1852, and Wigfall to Bell, August 18, 1852, Governors' Papers, TSL. See also petition of members of the Peters Colony, July 31, 1852, petitions from Nacogdoches, Brenham, Bedi (a community that no longer exists), Dallas, and Laredo, August 1852, and J. W. Magoffin petition, August 5, 1852, Governors' Papers, TSL; Charles J. Webb to Bell, August 6, 1852, W. Lund to Bell, August 6, 1852, M. B. Highsmith to Bell, August 11, 1852, and John M. Henderson to Bell, August 18, 1852, Texas Adjutant General's Papers, TSL. And in what must have amazed even Governor Bell, one John S. Hamilton (obviously saddened by the funeral procession) wrote from New York, offering to raise a company of rangers. Hamilton to Bell, October 4, 1852, Texas Adjutant General's Papers, BL. Hamilton's offer naturally arrived well after the crisis had passed.

25. Bell to Gillett, August 2, 1852, J. F. Crosby, S. Hart, and Rufus Doane to Bell, August 5, 1852, Bell to Millard Fillmore, August 20, 1852, H. R. Bee to Bell, August 26, 1852, Gillett to Bell, October 10, 1852, E. F. Calhoun to Bell, August 27, 1852, and Owen Shaw to Bell, September 22, 1852, Governors' Papers, TSL; Bell to Gillette, August 2, 1852, *Journals of the Senate of the State of Texas. Fourth Legislature—Extra Session* (Austin: J. W. Hampton, 1853), 32–35. A letter written from Laredo and published in the *[Austin] South-western American,* October 4, 1852, claimed that all of southern Texas would fall to Indians if the rangers were withdrawn. Shaw later refused Bell's request to turn the animals over to the government. See Shaw to Bell, December 27, 1852, Governors' Papers, TSL.

26. Sibley to Bell, August 9, 1852, Governors' Papers, TSL.

27. Sibley to Bell, August 9, 1852, and Secretary C. M. Conrad to Bell, September 30, 1852, Governors' Papers, TSL; Smith to Bell, August 9, 1852, NARG 393, LR, Western Division and Department, 1830, 1848–1853; Horace Capron to George Howard, August 12 and 27, 1852, and Howard to Bell, September 11, 1852, NARG 75, LR, Texas Agency.

28. Thomas J. Wood to Lieutenant Colonel St. George Cooke, December 30, 1852, NARG 94, LR, AGO; Horace Capron to Lea, January 23, 1853, NARG 75, LR, Texas Agency.

29. Cooke to assistant adjutant general, January 25, 1853, NARG 393, LR, Western Division and Department, 1830, 1848–1853.

30. Capron to Lea, February 18, 1853, Thomas H. Addicks to Howard, February 24, 1853, and Howard to Lea, March 18, 1853, NARG 75, LR, Texas Agency. It would appear that the Lipan Apaches did take vengeance on a small party of settlers headed back to the Texas settlements from El Paso later that summer. See Jane Adeline Wilson, *A Thrilling Narrative of the Sufferings of Mrs. Jane Adeline Wilson during Her Captivity among the Comanche Indians* (Fairfield, Wash.: Ye Galleon Press, 1971), 10–23. While Mrs. Wilson assumed her captors to be Comanches, the Mexican comancheros who later purchased her claimed that they were Lipan Apaches. Comancheros would have known the difference. See Sibley to Neighbors, October 8, 1853, NARG 75, LR, Texas Agency.

31. Pryor Lea to Luke Lea, February 17, 1852, George Howard to Luke Lea, March 23, 1852, R. A. Howard to George Howard, March 23, 1852, George Howard to Luke Lea, January 10 and (no date), 1853, George Howard to Luke Lea, March 1, 1853, and George Howard to Capron, April 23, 1853, NARG 75, LR, Texas Agency.

32. Stemm to Loomis, March 30, 1853, Stemm to Lea, March 31 and April 1, 1853, NARG 75, LR, Texas Agency.

33. The implementation of this removal and the debate over it can be found in Howard to George Manypenny, April 30, 1853, Robert McClelland to Manypenny, April 26, 1853, Neighbors to Manypenny, June 26, 1853, Howard to Manypenny, June 26, 1853, Neighbors to Manypenny, July 5, 1853, Capron to Manypenny, July (no date) 1853, A. Barnard to Neighbors,

July 5, 1853, Neighbors to Charles Mix, July 22, 1853, and Neighbors to Mix, July 22, 1853, NARG 75, LR, Texas Agency. While Neighbors suggested that too much money was spent to feed the removed Indians, a reasonable assessment given what he knew of it, in reality, at least two sources put the number of removed Indians at 300 and 200 respectively, suggesting that many dropped out of the caravan along the way. See "Journal of a Visit to the Northern frontier of Texas & the Gold Mines near Hamilton Valley," May 1853, Kuykendall Papers; Arnold to Neighbors, July 8, 1853, NARG 75, LR, Texas Agency.

34. Davis to Bell, September 19, 1853, Governors' Papers, TSL. Davis had drafted his letter after first soliciting information from General Smith, who confirmed that reservations, with agents in residence, would solve the problem in Texas. See Smith to Davis, September 4, 1853, NARG 94, LR, AGO.

35. Bell to the senate, November 9, 1853, *Journal [No. 5] of the Senate of the State of Texas. Fifth Legislature* (Austin: J. W. Hampton, 1853), 11–30; Neighbors to Manypenny, February 6, 1854, NARG 75, LR, Texas Agency; E. M. Pease to Davis, March 13, 1854, NARG 94, LR, AGO.

36. See contract papers, August 15, 1854, Reports Relating to Indian Affairs, RG005, TSL. A federal appropriation of money in 1928 allowed these Indians to expand their reservation to 4,351 acres, its current size. See Webb and Carroll, eds., *Handbook of Texas,* 1:19.

Chapter 17. Reservations or Concentration Camps?

1. See Thomas T. Smith, *The Old Army in Texas: A Research Guide to the United States Army in Nineteenth-Century Texas* (Austin: Texas State Historical Association, 1999), 94–97.

2. Smith, *Old Army in Texas,* 98–99.

3. Captain Henry H. Sibley to Brevet Lieutenant Colonel Hardee, January 22, 1853, and First Lieutenant J. M. Hawes to First Lieutenant G. F. Tyler, January 28, 1853, NARG 393, LR, Western Division and Department, 1830, 1848–1853. The Delaware leaders helped bring in 28 Mexican children to Neighbors. See "Names where taken, by whom taken, and place of residence of the Mexican captives surrendered by the Comanches and Lipan Indians under the Provisions of the Treaty of Guadalupe Hidalgo," 1853, Neighbors to Manypenny, January 23, 1854, and George Hill to Neighbors, March 26, 1854, NARG 75, LR, Texas Agency.

4. Just who killed the Forrester family was debated by army and Texas authorities. Neighbors and General Smith concluded that it was Lipans, while Howard, who was the Lipan agent, felt it was northern Comanches. It was most likely renegades, given Mr. Forrester's relaxed demeanor. See Christopher Luntzel report, February 14, 1854, extract of General Smith letter, April 8, 1854, Neighbors to E. M. Pease, April 10, 1854, Neighbors to Manypenny, April 18, 1854, NARG 75, LR, Texas Agency; Smith to Colonel Samuel Cooper, March 21, 1854, NARG 94, LR, AGO; Pease to Neighbors, March 24, 1854, public meeting of citizens in Webb County, April 5, 1854, and Neighbors to Pease, April 10 and 18, 1854, Governors' Papers, TSL.

5. Olmsted, *Journey Through Texas,* 294–295.

6. Neighbors to Pease, May 2, 1854, Governors' Papers, TSL; General Smith to Colonel Cooper, October 9, 1854, NARG 94, LR, AGO; Neighbors to Manypenny, May 2, 3, and 15 and September 10, 1854, Neighbors to General Smith, May 2, 1854, Howard to Manypenny, May 4, June 9 and 16, and July 20, 1854, and Secretary of Interior R. McClelland to commissioner of Indian affairs, August 17, 1854, NARG 75, LR, Texas Agency. The alcalde of Musquiz in Mexico reported that a band of armed Seminoles and African Americans had been active in defending his town in the spring of 1854 against Comanches. These Seminoles remained on duty for some time thereafter; the captains were identified as Gato del Monte (Wild Cat) and Coyote. Both

men died along with 15 others in September 1857 of smallpox. While the reports of the alcalde do not exonerate the Seminoles, they at least suggest that most Seminoles were not involved in the March raids. See extracts of the alcalde's correspondence in "Extractos y copias el documentos existentes en el Archivo del Ayuntamiento de la village Musquiz," letters for March 15, 1853, May 1, 1854, June 5, 1857, and September 6, 1857, Documentos de la Comision Pesquisidora de la Frontera del Norte, Archivo Relaciones Exteriores, Mexico City.

7. See report of Francis N. Page to assistant adjutant general, November 1, 1854, NARG 393, LR, Department of the West and Western Department, 1853–1861. Miller in *Coacoochee's Bones,* 139–155, offers the best account of Wild Cat's community in Mexico. Although this was not a pacifistic community, Miller found little evidence of Seminole raids into Texas. Likely it was a different story for the Kickapoos, Lipan Apaches, and Tonkawas, who had been forced from Texas.

8. Neighbors to Manypenny, March 4, 1854, Hill to Neighbors, July 8 and September 20, 1854, NARG 75, LR, Texas Agency. During the Neighbors-Howard debate, Neighbors used a statement from his new subagent, George Hill, to prove that "his" Comanches had been behaving themselves. See statement of G. H. Hill, June 29, 1854, Caddo Indian Papers, Oklahoma State Historical Society, Oklahoma City.

9. See census roll of Comanches, 1855, and additional census of Comanches, March 1855, NARG 75, LR, Texas Agency.

10. Howard to Manypenny, November 20, 1854, census for the Caddo, 1855, census for the Anadarko, 1855, census for the Tawakonis, 1855, census for the Wacos, 1855, census for the Tonkawas, 1855, and Hill to Neighbors, April 3, 1855, NARG 75, LR, Texas Agency. Moving the Tonkawas to the reserve also proved difficult, as a group of 18 whites, mostly ex-rangers, tried to run off their horses. Another confrontation resulted in the son of the Tonkawa chief being shot in the back by Texans near Fort Inge. See Howard to Manypenny, April 17, 1855, Smith to Cooper, May 26, 1855, and Neighbors to Manypenny, July 23, 1855, NARG 75, LR, Texas Agency.

11. March to Manypenny, September 30, 1854, Neighbors to Acting Commissioner Charles Mix, October 30, 1854, Howard to Manypenny, November 20, 1854, and Hill to Neighbors, December 15, 1854, NARG 75, LR, Texas Agency; Lieutenant Francis N. Page to assistant adjutant general, Department of the West and Western Department, 1853–1861.

12. For information on these groups during the mid-1850s, see Christopher Carson to D. Meriwether, July 26, 1855, NARG 75, LR, New Mexico Superintendency; John W. Whitfield to A. Cumming, August 1, 1855, NARG 75, LR, Upper Arkansas Agency; Neighbors to Manypenny, April 17, 1855, NARG 75, LR, Texas Agency; S. P. Ross to Neighbors, October 7, 1855, NARG 94, LR, AGO. Yet another excellent report on the Comanches, in particular, is Randolph Marcy's letter, January 15, 1855, NARG 94, LR, AGO. On this occasion, Marcy puts the "Middle Comanches" at 3,500 people, while giving less exact information on the "Northern Comanches."

13. Smith, *Old Army in Texas,* 138–139.

14. See John D. Unruh Jr., *The Plains Across: The Overland Emigrants and the Trans-Mississippi West, 1840–1860* (Urbana: University of Illinois Press, 1982), 170–171.

15. The *Handbook of Texas* (ed. Webb and Carroll) has good outlines for each of these forts and the troops assigned to them.

16. See petitions from Bosque and McLennan counties, April 14, 1854, J. B. Erath to Pease, April 17, 1854, William E. Jones to Pease, April 30, 1854, and petition of 5 citizens of Starr, Webb, and Nueces counties, July 27, 1854, Governors' Papers, TSL.

17. Petition of 5 citizens, July 27, 1854, Governors' Papers, TSL.

18. Pease to General Smith, August 8, 1854, Governors' Papers, TSL; Pease to secretary of war, September 23, 1854, Proclamations and Correspondence, Secretary of State Records, TSL.

19. Pease to John G. Walker, William Henry, and Charles E. Travis, November 6, 1854, and Pease to Jiles S. Boggess, William Fitzhugh, and Patrick H. Royer, November 6, 1854, Governors' Papers, TSL. Walter Prescott Webb seems to be totally unaware of Pease's efforts to organize rangers, describing the period 1852–1855 as one of "quiet." He also describes William Henry as "an adventurer," apparently unaware of Pease's order to Henry. See Webb, *Texas Rangers,* 145.

20. Captain J. S. Bollels to Pease, January 22, 1855, Governors' Papers, TSL.

21. Ford gave a revealing response to the offer: "The rangers will soon be out of service. They are ripe for anything in the shape of excitement!" Ford to Hugh McLeod, January 14, 1855, McLeod Papers, TSL.

22. General Smith to Cooper, March 14, 1855, NARG 94, LR, AGO. Henry's sacking of D'Hanis suggests that the religious conflict that existed between Catholics and Protestants back east had spread to Texas. See Olmsted, *Journey through Texas,* 280.

23. Assistant Adjutant General D. C. Buell to Captain W. J. Newton, January 30, 1855, NARG 75, LR, Texas Agency. Emphasis in original.

24. Major E. Steen to Captain Calhoun, January 10, 1855, Hill to Neighbors, January 23 and February 12, 1855, Neighbors to Manypenny, February 21 and April 2, 1855, Howard to Neighbors, February 21, 1855, and Major G. B. Crittenden to Howard, March 8, 1855, NARG 75, LR, Texas Agency.

25. Neighbors to commissioner of Indian affairs, January 8, 1855, Major E. Steen to Major D. C. Buell, March 3, 1855, Neighbors to Manypenny, March 20, 1855, Neighbors to Smith, March 27, 1855, and Neighbors to Howard, March 27, 1855, NARG 75, LR, Texas Agency; Smith to Cooper, March 10, 1855, NARG 94, LR, AGO.

26. General Smith to Cooper, May 28, 1855, NARG 94, LR, AGO.

27. Major E. Steen to Major E. C. Buell, March 3, 1855, NARG 75, LR, Texas Agency.

28. Neighbors to Pease, July 28, 1855, Governors' Papers, TSL; Neighbors to Mix, August 3 and September 20, 1855, and Hill to Neighbors, August 31, 1855, NARG 75, LR, Texas Agency; Neighbors to Major G. R. Paul, September 12, 1855, and Paul to Neighbors, September 15, 1855, NARG 94, LR, AGO.

29. Neighbors to Pease, September 20, 1855, and Ross to Neighbors, September 30, 1855, NARG 75, LR, Texas Agency; Ross to Neighbors, October 7, 1855, J. R. Baylor to Neighbors, October 7, 1855, and Paul to the assistant adjutant general, October 7, 1855, NARG 94, LR, AGO.

30. Petition from citizens of Guadalupe River, June 25, 1855, Pease to Callahan, July 5, 1855, Callahan to Pease, August 10, 1855, and Pease to Smith, September 5, 1855, Governors' Papers, TSL; Callahan to Burleson, August 15, 1855, and Burleson to Pease, September 8, 1855, Edward Burleson Papers, BL.

31. Captain Sidney Burbank to the assistant adjutant general, October 4 and 8, 1855, Ranger Records, TSL. William Kyle carried the call for reinforcements into San Antonio. See his letter, which optimistically describes the situation, in William Kyle to "Ed" (Burleson), October 7, 1855, Burleson Papers. Some Texans believed that 4,000 slaves (worth some $3,000,000) were living in the border towns south of the Rio Grande. See Ronnie C. Tyler, "The Callahan Expedition of 1855: Indians or Negroes?" *Southwestern Historical Quarterly* 70 (April 1967): 574–585; Webb, *Texas Rangers,* 146–147; Miller, *Coacoochee's Bones,* 168.

32. Smith to Lieutenant Colonel L. Thomas, October 14 and 17, 1855, NARG 94, LR, AGO.

33. Captain Burbank to assistant adjutant general, October 9, 1855, Smith to Lieutenant Colonel L. Thomas, October 14 and 17, 1855, NARG 94, LR, AGO; Smith to assistant adjutant general, October 17, 1855, Ranger Records, TSL.

34. Pease to Neighbors, October 20, 1855, Neighbors Papers, BL.

35. Captain Henry E. McCulloch to James S. Gillett, October 20, 1855, Pease to James W. Throckmorton, February 5, 1856, and Pease to Colonel A. M. M. Upshur, March 22, 1856, Ranger Records, TSL. Some of these ranger groups never did get paid, as Pease was urging the U.S. Congress to compensate them as late as August 1856. See Pease to Congress, August 4, 1856, Ranger Records, TSL.

36. See Miller, *Coacoochee's Bones,* 168–169.

37. List of men employed, May 31, 1855, Neighbors to Manypenny, June 10 and July 1 and 5, 1855, Neighbors to Mix, September 5 and 10, 1855, estimates for fiscal year ending June 30, 1857, and Ross to Neighbors, October 31, 1855, NARG 75, LR, Texas Agency; Ross to Neighbors, August 31, 1855, Neighbors Papers, BL.

38. Ross to Neighbors, January 1, February 1, April 1, and May 1, 1856, Neighbors to Mix, April 30, 1856, Neighbors to Manypenny, June 12, 1856, William R. Felder (farmer) to Ross, February 1, 1856, and joint resolution of the Texas Congress, February 4, 1856, NARG 75, LR, Texas Agency; Robert E. Lee to Neighbors, May 24, 1856, Neighbors Papers, BL; Neighbors to Pease, June 4, 1856, Governors' Papers, TSL. On Baylor's scrape with the law, see James D. Morrison, "Notes and Documents: Notes from the *Northern Standard,* 1842–1849," *Chronicles of Oklahoma* 19 (March 1941): 93.

39. McClelland to Mix, June 29, 1855, Neighbors to Mix, September 10, 1855, Ross to Neighbors, January 9 and 15, 1856, Baylor to Neighbors, January 17, March 10, May 3 and 17, June 30, and July 21, 1856, Joe Chandler to Ross, February 12, 1856, and Neighbors to Manypenny, February 20, March 7 and 18, and May 14, 1856, NARG 75, LR, Texas Agency; Baylor to Neighbors, January 12, 1856, and Baylor to Emy (his wife), April 3, 1856, Baylor Papers, Baylor University, Waco, Texas.

40. Neighbors to Manypenny, June 10 and July 1, 1855, Neighbors to Mix, September 10, 1855, Baylor to Neighbors, October 31, 1855, Ross to Neighbors, October 31, 1955, and Joe Chandler (Indian farmer) to Ross, February 12, 1856, NARG 75, LR, Texas Agency. The drought data come from Stahle and Cleaveland, "Texas Drought History Reconstructed."

41. Neighbors to Manypenny, March 7 and June 12, 1856, Baylor to Neighbors, May 3 and July 21, 1856, Ross to Neighbors, June 3, 1856, NARG 75, LR, Texas Agency; Baylor to Emy (his wife), April 3, 1856, Baylor Papers (transcripts in Barker Library); Neighbors to Pease, June 4, 1856, Governors' Papers, TSL.

42. Captain Gabriel René Paul to assistant adjutant general, October 21, 1855, NARG 94, LR, AGO; Baylor to Neighbors, October 31, 1855, NARG 75, LR, Texas Agency.

43. The First Cavalry did not arrive in Indian Territory until after the Mormon War. See James C. Milligan and L. David Norris, "Keeping the Peace: William H. Emory and the Command at Fort Arbuckle," *Chronicles of Oklahoma* 69 (Fall 1991): 256–281.

44. A good description of the organization of the Second Cavalry is found in Charles P. Roland, *Albert Sidney Johnston: Soldier of Three Republics* (Austin: University of Texas Press, 1964), 168–184.

45. Baylor to Neighbors, January 1 and 17 and March 31, 1856, Ross to Neighbors, January 15, 1856, and Neighbors to Manypenny, January 20 and April 8, 1856, NARG 75, LR, Texas Agency; Baylor to Fran, March 30, 1856, Baylor Family Papers, Baylor University.

46. Lee to his family, April 12, 1856, Lee Family, DeButts-Ely Collection, Library of Congress. Emphasis in original.

47. Ibid.

48. Baylor to Neighbors, May 10 and 24 and June 30, 1856, NARG 75, LR, Texas Agency.

49. Eastman to Neighbors, June 8, 1856, Neighbors to Manypenny, June 18, 1856, and Baylor to Neighbors, July 6, 1856, NARG 75, LR, Texas Agency; Lee to Baylor, June 19, 1856, Baylor Papers, Baylor University; D. C. Buell to Captain Eastman, June 16, 1856, NARG 393, LS, Department of Texas.

50. Baylor to Neighbors, May 1, 1856, NARG 75, LR, Texas Agency. Emphasis in original.

51. This view of the causes for declining bison herds, at least on the southern plains, runs counter to the new argument posed by Andrew C. Isenberg in *The Destruction of the Bison: An Environmental History, 1750–1920* (New York: Cambridge University Press, 2000). Despite the subtitle, Isenberg does little environmental history (ignoring tree-ring data, for example). He suggests that the major cause is overhunting. Evidence for the early decline, between 1650–1800, is found in Anderson, *The Indian Southwest*. There can be little doubt that drought was a major factor in the early period, since there were too few hunters to destroy the massive herds of those years.

52. Marcy report, January 15, 1855, NARG 94, LR, AGO.

53. Baylor to Neighbors, May 1 and July 6, 1856, NARG 75, LR, Texas Agency.

CHAPTER 18. THE PLAN

1. Johnston's order was sent under the hand of Assistant Adjutant General D. C. Buell to Lee, May 27, 1856, NARG 94, LR, AGO.

2. See Utley, *Frontiersmen in Blue,* 23–27.

3. Johnston to adjutant general, May 27, 1856, NARG 393, LS, Department of Texas; Baylor to Neighbors, July 12, 1856, and Ross to Neighbors, July 17, 1856, NARG 75, LR, Texas Agency.

4. Lee to Buell, July 24, 1856, and Johnston to Thomas, November 8, 1856, NARG 94, LR, AGO; Lee to family, July 28 and August 15, 1856, Lee Family, DeButts-Ely Collection, Library of Congress.

5. Brevet Lieutenant Colonel John Bankhead Magruder to Assistant Adjutant General Buell, April 15, 1856, and Captain James Oakes to Lieutenant Asher R. Eddy, September 8, 1856, NARG 94, LR, AGO; Buell to Magruder, May 17 and August 14, 1856, Buell to Lieutenant Colonel L. Thomas, November 8, 1856, and Johnston to Thomas, November 17, 1856, NARG 393, LS, Department of Texas.

6. Buell to Magruder, May 17, 1857, NARG 393, LS, Department of Texas.

7. The use of cottonwood bark as fodder for animals was reported on many occasions. James E. Sherow of Kansas State University first alerted me to this practice. Farther south, in the Brazos and Colorado River valleys, mesquite had become far more prominent. See Sherow, *Watering the Valley: Development Along the High Plains Arkansas River Valley, 1870–1950* (Lawrence: University of Kansas Press, 1990).

8. Johnston to Thomas, February 10, 1857, NARG 393, LS, Department of Texas.

9. Lieutenant R. N. Eagle to Captain J. N. Caldwell, November 25, 1856, Captain W. E. Prince to assistant adjutant general, December 8, 1856, General Johnston to Colonel Cooper, December 17, 1856, and Johnston to Colonel Cooper, February 10, 1857, NARG 393, LS, Department of Texas; Baylor to Pease, December 10, 1856, Governors' Papers, TSL; Baylor to Neighbors, December 31, 1856, and February 12 and March 31, 1857, and Captain J. N. Caldwell to assistant adjutant general, February 23, 1856, NARG 75, LR, Texas Agency; Baylor to Neighbors, March 21, 1857, NARG 75, LR, Wichita Agency.

10. Baylor to Neighbors, March 14, 28, and 31, 1857, Neighbors to Mix, May 8, 1857, Neighbors to Manypenny, January 10, 1857, Matthew Leeper to Neighbors, June 1, 1857, and W. H. Drinkard to J. Thompson, June 12, 1857, NARG 75, LR, Texas Agency.

11. See Coombes, *Diary of a Frontiersman,* October 7, 1858.

12. Ibid., October 8, 1858.

13. Ibid., October 15, 19, 23, 24, and 28, 1858, and January 21, 25, and 28 and February 18, 1859. Kenneth Franklin Neighbours, in his biography of his famous ancestor, Agent Neighbors (they are related despite the different spelling of the name), vehemently dismisses Coombes's charges, especially regarding the exploitation of Indian women by Neighbors, suggesting that if such had occurred, it would have been reported in the press and Neighbors dismissed. But exploitation was common in reservation villages, where gifts were used to entice women into relationships. Newspapermen had little interest in reporting such stories. Army soldiers were particularly troublesome. Interestingly, one of Coombes's schoolchildren was a young Caddo boy named "Sam Houston," born circa 1845, a year after Houston's negotiations with the upper Brazos River Indians. See Neighbours, *Robert Simpson Neighbors,* 214–216.

14. Petition of citizens near Fort Belknap, January 20, 1857, Leeper to Neighbors, June 30, 1857, and Ross to Neighbors, July 30, 1857, NARG 75, LR, Texas Agency; Kenneth F. Neighbours, "José Maria: Anadarko Chief," 254–274.

15. See Wilson and Fiske, *Appletons' Cyclopaedia of American Biography,* 1:201; Webb and Carroll, eds., *Handbook of Texas,* 1:123–125.

16. Major James Begler to Manypenny, January 19, 1857, NARG 75, LR, Texas Agency; Baylor to Fran, April 5 and 28, 1857, Baylor Papers, Baylor University; Fran (sister) to "Dearest Ned" (Ned Wharton), June 29, 1857, Special Collections, Hill Memorial Library, Louisiana State University, Baton Rouge. Neighbours suggests that it was Baylor's inability to handle the Comanche Indians that led to his dismissal. Apparently Agent Neighbors never put the charge of stealing into writing, since it surfaced only later in the Wharton correspondence. Baylor did have 150 head of cattle on his ranch by summer, a substantial herd given his salary. And Baylor had been in trouble in the past. He apparently was wanted for the murder of one Seaborn Hill in Indian Territory. See Morrison, "Notes and Documents," 93; Neighbours, *Robert Simpson Neighbors,* 181–182.

17. Memorandum of commissioner of Indian affairs to the secretary of the interior, May 22, 1857, and Jacob Thompson to John W. Denver, June 19, 1857, NARG 75, Southern Superintendency; Neighbors to Denver, July 15 and August 5, 1857, NARG 75, LR, Texas Agency; Elias Rector to Denver, July 25, 1857, NARG 75, LR, Wichita Agency; General David Twiggs to Colonel Thomas, August 3, 1857, NARG 393, LS, Department of Texas.

18. Wilson and Fiske, *Appletons' Cyclopaedia of American Biography,* 6:191.

19. General Twiggs to Colonel Thomas, May 27 and June 16, 1857, NARG 393, LS, Department of Texas; Lee letter to his family, June 29, 1857, Lee Family, DeButts-Ely Collection, Library of Congress.

20. General Twiggs to Colonel Lorenzo Thomas, June 11 and 15, 1857, and Assistant Adjutant General Thomas Withers to commanding officer at Fort McIntosh, June 15, 1857, NARG 393, LS, Department of Texas; General Twiggs to Colonel Thomas, June 1, 1857, NARG 94, LR, AGO.

21. Lieutenant J. B. Wood to post adjutant at Fort Mason, July 27, 1857, NARG 94, LR, AGO.

22. General Twiggs to Lieutenant Colonel Thomas, August 9 and October 8, 1857, NARG 393, LS, Department of Texas; Neighbors to Denver, August 5, 1857, NARG 75, LR, Texas Agency.

23. Isaiah A. Paschal to Pease, September 13, 1857, Governors' Papers, TSL.

24. J. A. Mieux to Pease, September 17, 1857, Governors' Papers, TSL.

25. See De León, *Tejano Community,* 14–16; Montejano, *Anglos and Mexicans in the Making of Texas,* 31.

26. See J. Fred Rippy, "Border Troubles along the Rio Grande, 1858–1860," *Southwestern Historical Quarterly* 23 (October 1919): 91–111. There is a brief account of the international implications of the violence in Webb and Carroll, eds., *Handbook of Texas,* 1:302.

27. General Twiggs to Lieutenant Colonel Thomas, August 9 and October 8, 1857, NARG 393, LS, Department of Texas; J. A. Paschall to Pease, September 13, 1857, and J. A. Mieux to Pease, September 17, 1857, Governors' Papers, TSL.

28. McKissick to Rector, October 21, 1857, NARG 75, LR, Wichita Agency.

29. John Smiley to Neighbors, November 3, 1857, and Neighbors to Denver, November 16, 1857, NARG 75, LR, Texas Agency.

30. Smiley to Neighbors, October 26, 1857, Leeper to Neighbors, November 20 and 27, 1857, and Neighbors to Denver, December 8, 1857, NARG 75, LR, Texas Agency; Will Robinson to Pease, November 3, 1857, M. Stephens to Harden Runnels, November 14, 1857, and George B. Erath to Pease, November 21, 1857, Governors' Papers, TSL. The claim of Mullins was likely an exaggeration or even possibly a fabrication. Mullins was a close associate of John Baylor. Nevertheless, Major Van Dorn reported that "large bands of Indians have swept the settlements," even though he was unable to catch or identify them. See Brevet Major Earl Van Dorn to Captain John Withers, November 1, 1857, NARG 94, LR, AGO.

31. Ross to Neighbors, December 1, 1857, and Captain Paul to Neighbors, December 3, 1857, NARG 75, LR, Texas Agency; Neighbors to Samuel A. Maverick, December 3, 1857, Neighbors to Major G. R. Paul, December 9, 1857, and Runnels to Twiggs, December 22, 1857, Governors' Papers, TSL.

32. Assistant Adjutant General Thomas Withers to commanding officer at Fort Belknap, December 23, 1857, NARG 393, LS, Department of Texas; Major Paul to commanding officer at Camp Cooper, January 8, 1858, NARG 75, Texas Agency.

33. Captain Stoneman to Captain Withers, December 4, 1857, Leeper to Neighbors, December 5, 1857, Leeper to Captain Stoneman, December 5, 1857, and Neighbors to General Twiggs, December 8, 1857, NARG 75, LR, Texas Agency.

34. Petition from Williamson County, December 13, 1857, and petition from citizens of Lampasas County, December 15, 1857, NARG 75, LR, Texas Agency.

35. Neighbors to editors of *[Austin] Texas Sentinel,* January 21, 1858, Neighbors Papers, BL.

36. General Twiggs to Colonel Thomas, January 20, 1858, NARG 393, LS, Department of Texas; Colonel Withers to commanding officers at Fort Belknap and Camp Cooper, NARG 75, LR, Texas Agency.

37. Captain Stoneman to Captain Withers, January 14, 1858, NARG 75, LR, Texas Agency; Captain Evans to Captain Withers, January 14, 1858, and Major Paul to assistant adjutant general, January 15, 1858, NARG 94, LR, AGO.

38. The ranching efforts of Paul and Givens are reported in a letter that Baylor writes to his sister, Fran, in which he indicates that both Paul and Givens had invited him to stay at their ranch houses while he put his herd of cattle, which numbered 150, in order. See Baylor to Fran, April 28, 1857, Baylor Papers, BL.

39. Captain Evans to Captain Withers, January 14, 1858, NARG 94, LR, AGO.

40. Captain Givens to Captain Withers, February 12, 1858, Neighbors Papers, BL.

41. Ibid. The Givens ranch was along Walnut Creek. Ty Cashion suggests that Givens used "diverted" army resources to build his ranch. Cashion also argues that General Albert Sidney Johnston was among the officers involved in ranch building along the upper Brazos, which may also explain Stoneman's role. See Cashion, *A Texas Frontier: The Clear Fork Country and Fort Griffin, 1849–1887* (Norman: University of Oklahoma Press, 1996), 50–52.

42. Neighbors to Mix, January 17, 1857, NARG 75, LR, Texas Agency.

43. Leeper to Neighbors, December 31, 1857, Neighbors to General Twiggs, January 18, 1858, and Neighbors to Mix, January 26, 1858, NARG 75, LR, Texas Agency.

44. General Twiggs to Pease, August 20 and 29, 1857, G. H. Nelson to Pease, October 14 and November 8, 1857, Pease to Twiggs, August 13 and October 3, 1857, Pease to G. M. Bryan and John H. Regan, November 3, 1857, Pease to John H. Conner, November 23, 1857, Pease to Neill Robinson, November 23, 1857, Pease to Thomas K. Cormack, November 23, 1857, Nelson to George B. Erath, January 4, 1858, Runnels to Twiggs, January 9, 1858, and John Forbes to Runnels, January 7, 1858, Governors' Papers, TSL; John S. Hodges to Runnels, January 9, 1858, Pease to Frost, December 7, 1857, and Runnels to John S. Ford, January 28, 1858, Ranger Records, TSL; joint resolution, November 17, 1857, and joint resolution, January 27, 1858, Frontier Protection Records, BL; Carmack to Runnels, January 11, 1858, and Frost to Runnels, January 8, 1858, NARG 75, LR, Texas Agency.

45. Conner to Pease, December 11, 1857; Carmack to Runnels, January 11, 1858, and Frost to Runnels, January 8, 1858, NARG 75, LR, Texas Agency.

46. W. G. Preston, J. B. Dawson, J. W. Curtis, H. McGhee, T. L. Stockton to Captain Givens, NARG 94, LR, AGO; secretary of interior to Mix, March 13, 1858, affidavit of John Chandler and David Seal, March 29, 1858, and affidavit of J. M. Gibbons and Thomas Lamshead, March 30, 1858, NARG 75, LR, Texas Agency; Baylor letter, April 1, 1858, *Dallas Herald*.

47. Francis M. Peveler to J. Evetts Haley, August 6, 1932, Peveler Papers, BL.

48. Neighbors to Mix, February 3 and 16, 1858, and Ross to Neighbors, February 12 and 17, 1858, NARG 75, LR, Texas Agency; Neighbors to General Twiggs, March 17, 1858, NARG 94, LR, AGO.

49. Neighbors to Mix, February 27, 1858, NARG 75, Texas Agency.

Chapter 19. Anarchy and "Total War"

1. A good sense of the frustration evident in the newspapers is an editorial dated May 19, 1858: "What is . . . [being done] toward raising the new regiment of Texas mounted rangers," the editor of the *[Austin] Southern Intelligencer* wrote. "One month has elapsed since the bill passed and not a note of preparation is heard. In the meantime, the U.S. regular troops are removed from the frontier, except one company, and our people are left to the mercy of the savages." See also *[Austin] Southern Intelligencer,* April 14, 1858, and *Dallas Herald,* April 1 and July 25, 1858.

2. See letter of Leeper with clipping from *Dallas Herald*. The Leeper letter is in undated, NARG 75, LR, Texas Agency.

3. Neighbors to Twiggs, March 29, 1858, NARG 75, LR, Texas Agency.

4. Leeper to Neighbors, April 2, 1858, Lieutenant Kenner Garrard to Neighbors, April 14, 1858, Leeper to Colonel John Wilson, May 1, 1858, and Captain Evans to Lieutenant Garrard, May 7, 1858, NARG 94, LR, AGO; Lieutenant Garrard to commanding officer at Camp Cooper, April 21, 1858, NARG 393, LS, Department of Texas; Leeper to Captain Evans, April 14, 1858, Captain Evans to Leeper, April 14, 1858, Neighbors to Colonel Wilson, April 20, 1858, Neighbors to Mix, April 22, 1858, and Leeper to Neighbors, March 27 and April 23, 1858, NARG 75, LR, Texas Agency; A. S. Jordan to Runnels, May 4, 1858, Governors' Papers, TSL.

5. Runnels to John S. Ford, January 28, 1858, Ranger Records, TSL; Runnels to Twiggs, February 2, 1858, Twiggs to Governor Runnels, February 3 and 7, 1858, Ford to Runnels, February 27, 1858, and Runnels to Ford, March 7, 1858, Governors' Papers, TSL.

6. John Ford affidavit, November 22, 1858, Edward Burleson statement, November 22, 1858, and Leeper letter dated July 25, 1858, in *Dallas Herald,* all in NARG 75, LR, Texas Agency.

7. Baylor to Runnels, April 23, 1858, and Ford to Runnels, April 26, 1858, Governors' Papers, TSL; Ross to Neighbors, February 28 and March 31, 1858, NARG 75, LR, Texas Agency.

8. Ford to Runnels, April 7 and 14, 1858, and Nelson to Captain Ford, April 13, 1858, Governors' Papers, TSL.

9. The best account of the expedition is Ford to Runnels, May 22, 1858, Governors' Papers, TSL. Other accounts of importance are Shapley P. Ross, "Life and Adventures of Capt. Shapley P. Ross, "A True Son of the Frontier of Texas in the Early Days with a True Account of Many Thrilling Indian Fights: Also a Biographical Sketch of the Romantic and Picturesque career of his Illustrious son, Lawrence Sullivan Ross," Ross Papers, Baylor Library. See also Nelson to Ford, May 21, 1858, Governors' Papers, TSL; C. E. Barnard to George Barnard, May 25, 1858, George Barnard to Neighbors, May 26, 1858, Ross to Neighbors, May 31 and June 30, 1858, and muster roll, July 15, 1858, NARG 75, LR, Texas Agency; Douglas H. Cooper to Rector, June 7, 1858, NARG 75, Southern Superintendency; *[Austin] Southern Intelligencer,* June 2, 1858; Rupert N. Richardson, *Comanche Barrier to the South Plains Settlements* (Glendale, Calif.: Arthur H. Clark, 1933), 234–237; William Y. Chalfant, *Without Quarter: The Wichita Expedition and the Fight on Crooked Creek* (Norman: University of Oklahoma Press, 1991), 36–37.

10. Neighbors to Leeper, April 23, 1858, and Neighbors to Mix, May 18, 1858, NARG 75, LR, Texas Agency; Neighbours, *Robert Simpson Neighbors,* 205.

11. Nelson to Buchanan, July 15, 1858, NARG 75, LR, Texas Agency.

12. Twiggs to Lieutenant Colonel L. Thomas, January 20, 1858, NARG 393, LS, Department of Texas; Neighbors to Mix, January 17, 1858, and Captain R. W. Johnson to assistant adjutant general, May 1, 1858, NARG 94, LR, AGO; J. Shirley to Charles Barnard, May 6, 1858, and Barnard to Neighbors, May 22, 1858, NARG 75, LR, Texas Agency; Runnels to Texas Delegation in Congress, May 28, 1858, Governors' Papers, TSL; Bedford, *Texas Indian Troubles,* 166–168.

13. Baylor to Barry, August 2, 1858, James Buckner Barry Papers, BL (emphasis in original). There is little evidence that President Buchanan gave Nelson's letter much attention.

14. John H. Reagan and Sam Houston to Mix, May 31, 1858, Jacob Thompson to commissioner of Indian affairs, August 12, 1858, Hawkins to Neighbors, September 18, 1858, Givens to Neighbors, September 22, 1858, Neighbors to Twiggs, September 23, 1858, Neighbors to Hawkins, October 9, 1858, Hawkins to Thompson, October 16, 1858, Hawkins to Mix, October 16, 1858, Nelson to Hawkins, October 26, 1858, and Baylor to Thompson, November 22, 1858, NARG 75, LR, Texas Agency; Hawkins to Barry, October 8, 1858, Barry Papers.

15. Leeper to Neighbors, June 18 and 30, 1858, Y. E. Combs to Ross, June 30, 1858, Neighbors to Mix, October 19, 1858, Hawkins to Mix, October 30, 1858, and affidavit of Jim Pockmark, Jack and Tai-ne-no, November 5, 1858, NARG 75, LR, Texas Agency.

16. Ford to Runnels, July 5, 1858, and William N. P. Martin to Runnels, September 12, 1858, Governors' Papers, TSL; Robert C. Miller to Colonel A. M. Robinson, July 20, 1858, and William Bent to Robinson, December 17, 1858, NARG 75, LR, Upper Arkansas Agency; D. H. Cooper to Elias Rector, July 21, 1858, Lieutenant J. E. Powell report, July 27, 1858, Thompson to John B. Floyd, August 19, 1858, and A. H. Jones to H. M. Brown, September 14, 1858, NARG 75, LR, Southern Superintendency; *[Austin] Southern Intelligencer,* September 1, 1958. Agent McKissick reported that while the northern tribes had reason to be angry, they were further

instigated by "Mormons" who supposedly were among them. See report by McKissick to Colonel R. P. Bulliam, April 15, 1858, NARG 75, LR, Wichita Agency.

17. Van Camp to assistant adjutant general, August 31 and September 2, 1858, and Leeper to Neighbors, August 31, 1858, NARG 94, LR, AGO; Leeper to Neighbors, August 31, 1858, NARG 75, LR, Texas Agency.

18. James Buckner Barry diary, September 5, 1858, BL; Neighbors to Mix, September 10, 1858, NARG 75, LR, Texas Agency; Neighbors to Runnels, September 14 and 15, 1858, Governors' Papers, TSL.

19. Runnels to Ford, July 6, 1858, and Runnels to the secretary of war, August 12, 1858, Proclamations and Correspondence of the Secretary of State and Governor, TSL; Runnels to John B. Floyd, secretary of war, July 10, 1858, and Neighbors to Runnels, September 8, 1858, Governors' Papers, TSL; [Austin] Southern Intelligencer, July 28, 1858.

20. Twiggs to Lieutenant Colonel L. Thomas, July 6, 12, and 27 and August 4 and 24, 1858, Governors' Papers, TSL.

21. Van Dorn to Captain John Withers, September 20, 1858, NARG 94, LR, AGO.

22. Twiggs to Thomas, September 17, 1858, NARG 94, LR, AGO.

23. Withers to commanding officer at Fort Belknap, September 21, 1858, Leeper to Neighbors, October 9, 1858, and Neighbors to Hawkins, November 26, 1858, NARG 75, LR, Texas Agency.

24. Van Dorn to commanding officer at Fort Belknap, October 5, 1858, and Van Dorn to Withers, October 11, 1858, NARG 94, LR, AGO.

25. Captain Charles J. Whiting to Lieutenant W. W. Lowe, October 2, 1858, Van Dorn to Withers, October 11 and November 16, 1858, Twiggs to Thomas, October 22, November 18 and 20, and December 13, 1858, NARG 94, LR, AGO; Ross to Neighbors, September 30, 1858, NARG 75, LR, Texas Agency; S. A. Blain to Mix, November 3, 1858, NARG 75, LR, Wichita Agency; A. H. Jones and H. M. Brown to Mix, November 30, 1858, NARG 75, Southern Superintendency; Neighbours, *Robert Simpson Neighbors,* 212–213. Some sources give a smaller number of dead Comanches. See Brad Agnew, "The 1858 War against the Comanches," *Chronicles of Oklahoma* 49 (Summer 1971): 223–229. The Van Dorn quotation is in James C. Milligan and L. David Norris, "Keeping the Peace: William H. Emory and the Command at Fort Arbuckle," *Chronicles of Oklahoma* 69 (Fall 1991): 264.

26. See Walter L. Buenger, "Unionism on the Texas Frontier, 1859–1861," *Arizona and the West* 22 (Autumn 1980): 237–254.

27. Baylor letter to the editor, April 15, 1858, NARG 75, LR, Texas Agency. Emphasis in original.

28. See James H. Swindell's letter, June 10, 1858, affidavit of Joseph Chandler, R. Oliphant, David Seal, and William Peterson, July 26, 1858, W. G. Preston affidavit, August 9, 1858, Baylor letter (in unidentified newspapers), August 30, 1858, and *Dallas Herald,* July 1858, NARG 75, LR, Texas Agency; petition from Lampasas County, October 14, 1858, and Benjamin Hubert to Runnels, October 14, 1858, Governors' Papers, TSL. On Texas politics during the late 1850s, see James Marten, *Texas Divided: Loyalty and Dissent in the Lone Star State, 1856–1874* (Lexington: University of Kentucky Press, 1990), 1–17.

29. The number of men who came to Texas after the army had restored order in Kansas is difficult if not impossible to determine. Most were involved in the horse and mule trade, supplying animals for the burgeoning market in Kansas, as well as for the army, which anticipated marching on Salt Lake City that spring. See Jay Monaghan, *Civil War on the Western Border, 1854–1865* (New York: Bonanza Books, 1955), 85–116.

30. Thomas Hawkin's journal, October 22, 1858, NARG 75, LR, Texas Agency.

31. Runnels to Ford, November 2, 1858, Proclamations and Correspondence of the Secretary of State and Governor, Secretary of State Records, TSL; Runnels to Ford, December 12, 1858, Governors' Papers, TSL.

32. J. J. Sturm to Ross, December 27 and 30, 1858, Records Relating to Indian Affairs, RG 005, TSL; *[Austin] Southern Intelligencer,* January 19, 1859; Ford to Runnels, December 28, 1858, and N. W. Battle to Runnels, February 14, 1859, Governors' Papers, TSL. A number of Texas sources, which emphasized Indian depredations, later tried to pin the attack on the peaceful Caddos and Wichitas. See, for example, Bedford, *Texas Indian Troubles,* 169–172, and James Buckner Barry commentary, January 2–3, 1859, Barry Papers. The name of a "Mr. Fondenburg" was later added to the list of men, Fondenburg being the man who led the others to the Indian camp.

33. Neighbors to Runnels, January 9, 1859, Records Relating to Indian Affairs, TSL; Erath to Runnels, January 10 and 15, 1859, S. J. Gurley to Runnels, February 3, 1859, Ford to Runnels, February 9 and 16, 1859, and Runnels to Ford, February 11, 1859, Governors' Papers, TSL. Neighbors had encouraged Ford to arrest the men and was duly disappointed on hearing of Ford's unwillingness to do so, especially after the assistance that the Indians had given Ford on his expeditions against the Comanches. Neighbors's angry reaction is recorded in Coombes, *Diary of a Frontiersman.*

34. See "Difficulties on Southwestern Frontier," 1859, in House Executive Document 52, 36th Cong., 1st sess., 1–82.

35. Ibid.

36. F. M. Harris to Ross, March 1, 1859, and Ross to Runnels, March 4, 1859, Records Relating to Indian Affairs, TSL.

37. W. R. Bradford to Ross, March 4, 1859, Major George H. Thomas to Ross, March 5, 1859, Ross to Neighbors, March 7, 1859, Runnels declaration, March 12, 1859, NARG 75, LR, Texas Agency; Neighbors to Runnels, March 1, 1859, Battle to Runnels, March 14, 1859, Withers to Runnels, March 19, 1859, and Twiggs to Runnels, March 23, 1859, Governors' Papers, TSL.

38. See Raymond Estep, ed., "Lieutenant William E. Burnet: Notes on Removal of the Indians from Texas to Indian Territory," *Chronicles of Oklahoma* 38 (Autumn 1960): 295–297.

39. Neighbors to Runnels, March 26, 1859, Governors' Papers, TSL; Neighbors to Twiggs, March 24, 1859, NARG 94, LR, AGO; Ross to Neighbors, March 25, 1859, and Neighbors to Denver, March 28, 1859, NARG 75, LR, Texas Agency; *[Austin] Southern Intelligencer,* March 16, 1859.

40. Quotation in *[Austin] Southern Intelligencer,* March 30, 1859. See also Neighbors to Runnels, March 28, 1859, Governors' Papers, TSL; Neighbors to Twiggs, March 28, 1859, and Captain T. H. King to Withers, March 28, 1859, NARG 94, LR, AGO; Charles E. Mix to Neighbors, March 30, 1859, and Mix to Jacob Thompson, March 30, 1859, Records Relating to Indian Affairs, TSL;

41. Ross to Neighbors, March 31, 1859, Sturm to Ross, March 31, 1859, and Neighbors to Mix, April 11, 1859, NARG 75, LR, Texas Agency; Ford to Colonel J. A. Wilcox, April 12, 1859, NARG 75, LR, Wichita Agency; Ford to Runnels, April 3 and 12, 1859, Governors' Papers, TSL; Van Dorn to Withers, May 13, 1859, and Van Dorn to Twiggs, May 31, 1859, NARG 94, LR, AGO; Grant Foreman, "Historical Background of the Kiowa-Comanche Reservation," *Chronicles of Oklahoma* 19 (June 1941): 133.

CHAPTER 20. THE FINAL EXODUS

1. Erath's comments are contained in a letter in which he expressed his desire not to be mentioned. See George Barnard to Runnels, May 4, 1859, Governors' Papers, TSL.

2. Neighbors to Mix, May 12, 1859, NARG 75, LR, Wichita Agency; Major Thomas to Captain John Withers, May 26, 1859, NARG 94, LR, AGO.

3. J. J. Sturm to Ross, May 8, 1859, and Ross to Neighbors, May 9, 1859, NARG 75, LR, Wichita Agency.

4. Sturm to Ross, May 8, 1859, Coombes to Neighbors, May 8, 1859, and Ross to Neighbors, May 9, 1859, NARG 75, LR, Wichita Agency.

5. Ross to Neighbors, May 8, 1859, and Neighbors to Mix, May 12, 1859, NARG 75, LR, Wichita Agency.

6. The Jacksboro manifesto is printed in the *[Austin] Southern Intelligencer,* May 25, 1859.

7. Plummer to assistant adjutant general, May 21 and 23, 1859, NARG 94, LR, AGO.

8. Plummer to assistant adjutant general, May 21 and 23, 1859, Major George Thomas to Captain John Withers, May 26, 1859, NARG 94, LR, AGO; Ross to Neighbors, May 26, 1859, and Neighbors to Ross, May 26, 1859, NARG 75, LR, Wichita Agency. Burnet's account of the battle is the best. See his letters in Estep, ed., "Lieutenant William E. Burnet Letters: Removal of the Texas Indians and the Founding of Fort Cobb," part 2, 371–374.

9. Runnels to Commissioners Erath, Coke, Smith, Brown, and Steiner, June 6, 1859, Governors' Papers, TSL. Neighbors had a right to be suspicious of the commission, given its makeup. Coke helped author the Dawes Severalty Act of 1887 (also known as the Allotment Act), a piece of legislation through which Indians lost two-thirds of their landholdings in the United States. On John Henry Brown, see *History of Texas from 1685 to 1892* and *Indian Wars and Pioneers of Texas.*

10. Neighbors to Ross, May 28, 1859, Neighbors to Charles Dobbs, United States commissioner, May 28, 1859, and Neighbors to R. B. Hubbard, United States district attorney, June 5, 1859, NARG 75, LR, Wichita Agency; Twiggs to Runnels, June 2, 1859, NARG 94, LR, AGO.

11. Erath, Smith, Coke, and Brown to Neighbors, June 16, 1859, and Neighbors to Erath, Smith, Coke, Brown, and Steiner, June 16, 1859, NARG 75, LR, Wichita Agency.

12. On the sale of stolen Indian stock, see Ross to Neighbors, August 25, 1859, NARG 75, LR, Wichita Agency,

13. See Neighbours, *John Simpson Neighbors,* 275, and Neighbors to his wife, August 8, 1859, Neighbors Papers, BL. For the trip, consult Brown to Neighbors, July 14, 19, and 29, 1859, Neighbors to Brown, July 17, 1859, Plummer to Brown, July 21, 1859, Brown to Runnels, July 22, 1859, and J. W. Nowlin to Brown, August 1, 1859, Governors' Papers, TSL; Plummer to Neighbors, July 16, 1859, Leeper to Greenwood, July 19, 1859, Neighbors to Greenwood, July 24 and 25, 1859, Leeper to Neighbors, July 24, 1859, and Neighbors to Brown, July 30, 1859, NARG 75, LR, Wichita Agency.

14. The Wichita Agency apparently moved several times before permanent buildings were erected. Its final location was just west of Fort Cobb, but Agent Blain indicated that originally the fort had been built some ten miles west of the agency. The unsettled situation in Indian Territory can be followed in Rector to Mix, May 14, 1859, Blain to Rector, May 14, 1859, Rector to Neighbors, June 14, 1859, Rector to Greenwood, June 15, August 15, and September 7, 1859, Neighbors to Greenwood, July 14, August 18, and September 2, 1859, Neighbors to Blain, August 24, 1859, Neighbors to Rector, September 2, 1859, Neighbors's report of removal, September 3, 1859, and Blain to Rector, October 25, 1859, NARG 75, LR, Wichita Agency. See also Raymond Estep, *The Removal of the Texas Indians and the Founding of Fort Cobb* (Oklahoma City: Oklahoma Historical Society), 1961.

15. The most disturbing report of depredations during September had been an attack on the Worman and Hunter families, who lived on an isolated ranch east of Eagle Pass. See "Difficulties on Southwestern Frontier," in House Executive Document 52, 36th Cong., 1st sess., 1–82.

16. There are many treatments of the Cortina War. See Montejano, *Anglos and Mexicans in the Making of Texas,* 32–33; Charles W. Goldfinch, *Juan N. Cortina, 1824–1892: A Re-Appraisal* (New York: Arno Press, 1974).

17. "Difficulties on Southwestern Frontier," House Executive Document 52, 36th Cong., 1st Sess., 1–82.

18. See Major S. P. Heintzelman to Captain John Withers, March 1, 1860, House Executive Document 81, 36th Cong., 1st sess., 1–82.

19. Ibid.

20. Estep, ed., "Lieutenant William E. Burnet Letters," part 2, 375–376.

21. John Henry Brown's reports to Runnels indicate the serious decline of support for the governor, even in West Texas. "As it is, all that can be done is to reduce Houston's majority. This will be considerabley [*sic*] done by changes to you, but more so by causing many not to vote who intended to vote for H [Houston]." See Brown to Runnels, July 22, 1859, Governors' Papers, TSL; Houston inaugural address, December 21, 1859, Frontier Protection Records, BL.

22. The increase in depredations can be followed in various letters in the Governors' Papers, TSL, as well in the following sources: James Buckner Barry diary, fall 1859, BL; Houston to John B. Floyd, March 12, 1860, Frontier Protection Records, BL; Ledbetter, *Fort Belknap,* 94–99; Cashion, *Texas Frontier,* 54–57.

23. Kenneth Neighbours gives the best account of the agent's assassination, in *Robert Simpson Neighbors,* 282–287. See also William Burkett to Mrs. Neighbors, September 14, 1859, Neighbors Papers, BL; Leeper to William Burkett, September 15, 1859, NARG 75, LR, Wichita Agency; Jeanne V. Harrison, "Matthew Leeper, Confederate Indian Agent at the Wichita Agency, Indian Territory," *Chronicles of Oklahoma* 47 (Autumn 1909): 249.

Chapter 21. Indians and the Civil War

1. See Stahle and Cleaveland, "Texas Drought History Reconstructed," 64. Using the June Palmer Drought Severity Index, the data show that both 1860 and 1862 were extremely dry years and that overall the drought that began so severely in 1855 continued until 1865, when rains finally reappeared on the plains. While it is always difficult to assess the impact of a drought that occurred over a hundred years ago, environmental historian Dan Flores agrees that the drought from 1855 to 1865 may have been the worst in plains history. Email discussion with Dan Flores, July 20–21, 2004.

2. Randolph B. Campbell's new textbook provides a good synthesis of this issue: "It is commonly said that Indian raiders rolled back the frontier fifty miles or more during the Civil War," the author wrote. "And there is no question that settlers suffered a great deal, having perhaps four hundred men, women, and children killed, wounded, or carried off." Campbell then offers as evidence the Elm Creek raid, in which seven Texans were killed and seven wounded. This was the worst attack by Indians during the war. After the war's conclusion, Indian agents in Kansas and Oklahoma ransomed about a dozen Texas women and children, which in reality represented the grand total taken. The number of Texans killed by Indians was likely between 20 and 30. See Campbell, *Gone to Texas,* 266–267.

3. Brown, the instigating Texas historian, led the assault on Neighbors and his program. "As to the pretended civilization of the Indians," Brown began in his final report to Governor Runnels after Neighbors's death, "since their location on the reserve, it is simply and palpably untrue. . . . I unhesitantly express the opinion . . . [that] they have retrograded." Brown's report, September 12, 1859, Governors' Papers, TSL.

4. Letter of J. G. Thomas in *[Seguin] Union Democrat,* October 8, 1859.

5. Neighbors to Greenwood, June 10, 1859, NARG 75, LR, Texas Agency.

6. Estep, ed., "Lieutenant William E. Burnet Letters," part 3, 19–25.

7. See Neighbours, *Robert Simpson Neighbors,* 280.

8. Murphy charged that a Tonkawa Indian named "Davis" had kidnapped Cornett's wife, but Agent Blain soon discovered that Mrs. Cornett was living in the Choctaw Nation with another man. See Z. E. Coombes to Neighbors, May 8, 1859, Murphy to Brown, August 4, 1859, statement of William McDougal, December 7, 1859, Murphy to Major Thomas, January 6, 1860, and Blain to Greenwood, February 3, 1860, NARG 75, LR, Wichita Agency; H. K. Vallentine to George Christopher, November 19, 1859, Governors' Papers, TSL.

9. See D.L.M. to "Dear Chum," December 15, 1859, Ranger Records, General Correspondence, 1852–1859, TSL; Webb, *Texas Rangers,* 97–215. The authenticity of the letter cannot be questioned; since the author eventually discussed the staged "kidnapping" of Cornett's wife, both Murphy and Cornett obviously had worked with the ring in one capacity or another.

10. Ford to Governor, February 24, 1859, Governors' Papers, TSL; Ford to Governor, February 29, 1859, NARG 94, LR, AGO.

11. D.L.M. to "Dear Chum," December 15, 1859, Ranger Records, TSL. Emphasis in original.

12. See Baylor to "Capt.," December 15, 1859, Governors' Papers, TSL. Baylor mentions the kidnapping of Cornett's wife but pretends to know nothing about its conspiratorial nature.

13. D.L.M. to "Dear Chum," December 15, 1859, Ranger Records, TSL.

14. Blain to Houston, May 29, 1860, Texas Adjutant General's Papers, TSL.

15. J. W. Swendell and others to Houston, March 27, 1860, Governors' Papers, TSL; Houston to Blain, April 16, 1860, Houston Papers, BL. Swendell wrote that Murphy was "making strenuous exertions to raise a [ranger] company," advocating strongly Houston's new policy. His recruits were "all, or nearly all, men of suspicious character—amongst them" Ed Cornett. Swendell concluded that the "Chum" to whom the D.L.M. letter was addressed was Ed Cornett.

16. See James Haworth to Enoch Hoag, November 14, 20, and 24 and December 27, 1873, NARG 75, LR, Kiowa Agency.

17. D.L.M.'s letter apparently arrived near Camp Cooper just after Christmas. It likely was taken from the body of Page, studied carefully, and sent on to Governor Houston. While it did not specifically mention names, it implicated Baylor, Givens, and others in the ring. Historian Walter Prescott Webb notes Houston's interest in raising ranger units to attack Mexico and start yet another Mexican war. The war would hopefully—at least in Webb's estimation—distract the country and unify it behind the Constitution. If any truth exists to this plot, it explains why Houston buried the letter in the Ranger Records. See Burleson to Houston, May 1 and 9, 1860, Burleson Papers. See also Lang, "My Wild Hunt after Indians: The Journal of Willis L. Lang, First Lieutenant, Waco Rangers, unpublished manuscript, 1860," May–August 1860, copy in the possession of Thomas W. Cutrer; Houston to John B. Floyd, March 8 and April 14, 1860, Frontier Protection Records, BL.

18. For detailed descriptions of this attack and for the petitions that evolved from it, see Milton Jack to President James Buchanan, February 4, 1860, and J. B. Standeft to Buchanan, March 4, 1860, NARG 75, LR, Wichita Agency; Lang, "My Wild Hunt after Indians."

19. The manufacturing of massive numbers of printed sources on the conflict in Texas in the nineteenth century led to the general belief that Comanches had committed all the atrocities, despite the evidence from the period collected by army personnel and Indian agents. Many authors, even of more recent books, have totally condemned the Comanches without looking carefully at the sources. A recent biography of ranger Lawrence Sullivan Ross (who later became a Civil

War hero, governor of Texas, and president of Texas A and M University) is indicative of how the mythic history of Texas became so overwhelming in the nineteenth century that it persists into the present. See Judith Ann Benner, *Sul Ross: Soldier, Statesman, Educator* (College Station: Texas A and M University Press, 1983). Benner depicts the raids in the fall of 1860 as being conducted by "the redoubtable war chief Peta Nacona," who with his Comanche followers "murdered, raped, robbed, and mutilated their way" across Texas. There is simply no evidence that Peta Nocona, the chief whom Ross claims to have killed, was involved in the raids that fall or that Comanches killed or raped anyone. See Benner, *Sul Ross,* 49.

20. Houston to John B. Floyd, March 8 and April 14, 1860, Frontier Protection Records, BL; Captain M. T. Johnson to Houston, May 16, 1860, Governors' Papers, TSL; Special Order No. 38, April 11, 1860, NARG 393, LR, Department of the West and Western Department, 1853–1861.

21. Rector to Greenwood, NARG 75, LR, Wichita Agency.

22. Johnson to Houston, July 29, August 26, and September 8, 1860, Governors' Papers, TSL; Rector to Greenwood, July 30, 1860, NARG 75, LR, Wichita Agency. A good description of the trip, including the conditions of the Indians, is found in Lang, "My Wild Hunt after Indians."

23. Bent to Greenwood, March 17, 1860, and Bent to A. M. Robinson, November 28, 1860, NARG 75, Upper Arkansas Agency. The hostility of the Kiowas was recorded by several visitors to the upper Arkansas River in the summer of 1860. Yet most of the raiding by the Kiowas was conducted along the Santa Fe Trail, a region of the country that they claimed as their hunting ground and were most familiar with. See Bent's letters above as well as George D. Bayard to Ettie, September 20, 1859, Bayard Papers, Missouri Historical Society, St. Louis; John Porter Hatch to his father, October 16, 1859, Hatch Papers, Library of Congress; J. L. Collins to Greenwood, July 10 and August 4, 1859, NARG 75, LR, New Mexico Agency.

24. Houston to Ross, December 6, 1860, Governors' Papers; Ross manuscript, "Life & Adventures," 1860, Ross Papers.

25. Ross, "Life & Adventures," Ross Papers. The story of the supposed killing of Peta Nocona has become legendary in Texas history. As Ross rose in politics, he became famous for the feat. Yet several authentic oral accounts from the Parker family, including that of Quanah Parker (who later became a famous chief in his own right), indicate that the man killed at the Pease River massacre was No-bah, a Mexican herder. For details of the controversy, see Benner, *Sul Ross,* 52–53; Mildred P. Mayhall, *Indian Wars of Texas* (Waco: Texian Press, 1965), 117–120; Rupert N. Richardson, ed., "The Death of Nacona and the Recovery of Cynthia Ann Parker," *Southwestern Historical Quarterly* 46 (July 1942): 15–21; Paul I. Wellman, "Cynthia Ann Parker," *Chronicles of Oklahoma* 12 (June 1934): 163–170. Wellman discovered that No-Bah had another name, supposedly Joe Nokoni, taken likely from Cynthia Ann's husband's name.

26. Governor Clark to Jefferson Davis, April 4, 1861, and William G. Webb to Clark, June 26, 1861, Frontier Protection Records, BL.

27. Lubbock to McCulloch, December 23 and 24, 1861, Lubbock to Colonel P. O. Herbert, September 25, 1862, Frontier Protection Records, BL.

28. DeWitt Clinton Peters to his sister, March 13, 1861, Peters Letters, Bancroft Library; William Hemphill Bell to "my dear mama," March 12, 1861, Ritch Papers.

29. N. H. Darnell to Clark, May 15, 1861, Frontier Protection Records, BL; Colonel Henry McCulloch to Colonel Van Dorn, June 8, 1861, Adjutant General's Papers, TSL; Major Edward Burleson to Captain J. M. Hemsley, August 13, 1861, Burleson Papers. The original Pike treaty, with the "Pen-etegh-ca Band or the Neum, Wichita, Caddo-ha-da-chos, Hue-cos [Wacos], etc.," August 12, 1861, is in the Edward Ayer Collection, Newberry Library, Chicago.

30. See treaty, August 12, 1861, Ayer Collection, Newberry Library. The records of this supply system are amazingly accurate and have been preserved as the Charles Johnson Papers, Edward Ayer Collection, Newberry Library, Chicago. It did take time to establish the system. See D. A. Bickel to J. J. Sturm, December 28, 1861, and January 4 and February 15, 1862, accounts charged to Matthew Leeper, October 1861–August 1861, John Grimes to Charles Johnson, November 18, 1861, and A. S. Page to Johnson, June 11, 1862, Johnson Papers; Jesse Marshall to Colonel Henry McCulloch, July 20, 1861, Burleson Papers.

31. George Barnard to Governor Lubbock, February 21, 1861, Governors' Papers, TSL.

32. Henry M. McCulloch "Circular," August 2, 1861, Burleson Papers.

33. Burleson to Captain J. M. Hemsley, August 13, 1861, Burleson Papers.

34. The two sons were apparently lost in the engagement with Burleson's men. A leading chief was also killed in the fight. See Boone to Dole, January 11, 1862, NARG 75, LR, Upper Arkansas Agency.

35. Report of patrol, November 24–December 1, 1861, and Leeper to Burleson, October 1, 1861, Burleson Papers.

36. E. H. Carruth to "sir," July 11, 1861, and Charles B. Keith to Colonel H. B. Branch, August 24, 1861, NARG 75, Southern Superintendency; Captain E. Otis to commissioner of Indian affairs, August 17, 1861, and A. G. Boone to William P. Dole, October 26, 1861, NARG 75, LR, Upper Arkansas Agency.

37. Boone to Dole, February 2 and March 1, 1862, and Samuel G. Colley to John Evans, June 30, 1862, NARG 75, LR, Upper Arkansas Agency; George W. Collamore to Dole, April 21, 1862, NARG 75, LR, Southern Superintendency.

38. Such an assertion is obviously difficult to prove. I have consulted tree-ring data and looked at the federal government's beef buy-out program for the plains states during the 1930s. Many of the cows and horses purchased by the federal government were simply destroyed, as they were nothing more than skin and bones. According to the tree-ring data for the period 1690–1980, the drought of 1855–1866 was the driest, longest-extended period on record. See Stahle and Cleaveland, "Texas Drought History Reconstructed"; Donald Worster, *The Dust Bowl: The Southern Plains in the 1930s* (New York: Oxford University Press, 1979), 112–115.

39. Colley to Dole, August 11 and December 31, 1862, and Colley to William Gilpin, December 19, 1862, NARG 75, Upper Arkansas Agency; E. H. Carruth to Dole, April 10, 1862, NARG 75, LR, Wichita Agency; S. G. Coffin to Dole, June 15, 1862, NARG 75, Southern Superintendency.

40. The destruction at Fort Cobb was exaggerated in Confederate reports. Still somewhat uncertain is how the Indians at the agency behaved, although most were apparently sympathetic with the Union. It must also be remembered that the Indian brigade that attacked the agency comprised, for the most part, relatives of the Indians living there. Information on the organization of the brigade and its orders are in E. H. Carruth to Dole, April 10, 1862, NARG 75, LR, Wichita Agency; W. G. Coffin to Dole, June 15, 1862. The best description of the brigade's makeup and its raid on Fort Cobb is F. Johnson to Dole, January 20, 1863, NARG 75, LR, Wichita Agency; reprinted in Annie Heloise Abel, *The American Indian as Slaveholder and Secessionist, an Omitted Chapter in the Diplomatic History of the Southern Confederacy* (Cleveland: Arthur H. Clark, 1915), 329–330. See also W. S. Nye, *Carbine and Lance: The Story of Old Fort Sill* (Norman: University of Oklahoma Press, 1937), 29–31; Lubbock to Baylor, November 10, 1962, Frontier Protection Records, BL.

41. J. J. Sturn to Charles B. Johnson, December 29, 1862, General D. H. Cooper to Johnson, January 12, 1863, and Major W. B. Blair to Johnson, February 18, 1863, Johnson Papers.

Some of the Tonkawa men scouted for Colonel James Barry, who had a small ranger force on the Red River. See Captain J. Ward to Barry, August 16, 1863, Barry Papers.

42. Captain Joseph Ward report, February 14, 1863, Adjutant General's Papers, TSL.

43. Lubbock to Captain S. F. Mains, March 12, 1863, Lubbock to Major J. A. Carroll, March 21, 1863, Lubbock to Lieutenant General E. Kirby Smith, August 31, 1863, Lubbock to General Henry McCulloch, September 2, 1863, and Lubbock's message to senate and house, November 3, 1863, Frontier Protection Records, BL.

44. Magruder wrote privately to Governor Pendleton Murrah, who had taken over for Lubbock in October, that he could only accept the regiment "unconditionally," but he gave his word that it would stay in the west. See Magruder to Murrah, November 20, 1863, Frontier Protection Records, BL. There are many good descriptions of the campaigns in Louisiana and Arkansas. See, for example, Richardson, Wallace, and Anderson, *Texas,* 220–222.

45. William Quayle to Governor Murrah, December 27, 1863, Adjutant General's Papers, TSL.

46. Rushing to Lubbock, August 12, 1863, Barry Papers. Ty Cashion, who studied the Clear Fork frontier, also found little evidence of raids in either 1862 or 1863. Cashion wrote, "Clear Fort ranchers were lucky; they spent more time worrying about Indians than fighting them." Cashion, *Texas Frontier,* 65.

47. Lubbock to General E. Kirby Smith, August 31, 1863, and Lubbock to Captain Ed. P. Turner, October 12, 1863, Frontier Protection Records, BL.

48. Coffin to Dole, February 24, 1863, NARG 75, Southern Superintendency.

49. Evans correspondence is found in his letterbooks at the Colorado Historical Society. Since he was also superintendent of Indian affairs, most of his early reports on attempted treaty making are addressed to Commissioner Dole. See also Colonel J. H. Leavenworth to Dole, June 27, 1863, NARG 75, LR, Upper Arkansas Agency.

50. Major George B. Erath to Colonel D. B. Culbertson, April 8, 1864, Major James M. Hunter "Report," May 18, 1864, Hunter to Culbertson, May 15, 1864, Brigadier General J. D. McAdoo to Culbertson, September (n.d.) 1864, and Major William Quayle to Culbertson, September 19, 1864, Adjutant General's Papers, TSL; Captain H. T. Edgar to Lieutenant Colonel A. G. Dickinson, May 11, 1864, and E. M. Downs to Dickinson, May 11, 1864, Frontier Protection Papers, BL.

51. Petition from Gillespie, Kerr, and Kimble counties, March 31, 1864, and Major James M. Hunter to Colonel D. B. Culberson, May 25, 1864, Adjutant General's Papers, TSL; Captain H. T. Edgar to Lieutenant Colonel A. G. Dickson, May 11, 1864, Frontier Protection Records, BL.

52. Good accounts of the Elk Creek raid are found in Cashion, *Texas Frontier,* 66–67, and in Ledbetter, *Fort Belknap,* 11–123.

53. For the Hungate massacre and its impact in Colorado, see Stan Hoig, *The Sand Creek Massacre* (Norman: University of Oklahoma Press, 1961), 56–59, 74–95.

54. Evans to Dole, August 9, 1864, Evans to Jesse Greenwood, August 13, 1864, and Evans to Captain A. G. Gell, of the "Colorado Rangers," August 24, 1864, Evans Letterbook, Colorado Historical Society, Denver.

55. Evans to General Curtis, April 11, May 24, June 16 and 22, and August 11 and 18, 1864, Evans to Dole, June 15, 1864, and Colley to Evans, July 26, 1864, Evans Letterbook, Colorado Historical Society, Denver.

56. For the council with Evans, see Hoig, *Sand Creek Massacre,* 114–127.

57. Evans to Colley, September 19 and 29, 1864, and Evans to William H. Seward, October 18, 1864, Evans Letterbook, Colorado Historical Society, Denver.

58. A good account of Carson's fight is George H. Pettis, *A Personal Narrative of the Battles of the Rebellion, No. 5: Kit Carson's Fight with the Comanche and Kiowa Indians* (Providence, R.I.: Sidney S. Rider, 1878), 8–43. See also "Bent's Fort," manuscript, Grinnell Papers; George Bent to George Hyde, December 13, 1905, Denver Public Library.

59. Hoig, *Sand Creek Massacre,* 145–162.

60. Leavenworth to Dole, February 19, 1865, NARG 75, LR, Kiowa Agency.

61. General Throckmorton to Murrah, January 13, 1865, and Throckmorton to Colonel John Burke, January 29, 1865, Frontier Protection Records, BL.

62. Brigadier General J. P. McAdoo to Colonel John Burke, February 28, 1865, Adjutant General's Papers, TSL.

63. Lieutenant Colonel Barry to adjutant general, January 20, 1865, Lieutenant George F. Adams to Colonel John Burke, January 23, 1865, Throckmorton to Murrah, January 29, 1865, Brigadier General J. P. McAdoo to Burke, February 20 and 28, 1865, Adjutant General's Papers, TSL; J. J. Callan to Murrah, February 15, 1865, Frontier Protection Records, BL.

64. Charles Bogy and W. R. Irvin to Louis V. Bogy, December 8, 1866, NARG 75, Documents Relating to Ratified and Unratified Treaties.

65. Milo Gookins to W. G. Coffin, October 17 and 20, 1864, NARG 75, LR, Wichita Agency.

66. Chisholm to Leavenworth, February 15 and July 14, 1865, Leavenworth to Dole, May 6 and 10, 1865, Leavenworth to General John B. Sanborn, August 1 and August 10, 1865, peace treaty, August 15, 1865, and Leavenworth to D. W. Dooley, November 9, 1865, NARG 75, LR, Kiowa Agency; Nye, *Carbine and Lance,* 39–40.

67. Leavenworth to Sanford, August 1, 1865, NARG 75, LR, Kiowa Agency.

68. Treaty with the Cheyenne and Arapahoe Indians, October 14, 1865, in Charles J. Kappler, ed., *Indian Treaties, 1778–1883* (New York: Interland Publishing, 1972), 887–891.

69. Treaty of October 18, 1865, in Kappler, *Indian Treaties,* 892–895. The best general discussion of the 1865 treaty and the situation in Indian Territory is William T. Hagan, *United States–Comanche Relations: The Reservation Years* (New Haven: Yale University Press, 1976), 19–26.

Chapter 22. The Final Ethnic Cleansing of Texas

1. The debate over the decline in bison populations and range is ongoing, as discussed earlier. See Isenberg, *Destruction of the Bison,* 124–142; Flores, "Bison Ecology and Bison Diplomacy"; David D. Smits, "The Frontier Army and the Destruction of the Buffalo: 1865–1883," *Western Historical Quarterly* 25 (Autumn 1994): 312–338.

2. All the Plains tribes were increasingly demanding coffee and sugar as part of their annuities from the federal government by the late 1860s, an indication of the changing lifestyle of these people. See the reports on annuities found in NARG 75, LR, Wichita and Kiowa Agencies, for the 1860s.

3. See Wooster, *Soldiers, Sutlers, and Settlers,* 13–25; Thomas T. Smith, *The U.S. Army and the Texas Frontier Economy, 1845–1900* (College Station: Texas A and M University Press, 1999), 40–41; Captain R. G. Carter, *On the Border with Mackenzie: or, Winning West Texas from the Comanches* (Washington, D.C.: Eynon Printing, 1935), 53–60; Leavenworth to D. N. Cooley, March 26, 1866, and Milo Gookins to Cooley, March 29, 1866, NARG 75, LR, Kiowa Agency; Major General Sheridan to Throckmorton, March 29, 1867, Governors' Papers, TSL. See also Paul Andrew Hutton, *Phil Sheridan and His Army* (Norman: University of Oklahoma Press, 1985).

4. General Griffin to Governor Pease, September 12, 1867, Governors' Papers, TSL.

5. Bent to Major Dryer, January 19, 1866, NARG 75, LR, Upper Arkansas Agency.

6. Leavenworth to D. N. Cooley, May 1 and June 5, 1866, and George A. Reynolds to N. G. Taylor, April 20, 1868, NARG 75, LR, Kiowa Agency.

7. A. A. Rankin to Colonel James Wortham, February 7, 1868, NARG 75, LR, Wichita Agency; Major W. A. Elderkin to E. S. Parker, December 22, 1869, NARG 75, LR, Kiowa Agency. After 1867, Buffalo Bill converted to Quakerism, even wearing a Quaker hat and coat. He did so to get a trade license from the agent who had replaced Leavenworth, Quaker Lawrie Tatum.

8. See report of council held at Fort Zarah, November 10, 1866, NARG 75, Documents Relating to Ratified and Unratified Treaties.

9. Phillip McCusky to Colonel Thomas Murphy, September 7, 1866, M. Goldbaum to General Carleton, June 7, 1866, and George Smith to E. Hoag, February 3, 1871, NARG 75, LR, Kiowa Agency; Sergeant W. Wilson to post adjutant, March 29, 1872, and Major Jonathan P. Hatch to acting adjutant general, March 30, 1872, NARG 94, LR, Adjutant General's Office. See also J. Evetts Haley, "The Comanchero Trade," *Southwestern Historical Quarterly* 38, no. 3 (January 1935): 157–176. The two rendezvous points were called Mucha Que and Quita Que by the comanchero traders. They were well known in New Mexico.

10. Anthropologists have tried to analyze the reorganization of Comanche band structure. See, for example, Thomas W. Kavanagh, "Comanche Population, Organization, and Reorganization, 1869–1901," part 2, *Plains Anthropologist* 34, no. 124 (May 1989): 99–111.

11. The best sources for information on all these men are the agency returns, at NARG 75, LR, Wichita Agency and Kiowa Agency.

12. While Texans would again report much higher losses from raids, by this time Indian agents and army officers were able to verify the numbers killed and ransom the captives, leading to an exact number. See the various reports, including Thomas Murphy to Cooley, January 22, 1866, Leavenworth to Murphy, December 14, 1866, and Leavenworth to Cooley, June 13 and August 23, 1866, NARG 75, LR, Kiowa Agency; John Field to E. Sells, April 20, 1866, NARG 75, LR, Wichita Agency.

13. See manuscript by Mrs. J. D. Bell (Bianca Babb), "A True Story of My Capture and Life with the Comanche Indians," Texas State Library, and Theodore Adolphus Babb, *In the Bosom of the Comanches* (Dallas: John F. Worley, 1912), 22–140. The army paid $333 for Bianca. See Nye, *Carbine and Lance,* 43–44.

14. See T. T. Mosby to Throckmorton, September 2, 1866, and J. H. Cox to Throckmorton, September 4, 1866, Governors' Papers, TSL.

15. Report of Second Lieutenant G. A. Hesselberger, September 29, 1866, Captain Andrew Sheridan to Brevet Major W. H. Harrison, October 1, 1866, G. H. Todd to Cooley, October 14, 1866, Mary Mathew Box statement, October 20, 1866, Browning to Cooley, October 2, 1866, NARG 75, LR, Kiowa Agency; Jesse Smith to Captain C. Bogy, November 12, 1866, and Bogy and W. R. Irwin to Commissioner of Indian Affairs Lewis V. Bogy, November 23, 1866, NARG 75, LR, Upper Arkansas Agency.

16. The statistics for these years come from gleaning the agency reports in Indian Territory and from various reliable accounts reported in Texas sources. See in particular Brown, *Indian Wars and Pioneers of Texas,* 119–123; *Dallas Herald,* March 7, 1868; Captain E. L. Smith to Colonel O. D. Green, February 16, 1867, Leavenworth to N. G. Taylor, April 23, 1867, First Lieutenant Mark Walker to assistant adjutant general, May 14, 1867, Leavenworth to Taylor, July 28 and 30, 1868, and Murphy to Charles Mix, August 28, 1868, NARG 75, LR, Kiowa Agency; Bedford, *Texas Indian Troubles,* 134–140.

17. J. W. Throckmorton to Reading W. Black, December 6, 1866, and Black to Throckmorton, January 6, 1867, Reading W. Black Papers, BL; Major A. J. Hogan to Captain J. C.

Baiden, January 12, 1867, and General Griffin to Governor Throckmorton, January 21, 1867, Governors' Papers, TSL; *Dallas Herald,* November 2 and 16, 1867.

18. General Hancock to Jesse Leavenworth, March 11, 1867, NARG 75, LR, Kiowa Agency. See the description of Hancock's actions in Wilbur Sturtevant Nye, *Plains Indian Raiders: The Final Phases of Warfare from the Arkansas to the Red River* (Norman: University of Oklahoma Press, 1968), 68–75.

19. Leavenworth to N. G. Taylor, May 2, 4, and 22, 1867, NARG 75, LR, Kiowa Agency.

20. A good overview of the commission is Prucha, *Great Father,* 1:485–533.

21. The treaty is found in Kappler, *Indian Treaties,* 977–982.

22. The supposition is here suggested that those chiefs who refused to attend opposed negotiating. It is of course difficult to document such opposition, the best evidence being later actions in which such chiefs voiced opposition to the reservation system, especially in the early 1870s.

23. The Cheyenne and Arapaho treaty is in Kappler, *Indian Treaties,* 984–989.

24. Even as late as 1868 there was still some question as to how many Indians were attached to the Kiowa/Comanche agency. Leavenworth accepted the numbers of 5,000 Comanches and 2,000 Kiowas, but Philip McCuster, a special agent assigned to investigate the agencies, thought those numbers too large. He estimated only 3,000 Comanches and 1,200 Kiowas. See Leavenworth to Taylor, May 4 and 16, 1867, and May 21 and June 30, 1868, Leavenworth to Mix, December 14, 1867, McCuster to commissioner of Indian affairs, June 5, 1868, and Henry Shanklin to Taylor, May 31, June 6, and June 15, 1868, NARG 75, LR, Kiowa Agency.

25. See the debate and the brewing troubles over annuities in Charles Bogy and W. R. Irwin to Lewis Bogy, November 26, 1866, Leavenworth to Colonel S. S. Bowers, February 22, 1866, Leavenworth to Taylor, May 16, 1867, and March 26, 1868, Leavenworth to Charles Mix, December 14 and 21, 1867, Leavenworth to commanding officer at Fort Arbuckle, April 3, 1868, Sheridan to Brevet Major General W. A. Nichols, May 22, 1868, and Philip McCuster to commissioner of Indian affairs, June 5, 1868, NARG 75, LR, Kiowa Agency; Henry Shanklin to Thomas A. Osborne, May 25, 1868, and Shanklin to Taylor, June 15, 1868, NARG 75, LR, Wichita Agency.

26. Commissioner of Indian affairs to Browning, July 1, 1868; Nye, *Plains Indian Raiders,* 129–137.

27. Robert Utley's biography does an excellent job of comparing Custer's Civil War and Plains service. See Utley, *Custer: Cavalier in Buckskin* (Norman: University of Oklahoma Press, 2001).

28. Nye, *Indian Plains Raiders,* 137–138; Robert C. Carriker, *Fort Supply, Indian Territory: Frontier Outpost on the Plains* (Norman: University of Oklahoma Press, 1970). The term "total war" comes from the Civil War. See Utley, *Custer,* 61–75. The Cheyennes and Arapahos later challenged the loss estimates, placing the number at 14 men, 12 women, and 6 children. Nye rejects this, arguing that Custer had plenty of time to count the dead on the ground before departing. Custer never did specify how many of the dead were men, women, or children. Likely, similar to Sand Creek, it was a mix of the three. See George Bent to George Bird Grinnell, October 2, 1913, Grinnell Papers, for those listed as killed by the Cheyennes and Arapahos.

29. A new study of the battle of the Washita focuses on the controversy within the Seventh Cavalry over Custer's abandonment of his men. See Jerome A. Greene, *Washita: The U.S. Army and the Southern Cheyennes, 1867–1869* (Norman: University of Oklahoma Press, 2004).

30. Much has been written on the peace policy. See, in particular, Robert Winston Mardock, *The Reformers and the American Indian* (Columbia: University of Missouri Press, 1971), 41–43 and the chapter entitled "The Peace Policy" in Prucha, *Great Father,* 1:479–483.

31. A marvelous account of the Quaker effort is found in Thomas C. Battey, *The Life and Adventures of a Quaker Among the Indians* (Boston: Lee, Shepard and Dillingham, 1875).

32. Tatum to E. S. Parker, July 24, 1869, and May 7, 1870, Tatum to Hoag, July 1 and September 1, 1870, and Colonel Benjamin Grierson to assistant adjutant general, September 25, 1869, and April 12, 1870, NARG 75, LR, Kiowa Agency.

33. Tatum to Hoag, August 19, September 6, and November 11, 1870, NARG 75, LR, Kiowa Agency.

34. Council notes at Fort Sill, July 4, 1870, Tatum to Hoag, October 27 and November 15, 1870, NARG 75, LR, Kiowa Agency.

35. Jones to Tatum, December 6, 1870, NARG 75, LR, Kiowa Agency.

36. Grierson to assistant adjutant general, May 13, 1871, NARG 75, LR, Kiowa Agency. Ironically, so many stories of Indian depredations had been published in Texas newspapers that some reprinted back East grossly exaggerated the problem. The *Dallas Herald* actually rebutted a story from the *New Orleans Picayune* that claimed that Comanche raiding parties of upwards of 300 warriors were devastating the state. See *Dallas Herald,* April 23, 1870.

37. Reports of the activities of these companies are found in Franklin Jones to James Davidson, August 8 and September 15, 1870, Jacob M. Harrell to James Davidson, September 1, 1870, H. J. Richarz to Davidson, October 15, 1870, John R. Kelson to Davidson, November 7, 1870, and Richarz to Davidson, December 4, 1870 and April 10, 1871, Adjutant General's Papers, TSL. As usual, army officers in Texas had little good to say about these ranger companies. See A. H. Cox to Governor Davis, October 29, 1870, Ranger Records, TSL.

38. See Sherman to Colonel William Wood, May 19, 1871, and Sherman to General John Pope, NARG 75, LR, Kiowa Agency; *Dallas Herald,* June 3, 1871. Grierson noted that three Indians were killed while the Indians made their attack, two died quickly thereafter, and two more had been mortally wounded, making seven in all. See Grierson to assistant adjutant general, June 1, 1871, NARG 75, LR, Kiowa Agency. Most of Colonel Mackenzie's correspondence relative to his early campaigns is found in Ernest Wallace, ed., *Ranald S. Mackenzie's Official Correspondence Relating to Texas, 1871–1873* (Lubbock: West Texas Museum Association, 1967).

39. Tatum to Hoag, May 25 and 28, 1871, June 10 and 17, 1871, July 1 and 22, 1871, Sherman to adjutant general, May 28, 1871, Tatum to Sherman, May 29, 1871, Grierson to assistant adjutant general, July 8, 1871, and Special Order No. 185, September 12, 1871, NARG 75, LR, Kiowa Agency; Robert G. Carter, *The Old Sergeant's Story: Winning the West from the Indians and Bad Men in 1870 to 1878* (New York: Frederick Hitchcock, 1926), 78–81.

40. Tatum to Hoag, February 21, 1872, NARG 75, LR, Kiowa Agency.

41. The best description of this expedition is in Carter, *On the Border with Mackenzie,* 157–176.

42. Colonel W. H. Wood to acting assistant adjutant general, June 13, 1872 and Major George Schofield to adjutant general, June 22, 1872, NARG 94, LR, AGO; Tatum to Hoag, June 22, 1872, NARG 75, LR, Kiowa Agency.

43. Schofield to assistant adjutant general, June 19, July 6, and August 5 and 19, 1872, and Delano to secretary of war, July 11, 1872, NARG 94, LR, AGO; Indian Peace Commission report, August 27, 1872, NARG 75, LR, Kiowa Agency.

44. Mackenzie's report, October 12, 1872, NARG 94, LR, AGO; Carter, *Old Sergeant's Story,* 82–89. Carter, *On the Border with Mackenzie,* 376–393, offers another description of the engagement, written much later. Carter came to believe in the early twentieth century that Quanah Parker, rather than Mowway, was actually the head of the Quahades. Quanah was likely there but would have been only in his mid-twenties then. Mackenzie identifies the village attacked in 1872 as that of Mowway, and Mowway was clearly the recognized chief. See pages 157 and 176 for a literary description of Quanah in the 1871 engagement with Mackenzie.

45. Cyrus Beede to John Walker, December 13, 1872, Tatum to Hoag, January 11 and March 31, 1873, Delano to Governor Davis, March 22, 1873, Beede to Hoag, April 4, 1873, Hoag to H. R. Clum, April 7, 1873, Haworth to Hoag, April 7, 1873, Delano to Davis, April 12, 1873, and Haworth to Beede, May 5, 1873, NARG 75, LR, Kiowa Agency.

46. Delano to Davis, May 27, 1873, Haworth to Hoag, June 9, 12, and 16, July 21, and September 8, 1873, Beede to Edward P. Smith, May 14, 1872, Lieutenant Colonel John R. Brooke to assistant adjutant general, September 4, 1873, Henry E. Alvord to Smith, September 20, 1873, and "Records of Indian Council," October 6, 1873, NARG 75, LR, Kiowa Agency; Hagan, *United States–Comanche Relations,* 94–99.

47. Mackenzie to assistant adjutant general, May 23, 1874, NARG 94, LR, AGO. According to Carter, who spoke with Mackenzie after he had met with General Sheridan, President Grant was aware of the need to cross the border into Mexico and gave his approbation. See Carter, *On the Border with Mackenzie,* 422–423.

48. Haworth to secretary of interior, December 15, 1873, NARG 75, LR, Kiowa Agency.

49. Haworth to secretary of interior, December 15, 1873, NARG 75, LR, Kiowa Agency. See also Hagan, *United States–Comanche Relations,* 102–105.

50. Haworth to Hoag, June 6, 8, and 27, 1874, NARG 75, LR, Kiowa Agency.

51. Haworth to Hoag, May 6, 1874, NARG 75, LR, Kiowa Agency.

52. Hagan, who researched the man's family, gave the spelling as Eschiti, or Coyote Droppings. George Bent offered another spelling: Isatac. See Hagan, *United States–Comanche Relations,* 105, and Bent to Hyde, October 24, 1913, George Bent Papers, Denver Public Library.

53. Lieutenant Colonel John R. Brooke to assistant adjutant general, June 15, 1874, and Colonel Davidson to assistant adjutant general, July 17, 1874, NARG 75, LR, Kiowa Agency; McCuster to Jones, July 20, 1874, NARG 94, LR, AGO; Hagan, *United States–Comanche Relations,* 108–109; Battey, *Quaker Among the Indians,* 302–303.

54. Captain G. K. Sanderson to post adjutant, August 9 and September 25, 1874, and Clark J. Connell to Benjamin Richards, August 22, 1874, NARG 75, LR, Kiowa Agency.

55. Miles to assistant adjutant general, September 1, 1874, Miles to General John Pope, September 5, 1874, Pope to Sheridan, September 18, 1874, and Sherman to General E. D. Townsend, October 14, 1874, NARG 94, LR, AGO; Carter, *On the Border with Mackenzie,* 473–523.

56. Lieutenant Colonel John Neill to assistant adjutant general, October 4, 1874, Sheridan to W. W. Belknap, October 5, 1874, Belknap to Sheridan, October 5, 1874, Mackenzie to General C. C. Augur, November 27, 1874, and Belknap memorandum, March 13, 1875, NARG 94, LR, AGO; Haworth to E. P. Smith, November 11, 1874, NARG 75, LR, Kiowa Agency; Hagan, *United States–Comanche Relations,* 110–117.

57. Jones to Adjutant General William Steele, of Texas, May 9, 1875, Adjutant General's Papers, TSL.

BIBLIOGRAPHY

Primary Sources—Archival

Ad-Interim Government. Records of the Secretary of State. Texas State Library (TSL), Austin.

Administrative Documents of Texas. Texas State Library (TSL), Austin.

Archivo de la Secretario de Gobierno del Estado. Barker Library Transcripts. Eugene C. Barker Library (BL), University of Texas, Austin.

Army Papers. Texas State Library (TSL), Austin.

Barry, James Buckner. Papers. Eugene C. Barker Library (BL), University of Texas, Austin.

Bayard, George D. Papers. Missouri Historical Society, St. Louis.

Baylor, John R. Papers. Baylor University Library, Waco, Texas.

———. Papers (transcripts). Eugene C. Barker Library (BL), University of Texas, Austin.

Bee, Bernard. Papers. Eugene C. Barker Library (BL), University of Texas, Austin.

Beeching, Robert. "Journal of a Trip from New York on the bark, 'Norumbega' to Galveston and then overland through Texas, Mexico, Arizona and southern California to San Diego." 1849. Henry E. Huntington Library, San Marino, California.

Bell, Mrs. J. D. (Bianca Babb). "A True Story of My Capture and Life with the Comanche Indians." Manuscript, Texas State Library (TSL), Austin.

Bent, George. Papers. Denver Public Library, Denver, Colorado.

Bexar Archives (BA). Eugene C. Barker Library (BL), University of Texas, Austin.

Bingham Family Papers. Western Manuscript Collection. University of Missouri, Columbia.

Black, Reading W. Papers. Eugene C. Barker Library (BL), University of Texas, Austin.

Blake, R. B. Papers. Eugene C. Barker Library (BL), University of Texas, Austin.

Bolton, Herbert Eugene. Papers. Bancroft Library, University of California, Berkeley.

Bonnell, George W. Papers. Edward Ayer Collection. Newberry Library, Chicago.

Burleson, Edward. Papers. Eugene C. Barker Library (BL), University of Texas, Austin.

Butler, Pierce M. Papers. Henry E. Huntington Library, San Marino, California.

————. Papers. Library of Congress, Washington, D.C.

Caddo Indian Papers. Oklahoma Historical Society, Oklahoma City.

Chouteau Family Papers. Missouri Historical Society, St. Louis.

Corbin, Harriet Turner (Porter), comp. "A History and Genealogy of Chief William McIntosh, Jr." Edited by Carl C. Burdick. Private collection.

Cox, Cornelius C. "Notes and Memoranda of an Overland Trip from Texas to California in the Year 1849." Henry E. Huntington Library, San Marino, California.

Dispatches from Consuls in Texas, 1825–1844. Eugene C. Barker Library (BL), University of Texas, Austin.

Documents Relating to the Committee of Vigilance and Safety at Nacogdoches. Eugene C. Barker Library (BL), University of Texas, Austin.

Douglas, K. H. Estate Papers. Starr Papers, Eugene C. Barker Library (BL), University of Texas, Austin.

Edwards, Hayden. Papers. Ralf W. Steen Library, Stephen F. Austin University, Nacogdoches, Texas.

Executive Department Journals, 1836. Texas State Library (TSL), Austin.

"Extractos y Copias el documentos existentes en el Archivo Documentos de la Comisíon Pesquisidora de la Frontera del Norte," 1852. Archivo Relaciones Exteriores, Mexico City.

Fomento-Colonización. Archivo General de la Nación (AGN), Mexico City. See also Transcripts, Eugene C. Barker Library (BL), University of Texas, Austin.

Frontier Protection Records. Eugene C. Barker Library (BL), University of Texas, Austin.

Governors' Papers. State of Texas. Texas State Library (TSL), Austin.

Grinnell, George Bird. Papers. Southwest Museum, Los Angeles, California.

Guerra y Marina. Archivo General de la Nación (AGN), Mexico City. See also Transcripts, Eugene C. Barker Library (BL), University of Texas, Austin.

Halton-Meisenheimer Papers. Ralph W. Steen Library, Stephen F. Austin State University, Nacogdoches, Texas.

Harris, Benjamin Butler. "Account of Journey from Panola, Co., Texas." 1849. Henry E. Huntington Library, San Marino, California.

Hatch, John Porter. Papers. Library of Congress, Washington, D.C.

Hereford, Thomas A. and Margaret S. Papers. Henry E. Huntington Library, San Marino, California.

Hill, C. C. Papers. Eugene C. Barker Library (BL), University of Texas, Austin.

Hornsby, Reuben. Family Papers. Texas State Library (TSL), Austin.

Houston, A. J. Papers. Texas State Library (TSL), Austin.

Houston, Sam. Papers. Eugene C. Barker Library (BL), University of Texas, Austin.

————. Papers. Gilcrease Library and Art Gallery, Tulsa, Oklahoma.

Hyde, George. Letters. Denver Public Library, Denver, Colorado.

Indian Papers. St. Louis Historical Society, St. Louis, Missouri.

Irion, R. A. Papers. Eugene C. Barker Library (BL), University of Texas, Austin.

Johnston, Albert Sidney. Papers. Texas State Library (TSL), Austin.

Johnston, Charles. Papers. Edward Ayer Collection. Newberry Library, Chicago.

Journal of the House. 1836. Texas State Library (TSL), Austin.

Karnes, Henry W. Papers. Texas State Library (TSL), Austin.

Kennett Family Papers. Missouri Historical Society, St. Louis.

Kuykendall, James and William. Papers. Ralf W. Steen Library, Stephen F. Austin State University, Nacogdoches, Texas.

Lang, Willis L. "My Wild Hunt after Indians: The Journal of Willis L. Lang, First Lieutenant, Waco Rangers." Unpublished manuscript, May–August 1860. Copy in possession of Thomas W. Cutrer.

Lasselle, Stanislaus. "Diary of an Overland Journey . . . by way of Ft. Smith, Ark., to Santa Fe, N.M. and the Spanish Trail in 1849, Feb. 6–Aug. 21." Henry E. Huntington Library, San Marino, California.

Lee, Robert E. Lee Family, DeButts-Ely Collection. Library of Congress, Washington, D.C.

Le Grand, Alexander. Papers. Texas State Library (TSL), Austin.

Lundy, Benjamin. Journal and Papers. Ohio Historical Society, Columbus.

Marmaduke, Merideth M. Papers. Western Historical Manuscript Collection. University of Missouri, Columbia.

Matamoros Archives. Eugene C. Barker Library (BL), University of Texas, Austin.

Matamoros Consul Papers. Microfilm. Eugene C. Barker Library (BL), University of Texas, Austin.

McLeod, Hugh. Papers. Texas State Library (TSL), Austin.

Messages and Proclamations of the Presidents. Letters Sent. Secretary of State Records. Texas State Library (TSL), Austin.

Milam, James. Diary. Bancroft Library, University of California, Berkeley.

Miller, Washington. Papers. Texas State Library (TSL), Austin.

Nacogdoches Archives (NA). Texas State Library (TSL), Austin.

National Archives Record Group (NARG) 75. Correspondence of the Bureau of Indian Affairs. National Archives, Washington, D.C.

National Archives Record Group (NARG) 75. Documents Relative to the Negotiation of Ratified and Unratified Treaties. National Archives, Washington, D.C.

National Archives Record Group (NARG) 94. Letters Received (LR), Adjutant General's Office (AGO). National Archives, Washington, D.C.

National Archives Record Group (NARG) 393. Correspondence and Reports Relating to Special Subjects, 1831–1851. National Archives, Washington, D.C.

National Archives Record Group (NARG) 393. United States Army Continental Commands, 1821–1920. National Archives, Washington, D.C.

Neighbors, Robert S. Papers. Library of Congress, Washington, D.C.

———. Papers. Eugene C. Barker Library (BL), University of Texas, Austin.

Notes from the Texan Legation in the United States, Consular Letters, 1836–1845. Microfilm. Eugene C. Barker Library (BL), University of Texas, Austin.

Onderdonk, Gilbert. "Stories of Early Texas Life." Eugene C. Barker Library (BL), University of Texas, Austin.

Owens, Elizabeth McAnulty. "The Story of My Life." Eugene C. Barker Library (BL), University of Texas, Austin.

Peveler, Francis M. Papers. Eugene C. Barker Library (BL), University of Texas, Austin.

Raguet, Henry. Papers. Eugene C. Barker Library (BL), University of Texas, Austin.

Ranger Records. General Correspondence, 1852–1859. Texas State Library (TSL), Austin.

Records Relating to Indian Affairs. Texas State Library (TSL), Austin.

Ritch, William Gillet. Papers. Henry E. Huntington Library, San Marino, California.

Robinson, Joel. Memoir. Ralf W. Steen Library, Stephen F. Austin State University, Nacogdoches, Texas.

Ross, Lawrence Sullivan. Papers. Baylor University Library, Waco, Texas.

Rueg, Henry. Papers. Eugene C. Barker Library (BL). University of Texas, Austin.

Rusk, Thomas Jefferson. Papers. Eugene C. Barker Library (BL), University of Texas, Austin.

Saltillo Archives. Transcripts. Eugene C. Barker Library (BL), University of Texas, Austin.

Secretary of State Records. Texas State Library (TSL), Austin.

Simpson, John. Memoir. Ralf W. Steen Library, Stephen F. Austin Library, Nacogdoches, Texas.

Smith, Ashbel. Papers. Eugene C. Barker Library (BL), University of Texas, Austin.

Spanish Archives of New Mexico (SANM). State of New Mexico Records Center, Santa Fe.

Special Collections (Wharton Correspondence). Hill Memorial Library, Louisiana State University, Baton Rouge.

Stuart, J. E. B. Letter. Western Manuscript Collections. University of Missouri, Columbia.

Taylor, Calvin. Papers. Louisiana State University Library Archives, Baton Rouge.

Texas Adjutant General's Papers. Texas State Library (TSL), Austin.

Texas Indian Papers. Texas State Library (TSL), Austin.

Thomas, George H. Papers. Henry E. Huntington Library, San Marino, California.

Trimble, William Allen. Papers. Ohio Historical Society, Columbus.

PRIMARY SOURCES—PUBLISHED

Abert, James W. *Through the Country of the Comanche Indians in the Fall of the Year 1845: The Journal of a U.S. Army Expedition Led by Lieutenant James W. Abert of the Topographical Engineers.* Ed. John Galvin. San Francisco: John Howell Books, 1970.

Adair, James. *Adair's History of the American Indians: Edited under the Auspices of the National Society of the Colonial Dames of America, in Tennessee.* New York: Promontory Press, 1930; reprint of 1775 edition.

Almonte, Juan Nepomuceno. "Statistical Report on Texas." Trans. Carlos Castañeda. *Southwestern Historical Quarterly* 28 (January 1925): 177–221.

American State Papers. 7 vols. Washington, D.C.: Gales and Seaton, 1832–1861.

Austin, Stephen F. *The Austin Papers.* Ed. Eugene C. Barker. Vols. 1 and 2 and Supplement. Washington, D.C.: American Historical Association, 1919–1928. Vol. 3. Austin: University of Texas Press, 1926.

Babb, Theodore Adolphus. *In the Bosom of the Comanches*. Dallas: John F. Worley, 1912.

Banta, William, and J. W. Caldwell. *Twenty-seven Years on the Texas Frontier; or fifty years in Texas*. Austin: Ben Jones, 1893.

Battey, Thomas C. *The Life and Adventures of a Quaker Among the Indians*. Boston: Lee, Shepard, and Dillingham, 1875.

Berlandier, Jean Louis. *The Indians of Texas in 1830*. Ed. John C. Ewers. Washington, D.C.: Smithsonian Institution Press, 1969.

Bieber, Ralph P., ed. *Marching with the Army of the West, 1846–1848*. Vol. 6 of The Southwest Historical Series. Glendale, Calif.: Arthur H. Clark, 1936.

Binkley, William C., ed. *The Official Correspondence of the Texas Revolution, 1835–1836*. 2 vols. New York: D. Appleton, 1936.

Brown, John Henry. *History of Texas from 1685–1892*. 2 vols. St. Louis: L. E. Daniell, 1893.

———. *Indian Wars and Pioneers of Texas*. Austin: L. E. Daniell, 1897.

Buffon, comte de [George Louis Leclerc]. *Histoire Naturelle, Générale et Particuliére*. Paris: Imprimerie Royale, 1774–1789.

Burnam, Jesse. "Reminiscences of Capt. Jesse Burnam." *Texas Historical Association Quarterly* 5 (1901): 12–18.

Calhoun, J. S. *The Official Correspondence of James S. Calhoun while Indian Agent at Santa Fe and Superintendent of Indian Affairs in New Mexico*. Ed. Annie H. Abel. Washington, D.C.: Government Printing Office, 1915.

Canales, Isidro Vizcaya, ed. *La Invasión de los Indios Bárbaros al Noreste de Mexico en los Ános de 1840 y 1841*. Monterey, Mexico: Instituto Tecnológico y de Estudias Superiores, 1968.

Carter, Clarence E., and John P. Bloom, eds. *Territorial Papers of the United States*. 28 vols. Washington, D.C.: Government Printing Office, 1934– .

Carter, Captain R. G. *The Old Sergeant's Story: Winning the West from the Indians and Bad Men in 1870 to 1878*. New York: Frederick Ritchcock, 1926.

———. *On the Border with Mackenzie: or, Winning West Texas from the Comanches*. Washington, D.C.: Eynon Printing, 1935.

Chacon, Rafael. *Legacy of Honor: The Life of Rafael Chacon, a Nineteenth Century New Mexican*. Ed. Jacqueline Dorgan Meketa. Albuquerque: University of New Mexico Press, 1982.

Coombes, Z. E. *The Diary of a Frontiersman, 1858–1859*. Ed. Barbara Neal Ledbetter. Privately printed, no date.

Daniell, Forrest. "Texas Pioneer Surveyors and Indians." *Southwestern Historical Quarterly* 60 (April 1957): 501–506.

de la Teja, Jesús F., ed. *A Revolution Remembered: The Memoirs and Selected Correspondence of Juan N. Seguín*. Austin: State House Press, 1991.

DeWees, William B. *Letters From An Early Settler of Texas*. Cincinnati, Ohio: Hull, 1853.

Dolbeare, Dr. Benjamin. *A Narrative of the Captivity and Suffering of Dolly Webster Among the Comanche Indians in Texas, with an account of the massacre of John Webster and his party, as related by Mrs. Webster*. Clarksburg, Va.: M'Granaghan and M'Carty, 1843; reprint, New Haven, Conn.: Yale University Library, 1986.

Domenech, Ábbe Emmanuel Henri Dieudonné. *Missionary Adventures in Texas and Mexico: A Personal Narrative of Six Years' Sojourn in These Regions.* London: Longman, Brown, Green, Longmans, and Roberts, 1858.

Duke, Thomas M. "Reminiscences of Early Texas: A Collection from the Austin Papers." *Texas State Historical Association Quarterly* 5 (July 1901): 236–253, and 7 (July 1903): 29–64.

Duval, John C. *The Adventures of Big-Foot Wallace, the Texas Ranger and Hunter.* Philadelphia: Claxton, Temsen, and Haffelfinger, 1871.

Estep, Raymond, ed. "Lieutenant William E. Burnet: Notes on Removal of the Indians from Texas to Indian Territory." *Chronicles of Oklahoma* 38 (Autumn 1960): 274–309.

———. "Lieutenant William E. Burnet Letters: Removal of the Texas Indians and the Founding of Fort Cobb," Part 2. *Chronicles of Oklahoma* 38 (Winter 1960–61): 369–396.

———. "Lieutenant William E. Burnet Letters: Removal of the Texas Indians and the Founding of Fort Cobb," Part 3. *Chronicles of Oklahoma* 39 (Spring 1961): 15–41.

Falconer, Thomas. *Letters and Notes on the Texan Santa Fe Expedition.* Ed. Frederick Webb Hodge. New York: Dauber and Pine, 1930.

Foreman, Grant. "The Journal of the Proceedings at our First Treaty with Wild Indians, 1835." *Chronicles of Oklahoma* 14 (December 1936): 393–413.

Fowler, Jacob. *The Journal of Jacob Fowler, Narrating an Adventure from Arkansas through the Indian Territory, Oklahoma, Kansas, Colorado, and New Mexico, to the Sources of the Rio Grande del Norte, 1821–1822.* Ed. Elliott Coues. New York: Francis P. Harper, 1898.

Fuller, Harlin M., and LeRoy Hagen. *The Journal of Captain John R. Bell: Official Journalist for the Stephen H. Long Expedition to the Rocky Mountains, 1820.* Glendale, Calif.: Arthur H. Clark, 1973.

Gaillardet, Frédéric. *Sketches of Early Texas and Louisiana.* Ed. and trans. James L. Shepherd III. Austin: University of Texas Press, 1966.

Harris, Benjamin Butler. *The Gila Trail: The Texas Argonauts and the California Gold Rush.* Ed. Richard N. Dillon. Norman: University of Oklahoma Press, 1960.

Harris, N. Sayre, ed. "Journal of a Tour in the Indian Territory." *Chronicles of Oklahoma* 10 (June 1932): 219–256.

Hicks, Elijah. "The Journal of Elijah Hicks." *Chronicles of Oklahoma* 13 (March 1935): 68–99.

House, E., ed. *A Narrative of the Captivity of Mrs. Horn and her Two Children with That of Mrs. Harris by the Camanche [sic] Indians.* St. Louis: C. Keemle, 1839.

Houston, Sam. *The Writings of Sam Houston.* 8 vols. Edited by Amelia W. Williams and Eugene C. Barker. Austin: University of Texas Press, 1938–1943.

Hunter, John Dunn. *Memoirs of a Captivity among the Indians of North America.* Ed. Richard Drinnon. New York: Schocken Books, 1973.

Jackson, Jack, and John Wheat, eds. *Texas by Terán.* Austin: University of Texas Press, 2000.

Jefferson, Thomas. *Notes on the State of Virginia.* Reprint, New York: Harper and Row, 1964.

Jones, Harold W. "Notes and Documents: The Diary of Assistant Surgeon Leonard McPhail on his Journey to the Southwest in 1835." *Chronicles of Oklahoma* 18 (September 1940): 281–292.

Journals of the Fourth Congress of the Republic of Texas, 1839–1840, to Which Are Added the Relief Laws. Ed. Harriet Smither. Austin: Von Boechmann-Jones, 1931.

Journals of the House of Representatives of the Republic of Texas: First Congress, First Session. Houston: Office of the Telegraph, 1838.

Journals of the House of Representatives of the Republic of Texas, at the Second Session of the First Congress, held by Adjournment at the City of Houston, and Commencing Monday May 1st, 1837. Houston: Telegraph Office, 1838.

Journals of the House of Representatives of the Republic of Texas: Called Session of September 25, 1837, and Regular Session, commencing November 6, 1837. Houston: National Banner Office, Niles and Co., 1838.

Journals of the House of Representatives of the Republic of Texas: Second Congress, Adjourned Session. Houston: Telegraph Office, 1838.

Journals of the House of Representatives of the Republic of Texas: Regular Session of the Third Congress, November 5, 1838. Houston: Intelligencer Office, S. Whiting, 1839.

Journals of the House of Representatives of the Republic of Texas: Fifth Congress, Appendix. Austin: Gazette Office, 1841.

Journals of the House of Representatives of the Seventh Congress of the Republic of Texas, Convened at Washington, on the 14th of Nov., 1842. Washington, Tex.: Thomas Johnson, 1843.

Journals of the House of Representatives of the Eighth Congress of the Republic of Texas. Houston: Cruger and Moore, 1844.

Journals of the House of Representatives of the State of Texas. Sessions One and Two. Clarksville, Tex.: Standard Office, 1848.

Journals of the House of Representatives of the State of Texas. Third Session. Austin: Gazette Office, 1849.

Journals of the Senate of the Republic of Texas: First Congress, First Session. Columbia: G. and T. H. Borden, 1836.

Journals of the Senate of the Republic of Texas: Adjourned Session, Second Congress. Houston: Telegraph Power Press, 1838.

Journals of the Senate of the Republic of Texas: Fifth Congress, First Session. Houston: Telegraph Office, 1841.

Journals of the Senate of the Republic of Texas: Sixth Congress. Austin: W. Whiting, 1842.

Journals of the Senate of the Ninth Congress of the Republic of Texas. Washington, Tex.: Miller and Cushney, 1845.

Journals of the Senate of the Extra Session, Ninth Congress of the Republic of Texas. Washington, Tex.: Miller and Cushney, 1845.

Journals of the Senate of the State of Texas, First Legislature. Houston: Telegraph Office, 1848.

Journals of the Senate of the State of Texas, Second Legislature. Houston: Telegraph Office, 1848.

Journals of the Senate of the State of Texas, Third Session. Austin: Gazette Office, 1849.

Journals of the Senate of the State of Texas. Extra Session—Third Legislature. Austin: Gazette Office, 1850.

Journals of the Senate of the State of Texas. Fourth Legislature. Austin: State Gazette Office, 1852.

Journals of the Senate of the State of Texas. Fourth Legislature—Extra Session. Austin: J. W. Hampton, 1853.

Journal [No. 5] of the Senate of the State of Texas. Fifth Legislature. Austin: J. W. Hampton, 1853.

Journals of the Sixth Congress of the Republic of Texas, 1841–1842. N.p.: Capital Printing, 1845.

Kappler, Charles J., ed. *Indian Treaties, 1778–1883.* New York: Interland Publishing, 1972.

Kennedy, William. *Texas, the rise, the progress and prospects of the Republic of Texas.* London: R. Hastings, 1841.

Lamar, Mirabeau B. *The Papers of Mirabeau B. Lamar* (cited as *Lamar Papers*). Ed. Charles A. Gulick, Jr., Katherine Elliott, and Harriet Smither. 6 vols. Austin: Von Boeckmann-Jones, 1921–1927.

Linn, John L. *Reminiscences of Fifty Years in Texas.* New York: Sadler, 1883.

Lundy, Benjamin. *The Life, Travels and Opinions of Benjamin Lundy, Including his Journeys to Texas and Mexico: With a Sketch of Contemporary Events, and a Motive of the Revolution in Hayti.* Philadelphia: William D. Purpish, 1847.

———. *The War in Texas: A Review of Facts and Circumstances, Showing that this contest is A Crusade Against Mexico, Set on Foot and Supported by Slaveholders, Land Speculators, etc., in order to Re-establish, Extend, and Perpetuate the System of Slavery and the Slave Trade.* Philadelphia: Merrihew and Gunn, 1837.

Miller, Hunter, ed. *Treaties and Other International Acts of the United States of America.* Washington, D.C.: Government Printing Office, 1933.

Montaignes, Francois des. *The Plains.* Ed. Nancy Alpert Mower and Don Russell. Norman: University of Oklahoma Press, 1972.

Morrison, W. B. "A Journey Across Oklahoma, Ninety Years Ago." *Chronicles of Oklahoma* 4 (December 1926): 333–337.

Olmsted, Frederick Law. *A Journey Through Texas; or, a Saddle-Trip on the Southwestern Frontier.* New York: Dixs, Edwards, 1857; reprint, Austin: University of Texas Press, 1978.

Oo-chee-ah (The Worm). "The Story of Sequoyah's Last Days." *Chronicles of Oklahoma* 12 (March 1934): 25–41.

Parker, A. A. *Trip to the West and Texas. Comprising A Journey of Eight Thousand Miles, Through New-York, Michigan, Illinois, Missouri, Louisiana, and Texas, in the Autumn and Winter of 1834–1835. Interspersed with Anecdotes, Incidents and Observations. With a Brief Sketch of the Texian War.* Boston: Benjamin B. Mussey, 1836; reprint, Austin and New York: Pemberton Press, 1968.

Parker, James W. *Narrative of the Perilous Adventures, Miraculous Escapes and Sufferings of Rev. James W. Parker, during a Frontier Residence in Texas, of Fifteen Years . . . To which is Appended a Narrative of the Capture and Subsequent Sufferings of Mrs. Rachael Plummer (His Daughter), During a Captivity of Twenty-one Months among the Cumanche [sic] Indians, with a Sketch of Their Manners, customs, Laws, etc.; with a Short Description of the Country over which She Travelled whilst with the Indians.* Louisville, Ky.: Morning Courier Office, 1844.

Perrine, Fred S., ed. "Hugh Evan's Journal of Colonel Henry Dodge's Expedition to the Rocky Mountains in 1835." *Mississippi Valley Historical Review* 14 (September 1927): 192–214.

Pettis, George H. *A Personal Narrative of the Battles of the Rebellion, No. 5: Kit Carson's Fight with the Comanche and Kiowa Indians.* Providence, R.I.: Sidney S. Rider, 1878.

Plummer, Rachel. *The Rachel Plummer Narrative: A Stirring Narrative of Adventure, Hardship, and Privation in the Early Days of Texas, Depicting Struggles with the Indians and Other Adventures.* N.p.: privately published, 1926; reprint, Austin: Jenkins Publishing, 1977.

Proceedings of the House of Representatives, From the 3d of October to the 23d of December. Columbia, Tex.: G. and T. H. Borden, 1836.

Rister, Carl Coke. *Comanche Bondage: Dr. John Charles Beales's Settlement of La Villa de Dolores on Las Moras Creek in Southern Texas in the 1830s, with an Annotated Reprint of Sarah Ann Horn's Narrative of Her Captivity Among the Comanches, Her Ransom by Traders in New Mexico, and Return Via the Santa Fe Trail.* Glendale, Calif.: Arthur H. Clark, 1955.

Sanchez, José Maria. "A Trip to Texas in 1828." *Southwestern Historical Quarterly* 29 (April 1926): 249–288.

Secret Journals of the Senate. Republic of Texas. Ed. Ernest W. Winkler. Austin: Austin Printing Company, 1911.

U.S. Congress, House and Senate Documents and Reports. Serial Set.

Wallace, Ernest, ed. "David G. Burnet's Letters Describing the Comanche Indians." *West Texas Historical Association Year Book* 30 (October 1954): 115–140.

———, ed. *Ranald S. Mackenzie's Official Correspondence Relating to Texas, 1871–1873.* Lubbock: West Texas Museum Association, 1967.

Wilbarger, John Wesley. *Depredations in Texas. Reliable Accounts of Battles, Wars, Adventures, Forays, Murders, Massacres, etc. etc., Together with Biographical Sketches of Many of the Most Noted Indian Fighters and Frontiersman of Texas.* Austin: Hutchins Printing, 1889.

Wilson, Adeline. *A Thrilling Narrative of the Sufferings of Mrs. Jane Adeline Wilson during Her Captivity among the Comanche Indians.* Fairfield, Wash.: Ye Galleon Press, 1971.

Wilson, Grant, and John Fiske. *Appletons' Cyclopedia of American Biography.* 6 vols. New York: D. Appleton, 1888.

Winfrey, Dorman H., and James M. Day, eds. *The Indian Papers of Texas and the Southwest, 1825–1916.* 5 vols. Austin: Pemberton Press, 1966.

Yoakum, Henderson. *History of Texas From the First Settlement in 1685 to Its Annexation to the United States in 1846.* 2 vols. New York: Redfield, 1855.

Newspapers

Arkansas Gazette, 1819–1836

Austin City Gazette, 1839–1843

Daily Bulletin (Austin), 1841

Daily Texian (Austin), 1841–1843

Dallas Herald, 1858–1859

Houston Weekly Times, 1840–1842

Niles Register, 1832–1835

Southern Intelligencer (Austin), 1858–1859

South-western American (Austin), 1852–1854

Telegraph and Texas Register (Houston), 1835–1846

Texas Gazette, 1830

Texas Sentinel (Austin), 1840–1858

Union Democrat (Seguin) 1858–1859

Secondary Sources

Abel, Annie Heloise. *The American Indian as Slaveholder and Secessionist, an Omitted Chapter in the Diplomatic History of the Southern Confederacy.* Cleveland: Arthur H. Clark, 1915.

Agnew, Brad. "The 1858 War against the Comanches." *Chronicles of Oklahoma* 49 (Summer 1971): 223–229.

———. *Fort Gibson: Terminal on the Trails of Tears.* Norman: University of Oklahoma Press, 1980.

Alessio Robles, Vito. *Coahuila y Texas: Desde La Consumacion de La Independencia Hasta El Tratado De Paz De Guadalupe Hidalgo.* 2 vols. Mexico City: Editorial Porrúa, 1979.

Alonzo, Armando C. *Tejano Legacy: Rancheros and Settlers in South Texas, 1734–1900* (Albuquerque: University of New Mexico Press, 1998).

Anderson, Gary Clayton. *The Indian Southwest: Ethnogenesis and Reinvention, 1580–1830.* Norman: University of Oklahoma Press, 1999.

———. *Kinsmen of Another Kind: Dakota-White Relations on the Upper Mississippi River, 1650–1862.* Lincoln: University of Nebraska Press, 1984.

Andreopoulos, George J. *Genocide: Conceptual and Historical Dimensions.* Philadelphia: University of Pennsylvania Press, 1994.

Anna, Timothy E. *Forging Mexico: 1821–1835.* Lincoln: University of Nebraska Press, 1998.

Axtell, James. *Beyond 1492: Encounters in Colonial North America.* New York: Oxford University Press, 1992.

Barker, Eugene C. *The Life of Stephen F. Austin.* Nashville and Dallas: Cokesbury, 1925.

———. "United States and Mexico, 1835–1837." *Mississippi Valley Historical Review* 1 (June 1914): 1–30.

Barr, Alwyn. *Black Texans: A History of African Americans in Texas, 1528–1995.* Austin: Jenkins Publishing, 1973.

Bedford, Hilory G. *Texas Indian Troubles: The Most Thrilling Events in the History of Texas.* Benjamin, Tex.: Hargreaves, 1905.

Benner, Judith Ann. *Sul Ross: Soldier, Statesman, Educator.* College Station: Texas A and M University Press, 1983.

Betty, Gerald. *Comanche Society: Before the Reservation.* College Station: Texas A and M University Press, 2002.

Binkley, W. C. "New Mexico and the Santa Fe Expedition." *Southwestern Historical Quarterly* 27 (October 1923): 85–107.

Brice, Donaly Edward. *The Great Comanche Raid: Boldest Indian Attack of the Texas Republic.* Austin: Eakin Publishers, 1987.

Brooks, James F. *Captives and Cousins: Slavery, Kinship, and Community in the Southwest Borderlands.* Chapel Hill: University of North Carolina Press, 2002.

Buenger, Walter L. "Unionism on the Texas Frontier." *Arizona and the West* 22 (Autumn 1980): 237–254.

———, and Robert A. Calvert, eds. *Texas Through Time: Evolving Interpretations.* College Station: Texas A and M University Press, 1991.

Campbell, Randolph B. *An Empire for Slavery: The Peculiar Institution in Texas, 1821–1865.* Baton Rouge: Louisiana State University Press, 1989.

———. *Gone to Texas: A History of the Lone Star State.* New York: Oxford University Press, 2002.

———. *Sam Houston and the American Southwest.* New York: HarperCollins, 1993.

Everett, Dianna, and Richard G. Lowe. *Wealth and Power in Antebellum Texas.* College Station: Texas A and M University Press, 1977.

Cantrell, Gregg. *Stephen F. Austin: Empresario of Texas.* New Haven, Conn.: Yale University Press, 1999.

Carlson, Paul H. *The Plains Indians.* College Station: Texas A and M University Press, 1999.

Carriker, Robert C. *Fort Supply, Indian Territory: Frontier Outpost on the Plains.* Norman: University of Oklahoma Press, 1970.

Cash, W. J. *The Mind of the South.* New York: Vintage Books, 1941.

Cashion, Ty. *A Texas Frontier: The Clear Fork Country and Fort Griffin, 1849–1887.* Norman: University of Oklahoma Press, 1996.

Chalfant, William Y. *Without Quarter: The Wichita Expedition and the Fight on Crooked Creek.* Norman: University of Oklahoma Press, 1991.

Chipman, Donald E. *Spanish Texas, 1519–1821.* Austin: University of Texas Press, 1992.

Clark, Mary Whatley. *Chief Bowles and the Texas Cherokees.* Norman: University of Oklahoma Press, 1971.

———. *David G. Burnet.* Austin and New York: Pemberton Press, 1969.

Costeloe, Michael P. *The Central Republic in Mexico, 1835–1846: Hombres de bien in the Age of Santa Anna.* New York: Cambridge University Press, 1993.

Davis, William C. *Three Roads to the Alamo: The Lives and Fortunes of David Crockett, James Bowie, and William Barret Travis.* New York: HarperCollins, 1998.

de la Teja, Jesús F. *San Antonio de Bexar: A Community on New Spain's Northern Frontier.* Albuquerque: University of New Mexico Press, 1995.

de la Teja, Jesús F., and John Wheat, eds. "Bexar: Profile of a Tejano Community, 1820–1832," *Southwestern Historical Quarterly* 89 (July 1985): 7–34.

De León, Arnoldo. *The Tejano Community, 1836–1900.* Albuquerque: University of New Mexico Press, 1982.

De León, Arnoldo, and Kenneth L. Stewart. *Tejanos and the Numbers Game: A Socio-Historical Interpretation from the Federal Census, 1850–1900.* Albuquerque: University of New Mexico Press, 1989.

Doughty, Robin W. *Wildlife and Man in Texas: Environmental Change and Conservation.* College Station: Texas A and M University Press, 1983.

Drinnon, Richard. *White Savage: The Case of John Dunn Hunter.* New York: Schocken Books, 1972.

Duval, John C. *The Adventures of Big-Foot Wallace, the Texas Ranger and Hunter.* Philadelphia: Claxton, Temsen, and Haffelfinger, 1871.

Estep, Raymond. *The Removal of the Texas Indians and the Founding of Fort Cobb.* Oklahoma City: Oklahoma Historical Society, 1961.

Everett, Dianna. *The Texas Cherokees: A People between Two Fires, 1819–1840.* Norman: University of Oklahoma Press, 1990.

Fehrenbach, T. R. *Lone Star: A History of Texas and the Texans.* New York: Macmillan, 1968.

Flores, Dan. "Bison Ecology and Bison Diplomacy: The Southern Plains from 1800 to 1850," *Journal of American History* 78 (September 1991): 465–485.

Foreman, Grant. "Historical Background of the Kiowa-Comanche Reservation." *Chronicles of Oklahoma* 19 (June 1941): 129–140.

Forman, Carolyn Thomas. "Black Beaver." *Chronicles of Oklahoma* 24 (Autumn 1946): 269–292.

———. "Colonel James B. Many: Commandant at Fort Gibson, Fort Towson, and Fort Smith." *Chronicles of Oklahoma* 19 (June 1941): 119–128.

———. "Nathan Boone: Trapper, Manufacturer, Surveyor, Militiaman, Legislator, Ranger, and Dragoon." *Chronicles of Oklahoma* 19 (December 1941): 322–247.

Forman, Frank. "Some New Lights on Houston's Life among the Cherokee Indians," *Chronicles of Oklahoma* 9 (June 1931): 139–157.

Foster, Morris. *Being Comanche: A Social History of an American Indian Community.* Tucson: University of Arizona Press, 1991.

Friend, Llerena B. *Sam Houston: The Great Designer.* Austin: University of Texas Press, 1954.

Garrett, Julia Kathryn. *Seven Flags Over Texas: A Story of the Last Years of Spain in Texas.* Austin: Pemberton Press Reprint, 1969.

Genovese, Eugene. *Roll, Jordan, Roll: The World the Slaves Made.* New York: Pantheon Books, 1974.

Gibson, Arrell Morgan. *The American Indian: Prehistory to the Present.* Lexington, Mass.: D. C. Heath, 1980.

Goldfinch, Charles W. *Juan N. Cortina, 1824–1892: A Re-Appraisal.* New York: Arno Press, 1974.

Greaser, Galen D., and Jesús F. de la Teja. "Quieting Title to Spanish and Mexican Land Grants in the Trans-Nueces: The Bourland and Miller Commission, 1850–1852." *Southwestern Historical Quarterly* 95 (April 1992): 445–464.

Green, Michael D. *The Politics of Indian Removal: Creek Government and Society in Crisis.* Lincoln: University of Nebraska Press, 1982.

Greene, Jerome A. *Washita: The U.S. Army and the Southern Cheyennes, 1867–1869.* Norman: University of Oklahoma Press, 2004.

Gregory, Jack, and Rennard Strickland. *Sam Houston and the Cherokee, 1829–1833.* Austin: University of Texas Press, 1967.

Gronet, Richard W. "The United States and the Invasion of Texas." *Americas* 25 (January 1969): 281–306.

Hagan, William T. *United States–Comanche Relations: The Reservation Years.* New York: Yale University Press, 1976.

Haley, James L. *Sam Houston.* Norman: University of Oklahoma Press, 2002.

Haley, J. Evetts. "The Comanchero Trade." *Southwestern Historical Quarterly* 38, no. 3 (January 1935): 157–176.

Hardin, J. Fair. "Fort Jesup—Fort Selden—Camp Sabine—Camp Salubrity: Four Forgotten Frontier Army Posts in Western Louisiana," *Louisiana Historical Quarterly* [part 1] 16 (January 1933): 5–26, [part 2] 16 (April 1933): 279–294, [part 3] 16 (July 1933): 441–453, [part 4] 16 (October 1933): 671–685.

Hardin, Stephen L. *Texian Iliad: A Military History of the Texas Revolution.* Austin: University of Texas Press, 1994.

Harrison, Jeanne V. "Matthew Leeper, Confederate Indian Agent at the Wichita Agency, Indian Territory." *Chronicles of Oklahoma* 47 (Autumn 1969): 242–257.

Haynes, Sam W. *Soldiers of Misfortune: The Somervell and Mier Expeditions.* Austin: University of Texas Press, 1990.

Henson, Margaret Swett. *Juan Davis Bradburn: A Reappraisal of the Mexican Commander of Anahuac.* College Station: Texas A and M University Press, 1982.

———. *Lorenzo de Zavala: The Pragmatic Idealist.* Fort Worth: Texas Christian University Press, 1996.

Hietala, Thomas. *Manifest Destiny: Anxious Aggrandizement in Late Jacksonian America.* Ithaca, N.Y.: Cornell University Press, 1985.

Higginbotham, R. Don. "The Martial Spirit in the Antebellum South: Some Further Speculations in a National Context." *Journal of Southern History* 58 (February 1992): 3–26.

Himmel, Kelly F. *The Conquest of the Karankawas and the Tonkawas, 1821–1859.* College Station: Texas A and M University Press, 1999.

Hoare, Quinton, and Geoggrey Nowell Smith. *Selections from the Prison Notebooks of Antonio Gramsci.* New York: International Publications, 1971.

Hodge, Frederick Webb. *Handbook of North American Indians North of Mexico,* in 2 parts. Washington, D.C.: Government Printing Office, 1910.

Hoerig, Karl A. "The Relationship between German Immigrants and the Native Peoples of Western Texas." *Southwestern Historical Quarterly* 97 (January 1994): 423–452.

Hoig, Stan. "Jesse Chisholm: Peace-maker, Trader, Forgotten Frontiersman." *Chronicles of Oklahoma* 66 (Winter 1988–89): 350–373.

———. *The Sand Creek Massacre.* Norman: University of Oklahoma Press, 1961.

Hollon, W. Eugene. *Beyond the Cross Timbers: The Travels of Randolph B. Marcy.* Norman: University of Oklahoma Press, 1955.

Howren, Alleine. "The Causes and Origins of the Decree of April 6, 1830." *Southwestern Historical Quarterly* 16 (April 1916): 395–398.

Huston, Cleburne. *Towering Texan: A Biography of Thomas J. Rusk.* Waco: Texian Press, 1971.

Hutton, Paul Andrew. *Phil Sheridan and His Army.* Norman: University of Oklahoma Press, 1985.

Isenberg, Andrew. *The Destruction of the Bison: An Environmental History, 1750–1920.* New York: Cambridge University Press, 2000.

James, Marquis. *The Raven: A Biography of Sam Houston.* Indianapolis: Bobbs-Merrill, 1929.

Jenkins, John H., and Kenneth Kesselus. *Edward Burleson: Texas Frontier Leader.* Austin: Jenkins Publishing, 1990.

Jones, Robert L., and Pauline H. Jones. "Houston's Politics and the Cherokee." *Chronicles of Oklahoma* 46 (Winter 1968–69): 418–432.

Jordan, Terry G. *German Seed in Texas Soil: Immigrant Farmers in Nineteenth-Century Texas.* Austin: University of Texas Press, 1966.

Kavanagh, Thomas W. "Comanche Population, Organization, and Reorganization, 1869–1901." [Part 2.] *Plains Anthropologist* 34, no. 124 (May 1989): 99–111.

Kennedy, William. *Texas: The Rise, Progress, and Prospects of the Republic of Texas. In One Volume.* Fort Worth, Tex.: Molyneaux Craftsmen, 1925.

Kessell, John L. *Kiva, Cross, and Crown: The Pecos Indians and New Mexico, 1540–1840.* Albuquerque: University of New Mexico Press, 1987.

Lack, Paul D. "The Córdova Revolt," in *Tejano Journey, 1770–1850,* ed. Gerald E. Poyo. Austin: University of Texas Press, 1996.

———. *The Texas Revolutionary Experience: A Political and Social History, 1835–1836.* College Station: Texas A and M University Press, 1992.

LaVere, David. *The Caddo Chiefdoms: Caddo Economics and Politics, 700–1835.* Lincoln: University of Nebraska Press, 1998.

———. *Contrary Neighbors: Southern Plains and Removed Indians in Indian Territory.* Norman: University of Oklahoma Press, 2000.

———. *Life among the Texas Indians: The WPA Narratives.* College Station: Texas A and M University Press, 1998.

Lay, Bennett. *The Lives of Ellis P. Bean.* Austin: University of Texas Press, 1960.

Lears, T. J. Jackson. *No Place of Grace: Antimodernism and the Transformation of American Culture, 1880–1920.* New York: Pantheon Books, 1881.

Lecompte, Janet. "Bent, St. Vrain & Co., among the Comanches and Kiowas." *Colorado Magazine of History* 44, no. 4 (Fall 1972): 273–293.

Ledbetter, Barbara A. Neal. *Fort Belknap, Frontier Saga: Indians, Negroes, and Anglo-Americans on the Texas Frontier.* Burnet, Tex.: Eakin Press, 1982.

Mardock, Robert Winston. *The Reformers and the American Indian.* Columbia: University of Missouri Press, 1971.

Marten, James. *Texas Divided: Loyalty and Dissent in the Lone Star State, 1856–1874.* Lexington: University of Kentucky Press, 1990.

Matovina, Timothy M. "Between Two Worlds," in *Tejano Journey, 1770–1850,* ed. Gerald E. Poyo. Austin: University of Texas Press, 1996.

Mayhall, Mildred P. *Indian Wars of Texas.* Waco: Texian Press, 1965.

McConnell, Joseph Carroll. *The West Texas Frontier, or a Descriptive History of Early Times in Western Texas.* Jacksboro, Tex.: Gazette Press, 1933.

McGraw, William Cochran. *Savage Scene: The Life and Times of Mountain Man James Kirker.* San Lorenzo, N.Mex.: High-Lonesome Books, 1972.

McKitrick, Reuben. *The Public Land System of Texas, 1823–1910.* Bulletin of the University of Wisconsin no. 905. Madison, 1918.

McWhiney, Grady. *Cracker Culture: Celtic Ways in the Old South.* Tuscaloosa: University of Alabama Press, 1988.

———. "Ethnic Roots of Southern Violence," in *A Master's Due: Essays in Honor of David Herbert Donald,* ed. William J. Cooper Jr., Michael F. Holt, and John McCardell. Baton Rouge: Louisiana State University Press, 1985.

McWhiney, Grady, and Perry D. Jamieson. *Attack and Die: Civil War Military Tactics and the Southern Heritage.* Tuscaloosa: University of Alabama Press, 1982.

Meketa, Jacqueline Dorgan, ed. *Legacy of Honor: The Life of Rafael Chacon, a Nineteenth-Century New Mexican.* Albuquerque: University of New Mexico Press, 1982.

Miller, Susan A. *Coacoochee's Bones: A Seminole Saga.* Lawrence: University of Kansas Press, 2003.

Miller, Thomas Lloyd. *The Public Lands of Texas, 1590–1970.* Norman: University of Oklahoma Press, 1971.

Milligan, James C., and L. David Norris. "Keeping the Peace: William H. Emory and the Command at Fort Arbuckle." *Chronicles of Oklahoma* 69 (Fall 1991): 256–281.

Monaghan, Jay. *Civil War on the Western Border, 1854–1865.* New York: Bonanza Books, 1955.

Montejano, David. *Anglos and Mexicans in the Making of Texas, 1836–1986.* Austin: University of Texas Press, 1987.

Morrison, James D. "Notes and Documents: Notes from the *Northern Standard,* 1842–1849." *Chronicles of Oklahoma* 19 (March 1941): 82–93.

Morrison, W. B. "Ft. Washita." *Chronicles of Oklahoma* 5 (June 1927): 251–258.

Muckleroy, Anna. "The Indian Policy of the Republic of Texas." *Southwestern Historical Quarterly* [part 1] 25 (April 1922): 229–260, [part 2] 26 (July 1922): 1–29, [part 3] 26 (October 1922): 128–148, and [part 4] 26 (January 1923): 184–206.

Mulroy, Kevin. *Freedom on the Border: The Seminole Maroons in Florida, the Indian Territory, Coahuila, and Texas.* Lubbock: Texas Tech University Press, 1993.

Naimark, Norman N. *Fires of Hatred: Ethnic Cleansing in Twentieth-Century Europe.* Cambridge, Mass.: Harvard University Press, 2001.

Nance, Joseph Milton. *After San Jacinto: The Texas-Mexican Frontier, 1836–1841.* Austin: University of Texas Press, 1963.

Neighbours, Kenneth. "José Maria: Anadarko Chief." *Chronicles of Oklahoma* 44 (Autumn 1966): 254–274.

———. *Robert Simpson Neighbors and the Texas Frontier, 1836–1859.* Waco: Texian Press, 1975.

Nye, W. S. *Carbine and Lance: The Story of Old Fort Sill.* Norman: University of Oklahoma Press, 1937.

———. *Plains Indian Raiders: The Final Phases of Warfare from the Arkansas to the Red River.* Norman: University of Oklahoma Press, 1968.

Oakes, James. *The Ruling Race: A History of American Slavery.* New York: Vintage Books, 1983.

Olson, James S. *A Line in the Sand: The Alamo in Blood and Memory.* New York: Free Press, 2001.

Orozco Zamora, Cynthia, and Rodolfo Rocha, eds. *Mexican Americans in Texas History.* Austin: Texas State Historical Society, 2000.

Parsons, Edmund M. "The Fredonian Rebellion." *Texana* 21 (Spring 1967): 11–52.

Pearce, Roy Harvey. *Savagism and Civilization: A Study of the Indian and the American Mind.* Baltimore, Md.: Johns Hopkins University Press, 1953.

———. "The Significance of the Captivity Narrative." *American Literature* 19 (1947): 1–20.

Perttula, Timothy K. *"The Caddo Nation": Archaeological and Ethnohistorical Prespectives.* Austin: University of Texas Press, 1992.

Pohl, James W., and Stephen Hardin. "The Military History of the Texas Revolution: An Overview." *Southwestern Historical Quarterly* 89 (March 1986): 269–308.

Poyo, Gerald E., ed. *Tejano Journey: 1770–1850.* Austin: University of Texas Press, 1996.

Prucha, Francis Paul. *American Indian Policy in the Formative Years: The Indian Trade and Intercourse Acts, 1790–1834.* Lincoln: University of Nebraska Press, 1962.

————. *The Great Father: The United States Government and the American Indians.* 2 vols. Lincoln: University of Nebraska Press, 1984.

————. *Sword of the Republic: The United States Army on the Frontier, 1783–1846.* London: Macmillan, 1969.

Purdue, Theda. *Cherokee Women.* Lincoln: University of Nebraska Press, 1998.

Reagan, John H. "The Expulsion of the Cherokee from East Texas." *Quarterly of the Texas State Historical Association* 1 (July 1897–April 1898): 38–46.

Richardson, R. N. *Comanche Barrier to the South Plains Settlements.* Glendale, Calif.: Arthur H. Clark, 1933.

————. *The Frontier of North West Texas, 1846–1876.* Glendale, Calif.: Authur H. Clark, 1963.

————, ed. "The Death of Nacona and the Recovery of Cynthia Ann Parker." *Southwestern Historical Quarterly* 46 (July 1942): 15–21.

Richardson, R. N., Ernest Wallace, and Adrian Anderson. *Texas: The Lone State.* Englewood Cliffs, N.J.: Prentice Hall, 1988.

Rippy, J. Fred. "Border Troubles along the Rio Grande, 1858–1860," *Southwestern Historical Quarterly* 23 (October 1919): 91–111.

————. "The Indians of the Southwest in the Diplomacy of the United States and Mexico, 1848–1853," *Hispanic American Historical Review* 2 (August 1919): 363–396.

Rodríguez O., Jaime E., and Kathryn Vincent. *Myths, Misdeeds, and Misunderstandings.* Wilmington, Del.: Scholarly Resources, 1997.

Roland, Charles P. *Albert Sidney Johnston: Soldier of Three Republics.* Austin: University of Texas Press, 1964.

Scott, James. *Domination and the Arts of Resistance: Hidden Transcripts.* New Haven, Conn.: Yale University Press, 1990.

Sheehan, Bernard. *Seeds of Extinction: Jeffersonian Philanthropy and the American Indian.* New York: W. W. Norton, 1974.

Sibley, Marilyn McAdams. "The Texas Cherokee War of 1839." *East Texas Historical Journal* 3 (March 1965): 18–33.

Siegel, Stanley. *The Poet President of Texas: The Life of Mirabeau B. Lamar, President of Texas.* Austin: Jenkins Publishing, 1977.

Sierra, Justo. *The Political Evolution of the Mexican People.* Trans. Charles Ramsdell. Austin: University of Texas Press, 1969.

Simpson, Lesley Byrd. *Many Mexicos.* Berkeley: University of California Press, 1964.

Slotkin, Richard. *Regeneration through Violence: The Mythology of the American Frontier, 1600–1860.* Middletown, Conn.: Wesleyan University Press, 1973.

Smith, Thomas T. *The Old Army in Texas: A Research Guide to the United States Army in Nineteenth-Century Texas.* Austin: University of Texas Press, 1999.

————. *The U.S. Army and the Texas Frontier Economy, 1845–1900.* College Station: Texas A and M University Press, 1999.

Smits, David D. "The Frontier Army and the Destruction of the Buffalo: 1865–1883." *Western Historical Quarterly* 25 (Autumn 1994): 312–338.

Stahle, David, and Malcolm K. Cleaveland. "Texas Drought History Reconstructed and Analyzed from 1698 to 1980." *Journal of Climate* 1 (January 1988): 59–74.

Stannard, David. *American Holocaust: The Conquest of the New World.* New York: Oxford University Press, 1992.

Starling, Suzanne. *Land Is the Cry! Warren Angus Ferris, Pioneer Texas Surveyor and Founder of Dallas County.* Austin: Texas State Historical Association, 1998.

Tate, Michael L. "Comanche Captives: People between Two Worlds." *Chronicles of Oklahoma* 72 (Fall 1994): 228–263.

———. *The Frontier Army in the Settlement of the West.* Norman: University of Oklahoma Press, 1999.

———. *The Indians of Texas: An Annotated Research Bibliography.* Metuchen, N.J.: Scarecrow Press, 1986.

Thornton, Russell. *American Indian Holocaust and Survival: A Population History since 1492.* Norman: University of Oklahoma Press, 1987.

Tijerina, Andrés. *Tejanos and Texas under the Mexican Flag, 1821–1836.* College Station: Texas A and M University Press, 1994.

Traylor, Maude Wallis. "Captain Samuel Highsmith." *Frontier Times* 17 (April 1940): 291–302.

Tyler, Ronnie C. "The Callahan Expedition of 1855: Indians or Negroes?" *Southwestern Historical Quarterly* 70 (April 1967): 574–585.

Tyler, Ronnie C., and Lawrence R. Murphy, eds. *The Slave Narratives of Texas.* Austin: Encino Press, 1974.

Unruh, John D. *The Plains Across: The Overland Emigrants and the Trans-Mississippi West, 1840–1860.* Urbana: University of Illinois Press, 1982.

Utley, Robert. *Custer: Cavalier in Buckskin.* Norman: University of Oklahoma Press, 2001.

———. *Frontiersmen in Blue: The United States Army and the Indians, 1848–1865.* New York: Macmillan, 1967.

———. *Lone Star Justice: The First Century of the Texas Rangers.* New York: Oxford University Press, 2002.

Vigness, D. M. "Indian Raids on the Lower Rio Grande, 1836–1837," *Southwestern Historical Quarterly* 59 (July 1955): 14–23.

———. *The Revolutionary Decades, 1810–1836.* Austin: Steck-Vaughn, 1965.

Wallace, Anthony F. C. *Jefferson and the Indians: The Tragic Fate of the First Americans.* Cambridge, Mass.: Harvard University Press, 1999.

Wallace, Ernest, and E. Adamson Hoebel. *The Comanches: Lords of the South Plains.* Norman: University of Oklahoma Press, 1952.

Webb, Walter Prescott. *The Texas Rangers: A Century of Frontier Defense.* Boston: Houghton Mifflin, 1935.

Webb, Walter Prescott, and H. Bailey Carroll. *The Handbook of Texas.* 2 vols. Austin: Texas State Historical Association, 1952.

Weber, David J. *The Mexican Frontier, 1821–1846: The American Southwest under Mexico.* Albuquerque: University of New Mexico Press, 1982.

———. *The Taos Trappers: The Fur Trade in the Far Southwest, 1540–1846.* Norman: University of Oklahoma Press, 1971.

Wellman, Paul I. "Cynthia Ann Parker." *Chronicles of Oklahoma* 12 (June 1934): 163–170.

Winfrey, Dorman. "Chief Bowles of the Texas Cherokee." *Chronicles of Oklahoma* 32 (Spring 1954): 29–41.

Wisehart, M. K. *Sam Houston: American Giant.* Washington, D.C.: Robert B. Luce, 1962.

Wolbert, Albert. "The Last of the Cherokees in Texas and the Life and Death of Chief Bowles." *Chronicles of Oklahoma* 1 (January 1921): 179–226.

Wooster, Robert. *Soldiers, Sutlers, and Settlers: Garrison Life on the Texas Frontier.* College Station: Texas A and M University Press, 1987.

Worster, Donald. *The Dust Bowl: The Southern Plains in the 1930s.* New York: Oxford University Press, 1979.

Wright, J. Leitch. *William Agustus Bowles: Director General of the Creek Nation.* Athens: University of Georgia Press, 1967.

Wyatt-Brown, Bertram. *Honor and Violence in the Old South.* New York: Oxford University Press, 1986.

———. *The Shaping of Southern Culture: Honor, Grace, and War, 1760s–1890s.* Chapel Hill: University of North Carolina Press, 2001.

———. *Southern Honor: Ethics and Behavior in the Old South.* New York: Oxford University Press, 1982.

INDEX

Any Texan will tell you: they are quick to act in defense of their honor. But what most Texans won't tell you—what they may not realize—is that Texas's early years do little to uphold that honor. In fact, they can best be described today as a time of ethnic cleansing.

The Conquest of Texas is not your grandfather's tale of how a courageous few made a righteous conquest of a wild land. Rather, this story explores race relations during the Mexican Republic, the Republic of Texas, and early statehood. Portraying nineteenth-century Texas as a cauldron of racist violence, Gary Clayton Anderson exposes the ethnic warfare that dominated that frontier.

This is the story of the struggle between Anglos and Indians for land—and Anderson places responsibility for most of the violence squarely on the Anglos. He tells how Scotch-Irish settlers clashed with Wichitas, Caddos, and other farming tribes and then challenged the Comanches and Kiowas for their hunting grounds. Next, the decade-long conflict with Mexico merged with war against Indians. For fifty years Texas remained in a virtual state of war—the longest continuous struggle of its kind in American history.

At the very heart of Texas mythology are the Texas Rangers. Until now most histories have justified their actions and vilified their opponents. But Anderson tells how the government encouraged the rangers